CROSSROADS
Integrated Reading and Writing

Second Edition

Pam Dusenberry, M.Ed.
Shoreline Community College

Julie O'Donnell Moore, MA
Green River Community College

Boston Columbus Indianapolis New York San Francisco Upper Saddle River
Amsterdam Cape Town Dubai London Madrid Milan Munich Paris Montréal Toronto
Delhi Mexico City São Paulo Sydney Hong Kong Seoul Singapore Taipei Tokyo

Executive Editor: Matthew Wright
Senior Development Editor: Gill Cook
Executive Marketing Manager: Roxanne McCarley
Executive Digital Producer: Stefanie A. Snajder
Digital Editor: Sara Gordus
Content Specialist: Anne Leung
Senior Supplements Editor: Donna Campion
Production Manager: Savoula Amanatidis
Project Coordination, Text Design, and Electronic Page Makeup: Integra Software Services

Cover Design Manager: John Callahan
Cover Designer: Maria Ilardi
Cover Image: © Mykola Mazuryk/fotolia
Photo Research: Integra Software Services
Senior Manufacturing Buyer: Dennis J. Para
Printer and Binder: Courier Corporation—Kendallville, IN
Cover Printer: Courier Corporation—Kendallville, IN

For permission to use copyrighted material, grateful acknowledgment is made to the copyright holders on p. 399, which are hereby made part of this copyright page.

Library of Congress Cataloging-in-Publication Data
Dusenberry, Pam.
  Crossroads : integrated reading and writing/Pam Dusenberry, M.Ed, Shoreline Community College;
Julie O'Donnell Moore, MA, Green River Community College.—2nd edition.
    pages. cm
  Includes bibliographical references and index.
  ISBN 978-0-321-91315-9 (alk. paper)
  1. English language—Rhetoric.   2. Report writing.   I. Moore, Julie.   II. Title.
  PE1408.D867 2014
  808'.0427—dc23

                                                                    2013049337

10 9 8 7 6 5 4 3 2—V0UD—18 17 16 15 14

www.pearsonhighered.com

ISBN-10:   0-321-91315-9
ISBN-13: 978-0-321-91315-9

Brief Contents

Detailed Contents

Part 4   Casebook: Reading and Writing Argumentative Texts   231

Chapter 11 **A Reading Process for Argumentative Texts**   236

Part 5   Reading Selections 311

Part 6   Grammar Essentials 375

Readings by Theme

Crossing Borders from Home

- *The Naked Culture*, by Vince Barnes
- *An Insider's Perspective: The Donna Beegle Story*, by Donna Beegle
- *The Crossing*, by Ruben Martinez
- *Allegory of the Cave*, by Plato
- *Aria*, by Richard Rodriguez
- *Whistlin' and Crowin' Women of Appalachia: Literacy Practices Since College*, by Katherine Kelleher Sohn
- *From* School Days of an Indian Girl, by Zitkala-Sa

Crossing Borders from High School

- *Learning Strategies in the Various Disciplines*, by Laurie Kimpton-Lorence
- *Now That You're Here*, by Sherrie L. Nist-Olejnik and Jodi Patrick Holschuh
- *On Being a Student*, by Donald E. Simanek
- *Reclaiming Native Education*, by Christina Twu

Crossing Borders of Gender

- *Don't Call Me a Hot Tamale*, by Judith Ortiz Cofer
- *Causes of Prejudice*, Vincent N. Parrillo
- *Whistlin' and Crowin' Women of Appalachia: Literacy Practices Since College*, by Katherine Kelleher Sohn

Crossing Borders of Social Class

- *The Naked Culture*, by Vincent Barnes
- *An Insider's Perspective: The Donna Beegle Story*, by Donna Beegle
- *Living in America: Challenges Facing New Immigrants and Refugees*, edited by Katherine Garrett, Robert Wood Johnson Foundation
- *Equalizing Opportunity*, by Richard Rothstein
- *On the Uses of a Liberal Education as a Weapon in the Hands of the Restless Poor*, by Earl Shorris
- *Whistlin' and Crowin' Women of Appalachia: Literacy Practices Since College*, by Katherine Kelleher Sohn
- *C. P. Ellis*, by Studs Terkel
- *Reclaiming Native Education*, by Christina Twu

Crossing Borders of Race, Ethnicity, or Culture

- *The Naked Culture*, by Vincent Barnes
- *Don't Call Me a Hot Tamale*, by Judith Ortiz Cofer
- *Learning to Read and Write*, by Frederick Douglass
- *Living in America: Challenges Facing New Immigrants and Refugees*, edited by Katherine Garrett, Robert Wood Johnson Foundation
- *Mute in an English Only World*, Chang-rae Lee
- *Assimilation through Education: Indian Boarding Schools in the Pacific Northwest*, by Carolyn Marr
- *Causes of Prejudice*, Vincent N. Parrillo
- *Aria*, by Richard Rodriguez
- *Reclaiming Native Education*, by Christina Twu
- *From* School Days of an Indian Girl, by Zitkala-Sa
- *C. P. Ellis*, by Studs Terkel

Preface

Integrated reading and writing instruction, high challenge–high support approaches, and acceleration are ideas sweeping the nation to improve developmental education outcomes. These approaches are held up as powerful solutions to helping better prepare students for college-level work and help them stay to graduate. To answer the call for improved results in developmental programs, *Crossroads* has been revised to more fully address many of these principles in its content and design.

The Common Core is another movement drawing the attention of educators in almost every state. The Common Core standards for K–12 set a high bar to ensure that most if not all high school students graduate ready to enter college. *Crossroads* matches the reading and writing goals laid out in the standards.

However, while *Crossroads* was written in part out of a nationwide need, its inception originated in the classroom where both authors, Dusenberry and Moore, have over 35 years of combined experience teaching precollege classes using a fully integrated approach. It is their experience with students that formed the backbone of revisions to the second edition of *Crossroads*, including a stronger emphasis on integrating textual evidence into student writing, reading college-level texts, engaging aspects of information literacy and critical thinking, and inviting students to explore a variety of types of supporting evidence in texts they read and write.

What Is New in the Second Edition

- **New full-color design:** A completely new, 4-color design makes instructional content easy to access and navigate, guiding readers through the reading and writing steps and supporting and reinforcing the content.
- **Additional themes:** College success and preparedness is still a key theme, but additional themes related to crossing the boundaries of college, race, class, culture, and gender have been integrated into the casebooks to offer students and instructors more diversity of topics.
- **Stronger emphasis on integrating textual evidence into students' writing:** Students see examples of how to integrate quoted and paraphrased materials into their writing, and this material comes from the reading they do in the book. This focus on textual support is key to preparing students for college writing, which often includes textual evidence. It also helps to reinforce the connection between reading and writing.
- **Flexibility of use of assignments:** While the text guides readers through concrete examples of reading to writing assignments in the Demonstrations, it offers flexibility within the assignments, so that instructors can tailor them to fit the needs of their students as well as their chosen readings from the textbook or other sources.
- **Acceleration options within writing assignments:** Assignments offer two tiers of challenge, so that students who are on an accelerated path or who want to push themselves have that option within the scope of the textbook.
- **Informational Literacy sections:** These sections introduce foundational elements of information literacy including finding and evaluating sources. The focus on information literacy is designed to help students build skills necessary to their college-level reading and writing success.
- *Critical Thinking* **sections:** These sections give new focus to elements of critical thinking such as analysis, synthesis, and reflection. They are woven into the reading and writing processes to help students consciously develop these skills.

- **Grammar instruction:** In addition to MySkillsLab, where students can get instruction on and practice with grammar, the second edition of *Crossroads* offers Part Six: Grammar Essentials, which focuses on key elements of grammar such as sentence basics, sentence boundaries, and punctuation. This will help instructors who want to highlight grammar instruction in their classes alongside MySkillsLab tutorial practice.
- **Fresh readings:** Nine new readings broaden and add depth to the themes in the book, providing additional opportunities for students to practice synthesizing and writing from sources.
- **Lexile levels for all readings** Lexile® measure—the most widely used reading metric in U.S. schools—provides valuable information about a student's reading ability and the complexity of text. It helps match students with reading resources and activities that are targeted to their ability level. Lexile measures indicate the reading levels of content in MyReadingLab and the longer selections in the Annotated Instructor's Editions of all Pearson's reading books. See the Annotated Instructor's Edition of *Crossroads* and the Instructor's Manual for more details.

MySkillsLab
- **Mastery tests** End of chapter assessment quizzes are included in the *Crossroads*, 2/e book-specific module in MySkillsLab.

Integrated Reading and Writing

Many instructors talk about the connections between reading and writing, but students rarely understand exactly what this means—how building strong reading skills will make them better writers, and how strong writing skills will make them better readers. Students need to know how to understand and analyze what they read so that they can apply it in their writing.

Crossroads offers instruction in the skills and strategies of both reading and writing, emphasizing the structural components of texts and the similarities of process that reading and writing share. Also, college writing across the curriculum often requires text-based writing, and *Crossroads* teaches students how to write using sources. In addition, with a focus on the theme of crossing borders, *Crossroads* helps prepare all students for college learning and culture.

Process Approach

Crossroads uses a *process approach* to reading and writing, which means students learn dozens of strategies for solving reading and writing problems. While there is no single process guaranteed to make students better readers and writers, there are steps that can be followed, rearranged, and repeated to help *all* writers and readers improve their skills. Chapters 1 and 2 introduce these key steps, and subsequent chapters offer demonstrations and explanations of how to use the reading and writing processes in different situations for varying purposes.

The similarities between the process approaches for reading and writing are consistently highlighted throughout the book in such features as the introductions to the parts, the Demonstrations and related Practices, and the organization of readings around themes to help students see the importance of background information. These elements emphasize not just the reading and writing connection, but the relationship between the *processes* of reading and writing.

A process approach prepares students for successful learning in college classes because it more closely approximates what they will do there. In a process approach, the skills of reading and writing are taught in the context of reading and writing whole, college-level texts. Students not only learn the sub-skills of reading and writing, but when and where to use them.

Theme-Based Contextualization

Many students who take developmental reading and writing classes are the first in their families to attend college, are new to the United States and college in the US, or are students who struggled to navigate the K–12 school system. With this in mind, *Crossroads* walks students through the reading and writing processes, using published and student writing presenting many different perspectives on the theme of crossing borders. Many students are crossing borders of some kind to enter and succeed in college: borders of language, of social class, of culture, or simply from high school.

Many readings relate to becoming educated, such as what it means to be a successful college student, what the purpose of a college education can be, and what college culture is like. Students build their reading and writing skills while learning about the environment and expectations of college and exploring the theme of crossing borders. The content themes are designed to meet students at their life experiences and help them transition into college learning and culture.

The readings are also organized into more focused themes such as "Crossing Borders into College" and "Crossing Borders of Immigration," and a thematic list of readings can be found on page xii.

High-Challenge Reading Selections

The reading selections in *Crossroads* range in level and most are challenging. The research in learning and best practices tells us that underprepared students must practice reading and writing college-level texts because if they practice only with simple texts, they are not prepared to do the work of college. The book's approach shifts responsibility for learning from the textbook and teacher toward the student.

Casebook Concept

Students encounter two main types of support when reading texts and writing papers for college classes: narrative evidence and informational evidence. Therefore, the textbook includes Casebooks, one that examines how to read and write texts that primarily use personal experience and/or narrative evidence (stories and biography) as support, and another that examines how to read and write texts that primarily use informational evidence (illustrations, descriptions, observations, facts, and statistics) as support.

A third casebook, on argumentation, addresses how writers may combine narrative and informational evidence to support a particular point of view. Each casebook also has a focused theme and includes two related readings to illustrate these two types of support. These two readings also supply content for students' own paragraphs and essays.

The goal of *Crossroads* is to help students see organizational structure as driven by supporting ideas; students should search for what they want and need to say, and then they should determine an appropriate organizational structure that best conveys this content.

How This Book Is Organized

Crossroads has six parts:

- **Part One** focuses on the foundational processes and structures of reading and writing. Chapter 1 introduces students to the academic reading process; Chapter 2 teaches students the steps involved in writing academic paragraphs and essays; Chapter 3 provides an overview of the basic components of the expository paragraph and essay; and Chapter 4 illustrates the various organizational modes used in the texts that students read and compose in college.

- **Part Two** introduces the narrative casebook with the theme of "Crossing Borders into College" and provides an overview of how narrative evidence is used as support in the academic texts students read and write in college. Within Part Two, Chapter 5 demonstrates the reading process for texts that use narrative or personal experience as their primary support; Chapter 6 introduces students to a process for writing paragraphs using narrative support; and Chapter 7 illustrates the process of writing essays using narration. The two texts used for reading and writing demonstration and practice are "An Insider's Perspective: The Donna Beegle Story" by Donna Beegle and "Whistlin' and Crowin' Women of Appalachia: Literacy Practices Since College" by Katherine Kelleher Sohn.
- **Part Three** constitutes an informational casebook with the theme "Crossing Borders of Prejudice." Chapters within Part Three focus on a second primary form of support or evidence that students encounter: information in the form of observation, description, facts, and statistics. Chapter 8 reviews a process for reading texts that use this type of support; Chapter 9 demonstrates the process of writing information-based paragraphs; and Chapter 10 helps students learn about and practice a process for writing descriptive and fact-based essays. The two texts used for reading and writing demonstration and practice are "Causes of Prejudice" by Vincent Parrillo and "C. P. Ellis" by Studs Terkel.
- **Part Four** explores the theme "Crossing Borders of Immigration" and uses texts and writing assignments in which authors argue a particular point of view. Chapter 11 focuses on strategies for reading arguments; Chapter 12 reviews a writing process that helps students develop, write, and polish argumentative paragraphs; and finally, Chapter 13 prepares students to write argumentative essays. The two texts here are "Living in America: Challenges Facing New Immigrants and Refugees" edited by Katherine Garrett for the Robert Wood Johnson Foundation, and "Aria" by Richard Rodriguez.
- **Part Five** offers a selection of additional readings on the theme of crossing borders for practicing the reading process and for use in writing text-based paragraphs and essays.
- **Part Six** provides instruction on the most common grammar and punctuation errors that students tend to make.

Chapter and Casebook Features

Chapters and Casebooks include the following features:

- **Learning Objectives** Each chapter starts with a list of learning objectives that indicates the topics students will be learning about.
- **Warm Ups** Each casebook and chapter opens with a photo and related activity designed to help students start thinking about the chapter topics and connect them to their prior experiences. The chapter Warm Ups can be completed online in the Crossroads 2/e MySkillsLab/eText book-specific module.
- **Information Literacy Sections** Information skills such as evaluating and integrating outside sources and using research to build background knowledge are critical to successful reading and writing. Throughout the text, there are sections on different aspects of information literacy and how they relate to chapter content.
- **Critical Thinking Sections** Reading and writing often call for higher-level thinking such as synthesis, evaluation, and reflection, and these skills are explored in relation to chapter content in many chapters.
- **Demonstrations** Nearly every step in the reading and writing process is illustrated with a demonstration of how a student has addressed specific reading and writing tasks. These serve as models for students as they learn and practice reading and writing techniques.
- **Practices** Instruction in each step in the reading and writing process is usually illustrated by a Demonstration immediately followed by an exercise, allowing students to practice the step and the skills inherent in it.

MySkillsLab

- **Chapter Quick Check** Each chapter ends with a review of the major concepts of the chapter in a question and answer format organized around the learning objectives listed on the opening page.
- **Introductions to Casebooks** Each casebook begins with an introduction to the focused theme of crossing a border and to the type of evidence or purpose of the reading and writing in the casebook.
- **Reading Assignment Flexibility** Each casebook provides two reading selections for demonstration and practice of reading and writing processes. However, instructors or students themselves can also select other or additional readings from thematic lists provided in the casebook introductions, which are available in Part Five, or from other relevant sources.
- **Students can test their understanding of chapter content right in MySkillsLab!** The *Crossroads*, 2/e, MySkillsLab/eText book-specific module contains end-of-chapter assessments that flow directly into the MySkillsLab instructor Gradebook.

MySkillsLab

Book-Specific Ancillaries

Crossroads is supported by a series of innovative teaching and learning supplements.

- The **Annotated Instructor's Edition** (ISBN 0-321-95573-0) is identical to the student text, but it includes answers printed directly on the pages where exercises appear.
- The downloadable **Instructor's Resource Manual** (ISBN 0-321-96208-7) includes teaching strategies, summaries of readings and suggested classroom activities to accompany the text. A separate **Answer Key** (ISBN 0-321-96050-5) is also available.
- A set of **PowerPoint slides** (ISBN 0-321-96059-9) accompanies the book and provides detailed instruction for each chapter.

Additional Resources

Pearson is pleased to offer a variety of support materials to help make teaching writing and reading easier for teachers and to help students excel in their coursework. Many of our student supplements are available free or at a greatly reduced price when packaged with Crossroads, 2/e. Visit www.pearsonhighereducation.com, contact your local Pearson sales representative, or review a detailed listing of the full supplements package in the Instructor's Resource Manual for more information.

MySkillsLab

MySkillsLab

MySkillsLab is where practice, application, and demonstration meet to improve reading and writing!

Efficiently blending the market-leading and proven practice from MyWritingLab and MyReadingLab into a single application, MySkillsLabs offers a wealth of practice opportunities and extensive progress tracking for combined reading-writing courses.

What makes the practice, application, and demonstration in MySkillsLab more effective?

- **Reading** MySkillsLab improves students' mastery of 26 reading skills across four levels of difficulty via mastery-based skill practice, and improves students' reading levels with the Lexile® framework (www.Lexile.com) to measure both reader ability and text difficulty on the same scale and pair students with readings within their Lexile range.

- **Writing** MySkillsLab offers skill remediation in grammar and punctuation, paragraph development, essay development, and research, and improves students' overall writing through automatic scoring by Pearson's proven Intelligent Essay Assessor (IEA).

- **The *Crossroads*, 2/e, eText and MSL module** The *Crossroads* eText is accessed through the *Crossroads*, 2/e, MySkillsLab/eText course. Students now have the eText at their fingertips while completing the various exercises and activities in MySkillsLab, including the assets and writing assignments in the new book-specific module within the *Crossroads*, 2e, MySkillsLab/eText course.

Authors' Acknowledgments

The editorial staff at Pearson Education was invaluable and fabulous to work with. We especially appreciate the help we received from our original acquisitions editor, Kate Edwards, and her assistant, Lindsey Allen. We would like to thank Nancy Blaine, our acquisitions editor for the second edition; Eric Stano, Editor-in-Chief, Developmental Reading and Writing, for his excellent oversight of the revision process; and Matthew Wright, Executive Editor, Developmental English, for his deep commitment to *Crossroads'* approach.

Gillian Cook, our development editor, receives our deep, heartfelt gratitude and admiration for guiding revisions for the second edition. We would also like to thank assistant editor Jamie Fortner for editing chapters, providing support, and managing the numerous tasks associated with revision, and editorial assistant Shannon Kobran for her invaluable assistance in preparing our manuscript for production. In addition, we would like to thank the staff at Integra for their excellent help during the production process.

Finally, we want to thank the following reviewers who read and commented on the manuscript; their feedback was essential:

Sylvia Boyd, Phillips CC of the University of Arkansas – Stuttgart; Joan Brickner, MSCTC (MN); Annemarie Chiarini, CC of Baltimore County; Stephanie Erin Denney, City College of San Francisco; Jon Drinnon, Merritt College; Ann Elliott, Merritt College; Aide Escamilla, Southwest Texas Junior College; Sonja Groves, Portland CC (OR); Ann Marshall, Weatherford College; Adriana Medina, University of North Carolina—Charlotte; Linda Moore, Skagit Valley College; Ellen Olmstead, Montgomery College; Pat Phillips, Highline CC; Julie Peluso Quinn, Northern Virginia CC; Christine Proctor, St. Louis CC—Merrimac; Nancy M. Risch, Caldwell CC; Wendy Swyt, Highline CC; Gina Teel, SEARK; Kathy Tyndall, Wake Tech CC; and Lori Vail, Green River CC.

Pam's Acknowledgments

I am very grateful to my family, Becky and Spencer, for their loving support, serious sacrifice, and excellent humor throughout the *Crossroads* adventure. Big thanks go to all the students I've taught over 30 years: they teach me as much as I teach them, sometimes more. Thanks go especially to the students in my English 090/Study Skills 100 classes at Shoreline Community College who use and critique *Crossroads* every quarter. Thanks to my colleagues: Laurie Kimpton-Lorence who helped shape the Shoreline developmental English philosophy underlying this text; Dutch Henry for his leadership at the college, state and national levels; and way too many others to name. To all the faculty, staff, and students at Shoreline: thank you for being my community. The most profound thanks go to Julie O'Donnell Moore: I am grateful to you for inviting me into this project and for your inspiration, insight, grace, creativity, productivity, and unerring fashion sense.

Julie's Acknowledgments

I'd like to thank my husband who gave up evenings, weekends, and breaks to let me write without distractions and who offered his editorial advice and support throughout the process. I'd also like to extend a huge thank you to my coauthor, Pam Dusenberry, who took a leap of faith to write the first edition of this book with me and whose tenacity and patience carried us through the second edition. Special thanks go to those who helped to inspire this book and its revision: Dutch Henry, with whom I team-taught my first developmental learning community and who helped me understand the importance of this learning experience for students; Lisa Hoonan-Trujillo, who worked with me to create developmental coordinated studies classes at Green River Community College; and Jill Alcorn, who team-taught with me a first accelerated class at Green River Community College. I'd also like to thank all of the students who have participated in the developmental coordinated studies classes I've taught at Green River Community College over the last 15 years, and who helped me to understand what helped them learn to be college-level readers and writers. Special thanks also go to two colleagues who inspired and encouraged me at every step, Marcie Sims and Jennifer Whetham. Finally, I would like to extend appreciation to Green River Community College and the English Department, who gave me the freedom to explore an integrated and accelerated approach to precollege reading and writing.

Pam Dusenberry
Julie O'Donnell Moore

Part One

Reading and Writing Different Types of Text

Introduction to Part One

Reading and writing are two of the most important tools you have for learning in college, and Part One of this book explains steps and techniques for reading and writing like an expert. It also explains the different styles of organizing information that you will find in college texts and will use in your college writing. By the end of Part One, you should have a strong foundation from which to read and write a variety of college materials. You will then apply your reading and writing skills more deeply to the focused themes in Parts Two through Four.

Chapters 1 and 2

The first chapter teaches a process for reading college-level materials. We then ask you to compare that to a process you can use to write paragraphs and essays for college, which is presented in the second chapter. While some steps in the reading and writing processes differ, you will find many similarities between what you do to read well and what you do to write effectively for college.

Chapters 3 and 4

Chapter 3 explains how to build paragraphs and essays for college. Chapter 4 identifies different types of organization for paragraphs and essays. For example, you will learn the differences between a text that compares and contrasts two things and one that analyzes one topic. This will help you to read texts that are organized in various patterns and to structure your writing to best fit the topic you are addressing.

Getting to Know the Academic Reading Process

LEARNING OBJECTIVES

In this chapter, you will learn to . . .

1   Understand the purposes of an academic reading process.

2   Preview before you read.

3   Read actively.

4   Consolidate your comprehension.

5   Practice the nine steps in a complete academic reading process.

Warm Up

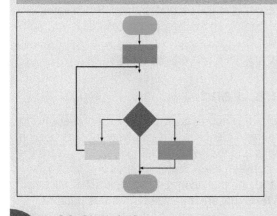

DIRECTIONS: Look at the picture. Then answer the following questions.

- How does the picture reflect a process or steps one takes to complete a task?
- Give an example of a time in life when you followed a process to get better at something.

MySkillsLab
Complete the Warm Up at
www.myskillslab.com

Introduction to the Academic Reading Process

Learning Objective 1
Understand the purposes of an academic reading process.

Think about a time that you learned something new. It could be playing a sport, learning to cook a new dish, or learning how to fix something mechanical. As you reflect, think about how part of learning to do this well included learning to follow a process. Whether you consulted an expert or coach to help you learn the process or whether you figured this out on your own, chances are good that your ability to do the task involved certain steps. As you grew in ability level, you might have realized how to combine parts of the process, and you might have gotten quicker at realizing what situations called for some steps rather than others, but the process—the steps—remained important no matter what.

Academic reading is similar: it also involves a process that can help you grow in your ability to read any type of college text well. As with many processes, the academic reading process includes a beginning, middle, and end. A comparison to exercising can serve as an illustration. Let us imagine that you were training for a 200-mile bike race from Seattle, WA, to Portland, OR. Each day you hit the road and increased your mileage, working to ride 80 miles a day for several days in a row prior to the big race. As you trained each day, you followed a process to help your body survive the rigors of training. You made sure to warm up for 10 minutes on your bike before stopping and doing some stretching, so your muscles were ready for the work ahead. You then dove into the ride, attacking hills and doing some flat work, so you exercised a variety of muscles. Finally, you cooled down with some lighter riding before ending with a final stretch of your muscles. Of course, throughout, you were sure to stay hydrated and eat regularly.

How is this similar to reading? Like bicycling, reading also involves a warm-up phase. During this part of the reading process, you prepare your mind for the work ahead of reading the text. For example, you might skim the text for key ideas, do some research on the topic to familiarize yourself with it, make sure you understand why you are reading and what you need to get out of the reading, and check your attitude about the reading assignment and topic. Reading also has a middle phase. Like the cyclist who had to train hard on hills and flats to build muscle, a reader also needs to dive into the reading and take certain steps like annotating, highlighting, checking vocabulary, and so on to ensure understanding of the text. Finally, just as the cyclist had to cool down, a reader needs to take final steps after reading a text. During this stage, a reader might check understanding by writing a summary or reflecting on feelings about the reading itself or the process of reading.

This chapter will introduce you to the reading process and help you see how it works. To practice the steps, you will use an essay by Frederick Douglass, "Learning to Read and Write," which you can find at the end of this part (p. 73). You will then spend the remainder of the term practicing this process on a variety of types of texts to gain mastery of it. We hope that by the class's end, you will be confident in applying this reading process to any text you read for college.

Academic Reading Process Phase One: Preview the Reading

Learning Objective 2
Preview before you read.

Author Julie Moore shares her experiences as a college student:

When I started college, I had not been taught a process for reading. I thought I would just open the text and start reading. Doing this had worked okay through high school, and I figured it would continue to work in college. Then I took a British Literature class and realized the error of my thinking. An instructor assigned *Beowulf*, a rather lengthy text that used older forms of English than I was used to reading. It was spring and the weather was nice, so I decided to procrastinate and put off the reading until 20 minutes before class. After all, a quick skim should do it, right? Wrong! I opened the text and started reading, quickly discovering my mistake. After 4–5 pages, I decided to look ahead to see how much more I had to read. It was then that I realized the text was over

20 pages long. There was no way I could finish in time, let alone understand what I had read. That day I learned a valuable lesson: preview the text, so you know how to plan for an effective reading of it.

There are a variety of things you can do to preview a text. Here are the steps that we suggest.

STEP 1: Get to Know the Text

To get a sense of what a reading is about—its main point and purpose—look over the whole text quickly, reading a few significant parts.

Scan the Reading

At this stage, your purpose is to get a sense of the whole text by briefly scanning it. When you **scan**, you look over the text quickly, reading a few words here and there so you get a feel for the topic, writing style and language, length, structure, and so on. Looking for the following information can help you to do this:

- **Title:** Look at the title to determine the topic and opinion of the text.
- **Author:** Find the author of the text. If there is information provided about the author, read it, as it will give you clues about the text he or she wrote.
- **Length:** Flip through the reading to assess its length.
- **Visual cues:** Look through the text, paying attention to bold headings, pictures, vocabulary words, and other features. Learn about the topic of the text through these visual cues.
- **Key words:** Run a finger down the middle of the page and let your eye pick up on words that stand out. This will give you some ideas about the topic of the reading.
- **Structure and organization:** Look at the structure of the text and the order in which ideas are presented. This will help you know how the information will be conveyed as well as how to take notes on the reading.

Skim the Reading

Skimming is quickly reading some of the words but not all of them. You are looking for main ideas in the text. The following steps can help you to do this:

- *Read the first and last paragraphs of the text as well as one or two key paragraphs in the middle.* This can give you a feel for the topic, tone, purpose, and structure of the text.
- *Read the first and last sentences of each paragraph in the text.* Often first sentences state main ideas and final sentences state concluding thoughts, so these can help you learn a lot about a text overall.

Information Literacy: Research Key Words

Once you have scanned and skimmed the text, you can deepen your understanding of the text's topic and better prepare yourself to read about it by learning more about the **key words** (repeated words related to the topic) you encountered. Select 3–4 key words that came up in the title, headings, and paragraphs with which you are not already familiar, and put them into a Google search or work with a librarian to find sources about them. You may find videos, pictures, maps, dictionary definitions, discussions, or arguments about the topics. These can provide background information that will help you better understand and remember the reading as well as enjoy it.

Information Literacy: Evaluate Sources

As you research your topic and prepare to read about it, be mindful of the quality of sources you find; not everything you find on the Internet is reliable. Therefore, it pays to be a careful consumer of information. Here are some questions you want to keep in mind when you research. We call them the **CRAAP** Test because we do not want you to end up with sources that are "CRAAP"; we want you to find quality and reliable information.

The CRAAP Test

To evaluate sources, ask the following questions about their *currency, relevance, authority, accuracy,* and *purpose*:

Currency: The timeliness of the information.
- When was the information published or posted?
- Has the information been revised or updated?
- If a website, are the links functional?

Relevance: The usefulness of the information for your needs.
- Does the information relate to your topic or answer your question?
- Who is the intended audience?
- Is the information at an appropriate level (i.e., not too elementary or advanced for your needs)?

Authority: The source of the information.
- Who is the author/publisher/source/sponsor?
- What are the author's credentials or organizational affiliations?
- Is the author qualified to write on the topic?
- Is there contact information, such as a publisher or email address?
- If on the web, does the URL reveal anything about the author or source (for example, *.com* indicates the site is commercial and designed to make a profit; *.edu* indicates the site is sponsored by a college or university, so the information is probably reliable; *.gov* means the information is posted by the government and facts and statistics should be accurate; and *.org* refers to an organization, often a nonprofit, which may or may not be biased)?

Accuracy: The reliability, truthfulness, and correctness of the content.
- Where does the information come from?
- Is the information supported by evidence?
- Can you verify any of the information in another source or from personal knowledge?
- Does the language or tone seem unbiased and free of emotion?
- Are there spelling, grammar, or typographical errors?

Purpose: The reason the information exists.
- What is the purpose of the information? Is it to inform, teach, sell, entertain, or persuade?
- Do the authors/sponsors make their intentions or purpose clear?
- Is the information fact, opinion, or propaganda?
- Does the point of view appear objective and impartial?
- Are there political, ideological, cultural, religious, institutional, or personal biases?

Demonstration   Getting to Know the Text

Here is an example of a student's answers to the previewing questions discussed on page 5 as they apply to this chapter. Use the example to help you answer the questions for Frederick Douglass's essay "Learning to Read and Write" in Practice 1.1.

1. **What does the title tell me?** This chapter will help me learn how to read better. Since it says "Academic Reading," it makes me think that there might be something different about reading for college.

2. **Who are the authors?** Pam Dusenberry and Julie Moore. I decided to use the information literacy step and look them up online. Pam Dusenberry teaches English for Shoreline Community College in Seattle, WA, and Julie Moore teaches English at Green River Community College in Auburn, WA. It sounds like they have some experience teaching about what this textbook is focusing on, which is great!

3. **What do the headings tell me?** The headings outline the different parts of the reading process and the various steps that I need to follow to be a stronger reader.

4. **What does the introduction tell me?** The introduction compares reading to learning new things as well as to a process a person goes through when exercising. It helps me to see that reading for college has different phases. These phases are familiar to me from cooking and playing sports.

5. **How are the ideas structured in this text?** The ideas are structured in order of the process. They are sequential. There are also places for me to practice what I am learning by doing exercises.

Practice 1.1   Getting to Know the Text

DIRECTIONS: Now you try answering the previewing questions for Frederick Douglass's essay "Learning to Read and Write" on page 73. Remember that you are only previewing, so do not start reading the full text yet. When you are done, you might want to compare your answers with those of other students in a small group discussion so you can learn with others about this text.

- **Look at the title.** Then write down what it tells you about the text's topic and focus.
- **Do research on the author and write down what you find out.** When did he live? What did he believe? What experiences were central to his life? *Hint! Remember to use the CRAAP test when doing research.*
- **Skim the text and write down what topic or topics the text is focusing on.** Also write down key words that seem central to the meaning of the text.
- **Choose 2–3 key words and do some research on them.** Write down what you learn about these words. *Hint! Remember to use the CRAAP test when doing research.*
- **Scan the reading and write down what you learn about the structure of the text.** How are ideas organized?

STEP 2: Check Your Attitude and Set Your Purpose

Our attitudes, or emotional states, seriously affect our ability to understand and remember. If you begin reading a story for a literature class or a chapter for chemistry with a negative attitude, thinking that the material will be boring, poorly written, or just flat out stupid, then you will get much less from it. On the other hand, if you are interested in or curious about the material and see its connection to your learning, you will understand and retain more of the ideas it offers. If you make your reason or purpose clear for doing the reading, it will usually be a better experience.

The following are some suggestions for finding a positive attitude and setting a clear purpose for reading.

Finding a Positive Attitude and Setting a Purpose for Reading

- **Relate the topic to your life.** You may do this by relating it to something you are already interested in or by relating it to a goal you have for yourself.
- **Clarify your purpose for reading the text.** Look over the course materials and understand how the reading connects to the course topic, themes, other readings, activities, assignments, and requirements.
- **Research the topic and learn more about it.** Sometimes we find a topic uninteresting because we do not know much about it. Research can help us learn how it is interesting and make us eager to know more.

Demonstration   Checking Attitude and Setting Purpose

Here is an example of a student's response to the questions on attitude and purpose as they relate to this chapter. Use these answers to help you answer the same questions for Frederick Douglass's essay "Learning to Read and Write" in Practice 1.2.

1. <u>Describe your attitude toward this reading.</u> My attitude is positive but nervous. I don't know if I will understand all this information. I also feel kind of hopeful that this reading process will help me earn better grades in my classes.

2. <u>Describe your purpose for reading.</u> The reason I am reading this chapter is because my teacher assigned it, and I plan to do all of my assignments on time. I also struggle with forgetting what I read, so maybe this will help me to remember what I read.

Practice 1.2   Checking Attitude and Setting Purpose

DIRECTIONS: Think about your brief preview of the article by Frederick Douglass titled "Learning to Read and Write." Check your attitude toward reading this selection, and write about it. Then describe your purpose for reading this selection. When you are done, consider comparing your comments with others in the class to learn how they are approaching the text.

STEP 3: Connect Experience and Background Knowledge with the Text

Imagine that you have just arrived home from a long day of work and classes. You are tired and just want to eat something and get a moment's rest before hitting the homework. You hang up your coat and head to the kitchen, but the hooks on the coat rack have fallen off. Your coat falls to the floor with a crash. Disheartened, you add that to your "to do" list: Fix the coat rack. Reading new information and having no hook upon which to put it in your brain is like this situation with the coat rack. The new information you learn will try to hook to something, but the hooks will be missing and the information will fall away, causing you to not remember what you learned. Activating background knowledge and prior experience on the text's topic will help you create these hooks in your brain, so the new information can stick to something and you can remember it.

To connect to the readings, do the following:

- Reflect on what you already know about the topic or author.
- Research the topic or author online.
- Ask others what they know about the topic or author.

Demonstration   Connecting with the Text

Following is an example of a student's response to the questions about background information as they relate to this chapter. Use this example to help you answer the questions for the Frederick Douglass essay in Practice 1.3.

1. **How is my experience related to this chapter?** My experiences with reading for school haven't been too positive. I enjoyed reading in grade school, but I hated the boring textbook assignments in HS. In 10th grade, we had to write a report every week on something from our history book. I usually got bad grades on those. Now I'm in college and have to take a pre-college reading class. It seems like I might be getting worse at reading the higher I go in my education! I like reading, though. I read novels all of the time.

2. **What background knowledge do I have?** I know how to read for pleasure, but it seems like this is different than reading for college. Maybe there is some crossover between the two? I often look through a new novel I'm going to read to see how long it is, and I always read the stuff on the cover and the first few pages before I buy it to see if I'll like it. This is kind of like previewing, I think.

Practice 1.3   Connecting with the Text

DIRECTIONS: Answer the following questions about Frederick Douglass's text. When you are done, you can share your ideas with others in class to get more ideas for how to connect to the text.

- How might my experience relate to Douglass's experience?
- What background knowledge do I have about Douglass or his story?

Academic Reading Process Phase Two: While Reading

Learning Objective 3
Read actively.

You have skimmed, scanned, researched, and prepared. Now it is time to dive in and start reading the full text! As you enter Phase Two of the academic reading process, remember that your purpose is to retain the information in the text so you can use it later for tests, papers, presentations, and even in your life outside of college. In order to help make this happen, your reading may slow down a bit. Do not worry about this as it is a sign you are reading more deeply. Expert readers know that good reading is not necessarily fast, but it is effective. Slowing down, then, is a sign that you are becoming a more expert reader.

For this section, we have given you several steps. These may be **recursive**, meaning that you may go back and forth between them as you read. Do not feel like you have to use the steps in sequential order as you may find vocabulary in the process of taking notes, or you may find an interesting idea while you look up vocabulary. It is okay if these next steps get combined as long as you do each of them as you read.

STEP 4: Write Down and Define Vocabulary

You must understand the words an author uses in order to comprehend his or her meaning. As vocabulary is the basis of knowledge and learning, it can be really frustrating to read a text that contains lots of unknown words. Therefore, it is very important that you recognize when you do not understand an important word or concept and take steps to learn its meaning.

Understanding vocabulary is also related to background information and information literacy. When you know a lot about a subject, you will probably understand the vocabulary. But when you lack background, you will encounter more words you do not know. Learning vocabulary builds the background that helps you comprehend what you are currently reading, and it helps you understand any reading you do later on that subject. Using information literacy by looking up words in online dictionaries or encyclopedias and researching topics online through videos and articles you explore can help you to develop a deeper understanding for words you are learning, allowing you to more fully comprehend them. To help you build vocabulary knowledge, do the following as you read:

- Identify and write down words you do not understand.
- Try to determine what the words mean by how they are used in the text.
- Look up words you do not know in a dictionary, encyclopedia, or with a librarian.
- Write down definitions in a vocabulary log or in the margins of the text you are reading.

Demonstration   **Writing Down and Defining Vocabulary**

The definitions of vocabulary words from the first part of this chapter that are listed below were taken from Merriam Webster's online dictionary. Use this as an example for your own vocabulary log for Frederick Douglass's essay in Practice 1.4.

hydrate: "To supply with ample fluid or moisture"

Beowulf: "A legendary Geatish warrior and hero of the old English poem Beowulf"

retain: "To keep in possession or use"

recursive: "Of, relating to, or constituting a process that can repeat itself indefinitely"

Practice 1.4   **Writing Down and Defining Vocabulary**

DIRECTIONS: As you read "Learning to Read and Write" by Frederick Douglass (p. 73), write down the words you do not understand and what you can tell about their meaning from how they are used in the sentence or paragraph. Then look up each one and write a definition for it.

STEP 5: Take Notes on Major Ideas and Important Details

Taking notes helps you comprehend the main points in a text. It also gives you a record to go back to after reading, so you can review the ideas in the text. In addition, it provides a quick cheat sheet that can be quite convenient for studying. Taking notes can keep you active and awake while you read by giving you something physical to do during the reading process.

Almost more important, though, is that taking notes makes you focus on what you are reading. You have to make decisions about what is important enough to write down; you do not want to write down too much. Making these decisions forces you to gain more from the text. One way to focus your notes is to write down the main idea and major supporting ideas in the text.

- **Main Idea:** The main idea is the overall topic of the text plus the author's opinion or stance on that topic. This may or may not be clearly stated.
- **Major Supporting Ideas:** Supporting information includes ideas and details. The ideas are the primary points that support the main idea. There may be only a few of these in the text. The details are the specifics about those ideas. There may be lots of details in a text. For your notes, focus on the ideas and not the details of the text you read.

There are many ways to take notes while you read. It is important to write notes in your own words, not just copy phrases or sentences directly from the material. Also, you can use abbreviations and symbols to make your note taking more efficient. Following are some note-taking techniques that we will illustrate throughout the chapters in this book.

Information Literacy: Avoiding Plagiarism When Taking Notes

Plagiarism is when a person does not give credit to the source of an idea or exact words taken from a text or online site. In your notes, you may occasionally want to copy a sentence exactly from what you are reading because the author says it so well. Also, such fabulous sentences could work as evidence in an essay or paragraph you might write. Whenever you take exact words out of a reading, *put those words inside quotation marks*. If you forget, then that sentence is plagiarized, even if *you* know the words are copied. Make it your habit always to put quotes around exact words taken from a reading and write down the details about the source they came from.

Note-Taking Techniques

- **Outlining:** Use an outline to record major and minor ideas in a text. This is the method we demonstrate in this chapter.
- **Annotating:** Use this in the margin of a reading to note major and minor points in the text. This technique is taught in Chapter 5.
- **Using Graphic Organizers:** A graphic organizer such as a "map" can help you organize major and minor ideas in a visual way. This approach is used in Chapters 5 and 8.
- **Formal Note Taking:** Use a formal note-taking technique such as Cornell Notes to record major and minor ideas. Look in Chapter 7 for instructions on using the Cornell method.

Demonstration   Taking Notes

Here is an example of notes in outline form based on this chapter. Use this as an example for your own notes on Frederick Douglass's essay in Practice 1.5.

Introduction/Academic Reading Process

In college we read to understand, learn, apply

   College reading is active reading

   Reading is a process with steps

   Reading process is like exercise

     1. Warm up before practicing something new

     2. Cool down after practicing

Phase One: Preview

   Step 1: Get to know the main point of the reading by skimming and scanning

   Step 2: Adjust my attitude to be positive and find a good reason for reading

   Step 3: Try to relate what I'm reading to what I already know or things that I've done in my life

Phase Two: While Reading

   Step 4: Write down the vocabulary words I don't understand and then write down their definitions

   Step 5: Take notes on main ideas and important details by outlining, annotating, using a graphic organizer, or using a formal format. Use my own words and don't write too much

Practice 1.5   Taking Notes

DIRECTIONS: As you read Frederick Douglass's essay "Learning to Read and Write," outline the process he goes through to learn to read and write, starting with his mistress's instruction and going through the instruction from those he encounters outside of his home. Then outline the pros and cons of his learning. What did he gain? What did he lose?

When you have finished your notes, share them with another student and/or use class discussion of this reading to check your understanding. Make additions or corrections to your notes as needed following discussion with others.

STEP 6: Record Your Thoughts and Reactions

Your own thoughts and reactions to the ideas in a reading are important: your ideas connect you to the reading and help you relate to and understand the author's meaning and intent. However, good readers are careful to separate their own ideas from the ideas of the author. Recording your own reactions and thinking in a separate place from notes on the reading helps you clearly separate what is actually in the reading from the ideas and feelings it generates in your mind. In addition, good readers pay attention to when they *do not* understand or are confused by an idea or detail, and they make a note of it.

Demonstration   Recording Your Thoughts and Reactions

Here is an example of a student's thoughts and reactions about this chapter. Use this as an example for writing your own thoughts and reactions to Frederick Douglass's essay in Practice 1.6.

- I never thought that the reading process was like other processes I use to do other things. In fact, I don't ever think I considered that most things actually follow a process and this process might be similar for different things I do. Interesting!
- I'm not sure I'm convinced that there is one process that will fit everyone's reading styles. Doesn't everyone read differently and need to do different things depending on their own style?
- The link between emotions and learning is interesting. It makes sense! Maybe this is why I do better in some classes than others. Maybe I'm more emotionally open to those subjects.
- I'm also feeling frustration right now because this chapter seems to have a lot of ideas in it and the steps seem like they will take a long time.

Practice 1.6   Recording Your Thoughts and Reactions

DIRECTIONS: As you read Douglass's essay "Learning to Read and Write" (p. 73), record the ideas in his text that seem confusing or interesting to you. Write them on a separate sheet of paper or in the margins of the essay next to the relevant passages. When you are done, share these with others in class to see how others reacted.

Academic Reading Process Phase Three: After You Read

Learning Objective 4
Consolidate your comprehension.

The first two phases of the reading process are vital to helping you read the full text to understand and retain the information in it, but the final phase of the reading process is crucial to enabling you to consolidate or solidify your understanding of the text's meaning, reflect on how it is important to you, and evaluate how you are growing as a reader. While it may be tempting to stop after Phase Two, resist that temptation! Here are some final steps that can help you complete the reading process with a strong finish.

STEP 7: Write a Summary

A **summary** is a condensed version of the original text in which you retell in your own words all of the most important ideas from a reading. Due to their condensed nature, summaries should focus on just the primary ideas and not the minor details included in the original text. While the length of summaries can vary, they are usually 1–2 paragraphs.

Summaries are important to write for a variety of reasons. First, they solidify your understanding of the reading by asking you to put into your own words what the author is saying as well as how the various parts of the reading relate to the larger, overall point. They also help you to check your understanding of the reading; if you cannot accurately summarize a text, it is likely that you do not understand it and need to return to the earlier phases of the reading process. Finally, summaries can be building blocks for essays and exams you write for college.

Information Literacy: Avoiding Plagiarism in Summaries

Remember that **plagiarism** is when a person does not give credit to the author of an idea or to his or her words copied from a text. In college, you need to tell whose idea or sentence you may use in your writing—even when you put the ideas in your own words. That is why you start summaries with the title and author of the text. If you do not include them, the summary appears to be your own ideas and thinking. This is considered plagiarism—stealing—in the academic world.

When you write a summary of a college reading, your professors expect you to use your own words or to put copied phrases or sentences inside quotation marks. Here is a checklist for writing a strong summary.

Checklist for Writing a Strong Summary

- **Find the author's thesis or main point.** An author's thesis or main point is the primary topic of the entire text *plus* his or her opinion or stance about that topic. To find this, ask these questions.
  - *What is the one overall topic that this text is talking about?*
  - *What message is it communicating or saying about that topic?*
  Use your reading process notes to help you here.
- **Find the main ideas the author uses to support or illustrate the thesis or purpose.** If you have taken good notes on the reading, you should have identified the major ideas. You also can look at the headings in the text (if the text has these)—headings often express main ideas.
- **Include the name of the author, title, and thesis/purpose statement of the reading in the first sentence.**
- **Restate briefly and accurately the main ideas in the text in the order they appear.** Make sure you are comprehensive and address all of the major points. Only quote a phrase or sentence if it is really important. Try to keep your overall summary to 1–2 paragraphs total.
- **Remember to stay objective.** Do not put your opinion or feelings into the summary.

Demonstration   Writing a Summary

Here is a student example of a summary of this chapter. Use this as an example for your own summary of Frederick Douglass's essay in Practice 1.7.

In Chapter 1 of Crossroads, the authors Julie Moore and Pam Dusenberry explain how college reading should follow a process with clear steps and activities. Reading for college must be active. The first phase of the reading process is previewing before you actually read. This involves looking over the whole thing, trying to see what it is all about, asking questions, and making sure you have a good attitude. The second phase is while you read, and it is important to pay attention. Taking notes while you read helps you understand and decide what's important to remember. Vocabulary words you don't understand should be looked up in a dictionary. You should pay attention to the thoughts that come into your head while you read, and write them down. The last phase is after you read, and you write a summary in a paragraph. Then, you write down how you felt about the reading. This is the reading process.

Practice 1.7   Writing a Summary

DIRECTIONS: Write a summary of Frederick Douglass's essay "Learning to Read and Write" (p. 73). Use the Checklist for Writing a Strong Summary to help you complete this step. When you are done, share it with other students to see what information they included in their summaries. Having a conversation about it can help you write better summaries in the future.

STEP 8: Respond to the Reading

The purpose of responding to a reading is to make an author's ideas your own by connecting them to your life or the ideas you hold. You can respond in a variety of ways such as the following:

- Choose an interesting or confusing idea you noted in Step 6, and write more about it. Why did it confuse you or interest you?
- Respond to the structure of the writing: how the ideas are organized.
- Respond to how the writer constructed sentences, the type of vocabulary used, or the tone or feeling of the writing.
- Write about the images the writing paints in your mind.

Critical Thinking: Analysis

Writing about how the ideas in one part of a text connect to ideas in another part of the text allows you to practice the aspect of critical thinking that involves **analysis**—examining the parts of a text to better understand the whole text. For example, you might write about how one scene at the beginning of a text connects to another scene later. Using analysis is a good way to respond to a reading.

Critical Thinking: Synthesis

Looking for relationships among the ideas within a course, or even between two different classes, deepens your understanding and ability to make use of your learning. It also allows you to **synthesize**, or combine, ideas from different texts to develop new ideas that contain elements from all of them. Synthesizing ideas from two course readings makes an excellent response.

Demonstration   Responding to the Reading

Use this student's response to the ideas in this chapter as an example for your own response to the ideas in Frederick Douglass's essay in Practice 1.8.

> I am going to respond by analyzing the structure of this chapter and how the ideas are organized. Organizing the reading process into three main phases with steps in each phase is helping me make sense out of what felt like chaos at first. When I usually sit down to read, I don't really know where to start. I've heard that there are strategies I can use to help me, but when friends have told me about these, the strategies always seem like a bunch of random tools that I don't know how to use. This chapter is helping me to put those tools into an order that I can understand and that makes sense. It's making me feel more excited to read because I feel like I might be able to be good at this! I also feel less overwhelmed. All I have to remember is that there are three main phases. If I can do a "before," a "during," and an "after," I will be a better reader. Yeah!

Practice 1.8   Responding to the Reading

DIRECTIONS: Write a response to Frederick Douglass's text on page 73.

STEP 9: Reflect on Your Reading Process

Did you know that your brain operates regularly with two different types of thinking? Critical-thinking scholars have studied this, and they say that we routinely use "Green Light Thinking" and "Red Light Thinking." **"Green Light Thinking"** is what allows us to function quickly and automatically. For example, we are driving and we see a green light, so we go. We do not stop to wonder why or if this is the best choice. We just move forward. While this type of thinking is crucial, it does not allow us to learn or make decisions based on best practices. That is the purpose of **"Red Light Thinking,"** the type of thinking that has us stop and ask ourselves if our choice is the best one, if what we are doing is right for us, and if we would do this again or make a different decision. "Red Light Thinking" is designed to help us grow and learn.

For this final step, we want you to do some "Red Light Thinking" about your process of reading. We want you to ask yourself what worked well about this reading process and what did not work as well—and why. This will help you monitor your own growth as a reader as well as help you make future decisions about your reading process based on what works for you.

Demonstration   Reflecting on Your Reading Process

Use this student's reflection about reading Chapter 1 as an example for your own reflection on your reading of Frederick Douglass's essay "Learning to Read and Write" in Practice 1.9.

1. **Which steps did you like the best? Which ones seemed most useful?** I have never used a process to read before—or if I did I didn't realize it. I usually just sit down and run my eyes over the page and give up when I get lost or bored. I am realizing that this probably isn't the best approach. This new reading process might really help me.

   I liked the online research step best. I found some YouTube videos that helped me to learn more about Frederick Douglass, and they helped me to stay interested in his story even when it was hard to understand him—lots of big words! I also didn't know much about slavery, so I searched the Internet and found some information about that, too. I liked how I found videos and pictures that helped me understand the reading better.

2. **Which steps were more difficult? Why?** The summary—definitely! It was much harder than I expected. I thought I had his main ideas, but when I compared my summary to Liam's, I realized I had missed a whole section of text. Whoops! I'm going to have to take better notes next time, so I am more ready to write the summary.

3. **What do you intend to keep the same about your reading process? Why?** I want to keep everything the same because I feel that I need more practice with the steps. Maybe as I get more practice I will have more to say here, but right now I'm still learning the process and I want to continue to get better at doing it.

4. **What would you like to change or adapt about your reading process? Why?** I'd like to get better at taking notes and summarizing, so I'll focus on those steps more next time.

Practice 1.9   Reflecting on Your Reading Process

DIRECTIONS: Reflect on the reading process you followed, using the exercises in this chapter, for reading "Learning to Read and Write" by answering the following questions.

- Which steps did you like the best? Which ones seemed most useful?
- Which steps were more difficult? Why?
- What do you intend to keep the same about your reading process? Why?
- What would you like to change or adapt about your reading process? Why?

The Academic Reading Process: Putting it Together

Learning Objective 5
Practice the nine steps in a complete academic reading process.

You have now practiced the steps of an active reading process. By separating out each step, you were able to see them individually, but as you read for college, you want to do all of these steps together for each text you read. Practicing all the steps will ensure that you fully comprehend your college reading assignments and that you can make use of your understanding on tests and in essays and other assignments.

We encourage you to keep a journal of these steps for each text you read in this class; we will refer to this as a *Reading Process Journal* throughout this book. Using this process and writing out all the steps every time you read for this class will improve your reading and provide you with lots of material to use when you write. We also suggest that you share your reading process steps with other students in your class. Talking with others about your reading helps you deepen your understanding of the reading and of your own reading process.

For future reference, the following is a template of the reading process steps. You can use this to complete your *Reading Process Journal* for your reading assignments in this class.

Reading Process Template

Phase One: Preview the Reading

1. **Get to know the text ...**
   - ☐ What do the title and author tell me?
   - ☐ What is the source of the reading, and when was it written?
   - ☐ If there are headings, what are they about?
   - ☐ Is there an introduction before the text begins? What is it about?
   - ☐ In what order are ideas presented? How is this text structured?

2. **Check your attitude and set your purpose ...**
   - ☐ How do I feel about the ideas I am encountering in this text?
   - ☐ What is my attitude toward this assignment?
   - ☐ What is my purpose for reading this assignment?

3. **Connect your experience and background knowledge with the text ...**
   - ☐ What experiences have I had that relate to the topic of the reading?
   - ☐ What do I know about this topic?

Phase Two: While Reading

4. **Write down and define vocabulary ...**
   - ☐ What words and phrases do I not understand?
   - ☐ What do these words seem to mean based on how they are used?
   - ☐ What are the dictionary definitions of these unknown words?

5. **Take notes on major ideas and important details; use one or more of the following methods ...**
   - ☐ Annotate (take notes in the margins of the text).
   - ☐ Make a map of the major points.
   - ☐ Take informal notes by writing main ideas and major details in your own phrases.
   - ☐ Use a formal strategy like the Cornell Method.

6. **Write down your thoughts and reactions ...**
   - ☐ What related thoughts and feelings go through my mind while I read this?

Phase Three: After You Read

7. **Write a summary ...**
   - ☐ Write a paragraph that begins with the thesis of the reading and continues in complete sentences to relay the most important points in the piece.

8. **Respond to the reading ...**
   - ☐ Write about your emotional reaction to *the ideas* in the text; or about confusing, exciting, or interesting ideas; or about a memory the text sparks.

9. **Reflect ...**
   - ☐ Think back over *your process* of reading this text. Write about what steps seemed most helpful or which caused difficulty; consider what you will do differently in the future.

Chapter Quick Check   MySkillsLab   Complete the mastery test for this chapter in MySkillsLab.

Use the following questions and answers to check your understanding of this chapter.

QUESTION	ANSWER
Learning Objective 1: Understand the purposes of an academic reading process. *Why is it important to follow a reading process?*	✔ It is important to follow a reading process because it allows you to more fully understand and remember what you read and successfully complete your reading assignments for college classes.
Learning Objective 2: Preview before you read. *What steps are included in the first phase of the reading process, "Preview the Reading," that help familiarize you with the text?*	The steps for previewing include . . . ✔ Skimming, scanning, looking at the title, or looking at headings in order to find out more about the content of the text. ✔ Identifying key words and researching them on the Internet. ✔ Using the CRAAP Test to make sure sources of information are reliable. ✔ Checking your attitude about reading the text. ✔ Setting your purpose for reading the text. ✔ Activating your background knowledge by thinking about what you already know about the topic(s) in the text.
Learning Objective 3: Read actively. *What steps are included in the second phase of the reading process, "While Reading," that help you fully understand academic texts?*	The steps for Phase Two, while reading, include . . . ✔ Writing down vocabulary words that you do not understand and looking them up in a dictionary. ✔ Taking notes about main ideas in the text. ✔ Writing down interesting or confusing ideas from the reading. ✔ Discussing the reading with your peers.
Learning Objective 4: Consolidate your comprehension. *What steps are included in the third phase of the reading process, "After You Read," that help you consolidate your understanding?*	You can consolidate your understanding by . . . ✔ Writing a summary of the main ideas in the reading. ✔ Responding to the content in the reading, including your emotional reaction. ✔ Reflecting on the effectiveness of your reading process.
Learning Objective 5: Practice the nine steps in a complete academic reading process. *Why is it important to practice all nine steps of the academic reading process?*	It is important to practice the steps of the reading process . . . ✔ To fully understand college reading assignments. ✔ To be able to use knowledge from college reading on tests and in written assignments.

Getting to Know the Academic Writing Process

2

LEARNING OBJECTIVES

In this chapter, you will learn to . . .

1   Understand the purposes and steps of the academic writing process.
2   Prewrite to generate, develop, and organize ideas and details.
3   Draft a paragraph.
4   Revise and polish your writing.

Warm Up

MySkillsLab
Complete the Warm Up at
www.myskillslab.com

DIRECTIONS: Look at the picture and answer the following questions.

- During an average week, what sorts of things do you write? For example, do you text? Write e-mails? Write in a personal journal? Write essays for school? Other?

- Now describe your process for writing those texts. What is involved? For example, does it require that you first read something so you can respond to it? Do you draft and polish what you write, or do you write just one draft? Do you have others look at your writing to give you feedback on it? Other?

- Is your writing process the same for all things you write, or does it differ depending on the writing task? Explain.

- Finally, talk about the time of day you prefer to write. Do you write at a certain time of day? Throughout the day? Does this depend on the type of writing you are doing? Explain.

Why Do I Need to Know About the Academic Writing Process?

Learning Objective 1
Understand the purposes and steps of the academic writing process.

Author Julie Moore shares her experiences as a college student:

In my freshman year of college, I was taking English 101, College Writing. When the first paper was assigned, I decided to follow my routine from high school, which was to wait until the night before the paper was due, sit in a comfortable spot, and wait for inspiration to come. I was pretty sure that all good writing came from a muse—some spirit-like being who came upon you and filled you with great words for your paper. Unfortunately,

19

I waited until 3 A.M. that night, sitting on a well-worn, orange couch in my college dorm, scribbling on my paper and trying not to panic before finally coming to the conclusion that, unless a miracle happened, this paper was not going to get done. It was then that I realized I needed to learn more about how to put together a paper. I needed to have more tools to work with, especially for those times that my usual process did not work.

Having different ways to approach writing is like knowing multiple routes you can use to get to a certain destination; if one road is blocked by an accident, you are not stuck because you know of another route you can take to get there. My problem with that paper in my freshman writing class was that I did not know of any other routes to take to finish the assignment. I hit a wall and did not know where to go from there. If you have ever experienced a time where you could not write or a writing assignment was difficult for you, think about how using a process, a series of steps and strategies, can be helpful. The process in this chapter is meant to provide you with those strategies that you can use to write successfully for college.

Most college writing assignments ask you to use information you have gained in the course—through lectures and reading. In the writing process taught in this chapter, you will practice writing about your own experience as well as about Frederick Douglass's in "Learning to Read and Write." You will want to read this now if you have not already (see p. 73).

What Is the Academic Writing Process?

Just as a structured reading process helps you be a stronger reader, an academic writing process helps you be a stronger writer. Writers should allow themselves time to warm up to the ideas about which they will write. Then, after writing a first draft, they should review that writing to see how to make it better for the final draft they will submit to the instructor. Following a process allows the mind to perform to its best ability. It sets you up to succeed.

The following are the main phases and steps in the writing process. You may notice a similarity between these steps and those in the last chapter on the reading process. The processes are similar—all learning involves a warm-up phase, a practice phase, and a cool-down or reflection phase. Reading and writing processes are also different from each other, too. Reading is about taking in new ideas and others' experiences while writing is about putting out ideas and experiences. They are two sides of a coin.

To introduce you to the writing process, this chapter demonstrates the process for writing a paragraph. Chapters 7, 10 and 13 demonstrate a writing process for composing different types of essays.

Academic Writing Process Phase One: Prewrite

Learning Objective 2
Prewrite to generate, develop, and organize ideas and details.

Just as you take certain steps to prepare to read, you also take certain steps to prepare to write. Both pre-reading and pre-writing are the foundations for gaining meaning from reading and expressing meaning in writing. The steps in this first phase of the writing process include the following:

- Analyze the assignment.
- Generate ideas.
- Focus your topic.
- Develop your ideas.
- Organize your ideas.

STEP 1: Analyze the Assignment

The first step in preparing to write a paragraph or essay is to look closely at your writing assignment.

Practice 2.1   Analyzing the Assignment

DIRECTIONS: Read the paragraph assignment below and then answer the questions that follow. The narrative by Frederick Douglass, "Learning to Read and Write," that is used throughout this chapter can be found on page 73.

Paragraph Assignment

PURPOSES Two purposes of this assignment are to learn how to write a paragraph for an academic audience and to reflect on why you want to improve your reading skills in this class. An additional and important purpose is to write about the experience of an author, in this case Frederick Douglass in "Learning to Read and Write."

ASSIGNMENT For this assignment, you will write two paragraphs of 10 or more sentences each. One paragraph should focus on your own experience as a reader and why it is significant to you. The second paragraph will focus on the reading experience of Frederick Douglass in his narrative "Learning to Read and Write." Each paragraph should have the following components of strong paragraph structure:

- Include a clear topic sentence that provides a focused point about how reading has impacted or been significant to the life of the reader.
- Support your topic sentence with ideas and details that illustrate the idea expressed in your topic sentence.
- End your paragraph with a sentence or two explaining your evidence; write how your ideas and details support your topic sentence.
- Write your paragraph for an audience of people you know but who are not in this class.
- Edit your writing.

Critically Reading the Assignment

1. What is the purpose, goal, or objective of this assignment?
2. Who is the intended audience for this writing?
3. What is the central topic you will need to write about?
4. Can you imagine meaningful things to say about this topic?
5. What information are you supposed to use as support in this paper?
6. What organizational structure will you need to use for this paper?
7. How do you feel about responding to this assignment (eager and ready, afraid, unsure)?
8. What questions do you have about this assignment?

STEP 2: Generate Ideas

In this step, you are trying to discover what you have to say about a given topic. During this part of the writing process, it is best to let all ideas out and write them down—even the stupid ones—because often the best idea comes right after a bad one. The frame of mind that allows ideas to flow is not critical and judgmental; rather it is creative and accepting. You may be tempted to find an easy idea or one that does not excite you but will "do." Resist this urge. Find your best idea that excites you. It will help you produce a strong paper that you enjoy writing.

Also keep in mind that finding a topic based on your own experiences is often easier than finding a topic from a text like Douglass's. When you are generating topics from a text, you have the added challenge of comprehending the text. This is where close reading is important. If you find that you do not understand a text well enough to write about it, return to the reading steps outlined in the first chapter to boost your comprehension. If you have carefully read the text and followed a reading process, then review your notes and responses to stimulate your memory of its ideas and details.

Brainstorming Techniques

You can use many methods to generate ideas, and all of them should be done quickly and without judgment. When you are brainstorming, try to let go of concerns about spelling, correctness, perfect wording, and how ideas will be supported in your writing. Just write fast, letting your mind think of whatever it wants and getting it down on paper.

- **List:** Write a list of phrases based on the topic from your assignment. Ten items on your list is a good goal, but you can aim for more, twenty or even thirty. You can see an example of listing in the demonstration that follows.
- **Cluster:** Start with your assignment topic circled in the middle of a page. Next, branch ideas off the central circle—you can enclose those in circles, too. You can show relationships among your ideas by using lines to connect them (see p. 198 for an example).
- **Freewrite:** This is like listing, only you write sentences instead of phrases. You can freewrite on a computer or on paper. Put your topic at the top of the page, then write what comes into your mind. Do not stop even if your mind goes blank—write that down, too. Freewrite for five minutes or longer and see what flows out. Usually freewriting results in some good ideas—ones you did not even know you had—and even sentences you can use later in your draft.
- **Map:** More structured than a cluster, a map helps you plot ideas and details in a timeline or diagram. For a good example, see page 88 in Chapter 5.
- **Create and answer questions:** Here is a list of ten questions that you can answer by listing or freewriting. Almost always they will result in ideas or details to use in your writing.

    1. What do I love about this topic?
    2. What irritates me about it?
    3. What are the "what, where, when, why, and how" of this topic?
    4. What sensory details (sight, sound, touch, smell, taste) arise from this topic?
    5. What stereotypes arise around this topic, and how can I be more open-minded about it?
    6. What group or category does this topic belong to?
    7. What similarities and differences arise when comparing or contrasting this topic with something?
    8. What audience might be interested in reading about this topic?
    9. What other points of view are there about this topic that differ from mine?
    10. What movie or song or book does this topic remind me of, and why?

As you experiment with these different brainstorming methods, see what ones work best for you. Then, use them regularly.

Demonstration   Listing to Generate Ideas About Personal Experience

Here is an example of part of student writer Kathy's list of how reading impacted her life.

Gained more knowledge about how to be a better parent
Able to earn high enough grades to get into college
Able to model reading to my children
Realized reading could help me understand other times and places
Science fiction helps me see how our world could be different

Practice 2.2   Listing to Generate Ideas *About Your Own Experience*

DIRECTIONS: Make a list of all of the ways that reading has been significant or made an impact on your life.

Demonstration Listing to Generate Ideas About a Text

Here are two ways Douglass's life was impacted by learning to read that Kathy learned from reading "Learning to Read and Write."

Learned about aspects of slavery he wasn't aware of before

Learned that there were abolitionists who were fighting against slavery

Practice 2.3 Listing to Generate *Your Ideas About Douglass's Text*

DIRECTIONS: Add several more items to the list we started above that identify additional ways that Douglass's life was impacted by being able to read.

STEP 3: Focus Your Topic

During this stage, you draw from the ideas you generated and narrow them down to one key focus for your writing. Narrowing may involve a few steps which could include choosing one topic out of several you brainstormed, checking to see that it is focused enough, and developing a sentence that clearly states this focus. This sentence can later form your topic sentence (for a paragraph) or a thesis statement (for an essay).

Finding a Focus

One way you can narrow a longer list of ideas into just one that you want to focus on in your writing is to freewrite. This allows you to explore the top 2–3 topics you initially listed, as well as to choose your favorite topic overall. Once you complete your freewriting, ask these questions:

1. What is my favorite idea—what excites me?
2. What idea can I best develop with supporting examples?
3. Will my focus allow me to meet the needs of this assignment?
4. Is my idea narrow enough for this assignment but broad enough to give me enough to say about it?
5. Do I have ideas that are good but could be saved for another assignment in this or another class?

Demonstration Finding a Focus Using Personal Experience

Kathy freewrote about her experiences with reading and then answered the questions listed above in order to narrow her topic to one idea.

Reading has impacted me in many ways, but the one I feel is most significant is being able to model reading and teach my children to be strong readers. My parents never read to me when I was a child, and I think that is partly why I struggled with reading in school. It makes me feel good

(continued)

to be able to help my children early on, so they won't go into school without knowing about reading or valuing reading. My children also see me reading when I do my homework. They can see that reading is important to learning in school. I have started reading the newspaper each day, so I know what is happening in the world, which is helping my schoolwork.

Another impact reading has had on me is allowing me to go to college. I am the first person in my family to go to college, so this is a big deal. Without reading, I wouldn't be able to make it through my classes.

Reading has made me a better person in lots of ways. I think I'm a better parent because I read to my children and they see me reading. I hope this helps them to see reading is important and will help them become better readers. I think I'm a better friend, because reading has taught me about different experiences and perspectives on life, so I can be there for my friends who are going through bad things. Reading has made me a better person in my community as well. I have read about social issues like voting and immigration and education and what I've learned has helped me in local community meetings, especially in PTA meetings.

What is my favorite idea—what excites me? I think I generated a lot of ideas that excite me. I didn't realize how valuable reading is in my life! I think the one that most excites me, though, is the first one on how reading is something I can model to my children.

What idea can I best develop with supporting examples? I can develop the ideas in my first and final paragraphs with the best examples. I like the idea in the middle paragraph, but since I haven't really been at college very long, I don't have much to say about this yet.

Will my focus allow me to meet the needs of this assignment? I think any of these topics will work with the assignment, yes.

Is my idea narrow enough for this assignment but broad enough to give me enough to say about it? I like all of the ideas in my final paragraph, but I think the topic of "become a better person" may be too big—I have so many ideas this could almost be a whole paper. The first paragraph about modeling reading to my children is more focused.

Do I have ideas that are good but could be saved for another assignment in this or another class? My middle paragraph. I love this idea, but I need to have more experiences in order to be able to discuss it fully.

Kathy ended by going back to her freewriting and underlining one sentence in paragraph 1 that she felt captured her key idea. She will use this as she continues on and forms a topic sentence.

Practice 2.4 Finding a Focus Using *Your Own Experience*

DIRECTIONS

1. Choose 2–3 of the ideas you generated about your own experience in Step 2, and free-write about them.
2. After you have written, answer the questions on page 23 (modeled in the Demonstration) in order to evaluate what you wrote and choose a topic that is the strongest.
3. Finally, go back through the freewriting on the topic you chose and see if you can find one sentence that has the topic clearly stated. If you struggle to find a full sentence, see if you can find one word or short phrase that identifies a topic you would like to make your focus. Underline this as you can use it later to build a topic sentence.

Demonstration Finding a Focus Using Douglass

Here is an example of Kathy's freewrite on the two ideas she brainstormed for Douglass's text on page 24. Again, she used freewriting to see which idea was the strongest one and about which she had the most to say.

<u>When he learned to read, Douglass learned about aspects of slavery he wasn't aware of before.</u> He learned that slavery existed and that he was a slave for life. He also learned that slavery changed people, like his Mistress, from someone who was kind to someone who was hard hearted. He learned that people were writing about slavery and that not everyone agreed with it. He learned that it was illegal for him to learn to read and to write. He also learned that he didn't have any real options to become free, and this depressed him.

Douglass also learned that there were abolitionists who were fighting against slavery. He heard this word spoken and wanted to find out what it meant, so he looked it up in a dictionary. There wasn't a good definition that could help him, though, because they all used "abolish" in the definition, and he didn't know what that meant. He had to listen to people who used the word instead and try to figure it out from context.

What is my favorite idea—what excites me? The idea in the first paragraph excites me—I like the theme of awareness and learning in his story. Abolitionists were important but I'm not sure I fully understand the topic, so I'm not comfortable writing about it.

What idea can I best develop with supporting examples? I can definitely talk about Douglass's growing awareness of slavery. The story didn't say as much about abolitionists. It was a word that Douglass heard others talk about, but there isn't a strong connection between what he learns about it through reading.

(continued)

Will my focus allow me to meet the needs of this assignment? Either topic could work—if I have enough to say about them.

Is my idea narrow enough for this assignment but broad enough to give me enough to say about it? The second topic may be too narrow as there isn't a lot in his story about what he learns about abolitionists through reading.

Do I have ideas that are good but could be saved for another assignment in this or another class? I'd like to learn more about abolitionists in another class, so I could write more about this topic.

Kathy ended by going back to her freewriting and underlining one sentence in paragraph 1 that she felt captured her key idea. She will use this as she continues on and forms a topic sentence.

Practice 2.5   Finding *Your Own Focus* Using Douglass's Essay

DIRECTIONS

1. Choose 2–3 of the ideas you added to your brainstorm list about Douglass's essay in Step 2, and freewrite about them.
2. After you have written, answer the questions on page 23 (modeled in the Demonstration) in order to evaluate what you wrote and choose a topic that is the strongest.
3. Finally, go back through the freewriting on the topic you chose and see if you can find one sentence that has the topic clearly stated. If you struggle to find a full sentence, see if you can find one word or short phrase that identifies a topic you would like to make your focus. Underline this as you can use it later to build a topic sentence.

Drafting a Topic Sentence

Each paragraph needs a controlling idea that all the other ideas connect to and support. In academic writing, it is most often expected that you will state this point clearly in a topic sentence. As a general rule, a topic sentence should include your topic and your opinion or argument about it:

Topic sentence = *topic* + <u>opinion/stance/argument about that topic</u>

During the writing process, there are several times when you can draft your topic sentence. You may do so in prewriting as you generate ideas. You may do so in the outlining phase. You may even have to draft the entire paragraph to find what you want to say in your topic sentence. Finally, you may write a topic sentence and then later change it as you discover exactly what you want to say in your writing. Ask these questions to help you develop a topic sentence:

1. What is the topic of my paragraph?
2. What opinion or argument do I want to make about this topic?
3. How can I combine my topic and opinion about it into one sentence?

Demonstration   Drafting a Topic Sentence

Here Kathy develops topic sentences for her paragraphs on her personal experiences with reading and Douglass's experience with reading.

Personal Experience

1. **What is the topic of my paragraph?** It will be about how I can model reading to my children.

2. **What opinion or argument do I want to make about this topic?** Modeling reading will help my children become stronger readers themselves.

3. **How can I combine my topic and opinion about it into one sentence?**

      topic   opinion

Modeling reading to my children is allowing me to help them become stronger readers.

Douglass's essay

1. **What is the topic of my paragraph?** What happened when Douglass learned to read.

2. **What opinion or argument do I want to make about this topic?** He became more aware of aspects of slavery.

3. **How can I combine my topic and opinion about it into one sentence?**

           topic   opinion

Learning to read allowed Frederick Douglass to become more aware of aspects of slavery.

Practice 2.6   Drafting a Topic Sentence

DIRECTIONS: Write a topic sentence for each of your paragraphs using these questions.

- What is the topic of my paragraph?
- What opinion or argument do I want to make about this topic?
- How can I combine my topic and opinion about it into one sentence?

STEP 4: Develop Your Ideas

Once you have a focus, you need to develop supporting ideas for that focus. This is a natural progression that nearly everything in nature follows. Think of a tree, for example: it develops branches and fills out as it grows; it develops. Like a tree, you want to develop your main idea by adding ideas and details that tell more about it.

- *Ideas* are main concepts that support, illustrate, or prove your overall focus.
- *Details* are the pieces of information you provide about each idea to further explain and illustrate it.

Your writing will be well developed when it has a variety of clear, concrete ideas and details that illustrate the main focus. Developing these elements from your own personal experience can be a fun and creative part of the writing process because you get to brainstorm specific support, stories, and facts to help your reader understand your point. Developing these elements from a text you have read can also be engaging as it can be like a scavenger hunt where you find ideas that illustrate what you want to say. One way to develop ideas and details is to brainstorm.

Demonstration   Brainstorming for Ideas Based on Personal Experience

Here is Kathy's brainstorm on the topic of how knowing how to read has impacted her ability to model reading for her children.

Topic: Reading has impacted me by allowing me to model this skill to my children

Supporting Ideas

— Read the newspaper

— Read to them before bedtime

— When I do homework, I show them that I'm a reader (and they can be too!)

— Encourage them to read for pleasure

— Read/do homework together as a family

Practice 2.7   Brainstorming for Ideas Based on *Your* Personal Experience

DIRECTIONS

1. At the top of a sheet of paper, put the topic that will be the focus of your paragraph on your own experience.
2. Below that topic, list as many ideas as you can that explain to your reader how you have been impacted by knowing how to read. If this is too difficult, remember that you can alter your focus to make it broader if you need to do so. Do not stop before you have at least three ideas that illustrate your overall focus.

Once you have a list of ideas, you can brainstorm further for details to support them.

Demonstration   Developing Details Based on Personal Experience

Here is an example of how Kathy created details for two of the supporting ideas listed above:

1. Read to them before bedtime

   • My youngest, Jennifer, loves to have me read to her every night before bed.

   • We are currently reading a Goosebumps story, which is a little higher level than she is reading, but she loves the story.

- When I read, I try to do the voices of the characters, so Jennifer enjoys the process.
- Sometimes I let her try to read a sentence I just read, so she can get practice trying this on her own.

2. <u>When I do homework, I show them that I'm a reader (and they can be too!)</u>

- Instead of doing homework in a closed room, I do it in the living room or dining room where they can see me doing it.
- If the kids have questions about what I'm reading, I share it with them. I'll even read to them from my textbooks sometimes.
- I always have highlighting pens, sticky notes for annotations, and my reading journal with me when I do my homework. This helps me, but it also shows them that reading is an active, hands-on activity.

Practice 2.8   Developing Details Based on *Your* Personal Experience

DIRECTIONS: Choose your favorite two supporting ideas. Put each one at the top of a sheet of paper. Then, list several details about each one.

Demonstration   Developing Ideas Based on Douglass's Text

Here is an example of Kathy's brainstorm for ideas about how reading impacted Frederick Douglass. Two ideas are listed here; add to this list in the exercise that follows.

<u>Topic:</u> Reading impacted Douglass by allowing him to learn about slavery.

<u>Supporting Ideas</u>

- Slavery changed white people like his mistress for the worse, which he saw through the process of her teaching him to read.
- Not everyone agreed that slavery was good, which he realized when he read texts from *The Columbian Orator.*

Practice 2.9   **Developing *Your* Ideas Based on Douglass's Text**

DIRECTIONS: Reread Douglass's story and see if you can find 2–3 more ideas that he learned about slavery not already listed on page 29.

Information Literacy: Quotations and Paraphrases

When you use ideas from a text you have read, you either quote exactly or paraphrase the idea in your own words.

What is a quotation and how is it used in writing? A quotation is a short passage taken word for word from a text. It is either introduced with the author's name and/or the title of the text. The exact words are placed in quotation marks and followed by an in-text citation that provides the page number (and the author's name if it has not been given in the introduction). In-text citations are placed in parentheses immediately before the end punctuation of the quotation. Here are two examples from Douglass:

> According to Douglass, "Slavery soon proved its ability to divest her of these heavenly qualities. Under its influence, the tender heart became stone, and the lamb-like disposition gave way to one of tiger-like fierceness. The first step in her downward course was in her ceasing to instruct me" (262).

> "Slavery soon proved its ability to divest her of these heavenly qualities. Under its influence, the tender heart became stone, and the lamb-like disposition gave way to one of tiger-like fierceness. The first step in her downward course was in her ceasing to instruct me" (Douglass 262).

Quotations are used as support within papers. They back up or illustrate what you have said to show the reader that it is indeed true. Anytime you take material word for word from another person's writing, you need to quote it. Otherwise, you are plagiarizing.

What is a paraphrase and how is it used in writing? A paraphrase is when a writer takes a short part of a text and puts it in his or her own words while keeping the exact meaning of the original. A paraphrase does not need to have quotation marks around it since it is not copied word for word, but it does need to be introduced and cited with the author and page number.

How do I paraphrase? The challenge of paraphrasing is that you have to convey the meaning of the original sentence while putting it in your own words. Paraphrases need to include the author's name and the page number like a quotation, but you omit the quotation marks because the text is in your own words and not the exact words of the author. It is essential that you accurately state the ideas in the original text.

Guidelines for Paraphrasing

- **Read the original sentence or passage and make sure you understand it.** Identify vocabulary words you do not understand and look them up, outline the key ideas in the text, and take notes.
- **Bullet the key points in the passage you want to paraphrase on a separate sheet of paper.** Double check that you have captured all of the key ideas.

- **Close the book and use your bullet points to write what the author said *using your own words.*** Use your own writing style, words, and synonyms.
- **Open the book again and compare your paraphrase to the original text.** Make sure you have accurately captured all the key ideas in the original but that you did not use the same words as the original.

Quotation: "What I got from Sheridan was a bold denunciation of slavery, and a powerful vindication of human rights" (Douglass 263).

Paraphrase of quotation: Sheridan's writing said slavery was to be ended. It was a strong piece about how human rights should be placed first (Douglass 263).

Practice 2.10   Developing Additional Details, *Douglass's Text*

DIRECTIONS: Reread Douglass's story to find passages that support or illustrate other ideas he learned from reading about slavery. Then practice either quoting or paraphrasing these passages. Remember to cite using the author and page number in parentheses after your quote or paraphrase.

STEP 5: Organize Your Ideas

This step of the writing process asks you to establish the order in which you will present ideas in your written piece. If you take time to organize your ideas, the drafting process will be easier because you have the ideas you generated in the correct order when you are ready to write about them. Often instructors will ask you to outline your ideas as part of this step, but you can also create an organizational map of your ideas (see Chapter 6, p. 103 for an example). The point is to write down your blueprint—or organizational plan—of your paper.

There are many different ways to organize your ideas, and organization often depends on your purpose for writing and on the audience who will read it. Review Chapters 3 and 4 on organization and structure to explore the different ways you can arrange your ideas. Then, think about what structure or combination of structures is best given what you want to say and whom you are addressing. Then, arrange your ideas in that order in your draft.

Emotionally, you may feel a sense of accomplishment when you organize your ideas because organizing allows you to see what you have generated and helps you realize that you are ready to put together all of these ideas into a complete piece of writing.

Demonstration   Organizing Ideas

Here is an example of how Kathy used an outline to organize her ideas before writing. She has chosen the deductive, or general-to-specific, mode of organizing (see Chapter 4, p. 58).

I. **Topic Sentence:** The most significant impact that reading has had on my life is allowing me to model reading to my kids.

(continued)

II. <u>One way I do this is by reading to them before bedtime</u>

   a. My youngest, Jennifer, loves to have me read to her every night before bed.

   b. We are currently reading a Goosebumps story, which is a little higher level than she is reading, but she loves the story.

   c. When I read, I try to do the voices of the characters, so Jennifer enjoys the process.

   d. Sometimes I let her try to read a sentence I just read, so she can get practice trying this on her own.

III. <u>Another way I do this is when I do homework, I show them that I'm a reader (and they can be too!)</u>

   a. Instead of doing homework in a closed room, I do it in the living room or dining room where they can see me doing this.

   b. If the kids have questions about what I'm reading, I share that with them. I'll even read to them from my textbooks sometimes.

   c. I always have highlighting pens, sticky notes for annotations, and my reading journal with me when I do my homework. This helps me, but it also shows them that reading is an active, hands-on activity.

Practice 2.11   Organizing *Your* Ideas

DIRECTIONS: Using the example above, outline a paragraph that either details your own experience with reading or details how reading impacted Douglass. Use these steps to help you.

1. Put your overall focus or topic at the top of a clean sheet of paper.
2. Then, outline your supporting ideas and the details that illustrate those ideas in the order you want to write about them. Think about your readers here. What information would be best to write about first? Second? Third? What order do you think makes logical sense?

Academic Writing Process Phase Two: Draft

Learning Objective 3
Draft a paragraph.

After finding a topic, gathering evidence, and getting organized, it is time to write out what you have to say in a full draft form. As you do so, do not forget what you did in the first phase of writing. For example, as you write, have your outline in front of you. It will help to keep you on track and give you ideas for what to say as you write. Also know that this second stage of the writing process—like reading—can be recursive.

For example, you may need to go back to earlier stages of the writing process to develop more ideas if you run out of things to say. This is okay; writing often folds back on itself. You may need to return to brainstorming or outlining in order to move forward as you draft, especially if a new idea emerges during the drafting process.

STEP 6: Draft

Drafting is where you give birth to your full written piece. It is where you use what you generated in brainstorming, focusing, developing, and organizing to write your paper. While this is a first draft, it should be the best you can do at this point. If your first draft is your best, it allows you to make it even better as you go through the rest of the process.

Drafting can bring a range of emotions. Sometimes if the prewriting phase went well and you come to drafting with a lot of ideas, drafting can be a smooth and fun process. Other times, though, it can be difficult to put into paragraph form what you brainstormed earlier. Each draft is different in how it will feel to write, and you should not feel bad if one draft is more difficult than another to produce. Know, too, that this is your first draft, not your final one. It does not have to be perfect at this point.

Demonstration   Drafting

Here is the draft paragraph Kathy wrote about her personal experience of writing based on her outline for Step 5 (see p. 32).

The most significant impact that reading has had on my life is allowing me to model reading to my kids. One way I do this is by reading to them before bedtime. My youngest, Jennifer, loves to have me read to her every night before bed. We are currently reading a Goosebumps story, which is a little higher level than she is reading, but she loves the story. When I read, I try to do the voices of the characters, so Jennifer enjoys the process. Sometimes I let her try to read a sentence I just read, so she can get practice trying this on her own. Another way I do this is when I do homework, I show them that I'm a reader (and they can be too!). Instead of doing homework in a closed room, I do it in the living room or dining room where they can see me doing this. If the kids have questions about what I'm reading, I share that with them. I'll even read to them from my textbooks sometimes. I always have highlighting pens, sticky notes for annotations, and my reading journal with me when I do my homework. This helps me, but it also shows them that reading is an active, hands-on activity. All of these activities have allowed me to give my kids what my parents could not give me: a solid foundation in reading that will help them be successful in school, work, and life.

Practice 2.12   Drafting

DIRECTIONS: Use the ideas you generated in the prewriting stage to write two paragraphs. One should be about the significance of reading in your life. The other should be about the significance of reading to Frederick Douglass.

Academic Writing Process Phase Three: Polish

Learning Objective 4
Revise and polish your writing.

Author Julie Moore shares her college writing process mistakes: When I was a writer early in my college career, I was confused by revision. I was convinced that I wrote my best work the first time and that revision was not needed. An instructor in a college writing class helped me to see how wrong I was! With her help, I came to see that parts of my writing I thought were clear were really only clear to *me* and not to my reader.

As I progressed in my college career, I realized that what my college writing teacher taught me about revision is also supported by research on how we write. For example, one scholar, Linda Flowers, said that writers have two main types of writing: Writer-based Prose and Reader-based Prose. She said that no matter how long one has been writing, one's first draft reflects Writer-based Prose. It is a piece that makes sense to the writer but does not make as much sense to the reader. For example, the topics might not be clear yet, explanations might not show how ideas connect, or there may be references to "he" or "she" that don't point to anyone. These are all normal parts of a first draft; every writer does this. What sets good writers apart, Flowers says, is that good writers know they need to revise in order to transform their text into Reader-based Prose, or writing that makes sense to their reader. In order to do this, writers need to get feedback from others and double check aspects of their writing on their own in order to make sure it makes sense to an outside reader. The polishing phase is focused on helping you move your draft from Writer-based Prose to Reader-based Prose.

STEP 7: Revise

Revision is crucial to good writing.

- **Revision** is improving your first draft to make it clearer and easier to understand for your reader.
- **Revision** is the process of re-seeing ("re-visioning") your paper through the eyes of an outside reader; it is the process of asking, "Would this make sense to a reader?"
- **Revision** focuses on content and structure in your paper, not on grammar. (However, sometimes the grammar can make it hard to understand the content. If this is the case, then you may also need to improve the grammar when you revise.)

You may feel a sense of elation after having finished the first draft only to have that feeling replaced with a sense of frustration at having to change certain things in your draft that do not make sense to the reader. Allow yourself time to feel angry, frustrated, and defeated. Then dig in and get to the work of revising, so your written piece makes sense to both you *and* the reader.

Critical Thinking: Evaluation

Revision asks the writer to practice the critical thinking skill of evaluating ideas and structures in writing. Here, evaluation means comparing your writing or that of a classmate to certain standards of college writing. In the example below, a student uses the writing assignment directions as the standards of evaluation.

Revising Using a Checklist

In the following example, Kathy gave her draft to her classmate, Antonio, for feedback. Antonio used a peer review checklist to make sure he carefully evaluated her paragraph.

Peer Review Checklist

Course: ENG090

Date: 9/18/13

Writer's name: Kathy

Reader's name: Antonio

1. Does the paragraph address the assignment by focusing on and explaining how reading impacted the reader in a significant way?

   Yes, I think this paragraph does a good job of talking about what the assignment asked. It focuses on how reading has helped you to model that for your kids. This is a great idea. I'll have to remember this for when I have kids!

2. Does the paragraph start with a clear topic sentence that identifies how reading has impacted the reader?

   Yes, I would say that the first sentence is pretty good at saying what the paragraph will be about.

3. Do the sentences that follow provide supporting ideas or details for how reading has been significant in the life of the reader?

   Yes—and I love all of the details such as how you do your homework with highlighters, sticky notes, etc. Your support actually gave me some great ideas for how to read more effectively—thank you! ☺

4. Are the paragraphs well developed with ample supporting points and discussion of those points?

   Your paragraph seems long enough and gives lots of details. If anything, I wonder if it's too long? You might ask our teacher about that as I think the paragraph was only supposed to be 10 sentences long and yours is longer than that.

5. Are spelling, grammar, and punctuation clear enough that the reader can understand the meaning of the text? If quotes or paraphrases are used, are they cited with author and page number?

   I could clearly understand what you are saying. I think there might have been some minor errors in places, though. Try reading this out loud to yourself to see if you can hear any missing words or other mistakes.

Kathy can decide for herself if she will make the changes that Antonio suggested. None of his criticism is passionate or strong, but Kathy may decide to rewrite using his observations.

Revising Using a Checklist

DIRECTIONS: Find someone in your class whom you do not know very well. Exchange your paragraphs about the impacts of knowing how to read. Ask your partner to mark on your paper or on the checklist the changes that might help improve the writing. Have your partner mark any sentences, words, or ideas that don't make sense to him or her. Do the same for your partner's paper. When you are done, meet with your partner to review the feedback. Then see if you can revise parts of your writing to be clearer to your reader. The following are the questions you need to answer for your partner's writing.

Response Checklist Based on the Assignment

1. Does the paragraph address the assignment by focusing on and explaining how reading impacted the reader in a significant way?
2. Does the paragraph start with a clear topic sentence that identifies how reading has impacted the reader?
3. Do the sentences that follow provide supporting ideas and details for how reading has been significant in the life of the reader?
4. Is the paragraph well developed enough with ample supporting points and discussion of those points?
5. Are spelling, grammar, and punctuation clear enough that the reader can understand the meaning of the text? If quotes or paraphrases are used, are they correctly cited with author and page number?

STEP 8: Edit and Proofread

Taking time to edit and proofread is an important step in communicating to your reader. **Editing and proofreading** means checking the grammar, punctuation, spelling, word choice, and citations in your writing.

When should you do this? It should be the final step you take before you submit your paragraphs to an instructor; it provides the final polish.

How should you edit?

- **Double-check spelling and grammar by reading for errors on your own or getting help from a tutor.** (For example, spell checkers cannot tell the difference between the correct use of homonyms, or sound-alike words, such as "there," "they're," and "their." Similarly, many grammar checkers will sometimes give you incorrect information.)
- **Read the paragraphs from last sentence to first sentence to expose errors in sentence structure.** Read them out loud for the most benefit as your brain will not be able to automatically fill in missing words or make sense of confusing ideas when you read silently.
- **Circle all quotations, paraphrases, and citations in your paper and double check that you have put author and page number(s) for each one.** Also double check that punctuation around the quotes is correct.

Why should you edit? Consider the impact that editing and proofreading will have on your reader. If your written product has a lot of errors in it, that shows you did not care enough to fix them, and your reader may not take you seriously. Use the following Editing and Proofreading Checklist to correct errors in your writing.

Editing and Proofreading Checklist

- **Sentence Structure:** Are all of your sentences complete? Do they have a subject, verb, and complete idea expressed? Underline any that you think may need editing. Then try to correct them on your own or with a tutor or instructor.
- **Spelling:** Run the spell check on your word processing program and see what it shows as incorrect. Use a dictionary to check all words that are identified as incorrect.

Then go through your draft and highlight any sound-alike words that the spell checker wouldn't catch. These include words like too/to/two, their/there/*they're, our/are,* and *then/than.* Double check that you have the correct word in each case.

- **Citations:** Go through your draft and circle each quotation or paraphrase. Then go back and make sure you have author and page number listed for each one. Also check that you have put quotes and punctuation correctly around each of these.

Practice 2.14　Editing and Proofreading

DIRECTIONS: Read your paragraphs out loud to yourself. Read from the last sentence to the first sentence. As you do so, use the Editing and Proofreading Checklist to do a final edit of your paragraphs.

STEP 9: Reflect on Your Writing Process

Reflection is the process of stopping and asking yourself the following questions about what you wrote using the writing process:

- What about this process worked well for me?
- What about this process did not work well for me?
- What would I like to do the same next time I write?
- What would I like to change or work on more next time I write?

Why reflect? It is important to stop and reflect on your writing, so you can learn whether or not all parts of the writing process are working for you and what you would like to do the same or differently next time you write.

Critical Thinking: Reflection

Reflection is the step that asks you to think critically about *how* you wrote. Those who study critical thinking have found that there are two main ways we think as we go through life as well as approach writing: *green-light thinking* and *red-light thinking.*

- **Green-light thinking is our automatic thinking mode.** It is the type of thinking that allows us to function automatically, without really checking to see if our choices are the best ones. For example, when we are shopping for food and we see a cereal we like, green-light thinking says, "Buy it!" and we do. While green-light thinking helps us move through life, it does not allow us to learn very much. Green-light thinking is not critical thinking.
- **Red-light thinking happens when we stop and analyze what we are doing.** Learning takes place when we engage in this type of thinking. For example, it may make you ask questions about cereal you are about to buy, like, "Is this cereal a good choice in terms of cost? Nutrition? Taste?" Red-light thinking is critical thinking.

While we do not always have time to do red-light thinking, it is important to do so periodically, so we can tell if we are doing the best we can and to see if we need to adjust our behavior. Reflection is when we do red-light thinking about our writing.

Practice 2.15   Reflecting on the Writing Process

DIRECTIONS: Write as much as you can about the following questions. Use your answers to learn about how you want to approach the writing process in future assignments.

- What exercises in this chapter worked well for me? Why?
- What exercises in this chapter did not work well for me? Why?
- What parts of the writing process would I like to do the same next time I write?
- What parts of the writing process would I like to change or work on more next time I write?

The Academic Writing Process: Putting It Together

You have just practiced the steps of a complete writing process that resulted in a well-structured, fully developed paragraph. These nine steps are the same you will use in later chapters to compose other paragraphs and essays. Once you master the steps, you will be able to tackle most writing assignments that college professors might give you.

You may notice that the writing process and the reading process from Chapter 1 have nine steps, and before, during and after phases. Read the chart below to see the similarities and differences between them, and to see how your reading can help you write well, and your writing can help you read well.

Connections between the Reading and Writing Processes

	Reading Process	Writing Process
Before	• **Purpose**: to get ready to learn from reading	• **Purpose**: to explore what you have to say

	• **Preview**
	  • Get an overview
	  • Check your attitude
	  • Set your purpose
	  • Be aware of what you know (background knowledge)
		• **Prewrite**
		  • Analyze the assignment
		  • Brainstorm
		  • Focus
		  • Develop ideas and details
		  • Organize

	• **Emotion**: be curious	• **Emotion**: be open and let all ideas out; tolerate chaos
During	• **Purpose**: to create an accurate understanding of the author's meaning; to take notes to help you understand and remember	• **Purpose**: to create a first draft of your meaning that is somewhat organized

	• **Read**
	  • Take notes on major ideas and details
	  • Find definitions of unknown vocabulary
	  • Note interesting or emotion-generating ideas
		• **Draft**
		Write a first draft

	• **Emotion**: be curious and persistent; tolerate frustration	• **Emotion**: be persistent and curious to find what you truly have to say

	Reading Process	Writing Process
After	• **Purpose**: to make sure you understand what you have read; to create a means to remember what you have read	• **Purpose**: to make your writing very clear to other readers

	• **After reading**
	  • Write a summary
	  • Respond to the reading
	  • Reflect on the reading process
		• **Polishing**
		  • Revise
		  • Edit and proofread
		  • Reflect on the writing process

	• **Emotion**: be thoughtful and reflective	• **Emotion**: be persistent and focused; try to put yourself in the minds of your readers

For future reference, the following is a template of the writing process steps. You can use this for the writing assignments you have in this class and in future classes.

Writing Process Template

Phase One: Prewriting

Step 1: Analyze the Assignment
- ☐ What is the purpose, goal, or objective of this assignment, and who is its intended audience? Can you imagine meaningful things to say about this topic?
- ☐ What is the central topic you will need to write about? What information are you supposed to use as support in this paper? What organizational structure will you need to use for this paper? How do you feel about responding to the assignment? What questions do you have about this assignment?

Step 2: Generate Ideas
- ☐ Brainstorm all of the ideas, details, experiences, and insights that you can think of that could relate to the assignment.
- ☐ Choose several of the best ideas, and freewrite about them.

Step 3: Focus Your Topic
- ☐ Choose the idea from your brainstorming that you like the best and that answers the assignment well. Underline this idea, and freewrite about it. Develop a one-sentence statement that captures this idea.

Step 4: Develop Your Ideas
- ☐ Brainstorm or cluster-map as many details as possible that help support or prove the idea you chose as your focus. This may be your own experiences or textual support from an essay you read.

Step 5: Organize Your Ideas
- ☐ Write an outline indicating the order you want your ideas and details to follow.

Phase Two: Draft

Step 6: Draft
- ☐ Write a first full draft of your composition, whether it be a paragraph or a full essay.

Phase Three: Polish

Step 7: Revise
- ☐ Review and revise your paper based on the assignment directions and on paragraph and essay structure.
- ☐ Reread your paper several times with specific questions in mind about its content and structure.
- ☐ Have another student or group of students read your paper and give you feedback.

(continued)

Step 8: **Edit and Proofread**

    ☐ Edit your paper for clear sentences and careful word choice.

    ☐ Proofread to find small errors in punctuation, spelling, citations, and other correctness issues.

Step 9: **Reflect**

    ☐ Think back over each step you took in preparing to write, writing, and polishing your composition. Which steps were the most helpful? Which were the most difficult? What will you do differently next time?

✔ Chapter **Quick Check**   **MySkillsLab**   Complete the mastery test for this chapter in MySkillsLab.

Use the following questions and answers to check your understanding of this chapter.

QUESTION	ANSWER
Learning Objective 1: Understand the purposes and steps of the academic writing process. *What are the major purposes of following the academic writing process?*	✔ When you follow a writing process, it allows you to write to your full potential. You give your brain time to find what it wants to say, say it, and polish those ideas for the reader.
Learning Objective 2: Prewrite to generate, develop, and organize ideas and details. *What steps are included in the first phase of the writing process?*	The steps in prewriting include... ✔ 1. Analyzing the assignment to understand your instructor's expectations. ✔ 2. Brainstorming to generate ideas about which to write. ✔ 3. Focusing those ideas, so you have a topic that fits your purpose for writing. ✔ 4. Developing and organizing your ideas so that you are ready to write about them in a linear form. ✔ 5. Using quotations and paraphrases effectively as support; following citation rules to avoid plagiarism.
Learning Objective 3: Draft a paragraph or essay. *What is the focus of the second phase of the writing process, "Draft"?*	✔ 6. Drafting your paragraph using the ideas and details you generated by brainstorming, focusing, developing, and organizing information as you read.
Learning Objective 4: Revise and polish your writing. *What steps do you take to revise and polish your draft?*	The steps for revising and polishing writing include... ✔ 7. Re-examining your draft, perhaps with a classmate, to check its focus, development, and organization. ✔ 8. Editing and proofreading sentences to correct punctuation, spelling, and grammar. ✔ 9. Reflecting on which steps were the most helpful and the most difficult and what you will do differently next time.

Structuring Paragraphs and Essays

3

LEARNING OBJECTIVES

In this chapter, you will learn to...

1 Identify yourself as both a reader and a writer.

2 Recognize the structure and parts of a paragraph.

3 Recognize the structure and parts of an essay.

Warm Up

DIRECTIONS: Look closely at the picture. Then answer the following questions.

- What do the individual parts in the art piece look like to you? What do they mean or symbolize on their own as individual parts?

- Now look at the picture again and this time approach it as a whole with different parts that each contribute to a larger composition. How does this change the meaning of the art piece? How are the individual pieces working together to form a whole?

- Compare this to your writing. When you write, do you have individual parts that can be combined to form a larger whole? Explain.

MySkillsLab
Complete the Warm Up at
www.myskillslab.com

Seeing Yourself as both Reader and Writer

Learning Objective 1
Identify yourself as both a reader and a writer.

As you read this chapter, think of yourself as both a reader and a writer. Understanding structure helps you to read and understand texts as well as compose strong texts of your own. Also keep in mind that both reading and writing have smaller parts that can work together to form a whole. As in the picture above, smaller parts, such as paragraphs in a text, can come together with other smaller parts to form a larger unit of information. When you read, seeing how the parts of a text contribute to the whole deepens your comprehension. Similarly, understanding the parts of a paragraph or essay will help you write better papers.

Writing Process Versus Writing Product

Unlike Chapter 2 on writing *process*, this chapter on structure and organization will focus primarily on the *product* of your writing. It will show you structures you can use to present your ideas. The product of your writing is *related* to the process you follow to write it, but it should not be confused with the process, or the steps you take to get to your paragraph or essay. It can be easy to confuse the two by thinking that, if you have a structure for your ideas, then all you have to do is plug ideas into that structure. Strong writing rarely results from doing this. Rather, strong writing results from utilizing the full writing process to find out what you want to say and then exploring the clearest and most reader-friendly way to structure and present those ideas.

Organization Versus Content

Organization should help make your content clear to a reader. The organization you use should also fit the content; they should complement one another. We encourage you to begin with your content. Find what you want to say. Then think about the clearest and most appropriate organizational structure that will help you communicate that content. As you do so, think of the needs of your audience. What structure will help them best understand your content? Because your instructor is also your audience, make sure to read an assignment closely. Has your instructor specified an organizational structure you should use? If so, make sure your writing is structured accordingly.

Consider this simile for thinking about organization: The size and type of clothes you wear are like the organization of your writing. Just as your clothes should fit your body and the occasion for which you are wearing them, so, too, should the organizational structure you use for your writing fit the content of your writing and the audience and purpose for which you write. For example, you would not wear size 2 jeans if your body were a size 8. The jeans would not fit. Similarly, you should not try to squeeze eight paragraphs of ideas into a five-paragraph essay structure. Rather, you should expand the structure to fit the content.

Furthermore, both your clothes and your writing should fit with your audience. You would not wear the same clothes to a funeral as you would to your college classes. You change your clothes to fit the occasion. Similarly, you want to change the structure of your writing to fit the occasion of that writing; you want your structure to address your audience in an appropriate manner. For example, you would write an e-mail asking to borrow money differently if the audience were a friend versus a bank.

Structures You Read Versus Those You Write

Finally, as you read this chapter, you will see that there are some similarities and some differences between texts you read for college and those you write for college. For example, both texts you read and write for college will have paragraphs. Most will have an overall purpose or argument. However, there may be some differences, too. For example, instructors in college often want you to write an explicit topic sentence for a paragraph, but many articles you read for college may not have explicit topic sentences. Do not expect texts you read and write for college to be identical in structure, and do not be confused by the differences you see in texts you read and write for college. Keep in mind that there are some similarities between these texts that can help you simultaneously become a stronger reader and writer.

Basic Components of Paragraphs You Read and Write

Learning Objective 2
Recognize the structure and parts of a paragraph.

We begin this chapter by looking at the basic components of the paragraph. These components should be in most paragraphs except for those that serve a special purpose such as the introduction and conclusion in an essay. A paragraph has nearly all of the same elements as an essay; therefore, learning the components of a paragraph will help you better understand the structure of an essay. We also outline different organizational patterns for paragraphs.

Paragraphs are like hamburgers. Just as a hamburger needs a top bun, meat, and a bottom bun in order to be considered a proper hamburger, so a paragraph needs certain ingredients such as a topic sentence, support, and analysis in order to be complete. While paragraphs can be structured in different ways, all paragraphs need to have the following basic parts.

A Topic Sentence Is Like the Top Bun of a Hamburger

A **topic sentence** is the main idea of a paragraph put into the form of a sentence.

Topic sentence = *topic of paragraph* + opinion/reaction/argument/stance about that topic.

This is very similar to a main idea in a reading, which also includes the topic of the text plus the author's stance or opinion about that topic. Keep in mind that a topic sentence should be focused enough so you can write about it in five to ten sentences. A paragraph is not long, so make sure the topic sentence fits the length of a paragraph.

Purpose of a Topic Sentence

In general, a topic sentence tells the main idea of a paragraph. It helps the reader to know what is coming and prepares the reader's mind to receive that information. A topic sentence is similar to a driver of a car who uses the turn signal to indicate her direction. The turn signal is not for the driver; she knows where she is going. The signal is for other drivers—those trying to "read" where she is going—so they can react appropriately. Similarly, your topic sentence helps your reader anticipate the direction in which your writing will go in your paragraph.

Location of a Topic Sentence

The topic sentence is often placed at the beginning of a paragraph, but depending on a paragraph's structure, it can also come at the end or even in the middle. In paragraphs that you read, it may come anywhere in the paragraph—beginning, middle, or end. In some texts you *read* for college, there will not be an explicit topic sentence. Instead, it will be implied. The writer wants you to put together the clues in the paragraph to figure out the main idea. You will rarely *write* paragraphs for college that have an implied topic sentence, though. Topic sentences in your writing should be clear and explicit.

Practice 3.1   Identifying a Topic Sentence

DIRECTIONS: Read the following paragraph, written by student Troy LaVance. Then, answer the questions that follow.

In many ways the parking at Green River Community College (GRCC) can interfere with a student's learning. For example, on my first day at GRCC, I had to drive around the parking lots for about 15 minutes, which made me late to my first class. In addition, the majority of the students I talk to say that is their main reason to be late to class no matter what time the class starts. When students are 10 or 15 minutes late, it affects their learning because sometimes they do not know what they missed in the class they are late to. Also most teachers will not go back over the subject again. So it is hard for them to find out what they missed, and now they are behind. Most people will argue that students should just come early, but that is not an option for most people because they may have work or they may have kids or little brothers and sisters that they have to take to day care. Also there may be times where students do not drive and the time they carpool with a friend may be the only opportunity for them to catch a ride. Finally, it can affect students' grades because if they are marked late or absent, that can impact their grade. Somehow we need to put a stop to this wild and crazy traffic so we can prevent the amount of late students.

1. With a highlighter, identify the topic sentence. Within that sentence, use a regular pen and circle the topic of the paragraph. Then underline the argument, stance, or opinion about that topic.
2. Explain why you chose the topic sentence you did.
3. How did the topic sentence help you prepare to read the paragraph?

Support Is Like the Meat of the Hamburger

The purpose of **support** is to provide evidence for the topic sentence. Writers use support to prove what they claim in their topic sentence and/or to illustrate the central point of their paragraph, so the reader better understands it. The majority of the content of a paragraph will be sentences that support the topic sentence.

Types of Support

Depending on the purpose and structure of the paragraph, support can be many different things. For example, it could be the details of a story, explanation, examples, statistics, facts, quotations, illustrations, definitions, or descriptive details. The following are some common types of support:

- **Ideas** are the primary points about the main idea or topic sentence. For example if you were writing about why golden retrievers make good family pets, your supporting ideas might be that they are loyal, easy to train, and bond well with both children and adults.

- **Details** give more specific information about each of the ideas; they are sub-points. In the golden retriever paragraph, supporting details could be examples, descriptions, or brief stories of loyalty, training ease, and bonding. Supporting ideas and details work together to help your reader more fully understand your topic sentence or main idea.

- **Logos, Pathos, and Ethos:** As writers develop ideas and details, they want to do so with different angles in mind, so they capture different interests of their readers. These different angles, or appeals, are called *logos, pathos*, and *ethos*:
  - *Logos* is support that appeals to a reader's logical side (facts, statistics, studies).
  - *Pathos* is support that appeals to a reader's emotions (personal stories, testimonies, case studies).
  - *Ethos* refers to the way that a text establishes a writer's credibility, character, or trustworthiness—how fair and ethical the writer is in approaching the topic and in appealing to the audience.

  A text that uses a combination of these appeals has stronger support than those texts that only use one of them.

- **Quotations, Paraphrases, and Summaries:** Authors also need to consider when it is appropriate to use quotations, paraphrases, and summaries. Quotations are more exact and reliable because they record exactly what an author has said. A paraphrase is when you put an author's idea into your own words; paraphrases also create strong support, but a reader may not consider them as reliable because the writer has put ideas from a text into her or his own words. There is more room for inaccuracy here. Summaries are useful as well, but they are more general and broad, so less precise when used as support.

Location of Support

Support can come in a variety of places in a paragraph depending on its structure and content. For example, if a paragraph begins with a topic sentence, the support will follow it. If a paragraph ends with a topic sentence, the paragraph may begin with support that leads into the topic sentence at the end. Writers also can weave different types of support throughout a paragraph, alternating the types of support used with analysis (a component of the paragraph that we will talk about in the next section).

Practice 3.2   **Identifying and Evaluating Supporting Ideas and Details**

DIRECTIONS: Read the following paragraph, written by student Christine Wong. Then, answer the questions that follow.

Students should get more involved with programs on campus in order to capitalize on this community of learning. Joining more programs on campus has lots of advantages, such as decreased stress from study, making more friends, learning how to organize a program, and so on. First of all, study can be stressful. Sometimes it will even cause you to give up. Getting involved with some programs can decrease your stress by helping you relax. It allows you to rest your brain and calm down in order to have better motivation to go back to study. Some may say

(continued)

college life is too busy to join extra activities. However, I think joining programs allows you to make a lot of friends. These college friends are not just friends that you go hang out with. They are friends who can help and give you suggestions. Since they are also in college, they understand your situation. You might even be able to study together and get some help. Last but not least, you can learn how to organize a program by joining one. You can also learn social skills through these programs. These are skills that you cannot learn in class but could be useful in your future career. All in all, I think students should get involved in more programs on campus.

1. Highlight the topic sentence. Within that sentence, use a regular pen to circle the topic of the paragraph. Then underline the argument, stance, or opinion about that topic.
2. Using two different-colored highlighters, identify supporting ideas in one color and supporting details in the other color.
3. Analyze the types of support that the writer uses. Do you see supporting ideas or details that show logos? Pathos? Ethos? Do you see any quotes or paraphrases?
4. Write in the margin next to the support (or on a separate sheet of paper) an evaluation of that support.
   - How do the supporting ideas and details help you as a reader to understand the point stated in the topic sentence?
   - Would this paragraph have been as effective if it had included only supporting ideas and not supporting details?
   - What types of support could this writer add to make this a stronger paragraph?
   - Why would these additions make it stronger?

Analysis Is Like the Bottom Bun of the Hamburger

The purpose of **analysis** is to help the reader understand the meaning of the supporting ideas and details in a paragraph, especially as they relate to the author's main idea or topic sentence. Writers often assume that their readers will comprehend information in the same way they do. Therefore, a writer may ask, "Why do I need to explain what the support means? Isn't it obvious?" It may be obvious—to *you*. However, the reader is not you. Therefore, to make your meaning clear, you need to explain what the support means and why you included it in your paragraph. This will help the reader to make the same connections that you made. Like the bottom bun of a hamburger, analysis provides the final layer that holds the whole paragraph together.

Types of Analysis

Analysis can be provided in several ways, but no matter the method, it should help the reader understand your support as well as why you used that support in your paragraph. Here are some ways writers develop analysis:

- **Interpretation** Analysis can be a writer's interpretation of the support he or she provides. In this case, the writer explains what the support means. It is like explaining the moral of a story. The moral is what the supporting details of the story add up to or mean.
- **Connecting Different Supporting Ideas** Analysis can also explain to the reader how different supporting points connect to each other. For example, if a writer includes statistics and examples as support in a paragraph, the analysis could explain how these two different types of support work together and complement one another.
- **Connecting Back to the Overall Point** Analysis could also explain to the reader how the support comes back to the larger point in the paragraph. For example, if a writer has made an argument in a topic sentence, the analysis could spell out for the reader how the support backs up the argument.

Location of Analysis

Where analysis is located depends on where the support comes in the paragraph, because analysis is there to explain the meaning and purpose of the support. The following are a couple of places that analysis most often appears in a paragraph.

- **At the end of the paragraph, after the support** In a traditional paragraph that begins with a topic sentence and then moves to support, the analysis should come at the end. Like the bottom bun of the hamburger, it is there to hold everything together.
- **Woven throughout the paragraph** If a paragraph contains several supporting ideas, each with details, analysis may be woven throughout the paragraph. In other words, there may be support and then analysis followed by more support and more analysis. Think of this as a Big Mac. You are layering the "meat," or support, with the "buns," or analysis.

Practice 3.3 Identifying and Evaluating Analysis

DIRECTIONS: Read the following paragraph, written by student Chirhiro Saito. Then, answer the questions that follow.

Anna, in the movie <u>Real Women Have Curves</u>, is a good example of how college gives a person a chance to decide her own life. Anna comes from a working class Mexican family. Her family, especially her mother, expected her to follow in their footsteps by working in the family's dress factory after she graduated from high school. She intended to bow to her mother's wishes. Though she wanted to go to college, she knew her family needed her. However, after she was accepted into Columbia, she started to think about her own future, and she decided to go to college even though her mother opposed it. She chose to go to college to get an education instead of working for her family. It was at that time she started to live her own life. If she didn't go to college, she would just follow her mother's opinions. She might live her life without thinking what she wanted to do, and she might give up having the hope of her future. College was a way to think about her life and spend more time for her. She could have the options of her career and her opinion about her life. She made her way by herself, and it changed her life and made it more valuable.

1. Highlight the topic sentence. Within that sentence, use a regular pen and circle the topic of the paragraph. Then underline the argument, stance, or opinion about that topic.
2. With a second color highlighter, identify the support in the paragraph. Then write an evaluation of that support in the margin next to it (or on a separate sheet of paper). You might answer these questions: What type of support did this author use? Did the author give enough ideas and details?
3. With a third color highlighter, identify the analysis in the paragraph. Then write an evaluation of the analysis in the margin next to it (or on a separate sheet of paper). You might answer these questions:
   - How does the analysis help you understand the meaning of the support in the paragraph?
   - How does the analysis help you understand how the support connects to the overall argument in the topic sentence?
   - Do you think this paragraph would have been as effective without the analysis?

Transitional Words Are Like Condiments (Ketchup, Mayonnaise, Onions) in a Hamburger

The purpose of **transitional words** is to link ideas and details together. They show the reader how an idea in one sentence connects to an idea or detail in a sentence before or after it. Transitional words can also help show changes in an argument or approach to a topic.

Types of Transitional Words

Transitional words include words such as the following:

Word	Meaning
also	in addition
therefore	a result or conclusion
however	change in position or stance to your topic
on the other hand	a contrasting point
for example	an illustration of an idea
in addition	another point you want to make
similarly	another idea or detail that is like a previous one
in contrast	a point that differs from a previous one

Practice 3.4   Identifying Transitions

DIRECTIONS: Read the following paragraph, written by student Yelena Bokova. Then, answer the questions that follow.

In my husband's story, we will see how he tried to go toward his dream, although his parents did not share his decision. He lived in a village, and his parents were farmers. When he graduated from high school, he had to decide what to do. He wanted to go to college and then to university to be a teacher. Another one of his dreams was to be a technology specialist. The last option was to stay at home with his parents and work on his family's farm. No one in his family could help him or support his decision because they had no idea about higher education. They wanted to see him as a specialist in their sphere of life. Despite their opinion, he chose to go toward his dream and went to college. After 10 years of studies, both of his dreams came true, and he got a master's degree. If he chose his parent's direction, he would never achieve his goals or be what he is now. In short, college helped him to accomplish his dream, in spite of his lovely parents' opinion.

1. Highlight the topic sentence. Within that sentence, use a regular pen and circle the topic of the paragraph. Then underline the argument, stance, or opinion about that topic.
2. With a second color highlighter, identify the support in the paragraph. Then write an evaluation of that support in the margin next to it (or on a separate sheet of paper). You might answer these questions: What type of support did this author use? Did the author give enough ideas and details?
3. With a third color highlighter, identify the analysis in the paragraph. Then write an evaluation of the analysis in the margin next to it (or on a separate sheet of paper). You might answer these questions:
   - How does the analysis help you understand the meaning of the support in the paragraph?
   - How does the analysis help you understand how the support connects to the overall argument in the topic sentence?
   - Do you think this paragraph would have been as effective without the analysis?
4. Finally, circle the transitional words. How do they help clarify the paragraph's content to you, the reader? How do they help link ideas in the paragraph?

Putting It Together

Whether you are writing a paragraph by itself or a body paragraph within a larger work such as an essay, it should have the basic components of *topic sentence, support,* and *analysis* and use *transitional words* to link ideas and make the content clear to your reader. Similarly, when you are reading, looking for these basic components can help you to decipher the meaning, find the author's purpose, and take notes.

The following chart shows the similarities and differences between the components of paragraphs you read and write.

Similarities between Texts You Read and Those You Write in College	Differences between Texts You Read and Those You Write in College
The components of main idea or topic sentence, support, and analysis usually exist in texts you read for college and those you write for college.	The components of topic sentence, support, and analysis may be omitted or arranged in a variety of organizational patterns in texts you *read* for college. Instructors expect you to have all three components in paragraphs you *write* for college, and these should follow a clear organizational pattern.
Paragraphs should stick to a clear and consistent idea.	Topic sentences can be stated or implied in texts you *read* in college. However, they should be clearly stated in paragraphs you *write* for college.
Texts you read and write for college will both use paragraphs.	The length of paragraphs you *read* for college will vary. Some paragraphs you read will be only two or three sentences long while others will be much longer. The length of paragraphs you *write* for college will usually be six to ten sentences.

The Basic Components of an Essay

Learning Objective 3
Recognize the structure and parts of an essay.

Like paragraphs, essays can be organized in many different ways. (See Chapter 4 for some of the options.) Regardless of whether they are comparison, process, or even a mix of various organizational modes, all essays need to have certain common components or parts. These include *an introduction, a thesis, body paragraphs*, and *a conclusion*. As you read about the components of an essay, note the similarities between a paragraph and an essay; a paragraph is like a smaller version of an essay.

Thesis Statement

The purpose of the **thesis statement** is to provide direction for a paper. Just as you have a destination when you take a vacation, there must be a goal, or destination, for an essay. The thesis also can preview the structure of the essay. When a thesis identifies the supporting ideas that will follow in the essay, it tells the reader to expect those topics to be addressed in that order within the body of the essay. The thesis is important for the writer, too: it gives the writer a larger idea to which he or she can connect the supporting ideas and details in the paper.

Thesis Statement Defined

The thesis in an essay is similar to a topic sentence in a paragraph. It provides a one-sentence statement that tells the topic of the essay plus the writer's opinion, stance, or argument about that topic. However, while the focus of the topic sentence in a paragraph is narrow, so it can be addressed in about six to ten sentences, the focus of the thesis statement should be broader, so it can be addressed with multiple paragraphs. Furthermore, a thesis statement may preview the main supporting points and their order.

The following are two common ways to structure a thesis statement; one is brief, and the other includes the supporting points the writer will use to develop the essay. Notice, however, that both options include the topic of the essay and the writer's opinion, stance, or argument about the topic, which are essential to a thesis statement.

1. *Topic of essay* + opinion/argument/stance about the topic.

opinion   topic   opinion

The best way to *read college texts* is to use a full reading process.

2. *Topic of essay* + opinion/argument/stance about the topic + *supporting idea 1* + *supporting idea 2* + *supporting idea 3* (and so on).

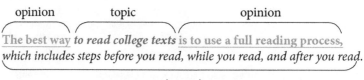

opinion   topic   opinion

The best way *to read college texts* is to use a full reading process, *which includes steps before you read, while you read, and after you read.*

supporting points

Location of Thesis Statement

The thesis statement may come in different places depending on the type of essay. In a traditional college essay, the thesis comes as the first or final sentence of the introductory paragraph. However, some college writing assignments may ask for the thesis in a section at the end titled "conclusions." This is particularly true of writing in science and social science classes. It may also be true of narrative essays in which you tell a story followed by the moral—or thesis.

As you read college texts, thesis statements may come at the beginning, end, or even in the middle. In some cases, there will be no thesis statement at all. The text may be informational and will not present an argument or opinion, or the text may present an implied thesis and ask the reader to figure it out using the clues provided throughout the text.

Common Mistakes in Writing Thesis Statements

As you write thesis statements for your own essays, be careful to avoid the following mistakes:

- **Too Broad** Your thesis must define an idea that is supportable in a college essay of two to four pages (for the purposes of this class). A common mistake is to choose a thesis that is too broad for a short paper. For example, a thesis such as "how to build a house" is too broad; there are whole books written on that topic. In a short college essay, it would be more appropriate to narrow the topic to how to build a level floor or how to install windows properly.
- **Too Narrow** However, be careful not to choose a thesis that is too narrow, or you will not have enough to say in the paper. For example, a thesis on the topic "the color of my car" would be too narrow as it would be difficult to develop multiple paragraphs about that subject.
- **Announces Intention** It is best to avoid announcing your intention with statements like, "In this essay I will…" or "This essay proves that…."

Practice 3.5   Analyzing the Structure of Thesis Statements

DIRECTIONS: The following are sample thesis statements. Highlight the topic in one color, and highlight the argument, opinion, or stance in a second color. If the thesis includes supporting points, highlight those in a third color.

1. College can change you by helping you reach your potential.
2. The purpose of college is to help you get a better job, as shown through my own experience, Laurie Sison's story in "Reclaiming Native Education," and my dad's experience.
3. College can change you by helping you find your identity in your career, in your relationships with loved ones, and as a citizen.

Introduction to an Essay

Think of the introduction as an invitation to a big party. An invitation should give the logistics—the *"what, when, where"*—but it should also get you excited to go to the party. Likewise, the **introduction** should give the reader a clear sense of what your paper will be about, but it should also excite the reader's interest in the essay.

Components of the Introduction

First, an introduction should include something that catches the reader's attention and invites the reader into the paper. Second, the introduction should set up and preview the topic for the paper. Third, it should include a thesis. The thesis traditionally comes as either the first or final sentence in the introduction. The following is a quick equation to help you remember the components of a strong introduction.

$$
\begin{array}{l}
\text{Catch Reader's Attention} \\
+ \text{Introduce Paper's Topic} \\
+ \text{Thesis} \\
\hline
= \text{Introduction}
\end{array}
$$

As you read essays, pay attention to things the writers do to catch the reader's attention. Make a note of what works, so you can use these strategies in your own introductions. In addition, play with some of the following suggestions, combining them as needed to develop your introduction. Be creative, have fun, and think of what will get your reader most excited about and prepared for reading your essay.

- **Story** Tell a story about a time in your own life or a friend's life that relates to the topic of your paper. Do not be afraid to add plenty of details to help make the story more vivid.

  Example: *If your paper is about how college changes relationships with family members who did not go to school, you might start with a story about a friend of yours who became a role model for his siblings after earning his associate's degree in accounting.*

- **Simile** Start with a simile that represents your paper's topic.

  Example: *If your paper is about how going to college can help you develop into a more complete person, you might start with a comparison to a butterfly, talking about how the butterfly can only become what it is meant to be by going through a chrysalis stage, or transformation. So, too, do people have to go through transformative experiences such as college to help them realize their potential.*

- **Background Information** Give background information about your topic.

  Example: *If you are writing about the value of coordinated studies classes, you might want to include some background information about coordinated studies classes and how they function, because your reader might not know what these are and how they differ from regular classes.*

- **Question** Ask a question.

  Example: *If you are writing about the usefulness of the Writing Center on your campus, you might start your introduction with a couple of questions. "Have you ever felt alone and in need of help when trying to write a paper for one of your college classes? Have you ever wondered where you could get specialized help with your writing?"*

Length of the Introduction

An introduction is usually one paragraph. However, you may find longer introductions in texts you read for college. You also may write longer introductions for papers you write in advanced college classes.

What to Avoid in an Introduction

There are several things that can cause an introduction to fail.

- **Overused Phrases** Overused phrases such as "throughout time" or "in our society today" do little to excite the imagination of the reader and pique his or her interest in the paper. They are also hard to support or illustrate in a paper. For example, it is next to impossible to tell what all people have thought throughout time and in every location within a two- to three-page paper. Avoid such phrases, and replace them with more engaging ideas that the paper can actually support.
- **Tangential Ideas** The introduction should not present ideas that the paper will not develop; rather, it should preview what will be discussed in the paper. Make sure your introduction fits the paper and focuses on ideas that will be talked about in the paper.
- **Lack of Thesis** Most college essay assignments will direct you to state your thesis in the introduction. Therefore, an introduction that fails to provide a thesis or that obscures the thesis will not fulfill your assignment.

Practice 3.6   Analyzing the Structure of Introductions

DIRECTIONS: Read through the following sample introductions written by students. Then answer the questions about these two introductions.

Introduction 1

Crawling along the scorching hot branch, looking for a worthy enough place to construct its cocoon, this caterpillar is trying to find a way, through many trials and tribulations, to go through metamorphosis and become a butterfly. Like this butterfly, many existing, as well as future, college students will develop and change the way they live life, entering into a more responsible and established lifestyle. When people go to college, their whole world changes in many aspects. Many people do not believe college is beneficial to a person's life. Contrary to such perceptions, college makes you more mature in the relationships you have with your family, expands on your horizons, and changes the values you hold.

Introduction 2

Are you struggling in math? Do you have math anxiety? Well I know someone who was struggling and having math anxiety. Her name was Jaime, and no matter how hard she tried and tried, she could not get math. Her teacher just did not have the time for her, and her classmates were trying to keep up on their own work. Her friend said, "If you are struggling, then the Math Center could be a very helpful tool." Jaime took her friend up on the offer. Jaime learned that the Math Center has many different ways that it can help you out in math, and it helped her succeed in her class. The Math Center is a useful resource for students who need help with their math.

1. What strategies did the authors use to catch your attention in each example introduction? Do you feel these worked? Why or why not?
2. How did each author introduce his or her thesis? Do you think each author gave enough information to allow you to get a feel for the topic of his or her thesis? Why or why not?
3. Where is the thesis statement in each example introduction? Was it easy to find each thesis statement? Why or why not?
4. What do you think are the strengths of these examples? What are the weaknesses?

Supporting Body Paragraphs

The purpose of support in an essay is similar to that of support in a paragraph: it explains and proves the thesis. While the thesis tells the reader what the essay will be about, the support illustrates, explains, and expands on the thesis.

Types of Support

Like support in a paragraph, support in an essay can be provided in many ways. It can be examples, stories, descriptions, facts, quotes, statistics, definitions, or illustrations. Any information that helps to prove your thesis is support in an essay.

Unless your instructor has specified that you include only certain types of support in your essay, your essay will be stronger and more fully developed if you include various types of support. A reader will understand your thesis in a deeper manner if you offer quotations, examples, descriptions, and statistics, and evidence that uses ethos, pathos, and logos. The reader might only partially understand your thesis if you offer only one or two of these types of support. Therefore, it is not only the amount of support that is important but also the variety of support.

Quantity and Variety of Support

Texts that are well supported are those that fully convince the reader of their thesis by using a variety of types of support. There is no easy equation for how much support is "enough"; if the support convinces the reader, it has achieved its purpose. As you write your own essays, the best rule of thumb is to get feedback from a reader who does not know you or your topic well. See if the support you have provided convinces that reader of your point as well as helps that reader understand your point. If not, you need more or different support.

Location of Support

The support should be provided in the body paragraphs of the essay and not in the introduction or conclusion. The structure of the essay will impact how the support is arranged in the body paragraphs, but it will always come after the introduction and before the conclusion.

Body Paragraph Structure

Body paragraphs can be structured in a variety of ways, but they should all have the basic components of topic sentence, support, and analysis that were outlined earlier in this chapter. For more examples of how to organize body paragraphs, refer to Chapter 4.

Transitions within an Essay

In a larger work such as an essay, the purpose of transitions is to help readers understand how body paragraphs relate to each other and to the thesis. You can use transitions when you are reading to help you understand how the parts of an article or essay lead to its thesis or main message. As a writer, you need to use transitions to help readers see how your body paragraphs are connected.

Types of Transitions

You can look for and use the transitional words for paragraphs listed on page 48 to identify relationships among paragraphs in what you read and to show relationships between paragraphs in what you write. You can also look for and use phrases that repeat a key idea to carry forward the reasoning from one paragraph to the next. You will see examples of transitions in the later chapters on writing essays (Chapters 7, 10 and 13). Usually, transitions that connect paragraphs come at the start of paragraphs, not at the end.

Conclusion of an Essay

If the introduction of an essay is like an invitation to a party, the conclusion is like the goodie bag that partygoers take with them when they leave. Like a goodie bag, the conclusion should send the reader off with some memories of the ideas they encountered while reading the paper as well as something he or she can do with those ideas.

Components of a Conclusion

The conclusion has two main parts. First, it should summarize or recap the main ideas in the essay. This helps the reader remember the thesis and main supporting points. Second, the conclusion should answer the question "so what?" The reader will want to know what is significant or important about the ideas in the paper, and the conclusion should explain this. The following is a quick "equation" to help you remember the components of a strong conclusion.

$$\text{Summarize Thesis and Supporting Points} + \text{Answer the Question "So What?"} = \textbf{Conclusion}$$

As you *read* essays, pay attention to what the authors do in their conclusions. Note what works well, so you can use their techniques in your own writing.

When you *write* essays for college, begin your conclusion with a summary of your paper by writing two or three sentences that restate your thesis and supporting ideas. Then select any one or more of the following ideas to address the question of "so what?" in your conclusion. This should form the final two to three sentences of your conclusion.

- **Call to Action** Give your readers a call to action, something to do with the information they have learned in your paper.

  Example: *If your paper is about the usefulness of the Writing Center on your college campus, you might end your conclusion by telling your readers to visit the Writing Center to get help with their next college writing assignment.*

- **Question** Just as you can start a paper with a question or series of questions, so, too, can you end a paper with questions to ponder.

  Example: *If you wrote a paper about how going to college can change your relationships with family members, you might ask the following questions at the end of your conclusion: "Could your act of going to college open doors for your younger siblings? Could it help others in your family see the importance of education? Could it be a decision that improves both your life and the lives of others in your family?"*

- **Story** If you started your introduction with a story, you might want to give the ending to the story in your conclusion.

  Example: *If you started your paper with a story about a friend of yours who became a role model for his siblings after earning his associate's degree in accounting, you could end it with a story about how his two sisters are now working toward degrees in teaching and nursing at their local community college.*

Length of a Conclusion

Like an introduction, a conclusion should be a paragraph in length. While you may see longer conclusions in texts you read for college, most college essays require no more than one paragraph as a conclusion.

What to Avoid in Conclusions

In order to have a strong conclusion, you want to avoid the following pitfalls:

- **Introducing New Ideas** The conclusion should sum up the paper, not introduce new ideas. Sometimes writers can introduce new ideas when they try to answer the question "so what?" Be careful that your answer to this question fits the topic of your paper.
- **Just Summarizing** Conclusions that just summarize and do not also answer the question "so what?" are a letdown to the reader. While summary is important, it is not enough by itself. You also need to tell the reader of the significance of the ideas in your paper.

Practice 3.7   Evaluating the Structure of Conclusions

DIRECTIONS: The following sample conclusions go with the sample introductions provided earlier (see pages 51–52). Read them, and then answer the questions that follow. This will give you ideas for writing your own conclusions.

Conclusion 1

Going to college can change a person in many ways. The hardest part about going to college is getting support from friends and family and actually taking the time to put all your effort into your education. Just like the butterfly, though, the transition may be hard and take time, but the end result is worth it and will be beautiful and enjoyed by many.

Conclusion 2

If you are struggling with math as Jaime was, then the Math Center is the right place for you to go. The Math Center can help ease some of your math anxiety. As you can see, the Math Center is a great reference place for people to go to, and if you have any questions, then the people in the offices can help you out.

1. Highlight in one color the sentences that summarize.
2. Highlight in a second color where the author addresses the question "so what?"
3. What do you think are the strengths of these examples? What are the weaknesses?

Chapter **Quick Check**   MySkillsLab   Complete the mastery test for this chapter in MySkillsLab.

Use the following questions and answers to check your understanding of this chapter.

QUESTION	ANSWER
Learning Objective 1: Identify yourself as both a reader and a writer.	
Why should you think of yourself as a writer and a reader?	✔ Understanding structure helps you to read and understand texts as well as compose strong texts of your own.
Learning Objective 2: Recognize the structure and parts of a paragraph.	
What are the four basic components of a paragraph?	✔ A paragraph should contain a *topic sentence, support, analysis,* and *transitions.*
What is the purpose of the topic sentence of a paragraph, and what should be included in this sentence?	✔ The *topic sentence* tells the reader what will be the focus of the paragraph. It should include the topic of the paragraph and your opinion, stance, or argument about that topic.
What types of support can you use in a paragraph?	✔ *Support* can consist of stories, descriptions, statistics, facts, illustrations, examples, quotations, or anything else that develops the topic of your writing.
What is analysis, and what should it do in one's writing?	✔ *Analysis* can be the writer's interpretation of the support; it can explain how multiple supporting ideas and details connect or how the support links back to the topic sentence. Its purpose is to help the reader understand the relationship between the support and main idea.
Learning Objective 3: Recognize the structure and parts of an essay.	
What are the four basic components of an essay?	✔ An essay needs an *introduction, thesis, body paragraphs,* and a *conclusion.*
What is the purpose of a thesis statement and how is it structured?	✔ A *thesis statement* gives direction to a paper by providing its topic plus the overall argument, opinion, or stance about that topic. A thesis may also include the supporting points the writer will discuss in the paper.
What should be included in the introduction to an essay?	✔ An *introduction* should include the thesis, an overview of the topic that will be discussed in the paper, and something that catches the reader's attention.
What should be included in the body paragraphs of my essays?	✔ The *body* is organized into paragraphs, each with one main idea that supports the essay's thesis. Body paragraphs also provide supporting ideas and details perhaps including quotations and paraphrases.
What should an essay's conclusion contain?	✔ A *conclusion* should include a summary of the thesis and main supporting points plus an answer to the question "so what?" in regards to your thesis.

Organizational Modes

4

LEARNING OBJECTIVES

In this chapter, you will learn to...

1   Understand modes used for organizing paragraphs and essays.

2   Recognize, understand, and use deductive structure.

3   Recognize, understand, and use inductive structure.

4   Recognize, understand, and use narrative structure.

5   Recognize, understand, and use descriptive structure.

6   Recognize, understand, and use process structure.

7   Recognize, understand, and use comparison–contrast structure.

8   Recognize, understand, and use analysis structure.

Warm Up

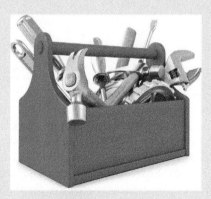

DIRECTIONS: Look closely at the picture and answer the following questions.

- Imagine that you have a carpentry job repairing a deck on a neighbor's house. What tools might you use for this job? Which ones would you leave in the box? Why?

- Why is it important to know how to use all of the tools in the box even if you do not use them for every repair job you might do? What does this knowledge allow you to do when you approach a new job?

MySkillsLab
Complete the Warm Up at
www.myskillslab.com

Organizational Modes Are Like Tools in Your Toolbox

Learning Objective 1
Understand modes used for organizing paragraphs and essays.

Different structures for paragraphs and essays are like tools in a toolbox; they each have distinct purposes and uses to achieve specific purposes. Learning how these different structures, or "tools," work can help you to be a stronger writer and reader. For example, if you were going to write about the process of repairing a deck, you would want to select an organizational structure in writing that helps you convey the information. A process structure would serve you well in this instance. In the case of reading, knowing the primary organizational structures that writers use will allow you to recognize more quickly how the text is organized. This will help you to navigate the ideas more easily as well as engage the reading process more smoothly, for example, by choosing what kind of note-taking technique will work best for the type of text.

Another way that tools and organizational structures are similar is that they can be used in combination to complete certain jobs or they can be used alone if the job is simpler. While this chapter will isolate different organizational structures, to show how each one is used, writers often combine these within a larger work, like an essay, using specific organizational modes in specific places within the text to accomplish certain purposes. For example, in an essay a writer might use narrative to catch a reader's attention in an introduction, contrast in a couple of body paragraphs to illustrate how one supporting point is stronger than another, and analysis in another paragraph or two to show the reader the different components of the thesis they are promoting in the overall essay. As you learn these organizational structures, keep in mind that they are flexible in how they can be used and combined. You can write paragraphs or essays that use a variety of structures, and you will read texts that also employ more than one structure to convey ideas.

Remember that the content of your writing comes before the structure you use to express it. Your best writing starts with what you have to say. When you know that, then you can choose to use the organizational modes to fit the content—or "job"—of your written piece.

Deductive Structure (General to Specific)

Learning Objective 2
Recognize, understand, and use deductive structure.

Deductive structure starts with the main idea in the beginning, and then the text supports the point in the following sentences. A graphic illustration of this structure looks like an upside-down triangle with the main idea at the top followed by the more specific evidence that supports that main idea.

This structure is useful when the writer wants the reader to know up front the overall topic and purpose of the paragraph. This can be especially effective for the reader who has little time and needs to know the point right off the bat.

> **Example** *If you defining a process such as how to apply for financial aid to an impatient and financially needy student, this structure would be useful because you state the topic of your paragraph up front. The friend knows right away that the information will be useful, increasing his or her odds of reading closely to what you had to say. Once you have your reader's attention, you can then give the details in the sentences that follow.*

Graphic Representation of Deductive Structure

Main idea/Topic sentence: Here is an effective process for applying for financial aid.

Support: Talk with the financial aid office about different options.

Support: Search online for scholarships and check if you meet the qualifications.

Support: Determine which scholarships you have the best chance of winning, fill out the applications, and ensure you submit all supporting documentation in a timely fashion.

Practice 4.1　Analyzing a Deductive Paragraph

DIRECTIONS: Read the following example of a deductive paragraph, written by student Kevin Chen. Then, answer the questions that follow.

> I think going to college changes people by making them more confident. "You can do it." This sentence contains a kind of huge strength, which is confidence. I used to be encouraged by others saying, "Try it." It was obvious that they wanted to encourage me to try to do something, but there was no certainty of success. I tried, but I did not change. However, my surroundings changed when I enrolled in college, and it changed me when I got used to the ambiance of colorful college life. People will have multiple opportunities and face different challenges when they take part in those activities in college. There are so many things they never believed they could do before.

1. Where is the writer's topic sentence in this paragraph?
2. How does the rest of the paragraph develop that topic sentence?
3. Compare this paragraph with the inductive one in the following section. Which organization do you think works best for this writer's topic? Why?

Practice 4.2　Writing a Deductive Paragraph

DIRECTIONS: Using the writing process introduced in Chapter 2, write a deductive paragraph. You can choose your own topic, or you can write about how college changes a person.

Inductive Structure (Specific to General)

Learning Objective 3
Recognize, understand, and use inductive structure.

Inductive structure begins with a specific supporting example and ends with a general main idea. A graphic representation of this structure looks like a right-side-up triangle. This structure allows the writer to build a case for the overall point before stating that point explicitly. Some readers, especially those who might be skeptical of the essay's ideas, are better convinced by the support than they are by the writer's explicit statement of purpose or main idea.

> **Example** *If you want to persuade a doubting student to visit the Writing Center, this structure allows you to first identify the benefits of going to the Writing Center. As the student considers these points, he or she can slowly come to the conclusion that the Writing Center is a great place to go to get help with writing. Your final concluding sentence, then, is the final, general statement of that point—the main idea or topic sentence. You lead them to your way of thinking, making them feel like the final conclusion is their idea rather than yours.*

Graphic Representation of Inductive Structure

Support: There are tutors at the Writing Center who help you work on assignments.

Support: The Writing Center has computers so that you can work on assignments and practice writing skills and techniques.

Support: With the help of the Writing Center I received an A on the last paper I worked on.

Main idea/Topic sentence: The Writing Center is a great place to go for help with writing.

Practice 4.3   Analyzing an Inductive Paragraph

DIRECTIONS: Read the following example of an inductive paragraph, written by student Kevin Chen. Then, answer the questions that follow.

> "You can do it." This sentence contains a kind of huge strength, which is confidence. I used to be encouraged by others saying, "Try it." It was obvious that they wanted to encourage me to try to do something, but there was no certainty of success. I tried, but I did not change. However, my surroundings changed when I enrolled in college, and it changed me when I got used to the ambiance of colorful college life. People will have multiple opportunities and face different challenges when they take part in those activities in college. There are so many things they never believed they could do before. I think going to college changes people by making them more confident.

1. How does the writer of this paragraph introduce his topic and invite you into the paragraph?
2. Where is the writer's topic sentence in this paragraph?

3. How does the beginning of the paragraph set up that topic sentence?

4. Compare this paragraph with the general-to-specific one on page 58. Which organization do you think works best for this writer's topic? Why?

Practice 4.4   Writing an Inductive Paragraph

DIRECTIONS: Using the writing process introduced in Chapter 2, write an inductive paragraph. You can choose your own topic, or you can rewrite your deductive paragraph into an inductive one by using the same topic.

Narrative Structure

Learning Objective 4
Recognize, understand, and use narrative structure.

Narrative structure is used when a writer wants to tell a story in order to illustrate a larger point he or she is making. The topic sentence or thesis in a narrative piece states the topic of the story and the writer's opinion, stance, or argument about the meaning or message of that story. The supporting ideas follow in chronological order, or the order in which the events took place. The only exception is if there is a flashback. In this case, the chronological order of events is interrupted with a flashback to something that took place earlier. If you do this in your own narrative writing, however, be careful to clearly indicate this to your reader, so he or she does not get confused.

Narrative structure uses third person (*he*, *she*, *they*, etc.) or first person (*I* or *we*). While you will want to avoid using first person in most writing you do for college, you need to use it in narrative writing if you are telling a story that is about you.

Graphic Representation of Narrative Structure

Practice 4.5   Analyzing a Narrative Paragraph

DIRECTIONS: Read the following example of a narrative paragraph, written by student Sonith Kun. Then, answer the questions that follow.

> I have two brothers. They are similar in some ways, but mainly they are different. It was a few years ago when I was in high school. I always heard my brothers talking about college. The first one thought that higher education would be the best for his future.

(continued)

The second one thought that if he could work without going to college and still earn the same amount of money as those who graduated from college, why would he want to waste the time on college? According to these two perspectives, I thought I would choose not to attend college and work right away after I graduated. I never understood why most people go to college if they can work. However, I ended up going to college, and it changed my perspective. It helped me understand that going to college is not just about earning a degree and working. It also helped me to improve my skills and learn valuable things for life that I could not learn anywhere else. Now I know that college is the best place to be, and I am planning to finish my AA and transfer to the University of Washington. This shows that college allows people to change their perspectives on life.

1. Where is the topic sentence of this paragraph?
2. According to this topic sentence, what does the writer promise to address in the paragraph? What is the writer's stance or opinion about this topic?
3. What details does the writer use to develop her story?
4. In what order are these details arranged?
5. Although this paragraph illustrates narrative writing, it also illustrates a structure we reviewed earlier in this chapter. Which structure does it illustrate? Why?

Practice 4.6   Writing a Narrative Paragraph

DIRECTIONS: Using the writing process introduced in Chapter 2, write a narrative paragraph. You can choose your own topic, or you can write a story about what led you to go to college.

Descriptive Structure

Learning Objective 5
Recognize, understand, and use descriptive structure.

Descriptive structure is used to describe a person, place, or thing. It can be used in an entire written piece to give a detailed description of something to a reader, or it can be used in part of a written piece to help a reader better understand a topic before the writer compares it to something else or tells a story about it.

The topic sentence or thesis of a descriptive piece includes the topic being described and the writer's opinion, stance, or argument about that topic. Descriptive structure describes a topic as it is frozen in time. You want to provide a sensory experience for your reader, telling him or her what the topic of your writing looks like, smells like, tastes like, and so on. There are two types of support commonly used in descriptive writing: sensory details and spatial details.

1. *Sensory details* are those that address the five senses. They describe how the topic smells, sounds, looks, feels, and tastes.
2. *Spatial details* relate to the topic in terms of space. For example, if you were describing a house using spatial details, you might start by describing the first room you see when you walk in the house. You would then describe the adjoining room, then the hallway, and finally the kitchen at the back of the house. Your written structure would follow the spatial structure of the house, thus making your writing spatially organized.

Graphic Representation of Descriptive Structure

Practice 4.7   Analyzing a Descriptive Paragraph

DIRECTIONS: Read the following example of a descriptive paragraph. Then, answer the questions that follow.

> The Writing Center is the best place to write your papers for college. It invites you in with soft beige walls, comfy chairs in the corner, posters about writers on the wall, and computers that surround the room. Once you enter the room and take a seat at one of the computers, you will find software that helps you compose your prose. Word for Windows, online links to dictionaries, and citation guidelines are at your fingertips if you need them. Tutors also mingle about the room, offering their assistance if you get stuck or need feedback. The sound of other students writing encourages you to focus on your own writing. It is as if their keystrokes are saying, "You can do it! You can do it!" Next time you face a writing assignment for one of your classes, visit the Writing Center. You'll be glad you did!

1. Where is the topic sentence of this paragraph?
2. According to this topic sentence, what overall topic does the writer promise to address in the paragraph? What is the writer's stance or opinion about this topic?
3. What details does the writer use to develop her description? List some of the spatial details. List some of the sensory details.
4. In what order are these details arranged?
5. Although this paragraph illustrates descriptive writing, it also illustrates a structure we reviewed earlier in this chapter. Which structure does it illustrate? Why?

Practice 4.8   Writing a Descriptive Paragraph

DIRECTIONS: Using the writing process introduced in Chapter 2, write a descriptive paragraph. You can choose your own topic, or you can write a description of a favorite place on campus.

Process Structure

Learning Objective 6
Recognize, understand, and use process structure.

Process structure is used to describe a series of steps one takes to accomplish a goal. This structure is useful when a writer wants to share with a reader how to do something or how something works. Writers may use this structure to describe a process, to teach the reader something new, to argue about the best process for completing a task, to reflect on a process in order to determine its effectiveness, and so on.

The topic sentence or thesis of a process piece identifies the process and the writer's opinion, stance, or argument about that process. The support explains the steps in the process, starting with the first step and ending with the final step.

Graphic Representation of Process Structure

Practice 4.9   Analyzing a Process Paragraph

DIRECTIONS: Read the following example of a process paragraph. Then, answer the questions that follow.

When you revise a paper for a college writing assignment, there are certain steps you need to take. First, you need to examine the big ideas to make sure they are clear and organized in a way that makes the paper coherent. To do this, cut and paste your thesis and just the topic sentence from each body paragraph into a separate paragraph, so you can read them back in sequence. Review these sentences closely to make sure they all connect and the supporting points back up the thesis. Second, examine the supporting ideas in your body paragraphs. Read the support and ask yourself if you have given enough details to back up each point. Look for areas where you could add more, so your reader will better understand what you are saying. Third, reread just the introduction and conclusion to your paper. Does the introduction invite the reader into the paper and set up the thesis? Does the conclusion recap the paper's main topic and leave the reader with some point of significance? Finally, edit the paper for grammar and spelling mistakes. A good way to do this is to read the paper from the final sentence to the first sentence. By reversing the order, your eyes will better see mistakes. Following these steps will help you improve your grades in writing.

1. Where is the topic sentence of this paragraph?
2. According to this topic sentence, what overall topic does the writer promise to address in the paragraph? What is the writer's stance or opinion about this topic?
3. What steps does the writer use to develop his or her topic?
4. Does the writer use signal words to help the reader navigate this organization? If so, what signal words did you find?

Practice 4.10   Writing a Process Paragraph

DIRECTIONS: Using the writing process introduced in Chapter 2, write a process paragraph. You can choose your own topic, or you can write about the process of registering for your classes for next quarter.

Comparison–Contrast Structure

Learning Objective 7
Recognize, understand, and use comparison–contrast structure.

Comparison–contrast structure is used to examine similarities (comparison) and/or differences (contrast) between two topics. Sometimes the purpose is to describe these similarities or differences, while other times the purpose may be to use the similarities or differences to support a larger conclusion or argument about the two topics.

The topic sentence or thesis for a comparison–contrast piece will always include the two topics. In addition, the topic sentence or thesis should identify whether the text will compare, contrast, or do both, as well as the writer's opinion, stance, or argument about the two topics. The support in a comparison–contrast piece should be arranged around categories common to both of the topics. The text should talk about the same categories for each of the topics.

There are two main ways to organize supporting ideas and details in a comparison–contrast piece: *block structure* and *alternating structure*. Both methods cover the same content, but they arrange it differently. Either organizational structure is appropriate, but the text should stick to one throughout.

Following are two graphic representations of comparison–contrast structure. One shows the block method, and the other shows the alternating method. Note that both have a total of six points and that these points are the same. The difference is the order in which the points are given to the reader.

Block Structure

In the **block structure** method, the writer talks about all of the categories for comparison–contrast for the first topic and then all of the categories for the second topic. In other words, the writer discusses each topic in a block before moving to the next topic.

In the following example, the writer first discusses three categories (*curriculum*, *teachers*, and *class activities*) in relation to the topic of coordinated studies, and then the same three categories in relation to the topic of regular classes.

Graphic Representation of Block Method

Topic 1: Coordinated Studies

Category 1: Curriculum

Category 2: Teachers

Category 3: Class activities

Topic 2: Regular Classes

Category 1: Curriculum

Category 2: Teachers

Category 3: Class activities

Paragraph Contrasting Coordinated Studies Classes and Regular Classes

Topic 1: Coordinated Studies Classes

Category	Support
1. Curriculum	Coordinated studies classes integrate curriculum from two different classes. For example, in a class that combines art and geology, you might show your understanding of a geological topic by painting a picture of this topic.
2. Teachers	There are two teachers in coordinated studies classes, one from each of the classes being combined. They often teach together for the entire class.
3. Class Activities	Coordinated studies classes emphasize active and integrated learning. For example, students do group work such as group discussions or group projects that ask them to integrate what they learn about the class topics.

Topic 2: Regular Classes

Category	Support
1. Curriculum	Regular classes teach topics that focus on just the subject of the class. For example, you would learn about the Civil War in an American history class or animal types in a biology class.
2. Teachers	There is just one teacher in a regular class.
3. Class Activities	Regular classes can have many types of activities, but there tends to be less of an emphasis on engaging students actively in group projects and presentations. Most regular classes use lecture as a primary way to teach students.

Practice 4.11   Analyzing a Comparison–Contrast Block Method Paragraph

DIRECTIONS: Read the following example of a block comparison–contrast paragraph. Then, answer the questions that follow.

> Learning in high school is radically different from learning in college. In high school, you are often able to do homework in class, and there is not a lot of homework each day. If you need help with your homework, you may be able to get a tutor, but usually you need to get help from the teacher or on your own at home. In high school, the classes go at a slower pace, and the teacher provides you with a lot of reminders and support to help you with your learning. In college, however, there is a lot of homework each day, and it is expected that you will complete it outside of class. If you need help, there are tutoring centers available on campus that offer free tutoring in almost any subject. College classes move faster than high school classes; there is a lot that is covered each day in a college class. Finally, college classes require the student to be more responsible for his or her own learning. It is up to the student to stay on top of his or her work, ask for help when needed, and remember due dates. Therefore, when you make the transition from high school to college, expect quite a few differences in what is expected of you as a student.

1. Which is the topic sentence of this paragraph?
2. According to this topic sentence, what two topics does the writer promise to address in the paragraph? Will the writer compare or contrast these topics? What is the writer's stance or opinion about these topics?
3. What details does the writer use to develop this paragraph?
4. Highlight in one color all of the support about one topic. Then highlight in a second color all of the support for the other topic. After you highlight your support, what do you notice about how this support is organized?
5. Compare this paragraph with the one in Practice 4.13 (p. 69) titled "Analyze a Comparison–Contrast Alternating Method Paragraph." While these paragraphs both have the same content, how do their different organizational structures affect the way you as a reader are able to understand and process that content? For example, is one easier to understand than the other? Why?

Practice 4.12   Writing a Comparison–Contrast Block Method Paragraph

DIRECTIONS: Using the writing process introduced in Chapter 2, write a comparison–contrast block method paragraph. You can choose your own topic, or you can write a comparison between the learning environment at college and the learning environment at the place you studied prior to coming to college.

Alternating Structure

In the **alternating structure** method, the writer talks about the first category in relation to topic one and then topic two. He or she then proceeds to the second category for topic one and the second category for topic two. The support continues this pattern until there are no more supporting points. In other words, the writer switches back and forth between the two topics, focusing on each category at a time.

In the following example, the writer discusses three categories (*curriculum*, *teachers*, and *class activities*) to contrast coordinated studies and regular classes.

Graphic Representation of Alternating Method

Category 1: Curriculum
Topic 1: Coordinated studies
Topic 2: Regular classes

Category 2: Teachers
Topic 1: Coordinated studies
Topic 2: Regular classes

Category 3: Class Activities
Topic 1: Coordinated studies
Topic 2: Regular classes

Paragraph Contrasting Coordinated Studies Classes and Regular Classes

Category 1: Curriculum

Topic 1: Coordinated Studies Classes	Topic 2: Regular Classes
Coordinated studies classes integrate curriculum from two different classes. For example, in a class that combines art and geology, you might show your understanding of a geological topic by painting a picture of this topic.	Regular classes teach topics that focus on just the subject of the class. For example, you would learn about the Civil War in an American history class or animal types in a biology class.

Category 2: Teachers

Topic 1: Coordinated Studies Classes	Topic 2: Regular Classes
There are two teachers in coordinated studies classes, one from each of the classes being combined. They often teach together for the entire class.	There is just one teacher in a regular class.

Category 3: Class Activities

Topic 1: Coordinated Studies Classes	Topic 2: Regular Classes
Coordinated studies classes emphasize active and integrated learning. For example, students do group work such as group discussions or group projects that ask them to integrate what they learn about the class topics.	Regular classes can have many types of activities, but there tends to be less of an emphasis on engaging students actively in group projects and presentations. Most regular classes use lecture as a primary way to teach students.

Practice 4.13   Analyzing a Comparison–Contrast Alternating Method Paragraph

DIRECTIONS: Read the following example of an alternating comparison–contrast paragraph. Then, answer the questions that follow.

> Learning in high school is radically different from learning in college. In high school, you are often able to do homework in class, and there is not a lot of homework each day. In college, however, there is a lot of homework each day, and it is expected that you will complete it outside of class. If you need help with your homework in high school, you may be able to get a tutor, but usually you need to get help from the teacher or on your own at home. In college, though, if you need help, there are tutor centers available on campus that offer free tutoring in almost any subject. In high school, the classes go at a slower pace and the teacher provides you with a lot of reminders and support to help you with your learning. College classes move faster than high school classes; there is a lot that is covered each day in a college class. Furthermore, college classes require the student to be more responsible for his or her own learning. It is up to the student to stay on top of his or her work, ask for help when needed, and remember due dates. Therefore, when you make the transition from high school to college, expect quite a few differences in what is expected of you as a student.

1. Which is the topic sentence of this paragraph?
2. According to this topic sentence, what two topics does the writer promise to address in the paragraph? Will the writer compare or contrast these topics? What is the writer's stance or opinion about these topics?
3. What details does the writer use to develop this paragraph?
4. Highlight in one color all of the support about one topic. Then highlight in a second color all of the support for the other topic. After you highlight your support, what do you notice about how this support is organized?
5. Compare this paragraph with the previous one in Practice 4.11: Analyze a Comparison–Contrast Block Method Paragraph (p. 67). While these paragraphs both have the same content, how do their different organizational structures affect the way you as a reader are able to understand and process that content? For example, is one easier to understand than the other? Why?

Practice 4.14   Write a Comparison–Contrast Alternating Method Paragraph

DIRECTIONS: Using the writing process introduced in Chapter 2, write a comparison–contrast alternating method paragraph. You can choose your own topic, or you can rewrite your block method paragraph into an alternating one.

Analysis Structure

Learning Objective 8
Recognize, understand, and use analysis structure.

Analysis structure is used to break a large topic into parts to examine how each part works together to form the larger whole. Analysis structure is useful when a writer wants to look at a topic that has many parts, showing how each part supports a larger conclusion about the topic.

The topic sentence or thesis for an analysis piece states the topic the writer will analyze and the opinion, argument, stance, or conclusion that results from his or her analysis of that topic. The support in an analysis piece focuses on smaller parts of the overall topic. It discusses each part and how it relates to the larger whole.

Graphic Representation of Analysis Structure

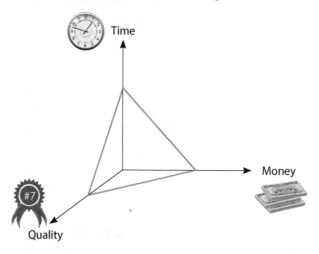

Practice 4.15   Analyzing an Analysis Paragraph

DIRECTIONS: Read the following example of an analysis paragraph. Then, answer the questions that follow.

> The poster advertising the course American Ethnic Literature helped me to determine that I want to take this course next quarter. First of all, the categories and pictures on the poster helped me to understand what American Ethnic Literature is. It included four different categories, which were "Native American Literature," "Latino/a American Literature," "African American Literature," and "Asian American Literature." Under each category, there were pictures of authors who wrote literature from that perspective. This was helpful because I put names and faces with larger categories the class would cover. Second, the poster included quotes from the various authors, which helped me to learn about the content of the course. By reading the different quotes, I could tell that the authors expressed their ideas in very different ways. Some even wrote like I talk with my friends, which surprised me. I learned from these quotes that I could relate to the literature. I am glad I saw this poster and was motivated to sign up for the class.

1. Which is the topic sentence of this paragraph?
2. According to this topic sentence, what topic does the writer promise to address in the paragraph? What is the writer's stance or opinion about this topic?
3. Highlight in one color the supporting details provided about the poster in this paragraph.
4. Then highlight in a second color the analysis, which is where the writer talks about what this support means in relation to her topic sentence.
5. How do both the support and analysis of this support (the two things you just highlighted) work together to develop the paragraph? Are both needed in the paragraph to hold it together? Why or why not?

Practice 4.16 **Writing an Analysis Paragraph**

DIRECTIONS: Using the writing process introduced in Chapter 2, write an analysis paragraph. You can choose your own topic, or you can write about the different elements of an ad you find in a magazine. (Analyze the color, images, and writing in the ad to come to a conclusion about its overall message.)

✔ Chapter **Quick Check**   **MySkillsLab**   Complete the mastery test for this chapter in MySkillsLab.

Use the following questions and answers to check your understanding of this chapter.

QUESTION	ANSWER
Learning Objective 1: Understand modes used for organizing paragraphs and essays. *What are organizational modes?*	✔ *Organizational modes* are methods for organizing information, and each is used to achieve specific purposes, for example, process structure is used to explain the steps in activity or how something works. Knowing the primary organizational structures that writers use will also help you to navigate their ideas more easily as you read.
Learning Objective 2: Recognize, understand, and use deductive structure. *What is deductive structure?*	✔ *Deductive structure* starts with the big idea and then provides specific evidence to support it. Use deductive structure when you want your reader to know immediately what your topic is and the point you want to make about it.
Learning Objective 3: Recognize, understand, and use inductive structure. *What is inductive structure?*	✔ *Inductive structure* starts with specific ideas and ends with a larger conclusion—the main idea or thesis. Use inductive structure when you want to convince a skeptical reader of your overall conclusion.
Learning Objective 4: Recognize, understand, and use narrative structure. *What is narrative structure?*	✔ *Narrative structure* tells a story or relates an experience in the order in which it happens. Use narrative structure when you want to include your own or someone else's personal experience as support for an idea.
Learning Objective 5: Recognize, understand, and use descriptive structure. *What is descriptive structure?*	✔ *Descriptive structure* uses sensory and spatial details to help readers experience the sights, sounds, tastes, smells, and physical touch related to the topic. You might use this structure to describe a place or a thing, like a favorite meal at an Italian restaurant.

(continued)

QUESTION	ANSWER
Learning Objective 6: Recognize, understand, and use process structure. *What is process structure?*	✔ *Process structure* is used to explain each step in how to do something or how something works. You might use this mode when explaining how to treat a pulled muscle or how Congress passes laws.
Learning Objective 7: Recognize, understand, and use comparison–contrast structure. *What is comparison–contrast structure?*	✔ *Comparison–contrast structure* involves explaining the similarities and/or differences of two ideas, objects, people, and so on in order to understand them. For example, you could contrast two different types of computers in order to persuade your reader to buy a certain type. Paragraphs using this structure can be organized using a block or alternating structure.
Learning Objective 8: Recognize, understand, and use analysis structure. *What is analysis structure?*	✔ *Analysis structure* involves breaking something into its parts, interpreting or evaluating the parts, and then saying how the parts contribute to the whole. You would use analysis of a movie for a film class or of a poem or novel for a literature class.

PART ONE READING SELECTION

Learning to Read and Write
Frederick Douglass

1   I lived in Master Hugh's family about seven years. During this time, I succeeded in learning to read and write. In accomplishing this, I was compelled to resort to various stratagems. I had no regular teacher. My mistress, who had kindly commenced to instruct me, had, in compliance with the advice and direction of her husband, not only ceased to instruct, but had set her face against my being instructed by any one else. It is due, however, to my mistress to say of her, that she did not adopt this course of treatment immediately. She at first lacked the depravity indispensable to shutting me up in mental darkness. It was at least necessary for her to have some training in the exercise of irresponsible power, to make her equal to the task of treating me as though I were a brute.

Frederick Douglass

2   My mistress was, as I have said, a kind and tender-hearted woman; and in the simplicity of her soul she commenced, when I first went to live with her, to treat me as she supposed one human being ought to treat another. In entering upon the duties of a slaveholder, she did not seem to perceive that I sustained to her the relation of a mere chattel, and that for her to treat me as a human being was not only wrong, but dangerously so. Slavery proved as injurious to her as it did to me. When I went there, she was a pious, warm, and tender-hearted woman. There was no sorrow or suffering for which she had not a tear. She had bread for the hungry, clothes for the naked, and comfort for every mourner that came within her reach. Slavery soon proved its ability to divest her of these heavenly qualities. Under its influence, the tender heart became stone, and the lamb-like disposition gave way to one of tiger-like fierceness. The first step in her downward course was in her ceasing to instruct me. She now commenced to practise her husband's precepts. She finally became even more violent in her opposition than her husband himself. She was not satisfied with simply doing as well as he had commanded; she seemed anxious to do better. Nothing seemed to make her more angry than to see me with a newspaper. She seemed to think that here lay the danger. I have had her rush at me with a face made all up of fury, and snatch from me a newspaper, in a manner that fully revealed her apprehension. She was an apt woman; and a little experience soon demonstrated, to her satisfaction, that education and slavery were incompatible with each other.

3   From this time I was most narrowly watched. If I was in a separate room any considerable length of time I was sure to be suspected of having a book, and was at once called to give an account of myself. All this, however, was too late. The first step had been taken. Mistress, in teaching me the alphabet, had given me the *inch*, and no precaution could prevent me from taking the *ell*.

4   The plan which I adopted, and the one by which I was most successful, was that of making friends of all the little white boys whom I met in the street. As many of these as I could, I converted into teachers. With their kindly aid, obtained at different times and in different places, I finally succeeded in learning to read. When I was sent on errands, I always took my book with me, and by going one part of my errand quickly, I found time to get a lesson before my return. I used also to carry bread with me, enough of which was always in the house, and to which I was always welcome; for I was much better off in this regard than many of the poor white children in our neighborhood. This bread I used to bestow upon the hungry little

urchins, who, in return, would give me that more valuable bread of knowledge. I am strongly tempted to give the names of two or three of those little boys, as a testimonial of the gratitude and affection I bear them; but prudence forbids;—not that it would injure me, but it might embarrass them; for it is almost an unpardonable offense to teach slaves to read in this Christian country. It is enough to say of the dear little fellows, that they lived on Philpot Street, very near Durgin and Bailey's shipyard. I used to talk this matter of slavery over with them. I would sometimes say to them, I wished I could be as free as they would be when they got to be men. "You will be free as soon as you are twenty-one, *but I am a slave for life!* Have not I as good a right to be free as you have?" These words used to trouble them; they would express for me the liveliest sympathy, and console me with the hope that something would occur by which I might be free.

5   I was now about twelve years old, and the thought of being *a slave for life* began to bear heavily upon my heart. Just about this time, I got hold of a book entitled "The Columbian Orator." Every opportunity I got, I used to read this book. Among much of other interesting matter, I found in it a dialogue between a master and his slave. The slave was represented as having run away from his master three times. The dialogue represented the conversation which took place between them, when the slave was retaken the third time. In this dialogue, the whole argument in behalf of slavery was brought forward by the master, all of which was disposed of by the slave. The slave was made to say some very smart as well as impressive things in reply to his master—things which had the desired though unexpected effect; for the conversation resulted in the voluntary emancipation of the slave on the part of the master.

6   In the same book, I met with one of Sheridan's mighty speeches on and in behalf of Catholic emancipation. These were choice documents to me. I read them over and over again with unabated interest. They gave tongue to interesting thoughts of my own soul, which had frequently flashed through my mind, and died away for want of utterance. The moral which I gained from the dialogue was the power of truth over the conscience of even a slaveholder. What I got from Sheridan was a bold denunciation of slavery, and a powerful vindication of human rights. The reading of these documents enabled me to utter my thoughts, and to meet the arguments brought forward to sustain slavery; but while they relieved me of one difficulty, they brought on another even more painful than the one of which I was relieved. The more I read, the more I was led to abhor and detest my enslavers. I could regard them in no other light than a band of successful robbers, who had left their homes, and gone to Africa, and stolen us from our homes, and in a strange land reduced us to slavery. I loathed them as being the meanest as well as the most wicked of men. As I read and contemplated the subject, behold! that very discontentment which Master Hugh had predicted would follow my learning to read had already come, to torment and sting my soul to unutterable anguish. As I writhed under it, I would at times feel that learning to read had been a curse rather than a blessing. It had given me a view of my wretched condition, without the remedy. It opened my eyes to the horrible pit, but to no ladder upon which to get out. In moments of agony, I envied my fellow-slaves for their stupidity. I have often wished myself a beast. I preferred the condition of the meanest reptile to my own. Any thing, no matter what, to get rid of thinking! It was this everlasting thinking of my condition that tormented me. There was no getting rid of it. It was pressed upon me by every object within sight or hearing, animate or inanimate. The silver trump of freedom had roused my soul to eternal wakefulness. Freedom now appeared, to disappear no more forever. It was heard in every sound, and seen in every thing. It was ever present to torment me with a sense of my wretched condition. I saw nothing without seeing it, I heard nothing without hearing it, and felt nothing without feeling it. It looked from every star, it smiled in every calm, breathed in every wind, and moved in every storm.

7   I often found myself regretting my own existence, and wishing myself dead; and but for the hope of being free, I have no doubt but that I should have killed myself, or

done something for which I should have been killed. While in this state of mind, I was eager to hear any one speak of slavery. I was a ready listener. Every little while, I could hear something about the abolitionists. It was some time before I found what the word meant. It was always used in such connections as to make it an interesting word to me. If a slave ran away and succeeded in getting clear, or if a slave killed his master, set fire to a barn, or did any thing very wrong in the mind of a slaveholder, it was spoken of as the fruit of ~abolition.~ Hearing the word in this connection very often, I set about learning what it meant. The dictionary afforded me little or no help. I found it was "the act of abolishing;" but then I did not know what was to be abolished. Here I was perplexed. I did not dare to ask any one about its meaning, for I was satisfied that it was something they wanted me to know very little about. After a patient waiting, I got one of our city papers, containing an account of the number of petitions from the north, praying for the abolition of slavery in the District of Columbia, and of the slave trade between the States. From this time I understood the words ~abolition~ and ~abolitionist,~ and always drew near when that word was spoken, expecting to hear something of importance to myself and fellow-slaves. The light broke in upon me by degrees. I went one day down on the wharf of Mr. Waters; and seeing two Irishmen unloading a scow of stone, I went, unasked, and helped them. When we had finished, one of them came to me and asked me if I were a slave. I told him I was. He asked, "Are ye a slave for life?" I told him that I was. The good Irishman seemed to be deeply affected by the statement. He said to the other that it was a pity so fine a little fellow as myself should be a slave for life. He said it was a shame to hold me. They both advised me to run away to the north; that I should find friends there, and that I should be free. I pretended not to be interested in what they said, and treated them as if I did not understand them; for I feared they might be treacherous. White men have been known to encourage slaves to escape, and then, to get the reward, catch them and return them to their masters. I was afraid that these seemingly good men might use me so; but I nevertheless remembered their advice, and from that time I resolved to run away. I looked forward to a time at which it would be safe for me to escape. I was too young to think of doing so immediately; besides, I wished to learn how to write, as I might have occasion to write my own pass. I consoled myself with the hope that I should one day find a good chance. Meanwhile, I would learn to write.

8   The idea as to how I might learn to write was suggested to me by being in Durgin and Bailey's ship-yard, and frequently seeing the ship carpenters, after hewing, and getting a piece of timber ready for use, write on the timber the name of that part of the ship for which it was intended. When a piece of timber was intended for the larboard side, it would be marked thus—"L." When a piece was for the starboard side, it would be marked thus—"S." A piece for the larboard side forward, would be marked thus— "L. F." When a piece was for starboard side forward, it would be marked thus—"S. F." For larboard aft, it would be marked thus—"L. A." For starboard aft, it would be marked thus—"S. A." I soon learned the names of these letters, and for what they were intended when placed upon a piece of timber in the ship-yard. I immediately commenced copying them, and in a short time was able to make the four letters named. After that, when I met with any boy who I knew could write, I would tell him I could write as well as he. The next word would be, "I don't believe you. Let me see you try it." I would then make the letters which I had been so fortunate as to learn, and ask him to beat that. In this way I got a good many lessons in writing, which it is quite possible I should never have gotten in any other way. During this time, my copy-book was the board fence, brick wall, and pavement; my pen and ink was a lump of chalk. With these, I learned mainly how to write. I then commenced and continued copying the Italics in Webster's Spelling Book, until I could make them all without looking on the book. By this time, my little Master Thomas had gone to school, and learned how to write, and had written over a

number of copy-books. These had been brought home, and shown to some of our near neighbors, and then laid aside. My mistress used to go to class meeting at the Wilk Street meetinghouse every Monday afternoon, and leave me to take care of the house. When left thus, I used to spend the time in writing in the spaces left in Master Thomas's copy-book, copying what he had written. I continued to do this until I could write a hand very similar to that of Master Thomas. Thus, after a long, tedious effort for years, I finally succeeded in learning how to write.

Part Two

Casebook: Reading and Writing Texts Using Narrative Evidence as Support

Crossing Borders into College

Introduction to Part Two

Part Two introduces the narrative evidence casebook with the theme of "Crossing Borders into College." This casebook demonstrates reading and writing texts that use narrative or personal experience evidence as support.

- **Chapter 5** demonstrates the reading process for texts using narrative or personal experience as their primary evidence.
- **Chapter 6** introduces students to a process for writing paragraphs using narrative evidence.
- **Chapter 7** illustrates the process of writing essays using narrative evidence.

At the end of Part 2 (p. 135), you will find the texts used for modelling the reading process and for use in text-based writing assignments: "Whistlin' and Crowin' Women of Appalachia: Literacy Practices Since College" by Katherine Kelleher Sohn and "An Insider's Perspective: The Donna Beegle Story" by Donna Beegle.

Introduction to the Casebook Theme: Crossing Borders into College

Author Julie Moore writes about her experience studying in England:

> I will always remember when I studied in London during my junior year of college. It was my first time abroad, and everything was new. While I understood the language in England because I was a native English speaker, the way the British used this language differed from how I'd used it in the U.S. I had to navigate the Tube, or underground transportation system, something completely new to me. My clothes set me apart. Even basic interactions with clerks in the grocery store or people on the streets differed from my past experiences in the U.S. I was a foreigner and had crossed a boundary into a new culture where everything I did seemed out of place.

As you begin college, you may feel a bit like Julie did when she studied abroad. The way your college is organized and separates subjects like English, Math, Business, and Science may differ from what you experienced in your previous learning institution. The way your college instructors talk may sound different; they may use words you have never heard before. You also may find that instructors and more experienced peers have expectations of you to behave in ways you have not seen before. If you feel this way, know that this is okay. College, like a different country, is a distinct place with a distinct culture. Part of your job as a student is learning the culture of college as you also learn the content in your classes. This casebook is focused on the topic of college culture, so you can see how other students, like you, have managed to cross this boundary and find success at college.

Casebook Texts

This casebook includes two reading selections, one by Donna Beegle (see p. 135) and another by Katherine Kelleher Sohn (see p. 145). Both of these texts use narrative evidence to tell the reader about the experience of crossing boundaries into college. Donna Beegle's story is a first-person account of how she moved out of generational poverty into a middle class life by getting a higher education. Katherine Keller Sohn is a researcher who collected stories of women in Appalachia who changed their lives by getting a college degree. Her article combines these different stories, and draws conclusions on what we can learn from these women. As you read and write about these texts, you will practice the full reading and writing processes to help you prepare to succeed as you cross the boundary into college.

This book also contains other texts on related themes of crossing borders, listed below, which you will find in the casebooks and Part Five. You may choose to use these readings to complete the reading and writing practices in this part of the book or your instructor may assign some of them.

Readings on the Casebook Theme of Crossing Borders into College

Crossing Borders of Social Class

"The Naked Culture" by Vincent Barnes p. 312

"Living in America: Challenges Facing New Immigrants and Refugees" edited by Katherine Garrett, Robert Wood Johnson Foundation p. 286

"The Crossing" by Rubén Martínez p. 328

"Equalizing Opportunity" by Richard Rothstein p. 342

"On the Uses of a Liberal Education as a Weapon in the Hands of the Restless Poor" by Earl Shorris p. 350

"C. P. Ellis" by Studs Terkel p. 223

"Reclaiming Native Education" by Christina Twu p. 362

Crossing Borders from High School

"Using Learning Strategies in the Various Discplines" by Laurie Kimpton-Lorence p. 317

"Now That You're Here" by Sherrie L. Nist-Olejnik and Jodi Patrick Holschuh p. 334

"On Being an Excellent Student" by Donald E. Simanek p. 360

"Reclaiming Native Education" by Christina Twu p. 362

Introduction to Narrative Evidence as Support

In this casebook, as you read and write about crossing the boundary into college, you will also learn about **narrative evidence**: using one's own experience or the experience of others as support for ideas.

Definition of Narrative Evidence

Most college reading and writing communicates one central idea called a thesis and then provides evidence to support or prove this thesis. One way to prove an idea is through narrative, or stories, or personal experience. A true story or experience helps you understand the idea an author is expressing, and telling a story can help you prove an idea in your own writing. In later chapters, you will also read and write material that uses facts, quotes, statistics, research, examples, and other means of support.

Purpose of Narrative Evidence

Narrative allows a writer to share feelings, impressions, insights, and other subjective material that helps a reader understand an experience on a personal level. In some areas of writing—in the sciences, for instance—narrative support is often seen as less reliable than other types of support such as facts, observations, examples, and statistics. However, it can actually be more reliable when the writer is trying to convey a feeling or emotion. Therefore, narrative allows the writer to capture different truths than other types of support.

Implicit and Explicit Main Idea or Thesis

Short stories or biographies that you will read for college rarely state their major point or thesis. Short stories relate personal experiences to suggest an overall meaning called a theme. As you read such a text, you have to put together the clues in the story to figure out its main message or theme—the **implicit main idea** or **thesis**. Often narratives you read have more than one theme.

However, the essays using narrative evidence that you write for your college classes will usually require an **explicit main idea** or **thesis**. The story or stories you use as support need to back up a larger point or thesis, and that point needs to be clearly stated to the reader.

Organization of Writing That Uses Narrative Evidence

Narratives are often told in **time order**, or chronological order, meaning that the details are given in the order in which they happened. Sometimes authors will use flashbacks to illustrate something important that happened earlier. To do this, the chronological order is interrupted as the author gives details about an event that took place earlier in time. After this flashback, the author resumes the story according to the original timeline. For the most part, however, narrative is organized according to the order in which the story or experience happened.

When you write a college essay using narrative evidence to support your ideas, you will organize your paper into paragraphs, each with its own main idea and narrative evidence as support. These paragraphs may be arranged in time order, or they may be organized by whose experience you are using, or according to the ideas your essay puts forward.

Types of Language

Narrative can be first person (*I* or *we*) or third person (*he, she, they*). Narratives are usually not written in second person (*you*) because they most often focus on events that happened to the writer (*I*) or those the writer observes (*he, she, they*). Also, narrative usually involves description of events, places, and people, so it includes specific, vivid language.

Vocabulary of Narrative Evidence

When talking about narratives, sometimes special vocabulary is used. "Plot" means the events of a story or narrative. "Characters" are the people who are in the story. "Setting" is when and where the narrative happens. "Theme" is the thesis, or main message, of a story.

A Reading Process for Texts Using Narrative Evidence as Support

5

LEARNING OBJECTIVES

In the chapter you will learn to...

1 Preview before you read texts using narrative evidence.

2 Actively read texts that use narrative evidence.

3 Consolidate your comprehension of texts that use narrative evidence.

Warm Up

DIRECTIONS: Look closely at the picture and answer the following questions.

1. In the picture, poverty is indicated by a direction. It is a path one might take in life. What things might cause a person to go in the direction of poverty? List the factors that could contribute to this including personal, social, family, and situational factors.

2. Likewise, the picture shows that wealth is a path one might take in life. What things might cause a person to go in the direction of wealth? List the factors—social, family, and situational—that could contribute.

3. Do you think that it is entirely a person's choice to go in the direction of either wealth or poverty? Given your lists for the first two questions in this activity, why might this be, or not be, a personal choice?

4. What impact do you think college has on a person's ability to go in either the direction of wealth or poverty?

MySkillsLab
Complete the Warm Up at
www.myskillslab.com

Phase One: Preview the Reading

Learning Objective 1
Preview before you read texts using narrative evidence.

The essays by Donna Beegle and Katherine Kelleher Sohn that are used in this chapter appear on pages 135 and 145. This chapter provides Demonstrations using Beegle's essay and asks you to complete Practices using Sohn's essay, an essay of your choice from Part Five (see the list of related themes and readings on p. 79), or one assigned by your instructor.

STEP 1: Get to Know the Text

Before you read, it is important to familiarize yourself with a text, to warm up your mind to learn and enjoy what you are reading. This is similar to how people pick up, shake, listen to, and feel a wrapped Christmas present under the tree. They want to get to know as much as possible about that present before ripping into it and finding out what is inside. Part of the fun of opening packages is to see if your guess was right. Similarly, you want to get to know a text before fully reading it.

To explore any text, you might ask yourself the following questions:

- **Title:** What is the title? What does it tell me about the content of the reading?
- **Author:** Who is the author? Do I know anything about him or her?
- **Source and Date:** What is the source of this reading? When was it written?
- **Organization and Headings:** How is this article organized? Does it have headings? If so, what can I learn about the reading from these headings?
- **Introduction:** Is there an introduction before the actual text begins? What is it about?
- **Text Structure and Order:** How is the text structured? In what order do ideas seem to be given in this reading?
- **Purpose:** What does the overall purpose of this article seem to be?
- **Audience:** Who is the intended audience for the reading?

Information Literacy: Using Online Sources

Remember to use information literacy tools such as the Internet and your college's library resources to help you in this stage of the reading process. For example, you might look up an author online or look up information in the library about the location in which the essay was set. As you do so, remember to check the reliability of the information you find by using the CRAAP Test in Chapter 1 (p. 5).

Demonstration   Getting to Know the Text

This example shows how one student answered the questions above about "An Insider's Perspective: The Donna Beegle Story" (p. 135).

1. <u>Title:</u> The title tells me that this essay is going to be about Donna Beegle. It sounds like it will be about her perspective. It also sounds like she is an insider to something, but I'm not sure what. The title is rather vague here.

2. <u>Author:</u> I don't know who Donna Beegle is or anything about her, so I searched for her on the Internet.

   <u>Information Literacy:</u> I found out quite a lot about her! There was even a video I could watch of her speaking about her experiences, which helped me to connect to her and the content of the story. Cool! She comes from generational poverty, meaning that she grew up in an extended family who had lived generation after generation in poverty. It surprised me that she was blond and blue eyed;

it's not a look I associated with poverty. She has a Ph.D. and started her own organization called Communication Across Barriers to help people out of poverty.

I used the CRAAP Test to evaluate the sources I found. The websites seemed reliable: they were all connected to her organization, Communications Across Barriers, and they provided contact information for this organization. The site was updated recently.

3. <u>Source and Date:</u> I looked up this title online, but I had a hard time finding the actual text. The title is listed as part of lectures and workshops she gives, e.g., one webpage shows it as the opening for a two-day workshop on poverty. It makes me think that this is her story and she uses it in lectures. She must have published it somewhere, too. I wonder if she continually updates it as she speaks, or if it's a script she wrote a while ago and continues to read? I'm getting more interested in reading the essay!

4. <u>Organization and Headings:</u> There are lots of headings. They seem to be in chronological order, beginning with her desire to be a mother and going on through the different phases of her education such as "Beginning my Education" and "Getting My GED." One of the headings confuses me: "Jennifer." This doesn't go with the other headings about her education. I wonder who Jennifer is and how she relates to the story. The final heading is "My Life and Family Today," so maybe Jennifer was the child referred to in the first heading about motherhood.

5. <u>Introduction:</u> No, the article does not have an introduction.

<u>Information Literacy:</u> It really helped to look up the author online, though, as it gave me a sort of introduction to the text.

6. <u>Text Structure and Order:</u> Mostly this seems chronological in order of how she got her education. Some of it seems to be about special information she wants to highlight within that chronology, though. For example, the part on "Jennifer" may be a focus on a specific person she knew during her process of getting an education and moving out of poverty.

7. <u>Purpose:</u> I think the author wants to tell us her story to help us understand how people can grow up in poverty, but how education can help them move out of that situation.

8. <u>Audience:</u> Since she shares this at workshops and lectures she delivers, the audience may be those who attend these sessions. I suppose, though, that anyone who wants to learn about poverty and how to overcome it could be her audience.

Practice 5.1   Getting to Know the Text

DIRECTIONS: Preview Katherine Kelleher Sohn's essay "Whistlin' and Crowin' Women of Appalachia: Literacy Practices Since College" on page 145, an essay of your choice, or one you have been assigned. Then answer the questions on page 82.

Information Literacy: Remember to use information literacy tools such as the Internet and your college's library resources to help you in this stage of the reading process. As you do so, remember to check the reliability of the information you find by using the CRAAP Test introduced in Chapter 1.

STEP 2: Check Your Attitude and Set Your Purpose

To further prepare for reading, you want to pay attention to how you feel about the topic(s) you discover. These feelings may cause you to read with certain preformed ideas, biases, or perspectives. You want to be aware of this as you begin to read the text, as it could affect your understanding of the material.

You may also want to notice your attitude toward the reading assignment. If you do not want to do it, you will learn a lot less from it than if you are eager to read. Many people think of all homework as a chore—as extra, unnecessary, boring practice. If your only reason for reading is because your teacher told you to, then you will understand and remember less of it. You can create your own personal reason for reading: because the topic interests you, because you already know something about it, or because it will teach you useful information. The reading will be easier and more fun if you find your *own* purpose for doing it.

Ask these questions, used in the following demonstration and practice, to guide your thinking about attitude and purpose:

- How do I feel about the ideas I am discovering in this text?
- What is my attitude toward reading right now?
- What is my purpose in reading?

Demonstration   Checking Attitude and Setting Purpose

This example shows how one student answered the questions above about "An Insider's Perspective: The Donna Beegle Story."

How do I feel about the ideas I'm discovering in this text? I'm feeling a few things. I'm a bit confused about some of the terms. I haven't learned that much about generational poverty. In fact, I had never even heard that term before I looked up Donna Beegle online and read about it there. I'm sure that I'll need to look up some words or maybe talk to my instructor to understand better what she is talking about in this article. I'm also feeling interested because my family has struggled with poverty at times. My mom suffers from bipolar disorder, and she would lose jobs because she was sick when I was growing up. I wonder if I will have some things in common with Donna Beegle. Donna Beegle's essay is long, but the headings make it seem like it will be easier to read.

What is my attitude toward reading right now? I know I need to develop stronger reading skills, so I'm excited to be doing that.

What is my purpose in reading? I know that part of my purpose in reading Beegle's essay is to also learn how to read better. It's going to be a lot to juggle as I have to pay attention to her content and my own reading strategies, but I think I can do it!

Practice 5.2 Checking Your Attitude and Set Your Purpose

DIRECTIONS: Answer the following questions about Katherine Kelleher Sohn's essay "Whistlin' and Crowin' Women of Appalachia: Literacy Practices Since College" on page 145, an essay of your choice, or one you have been assigned.

1. How do I feel about the ideas I am discovering in this text?
2. What is my attitude about the assignment?
3. What is my purpose for reading?

STEP 3: Connect Experience and Background Knowledge with the Text

Once you know the general idea of a text that uses narrative support, it can be helpful to connect your own experience to the topics being discussed. The result is that you will be more likely to remember the new information and your reading experience will probably be more enjoyable. A couple of questions you can use to connect personally with the text are:

- What experiences have I had that relate to the reading topic?
- What do I already know about this topic?

Your answers to these questions can also be used later when you write. Many assignments allow you to use your own personal experience as support or illustration for your topic. Your brainstorm now can act as a brainstorm for parts of your paper later. When you do this step for other reading assignments, be sure to save your work to use when you write your paragraph or essay.

Demonstration Connecting Experience and Background Knowledge

This example shows how one student answered questions about her own experiences as they relate to the topics in "An Insider's Perspective," so she could more easily connect to the text.

What experiences do you have with poverty? Well my mom suffers from mental illness, and this caused her to lose jobs frequently while I was growing up. Our family relied on her income, so it was always difficult to adjust when she lost a job. We experienced elements of poverty during those times. It also made it hard to save for college as any savings we had went to cover bills when she was sick.

Do you think that education can be a pathway that leads one out of poverty? Why or why not? I do think that education can be a way out of poverty. For example, my dad had a graduate degree, and it was this degree that allowed him to have a stable job that saw us through when my mom lost her jobs. If he hadn't had this education and job, I think we would've been in real trouble. However, education might not always be a way out of poverty. For example, my mom had a BA degree, but her mental illness periodically got in the way of her being able to hold onto a job. Therefore, it might not be just one's education that is important to getting out of poverty.

Practice 5.3   Connecting Experience and Background Knowledge with the Text

Look at Katherine Kelleher Sohn's essay "Whistlin' and Crowin' Women of Appalachia: Literacy Practices Since College" on page 145, an essay of your choice, or one you have been assigned. Then answer the following questions.

1. What experiences do you have with poverty?
2. Do you think that education can be a pathway that leads one out of poverty? Why or why not?
3. How might the location in which one lives impact one's ability to move out of poverty and/or to get an education?

Phase Two: While Reading

Learning Objective 2
Actively read texts that use narrative evidence.

The next phase of the reading process involves reading the text. As you do this, we ask you to take notes, work with vocabulary, and identify your thoughts and reactions. Doing these steps improves your attention, comprehension, and memory of the reading. It will also help you as you prepare to write. For example, information you map from a given article could help you outline a paragraph or essay about that article. Therefore, save all of your notes from this phase of reading because you may want to use them when you write.

STEP 4: Write Down and Define Vocabulary

Many texts you read for college will contain words that you do not understand or have never seen before. While it may be tempting to gloss over these words and ignore them, your understanding of the material will be limited if you do so. Learning new words and terms is central to learning new content in your courses.

There are different strategies you can use to learn new words. While any of these strategies can work alone, they are best used in combination. Here are some vocabulary strategies you can use as you read:

1. **Identify unknown words:** Scan the reading for words you do not know, and highlight the sentences where they appear. List these words on a piece of paper.
2. **Define by Context:** Look back at the sentence or sentences in which the words fall in the essay, and write down what you think they mean using the context of the sentences.
3. **Use a Dictionary:** Then look up the words in a dictionary, and write down their meanings. If you cannot find a meaning in the dictionary, note that you could not.
4. **Use the Internet:** Look up the words and any related terms on the Internet to learn additional information about them. Write down what you find. **Note**: This step is especially important if you could not find definitions of these words in a dictionary.

Demonstration   Writing Down and Defining Vocabulary

After scanning "An Insider's Perspective," this student listed the words he did not know and followed strategies 2–4, as shown below.

1. **Words I don't know**

   - predominantly
   - impoverished
   - below-subsistence wage

2. **Define by Context:** Look back at the sentence or sentences in which the words fall in the essay, and write down what you think they mean using the context of the sentences.

- predominantly: *This seems to mean "mostly" or "majority" because she is using it to talk about the generations of her family members.*
- impoverished: *I see "pover" in the middle of this word, which relates to "poverty" I think. Something to do with poverty?*
- below-subsistence wage: *The word "below" makes me think her wage was low. I'm not sure about "subsistence," though.*

3. **Use a Dictionary:** Then look up the words in a dictionary, and write down their meanings. If you cannot find a meaning in the dictionary, note that you could not.

- predominantly: *"For the most part: Mainly"*
- impoverished: *"Represented by a few species or individuals"*
- below-subsistence wage: *This wasn't in the dictionary*

4. **Use the Internet:** Look up the words and any related terms on the Internet to learn additional information about them. Write down what you find. **Note:** This step is especially important if you could not find definitions of these words in a dictionary.

- Below-subsistence wage: *I found a bit about minimum wage on Donna Beegle Web sites—might be related to my word? I looked "subsistence" up in the Merriam-Webster Dictionary. It means "the action or fact of maintaining or supporting one's self at a minimum level." Since the word "below" is in front of it, I think this must mean not making enough money to support yourself.*

Practice 5.4   Writing Down and Defining Vocabulary

DIRECTIONS: Read Katherine Kelleher Sohn's essay "Whistlin' and Crowin' Women of Appalachia: Literacy Practices Since College" on page 145, an essay of your choice, or one you have been assigned. While you read, apply the vocabulary strategies listed on pages 86–87.

STEP 5: Take Notes on Major Ideas and Important Details

Taking notes while you read is a powerful way to help you better understand a text. There are many ways to take notes and various purposes that notes can serve. In this casebook, we are going to show you two graphic forms of taking notes that work especially well with narrative evidence: *mapping* and *annotating*.

One of the most challenging parts of taking notes on texts using narrative support is deciding what essential information should be included and what can be left out. For the stories in this casebook, focus on primary ideas in the plot of each story. The points you include in your notes should be the major events that drive the action. For example, if you were taking notes on a story of a car chase, you would want to include where it took place, who was involved, how fast the cars were going, and whether anyone was hurt. You would omit details like the color of the car or what the passengers were wearing because these are minor points that are not essential to the plot.

Mapping

Mapping means you create a visual picture or diagram of the main ideas of the reading. When mapping, you use boxes, circles, and other shapes, as well as lines and arrows, to capture main ideas and show the relationships between these ideas. When you read a text that has headings, you can use those headings to help structure your map. The Demonstration on page 88 shows how you can do this.

Demonstration   **Taking Notes by Mapping**

This example of mapping diagrams the first two parts of Donna Beegle's story as outlined by the headings in her essay. Notice how this example uses color to show the difference between major ideas and supporting details. Color can be a powerful tool to customize your own notes, so they help you make sense of the text.

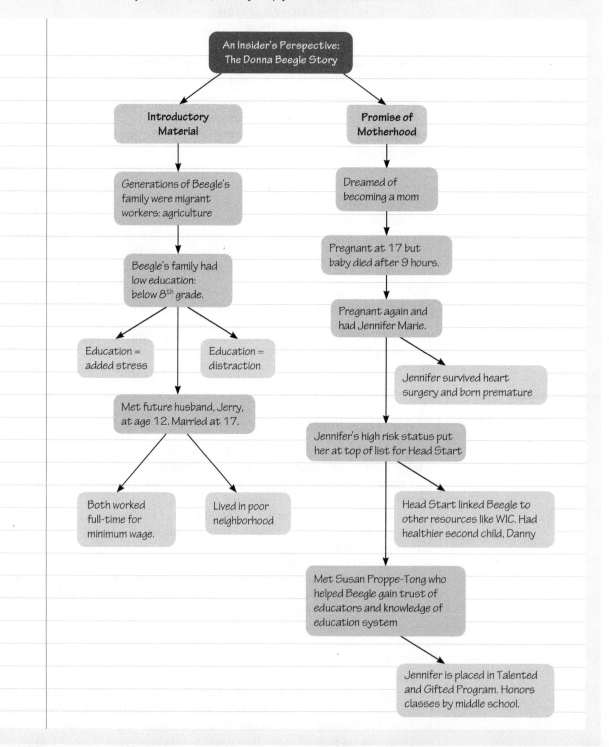

Annotating

Annotation is highlighting and taking notes on the actual pages of what you are reading. Annotating is especially helpful when reading texts that use narrative evidence: it helps you identify main events and important vocabulary as you are reading, and it helps you concentrate and stay focused on what you are reading. Margin notes and highlighting make the ideas of the reading easy to review, so you can go back and find an idea later without having to reread the whole text.

Many techniques can be used to annotate, and we hope you will practice annotating until you find the strategies and symbols that work best for you. Here are some suggestions for how to annotate effectively. The Demonstration below shows you how to annotate, using an excerpt from Donna Beegle's essay.

- **Identify main ideas:** Highlight or underline the main idea of each paragraph.
- **Summarize in margins:** Beside each paragraph or group of paragraphs, write a phrase that captures the topic of the paragraph or section.
- **Identify vocabulary:** Highlight in a different color or double-underline vocabulary words that are really important to understanding the reading.
- **Note important ideas to remember:** Put a star in the margin next to ideas or details that seem significant or that you want to remember.
- **Note areas of confusion and ask questions:** Put a question mark next to sentences that you cannot understand (try hard first). Ask questions. If you disagree with the author or are not sure he or she has sufficiently supported a point, write your questions in the margin.
- **Number lists or steps:** Use numbers to help identify lists or steps in a process.
- **Use abbreviations to help save time and space:** w/ for *with*, ed. for *education*, NA for *Native American*, and so on.
- **In your margin notes, use other symbols to save space:** Examples are as following: +, =, %, →, &, and so on.

Information Literacy: Using Outside Sources   Remember to take notes for texts you read from online or library sources, too.

Demonstration   Taking Notes by Annotating

Look at this sample annotation of a page from Donna Beegle's essay. Notice the underlining and the margin notes and symbols. Also notice how one color is used for vocabulary while another is used to note main ideas in the margins. The annotations are also organized so that vocabulary is in one margin and personal summaries and notes are in the other. As with mapping, the use of color and shapes can help you organize your annotations.

to ask to help Jennifer in elementary school. (I did not even know I could ask questions of school people. I thought we had to take whatever we got. That was what the world of poverty had taught me.) One of the questions Susan told me to ask was how Jennifer could be tested for the Talented and Gifted program. I asked that question, and Jennifer qualified for the program, subsequently getting extra educational support all through elementary school. In middle school, she was placed in honors classes.

Shows connection between poverty and educational disadvantages generations

(continued)

The Reality of Poverty

Very poor living conditions

14 By the age of twenty-two, I had been through four pregnancies and had two living children. We still had no health care and suffered from poor nutrition. Many nights our dinner was a spoonful of peanut butter. During those years, we subsisted on low-wage jobs or welfare—working in migrant labor, pizza parlors, retail, and manufacturing. We moved from place to place, hoping for a better life.

subsist-live on

Extra difficult for men in poverty

15 My marriage ended in 1986 after ten years. When Jerry and I divorced, my functionally illiterate ex-husband was living in a car that we had bought for $25 at an auction. Unfortunately for Jerry and men like him, there are few, if any, programs for males in poverty in the United States.

illiterate-can't read or write

!!!

16 I was now alone, trying to care for my six-year-old daughter (who was in the first grade) and two-year-old son. It was not long before we, too, were evicted and homeless. The difference for me and my children was that we could apply for welfare. We were given $408 per month plus minimal food stamps. With rent at $395, I had just $13 left each month for transportation, clothing, utilities, the Laundromat, soap, shampoo, and other basic necessities. I was constantly making impossible choices…pay the rent or pay the bills…have my utilities shut off or get evicted. My welfare worker told me I needed money management classes so I could stop being evicted. The message to me was clear: "Donna, you are doing something wrong. You need to get it together, to work harder. Do something!" But I did work hard. And guess what? None of the minimum-wage jobs provided me with a living wage for my little family. All work did for me was take me away from Jennifer and Daniel, who were my reason for being.

evicted-forced to leave

No way!

Beginning my Education

17 When my lights were turned off for nonpayment, I went to a Community Action Agency to ask for help. I was told about a pilot program that was connected to Mount Hood Community College (MHCC), near Portland, Oregon. The program, called Women in Transition (WIT), was designed to be a three-week life skills program for displaced homemakers. Its goal was to help single women gain an education or skills to earn a living for their families. I went to the program not thinking it would change anything, but not knowing what else to do. The director had the wisdom to know that it takes more than three weeks to interrupt poverty. She told the class the WIT staff would be there to support us whenever we needed them—even after the classes ended. I used their services for two years and then became a speaker and advocate on their behalf, sharing how much the program had made a difference in my life. Many of the strategies I teach today I learned in this program.

displaced-moved, removed

advocate-someone who makes a case for another person

WIT: A program that helps her move out of poverty through education

---

Practice 5.5   Taking Notes on Major Ideas and Important Details

DIRECTIONS: Look at Katherine Kelleher Sohn's essay "Whistlin' and Crowin' Women of Appalachia: Literacy Practices Since College" on page 145, an essay of your choice, or one you have been assigned. Then choose one of the two ways of taking notes (mapping or annotating) and take notes on the essay.

STEP 6: Write Down Your Thoughts and Reactions

Writing down your reactions to a reading *during* the process of reading it helps you to make meaning of what you read. It helps you to better understand the reading if you notice when you agree or disagree with what the author says, or when the reading reminds you of something. Further, your strong emotional reaction to what you read can influence your understanding. When you write down your feelings and thoughts, it is easier to keep your ideas separate from the author's.

To complete this step, you may elect to write your thoughts and reactions on a separate sheet of paper, or you may want to combine this with Step 5 and write them as annotations in the margins of your text. The important thing is that you are allowing yourself to interact with ideas in the text as you read.

Demonstration   **Writing Down Thoughts and Reactions**

This example shows how one student wrote down her thoughts and reactions to "An Insider's Perspective"

- Before I read this essay, I thought poverty meant the homeless person on the street. I thought that something usually contributed to this situation such as drug use or alcoholism. After reading Beegle's essay, though, my eyes have been opened to my own ignorance. I now realize that people can be born into poverty, just like they can be born into an abusive home or a wealthy home, etc. This gives them little choice about poverty since they are basically born with it.
- I also realized how much education can help a person get over poverty. I am going to college to get a better job and future for myself, but I now realize that college can lead to so much more than just a job. It is helping me to gain knowledge to be part of the middle class. I will learn things like how to speak and act in appropriate ways so that I can get a job but also be included in the culture of people who have good jobs.
- This essay helps me see how important social services like the WIT Program are to those who don't come from families or backgrounds that can help them. These programs are the only way out for some people.

Practice 5.6   **Writing Down Your Thoughts and Reactions**

DIRECTIONS: Write a reaction to one or more of the ideas in Sohn's essay, an essay of your choice, or one you have been assigned.

Phase Three: After You Read

Learning Objective 3
Consolidate your comprehension of texts that use narrative evidence.

After reading a text that uses narrative evidence, it is important to spend time strengthening your understanding by writing an effective summary, responding to the ideas supported by narrative evidence, and reflecting on your process of reading.

STEP 7: Write a Summary

A **summary** restates the ideas of an essay or article in your own words. A summary is usually one paragraph written in complete sentences that gives an accurate and complete overview of the author's main points. Summaries never include your opinion or feelings, only the author's ideas. The summary of a text using narrative evidence should explain the main points or events in the story to someone who has not read it.

Summarizing what you have read is a good final step because it allows you to make sure you understand the whole reading. It is also a good prewriting step because you may include parts of a summary in a paragraph or essay about a reading.

Guidelines for Writing the First Sentence of a Summary

A summary should start with a sentence that includes the author, title, and main message (thesis, theme, or main idea) of the reading. While you do not cite a page number for a summary, this first sentence is important because it identifies the source information and acts as citation for the entire summary.

Demonstration   Writing a Good First Sentence for a Summary

Here is an example of how to write the first sentence of a summary for Beegle's essay:

Author: Donna Beegle

Title: *"An Insider's Perspective: The Donna Beegle Story"*

Main Message: Education is vital to helping people overcome the culture of poverty

Putting it Together: Now we will combine these elements into one sentence:

> In "An Insider's Perspective: The Donna Beegle Story," Donna Beegle writes about how important education is to helping people like herself overcome the culture of poverty.

The mistakes in first sentences of summaries are usually because the main message is too narrow (specific) or too broad (general).

> **Too narrow:** In "An Insider's Perspective: The Donna Beegle Story," Donna Beegle writes about her family's experiences with poverty.

Beegle does talk about her family's experiences with poverty, but the article contains many more major ideas, so this thesis is too narrow.

> **Too broad:** In "An Insider's Perspective: The Donna Beegle Story," Donna Beegle writes about poverty.

Again, this statement is true, but this sentence tells only the *topic* of the article, not its major message, or opinion, about that overall topic.

Practice 5.7   Writing a Summary's First Sentence

DIRECTIONS: Look at your notes for Katherine Kelleher Sohn's essay "Whistlin' and Crowin' Women of Appalachia," an essay of your choice, or one you have been assigned." Then write the first sentence of your summary for that essay.

Guidelines for Writing an Effective Summary

After the all-important first sentence, you continue the summary, focusing only on very important information. Your summary should be shorter than your notes. Continue writing in complete sentences that capture the most important information all the way to the end of the article or story, using the following guidelines:

- Start with a sentence that includes the author, title, and main message (thesis, theme, or main idea) of the reading.
- Follow with several sentences that restate the main points of the reading in the order that they occur. Remember that, for narratives, these points will probably be the main events in the plot.
- Look back at your notes to guide you as you write your summary. Capture the main ideas from your notes.
- Put the ideas into your own words. Avoid copying from the reading. Also avoid quoting passages from the reading.
- Do not include your opinion. Just restate the points of the story.
- Connect the ideas to the author so it is clear that the author (and not you) came up with these ideas.

Demonstration   **Writing a Summary**

The following summarizes paragraphs 1–28 of "An Insider's Perspective: The Donna Beegle Story."

In "An Insider's Perspective: The Donna Beegle Story," Donna Beegle writes about how important education is to helping people like herself overcome the culture of poverty. She begins by telling her own story of growing up in generational poverty and then continuing on this path by marrying and having children into this culture of poverty. She then narrates how she moves out of poverty with the help of social services that connected her to education. She began by getting her GED and went from there to community college.

Practice 5.8   **Writing a Summary**

DIRECTIONS: Look at your notes for Katherine Kelleher Sohn's essay "Whistlin' and Crowin' Women of Appalachia," an essay of your choice, or one you have been assigned. " Then write a summary of that essay.

STEP 8: Respond to the Reading

Responding gives you the chance to think back about the ideas in the text. In a response, you can ask questions of the text, make connections to other texts or your own experience, or note a strong emotional reaction to the text. It is important, though, to keep your response clearly separate from the author's ideas. Responding also helps you remember what you have read by connecting it to your own thinking and feelings. While Step 6 asked for your thoughts and reactions during the reading process and to specific points in the essay, Step 8 asks that you write a comprehensive response to the entire reading as you learned from it overall.

Here are questions to stimulate your response to any reading:

- What ideas in the text confuse me?
- What ideas in the text anger or encourage me?
- What questions am I left with after reading this text?
- How does this text connect to something I know or have experienced?
- How do ideas in this text connect with ideas in other texts I have read?
- Will I use the ideas in my life in some way?

Critical Thinking: Synthesis

Synthesizing ideas asks you to connect ideas from multiple places or sources in order to come up with new meanings or ways of seeing things. Synthesizing is a part of critical thinking, and it is what college instructors will ask you to do with the ideas you learn in and out of your classes. As you practice Step 8 of the reading process, try synthesizing as a way of responding to a text. You can do this by answering any of the following questions.

- How do the texts I found online or at the library help me understand the class text better? What do these texts mean when put together or alongside one another?
- How do my life experiences add to or question the text?
- How do the ideas in this text relate to ideas I am learning in other classes I am taking or have taken in the past?

Demonstration   Writing a Response Using Synthesis

Here is an example of a response—using the critical thinking technique of synthesizing—to "An Insider's Perspective: The Donna Beegle Story":

> Watching Donna Beegle's online video of herself talking about her life impacted the way I thought about the text and about poverty in general. I realized that I had stereotypes about who would end up in poverty, and I also had stereotypes about who would be a migrant farm worker in poverty. I was shocked that she was a blond-haired, blue-eyed woman! I didn't realize before watching that video clip that I had already formed a picture in my head of what the author looked like, and she didn't look at all like the actual person who told her story in the online video. Using the outside resources available online forced me to confront stereotypes that I didn't even know I had. I also don't think the text alone would have forced me to confront these as I could have read the text with the existing picture in mind. This made me realize the value of doing outside research as it can change the impact of a text entirely!

Practice 5.9   Responding to the Reading

DIRECTIONS: Review your notes on (and reread if necessary) Katherine Kelleher Sohn's essay "Whistlin' and Crowin' Women of Appalachia," an essay of your choice, or one you have been assigned. Then write a response for that essay. If you looked up outside sources to help you understand her essay, feel free to write about how those helped you to better understand the text.

STEP 9: Reflect on Your Reading Process

We use the term "reflection" to mean thinking about how you read—your process—as opposed to the ideas you learned. **Reflecting** is looking back at an experience to realize what you did well, what could be done differently, and how the lessons learned can be used in the future. To reflect on your reading process, you might answer questions like the following:

- What steps of the reading process worked particularly well for me? Why?
- What steps of the reading process did not work as well for me? Why?
- How will I adapt or hone any of the steps to work better for me in the future?

Demonstration   Reflecting on the Reading Process

Here is an example of a reflection on the reading process for Beegle's essay:

> Donna Beegle's text was hard for me to read. It was one of the longest essays I've ever read, and I wanted to do a good job because this is a college class and I want to succeed. The reading process steps helped me, though, which was exciting. I found out I could do it; I could read a long essay! The steps that helped me the most were finding outside

sources and taking notes. The outside sources got me interested in reading before I started really tackling the essay. I wanted to read more because of that great video with Donna Bevegle talking. The notes were a labor, but they are so valuable—especially when you have to summarize later. I will force myself to always take good notes. I do want to work on different ways of taking notes, though. I wonder if there is a more efficient way of doing these, or if they will always take me such a long time?

Practice 5.10   Reflecting on Your Reading Process

DIRECTIONS: Reflect on the process you used to read Katherine Kelleher Sohn's essay "Whistlin' and Crowin' Women of Appalachia," an essay of your choice, or one you have been assigned. Then write down those reflections.

✓ Chapter **Quick Check**   MySkillsLab   Complete the mastery test for this chapter in MySkillsLab.

Use the following questions and answers to check your understanding of this chapter.

QUESTION	ANSWER
Learning Objective 1: Preview before you read texts using narrative support. *What steps are included in the first phase of the reading process that help familiarize you with the text?*	The steps for previewing include the following: ✔ Skim, scan, look at the title, or look at headings in order to find out more about the content of the text. ✔ Get to know the text by creating questions. ✔ Check your attitude about reading the text. ✔ Set your purpose for reading the text. ✔ Activate your background knowledge by thinking about how your own experiences might connect with the text.
Learning objective 2: Actively read texts that use narrative evidence. *What steps are included in the second phase of the reading process that help you fully understand texts that use narrative evidence?*	✔ Write down vocabulary words that you do not understand; use the context to understand them and look them up in a dictionary. ✔ Take notes about main events in the text. Mapping and annotating are two good ways to take notes on narrative evidence. ✔ Write down interesting or confusing ideas from the reading.
Learning objective 3: Consolidate your comprehension of texts that use narrative evidence. *What steps are included in the third phase of the reading process that help you consolidate your understanding?*	✔ Write a summary of the main ideas in the reading. ✔ Respond to the content in the reading, including your emotional reaction. ✔ Reflect on the effectiveness of your reading process.

6 A Writing Process for Paragraphs Using Narrative Evidence as Support

LEARNING OBJECTIVES

In this chapter, you will learn to...

1 Prewrite for a paragraph that uses narrative evidence.

2 Draft a paragraph that uses narrative evidence.

3 Revise and edit a paragraph that uses narrative evidence.

Warm Up

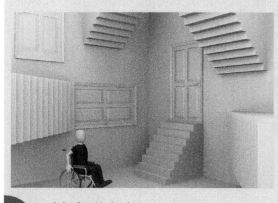

DIRECTIONS: Look closely at the picture and answer the following questions.

1. If the figure in the wheelchair were a real person, what goals might he have? What do you think he wants to accomplish given the details in this picture?

2. What are the different obstacles that stand in the way of his reaching these goals?

3. What resources does he have to overcome his obstacles and reach his goals? If you cannot identify any, list the resources that would help if they were added to this scene.

MySkillsLab
Complete the Warm Up at
www.myskillslab.com

Phase One: Prewriting

Learning Objective 1
Prewrite for a paragraph that uses narrative evidence.

The beginning phase of the writing process lets you concentrate on ideas and organization before you start to write your paragraph. It benefits you to separate the tasks of understanding your assignment, exploring ideas, focusing, gathering your narrative evidence, and organizing. When you spend time thinking (and writing) about each of these first, writing your paragraph is much easier—and you will earn a better grade on your work.

This chapter illustrates the writing process using narrative evidence from one student's experience, parts of "The Donna Beegle Story: An Insider's Perspective," and an outside source about Donna Beegle. You will be asked to complete the activities and the writing process for the paragraph by using either Beegle's (p. 135) and/or Sohn's (p. 145) essay. You could also choose to use a different essay from Part Five of this text (see list on p. 79) or use one assigned by your instructor.

STEP 1: Analyze the Assignment

The first step in preparing to write your own paragraph is to look closely at your assignment. Answering the following questions, either on paper or in your mind, will help you be sure you understand what is expected in your writing. If you are ever unsure about any of the answers to these questions, ask your instructor for help.

1. What is the purpose, goal, or objective of this assignment?
2. Who is the intended audience of the paper?
3. What is the central topic I will need to write about?
4. Can I imagine meaningful things to say about this topic?
5. What information am I supposed to use as support in this assignment?
6. What organizational structure will I need to use for this assignment?
7. How will this assignment be graded?
8. How do I feel about responding to this assignment (eager and ready, afraid, unsure, etc.)?
9. What questions do I have about this assignment?

Practice 6.1   Analyzing the Assignment

DIRECTIONS: Read the assignment below. Then answer the questions above to check your understanding of the assignment. If you have questions, ask your instructor for clarification.

Paragraph Assignment

PURPOSES The first purpose of this paragraph assignment is for you to explore the obstacles one might face when crossing the border into college, using your own experience and the experiences of Beegle, Sohn, or a writer from the list on page 79. The second purpose is for you to use a writing process. The third is for you to end up with two well-written paragraphs.

ASSIGNMENT Write these paragraphs for an academic audience. To envision who this might be, you can write for your instructor and your classmates.

Assignment
- Submit two paragraphs. Your paragraphs should each address the following question: *What obstacles can one face when crossing the border into college?*
- Each paragraph needs a clear topic sentence that provides both a focused topic for the paragraph as well as your reaction, opinion, or attitude about that topic.
- Each paragraph needs to support, or develop, the topic sentence using narrative details. One paragraph should use your personal experience as support. Another paragraph should use details from either Beegle's or Sohn's essays or one you chose from the list on page 79.

(continued)

- Each paragraph needs to stay with one main idea and be 7–10 or more sentences in length.
- Each paragraph needs to be edited for grammar and other mistakes.

How Your Paragraphs Will Be Graded

1. *Content* The paragraphs communicate a meaningful and significant idea about the obstacles one can face when crossing the border into college.
2. *Topic Sentence* Paragraphs each have an obvious topic sentence that is specific and focuses the paragraph's topic clearly. All other sentences in the paragraph relate to the topic of the topic sentence.
3. *Organization* The paragraphs are cohesive: Each sentence in each paragraph connects to the topic sentence. The paragraphs' sentences flow together and connect to one another. The details in the paragraphs are arranged in chronological order.
4. *Development and Support* The topic sentences are supported with narrative evidence. The details of experience should be vivid and chosen well to support the main idea. One paragraph should use your personal experience as evidence, and the other should use the experiences detailed in either Beegle's or Sohn's texts or one you chose from the list on page 79.
5. *Editing* The paragraph has been edited for grammar mistakes. It has also been proofread for missing words or unclear meaning.

STEP 2: Generate Ideas

The next step in the writing process is to generate ideas about which to write and details to support those ideas. There are numerous ways to generate ideas. You can list, freewrite, cluster brainstorm, and so forth. We illustrate two of these techniques in the Demonstration sections that follow. However, as you generate ideas, keep in mind the following two points.

Write from the Heart

One of the most important factors in how well you write is how much you believe in what you are writing about. Writing from the heart is the best writing to read, and, after all, your goal is to write something others want to read. Further, it is easier to write on something that you care deeply about.

How do you write from the heart? As you generate ideas for writing, it is very important to let all of your ideas flow out. If you let all of your thinking emerge in your brainstorming, then you have much more to choose from. Do not judge these first ideas and details that come to you. Write them down. From experience we have learned that the best ideas and the ones that students care most about often come out later rather than earlier. The more you brainstorm at this early stage, the more you will have to choose from that will truly communicate what you believe and know.

Draw from Your Reading Process

You have already created some ideas for your writing by following a process of reading. Therefore, gather your maps, information on vocabulary words, and any other writing you did while you read because they may have ideas that you can use in your writing.

Your instructor may have given you a different assignment than the one described in Practice 6-1, but for this casebook, we are going to use that assignment.

The first step is to generate ideas that respond to the question, *What obstacles can one face when crossing the border into college?* You can do that by brainstorming. In the following Demonstration, we show the first of a two-part process for brainstorming that begins with **listing**—writing out lists of ideas as you think of them without judging them—and ask you to further develop your ideas using listing in Practice 6.2.

Demonstration   Generating Ideas by Listing

1. **In your personal experience, what obstacles have you encountered as you have crossed the border into college?**

Lack of confidence in myself

Lack of skills (am I that bad at math?!)

Lack of family support

Lack of money

2. **What were some of the obstacles Donna Beegle experienced when she crossed the border into college?**

Lack of knowledge

Lack of language spoken in college/middle class

Difficulty balancing family and school

Lack of money

Lack of family understanding about her educational goals

Practice 6.2   Generating Ideas by Listing

DIRECTIONS: Using the Demonstration as a model, try generating ideas for your paragraphs. Use the two questions in the Demonstration above to generate obstacles from your own experience and then brainstorm obstacles that you read about in Beegle's or Sohn's essays or essays you have chosen or been assigned.

Freewriting is like listing because you write down every thought that comes into your mind, without judgment. However, you write complete sentences as opposed to making a list. You can use freewriting alone or in combination with listing as we have done here. When you use freewriting in combination with listing, choose one item from your list and freewrite about it to generate even more details about that specific idea or detail.

Demonstration Generating Ideas by Freewriting

1. **In your personal experience, what obstacles have you encountered as you have crossed the border into college?**

Lack of confidence in myself: I never have seen myself as a very good student or as smart enough to go to college. In high school, I made average grades, but I was never part of the college bound crowd. Teachers never talked to me about going to college. Nor did my family, which might be because no one in my family had gone. When my counsellor mentioned going to college, it was the first time I'd ever thought someone like me could actually get a college education. It has taken me a while to feel like I have the ability or the right to attend college. Even as I write this, I know I still doubt myself. Can I make it? Can I actually get a degree? I'm not sure I'm convinced of this yet.

2. **What were some of the obstacles Donna Beegle experienced when she crossed the border into college?**

Lack of knowledge: Donna Beegle wrote a lot about this. She had lack of knowledge in general because she dropped out before getting her high school degree. In fact, the first thing she had to do when she went back to college was get her GED. Even after getting that, though, she talks about how she has a lack of knowledge about how to speak the language of college. She refers to a mentor, Dr. Bob Fulford, who helped her learn how to speak the language of college and the middle class. I also learned from watching her video that she lacked the knowledge of how to behave in college. Many of the behaviors she'd learned growing up in a family of poverty didn't fit in the new college culture.

Practice 6.3 Generating Ideas by Freewriting

DIRECTIONS: Take a couple of items from the list you generated in Practice 6.2 and free-write about them to come up with more ideas about each topic. Remember that to address this assignment, you will need one paragraph about your own experience and another that draws from either Beegle or Sohn's essays or another text you have chosen or been assigned.

STEP 3: Focus Your Topic

Once you have generated lots of possible ideas to use in your writing, you need to find a focusing idea that you truly believe in and that fits the assignment. For a single paragraph, you want to make sure you have enough support to write ten or more sentences that illustrate your topic. To do this, first decide what you want to focus on, and then write that into one clear sentence, *a topic sentence*, for your paragraph.

Finding a Focus

In order to find a focus for your paragraph, look over your brainstorming and freewriting about the obstacles you encountered when crossing the border into college. Choose the one idea that means the most to you or the one that can best be supported with your own personal story. Then repeat this process for your brainstorming on Beegle's or Sohn's essay (or a text you have chosen or been assigned), so you can build a paragraph about evidence from one of these texts.

Demonstration   Finding a Focus for a Paragraph by Freewriting

Finding a Focus for a Paragraph on My Experience

I have a lot of obstacles that I have faced when crossing the border into college. However, after freewriting about it, I am realizing how big of an obstacle my own lack of confidence is. I didn't really realize that before freewriting about it. Therefore, I'd like to write about how lack of confidence is an obstacle I've faced when crossing the border into college.

Finding a Focus for a Paragraph Using Donna Beegle's Text

While I didn't fully relate to Donna Beegle's story because I haven't lived in that kind of poverty, I could relate to how she had to learn a different way of speaking when she came to college. Coming from an uneducated family myself, I have also experienced a difference in how my instructors want me to talk and how my family expects me to talk at home. I think I'd like to explore this idea in my paragraph about Donna Beegle by focusing on how she faced the obstacle of language when she went to college.

Practice 6.4   Finding a Focus for a Paragraph by Freewriting

DIRECTIONS: Freewrite about what focus you would like to take for each of your two paragraphs.

Drafting a Topic Sentence

Each paragraph needs a controlling idea that all other ideas in the writing connect to and support. In academic writing, it is most often expected that you will state this point clearly in a sentence. In a paragraph, you put this idea in a topic sentence. As a general rule, topic sentences should include the following:

Topic sentence = *topic* + <u>opinion/stance/argument about that topic</u>

During the writing process, there are several stages when you can draft your topic sentence. You may do so in prewriting as you generate ideas. You may do so in the outlining phase. You may even have to draft the entire paragraph to find what you want to say in a topic sentence. Finally, you may write a topic sentence and then later change it as you discover what you want to say in your writing.

Demonstration   Drafting Topic Sentences

Topic sentence for a paragraph about my experience

1. **What is the topic of your paragraph?** It will be about my own lack of confidence being an obstacle when I crossed the border into college.

2. **What opinion or argument do you want to make about this topic?** My lack of confidence made me doubt myself and got in the way of my ability to succeed.

3. **Write a topic sentence that combines these two things.**

        topic   opinion

The obstacle to my success as I crossed the border into college was my lack of confidence.

Topic for a paragraph about Donna Beegle's essay

1. **What is the topic of your paragraph?**

   Donna Beegle's crossing the border into college

2. **What opinion or argument do you want to make about this topic?**

   Beegle couldn't reach her educational goals if she didn't learn the language of college.

3. **Write a topic sentence that combines these two things.**

        opinion   topic

Donna Beegle had to learn the language of college in order to reach her goal of crossing the border into getting a higher education.

Practice 6.5   Drafting Topic Sentences

DIRECTIONS: Write a topic sentence for each of your paragraphs, using your answers to the following questions.

1. What is the topic of my paragraph?
2. What opinion or argument do I want to make about this topic?
3. Write a topic sentence that combines these two things.

STEP 4: Develop Supporting Details for a Paragraph

Once you have a focus for your paragraph, you need to develop ideas and details to support your focus. Again, the notes you took during the reading process can be a help here. For example, the map created in the last chapter could provide supporting ideas for a paragraph about Beegle's obstacles. (see p. 88).

However, while you may have generated some supporting details as a result of the reading process, you may still need to generate additional ones. You will also want to gather passages from the text you read so you can use them in your paragraph. To do this, determine the ideas for which you still need to develop support. Then, brainstorm about them using a map or freewriting, as illustrated in the following Demonstrations. Remember to find at least one passage you can quote directly to support your ideas in your second paragraph.

Demonstration   Developing Supporting Details

Paragraph with Support from My Own Experience

What supporting details have I already gathered from the reading or writing process?

I have some good ideas in step 2. I feel confident that I can write enough using these ideas I already brainstormed. I will try to expand them by giving stories that really show my reader about my lack of confidence. I will brainstorm that below.

Are these details relevant to my paragraph? I think they are all relevant.

Do I have enough of these details for my paragraph? Yes, I think so. If anything, I have too much information and will need to cut back when I write my paragraph.

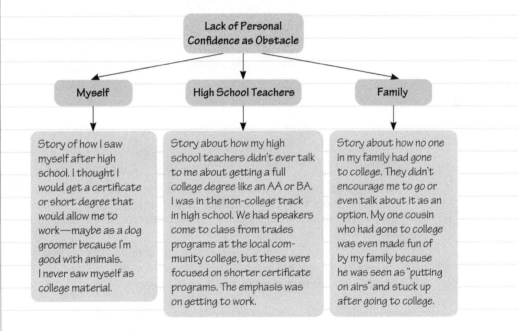

Lack of Personal Confidence as Obstacle

Myself → Story of how I saw myself after high school. I thought I would get a certificate or short degree that would allow me to work—maybe as a dog groomer because I'm good with animals. I never saw myself as college material.

High School Teachers → Story about how my high school teachers didn't ever talk to me about getting a full college degree like an AA or BA. I was in the non-college track in high school. We had speakers come to class from trades programs at the local community college, but these were focused on shorter certificate programs. The emphasis was on getting to work.

Family → Story about how no one in my family had gone to college. They didn't encourage me to go or even talk about it as an option. My one cousin who had gone to college was even made fun of by my family because he was seen as "putting on airs" and stuck up after going to college.

Paragraph with Support from Beegle's Text

What supporting details have I already gathered from the reading or writing process?

I have some great ideas in my reading notes from the section of Beegle's essay titled "Mentors, Middle-Class Language, and Meeting Me Where I Was—The Keys to My Educational Success."

I don't have any actual passages that I can quote from this section, though. I'm going to gather those by listing them now.

(continued)

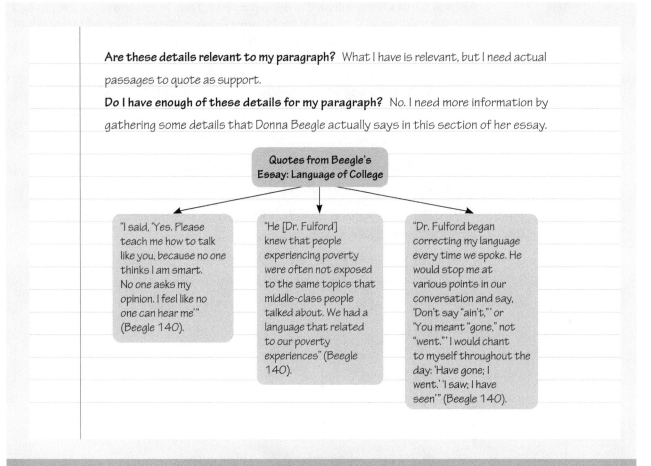

Are these details relevant to my paragraph? What I have is relevant, but I need actual passages to quote as support.

Do I have enough of these details for my paragraph? No. I need more information by gathering some details that Donna Beegle actually says in this section of her essay.

Quotes from Beegle's
Essay: Language of College

"I said, 'Yes. Please teach me how to talk like you, because no one thinks I am smart. No one asks my opinion. I feel like no one can hear me'" (Beegle 140).

"He [Dr. Fulford] knew that people experiencing poverty were often not exposed to the same topics that middle-class people talked about. We had a language that related to our poverty experiences" (Beegle 140).

"Dr. Fulford began correcting my language every time we spoke. He would stop me at various points in our conversation and say, 'Don't say "ain't,"' or 'You meant "gone," not "went."' I would chant to myself throughout the day: 'Have gone; I went.' 'I saw; I have seen'" (Beegle 140).

Practice 6.6   Developing Supporting Details

DIRECTIONS: Answer the following questions in regard to the supporting details in your paragraph about your own experience as well as your paragraph about either Beegle's or Sohn's text or a text you have chosen or been assigned. If you need to find more supporting evidence for either paragraph, do that here as well.

1. What supporting details have I already gathered from the reading or writing process?
2. Are these details relevant to my paragraph?
3. Do I have enough of these details for my paragraph?

STEP 5: Organize Your Ideas

Organization refers to the order and flow of the ideas and details in your writing. It is important to give thought to this before drafting, so that you have a roadmap of what to say. Planning now will save time and energy later when you start to write your full paragraph.

Narrative Structure

This casebook focuses on narrative evidence, and narratives are organized in **chronological order**; this means that the experiences in your paragraphs need to be presented in the order they happened. As noted earlier in the chapter on structuring paragraphs, sometimes you can use flashbacks to present details that happened earlier in time. However, you then want to return to chronological order as started prior to the flashback.

Coherence

Coherence means that a paragraph is organized so that the reader can easily follow what has been written and the relationships between ideas are clear. As you arrange your ideas and details, make sure all of the points you include support the topic sentence of your paragraph. This can be especially tricky when using narrative evidence because it can be easy to start to tell a story and then go off in a different direction. Your story then ends up saying something other than what you intended, or, worse yet, it does not ever get to the point. Therefore, as you arrange ideas and details in your paragraph, make sure each sentence builds on the one previous to it and goes with the main idea for the paragraph. You will double-check this in the final phase of revision, too.

One of the best ways to make sure your organization is strong and to prepare to draft a well-organized paper is to outline. Outlining provides a guide that you can follow as you draft your writing. The following Demonstration includes sample outlines. They are not the only method for organizing a paragraph with narrative support, but they offer one possible technique. Using a map like the ones illustrated on pages 103–104 can also be a useful organizing tool if you prefer a more visual layout.

Demonstration   Organizing Ideas by Outlining

<u>Outlining the Paragraph (My Experience)</u>

Topic Sentence: The obstacle to my success as I crossed the border into college was my lack of confidence.

Supporting Point 1: Myself

Evidence: Story about how I didn't ever see myself as a college student. I saw myself as learning a skill and going right to work. Ex: Dog Groomer

Supporting Point 2: High school teachers

Evidence: Story about how high school teachers never mentioned a full college degree such as an AA or BA as an option for me. Instead, we had guest speakers who emphasized technical certificates and "ready to work" degrees that were short and focused on a trade or skill.

Supporting Point 3: Family

Evidence: Story about how my family didn't encourage me to get a college degree. They made fun of my one cousin who went to college, accusing him of becoming stuck up after he got his degree.

Analysis A brief explanation of how this story shows how my lack of confidence was a major obstacle to my success as I crossed the border into college.

<u>Outlining the Paragraph (Donna Beegle "An Insider's Perspective")</u>

Topic Sentence: Donna Beegle had to learn the language of college in order to reach her goal of crossing the border into getting a higher education.

Supporting Point 1: Before she started getting help with her language from Dr. Fulford

(continued)

Evidence: "I said, 'Yes. Please teach me how to talk like you, because no one thinks I am smart. No one asks my opinion. I feel like no one can hear me'" (Beegle 140).

Supporting Point 2: While she started getting help with her language from Dr. Fulford

Evidence: "Dr. Fulford began correcting my language every time we spoke. He would stop me at various points in our conversation and say, 'Don't say "ain't," ' or 'You meant "gone," not "went." ' I would chant to myself throughout the day: 'Have gone; I went.' 'I saw; I have seen' " (Beegle 140).

Supporting Point 3: After she got help with her language from Dr. Fulford

Evidence: Donna Beegle eventually learned the language of college, and she was able to use it to not just get her Bachelor's Degree, but also her Master's and even her PhD.

Analysis A brief explanation of how Donna Beegle's story shows that language was an obstacle when she crossed the border into college to get her higher education.

Practice 6.7 Organizing Ideas by Outlining

DIRECTIONS: Use your prewriting from Steps 1–5 and outline the topic sentence, supporting points, evidence, and analysis for each of your paragraphs. Write your topic sentence first, followed by your first supporting point and the evidence to support it. Then repeat for points 2, 3, and so on. Use the Demonstration above as a model.

Phase Two: Draft

Learning Objective 2
Draft a paragraph that uses narrative evidence.

During the drafting stage, you need to put together all of the ideas and details generated during prewriting into one complete whole. Remember that this is a first and best attempt at creating a strong piece of writing, but it is not the final step. You will still have time to revise and edit your writing, so it reflects your best work.

STEP 6: Draft Your Paragraph

Through the demonstrations of Steps 1 through 5 in this chapter, two paragraphs, one personal and one based on the Beegle or Sohn or another text, have already been almost written. We hope you see how the steps of the prewriting phase help you write a good paragraph in the second phase of drafting. If you do all of these steps as you prepare to write a paragraph, you will have the ideas, details, and order you need to write some great paragraphs.

We invite you to refer to Chapter 3 on how to structure your paragraph. Remember that all paragraphs should have a topic sentence, support, and analysis. For additional examples of paragraph structure, look at the student papers in the highlighting workshop in the revision section (Step 7) of this chapter.

Information Literacy: Citing Sources

As you draft, it is important that you cite the sources for your supporting evidence from other texts. To learn more about how to punctuate these, refer to Part Six, "Grammar Essentials."

You will also want to be careful to introduce your source material in a way that makes sense to the reader. To do this, remember to provide an author's name before a quotation. It also can help if you give a brief description of what happened in the text prior to the quote. This allows your reader to follow the ideas, especially since your reader might not have read the text to which you refer. Look at the demonstrations below to see how to integrate source material. Then try this on your own.

Demonstration   Citing Sources

Here are two example paragraphs based on the prewriting activities in this chapter. Notice how the ideas are organized and how the writer has added some analysis in places after the supporting evidence to help the reader understand how the ideas connect.

Sample Paragraph 1: Personal Experience as Evidence

The obstacle to my success as I crossed the border into college was my lack of confidence. My own personal story contributed to this lack of confidence. For example, I never saw myself as earning a full college degree. Instead, I thought I wasn't smart enough and should instead find work right out of college. If I thought at all about going to college, it was to get a few classes, so I could work. For example, I thought I might be a dog groomer, which would require some specialized classes but nothing as big as an AA Degree. My high school teachers also encouraged my low confidence. I don't remember them ever asking if I was going to get a college degree. In fact, the only time they ever spoke of higher education was when we had a guest speaker come during my junior year and talk to us about certificate programs at the local community college that were focused on getting us skills so we could get work more easily. Maybe the biggest reason my confidence was low, though, was because of my family. No one in my immediate family had a degree, and they didn't talk about it as something that was good or that I should get. The only conversations I remember about college was when they made fun of my cousin who got his Bachelor's Degree. They said he got very stuck up after he graduated and was no fun at family events. All of these factors made me have low confidence about going to college, and this has been a huge obstacle as I crossed the border into college to work on my AA Degree.

Sample Paragraph 2: Donna Beegle's Essay as Evidence

Donna Beegle had to learn the language of college in order to reach her goal of crossing the border into getting a higher education. She first realized that she needed help with her language when her mentor, Dr. Fulford, offered to help her with this. She replied to his offer by

(continued)

saying, "'Yes. Please teach me how to talk like you, because no one thinks I am smart. No one asks my opinion. I feel like no one can hear me'" (140). Beegle realized that the way she talked was getting in the way of her success at college, and she jumped at the chance to get help. It wasn't easy to overcome this challenge, though. As she says, "Dr. Fulford began correcting my language every time we spoke. He would stop me at various points in our conversation and say, 'Don't say "ain't,"' or 'You meant "gone," not "went."' I would chant to myself throughout the day: 'Have gone; I went.' 'I saw; I have seen'" (140). Crossing the border into college wasn't an easy step that Beegle did in one leap. Instead, she had to get constant mentoring and she had to practice what she was learning. It paid off, though, because Beegle eventually learned the language of college, and she was able to use it to not just get her Bachelor's Degree, but also her Master's and even her PhD. While language was an obstacle, or barrier, for Beegle at first, it didn't end up causing her to fail. She found a way to overcome this and be successful. Finding a mentor and dedicating her time and energy to learning were important aspects of her success.

Practice 6.8   Drafting Your Paragraph

DIRECTIONS: Use the examples above as well as your prewriting to guide you. Then draft two full paragraphs, one using your experience as evidence, and another using the experiences of those you have read about as evidence.

Phase Three: Polish

Learning Objective 3
Revise and edit a paragraph that uses narrative evidence.

The last three steps of the writing process ask you to reread your writing as a reader rather than a writer. If you take the stance of a person who has never seen what you have written, then you can experience your writing like your readers do. This frame of mind helps you realize where the structure or content of your paragraphs can be improved, and in the editing stage, how your sentences can be more correct and effective.

STEP 7: Revise

There are many techniques for revising your writing. In this casebook, we illustrate a technique called the Highlighting Workshop. You can do the workshop on your own or with one or two classmates. It is an effective way to see if the ideas in your writing have enough supporting details and are well organized.

Highlighting Workshop

Evaluate the Strength of the Topic Sentence

1. *Take one color highlighter and highlight your topic sentence.*
2. *Using a ballpoint pen, draw a box around the topic in your topic sentence and underline your opinion or argument about that topic.* (If you cannot find one or the other of these things, you need to add them.)
3. *When you have finished, answer the following questions.* As you answer these questions, make notes of revisions you realize you will need to make.
    a. Do you have a topic sentence?
    b. Does your topic sentence include a focused topic for the paragraph?
    c. Does your topic sentence include an argument, opinion, or stance about that topic?
    d. Is the wording of your topic sentence clear? Would it make sense to a reader?

Evaluate the Strength and Coherence of the Support

4. *Take a second color highlighter and highlight all of the support in your paragraph.* This should be the details of the story you told in your paragraph.
5. *Remember that you can highlight each sentence in only one color.* Support cannot be the same as a topic sentence.
6. *When you have finished highlighting your support, answer the following questions.* Make notes of revisions you realize you will need to make as you review your work.
    a. Compare your topic sentence with the support in your paragraph. Do they match? Does the support actually back up the topic sentence? You are checking for coherence here.
    b. Visually assess the amount of support you have in your paragraph. Does it seem like enough just looking at it? (If a paragraph only has a couple sentences of support, it will need more.)

Evaluate the Strength and Coherence of the Analysis

7. *Take a third color highlighter and highlight the analysis in your paragraph.* This should be the sentences where you tell what your support means in relation to your topic sentence. This is not the actual support but rather where you talk about the meaning of the support.
8. *Remember that each sentence can only be highlighted with one color.*
9. *When you have finished highlighting, answer the following questions.* Make notes to yourself of revisions that you will need to make.
    a. Do you have analysis in your paragraph? (Hint: If you do not have three colors highlighted in your paragraph, you are missing the topic sentence, support, or analysis.)
    b. Do you have enough analysis? Each paragraph should have several sentences of analysis.
    c. Does the analysis go with the topic sentence and support in your paragraph? Make sure the paragraph is still coherent.

Check the Accuracy of Citations

10. *Take a pen and circle the introduction to each quotation or paraphrase in your paragraph.* This should include what you say to introduce the quote as well as the punctuation you use. Check for the following elements in this material you circled:
    a. Did you introduce the quote by telling who is speaking?
    b. Did you give some introductory description of what has happened in the text so far, so the quote makes sense to the reader?
    c. Did you provide a comma directly before the quotation began?
    d. Did you put quotation marks around the material you quoted?
11. *Underline the words you quoted from the text.* Then check for the following things within the parts you underlined:
    a. Did you copy the words correctly, not leaving out anything and spelling everything correctly?
    b. If the quoted material includes a reference to someone not named clearly in the quote, did you add this reference in brackets [ ]?

(continued)

c. If the quote has a quote within it, did you follow the rule of starting with a double quotation mark, then going to a single quotation for the quote within the quotation? Remember to end both the single and double quotation marks, too!

12. *Then take your pen and circle the punctuation and citation at the end of the quotation.* Check for the following elements in this material you circled:

a. Did you end with a quotation mark directly after the last word of the quote?

b. Did you include the citation in parentheses with the author's last name (if not already given in the paragraphs) and the page number before the final punctuation mark?

c. Did you end with the final mark of punctuation for the sentence (usually a period)?

Demonstration   Using the Highlighting Workshop

In this example, a student has followed the Highlighting Workshop, highlighting the topic sentence in orange, evidence in purple, and analysis in pink, and marking the topic sentence and quotations.

Donna Beegle had to learn the language of college in order to reach her goal of crossing the border into getting a higher education. She first realized that she needed help with her language when her mentor, Dr. Fulford, offered to help her with this. She replied to his offer by saying, "Yes. Please teach me how to talk like you, because no one thinks I am smart. No one asks my opinion. I feel like no one can hear me'" (Beegle 140). Beegle realized that the way she talked was getting in the way of her success at college, and she jumped at the chance to get help. It wasn't easy to overcome this challenge, though. As she says, "Dr. Fulford began correcting my language every time we spoke. He would stop me at various points in our conversation and say, 'Don't say "ain't."' or 'You meant "gone," not "went."' I would chant to myself throughout the day: 'Have gone; I went.' 'I saw; I have seen'" (Beegle 140). Crossing the border into college wasn't an easy step that Beegle did in one leap. Instead, she had to get constant mentoring, and she had to practice what she was learning. It paid off, though, because Beegle eventually learned the language of college, and she was able to use it to not just get her Bachelor's Degree, but also her Master's and even her PhD. While language was an obstacle, or barrier, for Beegle at first, it didn't end up causing her to fail. She found a way to overcome this and be successful. Finding a mentor and dedicating her time and energy to learning were important aspects of her success.

Reflections on topic sentence questions: I feel that my topic sentence is clear and that it fits what I wanted to say about Beegle's struggle to cross the boundary into college.

Reflections on support questions: I have never used more than one quotation in a paragraph before, but I'm happy with how this turned out. I think adding the second quotation helped me to more fully talk about Beegle's experiences. Using her words makes the paragraph stronger, too. It's not just me describing what she said. It's actually her speaking. I think the reader will like this. I hope it's okay that I didn't use a quotation for my third point, though. It just seemed like too much for one paragraph. I'm going to ask my instructor about this to double check, though.

Reflections on analysis questions: In my first draft of this paragraph, I put all of the analysis at the end, but then it looked like a bunch of quotations all slammed together. That didn't seem right. I tried putting a little explanation after each one instead, and I think it works better. I think this is especially important when using quotations because the reader needs time to hear me in between them. I also think everything goes together better this way. The analysis helps me to stay to my point throughout the paragraph and not get off topic.

Practice 6.9 — Using the Highlighting Workshop

DIRECTIONS: Complete the Highlighting Workshop on page 109 for your own paragraphs. Remember to do the highlighting and underlining as well as the reflection questions for each workshop.

STEP 8: Edit and Proofread

Once you have revised your paragraph by looking at global issues such as the topic sentence, support, and organization, it is time to do a final polish; it is time to edit for grammar and spelling errors. Try any of the following suggestions:

1. **Read your paragraph out loud to yourself.** Read slowly, and read every word. You will probably find some sentences that do not make sense or words that are missing. Fix these.
2. **Have another person read your writing.** This should be someone who has not previously seen the paper. Have that person mark any sentences or words that do not make sense to them. While this person might not be a grammar expert, he or she can give you feedback about sentences that are not "reader friendly" and therefore could use editing. Make sure the reader identifies your errors but does not correct your errors for you.
3. **Work with a tutor in your school's writing center or other tutoring center.** Have this person read your writing and work with you to revise any sentences that are not clear.
4. **Have your instructor look at your paragraph and mark for grammar and spelling errors.** Then, look at his or her marks. Try to find similar errors in any remaining paragraphs and fix them.

Practice 6.10 — Editing and Proofreading

DIRECTIONS: Pair up with a partner in class and read your paper out loud to that person. As you do so, listen for any errors and circle or highlight them. Then work on your own or with a tutor to correct those errors.

STEP 9: Reflect on Your Writing Process

The final stage in the writing process is to reflect on the process itself. You want to ask yourself some questions so that the next time you write you can change what did not work or repeat what did work. Therefore, before you begin on your next writing assignment, write a reflection of your process for composing. Also remember that this is an important critical thinking element of the writing process. Here are sample reflections questions you can ask yourself:

1. **What did you learn from thinking about the topic of this assignment?** Did reading and writing about the obstacles one faces when crossing the border into college help you realize things about yourself?

2. **How did you grow as a writer through the process of writing?** (For example, did you take on any new challenges? Did you discover any new goals you would like to work on in the future? Did you find that using a writing process worked for you or not?)

3. **How did your act of writing help you grow as a reader?** (For example, did the process of writing this help you to read texts written in similar styles? Did you better retain the information that you read? Was it hard to write about ideas in readings?)

4. **Discuss what you see as the strengths of your writing,** starting first with content (ideas and information) and then going to style (organization, language, voice, etc.).

5. **Discuss what you think are the weaknesses of your writing.**

6. If you had more time or inclination, would you do anything else to your writing? If so, what?

Practice 6.11   Reflecting

DIRECTIONS: Answer the questions above in order to reflect on your writing experience in this chapter.

✔ Chapter **Quick Check**   MySkillsLab   Complete the mastery test for this chapter in MySkillsLab.

Use the following questions and answers to check your understanding of this chapter.

QUESTION	ANSWER
Learning Objective 1: Prewrite for a paragraph that uses narrative evidence. *How do I create a topic sentence and gather narrative evidence for a paragraph?*	To create a topic sentence and gather narrative evidence for an assignment... ✔ Make sure you understand the assignment, brainstorm, freewrite, and review reading notes and summaries. ✔ Focus on the ideas most meaningful to you and create a topic sentence containing a focused topic and opinion or argument about the topic. ✔ Develop evidence by reviewing reading notes and reflecting on your own experience by listing and freewriting.
Learning Objective 2: Draft a paragraph that uses narrative support. *How do I draft a well-organized paragraph that uses narrative as support?*	✔ Write stories from your own experience or the experiences of others you have read about. Write paragraphs from an outline of supporting points.
Learning Objective 3: Revise and edit a paragraph that uses narrative evidence. *How do I revise and edit paragraphs that use narrative as support?* *What reflection can I do that will help me learn a good process for writing narrative support paragraphs?*	To revise and edit paragraphs using narrative support... ✔ Use workshop techniques such as highlighting. ✔ Have your teacher or a writing center tutor check your work to identify types of errors you make. ✔ Get to know the types of sentence errors you tend to make. ✔ Use a set of questions that help you see how you can use what you have learned. ✔ Write, and talk to others, about your writing experience.

A Writing Process for Essays Using Narrative Evidence as Support

7

LEARNING OBJECTIVES

In this chapter you will learn to . . .

1 Prewrite for an essay that uses narrative evidence.

2 Draft an essay using narrative evidence.

3 Revise and edit an essay that uses narrative evidence.

Warm Up

MySkillsLab
Complete the Warm Up at
www.myskillslab.com

DIRECTIONS: Look at the picture, which shows the basic building blocks of the solar system: a sun and planets. Then answer the following questions.

1. Consider the picture of our solar system.
   - How is the sun like a thesis statement?
   - How are the planets like supporting body paragraphs?
   - How is the overall system similar to the organization of an essay?

2. The picture focuses on just our solar system, but this is not the extent of our galaxy. The Milky Way contains billions of suns and planets. Consider how this relationship compares to an essay.
   - Is the Milky Way a good metaphor for an essay? Why or why not?

Phase One: Prewriting

Learning Objective 1
Prewrite for an essay that uses narrative evidence.

When confronted with an academic essay assignment, it is easy to feel overwhelmed. Essays contain a lot of parts, and knowing where to begin is hard. Writing an essay might seem like a brand new task that differs from writing a paragraph or reading a journal. However, remembering paragraph structure as well as the steps in the writing and reading processes will help you write a full essay. The basics remain the same whether you are writing a shorter piece with several supporting sentences or a longer piece with multiple supporting paragraphs. While the scope of your topic and the depth of what you will say about it will change, all of the other building blocks remain the same.

This chapter illustrates the process of moving from a paragraph to an essay as well as the process of moving from a basic essay to a more extensive one. To do this, we will build from the sample paragraphs from Chapter 6 to form an essay. We will then go a step further by adding outside sources to the essay in order to build it into a longer piece.

STEP 1: Analyze the Assignment

As with writing a paragraph, the first step in preparing to write an essay is to look closely at the assignment. Answering the following questions about an assignment will help ensure you understand what is expected in your writing. If you are ever unsure about the answers to any of these questions, ask your instructor for help.

1. What is the purpose, goal, or objective of this assignment?
2. Who is the intended audience of the paper?
3. What is the central topic I will need to write about?
4. Can I imagine meaningful things to say about this topic?
5. What information am I supposed to use as support in this assignment?
6. What organizational structure will I need to use?
7. How will this assignment be graded?
8. How do I feel about responding to this assignment (eager and ready, afraid, unsure, etc.)?

Practice 7.1   Analyzing the Assignment

DIRECTIONS: Read the assignment below. Then answer the questions above to check your understanding of the assignment. If you have questions, ask your instructor for clarification.

Essay Assignment

PURPOSES: This essay asks you to make connections between obstacles you faced when crossing the border into college and the obstacles faced by other people that you have read about. This helps you understand how reading adds to your knowledge base for use in your writing. Finally, it asks you to use what you learn about essay structure and paragraphs to create a meaningful essay.

AUDIENCE: Write this essay for an academic audience. To envision who this might be, write for your instructor and your classmates.

Assignment

Discuss what you consider to be the primary obstacle one faces when crossing the border into college, and support your thesis with information from your own experience and material you have read. The details of this assignment are listed below and include options for ways to extend your writing if you want to aim towards a higher level of complexity:

- **Thesis** Your essay will need a thesis statement that answers this question: *What is the primary obstacle one faces when crossing the border into college?*
- **Support and Development** Your essay will need to provide a minimum of three supporting body paragraphs. These paragraphs should use narrative details to illustrate and support your thesis. For example, you may want to use stories from your own experience and/or summaries of the stories you have read by Beegle, Sohn, or other writers to develop body paragraphs. Each body paragraph will need to illustrate strong paragraph structure.

  Option to Extend: Add evidence from 1–2 additional sources that you find outside of class. They might be from library or Internet sources you used during your reading process, for example. This evidence should extend or deepen what you say about the class text and should help you to develop your ideas in more depth.

- **Organization** This paper should illustrate basic essay structure by providing an introduction containing your thesis, at least three body paragraphs that support your thesis, and a conclusion. In your paper, you should use transitions to create connections between ideas. You should also make sure that all the paragraphs clearly relate to your thesis, therefore creating a coherent essay. Finally, each body paragraph should illustrate strong structure with a clear and focused main idea, concrete narrative details, analysis of the evidence, and coherent organization.
  - *Option to Extend:* Move beyond three body paragraphs by integrating additional source material. This may mean you add more supporting body paragraphs about distinct and additional points in support of your thesis, or it may mean that you add additional paragraphs that further develop one of your supporting points. You are expanding your organization to fit your larger content.
- **Format** Your paper should be between 1½ and 2 pages long, typed, double-spaced, in 12-point font, with one-inch margins. No cover pages are needed. Put your name and the class number at the top.
  - *Option to Extend:* Your paper will be 3–4 pages in length. All other requirements for formatting remain.
- **Mechanics:** Your paper needs to be proofread and edited for spelling, grammar, and mechanics and use the correct format for in-text citations.

How Your Essay Will Be Graded

1. *Content* The essay communicates a meaningful and significant idea about a major obstacle that exists when crossing the border into college.
2. *Thesis* The essay has a clear thesis that answers the assigned question in one clear sentence.
3. *Support and Development* The essay supports the thesis with concrete examples from your own life and/or those of the people we read about in this unit. There is enough narrative evidence to fully support your thesis.
4. *Organization* The essay follows basic essay structure (introduction, body, conclusion). Each paragraph connects to the one previous to it and to the thesis statement. Transitions are used to show connections between ideas.
   - *Introduction and Conclusion* The introduction and conclusion are present. The introduction catches the reader's attention and states the thesis. The conclusion summarizes what was said in the essay and leaves the reader with something to think about in relation to the paper topic.
   - *Paragraph Organization* The paper has clear and effective paragraphs with topic sentences and well-developed narrative details. Each paragraph focuses on just one idea that supports the thesis.
5. *Format* The paper is correctly formatted according to the assignment instructions.
6. *Mechanics* The paper is well edited and proofread for the grammar and mechanics conventions. The sentences convey meaning clearly to the reader.

STEP 2: Generate Ideas

The next step in the writing process is to generate ideas and details to find out what you have to say about the topic. You can list, freewrite, cluster brainstorm, and so on, to explore possibilities for your paper. We illustrate two techniques in the Demonstration sections that follow. In each case, we build on the ideas we generated in the previous chapter, so we can move from a paragraph to an essay.

As with the previous chapter, as you generate ideas, keep in mind the following two points.

Write from the Heart

One of the most important factors in how well you write is how much you believe in what you are writing about. Writing from the heart is the best writing to read, and, after all, your goal is to write something others want to read. Further, it is easier to write about something you have an emotional connection to, that you deeply care about. As you generate ideas, let all of your ideas come out first, so you can choose the ones that are most compelling to you.

Draw from Your Reading Process

Remember that the reading and writing processes are connected. The ideas you generate, the questions you ask, and the information you gather when you read can often be used when you write, so you want to have your reading materials with you as you move through the writing process.

One technique for finding ideas to write about is listing all the ideas you can think of without judging them. As you generate ideas for an essay, also remember that you want an idea that is large enough to explore in a full essay that includes multiple supporting paragraphs. Since this assignment is asking for different sources of support (personal experience, narrative evidence from texts, and support from outside sources), brainstorming with these requirements in mind will help you stay on track.

Demonstration   Generating Ideas by *Listing*

1. **In your personal experience, what have been some obstacles you faced when you crossed the border into college?**

Lack of confidence in myself
Lack of knowledge or skills (am I that bad at math?!)
Lack of family support
Lack of money

2. **What were some of the obstacles Donna Beegle experienced when she started college?**

Lack of knowledge
Lack of language spoken in college/middle class
Difficulty balancing family and school
Lack of money
Lack of family understanding about her educational goals

3. **What did you learn in your outside research about the obstacles people faced when they crossed the border into college?**

Lack of money
Social pressures from family and social groups
Lack of knowledge
Lack of self-esteem
Lack of mentors
Institutional barriers
Lack of value placed on education

Practice 7.2   Generating Ideas by Listing

DIRECTIONS: Using the Demonstration as a model, try generating ideas for your essay. Start with your own experience and then brainstorm obstacles that you read about in Beegle or Sohn's essays or another reading you chose or were assigned. You also might draw on research you did in Chapter 5 during Step 1: Getting to Know the Text, or if you have not researched the authors, you could do that now to generate additional ideas.

1. In your personal experience, what obstacles have you faced when you crossed the border into college?
2. What were some of the obstacles the women in Beegle and Sohn's essays (and the writer of the text you chose or were assigned) experienced when they started college?
3. What did you learn in your outside research about the obstacles people faced when they crossed the border into college?

STEP 3: Focus Your Topic

Once you have generated lots of possible ideas to use in your writing, you need to find a focusing idea that you truly believe in and that fits the assignment. Once you identify this focus, you can develop it into a thesis statement. When you are writing an essay, you need a thesis statement that can be fully supported in three or four paragraphs.

Start by reviewing your brainstorm list. Look for ideas that are repeated under different headings. For example, maybe you listed something under your own experiences that is similar to something you wrote under the section for an essay you read or research you did. This would be a good topic to select because you have a variety of supporting points that connect to it.

The following Demonstration offers an example of finding a focus and a thesis statement for the sample essay assignment through freewriting.

Demonstration   Finding a Focus for an Essay by Freewriting

Freewriting Prompt: Freewrite to find out which topic you want to make the focus of your whole paper. This topic should address the question, *What is the primary obstacle one faces when crossing the border into college?*

I am surprised by how many ideas came up that were similar in my three brainstorm lists! I thought there would be very different ideas for each section, but I'm seeing that there are some similar barriers that many people have in common when they cross the border into college. This makes me feel less alone in my struggles!

I have to narrow and choose just one topic as my focus. This is going to be tough. Lack of money comes up on all my lists, but I don't really want to write a whole paper about it—it

(continued)

might get repetitive. Lack of knowledge and/or skills also comes up on all of the lists. That might be a good topic because the skills I lacked were different from those of Donna Beegle. It would allow me to say a variety of things and not be so boring. The topic of family and social pressures also comes up a lot. That could be interesting to talk about, too, and it would also allow me to talk about different ideas because everyone's family differs a bit. Hmmm…I think I will go with the obstacle of knowledge for my paper. I feel like I can write a lot about that, and I understood what Donna Beegle was saying about this when I read her essay. I also think it is a major hurdle. I mean, people can move away from their family or social group if they need to and that can help address that obstacle to their college success. However, they can't avoid or escape their lack of knowledge. It has to be faced and addressed. Therefore, the topic of my paper is going to be about how a major obstacle one faces when crossing the border into college is lack of knowledge.

Practice 7.3 Finding a Focus for an Essay by Freewriting

DIRECTIONS: Begin by identifying the ideas common to two or more of your brainstorm lists. Then freewrite in response to the following prompt, so you can narrow to one idea you want to focus on in your essay.

Freewriting Prompt: Freewrite to find out which topic you want to make the focus of your whole paper. This topic should address the question *What is a primary obstacle one faces when crossing the border into college?* It should also be something you can address with support from your own experience as well as from Beegle's or Sohn's essays—or an essay you chose or were assigned—and your research about that essay.

Create a Thesis Statement

The **thesis statement** is the sentence that expresses the focused, overall idea of an essay. Every essay needs this controlling idea, and all the other ideas and details in the writing must support and connect to the thesis. When you write a paragraph, you put the controlling idea in a topic sentence. A thesis statement and a topic sentence are very similar in purpose and content. Their biggest difference is in scope: the idea in a topic sentence should be small enough to address in a paragraph whereas the idea in a thesis should be appropriate for the length of an essay.

Essays will almost always have a thesis sentence that provides direction for the overall essay. (Some instructors may not ask for an explicit thesis in narrative writing, so double-check your assignment guidelines regarding thesis statements.) When your essay assignment does call for a stated thesis, each part of the essay should connect to and develop the idea in the thesis. A thesis statement should be a one-sentence statement. It may include just the "root" or "root + supporting points." Ask your instructor which model he or she prefers for your papers.

Root of Thesis = *topic of overall paper* + argument/opinion/stance about the topic

Root of Thesis + **Supporting Points** = *topic of overall paper* + argument/opinion/stance about this topic + *supporting point 1* + *supporting point 2* + *supporting point 3*

During the writing process, there are several points at which you can draft your thesis statement. You may do so in prewriting as you generate ideas. You may do so in the outlining phase. You may have to draft the entire paper to find what you want to say in a thesis. Finally, you may write a thesis and then later change it as you discover what you want to say in your writing.

Demonstration   Drafting a Thesis Statement

1. **What is the topic of your paper?** An obstacle one faces when crossing the border into college is lack of knowledge.
2. **What opinion or argument do you want to make about this topic?** Lack of knowledge is the biggest obstacle one faces—it is the most significant.
3. **What three (or more) supporting points will you write about in your paper to support your topic and argument?** My own lack of basic reading, writing, and math skills, Donna Beegle's lack of knowledge about middle-class language, and my research about Donna Beegle from an online article I read from her Web site Communication Across Barriers
4. **Write a thesis sentence that combines these:**

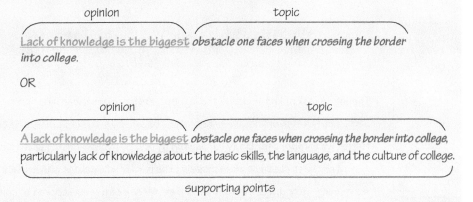

Practice 7.4   Drafting and Evaluating a Thesis

DIRECTIONS: Write out your answers to the four questions in the Demonstration above to help you create a clear thesis for your essay. Once you have drafted your thesis, answer the questions on the Thesis Evaluation Checklist p. 120 to help you assess the strength of your thesis.

Thesis Evaluation Checklist

1. Is your thesis written as one complete sentence? Is it a statement (not a question)?
2. Does your thesis have a clear topic that matches the assignment?
3. Does your thesis provide an argument or opinion or stance about the topic?
4. Does your thesis include supporting points, and if so, are these linked to the overall topic so they appear as support and not new topics?
5. Does your thesis include enough information so it makes sense to an outside reader? (You want to avoid having vague references like "he" or "it" as your reader will not know what you are talking about. Make sure to include all needed information in your thesis so it makes sense all by itself, without added information around it.)

STEP 4: Develop Your Ideas

Once you have a thesis for your essay, you need to develop narrative evidence to support it. Again, the notes you took during the reading process can be a help here. However, while you may have gathered some supporting ideas and details during the reading process, you may still need to generate additional ones. Furthermore, information you wrote about in your paragraphs for Chapter 6 might also be helpful. You may be able to expand upon one or more of those paragraphs in your full essay.

To generate narrative support for your body paragraphs, make sure each supporting example helps prove or explain the thesis statement. You can use a variety of brainstorming techniques, as shown in the following Demonstration, or you can use just one technique such as freewriting or mapping. As you review the Demonstration and later when you are developing support for your own essay, keep in mind the following questions:

- Are these supporting ideas and details relevant to my essay?
- Do I have enough ideas and details for several paragraphs in my essay?

Demonstration   Developing Your Ideas

Thesis: A lack of knowledge is the biggest obstacle one faces when crossing the border into college, particularly a lack of knowledge about the basic skills, the language, and the culture of college.

Narrative Support for Body Paragraph 1: My own experience (Freewrite)

My biggest obstacle when crossing the border into college was my lack of knowledge of basic skills like reading, writing, and math. I took the entrance exam when I applied to community college, and I found out I needed a lot of extra work on reading and math especially. Not too surprising—I wasn't in a college track in high school, and I stopped taking math after sophomore year. I was surprised by how low my reading skills were, but I guess college work is at a higher level. I realized how important these skills were my first quarter. I registered for a class I always wanted to take in high school, physics. I was so excited! But, after the first two weeks, I realized I didn't have the knowledge I needed to succeed. The textbook was a mystery to me. I would try to read it, but I didn't understand much. The pictures kind of helped, but it seemed like a foreign language when I read the words. When the class started to use math, I realized I was in big trouble. I dropped the class and registered for reading and math instead. I hope this will help.

Narrative Support for Body Paragraph 2: Donna Beegle's lack of knowledge of language from "An Insider's Perspective: The Donna Beegle Story." (Map)

> **Lack of Knowledge of Language:**
> **Donna Beegle's Essay**

> "I said, 'Yes. Please teach me how to talk like you, because no one thinks I am smart. No one asks my opinion. I feel like no one can hear me'" (Beegle 140).

> "Dr. Fulford began correcting my language every time we spoke. He would stop me at various points in our conversation and say, 'Don't say "ain't,"' or 'You meant "gone," not "went."'" I would chant to myself throughout the day: 'Have gone; I went.' 'I saw; I have seen'" (Beegle 140).

Narrative Support for Body Paragraph 3: Donna Beegle's lack of general middle-class "culture of college" knowledge from "An Insider's Perspective." (Listing)

- Lack of knowledge of history and events made it hard for her to understand ideas in her college classes.
  - **Quotation:** "For instance, I did not have context for subjects such as Watergate. People at the college would often say to me, 'How can you not know this? Aren't you American?'" (Beegle 139).
- Impoverished schools didn't teach her middle-class knowledge or values.
  - **Quotation:** "I had attended impoverished schools where the resources were minimal and the teachers were overwhelmed, an environment that was rarely conducive to learning" (Beegle 139).

Extension: Narrative Support I Could Use to Extend Ideas (Listing)

- **Source:** Article titled "The Crossing" by Todd Schwartz about Donna Beegle's experiences growing up in poverty (online article on the Web site Communication Across Barriers)
- **Information:** Beegle's first step from poverty into an education and the middle class was through a program called Women in Transition (WIT). In "The Crossing," Schwartz relates how she felt on her first day of this program. "She had no illusions that this was some heaven-sent second chance, in fact she had no interest whatsoever—except for the low-income housing certificate that came with the deal. That was gold in her country" (Schwartz 32).

Practice 7.5　Developing Your Ideas

DIRECTIONS: Using any form of brainstorming that is comfortable to you, develop narrative evidence for each of the supporting ideas in your paper. Quotations are stronger evidence than are general descriptions of what happened in a text, so, if possible, find quotations from texts to support your ideas.

Extend If you plan to do the extensions in the assignment, try developing ideas and gathering information from outside sources as well, so you have additional narrative evidence to use in your paper.

STEP 5: Organize Your Ideas

One of the easiest ways to make sure your organization is strong and to set yourself up to draft a well-organized essay is to outline before writing. Outlining provides a map that you can follow as you draft your essay. The following Demonstration provides a sample outline.

Demonstration　Organizing Your Ideas: Outlining an Essay

I. **Introduction**

  a. Attention Getter

  b. Introduction to my topic/background information

  c. **Thesis:** A lack of knowledge is the biggest obstacle one faces when crossing the border into college, particularly a lack of knowledge about the basic skills, the language, and the culture of college.

II. **Body Paragraph:** My experience as evidence

  a. **Topic Sentence:** My own experience crossing the border into college shows that a lack of knowledge is a major obstacle one has to overcome.

  b. **Support:** My story of taking a Physics class my first quarter at college and realizing that my low reading and math skills were barriers to my success. I lacked these skills needed to be able to pass the class.

  c. **Analysis:** I will explain how my example shows how lack of knowledge is the biggest obstacle I faced when crossing the border into college.

III. **Body Paragraph:** Donna Beegle's discussion of language in her essay "An Insider's Perspective: The Donna Beegle Story" as evidence

  a. **Topic Sentence:** Donna Beegle's ignorance of academic language shows how a lack of knowledge is a major obstacle when one crosses the border into college.

b. **Supporting Quotation 1:** "I said, 'Yes. Please teach me how to talk like you, because no one thinks I am smart. No one asks my opinion. I feel like no one can hear me'" (Beegle 140).

c. **Analysis:** Explain how this quotation shows she realizes that she lacks knowledge needed to successfully cross the border into college, and she eagerly seeks out how she will gain that knowledge.

d. **Supporting Quotation 2:** "Dr. Fulford began correcting my language every time we spoke. He would stop me at various points in our conversation and say, 'Don't say "ain't,"' or 'You meant "gone," not "went."' I would chant to myself throughout the day: 'Have gone; I went.' 'I saw; I have seen'" (Beegle 140).

e. **Analysis:** Explain how this shows how she worked to gain the knowledge she needed, but this wasn't an easy process. Crossing the border into college is possible, but it takes the work of gaining missing knowledge, so you can succeed.

IV. **Body Paragraph:** Donna Beegle's lack of general, middle-class "culture of college" knowledge as discussed in her essay "An Insider's Perspective: The Donna Beegle Story"

a. **Topic Sentence:** Donna Beegle's lack of middle-class "culture of college" knowledge shows how a lack of knowledge is a major obstacle when one crosses the border into college.

b. **Supporting Quotation 1:** "I had attended impoverished schools where the resources were minimal and the teachers were overwhelmed, an environment that was rarely conducive to learning" (Beegle 139).

c. **Analysis:** Explain how Beegle lacked needed knowledge to cross the border to college because the schools she had attended didn't provide this knowledge.

d. **Supporting Quotation 2:** "For instance, I did not have context for subjects such as Watergate. People at the college would often say to me, 'How can you not know this? Aren't you American?'" (Beegle 139).

e. **Analysis:** Discuss how this quote is an example of the information she was missing from the impoverished schools she attended—missing information that caused her to lack knowledge needed to cross the border into college.

V. **Extension Idea:** Donna Beegle's lack of knowledge about the value of education as discussed in "The Crossing" by Todd Schwartz (online article on the Web site Communication Across Barriers). **Note:** Adding the extension idea would mean changing the thesis to cover the additional point: A lack of knowledge is the biggest obstacle one faces when crossing the border

(continued)

into college, particularly a lack of knowledge about the basic skills, the language, the culture, and the value of college.

    a. <u>**Topic Sentence:**</u> Donna Beegle's lack of knowledge about the value of education was a major obstacle when she crossed the border into college.

    b. <u>**Support:**</u> Beegle's first step from poverty into an education and the middle class was through a program called Women in Transition (WIT). In "The Crossing," Schwartz relates how she felt on her first day of this program. "She had no illusions that this was some heaven-sent second chance, in fact she had no interest whatsoever—except for the low-income housing certificate that came with the deal. That was gold in her country" (Schwartz 32).

    c. <u>**Analysis:**</u> Discuss how this quote shows that she lacked knowledge of how valuable an educational program like WIT could be because she was so focused on meeting her basic needs.

VI. <u>Conclusion</u>

    a. Summary of Thesis and Main Points

    b. Point of Significance or Call to Action

Practice 7.6   Organizing Your Ideas

DIRECTIONS: Using all of your notes from your writing process so far, write an outline of your paper. You can do a formal outline like the one shown above, or you can map your ideas if you want a more visual outline. If you are extending ideas in your essay to address that part of the assignment, make sure to include those ideas in your outline and thesis as well.

Phase Two: Draft

Learning Objective 2
Draft an essay using narrative evidence.

This is the phase when you actually write out your complete essay. If you have actively engaged in the prewriting steps, this part should flow easily: since you have done your thinking and organizing, all you have to attend to now is composing your sentences and paragraphs.

STEP 6: Draft Your Essay

During the drafting stage, you need to put together all of the ideas you have generated during prewriting into one complete whole. Remember that this is a first attempt at creating a strong piece of writing, but it is not the final step. As mentioned in previous chapters, you will still have time to polish your writing so that it reflects your best work. If you are nervous as you begin to write, remember this. You will have a chance to make it better through revision and editing. While you have already gathered and organized many parts of your essay, you may still be wondering how to write an introduction, conclusion, and body paragraphs. We will give you some tips and examples here to get you started on your own work.

Introductory Paragraph

Chapter 3 on structuring essays explains the basics of writing an introduction for a college paper (see p. 51). However, you may have some questions about how to write an introduction for an essay that uses narrative evidence. The following Demonstration shows how you can move from brainstorming to drafting an introduction. If you have not brainstormed ideas for your introduction earlier in the writing process, it is important to do so before drafting. Remember that writing is recursive, meaning that you might repeat earlier steps in order to have ideas about which to write during drafting.

Demonstration   Brainstorming and Drafting an Introductory Paragraph

Here, the student brainstorms to develop ideas for an introduction, and then uses the brainstorming to draft an introductory paragraph.

The Attention Getter

1. **Brainstorm a list of stories you could tell** (that will not be used in the supporting body paragraphs of your paper) to introduce your paper topic.

- A story about how I crossed a border into a new culture when I lived in England for 6 months, and how I lacked knowledge to fit in there. Connect this to the idea of crossing borders into college.

- A story about how I had to take the COMPASS test when I entered community college and how it showed I lacked basic knowledge to do well in college classes. Talk about how this was my first introduction to how I lacked knowledge to cross the border into college.

2. **Brainstorm a list of questions you could use to begin your introduction.** This should lead into either your story or your thesis.

- Have you ever considered that going to college is like crossing a boundary?

- If you were going to cross a border into a new country, what knowledge would you want to have in order to do this?

- What does one need to know in order to cross into college successfully?

3. **Extension Idea:** Use the research you did while reading and preparing to write this paper and find either a quotation or paraphrase to start your introduction.

- Quote from "The Crossing" by Todd Schwartz (online article on the Web site Communication Across Barriers), "Across the ocean, on the far horizon, the clouds parted for a moment....Slowly, Beegle began to build a boat. It would take her nine years to complete the crossing" (Schwartz 32).

Background Information

Write one-sentence summaries of each of the texts you will write about in your paper. This background information helps introduce your reader to these texts. If you wrote summaries for any or all of these texts during your reading process, you can copy the first sentences for use here.

(continued)

1. **"An Insider's Perspective: The Donna Beegle Story":** This narrative by Donna Beegle tells her own story of moving from generational poverty to the middle class, and how education was key to making that transition.

2. **"The Crossing":** This online article about Donna Beegle shares parts of her personal story along with facts and statistics about poverty in order to explain how people can cross from poverty into the middle class.

The Thesis Statement

A lack of knowledge is the biggest obstacle one faces when crossing the border into college, particularly a lack of knowledge about the basic skills, the language, and the background information of college.

Draft Paragraph

"Across the ocean, on the far horizon, the clouds parted for a moment . . . Slowly, Beegle began to build a boat. It would take her nine years to complete the crossing" (Schwartz 32). Have you ever considered that going to college is like crossing an ocean to a new land? For Donna Beegle, who grew up in generational poverty and shared about her experiences in texts like "An Insider's Perspective: The Donna Beegle Story" and "The Crossing," going to college was like traveling to a new land, a land she knew nothing about and for which she lacked the knowledge to participate successfully. I also experienced a feeling of crossing a border when I entered college. I, too, found that I lacked knowledge of this new place and how to succeed in it. What this shows is that a lack of knowledge is the biggest obstacle one faces when crossing the border into college as shown by my own experience and that of Donna Beegle in her story "An Insider's Perspective: The Donna Beegle Story" as well as online texts where she shares about her experiences.

Practice 7.7   Brainstorming and Drafting an Introductory Paragraph

DIRECTIONS: Complete the following activities to prepare to write your introduction. Then, using the ideas you brainstormed, write a draft of your introductory paragraph.

1. Brainstorm a list of stories, questions, and quotes you could use as attention getters. Then choose your favorite to develop in your introduction.
2. Brainstorm one-sentence summaries of each of the texts you will write about in your paper, including those you found through research. You will use these to introduce your texts to your readers.
3. Do not forget that your thesis will also go in your introduction. It is usually the first or final sentence in the introduction.

Basic Structure for Body Paragraphs in an Essay

You may want to review Chapter 3 on structuring essays, which presents the basics of structuring a good paragraph (see p. 53). Remember that all paragraphs should have a topic sentence, supporting ideas and details, and analysis. If you have completed the steps demonstrated in this chapter, you have nearly written the introduction and body paragraphs of your essay. Use the following example body paragraph to guide you as you write your own body paragraphs.

Demonstration   Writing Body Paragraphs

This example draws from Chapter 6 where we demonstrated how to write paragraphs for the body of an essay.

Donna Beegle had to learn the language of college in order to reach her goal of crossing the border into getting a higher education. She first realized that she needed help with her language when her mentor, Dr. Fulford, offered to help her with this. She replied to his offer by saying, "'Yes. Please teach me how to talk like you, because no one thinks I am smart. No one asks my opinion. I feel like no one can hear me'" (Beegle 140). Beegle realized that the way she talked was getting in the way of her success at college, and she jumped at the chance to get help. It wasn't easy to overcome this challenge, though. As she says, "Dr. Fulford began correcting my language every time we spoke. He would stop me at various points in our conversation and say, 'Don't say "ain't,"' or 'You meant "gone," not "went."' I would chant to myself throughout the day: 'Have gone; I went.' 'I saw; I have seen'" (Beegle 140). Crossing the border into college wasn't an easy step that Beegle did in one leap. Instead, she had to get constant mentoring and she had to practice what she was learning. It paid off, though, because Beegle eventually learned the language of college, and she was able to use it to not just get her Bachelor's Degree, but also her Master's and even her PhD. While language was an obstacle, or barrier, for Beegle at first, it didn't end up causing her to fail. She found a way to overcome this and be successful. Finding a mentor and dedicating her time and energy to learning were important aspects of her success.

Practice 7.8   Drafting Body Paragraphs

DIRECTIONS: Use your outline and other prewriting to draft the body paragraphs of your paper.

Information Literacy: Citing Sources As you draft your body paragraphs, remember to cite all of your quotations and paraphrases by giving the author and page number and including proper punctuation.

Conclusion

To review the purpose of concluding paragraphs and techniques for writing them, review Chapter 3 (p. 54). Three things you can do in a conclusion are:

- summarize the thesis and your supporting main ideas,
- ask a question,
- or suggest what the reader can do after reading your paper.

The following Demonstration offers brainstorming ideas and an example of a conclusion specifically for an essay using narrative evidence.

Demonstration   Brainstorming and Writing a Conclusion Paragraph

Summarize the thesis and main points: Write a three- to four-sentence summary of the thesis and main ideas in your paper. This should be a brief overview of what you have said in your paper, but you should say it using different words and sentences.

Going to college is like crossing a border into a new land, and certain knowledge is required to do well. For many college students such as Donna Beegle and myself, this knowledge is lacking and becomes an obstacle to making a positive crossing. Specifically, a lack of knowledge of basic skills like reading and math hindered my ability to cross into college. For Donna, her lack of knowledge of middle-class language and cultural knowledge as well as her lack of knowledge of the language and the value of education stood in the way of her crossing into college.

Answer the question "So what?" Write a final question for the reader to consider.

- Do you have the knowledge needed to cross the border into the land of college?
- What can you do when you find out you lack the knowledge needed to cross the border into the land of college?

Point of Significance Give the reader something to do as a result of having read your paper.

- Be a mentor and help others who lack the knowledge they need to cross the border into college.
- Seek out help if you find out you lack the knowledge you need to successfully cross the border into college.

Conclusion Paragraph

Going to college is like crossing a border into a new land, and certain knowledge is required to do well. For many college students such as Donna Beegle and myself, this knowledge is lacking and becomes an obstacle to making a positive crossing. Specifically, a lack of knowledge of basic skills like reading and math hindered my ability to cross into college. For Donna, her lack of knowledge of middle-class language and cultural knowledge as well as her lack of knowledge of the value of education stood in the way of her crossing into college. As you embark on your own crossing into college, ask yourself this question. Do you have the knowledge needed to cross the border into the land of college? If not, seek out the mentors and guidance to help you get that knowledge. It worked for Donna Beegle and for me. It can work for you, too!

Practice 7.9 **Brainstorming and Writing a Conclusion Paragraph**

DIRECTIONS: Follow these steps to generate ideas for your conclusion.

1. Write a 1–4 sentence summary of your thesis and main supporting points.
2. Write a final question for the reader to consider.
3. Give the reader something to do as a result of having read your paper.
   Using the ideas you brainstormed, write a full draft of your concluding paragraph.

Phase Three: Polish

Learning Objective 3
Revise and edit an essay that uses narrative evidence.

The final phase of the writing process is to review your rough draft to make improvements to content, organization, grammar, and mechanics, and to reflect on your writing process to see how you might compose more effectively next time.

STEP 7: Revise

Revision means "re-seeing," and the purpose of revision is to work carefully on an essay to improve its content and structure. When you revise, you work on major issues like the thesis, organization, and development. (Spelling and punctuation are important, too, but it makes sense to attend to these later. Why work hard on correcting a sentence that you may end up cutting?)

An effective revision technique is to ask questions about the purpose of almost every sentence. The following "Highlighting Workshop" demonstrates a revision strategy you can do on your own or with your class. It is a powerful way to see if the ideas in your writing are well organized and developed. The steps are outlined and then demonstrated below and on the next page.

Highlighting Workshop

Evaluate the Strength of the Thesis, Overall Coherence, and Topic Sentences

1. *Take one color highlighter, and highlight your thesis.*
2. *Using a ballpoint pen, put a box around the topic in your thesis, and underline your opinion or argument about that topic.* (If you cannot find one of these elements, you need to add it.) If you have included supporting ideas in your thesis, put a squiggly line under these.
3. *Take the same color highlighter with which you highlighted your thesis, and highlight the topic sentence in each body paragraph.*
4. *When you have finished highlighting, answer the following questions.* Make notes of revisions you realize you will need to make as you review your work.
   - Compare each topic sentence against the thesis. Remember that a good topic sentence should have both the main idea for the paragraph and a connection back to the argument made in the thesis. Do you see this connection to the thesis in each topic sentence?
   - Also, if you listed supporting points in your thesis, do your body paragraphs follow the order of these ideas as they appear in your thesis?

Evaluate the Strength and Coherence of the Support

5. *Take a second color highlighter, and highlight all of your supporting ideas and details in each body paragraph.*
6. *Remember that you can highlight each sentence in only one color.* Supporting sentences cannot be the same as a topic sentence.

(continued)

7. *When you have finished highlighting your support, answer the following questions.* Make notes of revisions you realize you will need to make as you review your work.
   - Compare each topic sentence with its support in each body paragraph. Does the support back up the topic sentence? You are checking for coherence here.
   - Visually assess the amount of support you have in each paragraph. Does it seem like enough? (If a paragraph only has a couple of sentences of support, it will need more.)

Evaluate the Strength and Coherence of the Analysis

8. *Take a third color highlighter, and highlight the analysis in each body paragraph.* These are the sentences where you tell what your support means in relation to your thesis. This is not the actual support but rather where you are talking about the meaning of the support.
9. *Remember that each sentence can only be highlighted with one color.*
10. *When you have finished highlighting, answer the following questions.* Make notes to yourself of revisions you realize you will need to make.
    - Do you have analysis in each body paragraph? Each body paragraph needs to have all three colors, analysis included.
    - Do you have enough analysis? Each body paragraph should have at least one or two sentences of analysis.
    - Does the analysis fit with the topic sentence and support in your paragraph? Make sure the paragraph is still coherent.

Evaluate the Strength of the Introduction and Conclusion

11. *Re-read your introduction in comparison to your thesis.*
12. *Then, answer the following questions:*
    - Does the introduction draw the reader into the paper?
    - Does the introduction set up the ideas in the thesis?
    - Does the introduction state the thesis (usually in the first or final sentence)?
13. *Re-read your conclusion.*
14. *Then, answer the following questions.* Make notes to yourself of revisions that you need to make.
    - Does your conclusion summarize the main ideas in your paper?
    - Does your conclusion leave the reader with a point of significance, an action to take in response to what you said in your paper, or an answer to the question, "So what?"

Check the Accuracy of Citations

15. *Take a pen and circle the introduction to each quotation or paraphrase in your paper.* This should include what you say to introduce the quotation as well as the punctuation you use. Check for the following elements in this material you circled:
    - Did you introduce the quotation by telling who is speaking?
    - Did you give some introductory description of what has happened in the text so far, so the quotation makes sense to the reader?
    - Did you provide a comma directly before the quotation began?
    - Did you put quotation marks around the material you quoted?
16. *Underline the words you quoted from the text.* Then check for the following:
    - Did you copy the words correctly, not leaving out any words and spelling them correctly?
    - If the quoted material includes a reference to someone not named clearly in the quotation, did you add this reference in parentheses ( )?
    - If the quotation has a quote within it, did you follow the rule of starting with double quotation marks, then going to single quotation marks for the quote within the quotation? *Remember to end both the single and double quotation marks, too.*
17. *Then take your pen and circle the punctuation and citation at the end of the quotation.* Check for the following elements in this material you circled:
    - Did you end with a quotation mark directly after the last word of the quotation?
    - Did you include the citation in parentheses with the author's last name (if not already noted) and the page number?
    - Did you end with the final mark of punctuation for the sentence (usually a period)?

Demonstration   **Using the Highlighting Workshop**

Read the following *excerpt* from a sample essay for this chapter's assignment for which a student has completed the Highlighting Workshop for the introduction and first two body paragraphs, and look at the answers to the questions for the workshop described previously. (Note that the errors in grammar and punctuation will be fixed in the next section.) Use this as an example for your own highlighting workshop.

CROSSING BORDERS INTO NEW LANDS

"Across the ocean, on the far horizon, the clouds parted for a moment…Slowly, Beegle began to build a boat. It would take her nine years to complete the crossing" *(Schwartz 32)*. Have you ever considered that going to college is like crossing an ocean to another land? For Donna Beegle who grew up in generational poverty and shared about her experiences in texts like "An Insider's Perspective: The Donna Beegle Story" and "The Crossing," going to college was like traveling to a new land, a land she knew nothing about and for which she lacked the knowledge to participate successfully. I also experienced a feeling of crossing a border when I entered college. I, too, found that I lacked knowledge of this new place and how to succeed in it. A lack of knowledge is the biggest obstacle one faces when crossing the border into college, particularly the lack of knowledge about the basic skills, the language, and the background information of college.

I realized my biggest obstacle when crossing the border into college was my own lack of knowledge of basic skills like reading, writing, and math. I took the entrance exam when I applied to my community college, and I found out that I needed a lot of extra work on reading and math especially. I realized how important these skills were when I took my first quarter of college. I decided to follow my passion and register for a class I always wanted to take in high school, physics. I was so excited! However, after the first two weeks, I realized that I didn't have the knowledge I needed to succeed. The textbook was a mystery to me. I would try to read it, but I didn't understand much. The pictures kind of helped, but it seemed like a foreign language when I read the words. When the class started to use math, I realized I was in trouble. I dropped the class and registered for reading and math instead. This experience caused me to hit my head hard against the reality of low knowledge in basic skills of reading and math. I realized that I couldn't cross the border to college successfully until I gained that knowledge.

Donna Beegle had to learn the language of college in order to reach her goal of crossing the border into getting a higher education. She first realized that she needed help with her language when her mentor, Dr. Fulford offered to help her with this. She replied to his offer by saying, "Yes. Please teach me how to talk like you, because no one thinks I am smart. No one asks my opinion. I feel like no one can hear me" (140). Beegle realized that the way she talked was getting in the way of her success at college, and she jumped at the chance to get help. It wasn't easy to overcome this challenge, though. As she says, "Dr. Fulford began correcting my language every time we spoke. He would stop me at various points in our conversation and say, 'Don't say "ain't,"' or 'You meant "gone," not "went."' I would chant to myself throughout the day: 'Have gone; I went.' 'I saw; I have seen'" (140).

(continued)

Crossing the border into college wasn't an easy step that Beegle did in one leap. Instead, she had to get constant mentoring and she had to practice what she was learning. It paid off, though because Beegle eventually learned the language of college, and she was able to use it to not just get her Bachelor's Degree, but also her Master's and even her Ph.D. While language was an obstacle, or barrier, for Beegle at first, it didn't end up causing her to fail. She found a way to overcome this and be successful. Finding a mentor and dedicating her time and energy to learning were important aspects of her success.

Going to college is like crossing a border into a new land, and certain knowledge is required to do well. For many college students such as Donna Beegle and myself, this knowledge is lacking and becomes an obstacle to making a positive crossing. Specifically, a lack of knowledge of basic skills like reading and math hindered my ability to cross into college. For Donna, her lack of knowledge of middle class language and cultural knowledge as well as her lack of knowledge of the value of education stood in the way of her crossing into college. As you embark on your own crossing into college, ask yourself this question. Do you have the knowledge needed to cross the border into the land of college? If not, seek out the mentors and guidance to help you get that knowledge. It worked for Donna Beegle and for me. It can work for you, too!

Reflection on the thesis, topic sentences, and coherence: There is a lot of repetition between my thesis and topic sentences. I keep saying "crossing the border into college" over and over again. I guess this is good, though, because it connects all of the body paragraphs to this point, which is my main argument for the whole paper.

Reflection on the support questions: I'm proud of how I used narrative support from our readings and from my own experience, and I think this strengthens my overall support. Everything seems to go together and fit my thesis pretty well. I realize that I need to add two more paragraphs, though. I ran out of time to finish these, but I do have them in my outline, so I will finish those tonight.

Reflection on the analysis questions: I'm proud of myself for having analysis in each body paragraph, but I think I could probably expand this a bit. I'd like to add more because it would also help me develop my paragraphs more.

Reflection on the introduction/conclusion questions: I'm really happy with my introduction! I loved the quote I found from my research on Donna Beegle, and I was glad I could use it in my introduction. I'm not sure about my conclusion, though. I think the final sentence might be too optimistic. My instructor said to avoid pat endings or easy answers in the conclusion, and I think I might have done this. I'd like to think of a better final sentence for my conclusion.

Reflection on the citation questions: I think I did my citations correctly. These are really hard!

Practice 7.10   Using the Highlighting Workshop

DIRECTIONS: Complete the Highlighting Workshop for your essay. Remember to do the highlighting and underlining as well as the reflection questions for each workshop.

STEP 8: Edit and Proofread

Once you have revised your paragraph or essay by looking at content and structural issues such as the thesis, support, and organization, it is time to do a final polish, to edit your sentences for grammar and spelling errors. To edit your paper, try any of the following suggestions.

1. **Read your paper out loud to yourself.** Read slowly, and read every word. You will probably find some sentences that do not make sense or words that are missing. Fix these.
2. **Read your paper aloud, *starting at the end of the paper.*** Read the last sentence first, and then the sentence before that. Make corrections as you go. This works well because you are interrupting the flow of thought, so you are more likely to read what is actually on the page, rather than what you want it to say.
3. **Have another person read your paper.** This should be someone who has not previously seen it. Have that person mark any sentences or words that do not make sense to him or her. While this person might not be a grammar expert, he or she can give you feedback about sentences that are not "reader friendly" and therefore could use editing. Make sure the reader identifies your errors but does not correct your errors for you.
4. **Work with a tutor in your school's Writing Center or other tutoring center.** Have the tutor read your paper and work with you to revise any sentences that are incorrect or not clear.
5. **Have your instructor look at your paper and mark it for grammar and spelling in one paragraph.** Then, look at your instructor's marks. Try to find similar errors in the remaining paragraphs and fix them.

Practice 7.11 Editing and Proofreading

DIRECTIONS: Try two of the editing methods listed above to find and fix sentence errors in your paper.

STEP 9: Reflect on Your Writing Process

The final stage in the writing process is to reflect on the process itself. You want to ask yourself some questions so that the next time you write you can change what did not work or repeat what did work. Here are some sample reflection questions you can ask yourself before starting your next writing assignment.

1. **What did I learn from thinking about the topic of this paper?** Did reading and writing about the obstacles to crossing into college help you or change you in any way?
2. **How did I grow as a writer through the process of writing?** (For example, did you take on any new challenges? Did you discover any new places you would like to work on in the future? Did you find that using a writing process worked for you or not?)
3. **If you did extensions: How was the experience of doing research on my topic and adding the information I discovered to my paper?** What challenges did you face? What will you do the same or differently next time?
4. **How did the act of writing help me grow as a reader?** (For example, did the process of writing help you to read texts written in similar styles? Did you better retain the information that you read? Was it hard to write about ideas in readings?)
5. **What are the strengths of my writing?** Start with content (ideas and information) and then go to style (organization, language, voice, etc.)
6. **What are the weaknesses of my writing?**
7. **If I had more time or inclination, would I do anything else to my writing?** If so, what?

Practice 7.12   Reflecting on Your Writing Purpose

DIRECTIONS: Answer the questions on page 133 to reflect on your writing process.

✅ Chapter **Quick Check**   MySkillsLab   Complete the mastery test for this chapter in MySkillsLab.

Use the following questions and answers to check your understanding of this chapter.

QUESTION	ANSWER
Learning Objective 1: Prewrite for an essay that uses narrative evidence. *How do I gather information and generate ideas for an essay that uses narrative as support?* *How do I develop a thesis for an essay that uses narrative for support?*	To gather information, generate ideas, and develop a thesis... ✔ Make sure you understand the assignment, brainstorm, freewrite, and review your reading notes and summaries. ✔ Focus your essay by choosing the ideas most meaningful to you. Create a thesis containing the topic plus your opinion or containing the topic, your opinion, and the main supporting points.
Learning Objective 2: Draft an essay using narrative evidence. *How do I draft an essay that uses narrative as support?*	To draft an essay using narrative evidence as support, do the following... ✔ Write an introduction that is interesting to readers, provides enough background information, and states your thesis. ✔ Write body paragraphs from an outline of your topic sentence and supporting narrative stories. ✔ Write a conclusion that reflects the ideas in your essay and thoughtfully ends the paper.
Learning Objective 3: Revise and edit an essay that uses narrative evidence. *How do I revise essays that use narrative as support?* *What do I do to edit and proofread my writing?* *What reflection can I do that will help me learn a good process for writing narrative support essays?*	✔ To revise essays using narrative evidence as support, use workshop techniques such as highlighting for thesis, overall structure, development, and organization. To edit and proofread an essay... ✔ Ask your teacher or a Writing Center tutor check your work to identify types of errors you make. ✔ Get to know the types of sentence errors you tend to make so you can look for them to correct. ✔ Use a set of questions that help you see how you can use what you have learned about your process for writing. Write and talk to others about your writing experience.

PART TWO READING SELECTIONS

An Insider's Perspective: The Donna Beegle Story

Donna Beegle

Donna Beegle

1   For generations, my family has subsisted on minimum-wage employment and migrant work. We have never been landowners—always workers of the land. My grandparents and parents were cotton pickers. My family members were predominantly migrant workers who followed the fruit seasons—picking cherries, berries, potatoes, grapefruit, oranges, beans, and just about anything else that grew. Sometimes we would go into the woods and pull moss or bark off the trees and gather pinecones and mushrooms. We did work that didn't require an education or more skilled labor; jobs that did not require references or home telephone numbers. Although we worked hard doing migrant labor work and temporary minimum-wage jobs, we were constantly being evicted, going hungry, and struggling with poverty.

2   I was born into a family where no one had been educated beyond the eighth grade. My early experiences in impoverished schools shaped my views and my expectations for the future. In my world, education served as a distraction from being able to meet our daily basic needs or from being close to my family, the only thing I had. I learned early on that education meant additional "stress" to our family. The stress of trying to arrive on time, of having the right clothing, shoes, lunch, and materials for homework projects—all these stresses created a perception that education was not for people like me. I remember silently crying when teachers did not protect me from teasing and ridicule over my ragged clothes, shoes, and lack of middle-class knowledge. Thinking of these early educational experiences evokes memories of violence, humiliation, and the fear of not fitting in.

3   At twelve years old, I met my future husband, Jerry, who was also from generational poverty. At fifteen years old, I dropped out of school to get married. When I told my teacher I was planning to drop out, she told me, "Don't drop out. Someday you may want to get a job." The incentive she was providing to keep me in school—"a job"—had no meaning in the world I came from. At the time, meanings were not in words for me, but were in people, shaped by the context in which they lived. A "job" to me meant working long hours, not being respected, little or no hope for moving up, and being paid a below-subsistence wage. The American belief that "if you work hard, you'll move up" was a myth for me and others like me who had little education or training. I lived the experience that even though you work long and hard, you rarely move up, you still get evicted, and you often go hungry.

4   When we married, Jerry was seventeen years old and had only a seventh-grade education from impoverished schools. He could read and write at about a second-grade level. Jerry and I both began working full time for minimum wage at a foam rubber factory, but I had to lie about my age since it was illegal to hire a fifteen-year-old. We moved into a tiny, condemned one-bedroom house in a neighborhood rampant with poverty.

The Promise of Motherhood

5   My dream for as long as I could remember was to be a mom. If my teacher had known me better, she would have known the way to motivate me would have been through my desire to be a mother and be able to provide a good life for my family. My only role models had dropped out of school very young; every female I'd ever identified with had married very young and had babies. I did not know anyone who had done anything else, so I was going to do that, too. Thus, it is no surprise that my goal in life was to be a mom. For me, having children meant that I would love them, play with them, and that somehow we would find a way to get by and be happy!

6   I got pregnant right after turning seventeen. During my pregnancy, I rarely saw a doctor or had anyone to talk to about the upcoming birth. My first baby, Joyce Marie, was born with a head full of black hair and dark blue eyes. She weighed one pound, nine ounces, and was eight and a half inches long. She only lived for nine hours, since her lungs were just too tiny to survive. I was devastated by her death. Since I had no camera and no way to get one, I have no pictures of Joyce. All I have to show she even existed are a miniature hospital bracelet and a birth certificate showing her tiny footprint, which was the size of the tip of my little finger.

7   When I was eighteen and Jerry was twenty-one, we moved to an impoverished community with my mom, invalid dad, grandmother, uncle, brother Melvin, his wife Mary, their two daughters, and my brothers Wayne and Steve. The twelve of us moved into a small house with boarded-up windows. Since it only had two bedrooms, Jerry and I slept in the laundry room. Most of us slept on the floor.

8   My solution to the heartbreak of losing my daughter was to get pregnant as fast as possible so I could fulfill my dream. As with my first pregnancy, prenatal care was not part of my life. Welfare policy would not allow me to receive benefits if Jerry was in the home. So, when it got closer to the birth, I lied to my welfare caseworker. I told him that Jerry had left me so I could get a medical card in my fourth month of pregnancy.

9   On March 23, 1979, Jennifer Marie was born prematurely. She was immediately put on a respirator and had an IV inserted into her stomach. When she was eleven days old, the doctors said she had a hole in her heart and needed heart surgery right away. At this point, she weighed only four pounds. They told me she would have a 50 percent chance of surviving the surgery, and, if she lived, she would likely suffer from blindness and/or mental challenges. On the day of the surgery, I only remember sitting outside the surgery room crying. I was convinced she would die, just like her sister Joyce.

10   Jennifer survived the heart surgery and was kept on a respirator for two months. Every day, I would sit and rub her skin. I could not hold her, as she had too many wires attached to her, as well as recent stitches. She was a beautiful baby with long dark hair and blue eyes. The nurses moved the IV to her head, and each day they shaved a little of her hair to accommodate it. She could not make a sound because of the respirator in her throat. She would open her mouth to cry, but nothing came out. Deep sobs racked my body as I cried for her. I was terrified of losing my reason for being.

11   After two and a half months, the doctors told me she weighed five pounds and I could finally take her home. The University of Oregon Health Sciences University regularly followed the progress of preemie babies, so they did a free checkup on Jennifer every six months. Her only lingering problem from her premature birth was that she developed asthma.

12   Since she was considered high risk, Jennifer was placed at the top of the waiting list for Head Start, an education program for children in poverty. By this time, I had lost another baby and was pregnant with my son Danny. Jennifer's teacher at Head Start, Ms. Susan Proppe-Tong, made every effort to link our family to resources. She told me about the Women, Infants, and Children (WIC) nutrition program, and I was able to get juice and milk and healthy foods. I am convinced that it is due to these resources that my son Danny was born healthy and weighed almost six pounds.

13   Because of my own experiences, I had no trust for educators and was suspicious of Jennifer's teacher even though she had done so much for us. She consistently went out of her way to connect with me. When I arrived to drop Jennifer off or to pick her up, Susan made sure to notice me and to compliment Jennifer. When someone brags on your child that much, you have to like her! She established some trust by connecting me to the resources I was desperate for, and, as I gained trust, I confided to her our family needs. She showed me—and told me—in every way that she loved my little girl; thus, I began to feel safe and view her as a partner in getting Jennifer's needs met. I was able to hear her ideas about how I could help Jennifer learn. She even taught me what questions to ask to help Jennifer in elementary school. (I did not even know I could ask questions of school people. I thought we had to take whatever we got. That was what the world of poverty had taught me.) One of the questions Susan told me to ask was how Jennifer could be tested for the Talented and Gifted program. I asked that question, and Jennifer qualified for the program, subsequently getting extra educational support all through elementary school. In middle school, she was placed in honors classes.

The Reality of Poverty

14   By the age of twenty-two, I had been through four pregnancies and had two living children. We still had no health care and suffered from poor nutrition. Many nights our dinner was a spoonful of peanut butter. During those years, we subsisted on low-wage jobs or welfare—working in migrant labor, pizza parlors, retail, and manufacturing. We moved from place to place, hoping for a better life.

15   My marriage ended in 1986 after ten years. When Jerry and I divorced, my functionally illiterate ex-husband was living in a car that we had bought for $25 at an auction. Unfortunately for Jerry and men like him, there are few, if any, programs for males in poverty in the United States.

16   I was now alone, trying to care for my six-year-old daughter (who was in the first grade) and two-year-old son. It was not long before we, too, were evicted and homeless. The difference for me and my children was that we could apply for welfare. We were given $408 per month plus minimal food stamps. With rent at $395, I had just $13 left each month for transportation, clothing, utilities, the Laundromat, soap, shampoo, and other basic necessities. I was constantly making impossible choices…pay the rent or pay the bills…have my utilities shut off or get evicted. My welfare worker told me I needed money management classes so I could stop being evicted. The message to me was clear: "Donna, you are doing something wrong. You need to get it together, to work harder. Do something!" But I did work hard. And guess what? None of the minimum-wage jobs provided me with a living wage for my little family. All work did for me was take me away from Jennifer and Daniel, who were my reason for being.

Beginning My Education

17   When my lights were turned off for non-payment, I went to a Community Action Agency to ask for help. I was told about a pilot program that was connected to Mount Hood Community College (MHCC), near Portland, Oregon. The program, called Women in Transition (WIT), was designed to be a three-week life skills program for displaced homemakers. Its goal was to help single women gain an education or skills to earn a living for their families. I went to the program not thinking it would change anything, but not knowing what else to do. The director had the wisdom to know that it takes more than three weeks to interrupt poverty. She told the class the WIT staff would be there to support us whenever we needed them—even after the classes ended. I used their services for two years and then became a speaker and advocate on their behalf, sharing how much the program had made a difference in my life. Many of the strategies I teach today I learned in this program.

18   The four-member program staff began by sharing their own life experiences. I was amazed. I had never heard the life story of a middle-class person before. I had been so isolated that I had only known people from generational poverty. I learned that most of the WIT staff members had gone to the same school for more than three or four months, something I had never done. I learned that they had never gone hungry, nor been evicted, nor watched family members treated badly or arrested. At the same time, I came to realize that they were not better than me. They were people just like me who had different opportunities. And conversely, I was someone just like them, but I had had fewer opportunities. This was so empowering. If they weren't better than me, then maybe I, too, could create the kind of life I wanted for me and my children!

19   The WIT staff took the time to get to know me and to find out what was important to me. They taught me by using examples from my life to illustrate the concepts they were introducing. They also worked hard on improving my self-concept by teaching me that I was somebody, that I was special. They pointed out that I had accomplished amazing things during my years in poverty, and they praised my resourcefulness. They began exposing me to possibilities for a different future than the one that faced me in poverty.

20   The staff helped me with my most pressing needs. With a single phone call, they handled a crisis that would have taken me weeks to deal with. They linked me with other programs and built my capacity to have the luxury of learning. I had no idea how much of my brainpower and energy were devoted to crisis needs until some of those needs were met.

Getting My GED

21 I came out of the WIT program believing that I had something to offer. At last, I had hope. I wrote my dream in my diary: "I want to get a GED (general equivalency diploma) and maybe someday take a journalism class. Then I will be somebody and be able to take care of Jennifer and Daniel." My passionate motivation to take care of my two children remained constant throughout my educational journey.

22   My emergence from poverty began with my GED. The WIT staff took me to the main campus of MHCC and helped me to establish relationships with faculty, support staff, and resource personnel at the college. They knew that going on my own would have been too far out of my comfort zone. The WIT staff, along with the staff from the GED program, provided me with a tremendous amount of personal one-on-one teaching. Supported with government resources to meet my family's basic needs, I was able to reach a milestone and attain my GED.

23   Graduating with my GED was a huge moment for my family and me. My grandmother, parents, and brothers all came to the graduation. The ripple effect of my education on my family began shortly after that time, when my brother began work on his GED. I remember thinking that the GED wasn't so bad, that maybe I could get a two-year degree and then I could take even better care of my two children. I had now been exposed to college and to people who were going to college. Once again, I met people who were not that different from me or better than me—just people with different experiences and opportunities.

Overcoming Barriers to Education

24 Shortly after my GED graduation, I went to my welfare worker and told her I wanted to try to get a two-year degree so I would not need government assistance anymore. She quickly told me that the state and federal welfare policies dictate that in order to qualify for welfare I needed to be available for any minimum-wage job. If I were in school, I would not be available. If I went to school, the government would sanction me and cut my welfare check from $408 to $258. This policy is still in effect in all but five states today. The one thing that kept me from giving up was the "Section 8" public housing certificate from the Portland Housing Authority given to me by the WIT program. My class was the only group these

certificates had been available to within the WIT program; public housing assistance is currently available to only 14 percent of those who qualify.

25   As I sat there crying in the welfare office, I began calculating how my kids and I could survive on $258 a month. Not having to worry about being evicted was a huge comfort. I knew I could sell my food stamps for 50 cents per dollar, which would help me pay the utility bills, go to the Laundromat, and buy shampoo and toilet paper. Still, that life was all too familiar to me. I did not know what was ahead, but I knew I did not want to stay in the world of welfare and poverty. I told the welfare worker to "go ahead and cut my check" if that's what she had to do, but I was going to school. My welfare check was reduced to $258, but I still managed to survive by continuing to implement the survival strategies that I knew well: I went to food banks, clothing closets, and Community Action Agencies.

26   When the WIT staff connected me with the financial aid office at MHCC, I learned that someone like me could get money to pay for school. When the community college advisor told me that I could get financial aid to pay for college, I said, "Why don't you pull me up on your fancy-pantsy computer and look at my credit history. Then you won't want to help me at all." I had an attitude, a smart mouth—something you get from not having your basic needs met.

27   "We don't look at credit for financial aid," said the advisor. Astonished, I replied, "Huh? You give people money, and you don't look at their credit?" I didn't live in that world. I lived in a world where I couldn't get anything because I had bad credit. That was my frame of reference.

Furthering My Education

28   With an enormous amount of support from the WIT program staff and my family, I entered the community college to work on a two-year degree. I was absolutely terrified. I could not write a complete sentence. The professors wrote words such as "fragment," "double negative," and "run on" on my papers. I did not know what those comments meant, but I knew from the red ink that they were bad. I was also baffled by most of the words in the incredibly expensive textbooks. The dictionary was no help; it only gave me more words I did not know. I did not learn what continent I lived on until I was a junior in college. My knowledge gaps were large and served to reinforce my internal feeling that I did not belong in college.

29   Students from poverty are often placed in special-education classes. If they do not know words or concepts, assumptions are made that they are unable to know them—often equating knowing the meaning of a word or subject with intelligence. This happens far too often to children in poverty conditions. But if no one around you uses those words or talks about those subjects, you're not likely to understand them. Thus, my ignorance, much like that of all students from poverty, had nothing to do with intelligence, but everything to do with growing up in poverty. For instance, I did not have context for subjects such as Watergate. People at the college would often say to me, "How can you not know this? Aren't you American?" They did not understand that while living in poverty, I was in an environment in which hunger and homelessness forced me to focus on meeting basic needs. Nor did they comprehend that I had attended impoverished schools where the resources were minimal and the teachers were overwhelmed, an environment that was rarely conducive to learning.

30   My language also created difficulties in the education environment. I used the word "ain't" in practically every other sentence. I did not know when it was proper to say "gone" or "went" or "seen" or "saw." I did not know I was not speaking Standard English. My only clue that my speech was different was related to my perception that people judged me as unintelligent. I was rarely asked for my opinions or thoughts, and, when I did try to share them, it seemed no one could hear me. I was invisible and, to many people, expendable. I did not look "right", talk "right", or have the "right" family.

31   Despite not having the "right" family, my brother Wayne provided support that helped me complete my two-year degree. Wayne had spent the last twelve years in prison reading and was amazingly literate. I would write him questions about a subject I was studying, and he would respond with twenty-five pages or so, using words and examples from our background to explain the subject matter. I could relate to the examples he gave me because they were in our language and were drawn from our life experiences. I rarely read my textbooks; instead I read his letters, and for the most part I did well in my classes.

32   One day during lunch at MHCC, I stumbled on a college fair. Recruiters from four-year universities were passing out information. A recruiter from the University of Portland asked, "What's your grade point average?" I told him, and he said, "I'll waive the application fee if you would like to apply." My thoughts immediately flew to my kids. Wow, if I could get a four-year degree, I could really take care of Jennifer and Daniel. Because of the location of the University of Portland, I knew I could still rely on my mom and dad to take care of my kids while I attended classes and studied. I could also count on my brothers to help out any way they could. I applied to the University of Portland and received an acceptance letter shortly after. At this time, the primary supports that kept me moving forward in the educational system were the safety of having my housing needs met, the continued support of my family, and having mentors from the WIT program and MHCC who believed in me and encouraged me.

Mentors, Middle-Class Language, and Meeting Me Where I Was—The Keys to My Educational Success

33   My junior year in college, I began attending the University of Portland. In one of my first classes there, a professor, Dr. Bob Fulford, asked me if I wanted him to correct my grammar. By this time I had lost my smart mouth and attitude, so instead of responding sarcastically, I said, "Yes. Please teach me how to talk like you, because no one thinks I am smart. No one asks my opinion. I feel like no one can hear me." Dr. Fulford was a language specialist and had done extensive work on social-class barriers. He did not tell me to go learn nouns, adjectives, and verbs, as other teachers had done. He knew that what I was doing was, in effect, learning a second language. He knew that people experiencing poverty were often not exposed to the same topics that middle-class people talked about. We had a language that related to our poverty experiences. He knew that we did not say things incorrectly, but rather in ways that differed from ways the middle class said things—speaking with a sentence structure and language that was clear and consistent but did not match what was expected of us in school. He knew that for me to learn the meaning of a word, the word needed to be used in a context that was familiar to me.

34   Dr. Fulford began correcting my language every time we spoke. He would stop me at various points in our conversation and say, "Don't say 'ain't,'" or "You meant 'gone,' not 'went.'" I would chant to myself throughout the day: "Have gone; I went." "I saw; I have seen." After some time, he stopped giving me the correct word. He would simply shake his head. I would reiterate my point, thinking he did not understand, but again he would shake his head, or say, "No." Finally, I would realize I was using dialectical grammar and would ask for the appropriate wording.

35   Dr. Fulford also insisted that I read the newspaper. I protested that I did not know the concepts or many of the words used in the articles. It wasn't that I could not understand; it was that in my education, certain concepts and words had not been taught to me in a way that was relevant to my life in poverty. He said I should circle what I did not know or understand and come see him in his office. Then, he would explain—using familiar language and giving examples I could relate to—until I understood it. Dr. Fulford also hired me to grade papers. I now know that he had to grade them again after I had finished them, but the fact that he believed in and trusted me made me try so hard. Because of him, I learned

to write. I also learned that the other university students made mistakes, too. Before reading their papers, I had thought that they were perfect students.

36   After months of intense mentoring from Dr. Fulford, I became fluent in middle-class language. Now, I am "bilingual." I speak the language of generational poverty (oral culture), and I speak middle-class (print-culture) language. Speaking a language requires being literate about the culture and experiences that are associated with it.

37   With subsidized housing, food stamps, mentoring from numerous people, and the support and encouragement of family and agencies, I was able to move forward and become educated. Today, I can discuss topics frequently discussed by middle-class people, such as literature, politics, food, and travel, or I can return to my original culture, where the main topics are people, relationships, and survival issues. Prior to becoming bilingual, I did not understand middle-class jokes. The references made in the jokes were unfamiliar to me. The feeling was similar to the one I had when I went to a British comedy club in London during my university studies. British people were laughing, and there I sat, confused about what was funny.

38   Dr. Fulford also linked me with other professors at the university who he knew would "take care of me" and mentor me to success. One professor, Rick Seifert, a former newspaper reporter, worked with me extensively on my writing skills. Dr. Barbara Gayle, a speech teacher, encouraged me to speak about my experiences at conferences. She often spent hours working with me and found resources to pay for my trips. Cat Warren, a journalism professor, encouraged me to share my life story and helped me to let go of the shame of being born into poverty. Because of Cat's mentoring, I published my first newspaper article, in Portland's local newspaper, *The Oregonian*. The story went out over the Associated Press wire service and was printed all over the nation.

39   The doors of opportunity were continually opened for me. Because Dr. Fulford believed I was special and treated me that way, I was noticed on campus. I was selected for special activities and opportunities. He even got to know my family and helped my children get scholarships to athletic camps. When he found out that my dad loved Johnny Cash, he bought tickets for our whole family to go see his concert. When he discovered that I had never really eaten in a restaurant, he made it part of my learning to try ethnic food (now my favorite!). He visited my brother in prison and went to the parole board to help gain his release. Bob Fulford was the essential model of a mentor. He believed in me. He believed there was a way out of poverty. He met me where I was, never judging but always moving me forward. Perhaps most important, he linked me to a network of professionals in the community who continued to widen my range of possibilities.

40   Part of this mentoring meant encouraging me not to stop with a bachelor's degree. My mentors encouraged me to go for a master's degree. I said, "No way; that's for smart people." It took a long time to undo the messages that I was not smart. I began meeting people in the university setting, and I would say, "What did you study?" They would reply that they had a master's in psychology or some other discipline. I would talk with them for a while and realize that I was fundamentally like them, despite our different backgrounds. Once again, I was empowered by the feeling that I could continue my education. The pattern persisted: When I attained my master's degree, my professors and mentors encouraged me to go all the way to the doctoral level. As a doctoral student, I learned how to conduct research and use knowledge to better understand and address the poverty conditions that once had prevented me from getting a good education.

Family Support

41   Whenever I told my family I was taking more classes, they would say to me, "When are you getting out?" in the same tone of voice they used with my brother who had been in prison for twelve years. My family members had never known anybody who had benefited from education. They had no frame of reference for believing that education can be a good thing

or even a possibility for people like them. That did not mean they did not love me or want the best for me. They just did not have experiences that indicated that education was the best option for being successful in life.

42   It is a commonly held belief among educators that families living in poverty are not supportive of their children and their education. My research and my personal experiences indicate otherwise. Families living in poverty may have no frame of reference for education being a positive influence in their lives, but they overwhelmingly want what they see as "best" for their children. Support may mean something very different to those in poverty than it does to those in middle-class society. My family supported me in many ways. They loved me. My mom and dad watched my kids while I was in school and often did my laundry and cooked for us. My dad talked with me when I was troubled and helped me parent my kids. My brothers fixed my broken-down cars or did repairs at my house. My cousins, uncles, aunts, and grandma all pitched in wherever and whenever they could. There was no one prouder than they were when I received my doctorate. My entire family knows that without their contributions, I would not be Dr. Beegle. My family is living proof that it takes all kinds of support to educate students who are living in poverty.

43   I do not agree with the notion that people from poverty have to leave their family behind to become educated or middle-class. Harriet Goldhor Lerner (1989) writes that you cannot "not communicate with your family." She says it will impair other relationships in your life. I did have to violate some of the values I grew up with. I was taught that if I had space on my floor, someone should be able to sleep there. If I had extra beans, someone should be eating them. If I had two dollars and you needed one, I should give one to you. When my financial aid came, I often had to lie to my family and tell them I had no money. If I had given them the financial aid granted for my educational expenses, I would not have had gas to get to school or money to buy my books. Many nights I cried myself to sleep knowing that my brother's heat was shut off or my mom was out of milk and bread. I stayed sane by promising myself that someday I would be in a position to help my entire family get ahead—not just Jennifer, Daniel, and me. If I did not say no, we would all stay trapped. Even though I did have to abandon some of my values, I never abandoned my family and they never abandoned me.

Jennifer

44   While I was getting my education, my daughter was also getting hers—both in school and out. As a freshman in high school, Jennifer was offered a scholarship to an elite Portland-area private school, Catlin Gabel. There, Jennifer became fluent in French and traveled to France—twice. Jennifer found a way to fit in with very privileged kids through joining the volleyball team (and later becoming captain) and through acting in and directing plays. She often told me it wasn't easy fitting in with those who had so much more than we did. She would say things to the students from privilege like, "You paid what for that sweater? Do you realize that would buy someone's utilities for two months?" "Look at our science class and all this equipment. There are only seven of us in the class. In my old school, there were forty-five kids, no equipment, and we shared one textbook." Jennifer knew poverty firsthand. She was fourteen when we finally got out of public housing and off food stamps. She had so many people she loved still living in poverty that she was compelled to help raise awareness that not everyone has the same opportunities.

45   At seventeen and a half, Jennifer was invited to interview at Columbia University. I tried to convince her that she didn't want to go to New York. I gave her a long list of reasons why she would not like it. I did not want her to leave Oregon. She pleaded with me and showed me how she could get financial assistance to pay for the trip. Jennifer spent a week in New York. She called me after a few days and said, "Mom, I have crossed off all the reasons on your list for not liking New York. I even talked with the admissions director for two hours about poverty. I love the school. I have been writing poetry in the

outdoor cafes, and I have been going to the theater. I LOVE NEW YORK! This is where I want to go to college."

46   One week after Jennifer came home from New York, she was killed in a car wreck. She was traveling 30 miles an hour in a 1962 Volvo on a bridge with metal grating. It was raining, and when she hit the brakes, her back tires slid, causing her to spin into the other lane. She was hit by a raised truck and did not have a chance. When I lost my daughter, I also lost a huge part of me. I ache for the loss her death represents, for the changes I believe she would have made to this planet, because, in many ways, Jennifer was much wiser than I am about how we could be a more inclusive society and treat all people more humanely.

47   I am eternally grateful that I had Jennifer for seventeen and a half years. I am also grateful for all the people who helped our family move out of poverty—people who went beyond their job descriptions and did not judge, but truly helped us to access resources and to envision possibilities. Without them, I know Jennifer would never have attained the potential she realized. Most people in poverty never get to know they love theater, or enjoy writing poetry, or have the pleasure of traveling to France. Few get an opportunity to be all they can be. My Jennifer did. I share her story to challenge anyone working with people in poverty to look for the "Jennifers" in their life.

My Life and Family Today

48   Today, I live in Tigard, Oregon, with my husband, Chuck, and my two youngest children, Austin (who is nine) and Juliette (who is eight). My favorite thing in the world is talking and playing with my kids.

49   My son Daniel, now twenty-four, lives minutes away. I really enjoy watching him mature and pursue his dreams. When Daniel was fourteen, he was counting silently on his fingers. I said, "Danny, what are you doing?" He said, "Mom, in fourteen years, I should have my doctorate." Danny's dad has a seventh-grade education. Danny struggles with learning difficulties, but he believes in himself and is surrounded by the support needed to succeed in education.

50   Two of my brothers have received bachelor's degrees. Three still struggle with literacy, but they now know they can learn, because their sister did. I have cousins, nieces, and nephews who are becoming educated. I have a number of cousins who grew up homeless who now have bachelor's degrees; some are entering graduate school. I have a niece who wants to be a pediatrician (not a word my family even knew before—and not someone we had ever taken our kids to!). For most of my family members, education has a new meaning. It used to mean only stress, but now it means opportunity.

51   Though some family members have moved out of poverty, there are still those who live on disability checks of $600 per month and temporary and minimum-wage jobs. I love my family and am very close to them. I practice what I teach in my relationships with family—I help them with everything I personally can, and I build resources by connecting them to mentors and new opportunities. I am their advocate when systems that are set up to help them are not meeting their needs.

52   Professionally, all of my work is devoted to ending poverty. I am president of Communication Across Barriers[TM], a consulting firm devoted to improving relationships and communication across class, race, and gender barriers. I am also the founder and CEO of PovertyBridge, a Portland-based non-profit organization that is focused on providing opportunities for people in poverty. I speak, train, and consult nationwide with anyone who works with or is interested in making a difference for people from poverty backgrounds and those who are currently living in poverty. I combine life experience, eighteen years of working on poverty issues, and my research to help people and organizations gain better knowledge about what they can do to make a genuine difference for those they serve.

53   When asked why I do this work, my response is always the same: "How can I not do it? I know too much to be silent." I know what it is like to go through life feeling like there

is no hope and like no one cares. I grew up watching the people I loved not being treated very well by people in organizations that were supposed to help them. I saw my mom cry time after time when she was told she did not have the right paperwork or correct identification to get food or shelter. I saw my dad work sixteen hours a day and saw him cry when his pay would not cover the rent and groceries for our family. I saw my grandma sleep on the ground in a cherry field, exhausted from picking since 3:00 a.m. I watched my brothers try to hide their fear and anger when they saw our parents could not get any help to feed us—the fear and anger that eventually led some of them to incarceration. I cried my heart out when the judge sentenced my beloved middle brother and best friend to prison. I hurt to my core when I saw the fear on my six-year-old child's face when we were evicted and became homeless. I will always do work that makes a difference for those who have not had genuine opportunity. I learned this not only from my experience, but from the example set by my friend and mentor Dr. Bob Fulford.

54   Dr. Bob Fulford died of a heart attack the day I received my doctoral degree. At his service were many of Bob's previous students who were like me: steeped in an oral culture, mostly from poverty, ill equipped for the traditional education system. One after another, those students told stories of Bob making them feel smart, making them believe they could succeed, building the supports and networks to make it happen, and seeing only their strengths and not their weaknesses. Many people would say that it was not Bob Fulford's job to teach a junior in college not to say "ain't" and how to write a sentence. Bob often said, "I go to work every day to educate. For Donna Beegle, that meant something a little different than for other students. It meant starting where she was and keeping the high expectation that she would become educated." He would then tell anyone who would listen, "The real question is, did she get educated?" With a grin, he'd nod and say, "And then some."

55   I share my successes, and my gratitude for the help of Bob Fulford and the many others along the way who stepped outside of their job descriptions, because I know that too many people in poverty never have these chances. Every day, their potential is thrown away when we do not think outside of the box, or consider the context of poverty and ask, "Am I setting people up for success?" Herbert Gans (1995) says in his book *War on the Poor* that we keep asking people in poverty conditions to act middle class when they do not have the resources to do so. What we have to do to help people in poverty reach their potential may not be in our job description. It may not be what we are trained to do. But if we are clear about why we are in a helping profession, we are much more likely to do the right thing as opposed to doing what we have always done. If we are clear about why we go to work and what outcomes we seek to achieve, we will do what Lisbeth Schorr (1988) advocates in her book *Within Our Reach: Breaking the Cycle of Disadvantage*: We will provide a comprehensive, flexible approach that meets people where they are, not where we want them to be.

Whistlin' and Crowin' Women of Appalachia: Literacy Practices Since College
Katherine Kelleher Sohn

Whistlin' women and crowin' hens, always come to no good ends. (Appalachian folk adage)

You can't be a voice box for your own feelings and experiences, much less for those of your place, if you've accepted that your first speech was wrong. For if you abandon or ridicule your voiceplace, you forfeit a deep spiritual connection. (Lyon 174)

Katherine Kelleher Sohn

1   I invite you to consider this narrative of silence, identity, and voice. It begins with my moving to Appalachia in 1975 and finding a spiritual home. It moves ahead to the time when, after many years of silence as a part-time composition teacher, I hungered for education and completed my doctorate in rhetoric and linguistics at the age of fifty-three. Finding my voice, I became curious about the former students in my classrooms who began each semester in silence. From my research with eight female nontraditional students, I found common ground and learned about the consequences of teaching and learning, findings that turned my teaching upside down and that demonstrated the positive effects of literacy on women. These mothers, coal miners' wives, and high school dropouts—Mary, Lucy, Jean, Sarah, Hope, Judith, Faith, and Polly— turned discomfort with academic literacy into the bluster of confidence and improved self-esteem as they progressed through the academic program. After graduation, they took literacy into their homes, jobs, and communities as teachers, social workers, nurses, and community members—achievements that would not have happened without the degree. Ultimately, the participants and this author disprove the Appalachian adage that "Whistlin' women and crowin' hens, always come to no good ends" as we moved from silence in the academy to voice in our communities to more self-confident identity.

The Appalachian Region

2   Though the women in my study do not use the term Appalachian to describe themselves because they are residents of their hollow, town, or county, they help me to identify some commonalties of a region that is not monolithic and not so easily defined (Hanna). This representation is not meant to be generalizable; this is our view, me as an acculturated outsider, the views of the study participants who are native Appalachians, and some added Appalachian sources. This is the cultural stage on which the women act out their literacy.

3   During the twenty-seven years we have lived here, my husband and I have learned to open our minds and hearts to our neighbors and to recognize their virtues—love of the place, sense of humor, independence, religious values, and closeness of family. These values contrast with the invention of Appalachia by outside media: the ignorance and meanness of *Deliverance* or the combination of ignorance and common sense in the characters of Grandma and Ellie Mae in *The Beverly Hillbillies*. Acting on those images, missionaries, politicians, and federal program administrators for years have brought programs of uplift, setting Appalachia apart from mainstream America (Batteau; Billings, Norman, and Ledford; Jones; McNeil; Shapiro). Though their intentions may have been pure, these programs were often fired by "an ethnocentric conviction that bringing 'advanced'...civilization to social and cultural premoderns was humane and enlightened despite its physical,

social, and cultural costs to the indigenous population" (Whisnant 257). The attitude of the women in this study is reflected in Lucy's statement, "We're basically like everyone else. We're not outstanding, but we're not really stupid" (February 11, 1999).

4   When I asked the women to define the region, they centered on the reasons they remain here: close family ties, neighborliness, lack of crime, and so on. For Jean, "It's hard to leave the area. It's like a security blanket, really. You know everybody and get along so well" (April 29, 1999). All agreed that family takes the center position and reflects research which shows that Appalachian people "are more truly themselves when within the family circle" (Jones, *Values* 75), a "united front to the outside world" (Fiene 38).

5   The women lived in Preston County (a fictional name), one of forty-nine distressed counties with an overall poverty rate of 29 percent, located in the central Appalachian mountain range, which contains portions of Kentucky, West Virginia, and Tennessee. This section is "the smallest, poorest, and least populous subregion" of the Appalachian Regional Commission (Isserman; Wood and Bischak). The largest geographic land area in the state, the county sits at the edge of the state bordered by West Virginia and Virginia. The women shopped, visited doctors, and retained attorneys as needed in the county seat of Preston, which has 6,500 residents. They resided in the county amid rugged and steep mountains that allowed little flat space for building, often living with their families up and down the hollows and creek bottoms in places like the Right Fork of Cowpen Creek, Stone Coal, and Big Hackney's Creek.

6   Winding roads slow travel time; driving thirty miles may take an hour, though longer if the traveler gets stuck behind a coal truck. The women would say that the remoteness, which might frustrate a city dweller, is desirable because of the freedom it gives them. They caution against the interpretation that isolation somehow implies lack of culture or lack of intelligence, and they poke fun at the common stereotypes of barefoot and pregnant women striding behind men in coveralls toting a rifle in one hand and a jug of moonshine in the other. In other words, the women in this study are content to live in the region. Michael Montgomery observes,

> What outsiders view as "isolation," local people often see as "independence".... Traditional mountain society has always been aware of the larger society. Far from being passive recipients of outside language and culture, mountain people have actively chosen and negotiated how much and what kind of interaction they want to have with the society at large. (12)

7   The study participants grew up where the primary source of employment was coal mining. Their fathers supported their families with mining or mine-related work, and they married men who worked in the mines, with the exception of Faith whose husband was postmaster in their small town. Like the coal miners' wives in Carol Giesen's study, the Preston County women lived daily with the threat of "death...strikes, layoffs, and the seemingly inevitable black lung [disease]" (2). In fact, four of the eight women in the study came to college because they needed to supplement their husband's mining disability payments. Currently, increased mechanization and lack of demand for coal have decreased employment opportunities. Even when mining was profitable, the women saw mining profits flow "out of the region as a result of ownership in the industry being predominated by distant individuals and corporations, thereby exacerbating the economic uncertainty inherent in coal extraction" (Puckett, "Recent" 8).

8   Mothers of the women in my study worked primarily as homemakers but took odd jobs such as hospital dietician, school bus driver, small grocery store owner, aide in a federal program, and house cleaner. All provided basic needs for their children, though times were rough especially in large families. Other major employers in the region are the post office, the county school board, two hospitals, large and small retail outlets like Wal-Mart and Lowes, banks, county government, and the college (Preston County).

9   The women in this study reported their frustration with the county educational system, part of the Kentucky school system, which at the time of this study was ranked near the

bottom among the fifty states. Current statistics reveal that despite a large improvement in adults who finished high school from 1970 to 1990, "Appalachia still lags the nation in educational attainment...7 percentage points behind the nation" (Isserman 4). Two women dropped out—one in eighth grade, the other in tenth grade. The most visible case of how public schools marginalized working-class students was Lucy whose "generational teachers" [teachers who came from the same family and taught in the same school for generations] made fun of the clothes she wore to school. The middle of seven children, Lucy was obese and poor. She observed that the teachers had their pets who were usually middle-class students (Lucy, February 11, 1999). In fact, public schools are often seen as a place that "perpetuated demeaning stereotypes about working-class Appalachian people," especially when schools became consolidated (Seitz 119–20). Although Kentucky school reform is seeking to address educational inequities, the women in this study felt that the schools their children attended were still not doing as well as schools in other parts of Kentucky.

10   Language and dialect figure strongly in the women's definition of themselves. Because they grew up hearing and speaking forms of standard American English and nonstandard Appalachian English, "a highly stigmatized variety of American English" (Puckett, *Seldom* xiii), they were self-conscious about their speech. Jean, one of the participants, edited her transcript because she wanted to sound better. Mountain women like Jean are aware of the difference between their speech and the more "proper" speech "spoken by more educated people, usually outsiders" (23), but they want respect for their way of speaking whatever form it takes (Donehower).

11   Though they stated in their interviews that they did not attend church as regularly as they used to, religion is central in their lives, for they use Christian principles to run their lives, and "[they] are religious in the sense that most of [their] values and the meaning [they] find in life spring from the Bible. To understand mountaineers, one must understand [their] religion" (Jones, *Values* 39). Secular events they attended such as club meetings, ball games, or political gatherings always began with a prayer. The Bible was central to the early literacy lives of these women. They tell stories of reading it with their grandparents around the kitchen table, supporting Loyal Jones's observation that "ordinary people have dealt with the complexities of theology and use the Scriptures and lore from their culture to find meaning in life" (*Faith* 203).

12   This is the cultural setting in which the eight women developed their literacy.

The Preston County Study

13   Because I wanted to do research that would "validate and improve women's lives, not simply observe and describe them" (Kirsch and Mortensen xxi), I decided to elicit information through qualitative interviews. To select participants for the study, I studied old class lists and selected women based on their fulfillment of four criteria. Because I wanted to challenge stereotypes about Appalachian women being ignorant, I chose women who were Appalachian born for two or more generations. Since the women constantly mentioned in class how they hoped they were modeling education so that their children might come to college after high school, I chose women who were married or divorced with children. Having completed my master's degree in rhetoric and composition at Northern Arizona University in August 1989, I wanted students who benefited from the knowledge I gained, so I chose students who were in my composition classes after that time. Although it would have been interesting to include women who had dropped out for one reason or another, I was mainly curious about women who had graduated from Preston College by the time of this study in January 1999. Many of us wonder what happens to our graduates; I especially wanted to know if and how academic literacy enhanced their lives. I wanted to determine literacy practices since college for Appalachian women who had defied the cultural norm and come to college.

14   I came up with a list of thirty-four women, which I narrowed to seventeen and eventually to eight by working with the Preston College Alumni Office to get current addresses

and telephone numbers. The final eight participants ranged in age from early-30s to mid-40s and graduated between May 1993 and May 1997, with five of the eight choosing education majors (reflecting the overwhelming choice next to nursing of nontraditional women), one in art, one in nursing, and one in psychology/human services. The time out of school from after they left high school until they came to college ranged from seven to twenty-four years. They were raised in families that ranged in number from one child to three families with six, seven, and nine children. All families were working class, and none had college-educated parents. At the time of the study, Judith taught middle school math; Hope taught special education; Lucy's cystic fibrotic child prevented her from full-time work; Mary was a data entry clerk for an environmental lab; Sarah worked as a foster care worker; Jean worked as a nurse in the ICU ward at our local hospital; Faith taught as an assistant teacher for a Title I program; and Polly was appointed city clerk of a small town near Preston one month before this project. Table I provides composite data about the eight participants.

15   The primary research site for this study was Preston College, though this study was not classroom based. The four-year liberal arts college from which the participants graduated is located in eastern Kentucky on a hill in the middle of Preston, a town of 6,500 in a county with a population of 75,000. The ninety-nine steps (and in 1998, an elevator) leading from the town to the college signify the literal and figurative journey the women took to come to college. Founded by religious missionaries, this private, Presbyterian college has served the Appalachian region with a Christian emphasis in higher education for over one hundred years. At the time of their attendance, 90 percent of the undergraduate enrollment of 800 came from within a 100-mile radius of the college, and 96 percent were on some sort of financial aid.

16   After identifying the women, I scheduled interviews during January and February 1999. When I called them, I said how much they impressed me personally and academically during the time I taught them and how much I wanted to tell their stories to those outside the region, said that I would like to ask them questions about how they were using the reading and writing in their jobs, homes, and communities. I told them about my plans to eventually choose three of the original eight women to do in-depth case studies, shadowing them on their jobs, interviewing a family member about literacy's effect on the family, and interviewing them again with more questions based on the findings above. During the actual interview, I spent time becoming reacquainted with each woman, reviewing the importance of the informed consent forms and other administrative matters.

17   A curious thing happened when I reviewed the Informed Consent Form and asked them to sign it. Each woman grinned at me as I went over the need for their protection as human subjects as if to say, "I trust you. I'll fill this out to make you happy, but we already have a relationship of trust." Though I believe in the participants' right to know about the full nature of the research project, how they will be involved, and their right to withdraw, I resonated with sociologist Murray Wax's concept of a covenant of trust. Unlike biomedical research where the subject needs protection, "the potential host community [of the qualitative researcher] does not typically require protection from the researcher; and, since neither party yet knows the consequences of the intrusion, 'informed consent' becomes a fantasy" (28). Qualitative research is based on relationships and connectedness; I had been their teacher, so we had established relationships before the research. During the study, the eight women and I found common ground and trust as I sought to learn about their literacy practices since college.

18   I began the interviews with a broad definition of literacy as the use of symbol systems in our culture, which included traditionally understood reading and writing as well as literacy in context: grocery lists, recipes, catalogs, and so on. I divided the questions into three sections: pre-, during, and postcollege. In the precollege section I asked what sort of reading and writing they and their families did, who or what influenced them to come to college, and whether they were the first in their family to attend. These questions gave

me some ideas about their literate background and their motivation for coming to college. The second section focused on reflections and evaluation of their college experiences in relation to managing academic discourse within the college and balancing college work with other obligations. I asked how they changed their home literacy habits to suit college demands; what changes they noted in themselves from freshman to senior year; what was most or least helpful in college; how being in college affected their families, their home life, and their children; and how they viewed the writing they did in my class. Their answers informed me about their lives within and without the college during their time there. The final section focused on their postcollege literacy practices in home, community, and work and sought information about achievement of the hopes and dreams expressed in class; their activities since graduation; their evaluation of how and if college prepared them for their jobs; what sort of reading and writing they did at home, in their communities, and on the job; whether their children who had graduated from high school had gone on to college; and their evaluation of the total college experience. These interviews generally took one hour and took place at their job site or in my college office. As indicated earlier, I then chose Sarah, Lucy, and Jean to do case studies. This article focuses on the original eight interviews.

19   When I completed writing, I involved the participants by having them read over their transcripts. In addition, I engaged two native-born, college-educated Appalachian women to assist me in my research. Tina Collins, who transcribed all the interviews, spent hours with me discussing the women and their stories from her perspective as a high school and college honors student. More importantly, my neighbor, Connie Wagner who had a master's degree in English education helped me by checking my biases and by acting as informant, editor, peer debriefer, naïve observer, and outsider in the professional sense. With everyone's help, I completed my research and looked with amazement at what I learned.

Literacy Scholarship

20   Although there has been some scholarship on literacy including those outside the mainstream (Guerra et al.; Holzman et al.), no literacy study so far has followed the reading and writing of former students after graduation to determine literacy practices in the home, community, and workplace. Following the lead of Mary Field Belenky et al. and other scholars (Brandt, Neilsen, and Flynn), I create an awareness of women coming to voice in and out of the academy. Like other works about working-class women (Lunneborg et al.; Pascall and Cox), I illustrate the transformative as well as the destructive sides of literacy. The women in this study also challenge Appalachian stereotypes in particular as have other authors (Donehower et al.; Egan et al.). Like other scholars who have studied literacy in context (Barton; Hamilton et al.), I hope compositionists remember that we are just one part of the literacy in students' lives and not necessarily the most important.

Literacy Practices Since College

21   As the former teacher of these women, my main goal in this study was to investigate how literacy had developed since college; what sort of literate practices they used on the job, at home, in the community; what effects their education had on their children; and whether their college-enhanced literacy helped them achieve the hopes they had when they came to college, in other words to see if the whistlin' and crowin' women had come to good ends.

22   The findings of this study have humbled me, have upset my ethnocentric attitudes about the primacy of academic literacy as a vehicle for upward mobility, and have educated me about working-class students in the academy. Acknowledging once again that these findings are not generalizable, I highlight the major arguments.

23 ***Literacy for the Appalachian women in this study served different purposes than it might in the larger population.***

> If I couldn't read, I would have to get into some kind of literacy program. I would *have* to learn to read. I just don't know how people can live without it. And to read well is wonderful (Polly, January 21, 1999).

Polly conveys her love of reading which her college education enhanced. She and the other women described early scenes of literacy that fit traditional definitions of literacy but which also included literacy in context. Hope reported seeing her mother teach her dad to read; Faith saw her father reading Louis L'Amour westerns and *National Geographic;* Sarah's mother traveled to the public library monthly to bring home a box of books, especially Biblical commentaries; and all participants were actively involved with extended family in reading the Bible. Lucy remembered her mother's poetry, and Judith's mother wrote letters to relatives away from Preston County. Despite not having college-educated parents, the women saw literacy modeled for them.

24 Their main fear about acquiring additional literacy was losing the common sense they valued. Commenting on her unschooled grandparents, Mary notes: "Most of these people are so talented in so many different ways, and they feel less of a person because they don't have that education. But sometimes I think I would not trade mine for their wisdom, you know?" (February 2, 1999). Because of poor public school experiences, the women may have had some doubts about higher education and social mobility since they have often seen literacy's promises divide society into "masters" and "servants" (Trimbur), and they would choose preservation of mountain values over upward mobility in any case.

25 The women in this study illustrated that literacy is gender related. Men in the region are generally more suspicious of literacy, and more women than men finish high school, though only 5 percent of women in the five-county administrative district graduate from college. As reported in Shirley Brice Heath's work in Roadville (a community with Appalachian roots), writing was used by women for memory aids, substitutes for oral messages, and social-interactional ("to give information and extend courtesies") (218). In fact, Anita Puckett's study of literacy in rural eastern Kentucky reveals that "literate practices are God-given attributes of women's 'nature'...provid[ing] contexts in which a woman can negotiate her social, religious, and cultural identity" ("Let" 137). Though women can acquire literacy, they are bound by cultural roles not to get "above their raisings," another variation of the saying that "whistlin' women and crowin' hens, always come to no good ends." Puckett observes about her southeastern Kentucky women:

> Ash Creek women walk a literate tightrope, called upon to assert an identity that affirms "good" reading and writing skills but constrained by cultural norms and social practices in the directions and forms their writing can successfully assume to maintain social propriety and their family name. (143)

The women in this study would agree with Puckett's findings, but they pushed the cultural norms further by coming to college.

26 ***Academic literacy in the form of expressivist writing enabled the women after some initial difficulties to tell stories they had not been able to tell, moving them from silence to voice.***

> At first I thought it [writing] would be difficult, but once I started learning some patterns about writing, how to get across what I wanted to, because you can't just write something down on paper, [it was not so hard]. There are certain steps you've got to take. And I was never taught those steps. (Mary, February 2, 1999)

Mary reflects on the process of academic writing; she wrote poetry before she enrolled in college but was unfamiliar with the expository essay. When Mary and the others were enrolled in my classes, I was impressed by their discovery of writing as a means of personal expression and the palpable excitement at being able to reflect on their stories. What surprised me in these interviews was how they disparaged their writing skills, though I found their essays were far superior to the traditional-aged students' work. Some who had been out of high school for years needed work on writing skills, but they caught on quickly and had no trouble with content because of their life experiences. Like most teachers, my primary role was boosting confidence, which Judith described, "When I would do my writings, because I know some of them were probably pathetic, you gave me the encouragement to say, 'You can do it' " (February 5, 1999). Because it had been so long since she had done any writing, Jean reflects the feelings of several women when she says, "I didn't know what words to put where, how to express it or anything. But I can say that in your class, I learned how to express it and how to put it together: the introduction, the body, the conclusion. I learned what you look for and how to do it" (February 11, 1999).

27   Many of the women, despite their unfounded worry about what poor writers they were, ended up having their essay(s) printed in the English department book of student essays, *Voices from the Hill*. Those included Mary's essay on "Making an Apple Stack Cake" and Jean's essay on "Making Chocolate Gravy," both creatively describing the process of making traditional Appalachian recipes. In another essay, Sarah challenged the stereotypical portrait of this area in *48 Hours*, a CBS documentary aired in 1988. Lucy's essay in *Voices* described her childhood as the middle of seven children growing up on the Right Fork of Cowpen. For their research papers, the women wrote about date rape, spouse abuse, and other issues that affected their lives as well. Like Eileen Ferretti's students, the women's "ways of learning and knowing [as mothers and workers]...[were] more rooted in the interpersonal relationships and caretaking activities they participate in at home and [were] limited by the subordinate roles they play in the workplace...inscrib[ing] their life experiences as wives, mothers, and working women" (84). Deborah Piper adds that the women in her classes built on their life experiences and revealed "incredible talents and strengths...as they wrote of finding ways to advocate for themselves and their communities...All became empowered by their own stories" (289–90). These authors would agree that writing has the potential for being "the greatest force for empowering, validating, and affirming [the women] and [their] self-worth" (Harrienger 151), a vehicle for opening up voices that are often "suppressed, silenced, marginalized, written out of what counts for authoritative knowledge" (Flynn 551). Without essentializing, we know from Elizabeth Flynn's study that women respond to developmental and interpersonal writing, which is not as privileged in the academy as male discourse. Obviously we want to bridge the gap from personal to academic writing, but beginning with the personal is a good first step, especially for nontraditional women.

28   ***The women in this study illustrate the intergenerational effects of literacy in multiple directions.***

> I guess the one thing that made it [going to college] all seem worth it to me was on graduation day when my mom got to stand there and watch the dream come true.
> And just as soon as they started playing the music, my mom started crying. So that is what I worked hard for. Her dream and my dream. (Sarah, January 25, 1999)

Knowing that education begets education and that "highly educated parents are more likely than their less-educated counterparts to raise children who themselves recognize the value of education" (Pascarella and Terenzini 414), I wondered about the education of these women's parents. I learned that more mothers than fathers finished high school; six fathers did not complete higher than an eighth grade education because they went into the mines; five of the mothers completed high school.

29   [Sarah's mother, Naomi, to whom she refers above, was just one of many mothers who may have been unable to attend college, but who modeled literacy during their daughters' formative years and who strongly encouraged their daughters to attend college. In fact, for

three of the mothers, their daughters' going to college was an achievement for them as well. With only an eighth grade education, Naomi had saved $10,000 from her monthly social security allowance to make sure that Sarah could go to college. Sarah remembers that her mom "push[ed] me to have something better than what she had—a very limited education, limited abilities. I guess ever since I was little I can remember her going over and over how important education was" (January 25, 1999). Judith's mother encouraged her by saying, "I didn't get this opportunity because when I grew up, the family was only concerned with the boys. Only the boys got to go on to high school and to college. It's [going to college] just too important not to do" (February 5, 1999). Hope's mother, a hospital dietitian who died before she saw her daughter graduate, repeated constantly to Hope when she was in high school, "Go to school and be a teacher" (January 20, 1999). After her mother's death, her dad actively supported her and offered financial help for summer school and other educational expenses. These mothers support C. L. Barney Law's observation that parents of working-class children hope that education will help their children realize their dreams, but they want them to "come home essentially the same" (5).

30   Continuing the generational effect, the women in this study hoped that coming to school would model the importance of a college education, so that their children would enroll immediately after high school instead of waiting as long as they had. Jean remarked, "they [the children] have seen that if you don't get it [college education] now, it's a lot harder to get it later" (April 29, 1999). Curious about how that modeling worked out, I learned from the women that of the seven children who had graduated from high school (including one who had dropped out), only one had attended a technical school, but none of the others had attended a community or a four-year college, a factor that frustrated their mothers like Polly who said, "How do you encourage kids? How do you get them to [go to college]? Because I always wanted mine to, but they just never did" (January 21, 1999). Among the reasons for this low percentage, I speculate that five of the seven children were males who generally consider education a more acceptably feminine pursuit. Also, the children may have seen the sacrifices their mothers made and decided it was not worth it, like the participants in Deborah Brandau's study in upstate New York. Some may, in fact, enroll in college as they get older just as their mothers did. For the children who were still at home, it was too soon to tell. In any case, the effects on their children do not end with whether they go to college or not. As Lucy reports, "Going to college helped me personally to really find myself, and it even helped in raising my children" (April 22, 1999). Having the women set the example of finishing what they started influenced many around them, including their children.

31   *The women in this study chose traditional occupations because not many nontraditional jobs exist in the immediate region, because a depressed economy does not offer many jobs for either gender, and because in doing so, they were able to preserve their families.*

> I think it's a lot different for the girls than it is the boys. The boys can always get out and make a living. They can do something somewhere, somehow. Driving a coal truck, driving something, they can still make the money. But for a girl it's very hard. They can't get out and do what they want. And who wants to house clean for $5 an hour the rest of your life? It's fine; I've done it before. It's good. But you don't want to stay there the rest of your life. (Jean, April 29, 1999)

Discussing this research, a colleague asked me why these women had chosen traditional jobs. My answer was that working-class people generally do not have choices, particularly in a depressed economy. They generally come from backgrounds where a college education is not modeled, and "they typically harbor some resentment toward highly educated professional women, and they cringe at the word 'feminism.' Although most of them came of age during the recent women's movement, they did not have access to the wider educational and professional options that their middle-class counterparts fought for" (Ferretti 78). For the women in this study, being in minimum wage jobs is not seen as "gender oppression but primarily as a result of economic conditions that have negatively impacted the working-class. Their worker husbands, no longer earning enough to support the family, have sent them out to work or have left them (turning them into single mothers)" (78).

32   So the women in this study became nurses, teachers, and social workers. Because of the depressed economy, they were fortunate to find jobs. Of the seven women employed outside the home, not all were working in the occupation they set out to attain. The only unemployed participant, Lucy, took care of her daughter with cystic fibrosis, a fatal genetic disease requiring constant care. Hope was teaching special education for kindergarten through fifth grade, though she had a 45-mile and seventy-minute commute from her home (not common in this region where distances to work are minimal) because there were no positions open in schools within her town. Another education major, Faith, after graduating in December 1993, took a series of substitute positions, finally getting a nonpermanent position as Title 1 assistant teacher. Judith was employed faster than any of the others; after graduating in December 1997, she landed a job as a junior high math teacher in October 1998.

33   Eventually, two of the eight women ended up in noneducation jobs. Mary, who graduated in May 1993, took odd jobs as photographer at K-Mart and substitute teacher until she found her position at the time of the study as a lab assistant for an environmental consulting firm that saw her capabilities. She was being trained to move beyond the clerical job. Polly had taken substitute-teaching jobs to carry her from graduation in May 1995 until January 1999. Then she was offered the city clerk position in a nearby town, which she took because of the instability of substitute teaching. In the meantime, she helped her father and her second husband with bookkeeping for their sanitation business.

34   When asked what they would be doing had they not gone to college, most talked about being bored, wasting their time, carping at their husbands, or making minimum-wage salaries at jobs they hate. So they chose traditional professions, moving from minimum-wage jobs to salaried positions as teachers, nurses, and social workers. Looking at Anne Aronson's concept of "downward mobility" for many working-class nontraditional students, "the promise that all Americans can move up the socioeconomic ladder if they work hard enough—is not a reality," (39–40), I believe that even downward mobility was an improvement in some of their lives.

35   *Achieving academic literacy for working-class nontraditional women is a double-edged sword, fraught with obstacles that might seem insurmountable to traditional students, but one that ultimately liberates women from abuse and other ills.*

> [My husband] was uneducated. He couldn't read and write…He just didn't see the need of it [college]….I was not allowed to bring my [college] books into the house. (Lucy, Feb. 4, 1999)

Lucy's husband felt threatened by her literacy to the point of not allowing any printed material in the house; in addition, he physically abused her. Though some women in the study had supportive spouses and relatives, Lucy's situation and others demonstrated that literacy becomes a two-edged sword (Lauer): positive in that the women were improving themselves, negative in that this improvement threatened others around them.

36   In this study, Lucy and Sarah directly connected their divorces to their increased education: Lucy divorced her husband when his abuse became too bad. Sarah's ex-husband said she was becoming too independent. Other women experienced objections from their families. Polly relates her family's reaction: "They didn't think that I was smart enough or that my grades would be good, or that I could do it. 'You've got three children. You need to be here and take care of them. You can't handle both of them'" (January 21, 1999). If the immediate family did not object, sometimes their husbands' families objected. Hope talks about the silence of her sisters-in-law when she decided to come to college. When asked

how they showed their objections, she said, "They didn't say anything. That was it; they just avoided the subject" (January 20, 1999). Jean's in-laws were more vocal. They gave her all kinds of trouble, making her feel like a bad mother for returning to school even though she, her husband, and children managed the situation.

37   These negative responses may have occurred for several reasons. Because outsiders have caricatured Appalachian speech and culture and implied religious and cultural superiority, mountain people have adopted defensive attitudes about formal education and social mobility. Men especially are often trapped in a world that is not always of their choice, especially if they are the primary breadwinners. Many did not have the choice of higher education, for according to the coal miners' wives in Giesen's study, "It was school or food on the table, and what choice was there?" (26). The promises of literacy are not the same for all, especially the working class.

38   In addition, some of the antieducation attitudes may have been shaped by deep religious values. Some Appalachian churches preach against the dangers of education, such as this Primitive Baptist minister who wrote, "With every *progress* in culture, science, commerce, manufacture, education…each resulted in another subtle but sure means of undermining and weakening the foundations and bulwarks of marriage, family, and local community" (Berry quoted in Jones, *Faith* 29). Puckett in her linguistic study of an Appalachian community, states that during several church services she attended, "I found myself being 'preached at' during religious services as preachers condemned the kinds of behavioral pitfalls education can lead one into" ("Let" 137). In the interviews, some of the women whom I had remembered as religious surprised me by telling me that they had stopped attending church because they began to see areas of gray among the black-and-white church teachings as they progressed through college. Their family members had not experienced the same thing.

39   Other studies support these findings about the multiple effects of literacy. Sharon Hamilton's literacy transformation from a person labeled as disobedient, uneducable, and socially maladjusted to a literate person equipped with "knowledge and confidence to decide how I would live my life as the kind of person I wanted to be" (xiv) led to her divorce. Sandra Rodriguez's community college student, Mamie, overcomes drug and spouse abuse and a nonsupportive husband to graduate from college. S. Hammons-Bryner observes that experiences like the traumatic relationships with fathers or husbands seem to "spark and strengthen [the African American women's] determination to get a college degree and professional status. For them, education is the main avenue for escaping dependence on men, a situation that they viewed as unpleasant and undesirable" (14).

40   In most cases, the women divorced their nonsupportive husbands so that they could finish college and get jobs to support their single families. Those relatives who objected came around after the participants' graduations from college.

41   ***Academic literacy did not destroy community for the women in this study. They overcame poor public school experiences, constraints of gender, and dead-end jobs to get a college education, adapting academic literacy to their own purposes, and maintaining the common sense they valued.***

> I think the major thing is the community. It's a lot of families. They're close. And not only just the close family but extended family. You also consider your neighbor as part of your family. There are times that you can go out and if your neighbor needs something done and you see them out working and you know they haven't been feeling good, you'll go over and do it for them. (Jean, April 29, 1999)

Jean illustrates that her education has not severed her from her community; she operates much as she had before her college education. Unlike many nonmainstream groups who are alienated from their cultural moorings because of acquired academic literacy, I found that literacy did not create a disjunction between these women and their community, challenging previous writings by R. Rodriguez, Patricia Bizzell, Carolyn Dews and Barney Law, Sherry Linkon, Ira Shor, and others. Dews co-edits *This Fine Place So Far from Home,* essays of working-class academics who echo her feeling that the academy "has always erased our stories…[and] *has* destroyed something even while it has been re-creating me in its own image" (1). For many immigrant groups, education creates "the clash and dislocation in our communities" (Rose 226), most notably depicted by R. Rodriguez as he describes his estrangement from his home and native tongue, Spanish, as a result of his education. Not all academics feel this way. Kentucky-born author Linda Scott DeRosier states that she is at home in both communities [academic position as professor at the University of Montana and daughter of a Kentucky coal miner in eastern Kentucky], though she watches her speech so as not to offend her Kentucky relatives. She says, "My sense of who I am comes from my identity as a hillbilly woman, and I do not see that ever changing.…To maintain a sense of wholeness and of loyalty to the community that I was brought up in, I have held on to an accent that is too often mistakenly seen as an indication of lower intelligence than many other accents in the US" (66–67).

42   Those who do not know how close families are may suggest that if the women had a way out of poverty, then they could have looked elsewhere for better opportunities and increased income. However, a colleague who formerly lived in eastern Kentucky with her professor husband and was a nontraditional student in the Preston College English program, points out to me the evolution of her thinking about people preferring to remain "disadvantaged":

> But the magnificent, awe-inspiring beauty of Kentucky's hills and "hollers" and the sense of familial commitment made me see "wealth" and "resources" differently. Having been ping-ponged as academic gypsies, back-and-forth these past many years and realizing too late the negative impact that has on family, I know that "poverty" of soul and poverty of social ties are much worse than poverty of "stuff." (Knudson)

43   The women in this study prefer to live in the mountains than to uproot their entire families just to be more upwardly mobile. In fact, preliminary findings of a study of the alumni of the thirty-three colleges that make up the Appalachian College Association reveal that most graduates of their colleges of any age remain in the area. This study by Ernest Pascarella et al. supports my findings.

44   That the women were able to return to their communities points to several observations. I believe with Caroline Pari that educators need to examine our elitist attitudes which assume that all working-class students aspire to middle-class values and want to move out of their surroundings. Secondly, I believe that we need to be more aware of class so that we can help our students "understand and deal with the life context that contributes to their hopelessness, their anger, and the manifestations of those feelings" (Piper 291). As we do with marginalized people of color, we can bring working-class

> languages, cultures and knowledge at the center of the writing classroom [which] can enrich and improve the learning experiences of…marginalized groups.…I do not believe that academic success depends upon breaking our students' ties with their communities or that the denial of a working-class background is the price to pay for academic success and upward mobility. (Pari 140–41)

Ferretti echoes this feeling about the women in her class who found "a voice of their own" in higher learning: "I do not believe that the construction of a student identity…necessitates the erasure of other existing identities" (84). In her study of four working-class proficient students, Hannah Ashley argues that rather than experiencing loss, her writers took control of academic writing and learned how to "trick" teachers by producing acceptable texts. She objects to the automatic assumption that working-class students are poor writers.

45   The women in my study may have been afraid of "getting above their raisin's" and did meet some resistance to the academic process from relatives, but after graduation the women managed to fit their newly acquired literacy into the community from which they came, offering a contrast to the image of upwardly mobile graduates who move away from their communities. They have used academic literacy to make a better life for themselves, shaping it to community values. The narratives of women in this study illustrate that "the modernist promise of literacy...is inequitably fulfilled. But they [little narratives] also show that some people use literacy to make their lives more meaningful, no matter what their economic and political circumstances are" (Daniell 404).

46   *Whether they got a job or not, the women continually praised the college for helping them to move from silence to voice.*

If I hadn't come to college, I wouldn't be the person I am now. I wouldn't trade that growth or the knowledge I've gained. Yeah, I'm glad I did that. I'm glad I did that. It made me a better person. (Mary, February 2, 1999)

Having seen so many graduates working the cash register at Wal-Mart or waiting tables at Jerry's Restaurant, I wondered before the research whether college literacy had changed the lives of the study participants and whether they might not be extremely upset with Preston College because their diplomas were gathering dust. I was surprised when all participants, regardless of their status, praised the college for enabling them to finish their degree programs, for providing models for their children, and for increasing their self-esteem. The experience gave them the chance to be "somebody" (Luttrell), and moved them "from a passive to an active role...to see themselves as...instrument[s] of knowledge and influence" (Neilsen 132).

47   Those who did not get jobs in their major did not blame the college; they were frustrated with the job market, with perceived gender and age discrimination (younger women were being hired over them), and with not being able to use talents they developed during their four years at the college. The key difference between their precollege experience and college appeared to be that the women were "instrumental in shaping...their destiny" (Fiene 53). The most important achievement of these nontraditional women seems to be "the sense of self-respect and worth gained from taking that first step into college and sticking it out until they finish" (Shiber 2).

48   That sense of self-respect is one the list of life-changing experiences at Preston College reported by the women: undiscovered special talents; multiple skills for living life; specific knowledge in content areas like nursing, psychology, computers, and science labs; and practice of job-related skills. It appears that those benefits outweigh conditions like the job market, something that cannot be specifically controlled by the college.

49   *The women are making their voices heard by using literacy in their jobs, community, and homes. Knowing the power of literacy, they are invested in the concept of lifelong learning.*

Literacy permeated the lives of the women in this study, especially in their jobs. Judith, Hope, and Faith wrote lesson plans as well as read materials to prepare for teaching. In addition, Judith taught reading and writing in her homeroom even though the rest of her load was mathematics. Hope taught anything from language arts to math, based on what the central office testing staff designated as the special education students' needs. She developed written individual education plans for each student in grades kindergarten through fifth grade. Faith filled out curriculum guidelines but did more reading than writing since she was teaching in the math and science area rather than in the language arts for which she was trained.

50   As city clerk, Polly learned the bookkeeping system of the woman who preceded her. She screened the mayor's calls, wrote messages, sent out bills and property taxes to residents, kept the books, and read ordinances and minutes of city council meetings. She felt

that her college education impressed the hiring committee and provided the background to make her trainable. Mary, a data-entry clerk for the environmental testing lab, used reading to look up information related to lab samples that came in and used writing to write up the report for the client. She posted results on the computer and developed quarterly reports for test results from the ponds which the lab tests regularly.

51   The women used reading and writing for enjoyment and personal expression at home. All of the women who had children at home read to them and helped them with their homework. Many spent time reading material on the computer. Polly wrote reminders to herself. She loved vocabulary and used the dictionary constantly, urging her children to do the same when they asked her the meaning of a word. She also used encyclopedias to look up something she did not know since "I don't want to take what somebody else says because I might not believe them" (Polly, January 21, 1999). Besides those sources, she referred to her copy of a *Physician's Desk Reference* to look up drugs when she returned from the doctor's office. She wrote poetry as a direct result of having written in language arts classes; a folder contains her poetry.

52   Mary reported that she read more than she watched TV and liked John Grisham, Danielle Steel, John Steinbeck, and all the Appalachian writers. She also wrote poetry and her thoughts out in a journal of sorts on the computer when something bothers her; "if you don't want to talk to somebody about it, it helps to write about it" (February 2, 1999).

53   Like so many working-class people, the women in this study were generally so exhausted and pressured when they got home from work that they had very little leisure time for reading more than the newspaper or for writing more than a grocery list. Judith and Hope talked about reading for themselves in the summer when school wasn't in session, but they did take time to read to their grandchildren when they got a chance. Polly said that she read more than before she went to college. In addition, they were involved in more activities outside their jobs like writing letters to communicate with people they did not have time to contact during the work week, keeping journals to record and sort through their feelings, reading nursing journals, and consulting the textbooks that lined their shelves at home. Although I realized there was no quantitative measure of literacy development, women developed literacy to handle the demands of their jobs, a kind of reading and writing none of them had done before college. College made them more aware of literacy than they had been before they came.

54   Another literacy tool that the women mastered since college is the use of computers. During the time they were in college, computers and computer courses were not as widespread as they might have been on many urban campuses. In the interviews, the women talked about having recently purchased computers for their families, which they used in their personal and professional lives. Owning a personal computer was also an indicator of how well some of them were doing financially in comparison to the homes they grew up in. Sarah used the computer to communicate with other professionals: "I'll sit down and do a letter form on the computer and do my own letterhead and design my own thing because usually by the time I get home, everybody is closed, and so I just write them letters" (February 5, 1999). At work she used the counseling center's laptop to do her daily, monthly, quarterly, and annual reports on her assigned foster care families. Polly's family played strategy games on the computer, and she used it for e-mails. Mary reported that her computer skills were one of the most valuable things she learned at Preston College; it enabled her to post lab reports and take care of other communication related to the laboratory tests performed at her place of work. Since college, Mary has developed a Web page with links to family photographs, to her poetry, and to a national poetry Web site, making her voice heard across the Web. Jean used the computer to check on medicines for the patients to whom she was assigned and to order new ones from the pharmacy if needed. Judith used the computer for lesson plans and other school activities. On the other hand, Lucy said that her mother with an eighth-grade education could operate a computer

beautifully, and she with her college education could not handle anything more difficult than a microwave.

55   Not content to remain in one position for too long, most of the employed women talked about job advancement. Mary, working in the lab at the time of this study, wanted to get a degree in English and work for a master's degree, "and maybe someday, I'll get to teach on the college level" (February 2, 1999). Hope was planning in summer 1999 to go back for her master's degree, either in special education or in teaching reading on the elementary level, education that helps her move up the salary scale in the Preston County schools. When Judith finished her internship, she was planning to pursue graduate school. Jean's plans included getting numerous nursing certifications and working for her master's degree in critical care nursing through correspondence. Sarah was working to get a master's degree in social work. Since Preston College is only a four-year institution, they do not have many options. To pursue graduate work, women have to travel more than 100 miles to get graduate classes or attend satellite programs from regional universities and correspondence courses. What impressed me about the women is their belief that their education is a lifelong process. They illustrate that literacy is social practice that "demonstrates the changing demands that people experience at different stages of their lives and offers convincing evidence of the need for lifelong learning systems which people can access at critical points when they need to respond to new demands" (Barton and Hamilton 282).

Whistlin' and Crowin' Women

56   One year ago, Mary called to see if I could help her find a publisher for her poems. In the middle of the conversation, she described the hours she had spent constructing a Web page and went on to say, "After the interview with you [winter 1999], I realized how much I missed writing, so I began writing poetry again." In addition to the poems, she has written for a local newspaper about local bluegrass artists. Having worked for several years as an environmental lab assistant during the study, she quit to get back into teaching, which she always loved to do. Still, she says, she cannot get a job, though the school principals she works for are pleased with her work. "When a job opens, somebody's cousin gets the job!" she states, describing the state of nepotism in the county teaching system. Her conversation with me and numerous others I meet in our small town confirm for me the continuing importance of literacy in the lives of these women.

57   Accepting the broad definition of literacy as social practice, the women in this study came to college literate. Despite attending schools with inconsistent educational services, especially for marginal students who were not on the "college track," the women spoke of reading willingly and often. With college completed, the women could apply for higher than minimum-wage jobs, work in fields they studied for and loved, develop literacy in their fields, and seek to advance themselves personally and professionally. In this study, college exposed them to technology and other life skills by nourishing the hunger for more knowledge. The women illustrated that they could "negotiate the secondary effects of both gender and class and use educational opportunities to create social and economic opportunities" (Pascall and Cox).

58   At the time of this study, among the participants, some achieved financial security they had never known, though most of them could earn higher wages away from the region. Even Lucy, on supplementary income, maintained that she had enough financial help to buy a car so that she could transport herself and her young children without depending on others. Sarah as a single parent had been able to buy a new car and to pay her bills. After existing on financial aid and his disability check when she was in school, Jean and her husband were talking about buying a retirement cabin in Tennessee.

59   Not all dreams are financial, either. Many seemed content with their lives, some working to pursue advanced degrees that did not automatically equate to increased pay. Lucy used her literacy skills to help others who were in trouble, such as a friend whose trailer

had burned down. She knew the agencies and merchants who would help out and what written proof about the crisis the agency needed. In this case, she speeded up the time within which her friend received help and acted in the role of "local expertise" (Barton and Hamilton 243). All considered themselves literate, educated persons who contributed to the well-being of their communities. All exhibited a solid sense of independence and the ability to teach themselves (Bencich). Though just one part of their accumulating literacies (Brandt), college literacy enabled them to get the credentials they needed and life skills to continue building on throughout their lives.

60   It appears that academic literacy in the form of a college education enabled these strong and inherent survivors to build on the talents they brought to the classroom, taking it and fitting it to their practical purposes so that it caused only minor discomfort and allowed them to remain in the region they call home. Their voices crow in individual ways. Lucy roars that going to college was originally to prepare herself for a job, but "after I got into it, it got to be more for me, to make me feel better about *me*" (April 22, 1999). Jean, passing on a legacy to her grandchildren, bellows that making a difference in her world would be "better than running for president" (April 29, 1999). Sarah's voice shouts: "I am bound and determined I will be successful" (May 4, 1999). They know that if they do not seek solutions to their problems, then those from the outside will step in (Bailey).

61   I hope that these stories will create an awareness of class in our multicultural discussions, for "without acknowledging the struggles inherent in the class system," we have an incomplete and idealistic view of reality (Villanueva 114). In fact, our "genuine concern for diversity should lead us to question the selective functions of the academy and the role of composition in maintaining them" (Soliday 731). We must be aware of "this exclusionary function [which]…reflects [what]…reproduce[s] the existing social structure by screening out students from the working-class and consequently reserving for the children of the professional and managerial classes the privileges that attend academic success" (Peckham 263). Often we penalize those with differences, especially in composition classes.

62   In addition to discrimination on the basis of class, the women in this study suffered discrimination because of their Appalachian birthplace. As compositionists, we can learn that "to stereotype is to dehumanize; to make ridiculous; to ignore history, politics, economics, and culture.…[It] serve[s] to dismiss legitimate complaints about discrimination and to deflect potentially disturbing questions about who has money and power, who doesn't, and why" (Shelby 158). Maybe, like Henry D. Shapiro says, we can come to an altered definition of our nation as "pluralist and regional rather than nationalist" (xix) so that differences among regions can be respected rather than obliterated.

63   My reconnection with my former students—Mary, Polly, Faith, Judith, Lucy, Sarah, Jean, and Hope—made me speechless, and as I listened, I realized what a precious gift they gave me, their time and generosity, countless riches that have changed my teaching and my life. I thank them for the honor of their trust; their treasures fill my heart. I hope my representation of them makes their whistlin' and crowin' voices reverberate throughout the land, for they have indeed come to good ends.

Acknowledgments

64   Special thanks to the eight women in this study who gave me the words that grace these pages.

Part Three

Casebook: Reading and Writing Texts Using Informational Evidence as Support

Crossing Borders of Prejudice

Introduction to Part Three

Part Three constitutes an evidence casebook with the theme "Crossing Borders of Prejudice." Chapters within Part Three focus on a second primary form of support or evidence that students encounter: information in the form of observation, description, facts, and statistics.

- **Chapter 8** reviews a process for reading texts that use this type of support.
- **Chapter 9** demonstrates the process of writing information-based paragraphs.
- **Chapter 10** helps students learn about and practice a process for writing descriptive and fact-based essays.

At the end of Part 3 (p. 213), you will find the texts used for modelling the reading process and for students to use in their text-based writing assignments: "The Causes of Prejudice" by Vincent Parrillo and "C. P. Ellis" by Studs Terkel.

Introduction to the Casebook Theme: Crossing Borders of Prejudice

DIRECTIONS: Look at the picture and answer the questions that follow.

1. The man in the picture is literally blindfolded and unable to see his surroundings. Describe a time when you were blinded in a similar way and literally unable to see something. (For example, have you ever experienced another car in your blind spot while you were driving? Have you ever bumped into something in the night when you could not see?)

2. We can also be blind to things that are less literal. For example, we may use a word or term that is hurtful to others without realizing it, or we may take actions that we think are "cool" without realizing their full and hurtful consequence on others. Describe a time when you realized you were blind to the full meaning or consequences of something you did or said.

3. Compare these two situations of being literally blind and unintentionally oblivious. How were they similar in terms of your feelings and realizations? How were they differ?

Like the man in the picture above, we all have certain blind spots that can lead to our being prejudiced about others. While it is a common assumption to think that prejudice means racism, remember that prejudice is larger than this. It includes racism, but it can also address biases like sexism, ageism, and heterosexism. Furthermore, we are often unaware of our own prejudices until we are confronted with them—or someone else confronts us about them.

College can be the place where we first learn about our own prejudices or those of our community or nation. Your college classes may be the first time you find yourself in a room and interacting with a more diverse population than you have done previously. You also may take classes that expose you to different ideas, histories, perspectives, and theories and be asked to question your own biases and assumptions. Both of these can lead you to confront your own prejudices or those you have experienced in your family or peer groups.

Casebook Texts

This casebook invites you to explore two texts that inform you about prejudice, and it will also introduce you to techniques for reading nonfiction, or informational, texts. The first text by Vincent Parrillo is written from a Social Sciences perspective. He outlines major causes of prejudice from a sociological viewpoint and from a psychological viewpoint. His text is taken from a textbook, so the casebook will show you reading techniques that will help you navigate this type of material. The second reading, by Studs Terkel, provides an example of prejudice through the lived experience of C. P. Ellis. This text is more narrative in style and will help you practice what you learned in the previous casebook while you build new skills around reading informational texts.

This book also contains other texts on related themes of crossing borders of prejudice, listed below, which you will find in the casebooks and Part Five. You may choose to use these readings to complete the reading and writing practices in this casebook or your instructor may assign one of them.

Readings on the Casebook Theme of Crossing Borders of Prejudice

Introduction to Informational Evidence

In the Part Two "Narrative Casebook," we introduced you to using narrative or personal experience as an important means of supporting your ideas—of giving evidence to prove your points. Here in the Part Three "Information Casebook," we look closely at the second type of evidence used in most college-level texts, what we call **information**, which includes *facts, examples, theories, models, statistics, descriptions, observations,* and *quotes.* Its most defining feature is the organization of ideas and details, which is very different from narrative or chronological order.

Authors use information as supporting evidence to teach readers about a topic. It is different from narrative because it does not tell a story or experience in the order in which it happened. Instead, informational writing offers factual details to support an idea. This kind of writing is often more difficult to read because the order of information flows differently than in a story. Textbooks use informational support as do encyclopaedias, college catalogs, dictionaries, and many other texts you will use in college. Web sites, almanacs, newspapers, and magazines also commonly use this type of support. Argumentative texts, those that seek to convince a reader of a certain point of view, also use information as support; argumentation is covered in depth in the next casebook.

Purpose of Informational Evidence

Authors use this type of support for a variety of reasons, usually to inform readers about a topic. It is sometimes considered more reliable than narrative support because it is more "**objective**," or more provable, than people's personal experiences. Factual information is seen in some academic subjects as the only reliable evidence.

Organization of Texts That Use Informational Evidence

Organizing informational evidence is more complicated than organizing narrative evidence. Narrative support usually follows the "natural" order of a story or experience, but with informational support a writer has to decide how to group information into paragraphs, and then decide on the order of those paragraphs. It helps your comprehension of informational texts when you understand how an author has organized his or her information.

There are a variety of ways to organize evidence that is informative. However, some of the main ways that this type of support is arranged is by *deductive* (*general to specific*), *inductive* (*specific to general*), *order of importance*, or *process*.

- **Deductive (General to Specific)** This pattern starts with a general statement and backs it up with specific informational details or examples. For example, a scientist might start with a general statement, such as "Most plants use a process of photosynthesis." That scientist would then support this general statement with specific informational details of how this is true. To review this structure in more detail, see "Deductive Structure" in Chapter 4 on page 58.

- **Inductive (Specific to General)** This pattern organizes ideas so that specific details come first and a general, concluding statement sums up these specific details or examples at the end of the text. For example, a literature instructor might begin a lecture by sharing several quotes where women speak in Shakespeare's plays. That instructor would then end with a general conclusion about women's roles in these plays. To review this structure in more detail, see "Inductive Structure" in Chapter 4 on page 60.

- **Order of Importance** This pattern organizes ideas in terms of their importance or strength. Some writers will organize starting with the most important and ending with the least important. Others will organize starting with the least important and ending with the most important. Finally, writers may "hide" the least important idea in the middle, hoping the reader will not notice.

  For example, a politician may start a speech about welfare reform by supporting it with an appealing and strong point about how the plan will reduce taxes for everyone. This is an important point that many listeners will appreciate and support. The politician then may "hide" a second and weaker point by saying it next. This speaker will hope you are still thinking about tax reduction as he or she quickly tells you how many poor people will need to find jobs if welfare payments are reduced. Finally, the speaker will end with a strong point. By ending with a supporting point such as "free more people from the welfare system," the politician is counting on you to remember that and vote for him or her.

- **Process Order** This pattern organizes ideas and details according to steps that lead to an outcome, such as in describing how to train for a marathon, or according to how a process works, for example the process of osmosis. To review this structure in more detail, see "Process Structure" in Chapter 4 on page 64.

Types of Language

Unlike narrative support that uses first person, informative support usually avoids using first person. In general, informative writing does not include personal experience as evidence of an idea. First-person writing can often weaken informative support by making it seem like someone's personal opinion rather than fact. Because informational writing provides evidence through facts, statistics, description, theoretical models, and other impersonal means, the writing often feels more formal and less conversational.

Explicit or Implicit Main Idea or Thesis

Most texts that use informative support will have an explicit and clear main idea or thesis. Unlike narrative writing, which may present an implied main idea or theme, writers who use informative support present their points clearly so readers will not be confused. For example, news reporters want to make sure their audience understands the ideas in their reports. They do not want audiences to have to guess. Likewise, textbook authors usually state very clearly what each chapter and section is about, because their purpose is to convey knowledge. Occasionally, however, you will come across an information-based article that never fully states its main point, so you will have to gather it from the evidence provided.

A Reading Process for Texts Using Informational Evidence as Support

LEARNING OBJECTIVES

In this chapter you will learn to...

1   Preview before you read texts using informational evidence.

2   Actively read texts that use informational evidence.

3   Consolidate your comprehension of texts that use informational evidence.

Warm Up

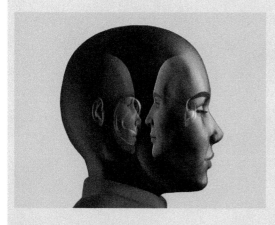

DIRECTIONS: Consider the pictures and answer the questions that follow.

1. Each of the two pictures focuses on people, but they do so in different ways. Describe the differences you see in how each picture looks at humans. For example, what human interactions does each picture focus on? What part of the human does each picture focus on? How many humans does each picture focus on?

2. These pictures relate to how certain disciplines—or subjects—at college view human development, actions, and relationships. One of these pictures represents a Psychological perspective and the other a Sociological perspective. Which picture do you think represents a Psychological perspective? Why? Which one represents more of a Sociological perspective? Why?

3. Often different disciplines each have their own explanation for a common situation or problem. How do you think psychologists might approach a problem like prejudice? How do you think sociologists might approach this same problem? Explain your answers.

MySkillsLab
Complete the Warm Up at
www.myskillslab.com

Phase One: Preview the Reading

Learning Objective 1
Preview before you read texts
using informational evidence.

Warming up to read informational texts might be even more important than doing it for narrative writing. Stories (narratives) are generally more interesting and therefore easier to read; we can all relate to human experience. It can be harder to relate to facts, statistics, and other seemingly dry material that is organized differently than a story. Before you read informational texts, spend time warming up your mind and generating interest so you can get the most possible from the material.

Refer to the end of this part where the essays by Vincent Parrillo (p. 213) and Studs Terkel (p. 223) appear. This chapter will provide demonstrations using Parrillo's essay and will ask you to complete the practice exercises using Terkel's essay, an essay of your choice from Part Five (see the list of related themes and readings on p. 163), or one assigned by your instructor.

STEP 1: Get to Know the Text

It is important to first familiarize yourself with texts that use information as support in order to see how they are structured, what topics they will make their focus, and to discover how you feel about the ideas in them. Avoid jumping straight into reading without first getting to know the text and exploring your reaction to it.

To explore an informational text, you might ask yourself the following questions, which differ from those you would ask about a narrative text:

1. **Title:** What is the title? What does it tell me about the content of the reading?
2. **Author:** Who is the author? Do I know anything about him or her?
3. **Source:** What is the source of this reading? When was it written?
4. **Purpose:** What does the overall purpose of this article seem to be?
5. **Audience:** Who is the intended audience for the reading?
6. **Structure and Organization:** Are there headings? What are they about? Is there an introduction before the actual text begins? What is it about? In what order do ideas seem to be given in this reading? How is it structured?
7. **Graphics:** Are there any pictures, graphs, or other visuals in the text? What do these tell me about the content of the text? What questions do I have about these images?
8. **Sidebars:** Are there sidebars with information such as vocabulary or key terms? What do these tell about the content of the text? What questions do I have about these?

Information Literacy: Evaluating Sources

Remember to use information literacy tools such as the Internet and your college's library resources to help you in this stage of the reading process. For example, you might look up an author online or look up information about key terms in the text or title. As you do so, remember to check the reliability of the information you find by using the CRAAP Test introduced in Chapter 1 (see p. 5).

Demonstration   Asking Questions to Explore a Text

This example shows how one student answered the questions above about "Causes of Prejudice by Parillo (p. 213)." Her use of information literacy during this process is labeled.

1. **What is the title? What does it tell me about the content of the reading?** The title is "Causes of Prejudice." It tells me that this reading is going to be about different reasons for why prejudice exists.

(continued)

2. <u>**Who is the author? Do I know anything about him or her?**</u> The author is Vincent Parrillo. I do not know much about him, so I looked him up online.

   • *Information Literacy on the Author:* I found one link to a webpage that showed photos of covers of books he wrote, and I searched for one book that came up a lot on the site titled <u>Strangers to These Shores</u>. According to Amazon, this book looks at over 50 different racial, ethnic, and religious groups and gives a broad review of ethnic and racial relations. Wikipedia said he's a sociology professor at William Paterson University. He wrote and produced two PBS documentaries and is a guest lecturer who travels around the nation and globe to share his work with others.

   • *Information Literacy on Key Terms:* Sociology and psychology are key terms in the text, so I looked them up as well. According to The Free Online Dictionary, <u>sociology</u> means, "The study of human social behaviour, especially the study of the origins, organization, institutions, and development of human society"

     According to The Free Online Dictionary, <u>psychology</u> is "The science that deals with mental processes and behaviour" When I searched for psychology online, I found some sites that combined sociology and psychology, for example, a site titled "Department of Psychology, Sociology, and Social Work." Another site talked about how psychology and sociology make a good double major. Both of these sites were college Web sites, so I think they are reputable. This makes me think that these two areas are distinct but still linked.

3. <u>**What is the source of this reading? When was it written?**</u> "Causes of Prejudice" is an excerpt from Parillo's book <u>Strangers to These Shores</u>.

4. <u>**What does the overall purpose of this article seem to be?**</u> The purpose seems to be to provide information on different causes of prejudice.

5. <u>**Who is the intended audience for the reading?**</u> I guess it would be the audience for his book <u>Strangers to These Shores</u>. From the Amazon description of the book, it sounds like a broad overview of different racial and ethnic relations between a lot of different groups—Native American, African American, etc. So, I think "Causes of Prejudice" is probably written to an audience who wants to learn more about prejudice but who might not know much to begin with—an introduction.

6. <u>**Structure/Organization: Are there headings? What are they about? Is there an introduction before the actual text begins? What is it about? In what order do ideas seem to be given in this reading? How is it structured?**</u> This text has a short introduction. The two main headings are "The Psychology of Prejudice" and "The Sociology of Prejudice." Under each heading are paragraphs with words in bold. These seem like key terms or vocabulary words. Given this, I think the text will look at the main causes of prejudice from two different perspectives—sociology and psychology.

7. <u>**Graphics: Are there any pictures, graphs, or other visuals in the text? What do these tell about the content of the text? What questions do I have about these images?**</u> There is an interesting cartoon in the middle of the text. It has six different pictures and goes back in time looking at how the US mainstream population has wanted to get rid of different immigrant groups like Mexicans, Italians, Chinese, Irish, and German immigrants during our history. I think the author is using this as an example of prejudice.

8. <u>**Sidebars: Are there sidebars with information such as vocabulary or key terms? What do they tell about the content of the text? What questions do I have about these?**</u> There aren't any sidebars.

Practice 8.1   Getting to Know the Text

DIRECTIONS: Look at Terkel's essay "C. P. Ellis" on page 223, an essay of your choice, or one you have been assigned. Then answer the questions on page 167.

Information Literacy Remember to use information literacy tools such as the Internet and your college's library resources to help you in this stage of the reading process. As you do so, remember to check the reliability of the information you find by using the CRAAP Test introduced in Chapter 1 on page 5.

STEP 2: Check Your Attitude and Set Your Purpose

To further prepare for reading, you want to pay attention to how you feel about the topic(s) you discover. These feelings may cause you to read with certain preformed ideas, biases, or perspectives. When reading about prejudice as we are here, you also may find yourself defending belief systems you hold close. Without realizing it, you may have emotional reactions to the content of a reading because it challenges deep values you hold. You want to be aware of this as you begin to read a text, as it could affect your understanding of the material.

You may also want to notice your attitude toward a reading assignment. If you do not want to do it, you will learn a lot less from it than if you are eager to read. Many people think of all homework as a chore—as extra, unnecessary, boring practice. If your only reason for reading is because your teacher told you to, then you will understand and remember less of it. You can create your own personal reason for reading: because the topic interests you, because you already know something about it, or because it will teach you useful information. The reading will be easier and more fun if you find your *own* purpose for doing it.

Ask these questions, used in the following demonstration and practice, to guide your thinking about attitude and purpose:

- How do I feel about the ideas I am discovering in this text?
- What is my attitude about the assignment?
- What is my purpose in reading?

Demonstration   Checking Your Attitude and Setting Your Purpose

This example shows how one student answered the following questions about "Causes of Prejudice by Parillo (p. 213)."

1. <u>**How do I feel about the ideas I am discovering in this text?**</u> I feel interested as prejudice is something that is everywhere. I'd like to learn more about it. I also am interested in learning about the differences between psychology and sociology. I want to take classes in these areas because I'm interested in going into social work, so this reading will help to introduce me to that area.

2. <u>**What is my attitude about the assignment?**</u> It is okay, but reading materials that aren't stories is harder for me. I struggled with textbooks in high school because I felt they were boring and I lost interest. I hope this chapter helps me get interested in this type of reading—or at least helps me be better at it. I know I will read a lot of texts like this in college, so it is probably a good idea to learn how to do this better.

3. <u>**What is my purpose for reading?**</u> I need to finish my assignment. I also want to learn more about prejudice, though, and the differences between sociology and psychology.

Practice 8.2   Checking Your Attitude and Setting Your Purpose

DIRECTIONS: Answer the following questions about Terkel's essay "C. P. Ellis" on page 223.

1. How do I feel about the ideas I am discovering in this text?
2. What is my attitude about the assignment?
3. What is my purpose for reading?

STEP 3: Connect Your Experience and Background Knowledge with the Text

Once you know the general idea of a text that uses narrative support, it can be helpful to connect your own experience to the topics being discussed. The result is that you will be more likely to remember the new information. A couple of questions you can use to connect personally with the text are:

1. What experiences have I had that relate to the reading topic?
2. What do I already know about this topic?

Your answers to these questions can also be used later when you write. Some assignments allow you to use your personal experience as support or illustration for your topic, or you may be able to use them as an attention getter in your introduction. Therefore, when you do this step for other reading assignments, be sure to save your work for later when you write a paragraph or essay.

Demonstration   Connecting Experience and Background Knowledge

This example shows how one student answered the questions about "Causes of Prejudice" that asked her to draw on her own experiences in relation to the topics in the article, so she could more easily connect to the text.

1. <u>**What experiences do you have with prejudice?**</u> I experienced prejudice when a friend of mine came out as a lesbian. While all of our close friends were fine with this, it became clear that the legal system was prejudiced against homosexuals. I think it is possible for prejudice to be held by a larger group like a government or a legal system, so I'd like to describe how I saw this work.

    When my friend came out, she was 22. We were in our last year of college, and many of the women in our circle were thinking about getting married, some were already engaged. I will always remember an evening when we were out for dinner with our close group of friends and one of the women announced her engagement. Everyone was excited and asking her questions about her ring, where she wanted to get married, what her dress would look like, where the honeymoon would be, etc. Then I looked at my friend who had just come out, and saw that her face was blank. She was not feeling the excitement of the group. She looked like she wanted to get up and leave. When I asked her about it later, she said she was really hurt at being always left out of this experience. Unless laws changed, she said, she could never look forward to marrying the love of her life. Marriage wasn't legal in our state for gays or lesbians, and she always felt like a second-rate citizen when friends got engaged. Being heterosexual, I had always taken it for granted that I could marry. Talking to my friend made me realize that this wasn't the case for everyone and that the laws around marriage were biased against some. This was a real introduction to prejudice.

2. **What do I already know about prejudice?** I usually think of racism when I think of prejudice. I think of the Ku Klux Klan (KKK) or of racial profiling. My experience with prejudice, though, shows that it can also be about other things like prejudice against those who are gay. I also tend to think about prejudice being about individuals. However, I guess it can happen between a group and an individual. The KKK, for example, is a group that holds prejudice against black people. My example about my lesbian friend also shows that prejudice can be in our laws. This is a pretty complex and deep topic!

Practice 8.3   Connecting Experience and Background Knowledge with the Text

DIRECTIONS: Answer the following questions that will help prepare you to read Terkel's essay "C. P. Ellis," an essay of your choice, or one you have been assigned.

1. What experiences do you have with prejudice?
2. What experiences do you have with the specific form of prejudice in the text you are reading? (This form is racism in Terkel's text.)
3. Have you ever experienced the process of unlearning a prejudice you held? Describe this and tell how you felt during this process.

Phase Two: While Reading

Learning Objective 2
Actively read texts that use informational evidence.

As you read informational texts, it is important to take notes and work with vocabulary. These steps are also prewriting strategies. For example, information you map for a given article could help you outline a paragraph or essay about that article. Therefore, save all of your notes from this phase of reading because you may want them when you write.

STEP 4: Write Down and Define Vocabulary

Many texts you read for college will contain words that you do not understand or have never seen before. While it may be tempting to gloss over these words and ignore them, your understanding of the material will be limited if you do so. Learning new words and terms is central to learning new content in your courses.

There are different strategies you can use to learn new words. While any of these strategies can work alone, they are best used in combination. Here are some vocabulary strategies you can use as you read:

1. **Identify unknown words:** Scan the reading for words you do not know, and highlight the sentences where they appear. List these words.
2. **Define by Context:** Look back at the sentence or paragraph where the words are used, and write down what you think they mean using context.
3. **Use a Dictionary:** Look up the words, and write down their meanings. Make a note if you could not find a definition.
4. **Use the Internet:** Look up the words and any related terms on the Internet to learn additional information about them. Write down what you find. **Note:** This step is especially important if you could not find dictionary definitions.

As you work with these strategies, remember that you can record vocabulary definitions in a separate vocabulary journal, in the margins of your text, or on sticky notes that you put in your text next to or beside the word. (If you have an online text, this can be especially useful as many e-readers have electronic sticky notes you can use to record vocabulary definitions or notes.)

Demonstration   Exploring Vocabulary

This example shows how one student explored some vocabulary in "Causes of Prejudice." After scanning the reading for words she did not know, she highlighted the words and the sentences they appeared in. She then followed the strategies shown below.

1. Words I don't know

   • perspective   • self-justification

   • ethnocentrism   • Jim Crow laws

2. **Define by Context:** Look back at the sentence or paragraph where the words are used, and write down what you think they mean using context.

   a. perspective: This seems to be about a specific focus or angle one has on a topic.

   b. ethnocentrism: The text's definition of this is kind of confusing. It talks about in groups and out groups. The part that made sense to me, though, was when it talked about how certain groups will reject others based on whether they are part of that group or not. I wonder if this is like the legal system rejecting legal marriage for those who are gay because homosexuals are not part of the mainstream group.

   c. self-justification: There are two words in the definition of this that do not make sense to me: "denigrate" and "maltreatment." I'm really not sure about this word as the context in the text just confused me more. I'm going to have to explore this more using an online dictionary.

   d. Jim Crow laws: I know that this is a set of laws that focused on segregation. The book says these were in place in the 1890s. I wonder if they are still around.

3. **Use a Dictionary:** Look up these words in the dictionary and write down their meanings. If you cannot find a meaning in the dictionary, simply note that you could not find the meaning. (This student used Merriam Webster's online dictionary.)

   a. perspective: "The interrelation in which a subject or its parts are mentally viewed: Point of view."

   b. ethnocentrism: The dictionary only had "Ethnocentric." It means "Characterized by or based on the attitude that one's own group is superior."

   c. self-justification: "The act or instance of making excuses for oneself."

   d. Jim Crow laws: This one wasn't in the dictionary.

4. **Use the Internet:** Look up the word(s) and any related terms on the Internet to learn additional information about them. Write down what you find about the words. (**Note:** This step is especially important if you could not find definitions of these words in a dictionary.

Jim Crow laws: The Encyclopaedia Britannica online site says that these were a set of laws that maintained racial segregation in the south from 1877 until the 1950s. Anyone who was considered "colored" had to use separate facilities. For example, they had to sit in different areas on buses. They had to use different bathrooms, go to different schools, and even be buried in different cemeteries. The Jim Crow laws were struck down in 1954 with Brown v. Board of Education Topeka. This case made it illegal to segregate schools, and this extended to other areas as well.

Practice 8.4 Writing Down and Defining Vocabulary

DIRECTIONS: Look at Terkel's "C. P. Ellis" on page 223, an essay of your choice, or one you have been assigned. Then apply the vocabulary strategies listed on page 171.

STEP 5: Take Notes on Major Ideas and Important Details

In this casebook, we build on what you have already learned about note taking. Cornell Notes, discussed below, work especially well with informational texts, and we will provide an example using Parillo's "Causes of Prejudice." Mapping can also be an effective strategy for taking notes on informational texts because you can use headings for the first branches with main ideas branching from them and supporting details branching off the main ideas.

When reading texts with informational support, choosing essential information for your notes can be especially difficult because every point can look important. For example, it can be hard to determine whether a statistic is or is not essential in a scientific study. A rule of thumb is that you want to include enough information in your notes so that you can explain the major ideas to someone else, without having to look back at the actual text.

In informative writing, information is often organized into sections with headings or titles. You can use these to identify important categories of information. Also helpful is that informational paragraphs almost always have one clear main point, and if you can identify it, then the most important supporting details are easier to understand and to select for your notes.

Cornell Notes

The **Cornell Note-Taking System** is remarkably simple, and it helps you to make decisions about how to organize information from a dense textbook, article, or report. Here is how it works. Take a piece of notebook paper and fold it so there is about one-third of the page on the left and two-thirds on the right. You can draw a line if you like at the fold. Then, at the bottom, mark off two to three inches for summarizing the ideas on that page. Some college bookstores sell paper with the lines printed in this manner; it is usually called "summary paper."

Write the thesis at the top of the first page of your notes. As you take notes, put big ideas on the left and more specific details on the right. Write a brief summary of your notes at the bottom of each page. It is a good idea to copy headings on both sides of the page, so you can follow the ideas even when you cover one column, which you will want to do when testing yourself and studying for exams. The format for your notes should look like this template.

Thesis: Only write the thesis of the overall text at the top of the first page.

Main Ideas Are General	Details Are Specific
Vocabulary word	Definition
Name of a theory	Explanation of the theory; Examples of the theory applied
Reasons	Evidence
Important person	Facts about the person
Important date	What happened on that date
Mathematical formula	Sample problems using the formula
Main ideas	Supporting details

Summary: In a sentence or two, summarize the main ideas on each page of notes.

One reason for taking notes in this way is to provide a clear differentiation between general information (the big ideas) and specific information (the details that explain or provide examples). Another reason for taking Cornell Notes is that it provides you with an excellent study tool. You can cover one or the other side of the page and try to recall either the big points or the details. The summary at the end helps you see the bigger picture in one chunk of your reading at a time. It also helps you write your summary of the whole reading at the end.

Demonstration   Using the Cornell Note-Taking System

This example of Cornell Notes covers the first couple of pages of Parrillo's text.

Thesis: Prejudice is a complex thing that has psychological and sociological causes.

Main Ideas (General)	Details (Specific)
Introduction	
Prejudice	A set of beliefs, attitudes, or actions about a certain group or groups of people. It can be negative or positive, but studies usually focus on the negative.

	Psychological perspective	Psychological perspective focuses on states of minds of people that contribute towards prejudice.
	Sociological perspective	Sociological perspective focuses on social forces and conditions of society that contribute towards prejudice.
	The Psychology of Prejudice Levels of prejudice	
	1. Cognitive Level	The cognitive level of prejudice is a person's beliefs or perceptions about another person or group. Example: The perception or belief that the Irish are heavy drinkers.
	Ethnocentrism	When people are ethnocentric, they reject all groups except their own. They are focused on their own group.
	2. Emotional Level	The emotional level of prejudice addresses the feelings/emotions that a minority group evokes. These emotions can be triggered by actual interactions or by the potential of an interaction with the minority group. Example: Whites fearing and being angry about integration of their schools with students from minority groups.
	3. Action-Orientation Level	The action-orientation level of prejudice is when a person is predisposed to acting out discriminatory behavior. Example: When members of one group exclude members of another from doing business with them.
	Self-Justification	Self-justification is when a person puts another person or group down to make him- or herself feel better about treating them poorly. We convince ourselves that another person or group is inferior and deserves our poor treatment. Self-justification can come before or after the poor treatment happens. Example: Puritans burning women who were witches Example: Whites enslaving Africans

Summary: There are psychological and sociological causes of prejudice. Psychological causes include four main areas of study. Levels of Prejudice and Self-Justification are two of these areas of study.

Practice 8.5   Taking Notes on Major Ideas and Important Details Using Cornell Notes

DIRECTIONS: For practice, finish Cornell Notes for Parrillo's essay (p. 213). Use ours to help you get started and then complete your own for the remainder of his essay. When you are done, use any of the note-taking methods we have introduced thus far (mapping, annotating, Cornell Notes) to take notes on Terkel's "C. P. Ellis" (p. 223), an essay of your choice, or one you have been assigned.

STEP 6: Write Down Your Thoughts and Reactions

Often the first couple of times that you read a text, you are focused on understanding the literal meaning. Additional readings can give you the chance to respond to the big ideas, ask questions, and make connections between this text and others you have read. Remember that this step is asking you to respond to smaller parts of the text as you are reading them. You will get the chance to respond to the overall reading in a more comprehensive manner later in Step 8.

Demonstration   Writing Down Thoughts and Reactions

This example shows how one student wrote down her thoughts and reactions to "Causes of Prejudice." This student decided to write her reactions on a separate sheet of paper.

Parillo's essay is one of the hardest essays I've ever read. I had to keep stopping and double checking myself. There were so many new vocabulary words that I had never seen before, and the definitions of them included words I didn't understand. I feel really accomplished for finishing this essay, but I still have a lot of questions about it. For example, I don't understand why the psychological perspective breaks down the levels of prejudice into thinking, feeling, and acting. Don't those things just happen all at once? When would a person feel but not act? Think but not feel? I'm also confused by the overlap between the psychological causes and the sociological causes. Some of these seem similar to me. For example, isn't scapegoating a social action? Why isn't this in the sociological perspective instead of the psychological one? Maybe this is why my Internet research on psychology and sociology said they were linked. There are a lot of similarities, I think!

I like learning about the different aspects of prejudice, though. This article is helping me better understand how complex prejudice is. I also like the examples in the article as they are helping me to better understand how prejudice happens.

Practice 8.6   Writing Down Your Thoughts and Reactions

DIRECTIONS: Look at Terkel's essay "C. P. Ellis" on page 223, an essay of your choice, or one you have been assigned. Then write a reaction to the ideas in that essay. Here are some questions to guide your writing:

1. What words, concepts, or ideas confuse you?
2. What concepts or ideas excite you?
3. What ideas do you particularly like? Why?
4. What questions arise for you as you read?

Phase Three: After You Read

Learning Objective 3
Consolidate your comprehension
of texts that use informational
evidence.

After you have finished reading a text, writing a summary, response and reflection ensures that you learn the material and improve on your reading process.

STEP 7: Write a Summary

Writing a summary serves several important purposes: writing about an informational article in your own words ensures that you understand what you have read. It also ensures that you think one more time about the main ideas, and therefore you are more likely to remember them later. Thirdly, writing a summary provides you with a clear record of what you have read so that you do not have to reread it to retrieve the main points. Finally, a summary can sometimes be used in the paragraphs and essays you write.

Writing summaries of informational texts can be different from writing them for narrative texts. For example, informational texts may have more vocabulary words and concepts in them than a narrative text, and it can be hard to determine what ideas to include in the summary and which ones to omit. Another difference is the organizational structure of informational texts and narrative ones. While narrative texts often follow a chronological order, making it easy to summarize the events in time order, informational texts often move in a different sequence. They may arrange ideas by order of importance, categories, or process. Therefore, as a writer, you need to analyze the structure of the text and determine how to best reflect that in your summary.

Cornell Notes are wonderful tools for summaries as they identify the main ideas and the order in which those ideas are arranged. They are essentially prewriting for a summary. To write a strong summary, try taking the ideas in the left column of your notes and summarizing them in your own words. This will help you test your understanding of the material as well as ensure that you capture all of the key ideas in the text. We do not recommend

Basic Steps for Writing a Summary

Here is a review of the basic steps for writing a summary:
- **Start with a sentence that includes the title, author (if there is one), and main message** (thesis, theme, or main idea) of the reading.
- **Follow that with the main ideas in the text**. (Hint: When using Cornell Notes to write your summary, be sure to include the bigger ideas on the left; consider carefully before including more specific information such as examples from the right side.)
- **Look back at your notes to guide you as you write your summary**.
- **Do not include your opinion about the writing**. Just restate the major points objectively.
- **Put the ideas into your own words**. Avoid quoting from the reading.
- Generally your summary can follow the same order as the information in the text.

Demonstration   Writing a Summary

The following summary of "Causes of Prejudice" is an excerpt from one by a student, Brooke King. Her example shows how to summarize the first half of Parrillo's essay, which focuses on the psychological causes of prejudice.

(continued)

In the essay "Causes of Prejudice," the author Vincent Parrillo talks about the causes of preju- dice in today's society; Parrillo describes the two main causes as the psychological side and the sociological side. The psychological side has four areas of study. The first one is the levels of preju- dice. The levels of prejudice include three things, which are the cognitive level, the emotional level, and the action-orientation level. The cognitive level refers to a person's beliefs or perceptions about the inferiority of another group/individual. The emotional level refers to a person's feelings of prejudice against a minority group/individual. The action-orientation level refers to a person's predisposition to act out against people for which they have prejudice. Ethnocentrism is the rejection of a par- ticular group. Another psychological area of study is self-justification. Self-justification is where someone reassures themselves that something is right and they are doing the right thing when they are not. The third area of study is personality. Personality is how the child is disciplined or brought up during life and is raised a certain way. The last area of study is frustration. When people talk about frustration, it means they can't do anything about something, so they get angry and frustrated. When someone is frustrated, they usually blame others, and this is known as scapegoating. This helps them justify what they are doing or thinking.

Practice 8.7   Writing a Summary

DIRECTIONS: Look at the Cornell Notes you finished for Parrillo's essay in Practice 8.5 (p. 175). Then finish the summary we started for Parrillo's essay by summarizing the section titled "The Sociology of Prejudice" (pp. 219–222). Remember to capture the ideas from the left side of your Cornell Notes in your summary. If you want added practice with summary, write one for Terkel's essay "C. P. Ellis," an essay of your choice, or one you have been assigned.

that you take the summary section at the bottom of each page of Cornell Notes and use that as your overall summary, though. The summary section of your Cornell Notes may not be detailed enough to provide a complete summary of an entire essay.

STEP 8: Respond to a Reading

Responding gives you the chance to think more about the ideas in a reading. In a response, you can ask questions of the text, make connections to other texts or your own experience, or note a strong emotional reaction. It is important, though, to keep your response clearly separate from the author's ideas. Responding also helps you remember what you have read by connecting it to your own thinking and feelings.

Critical Thinking: Synthesis

As we noted in Chapter 5, an element of critical thinking is called synthesis. According to Merriam Webster's Online Dictionary, synthesis is "the composition or combination of parts or elements so as to form a whole." This relates to reading because you can synthesize ideas in a text or between multiple texts to show how the different parts can form a new and more comprehensive way of seeing a topic. In this way, you are deepening your understanding by bringing together ideas from different places in one or more texts. This is also a great prewriting activity because synthesis can create significant ideas about which to write.

Demonstration   Synthesizing Ideas

The following is an example of a response using the critical thinking technique of synthesizing. The student has used a graphic organizer called a T-Chart to illustrate this synthesis. To create a **T-Chart**, divide a page in half and put ideas about one topic or text on one side mirrored by similar or contrasting ideas about a second topic or text on the other. This allows you to quickly see points of comparison or contrast between topics or texts, and it can be a great reading and prewriting tool. The student used this process to compare two points that were made in both Parrillo's and Terkel's essays and illustrates them with quotes from each essay.

Parrillo	Terkel
Relative Deprivation: "A lack of resources, or rewards, in one's standard of living in comparison with those of others in the society" (217).	Terkel illustrates **relative deprivation** when he says, "My father worked hard but never had enough money to buy decent clothes. When I went to school, I never seemed to have adequate clothes to wear. I always left school late afternoon with a sense of inferiority. The other kids had nice clothes, and I just had what Daddy could buy. I still got some of those inferiority feelin's now that I have to overcome once in a while" (223).
Scapegoating: "Blaming others for something that is not their fault" (218).	Terkel illustrates **scapegoating** when C. P. Ellis says, "I really began to get bitter. I didn't know who to blame. I tried to find somebody. I began to blame it on black people" (224).

Practice 8.8   Responding to the Reading and Synthesizing Ideas

DIRECTIONS: Review Parrillo's and Terkel's essays on pages 213 and 223. Then continue the work we started above in the T-Chart by finding 3–4 more examples of Parrillo's concepts in Terkel's essay and noting them in your own T-Chart. Find quotes to illustrate your ideas if possible. If you are working with texts other than Parrillo's and Terkel's, complete a T-Chart for those texts. *Save this as prewriting for Chapters 9 and 10.*

STEP 9: Reflect on Your Reading Process

We use the term "reflection" to mean thinking about how you read—your process—as opposed to the ideas you learned. Reflecting is looking back at an experience to realize what you did well, what could be done differently, and how the lessons learned can be used in the future. To reflect on your reading process, you might answer questions such as the following:

1. What steps of the reading process worked particularly well for me? Why?
2. What steps of the reading process did not work as well for me? Why?
3. How will I adapt or hone any of the steps to work better for me in the future?

Demonstration Reflecting on the Reading Process

The following is an example of a reflection on the reading process for Parrillo's essay.

Parrillo's text was definitely demanding and one of the hardest I have ever read. The reading step that helped me the most was Step 5. Cornell Notes take a long time, but they pay off! I had to concentrate while I read in order to take these notes, and taking notes helped check that I understood what I read. I could've easily dozed off during this reading or just gotten frustrated and given up, but the notes kept me focused and on track. They were really useful when I wrote my summary. It practically wrote itself from these notes—yay!! They even helped when I had to synthesize ideas between Parillo and Terkel in Step 8 of the reading process because I could easily find information in each text by using them. I'm going to keep practicing Cornell Notes. They might be useful for taking notes in a lecture, too. I have another class that is all lecture, so I'm going to give it a try; perhaps they will help me focus better.

Practice 8.9 Reflecting on the Reading Process

DIRECTIONS: Reflect on the process you used to read either Parrillo or Terkel's essays, an essay of your choice, or one you have been assigned, using the steps above. Then write down those reflections.

Chapter **Quick Check**   MySkillsLab   Complete the mastery test for this chapter in MySkillsLab.

Use the following questions and answers to check your understanding of this chapter.

QUESTION	ANSWER
Learning Objective 1: Preview before you read texts using informational evidence. *What steps are included in the first phase of the reading process, "Preview the Reading," that help familiarize you with an informational text?*	The steps in the first phase of writing that help you become familiar with informational text are… ✔ Skim, scan, and look at the title and headings in order to get a sense of the content and organization of the text. ✔ Notice visual elements such as pictures, graphs, charts, or sidebars. ✔ Check your attitude about and purpose for reading the informational text. ✔ Activate your background knowledge by thinking about what you already know about the topic(s) in the text.
Learning objective 2: Actively read texts that use informational evidence. *What steps are included in the second phase of the reading process, "While Reading" that help you fully understand texts that use informational evidence?*	The steps in the second phase of the reading process that help you fully understand informational evidence are… ✔ Write down vocabulary words that you do not understand and look them up in a dictionary or research them on the Internet. ✔ Take notes about major topics and main ideas in the text. The Cornell Note-Taking System is an effective way to take notes on texts that use informational evidence because it clearly separates big ideas from informational details. ✔ Make note of interesting or confusing information from the reading.
Learning objective 3: Consolidate your comprehension of texts that use informational evidence. *What steps are included in the third phase of the reading process, "After You Read," that help you consolidate your understanding?*	The steps in the third phase of the reading process that help you consolidate your understanding are… ✔ Write a summary of the main ideas in the reading. ✔ Respond to the content in the reading, including your emotional reaction. ✔ Reflect on the effectiveness of your reading process.

9 A Writing Process for Paragraphs Using Informational Evidence as Support

LEARNING OBJECTIVES

In this chapter, you will learn to . . .

1   Prewrite for a paragraph that uses informational evidence.

2   Draft a paragraph that uses informational evidence.

3   Revise and edit a paragraph that uses informational evidence.

Warm Up

DIRECTIONS: Look at the picture and answer the questions that follow.

1. Find one example in the picture that represents something you learned about prejudice in either Parrillo's or Terkel's essays from Chapter 8. Describe this example and link it to what either author said that explains this example of prejudice.

2. Reflect on your own learning about prejudice from Parrillo's or Terkel's essays. What new ideas did you learn in these texts? Did they surprise you? Explain.

MySkillsLab
Complete the Warm Up at
www.myskillslab.com

Phase One: Prewriting

Learning Objective 1
Prewrite for a paragraph that uses informational evidence.

Spending time prewriting before you draft is important for all types of academic writing, and the same applies to writing a paragraph that uses informational evidence. Perhaps it is even more important for this type of writing because grouping ideas and details is less obvious with information than with narrative or personal experience. The details of informational evidence can be sorted in many different ways, but there must always be an organizing principle at work—a reason why you put certain details together. Making such decisions (and others) before you write your first full draft results in a better paragraph.

In this chapter, we will illustrate the process of writing an informational paragraph using the essays by Parrillo and Terkel on pages 213 and 223. You can complete the practices in this chapter using these two casebook readings or find another example of prejudice from a reading in this text (see list on p. 163) or a resource such as a periodical. If you choose your own text, use Parrillo's essay to analyze an example of prejudice it discusses, as we have used Parrillo's text to analyze the examples found in Terkel's essay.

STEP 1: Analyze the Assignment

The first step in preparing to write your own paragraph is to look closely at your assignment to make sure that you understand your professor's instructions. Answering the following questions, either on paper or in your mind, will help you be sure you understand what is expected in your writing. If you are ever unsure about any of the answers to these questions, ask your instructor for help.

1. What is the purpose, goal, or objective of this assignment?
2. Who is the intended audience of the paper?
3. What is the central topic you will need to write about?
4. Can you imagine meaningful things to say about this topic?
5. What information are you supposed to use as support in this assignment?
6. What organizational structure will you need to use for this assignment?
7. How will this assignment be graded?
8. How do you feel about responding to this assignment (eager and ready, afraid, unsure, etc.)?
9. What questions do you have about this assignment?

Practice 9.1   Analyzing the Assignment

DIRECTIONS: Read the assignment below. Then answer the questions above to check your understanding of the assignment. If you have questions, ask your instructor for clarification.

Paragraph Assignment

PURPOSES The first purpose of this paragraph assignment is for you to connect ideas between two texts around the topic of prejudice. This will give you practice synthesizing and comparing ideas across texts. The second purpose is for you to continue to practice using a writing process. The third is for you to continue to practice building strong paragraphs.

AUDIENCE Write these paragraphs for an academic audience. Academic writing is usually expected to stand on its own, outside the context of the class in which it is written. Be sure to write for readers who are not in your class.

Assignment

• Submit two paragraphs that discuss ONE common cause of prejudice that is addressed by Parrillo and Terkel or Parrillo and another text of your choice. Together, your two paragraphs should show how this cause of prejudice is explained across the two texts.

(continued)

- Each paragraph needs a clear topic sentence that provides both a focused topic for the paragraph as well as your reaction, opinion, or attitude about that topic.
- Each paragraph needs to support, or develop, its topic sentence using informational details. One paragraph should use information from Parrillo's essay that illustrates and explains the cause of prejudice you have chosen. The second paragraph should use details from Terkel or a text of your choice as support that illustrates and explains the same cause of prejudice.
- Each paragraph needs to stay with one main idea and be 8–12 sentences in length.
- Each paragraph needs to be edited for grammar and other mistakes.

How Your Paragraphs Will Be Graded

1. *Content* The paragraphs focus on one common cause of prejudice and show how this is illustrated in Parrillo's and Terkel's texts or Parrillo's and a text of your choice.
2. *Topic Sentence* Paragraphs each have an obvious topic sentence that is specific and focuses the paragraph's topic clearly. All other sentences in the paragraph relate to the topic of the topic sentence.
3. *Organization* The paragraphs are cohesive: Each sentence in each paragraph connects to the topic sentence. The paragraphs' sentences flow together and connect to one another. The details in the paragraphs are arranged in chronological order.
4. *Development and Support* The topic sentences are supported with informational evidence from Parrillo's essay and Terkel's essay or Parrillo's essay and one of your choice. The supporting material should match the topic and develop the ideas in the paragraph in depth.
5. *Editing* The paragraph has been edited for grammar mistakes. It has also been proofread for missing words or unclear meaning. All quoted material is punctuated and cited correctly.

STEP 2: Generate Ideas

The next step in the writing process is to gather ideas about which to write. You have already done some of this by following a process of reading. Therefore, gather your maps, information on vocabulary words, and any other writing you did while you read, as these exercises may contain ideas that you can use to focus or develop your writing.

Find a Topic

The first step is to find a topic. To begin this process, we suggest you look at the T-Chart you created in Chapter 8 for Step 8 (p. 179) and use it to brainstorm ideas, as shown in the following Demonstration.

Demonstration   Finding a Topic

Here the student has taken his T-Chart from Chapter 8, Step 8 (p. 179), and added another column titled "Common Causes of Prejudice." He has also added more supporting ideas in the second and third columns that he found during this step in the writing process. While a T-Chart is a good way to respond to reading texts by synthesizing information in them, it also makes a powerful brainstorming tool, helping a writer to find examples from each text for certain common elements (in this case, causes of prejudice).

Common Causes of Prejudice	Parrillo	Terkel
Relative Deprivation	Relative Deprivation: "A lack of re-sources, or rewards, in one's standard of living in comparison with those of others in the society" (217).	Terkel illustrates relative deprivation when he says, "My father worked hard but never had enough money to buy decent clothes. When I went to school, I never seemed to have adequate clothes to wear. I always left school late afternoon with a sense of infe-riority. The other kids had nice clothes, and I just had what Daddy could buy. I still got some of those inferiority feelin's now that I have to overcome once in a while" (223).
Scapegoating	Scapegoating: "Blaming others for something that is not their fault" (218). "There have been many instances throughout world history of minority groups serving as scapegoats, includ-ing the Christians in ancient Rome, the Huguenots in France, the Jews in Europe and Russia, and the Puritans and Quakers in England" (218).	Terkel illustrates scapegoating when he says, "I really began to get bitter. I didn't know who to blame. I tried to find somebody. I began to blame it on black people" (224). "I had to hate somebody. Hatin' America is hard to do because you can't see it to hate it. You gotta have something to look at to hate....The natural person for me to hate would be black people, because my father be-fore me was a member of the Klan" (224).

Practice 9.2 Finding a Topic

DIRECTIONS: Create a T-Chart, using the template in the Demonstration above. Complete it, us-ing information from the T-Chart you created for Practice 8.8 (p. 179), for *three or more causes of prejudice*. Brainstorming about several ideas will help later if you end up hitting a dead end or need to switch topics later in the writing process. Also, *finding more than one quote for each cause of prejudice in both essays* will help you to develop your paragraph more fully.

If you have chosen an alternate essay, substitute the author's name for Terkel's and complete the column using ideas from that essay.

STEP 3: Focus Your Topic

Once you have generated several possible ideas to use in your writing, you will need to choose one you understand well, can write about in depth, and that fits the assignment. Remember that for each paragraph you want to make sure you have enough support to write 7–10 sentences that illustrate your topic.

In order to focus your topic, look over your T-Chart brainstorm in the previous step and answer the following questions about each of the causes you have identified. Using your answers to guide you, choose the strongest topic and circle it on your chart.

1. Have I identified one clear cause of prejudice? Is this succinct and accurately stated?
2. Have I found supporting evidence from each text that illustrates this cause of prejudice?

3. Do my supporting quotes accurately describe the cause of prejudice? (You may want to ask your instructor to double check this for you as accuracy of information is vital to your paragraph's success.)
4. Do you have enough support to write an entire paragraph about this topic?
5. Do you feel comfortable and knowledgeable about this topic? (This is important as it will help you write about it more easily.)

Demonstration   Focusing a Topic Using Evaluation Questions

In this Demonstration, the student who created the T-Chart on page 185 asked and answered the evaluation questions about the topic of scapegoating.

1. Have I identified one clear cause of prejudice? Is this succinct and accurately stated using the terms I learned in Parrillo's essay and Terkel's essay? Yes, I used Parrillo's term of "scapegoating" to make sure I was staying true to the causes of prejudice introduced in these readings.

2. Have I found supporting evidence from each text that illustrates this cause of prejudice? Yes.

3. Do my supporting quotes accurately describe the cause of prejudice? I feel like I understand scapegoating well, and I feel confident that my support goes together and is accurate.

4. Do you have enough support to write an entire paragraph about this topic? Yes, I feel I do. I like how I was able to get two quotes from Parrillo's and Terkel's essays, too. I think this will help me to develop those paragraphs well.

5. Do you feel comfortable and knowledgeable about this topic? I feel that I understand this cause well. I've learned about scapegoating before, so it's not an entirely new term. This helps me feel more comfortable explaining it in my paragraph.

Practice 9.3   Focusing a Topic Using Evaluation Questions

DIRECTIONS: Answer the evaluation questions on page 185 for each of the causes of prejudice that you identified in your T-Chart from Step 2. When you are done, look over your answers and use them to choose one of your topics that you want to make the focus of your paragraphs.

Draft a Topic Sentence

Each paragraph needs a controlling idea that all other ideas in the writing connect to and support. In academic writing, it is most often expected that you will state this point clearly in a sentence. In a paragraph, you put this idea in a topic sentence. As a general rule, topic sentences should include the following:

Topic sentence = *topic* + opinion/stance/argument about that topic

During the writing process, there are several places you can draft your topic sentence. You may do so in prewriting as you generate ideas. You may do so in the outlining phase. You may have to draft the entire paragraph to find what you want to say in a topic sentence. Finally, you may write a topic sentence and then later change it as you discover what you want to say in your writing.

Use these questions to help you write an effective topic sentence:
1. What is the topic of my paragraph?
2. What opinion or argument do I want to make about this topic?
3. How can I combine my topic and opinion in an effective a topic sentence?

Demonstration   Drafting a Topic Sentence

Topic sentence for a paragraph about a cause of prejudice in Parrillo's essay

1. What is the topic of my paragraph? *Scapegoating in Parrillo's essay "Causes of Prejudice."*
2. What opinion or argument do I want to make about this topic? *It is one of the many complex causes of prejudice.*
3. How can I combine my topic and opinion in an effective a topic sentence?

topic   opinion

4. *Scapegoating as explained in Parrillo's essay "Causes of Prejudice"* is one of the many complex causes of prejudice

opinion

Topic sentence for a paragraph about a cause of prejudice in Terkel's essay

1. What is the topic of my paragraph? *Scapegoating in Terkel's essay "C. P. Ellis."*
2. What opinion or argument do I want to make about this topic? *It is one of the many complex causes of prejudice.*
3. How can I combine my topic and opinion in an effective a topic sentence?

topic   opinion

Scapegoating as explained in Terkel's essay "C. P. Ellis" is one of the many complex causes of prejudice

opinion

Practice 9.4   Drafting a Topic Sentence

DIRECTIONS: Write a topic sentence for each of your paragraphs, using your answers to the following questions.

1. What is the topic of my paragraph?
2. What opinion or argument do I want to make about this topic?
3. How can I combine my topic and opinion in an effective a topic sentence?

STEP 4: Develop Supporting Details for a Paragraph

Once you have your topic, you want to gather information about it and deepen your understanding so you have enough to say about it. While you have already gathered some support in Step 2, you may want to return to each essay and do some research online or at your library to gather more supporting evidence. Use these steps to guide your online search:

1. Generate a list of key words.
2. Search the Internet using these key words.
3. Use the evaluation questions in the CRAAP Test (p. 5) to ensure quality sources.
4. Take notes.

Demonstration   Developing Supporting Details Using Information Literacy

In order to more fully understand the topic of scapegoating, this student decided to do some research online. To do this, she followed the steps on page 187, and generated a list of key words to guide the search. She used Parrillo's text to find key words, so notice how some of them come from examples in his essay. She used the CRAAP Test and took notes.

Key word: scapegoat (I got this information from Wikipedia. It's not known for being really reliable, but it was a good place to start. I'll do more checking.)

- scapegoating comes from a Hebrew word that ties it to Leviticus 16:8
- scapegoats were often lower members of society such as cripples, beggars, or criminals
- scapegoats would be blamed and then cast out of the society in response to disasters or other social ills

Key word: Day of Atonement (I found info on this from a variety of sources, including a primary source—the Bible.)

- comes from the Old Testament in Leviticus 16
- on the Day of Atonement, a goat was sacrificed to atone for the sins of the people
- the word "scapegoat" comes from this historical sacrifice of the goat on the Day of Atonement

Practice 9.5   Developing Supporting Details Using Information Literacy

DIRECTIONS: In order to more fully understand your paragraph topics, do some research online and/or in your library, using the steps listed on the previous page.

STEP 5: Organize Your Ideas

Organizing is an important step prior to drafting your paragraph. It allows you to select the ideas you want to include in your paper and plan where to put them. If you have many pages of prewriting, organizing before you start to draft can reduce stress. It will also make the writing process go faster and smoother because you will select the ideas and details you want to use and put away those you do not want to include.

As you organize your informational paragraphs, keep in mind that the order of ideas will differ from that of a paragraph that uses narrative as support. You will want to think about the order of ideas for your informational paragraph. Do you want to order ideas in terms of category? Source types? General to specific? Specific to general? Organizing can help you determine this order prior to writing; it gives space in the writing process for this thought process.

Also remember that all of your ideas need to relate to your topic sentences. If you did research for Step 4, you might have encountered some interesting information. However, you may not use all of this information in your paragraphs. It may not relate to your topic or it may be irrelevant to your actual paragraph. Again, organizing can help you determine what information should be included and what should be left out of your paragraph, so it remains coherent.

Outlining

One of the best ways to make sure your organization is strong and to prepare to draft a well-organized paper is to outline. Outlining provides a guide that you can follow as you draft your writing. The following are sample outlines. They are not the only method for organizing a paragraph with informational support, but they offer one possible technique. Using a map like the ones illustrated in Chapter 6 can also be a useful organizing tool if you prefer a more visual layout.

Demonstration   Outlining a Paragraph

Here is a student outline for a paragraph on a scapegoating as a cause of prejudice in Parrillo's essay.

<u>Topic Sentence</u>: Scapegoating as explained in Parrillo's essay "Causes of Prejudice" is one of the many complex causes of prejudice.

    <u>Supporting Point 1: Definition of scapegoating</u>

        <u>Evidence</u>: Parrillo defines scapegoating as, "Blaming others for something that is not their fault" (218).

    <u>Supporting Point 2: Historical background of scapegoating</u>

        <u>Evidence</u>: Scapegoating has its roots in the Bible in Leviticus 16:15–22 where it talks about the Day of Atonement. This was a day when sins were atoned for by killing a live goat. "And when he has made an end of atoning for the Holy Place, the tabernacle of meeting, and the altar, he shall bring the live goat. Aaron shall lay both his hands on the head of the live goat, confess over it all the iniquities of the children of Israel, and all their transgressions, concerning all their sins, putting them on the head of the goat, and shall send it away into the wilderness by the hand of a suitable man. The goat shall bear on itself all their iniquities to an uninhabited land; and he shall release the goat in the wilderness" (http://cofac.org/atonement.html).

<u>Analysis</u>: Scapegoating is something that comes from a historical practice of making amends, but in its current practice, it ends up being a cause of prejudice. In today's society, the goat of olden days is replaced by a person or group of people who are cast out or discriminated against because they are different.

<u>Supporting Point 3: Example of Scapegoating</u>

        <u>Evidence</u>: According to Parrillo, "There have been many instances throughout world history of minority groups serving as scapegoats, including the Christians in ancient Rome, the Huguenots in France, the Jews in Europe and Russia, and the Puritans and Quakers in England" (218).

<u>Analysis</u>: Blaming others, or making them a scapegoat, is a cause of prejudice that has been going on for centuries and is still taking place today.

Practice 9.6   Organizing Ideas Using an Outline

DIRECTIONS: Use your prewriting from Steps 1–5 and outline the topic sentence, supporting points, evidence, and analysis in each of your paragraphs.

Phase Two: Draft

Learning Objective 2
Draft a paragraph that uses informational support.

STEP 6: Draft Your Paragraph

During the drafting stage, you need to put together all of the ideas you have generated during prewriting into one complete whole. Remember that this is a first attempt at writing a strong paragraph, but it is not the final step. You will still have time later on to revise and polish your writing, so it reflects your best work.

We invite you to refer to Chapter 3 on how to structure paragraphs. Remember that all paragraphs should have a topic sentence, support, and analysis.

Demonstration   Drafting a Paragraph

Here is the student's draft of a paragraph based on the outline in the preceding Demonstration.

> Scapegoating as explained in Parrillo's essay "Causes of Prejudice" is one of the many complex causes of prejudice. Parrillo defines scapegoating as, "Blaming others for something that is not their fault" (218). This is an action that has its roots in Biblical times. For example, in Leviticus it talks about the Day of Atonement. This was a day when sins were atoned for by killing a live goat. The Bible says, "And when he has made an end of atoning for the Holy Place, the tabernacle of meeting, and the altar, he shall bring the live goat. Aaron shall lay both his hands on the head of the live goat, confess over it all the iniquities of the children of Israel, and all their transgressions, concerning all their sins, putting them on the head of the goat, and shall send it away into the wilderness by the hand of a suitable man. The goat shall bear on itself all their iniquities to an uninhabited land; and he shall release the goat in the wilderness" (Leviticus 16:15–22). Scapegoating is something that comes from a historical practice of making amends, but in its current practice, it ends up being a cause of prejudice. In today's society, the goat of olden days is replaced by a person or group of people who are cast out or discriminated against because they are different. According to Parrillo, "There have been many instances throughout world history of minority groups serving as scapegoats, including the Christians in ancient Rome, the Huguenots in France, the Jews in Europe and Russia, and the Puritans and Quakers in England" (218). Blaming others, or making them a scapegoat, is a cause of prejudice that has been going on for centuries and is still taking place today.

Practice 9.7   Drafting

DIRECTIONS: Use the examples shown as well as your prewriting to guide you. Then draft two full paragraphs, one using Parrillo's essay as evidence, and another using Terkel's essay, or the essay of your choice, as evidence.

Phase Three: Polish

Learning Objective 3
Revise and edit a paragraph that uses informational evidence.

An easy trap to fall into when writing for academic purposes is to think your paper is finished when your rough draft is written. This simply is not true. While you drafted, your attention was on saying what you had to say—getting it out and onto paper in a reasonably clear and organized way. In the polishing phase, your focus is on making sure that your content and structure are meaningful and effective, and your sentences are correct and stylish. These final steps are what make good writing great.

STEP 7: Revise

Peer review is a guided process that allows you to get feedback from another student in class on how to improve or revise your writing. Many peer-review questions are also questions that instructors ask when assessing your writing, so, as you do peer review, you will also practice looking for things that your teacher may look for when grading your paragraph. Use the following guidelines when reviewing a peer's writing:

Guidelines for Peer Review of a Paragraph

1. **Topic Sentence** Write the topic sentence for the paragraph on a sheet of paper. Then, evaluate it using the following questions:
   - Is the topic sentence easy to find in the paragraph? Was it obvious to the reader? (Make suggestions for revision if needed.)
   - Does this topic sentence include a focused topic and opinion or feeling about the topic? (Make suggestions for revision if needed.)
   - Does this topic sentence fully explain what the paragraph actually talks about?
2. **Development and Support** Is the topic sentence of the paragraph supported with sufficient and appropriate information (eight or more sentences of examples, facts, observations, etc.)? Is this support specific and detailed? Note which ideas need more support and which need more specific and vivid support.
3. **Cohesion** Does each sentence in the paragraph connect to the topic sentence? Read each sentence closely and compare it to the topic sentence to see if it matches. If not, make note of the sentences that do not match the topic sentence.
4. **Organization** Does the paragraph fit a logical organizational pattern? For example, does it go from specific to general? General to specific? Order of importance? Note any ideas in the paragraph that are out of order with the ideas in the rest of the paragraph.
5. **Voice and Tone** Does the tone or voice used in the paragraph fit the needs of the audience, and is it appropriate given the subject matter of the paragraph? Make a note if it seems too informal or inappropriate for an academic audience or if the tone doesn't fit the topic discussed in the paragraph.

Demonstration   Practicing Peer Review

Here is a sample peer review for the paragraph on Parrillo from Step 6. Use this as an example to guide your own peer review of a partner's paragraphs.

1. **Topic Sentence** Scapegoating as explained in Parrillo's essay "Causes of Prejudice" is one of the many complex causes of prejudice.
   - The topic sentence was very easy to find.
   - Yes, this topic sentence includes a focused topic and opinion or feeling about the topic.
   - I'm not sure that this topic sentence does a great job of fully explaining what the paragraph is about. A lot of the paragraph focuses on the Biblical roots of scapegoating, and the topic sentence doesn't fully address that. You might want to change it to something like this. "Parrillo's essay shows how scapegoating has been a cause of prejudice throughout history."

2. **Development/Support** This paragraph seems to have enough support. It includes six sentences of examples, facts, and observations. Bringing in history from the Bible was interesting. The only problem is that the biblical passage takes up a lot of space. It almost makes it look like your paragraph is about the history of scapegoating. Plus, your topic sentence says the paragraph will focus on Parrillo, and the Bible quote is not from his essay. I wonder if you could shorten the quote a little bit, so it is more balanced with the rest of the paragraph. You also might want to connect it to Parrillo better. Maybe you could connect it by saying it was an example he shared in his essay. Then you can give more information about that idea using your research from the Bible.

3. **Cohesion** Each sentence seems connected to the topic of scapegoating, but I think if you broaden your topic sentence a bit it will help to include the part from the Bible.

4. **Organization** I'm not sure if this paragraph follows a particular order, but the sentences flow okay and they make sense.

5. **Voice and Tone** The purpose of this paragraph is to inform the reader about scapegoating in Parrillo's essay. I didn't notice where the voice or tone was inappropriate.

Practice 9.8   Practicing Peer Review

DIRECTIONS: Trade paragraphs with a partner in class. Then answer the peer review questions on page 191. It may help to do two separate reviews, one for each paragraph. When you are done, debrief with your partner, so you can explain what you found, answer your partner's questions, and get feedback on your own writing from your partner. Finally, make notes about what you plan to revise given the feedback you received.

STEP 8: Edit and Proofread

Once you have looked at global issues—such as the topic sentence, support, and organization—it is time to check your sentences for grammar and spelling errors as well as citations. To edit your paper, try any of the following suggestions.

1. **Read your paper out loud to yourself.** Read slowly, and read every word. You will probably find some sentences that do not make sense or words that are missing. Fix these.
2. **Circle all of the punctuation, author names, and page numbers around each quotation you have used.** Check to see that you have given the correct information and that you have punctuated correctly.
3. **Have another person read the paper.** This should be someone who has not previously seen it. Have that person mark any sentences or words that do not make sense to him or her. While this person might not be a grammar expert, he or she can give you feedback about sentences that are not "reader friendly" and therefore could use editing.
4. **Work with a tutor in your school's writing center or other tutoring center.** Have this person read your paper and work with you to edit any sentences that are not clear.
5. **Have your instructor look at your paragraphs and mark for grammar and spelling in one paragraph.** Then, look at his or her marks. Try to find similar errors in the other paragraph and fix them.

Practice 9.9   Editing

DIRECTIONS: Do one or both of the following to find and fix errors in your paragraph.

1. **Pair up with a partner in class and read your paper out loud to that person.** As you do so, listen for any errors and circle or highlight them. Then work on your own or with a tutor to correct the errors.
2. **Ask your instructor to edit five lines of your paragraphs.** Then use your instructor's comments to look for patterns that will probably show up in the rest of your writing as well. See if you can find these and correct them on your own.

STEP 9: Reflect on Your Writing Process

In this final stage in the writing process, you reflect on the steps you took to arrive at your final, polished draft. Reviewing your process is helpful so that the next time you write, you can change what did not work or repeat what did work. Another approach is to discuss your process with a classmate. The following questions in Practice 9.10 can act as a guide for your reflection.

Practice 9.10   Reflecting on Your Writing Process

DIRECTIONS: Answer the following questions in order to reflect on your writing experience in this chapter.

1. **How did you grow as a writer through the process of writing?** (For example, did you take on any new challenges? Did you discover any new steps you would like to work on in the future? Did you find that using a writing process worked for you or not?)
2. **How did the act of writing help you grow as a reader?** (For example, did the process of writing this assignment help you to read texts written in similar styles? Did you better retain the information that you read? Was it hard to write about ideas in readings?)

(continued)

3. **Discuss what you see as the strengths of your writing**, starting with content (ideas and information) and then going to style (organization, language, tone, etc.)
4. **Discuss what you think are the weaknesses of your writing.**
5. If you had more time or inclination, would you make any additional changes to your writing? If so, what?

✅ Chapter **Quick Check**   **MySkillsLab**   Complete the mastery test for this chapter in MySkillsLab.

Use the following questions and answers to check your understanding of this chapter.

QUESTION	ANSWER
Learning Objective 1: Prewrite for a paragraph that uses informational evidence. *How do I prewrite for a paragraph that uses informational evidence?*	To prewrite for a paragraph using informational support… ✔ Make sure you understand the assignment. ✔ Brainstorm and freewrite. ✔ Gather information by reading, observing, interviewing experts and reviewing reading notes and summaries. ✔ Create a good informational topic sentence that includes the topic and an opinion or point of view about the topic.
Learning Objective 2: Draft a paragraph that uses informational support. *How do I draft a paragraph using informational support?*	To draft a paragraph using informational support… ✔ Write supporting sentences using a map or outline that lists your evidence.
Learning Objective 3: Revise and edit a paragraph that uses informational evidence. *How do I revise and edit a paragraph that uses informational evidence?*	To revise and edit a paragraph using informational support… ✔ Use workshop techniques such as peer review to get feedback on the paragraph's topic sentence, overall structure, development, and organization. ✔ Have your teacher or a Writing Center tutor check your work to identify types of errors you make. ✔ Get to know the types of sentence errors you tend to make. ✔ Practice fixing your sentence mistakes.

LEARNING OBJECTIVES

In this chapter, you will learn to...

1   Prewrite for an essay that uses informational evidence.

2   Draft an essay that uses informational evidence.

3   Revise and edit an essay that uses informational evidence.

Warm Up

DIRECTIONS: Look at the picture and answer these questions.

1. What is causing the line down the middle of the rocks? Is it just one thing? Several things working together?

2. How does this line relate to the causes of prejudice? For example, are they multiple? Varied? Dependent on one another? Explain.

MySkillsLab
Complete the Warm Up at
www.myskillslab.com

Phase One: Prewriting

Learning Objective 1
Prewrite for an essay that uses informational evidence.

Getting ready to write an essay that uses primarily informational evidence requires preparation—just like all academic writing. Following are prewriting steps that will help you create an interesting, well-organized essay.

In this chapter, we will illustrate the process of writing an informational essay using the texts by Parrillo and Terkel on pages 213 and 223. You can complete the practices in this chapter using these two casebook readings or find another example of prejudice from a different reading in this text (see list on p. 163) or a resource such as a periodical. If you choose your own text, use Parrillo's essay to analyze your examples of prejudice, as we have used it to analyze the examples in Terkel's essay.

STEP 1: Analyze the Assignment

The first step to prepare to write your essay is to look closely at your assignment to be sure you understand what is expected in your writing. Answer the following questions, either on paper or in your mind, to ensure you understand what is expected. If you are ever unsure about any of the answers to these questions, ask your instructor for help.

1. What is the purpose, goal, or objective of this assignment?
2. Who is the intended audience of the paper?
3. What is the central topic you will need to write about?
4. Can you imagine meaningful things to say about this topic?
5. What information are you supposed to use as support in this assignment?
6. What organizational structure will you need to use?
7. How will this assignment be graded?
8. How do you feel about responding to this assignment (eager and ready, afraid, unsure, etc.)?

Practice 10.1   Analyzing the Assignment

DIRECTIONS: Read the following assignment, and use the questions listed above to check whether you understand it. If you have any questions, ask your instructor to clarify.

> **Essay Assignment**
>
> **PURPOSE** This essay asks you to make connections between causes of prejudice in two different texts. It also asks you to apply what you have read to your writing. This helps you understand how reading adds to your knowledge base for use in your writing. Finally, it asks you to use what you are learning about essay structure and sentence grammar to create a coherent, well-organized, and thoughtful essay.
>
> **ASSIGNMENT** This essay will help your readers better understand the causes of prejudice. You will draw from Vincent Parrillo's "Causes of Prejudice" for defining the causes, and use Studs Terkel's "C. P. Ellis" or a different second text to provide additional support or examples for those defining causes. Use these readings to develop a paper that integrates information as support and tells your reader more about the causes of prejudice. Specifically, your paper needs to include the following:
> - **Thesis** Your paper will illustrate several causes of prejudice that are explained in Parrillo's text "Causes of Prejudice" and another text, possibly Terkel's "C. P. Ellis." Your paper needs to have a thesis statement that answers this question: *What are the primary causes of prejudice in Parrillo's and a second author's texts?*
> - **Support/Development** Your essay will need to provide a *minimum* of three supporting points that develop your thesis. Each supporting point should use quotes from Parrillo's text and either Terkel's or an alternate text to illustrate the cause or causes of prejudice you identify in your thesis. You may develop each point with multiple

paragraphs that illustrate that point with quotes and paraphrases from Parrillo and your chosen text.

> **Extension:** To build on what you learned in the previous casebook, add a paragraph for each supporting point that further illustrates that point with your own experience. This means that for each point in your paper, you will have support from Parrillo, Terkel (or alternate text), and your own lived experience.

- **Organization** This paper should have an introduction with your thesis, body paragraphs to develop *at least* three supporting points that support your thesis, and a conclusion. In your paper, you will want to use transitions to create connections between ideas. You will also want to make sure that all paragraphs support your thesis, thereby creating a coherent essay. You may use any of the following organizational structures for your essay: general to specific, specific to general, emphatic order (order of importance), or comparison–contrast.
- **Format** The length should be between 2 and 4 pages, typed, double-spaced, in a 12-point font, with one-inch margins. No cover pages are needed. Put your name and the class number at the top.

  > **Extension:** Your paper will be longer if you integrate your own experience as additional support. Plan on writing a paper that is 3–5 pages in length.

- **Mechanics:** Your paper needs to be proofread and edited for spelling, grammar, and mechanics. You also need to have correct in-text citations in your paper.

How Your Essay Will Be Graded

1. **Thesis** Does the paper have a clear thesis that answers the assigned question in one clear sentence?
2. **Support** Do the body paragraphs support your thesis with appropriate, accurate, and relevant support from Parrillo's and your second text? Is there enough support to develop the thesis?
3. **Paper Organization** Does the paper follow basic essay structure (introduction, body, conclusion)? Does each paragraph connect to the one previous to it and to the thesis? Are transitions used to show connections between ideas? Is the overall structure of the paper logical and consistent?
   - **Introduction and Conclusion** Are the introduction and conclusion present? Does the introduction catch the reader's attention and state the thesis? Does the conclusion review what was said in the essay?
   - **Paragraph Organization** Does the paper have clear and effective paragraphs that have topic sentences and are well developed with informational details? Does each paragraph focus on just one idea that supports the thesis?
4. **Format** Is the paper correctly formatted according to the assignment instructions?
5. **Grammar and Mechanics** Is the paper well edited and proofread for grammar and mechanics conventions? Do the sentences convey meaning clearly to the reader? Are quotes and paraphrases correctly cited?

STEP 2: Generate Ideas

The next step in the writing process is to generate ideas about which to write. You have already done some of this work in the reading process as well as the writing process for paragraphs. Therefore, gather your maps, information on vocabulary words, and any other writing you did while you read as well as your brainstorming, outlining, and final paragraphs because they may have ideas that you can use in your essay.

Cluster Brainstorming

One technique for finding ideas to write about is cluster brainstorming all the ideas you can think of without judging them. As you generate ideas for an essay, also remember that you want an idea that is large enough to explore in a full essay that includes multiple supporting paragraphs. Since this assignment is asking for support from different texts, brainstorming with that in mind will help you stay on track.

Demonstration   **Generating Ideas by *Cluster Brainstorming***

Here are a student's cluster brainstorms for Parrillo and Terkel.

Cluster Brainstorm for Parrillo

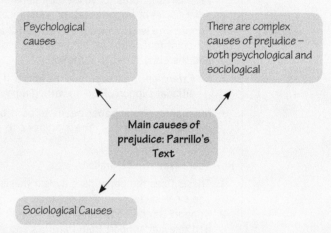

Cluster Brainstorm for Terkel

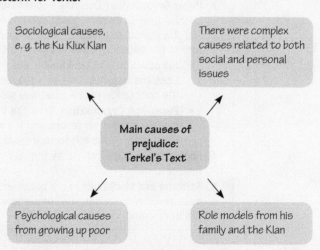

Practice 10.2   **Generating Ideas with Cluster Brainstorming**

DIRECTIONS: Do cluster brainstorms for the main causes of prejudice that you see in Parrillo's and Terkel's texts (or a text of your choice). If you are doing the extension for this paper, do a third cluster brainstorm for the main causes of prejudice that you have experienced.

STEP 3: Focus Your Topic

Once you have generated a number of possible ideas to use in your writing, you need to find a focusing idea that you truly believe in that fits the assignment. Once you have this focus, you will use it to develop a thesis. When you are writing an essay, you need a thesis that can be fully supported with your body paragraphs.

To focus your topic, start by reviewing your cluster brainstorms. Look for ideas that are repeated in each cluster. For example, maybe you listed something in the cluster brainstorm for Parrillo that is similar to something in the one for Terkel. This would be a good topic to select because you have a variety of supporting points that connect to it. If your cluster brainstorms share several similar ideas, use freewriting to explore which of the ideas is the strongest or easiest to write about and support.

Demonstration — Finding a Focus for an Essay by Freewriting

Here the student freewrote to identify his topic, using the following prompt.

Freewriting Prompt: Freewrite about what topic you want to make the focus of your whole paper. This topic should address the question, *What is the primary cause or causes of prejudice in Parrillo's and Terkel's texts?*

> I came up with very similar things in each of my cluster brainstorms. The question is which of these ideas do I want to make my focus? I think my two top choices are (1) how prejudice is caused by complex things and (2) how prejudice is caused by psychological causes. The first choice is good because it gives me a lot of room. I can talk about both sociological and psychological causes. My second choice could be good, too, though. Parrillo's text spends a lot of time focusing on psychological causes, so I think I could come up with more to say about that. Terkel's text also focuses on that quite a lot. I feel like I understand the psych causes better than the sociological ones. Hmm—I think I'll go with my second choice. It seems more focused than the one about prejudice being caused by complex causes, and my instructor says I need to focus more in my writing.

Practice 10.3 — Finding a Focus for an Essay by Freewriting

DIRECTIONS: Begin by identifying the common ideas from your cluster brainstorms. Then freewrite about what topic you want to make the focus of your whole paper. This topic should address the question, *What is the primary cause or causes of prejudice in Parrillo's and Terkel's texts (or one of your choice)?* It should also be an idea you can address with support from these texts as well as your own experience (if you are doing the extension of this assignment).

Create a Thesis

The following Demonstration shows how to form a thesis for an essay that uses information as support. Remember that you can adjust your thesis after you outline or write your paper if you find your ideas leading you in a different direction. However, drafting a thesis gives you a starting place for your outline and draft.

Essays almost always have a thesis that provides direction. Each part of the essay should connect to and develop the idea in the thesis. A thesis should be a one-sentence statement. It may include just the "root" or the "root + supporting points." Ask your instructor which model he or she prefers for your paper.

Root of Thesis = *topic of overall paper* + argument/opinion/stance about the topic

Root of Thesis + **Supporting Points** = *topic of overall paper* + argument/opinion/stance about this topic + *Supporting Point 1* + *Supporting Point 2* + *Supporting Point 3*

Demonstration   Drafting and Evaluating a Thesis Statement

1. **What is the topic of your paper?** main cause of prejudice in Parrillo's and Terkel's texts

2. **What opinion or argument do you want to make about this topic?** psychological causes are the main cause of prejudice

3. **What three (or more) supporting points will you write about in your paper to support your topic and argument?** I'm not sure yet. I'm going to fill this in later once I've gathered support and figured out which three psychological causes I will focus on. Right now, though, I think I might focus on relative deprivation, scapegoating, and displaced aggression. I'll use these as placeholders now in my thesis and change them later if I need to.

4. **Write a thesis sentence that combines these things.**

topic   opinion

The primary cause of prejudice in Parrillo's and Terkel's essays is psychological causes.

OR

topic   opinion   supporting details

The primary cause of prejudice is psychological causes *as shown by relative deprivation, scapegoating, and displaced aggression.*

supporting details

Practice 10.4   Drafting and Evaluating a Thesis

DIRECTIONS: Address the following questions in order to develop your thesis.

1. What is the topic of your paper?
2. What opinion or argument do you want to make about this topic?
3. What three (or more) supporting points will you write about in your paper to support your topic and argument?
4. Write a thesis sentence that combines these.

Once you have drafted your thesis, answer the questions on the Thesis Evaluation Checklist to help you assess the strength of your thesis.

Thesis Evaluation Checklist

1. Is your thesis written as one complete sentence? Is it a statement (not a question)?
2. Does your thesis have a clear topic that matches the assignment?
3. Does your thesis provide an argument or opinion or stance about that topic?
4. Does your thesis include supporting points, and if so, are these linked to the topic so they appear as support and not competing topics?
5. Does your thesis include enough information so it makes sense to an outside reader? (You want to avoid having vague references like "he" or "it" as your reader will not know what you are talking about. Make sure to include all needed information in your thesis so it makes sense all by itself and without added information around it.)

STEP 4: Develop Your Ideas

In this casebook, your writing is primarily informational, so the challenge of developing ideas is gathering that information. Your first step should be to return to your reading process notes as well as your prewriting for your paragraphs on prejudice. The Cornell Notes you took during the reading process as well as the T-Chart you developed while writing your paragraphs can be great sources of information to draw from when developing ideas for a full essay. Once you have these notes in front of you, highlight portions of them to use in your paper.

However, since this is a larger paper, you may need even more information. Therefore, it is also important to return to your texts and gather additional information in the form of quotes and examples. You may want to use your T-Chart again and expand it to include additional ideas as this will allow you to build onto existing notes and stay organized as you develop additional ideas.

Practice 10.5 | Developing Your Ideas Using Reading and Writing Notes

DIRECTIONS: Read through your notes from the reading process and the paragraph writing process in this casebook. Highlight any quotes or ideas that you think you may be able to use to develop support of your thesis.

Add to your T-Chart by gathering quotes from Parrillo's text and Terkel's (or one of your choice) that support your thesis. If you are able to find more than one quote for each idea, that is even better, but make sure that each quote you find connects to the idea in your thesis.

If you are writing the extension of this paper, brainstorm a supporting story or example from your own experience for each cause of prejudice you have listed in your T-Chart.

Information Literacy: Using Online Sources

Doing research online about prejudice as it has occurred nationally or in your community is also a great way to gather evidence that can be used to develop ideas in your paper. You might find information that you could use to extend an idea in your supporting paragraphs, or with which to develop your introduction.

STEP 5: Organize Your Ideas

Organizing is an important step prior to drafting. It allows you to select the ideas you want to include in your essay and plan where to put them. The writing process will go faster and smoother if you plan the order of the ideas you want to use and put away those you do not.

In this casebook, we will show you how to move from a graphic organizer like the T-Chart to a linear outline. The graphic organizer lends itself to outlining because it asks you to start organizing ideas in the reading and early prewriting stages. It also sets up a comparison–contrast structure nicely as it ensures that you have support for each main topic and point in your paper. Now you want to take that information and organize it into a plan you can use to draft your essay. An outline is a very effective tool for doing this.

Demonstration   Organizing from T-Chart to Outline

This student took his T-Chart from Step 2 (see Chapter 9, p. 185) and converted it into a linear outline. His outline reflects the alternating comparison structure that was reviewed in Chapter 4 (p. 67); that is, he discusses the same point, for example "relative deprivation," first for Parrillo in a full paragraph and then for Terkel in a full paragraph. Review his T-Chart notes and then read the following outline. The details for his first two body paragraphs are included to show how he drafted topic sentences for his paragraphs, planned to use the quotes he found, and outlined his analysis. The topic sentences are shown for the subsequent paragraphs.

Linear Outline

I. Introduction

   a. Attention getter

   b. Introduction to my topic/background information

   c. Thesis: The primary causes of prejudice are psychological as shown by relative deprivation, scapegoating, and economic competition.

II. Body Paragraph 1: Relative Deprivation in Parrillo

   a. Topic Sentence: One aspect of the psychological cause of prejudice in Parrillo's essay is relative deprivation.

   b. Support: Parrillo defines relative deprivation as, "A lack of resources, or rewards, in one's standard of living in comparison with those of others in the society" (217).

   c. Analysis: This can lead to prejudice as people can blame others for their deprivation.

III. Body Paragraph 2: Relative Deprivation in Terkel

   a. Topic Sentence: Terkel's essay further illustrates the psychological cause of relative deprivation.

   b. Supporting Quote: "My father worked hard but never had enough money to buy decent clothes. When I went to school, I never seemed to have adequate clothes to wear. I always left school late afternoon with a sense of inferiority. The other kids had nice clothes, and I just had what Daddy could buy. I still got some of those inferiority feelin's now that I have to overcome once in a while" (223).

   c. Analysis: Terkel's lack of money to buy clothes and feel good about himself through his outward appearance made him feel less than other kids who could buy nicer things to wear. This later contributed to his prejudice against those who he thought took away his ability to have enough money. It was a key stepping stone of his prejudice.

IV. <u>Body Paragraph 3: Scapegoating in Parrillo</u>

<u>Topic Sentence</u>: Another aspect of the psychological cause of prejudice in Parrillo's essay is scapegoating.

V. <u>Body Paragraph 4: Scapegoating in Terkel</u>

<u>Topic Sentence</u>; Scapegoating as a major psychological cause of prejudice is also shown in Terkel's essay.

VI. <u>Body Paragraph 5: Displaced Aggression in Parrillo</u>

<u>Topic Sentence</u>: Displaced aggression is further evidence of a psychological cause of prejudice, as illustrated in Parillo's essay.

VII. <u>Body Paragraph 6: Displaced Aggression in Terkel</u>

<u>Topic Sentence</u>: Terkels' story is evidence of Parrillo's point that displaced aggression is a psychological cause of prejudice.

VIII. <u>Conclusion</u>

a. Summary of thesis and main points

b. Leave the reader with something to do

Practice 10.6 Organizing Your Ideas

DIRECTIONS: Using all of your notes from your reading and writing processes so far, write an outline of your paper. Try to move from graphic organizers like a T-Chart or cluster brainstorm to a more formal and linear outline. If you are extending ideas in your essay to address that part of the assignment, make sure to also include those ideas in your essay.

Phase Two: Draft

Learning Objective 2
Draft an essay that uses informational evidence.

During the drafting stage, you put together all of the ideas you have generated during prewriting into one complete essay.

STEP 6: Draft Your Essay

Remember that this is a first attempt at creating a strong piece of writing, but it is not the final step. You will still have time to revise and edit your writing so it reflects your best work. While you have gathered and organized many parts of your essay, you may still be wondering how to write an introduction, conclusion, and cohesive paragraphs. We will give you some tips and examples here to get you started on your own work.

Introductory Paragraph

We invite you to reread Chapter 3 on organizing paragraphs and essays. This goes over the basics of writing an introduction for a college paper. In general, the introduction for an informational essay has the same purposes as those for other types of papers: It catches readers' attention, introduces your topic, and states the thesis. Allow the following demonstration to help you get started on your introduction.

Demonstration   Brainstorming and Drafting an Introductory Paragraph

Here, the student brainstorms to develop ideas for an introduction, and then uses the brainstorming to draft an introductory paragraph.

The Attention Getter

1. **Brainstorm a list of stories you could tell** (that aren't going to be in the supporting body paragraphs of your paper) to introduce your paper topic.

   a. A story about how a lesbian friend of mine taught me how much of a heterosexual privilege it is to be able to get married.

   b. *Information Literacy Tip:* Look up stories in my local news about prejudice in my community, and then choose one to summarize. For example, there has been a lot of debate around immigrants and their rights to get financial aid, a driver's license, etc. without fear of deportation.

2. **Brainstorm a list of questions you could use to begin your introduction.** This should lead into either your story or your thesis.

   a. Have you ever thought about what causes people to be prejudiced?

   b. Have you ever thought about how we are blind to our own prejudice?

   c. Have you ever held prejudice against another person or group?

3. **Brainstorm a list of similes you could make about prejudice.**

   a. Prejudice is like a blindfold that you don't know you are wearing. It blinds you to things you don't even realize you feel, think, and do against others.

   b. Prejudice is like armor a knight wears in battle. It shields you from having to confront difficult issues without having protection.

Background Information

Write one-sentence summaries of each of the texts you will write about in your paper. Use this in your introduction as background information to introduce your reader to the texts you will discuss in your paper.

1. "Causes of Prejudice" by Vincent Parrillo: This essay argues that psychological and sociological forces combine to create a complex network that causes prejudice.

2. "C. P. Ellis" by Studs Terkel: This essay is Terkel's interview with C. P. Ellis, a former Klansman who overcomes his prejudice towards African Americans, and it documents Ellis's transformation as he realizes the causes of his prejudice.

Thesis Statement: The primary causes of prejudice are psychological as shown by relative deprivation, scapegoating, and displaced aggression.

Draft Paragraph

I will always remember being out for dinner with a close group of friends from college, when one of the women announced her engagement. Everyone was excited and asking her questions about her ring, where she wanted to get married, what her dress would look like, and where the honeymoon would be. Then I looked at my friend who had just come out as a lesbian, and I noticed that her face was blank. She was not feeling the excitement of the group. She looked like she wanted to get up and leave. When I asked her about it later, she said she was really hurt at being always left out of this experience. Unless laws changed, she said she could never look forward to marrying the love of her life. Marriage was not legal in our state for gays and lesbians, and therefore she always felt like a second-rate citizen or somehow lesser when others got engaged and had the opportunity to get excited about this step in their life. Being heterosexual, I had always taken it for granted that I could marry. Talking to my friend made me realize that this wasn't the case for everyone and that the laws around marriage were biased. This was a real introduction to prejudice. Parrillo's text "Causes of Prejudice" helped me to learn more about this topic. His essay argues that psychological and sociological forces combine to create a complex network that causes prejudice. Another essay that helped to further explain Parrillo's ideas and illustrate prejudice in one person's experience was "C. P. Ellis" by Studs Terkel. C. P. Ellis was a former Klansman who overcame his prejudice towards African Americans, and this essay by Terkel documents Ellis's transformation as he realizes the causes of his prejudice. All of this has led me to ask, "What causes prejudice?" Given the essays by Parrillo and Terkel, the primary causes of prejudice are psychological as shown by relative deprivation, scapegoating, and displaced aggression.

Practice 10.7 Brainstorming and Drafting an Introductory Paragraph

DIRECTIONS: Complete the following activities to develop ideas for your introduction.

1. Brainstorm a list of stories, questions, and similes you could use as attention getters. Then choose your favorite to develop in your introduction.
2. Brainstorm one-sentence summaries of each of the texts you will write about in your paper. You will use this to introduce your texts to your readers.
3. Do not forget that your thesis will also go in your introduction. It usually goes as the first or final sentence in the introduction.

Using the ideas you brainstormed, put them together into one introductory paragraph.

Body Paragraphs

Remember that all paragraphs should have a topic sentence, support, and analysis (see Chapters 3 and 4). If you have completed the steps demonstrated in this chapter, you have nearly written the introduction and body paragraphs of your essay. Use your outline and other prewriting materials to draft your body paragraphs, and use the following Demonstration to guide you as you write.

Demonstration   Drafting a Body Paragraph

Here is a body paragraph of an essay written in response to the assignment for this chapter. The student's T-Chart is on page 185.

Scapegoating as explained in Terkel's essay "C. P. Ellis" is one of the psychological causes of prejudice. Ellis grew up in Durham, North Carolina. He was born before the Depression and experienced poverty his whole life. His father worked in a textile mill, bringing in barely enough for the family to live on. He died young and left Ellis with the burden of supporting his family, forcing Ellis to drop out of school after the eighth grade and work. Ellis's feelings of inferiority that were bred from growing up poor continued when he got married and had a family of his own. He worked every day, taking overtime and extra jobs, but he never had enough to pay the bills. It was this that caused him to get bitter and look for someone to blame for his situation. He says, "I really began to get bitter. I didn't know who to blame. I tried to find somebody" (224). He looked around and saw black people. They became an obvious focus for his blame. "I had to hate somebody. Hatin' America is hard to do because you can't see it to hate it. You gotta have something to look at to hate.... The natural person for me to hate would be black people, because my father before me was a member of the Klan" (224). Ellis's prejudice against blacks was a way of relieving the pressure of his situation. Having a scapegoat, or someone to blame, made him feel like there was a reason for his poverty; it helped to rationalize it and make it less painful. His story is a strong example of how scapegoating is a psychological cause of prejudice.

Practice 10.8   Drafting Body Paragraphs

DIRECTIONS: Use your outline and other prewriting to draft the body paragraphs of your paper.

Information Literacy: As you do so, remember to cite all of your quotes and paraphrases by giving the author and page number and including proper punctuation.

Conclusion

To review the purpose of concluding paragraphs and techniques for writing them, review Chapter 3. Two strategies you can use when writing a conclusion for an informational essay are:

- Write a three-sentence summary of the thesis and main ideas in your paper. (This should be a brief overview of what you have said in your paper.)
- Write a final question or give the reader something to do as a result of having read your paper. Indicate the significance or importance of the thesis and evidence presented in the essay.

Demonstration Brainstorming and Drafting a Conclusion Paragraph

1. Write a three- to four-sentence summary of the thesis and main ideas in your paper. This should be a brief overview of what you have said in your paper.

According to Parrillo and Terkel, psychological causes are the primary ones that contribute to prejudice. Relative deprivation is one element of psychological causes, as it is how we feel when we don't think we have adequate resources as compared to others in our community. Scapegoating can be a result of relative deprivation as we act on our feelings of not having enough by blaming others. Finally, displaced aggression (often against a scapegoat) is when a person acts out their anger against a group that didn't create the problem to begin with.

2. Write a final question, give the reader something to do as a result of having read your paper, and/or indicate the significance or importance of the thesis and evidence presented in the essay.

The causes of prejudice are complex and we are often blind to our own prejudices. Try taking off your own blindfolds, or analyzing them more closely to see if you hold prejudice against others. Then take steps to overcome this. Just like C. P. Ellis overcame his prejudice, so can you.

Conclusion Paragraph

According to Parrillo and Terkel, psychological causes are the primary ones that contribute to prejudice. Relative deprivation is one element of psychological causes, as it is how we feel when we don't think we have adequate resources as compared to others in our community. Scapegoating can be a result of relative deprivation as we act on our feelings of not having enough by blaming others. Finally, displaced aggression (often against a scapegoat) is when a person acts out their anger against a group that didn't create the problem to begin with. The causes of prejudice are complex and we are often blind to our own prejudices. Try taking off your own blindfolds, or analyzing them more closely to see if you hold prejudice against others. Then take steps to overcome this. Just like C. P. Ellis overcame his prejudice, so can you.

Practice 10.9 Brainstorming and Drafting a Conclusion Paragraph

DIRECTIONS: Follow these steps to generate ideas for your conclusion.

1. Write a one- to three-sentence summary of your thesis and main supporting points in your paper.
2. Brainstorm a final point of significance or answer to the question, *So What?* Use any of the following techniques to do this.
   - Write a final question for the reader to consider.
   - Give the reader something to do as a result of having read your paper.
3. Using the ideas you brainstormed, draft your conclusion.

Phase Three: Polish

Learning Objective 3
Revise and edit an essay that uses informational evidence.

The final phase of the writing process is always to revise to improve the essay's content and structure and edit sentences for mistakes.

STEP 7: Revise

Peer review is a guided process that allows you to get feedback from another student in class on how to improve or revise your writing. Many peer-review questions are also questions that instructors ask when assessing your writing, so, as you do peer review, you will also practice looking for things that your teacher may look for when grading your paragraph. Use the following guidelines when reviewing a peer's writing:

Guidelines for Peer Review of an Essay

1. **Thesis** Write the thesis for the essay on a sheet of paper. Then, evaluate it using the following questions:
   - Is it clear (i.e., can you understand it, and did it stand out to you as you read the paper)?
   - Does it provide a clear topic for the paper as well as an opinion about that topic?
   - Does it address the assignment?

2. **Body Paragraphs**
   - *Topic Sentences of Body Paragraphs* Write down the topic sentence of each body paragraph. Then, evaluate each one. Does each have one clear topic and a connection to the thesis? Note any topic sentences that are lacking one or two of these elements.
   - *Support* Does each body paragraph contain enough supporting evidence? If not, suggest ideas that the writer could add.
     - Does the evidence give enough information, so the audience will know what the writer is talking about even if they have not read the articles?
     - Is the support accurate; does it reflect the topics the writer is discussing?
     - Are all quotes or paraphrases cited?
   - *Analysis* Does each body paragraph include one or two sentences of analysis at the end and/or following each quote that tells how the supporting information connects to the thesis? If not, tell the writer where he or she needs to add this information.
   - *Body Paragraph Coherence* Does each supporting body paragraph stay on one topic? If not, note which ones do and which ones don't. Provide some suggestion for how to improve the paragraphs that need revision.

3. **Development of Ideas** Does the paper include enough supporting ideas and details to fully develop the thesis? As a reader, did you come away from the paper wanting to know more about the thesis? If so, what did you still want to know?

4. **Essay Structure**
   - *Introduction* Does the introduction invite you, the reader, into the paper in an interesting and engaging way? Does it make you want to read further? How could it be improved to do so?
   - *Paper Coherence* Does each supporting paragraph in the paper connect with the thesis statement? Note any paragraphs that don't seem to connect or that go off on a tangent.
   - *Conclusion* Does the conclusion summarize the thesis and main supporting points? Does it leave you, the reader, with a sense of significance (why you were told this information or what you should do with this information)?

5. **Language, Voice, and Tone** Does the tone or voice fit the needs of the audience, and is it appropriate given the subject matter of the essay? Make a note if it seems too informal or inappropriate for an academic audience or if the tone doesn't fit the topic.

Demonstration   **Practicing Peer Review**

The following is an example peer review for the introduction, one body paragraph, and conclusion we have demonstrated in this chapter.

1. <u>Thesis</u>

   a. <u>**Thesis Statement**</u> *"Given the essays by Parrillo and Terkel, the primary causes of prejudice are psychological as shown by relative deprivation, scapegoating, and displaced aggression."*

   b. <u>**Evaluate the thesis**</u> *I think it does a great job of addressing the assignment and being to the point. I really like how you included your supporting points, too. I struggle with that, so it's helpful to see an example.*

2. <u>Body Paragraphs</u>

   a. <u>**Topic Sentence**</u> *"Scapegoating as explained in Terkel's essay "C. P. Ellis" is one of the psychological causes of prejudice."*

   <u>**Evaluate the topic sentence**</u> *I think you did a great job here as well. You have the author (Terkel) and the supporting point (scapegoating), and you linked it to your thesis (psychological causes). Maybe you could use a transition from the previous paragraph on Parrillo, though. I might add to the beginning of the sentence something like this, "In comparison to Parrillo, . . ." That would give a transition of ideas better.*

   b. <u>**Evaluate support, analysis, and coherence:** **Support**</u> *I love how you introduced your support with a brief summary of Ellis's life. That really helped me to understand the quote, and I think it would especially help readers who didn't know the story. Your quote clearly shows scapegoating, too, so I think you are accurate in your support. You also have enough support to show your point.*

   <u>**Analysis**</u> *I think this is enough. You connect back to your thesis, which is great! You also explain the quote a bit. I struggle with analysis, so I'm not sure if my feedback is good here, but your analysis seems good to me!*

   c. <u>**Coherence**</u> *Yes, this paragraph stays on topic. Nice job!*

3. <u>Essay Structure</u>

   a. <u>**Introduction**</u> *I loved your story! It helped me feel how real the topic of prejudice is for you, and it drew me in to your paper because I wanted to know more about your story. Great idea! You also transitioned to the texts by Parrillo and Terkel easily and then your thesis. It flowed well. I never got lost or felt like it jumped around.*

   b. <u>**Conclusion**</u> *The conclusion includes a thorough summary of the paper, and then it uses Ellis's story to motivate the reader to change their prejudicial attitudes. Cool! I liked it.*

(continued)

Practice 10.9   Practicing Peer Review

DIRECTIONS

1. Trade papers with a partner in class. Then answer the peer review questions on page 208 for your partner's paper, and have your partner answer them for your essay. When you are done, talk with your partner, so you can explain what you found, answer your partner's questions, and get feedback on your own writing from your partner. Finally, make notes about what you plan to revise given the feedback you received.
2. Have another classmate—a peer—review your essay by answering peer review questions (p. 208) in writing. Then use this feedback to make improvements to your essay.

STEP 8: Edit and Proofread

Once you have looked at global issues—such as the thesis, support, and organization—it is time to do a final polish by editing your paper for grammar and spelling errors. To edit your paper, try any of the following suggestions.

1. **Read your paper out loud to yourself.** Read slowly and read every word. You will probably find some sentences that don't make sense or words that are missing. Fix these.
2. **Read your paper aloud,** *starting at the end of the paper.* Read the last sentence first and then the sentence before that. Make corrections as you go. This works well because you are interrupting the flow of thought so that you are more likely to read what is actually on the page, rather than what you want it to say.
3. **Have another person read the paper.** This should be someone who has not previously seen it. Have that person mark any sentences or words that do not make sense to him or her. While this person might not be a grammar expert, he or she can give you feedback about sentences that are not "reader friendly" and therefore could use editing.
4. **Work with a tutor in your school's Writing Center or other tutoring center.** Have this person read your paper and work with you to edit any sentences that are not clear or correct.
5. **Have your instructor look at your paper and mark one paragraph for grammar and spelling.** Then, look at his or her marks and note the types or patterns of errors you tend to make. Try to find similar errors in the remaining paragraphs and fix them.

Practice 10.10   Editing and Proofreading

DIRECTIONS: Do one or both of the following to edit your revised draft.

1. Pair up with a partner in class and read your paper out loud to that person. As you do so, listen for any errors and circle or highlight those. Then work on your own or with a tutor to correct those errors.
2. Ask your instructor to edit five lines of your paragraphs. Then use your instructor's comments to look for patterns that will probably show up in the rest of your writing as well. See if you can find these and correct them on your own.

STEP 9: Reflect on Your Writing Process

The final stage in the writing process is to reflect on the process itself. You want to ask yourself some questions so that the next time you write, you can change what did not work or repeat what did work. Here are sample reflection questions you can ask yourself before starting your next writing assignment:

1. **What did you learn from thinking about the topic of this paper?** Did reading and writing about prejudice help you or change you in any way?
2. **How did you grow as a writer through the process of writing?** (For example, did you take on any new challenges? Did you discover any new places you would like to work on in the future? Did you find that using a writing process worked for you or not?)
   - If you completed the extensions in the assignment, comment on this. How was the experience of doing research on your topic and then adding this to your paper? What challenges did you face? What will you do the same or differently next time?
3. **How did the act of writing help you grow as a reader?** (For example, did the process of writing help you to read texts written in similar styles? Did you better retain the information that you read? Was it hard to write about ideas in readings?)
4. **Discuss what you see as the strengths of your writing,** starting first with content (ideas and information) and then going to style (organization, language, voice, etc.).
5. **Discuss what you think are the weaknesses of your writing.** If you had more time or inclination, would you do anything else to your writing? If so, what?

Practice 10.11   **Reflecting on Your Writing Process**

DIRECTIONS: Answer the questions above to reflect on your writing process.

Chapter **Quick Check**   MySkillsLab   Complete the mastery test for this chapter in MySkillsLab.

Use the following questions and answers to check your understanding of this chapter.

QUESTION	ANSWER
Learning Objective 1: Prewrite for an essay that uses informational support. *How do I prewrite for an essay that uses informational support?*	To prewrite for an essay using informational support… ✔ Make sure you understand the assignment. ✔ Brainstorm and freewrite. ✔ Gather information by reading and researching. ✔ Review reading notes and summaries. ✔ Focus by choosing the most significant ideas and information about your topic. Include these ideas within your thesis. A good informational thesis includes the topic and an opinion or point of view about the topic, and it may also include the supporting main ideas.
Learning Objective 2: Draft an essay that uses informational support. *How do I draft an essay using informational support?*	To draft an essay using informational support… ✔ Write an introduction that is interesting to readers, provides enough background information, and states your thesis. ✔ Write body paragraphs from an outline of your topic sentence and supporting information. ✔ Write a conclusion that reflects the ideas in your essay and relays the importance of the thesis.
Learning Objective 3: Revise and edit an essay that uses informational support. *How do I revise and edit essays that use information as support?*	To revise and edit an essay using informational support… ✔ Use workshop techniques such as peer review to get feedback on the paper's thesis, overall structure, development, and organization. ✔ Have your teacher or a Writing Center tutor check your work to identify types of errors you make. ✔ Get to know the types of sentence errors you tend to make. ✔ Practice fixing your sentence mistakes.

PART THREE READING SELECTIONS

Causes of Prejudice
Vincent N. Parrillo

1. Prejudicial attitudes may be either positive or negative. Sociologists primarily study the latter, however, because only negative attitudes can lead to turbulent social relations between dominant and minority groups. Numerous writers, therefore, have defined *prejudice* as an attitudinal "system of negative beliefs, feelings, and action-orientations regarding a certain group or groups of people."[1] The status of the strangers is an important factor in the development of a negative attitude. Prejudicial attitudes exist among members of both dominant and minority groups. Thus, in the relations between dominant and minority groups, the antipathy felt by one group for another is quite often reciprocated.

2. Psychological perspectives on prejudice—whether behaviorist, cognitive, or psychoanalytic—focus on the subjective states of mind of individuals. In these perspectives, a person's prejudicial attitudes may result from imitation or conditioning (behaviorist),

Vincent T. Parillo

perceived similarity–dissimilarity of beliefs (cognitive), or specific personality characteristics (psychoanalytic). In contrast, sociological perspectives focus on the objective conditions of society as the social forces behind prejudicial attitudes and behind racial and ethnic relations. Individuals do not live in a vacuum; social reality affects their states of mind.

3. Both perspectives are necessary to understand prejudice. As psychologist Gordon Allport argued, besides needing a close study of habits, perceptions, motivation, and personality, we need an analysis of social settings, situational forces, demographic and ecological variables, and legal and economic trends.[2] Psychological and sociological perspectives complement each other in providing a fuller explanation about intergroup relations.

The Psychology of Prejudice

4. We can understand more about prejudice among individuals by focusing on four areas of study: levels of prejudice, self-justification, personality and frustration.

Levels of Prejudice

5. Bernard Kramer suggests that prejudice exists on three levels: cognitive, emotional, and action orientation.[3] The **cognitive level of prejudice** encompasses a person's beliefs and perceptions of a group as threatening or nonthreatening, inferior or equal (e.g., in terms

---

[1] Reported by Daniel Wilner, Rosabelle Price Walkley, and Stuart W. Cook, "Residential Proximity and Intergroup Relations in Public Housing Projects," *Journal of Social Issues* 8(1) (1952): 45. See also James W. Vander Zanden, *American Minority Relations,* 3d ed. (New York: Ronald Press. 1972). p. 21. [All notes are the author's.]

[2] Gordon W. Allport, "Prejudice: Is It Societal or Personal?" *Journal of Social Issues* 18 (1962): 129–30.

[3] Bernard M. Kramer, "Dimensions of Prejudice," *Journal of Psychology* 27 (April 1949 389–451.

of intellect, status, or biological composition), seclusive or intrusive, impulse-gratifying, acquisitive, or possessing other positive or negative characteristics. Mr. X's cognitive beliefs are that Jews are intrusive and acquisitive. Other illustrations of cognitive beliefs are that the Irish are heavy drinkers and fighters. African Americans are rhythmic and lazy, and the Poles are thick-headed and unintelligent. Generalizations shape both ethnocentric and prejudicial attitudes, but there is a difference. **Ethnocentrism** is a generalized rejection of all outgroups on the basis of an ingroup focus, whereas **prejudice** is a rejection of certain people solely on the basis of their membership in a particular group.

6   In many societies, members of the majority group may believe that a particular low-status minority group is dirty, immoral, violent, or law-breaking. In the United States, the Irish, Italians, African Americans, Mexicans, Chinese, Puerto Ricans, and others have at one time or another been labeled with most, if not all, of these adjectives. In most European countries and in the United States, the group lowest on the socioeconomic ladder has often been depicted in caricature as also lowest on the evolutionary ladder. The Irish and African Americans in the United States and the peasants and various ethnic groups in Europe have all been depicted in the past as apelike:

> The Victorian images of the Irish as "white Negro" and simian Celt, or a combination of the two, derived much of its force and inspiration from physiognomical beliefs…[but] every country in Europe had its equivalent of "white Negroes" and simianized men, whether or not they happened to be stereotypes of criminals, assassins, political radicals, revolutionaries, Slavs, gypsies, Jews, or peasants.[4]

7   The **emotional level of prejudice** refers to the feelings that a minority group arouses in an individual. Although these feelings may be based on stereotypes from the cognitive level, they represent a more intense stage of personal involvement. The emotional attitudes may be negative or positive, such as fear/envy, distrust/trust, disgust/admiration, or contempt/empathy. These feelings, based on beliefs about the group, may be triggered by social interaction or by the possibility of interaction. For example, whites might react with fear or anger to the integration of their schools or neighborhoods or Protestants might be jealous of the lifestyle of a highly successful Catholic business executive.

8   An **action-orientation level of prejudice** is the positive or negative predisposition to engage in discriminatory behavior. A person who harbors strong feelings about members of a certain racial or ethnic group may have a tendency to act for or against them—being aggressive or nonaggressive, offering assistance or withholding it. Such an individual would also be likely to want to exclude or include members of that group both in close, personal social relations and in peripheral social relations. For example, some people would want to exclude members of the disliked group from doing business with them or living in their neighborhood. Another manifestation of the action-orientation level of prejudice is the desire to change or maintain the status differential or inequality between the two groups, whether the area is economic, political, educational, social, or a combination. Note that an action orientation is a predisposition to act, not the action itself.

Self-Justification

9   **Self-justification** involves denigrating a person or group to justify maltreatment of them. In this situation, self-justification leads to prejudice and discrimination against members of another group.

10   Some philosophers argue that we are not so much rational creatures as we are rationalizing creatures. We require reassurance that the things we do and the lives we live are

---

[4]L. Perry Curtis, Jr., *Apes and Angels: The Irishman in Victorian Caricature* (Washington, D.C): Smithsonian Press, 1971).

proper, that good reasons for our actions exist. If we can convince ourselves that another group is inferior, immoral, or dangerous, we may feel justified in discriminating against its members, enslaving them, or even killing them.

11   History is filled with examples of people who thought their maltreatment of others was just and necessary: As defenders of the "true faith," the Crusaders killed "Christ-killers" (Jews) and "infidels" (Moslems). Participants in the Spanish Inquisition imprisoned, tortured, and executed "heretics," "the disciples of the Devil." Similarly, the Puritans burned witches, whose refusal to confess "proved they were evil"; pioneers exploited or killed Native Americans who were "heathen savages"; and whites mistreated, enslaved, or killed African Americans, who were "an inferior species." According to U.S. Army officers, the civilians in the Vietnamese village of My Lai were "probably" aiding the Vietcong; so in 1968 U.S. soldiers fighting in the Vietnam War felt justified in slaughtering over 300 unarmed people there, including women, children, and the elderly.

12   Some sociologists believe that self-justification works the other way around. That is, instead of self-justification serving as a basis for subjugating others, the subjugation occurs first and the self-justification follows, resulting in prejudice and continued discrimination.[5] The evolution of racism as a concept after the establishment of the African slave trade would seem to support this idea. Philip Mason offers an insight into this view:

> A specialized society is likely to defeat a simpler society and provide a lower tier still of enslaved and conquered peoples. The rulers and organizers sought security for themselves and their children; to perpetuate the power, the esteem, and the comfort they had achieved, it was necessary not only that the artisans and labourers should work contentedly but that the rulers should sleep without bad dreams. No one can say with certainty how the myths originated, but it is surely relevant that when one of the founders of Western thought set himself to frame an ideal state that would embody social justice, he—like the earliest city

---

[5]See Marvin B. Scott and Stanford M. Lyman, "Accounts," *American Sociological Review* 33 (February 1968): 40-62.

dwellers—not only devised a society stratified in tiers but believed it would be necessary to persuade the traders and work people that, by divine decree, they were made from brass and iron, while the warriors were made of silver and the rulers of gold.[6]

13   Another example of self-justification serving as a source of prejudice is the dominant group's assumption of an attitude of superiority over other groups. In this respect, establishing a prestige hierarchy—ranking the status of various ethnic groups—results in differential association. To enhance or maintain self-esteem, a person may avoid social contact with groups deemed inferior and associate only with those identified as being of high status. Through such behavior, self-justification may come to intensify the social distance between groups....*Social distance* refers to the degree to which ingroup members do not engage in social or primary relationships with members of various outgroups.

Personality

14   In 1950, in *The Authoritarian Personality*, T. W. Adorno and his colleagues reported a correlation between individuals' early childhood experiences of harsh parental discipline and their development of an **authoritarian personality** as adults.[7] If parents assume an excessively domineering posture in their relations with a child, exercising stern measures and threatening to withdraw love if the child does not respond with weakness and submission, the child tends to be insecure and to nurture much latent hostility against the parents. When such children become adults, they may demonstrate **displaced aggression,** directing their hostility against a powerless group to compensate for their feelings of insecurity and fear. Highly prejudiced individuals tend to come from families that emphasize obedience.

15   The authors identified authoritarianism by the use of a measuring instrument called an F scale (the *F* standing for potential fascism). Other tests included the A-S (anti-Semitism) and E (ethnocentrism) scales, the latter measuring attitudes toward various minorities. One of their major findings was that people who scored high on authoritarianism also consistently showed a high degree of prejudice against all minority groups. These highly prejudiced persons were characterized by rigidity of viewpoint, dislike for ambiguity, strict obedience to leaders, and intolerance of weakness in themselves and others.

16   No sooner did *The Authoritarian Personality* appear than controversy began. H. H. Hyman and P. B. Sheatsley challenged the methodology and analysis.[8] Solomon Asch questioned the assumptions that the F scale responses represented a belief system and that structural variables (such as ideologies, stratification, and mobility) do not play a role in shaping personality.[9] E. A. Shils argued that the authors were interested only in measuring authoritarianism of the political right while ignoring such tendencies in those at the other end of the political spectrum.[10] Other investigators sought alternative explanations for the authoritarian personality. D. Stewart and T. Hoult extended the framework beyond family childhood experiences to include other social factors.[11] H. C. Kelman and Janet Barclay pointed out that substantial evidence exists showing that lower intelligence and less education also correlate with high authoritarianism scores on the F scale.[12]

---

[6]Philip Mason, *Patterns of Dominance* (New York: Oxford University Press, 1970), p. 7. See also Philip Mason, *Race Relations* (New York: Oxford University Press, 1970), pp. 17–29.

[7]T. W. Adorno, Else Frankel-Brunswik, Daniel J. Levinson, and R. Nevitt Sanford, *The Authoritarian Personality* (New York: Harper & Row, 1950).

[8]H. H. Hyman and P. B. Sheatsley, "The Authoritarian Personality: A Methodological Critique," in R. Christie and M. Jahoda (eds.), *Studies in the Scope and Method of "The Authoritarian Personality"* (Glencoe, Ill.: Free Press, 1954).

[9]Solomon E. Asch, *Social Psychology* (Englewood Cliffs, N.J.: Prentice-Hall, 1952), p. 545.

[10]E. A. Shik, "Authoritarianism: Right and Left," in *Studies in the Scope and Method of "The Authoritarian Personality."*

[11]D. Stewart and T. Hoult, "A Social-Psychological Theory of 'The Authoritarian Personality.'" *American Journal of Sociology* 65 (1959): 274.

[12]H. C. Kelman and Janet Barclay, "The F Scale as a Measure of Breadth of Perspective," *Journal of Abnormal and Social Psychology* 67 (1963): 608-15.

17   Despite the critical attacks, the underlying conceptions of *The Authoritarian Personality* were important, and research into personality as a factor in prejudice has continued. Subsequent investigators refined and modified the original study. Correcting scores for response bias, they conducted cross-cultural studies. Respondents in Germany and Near East countries, where more authoritarian social structures exist, scored higher on authoritarianism and social distance between groups. In Japan, Germany, and the United States, authoritarianism and social distance were moderately related. Other studies suggested that an inverse relationship exists between social class and F scale scores: the higher the social class, the lower the authoritarianism.[13]

18   Although studies of authoritarian personality have helped us understand some aspects of prejudice, they have not provided a causal explanation. Most of the findings in this area show a correlation, but the findings do not prove, for example, that harsh discipline of children causes them to become prejudiced adults. Perhaps the strict parents were themselves prejudiced, and the child learned those attitudes from them. Or as George Simpson and J. Milton Yinger say:

> One must be careful not to assume too quickly that a certain tendency—rigidity of mind, for example—that is correlated with prejudice necessarily causes that prejudice.... The sequence may be the other way around.... It is more likely that both are related to more basic factors.[14]

19   For some people, prejudice may indeed be rooted in subconscious childhood tensions, but we simply do not know whether these tensions directly cause a high degree of prejudice in the adult or whether other powerful social forces are the determinants. Whatever the explanation, authoritarianism is a significant phenomenon worthy of continued investigation. Recent research, however, has stressed social and situational factors, rather than personality, as primary causes of prejudice and discrimination.[15]

20   Yet another dimension of the personality component is that people with low self-esteem are more prejudiced than those who feel good about themselves. Some researchers have argued that individuals with low self-esteem deprecate others to enhance their feelings about themselves.[16] One study asserts that "low self-esteem individuals seem to have a generally negative view of themselves, their ingroup, outgroups, and perhaps the world," and thus their tendency to be more prejudiced is not due to rating the outgroup negatively in comparison to their ingroup.[17]

Frustration

21   Frustration is the result of relative deprivation in which expectations remain unsatisfied. **Relative deprivation** is a lack of resources, or rewards, in one's standard of living in comparison with those of others in the society. A number of investigators have suggested that frustrations tend to increase aggression toward others.[18] Frustrated people may easily strike out

---

[13]For an excellent summary of authoritarian studies and literature, see John P. Kirscht and Ronald C. Dillehay, *Dimensions of Authoritarianism: A Review of Research and Theory* (Lexington: University of Kentucky Press, 1967).

[14]George E. Simpson and J. Milton Yinger, *Racial and Cultural Minorities: An Analysis of Prejudice and Discrimination* (New York: Harper & Row, 1953), p. 91.

[15]Ibid., pp. 62–79.

[16]Howard J. Ehrlich, *The Social Psychology of Prejudice* (New York: Wiley, 1974); G. Sherwood, "Self-Serving Biases in Person Perception," *Psychological Bulletin* 90 (1981): 445-59; T. A. Wills, "Downward Comparison Principles in Social Psychology," *Psychological Bulletin* 90 (1981): 245-71.

[17]Jennifer Croeker and Ian Schwartz, "Prejudice and Ingroup Favoritism in a Minimal Intergroup Situation: Effects of Self-Esteem," *Personality and Social Psychology Bulletin* 11 (4) (December 1985): 379–86.

[18]John Dollard, Leonard W. Doob, Neal E. Miller, O. H. Mowrer, and Robert P. Sears, *Frustration and Aggression* (New Haven, Conn.: Yale University Press, 1939); A. F. Henry and J. F. Short, Jr., *Suicide and Homicide* (New York: Free Press, 1954); Neal Miller and Richard Bugelski "Minor Studies in Aggression: The Influence of Frustration Imposed by the Ingroup on Attitudes Expressed Toward Out Groups." *Journal of Psychology* 25 (1948): 437–42; Stuart Palmer, *The Psychology of Murder* (New York: T. Y. Crowell. 1960); Brendan C. Rule and Elizabeth Percival, The Effects of Frustration and Attack on Physical Aggression," *Journal of Experimental Research on Personality* 5 (1971): 111-88.

against the perceived cause of their frustration. However, this reaction may not be possible because the true source of the frustration is often too nebulous to be identified or too powerful to act against. In such instances, the result may be displaced aggression; in this situation, the frustrated individual or group usually redirects anger against a more visible, vulnerable, and socially sanctioned target, one unable to strike back. Minorities meet these criteria and are thus frequently the recipients of displaced aggression by the dominant group.

22   Blaming others for something that is not their fault is known as **scapegoating.** The term comes from the ancient Hebrew custom of using a goat during the Day of Atonement as a symbol of the sins of the people. In an annual ceremony, a priest placed his hands on the head of a goat and listed the people's sins in a symbolic transference of guilt; he then chased the goat out of the community, thereby freeing the people of sin.[19] Since those times, the powerful group has usually punished the scapegoat group rather than allowing it to escape.

23   There have been many instances throughout world history of minority groups serving as scapegoats, including the Christians in ancient Rome, the Huguenots in France, the Jews in Europe and Russia, and the Puritans and Quakers in England. Gordon Allport suggests that certain characteristics are necessary for a group to become a suitable scapegoat. The group must be (1) highly visible in physical appearance or observable customs and actions; (2) not strong enough to strike back; (3) situated within easy access of the dominant group and, ideally, concentrated in one area; (4) a past target of hostility for whom latent hostility still exists; and (5) the symbol of an unpopular concept.[20]

24   Some groups fit this typology better than others, but minority racial and ethnic groups have been a perennial choice. Irish, Italians, Catholics, Jews, Quakers, Mormons, Chinese, Japanese, Blacks, Puerto Ricans, Chicanos, and Koreans have all been treated, at one time or another, as the scapegoat in the United States. Especially in times of economic hardship, societies tend to blame some group for the general conditions, which often leads to aggressive action against the group as an expression of frustration. For example, a study by Carl Hovland and Robert Sears found that, between 1882 and 1930, a definite correlation existed between a decline in the price of cotton and an increase in the number of lynchings of Blacks.[21]

25   In several controlled experiments, social scientists have attempted to measure the validity of the scapegoat theory. Neal Miller and Richard Bugelski tested a group of young men aged eighteen to twenty who were working in a government camp about their feelings toward various minority groups. The young men were reexamined about these feelings after experiencing frustration by being obliged to take a long, difficult test and being denied an opportunity to see a film at a local theater. This group showed some evidence of increased prejudicial feelings, whereas a control group, which did not experience any frustration, showed no change in prejudicial attitudes.[22]

26   Donald Weatherley conducted an experiment with a group of college students to measure the relationship between frustration and aggression against a specific disliked group.[23] After identifying students who were or were not highly anti-Semitic and subjecting them to a strongly frustrating experience, he asked the students to write stories about pictures shown to them. Some of the students were shown pictures of people who had been given Jewish names; other students were presented with pictures of unnamed people. When the pictures were unidentified, the stories of the anti-Semitic students did not differ from those of other students. When the pictures were identified, however, the anti-Semitic students wrote stories reflecting much more aggression against the Jews in the pictures than did the other students.

---

[19]Leviticus 16:5-22.

[20]Gordon W. Allport, *The Nature of Prejudice* (Cambridge, Mass.: Addison-Wesley, 1954), pp. 13–14.

[21]Carl I. Hovland and Robert R. Sears, "Minor Studies of Aggression: Correlation of Lynchings with Economic Indices," *Journal of Psychology 9* (Winter 1940): 301–10.

[22]Miller and Bugelski. "Minor Studies in Aggression," pp. 437–42.

[23]Donald Weatherley, "Anti-Semitism and the Expression of Fantasy Aggression," *Journal of Abnormal and Social Psychology 62* (1961): 454-57.

27   For over twenty years, Leonard Berkowitz and his associates studied and experimented with aggressive behavior. They concluded that, confronted with equally frustrating situations, highly prejudiced individuals are more likely to seek scapegoats than are non-prejudiced individuals. Another intervening variable is that personal frustrations (marital failure, injury, or mental illness) make people more likely to seek scapegoats than do shared frustrations (dangers of flood or hurricane).[24]

28   Some experiments have shown that aggression does not increase if the frustration is understandable.[25] Other experiments have found that people become aggressive only if the aggression directly relieves their frustration.[26] Still other studies have shown that anger is a more likely result if the person responsible for the frustrating situation could have acted otherwise.[27] Clearly, the results are mixed, depending on the variables within a given social situation.

29   Frustration–aggression theory, although helpful, is not completely satisfactory. It ignores the role of culture and the reality of actual social conflict and fails to show any causal relationship. Most of the responses measured in these studies were of people already biased. Why did one group rather than another become the object of the aggression? Moreover, frustration does not necessarily precede aggression, and aggression does not necessarily flow from frustration.

The Sociology of Prejudice

30   Sociologist Talcott Parsons provided one bridge between psychology and sociology by introducing social forces as a variable in frustration–aggression theory. He suggested that both the family and the occupational structure may produce anxieties and insecurities that create frustration.[28] According to this view, the growing-up process (gaining parental affection and approval, identifying with and imitating sexual role models, and competing with others in adulthood) sometimes involves severe emotional strain. The result is an adult personality with a large reservoir of repressed aggression that becomes *free-floating*—susceptible to redirection against convenient scapegoats. Similarly, the occupational system is a source of frustration: its emphasis on competitiveness and individual achievement, its function of conferring status, its requirement that people inhibit their natural impulses at work, and its ties to the state of the economy are among the factors that generate emotional anxieties. Parsons pessimistically concluded that minorities fulfill a functional "need" as targets for displaced aggression and therefore will remain targets.[29]

        Perhaps most influential in staking out the sociological position on prejudice was Herbert Blumer, who suggested that prejudice always involves the "sense of group position" in society. Agreeing with Kramer's delineation of three levels of prejudice, Blumer argued that prejudice can include beliefs, feelings, and a predisposition to action, thus motivating behavior that derives from the social hierarchy.[30] By emphasizing historically established group positions and relationships, Blumer shifted his focus away from the attitudes and personality compositions of individuals. As a social phenomenon, prejudice rises or falls according to issues that alter one group's position vis-à-vis that of another group.

---

[24]See Leonard Berkowitz, "Whatever Happened to the Frustration-Aggression Hypothesis?" *American Behavioral Scientist* 21 (1978): 691–708; L. Berkowitz, *Aggression: A Social Psychological Analysis* (New York: McGraw-Hill, 1962).

[25]D. Zillman, *Hostility and Aggression* (Hillsdale, N.J.: Laurence Erlbaum, 1979); R. A. Baron, *Human Aggression* (New York: Plenum Press, 1977); N. Pastore, "The Role of Arbitrariness in the Frustration-Aggression Hypothesis," *Journal of Abnormal and Social Psychology* 47 (1952): 728–31.

[26]A. H. Buss, "Instrumentality of Aggression, Feedback, and Frustration as Determinants of Physical Aggression," *Journal of Personality and Social Psychology* 3 (1966): 153–62.

[27]J. R. Averill, "Studies on Anger and Aggression: Implications for Theories of Emotion," *American Psychologist* 38 (1983): 1145-60.

[28]Talcott Parsons, "Certain Primary Sources and Patterns of Aggression in the Social Structure of the Western World," In *Essays in Sociological Theory* (New York: Free Press, 1964), pp. 298–322.

[29]For an excellent review of Parsonian theory in this area, see Stanford M. Lyman, *The Black American in Sociological Thought: A Failure of Perspective* (New York: Putnam, 1972), pp. 145–69.

[30]Herbert Blumer, "Race Prejudice as a Sense of Group Position." *Pacific Sociological Review* 1 (1958): 3-7.

Socialization

32   In the **socialization process,** individuals acquire the values, attitudes, beliefs, and perceptions of their culture or subculture, including religion, nationality, and social class. Generally, the child conforms to the parents' expectations in acquiring an understanding of the world and its people. Being impressionable and knowing of no alternative conceptions of the world, the child usually accepts these concepts without questioning. We thus learn the prejudices of our parents and others, which then become part of our values and beliefs. Even when based on false stereotypes, prejudices shape our perceptions of various peoples and influence our attitudes and actions toward particular groups. For example, if we develop negative attitudes about Jews because we are taught that they are shrewd, acquisitive, and clannish—all-too-familiar stereotypes—as adults we may refrain from business or social relationships with them. We may not even realize the reason for such avoidance, so subtle has been the prejudice instilled within us.

33   People may learn certain prejudices because of their pervasiveness. The cultural screen that we develop and through which we view the surrounding world is not always accurate, but it does permit transmission of shared values and attitudes, which are reinforced by others. Prejudice, like cultural values, is taught and learned through the socialization process. The prevailing prejudicial attitudes and actions may be deeply embedded in custom or law (e.g., the **Jim Crow laws** of the 1890s and the early twentieth century establishing segregated public facilities throughout the South, which subsequent generations accepted as proper, and maintained in their own adult lives).

34   Although socialization explains how prejudicial attitudes may be transmitted from one generation to the next, it does not explain their origin or why they intensify or diminish over the years. These aspects of prejudice must be explained in another way.

Economic Competition

35   People tend to be more hostile toward others when they feel that their security is threatened; thus many social scientists conclude that economic competition and conflict breed prejudice. Certainly, considerable evidence shows that negative stereotyping, prejudice, and discrimination increase markedly whenever competition for available jobs increases.

36   An excellent illustration relates to the Chinese sojourners in the nineteenth-century United States. Prior to the 1870s, the transcontinental railroad was being built, and the Chinese filled many of the jobs made available by this project in the sparsely populated West. Although they were expelled from the region's gold mines and schools and could obtain no redress of grievances in the courts, they managed to convey to some Whites the image of being a clean, hard-working, law-abiding people. The completion of the railroad, the flood of former Civil War soldiers into the job market, and the economic depression of 1873 worsened their situation. The Chinese became more frequent victims of open discrimination and hostility. Their positive stereotype among some Whites was widely displaced by a negative one: They were now "conniving," "crafty," "criminal," "the yellow menace." Only after they retreated into Chinatowns and entered specialty occupations that minimized their competition with Whites did the intense hostility abate.

37   One pioneer in the scientific study of prejudice, John Dollard, demonstrated how prejudice against the Germans, which had been virtually nonexistent, arose in a small U.S. industrial town when times got bad:

> Local Whites largely drawn from the surrounding farms manifested considerable direct aggression toward the newcomers. Scornful and derogatory opinions were expressed about the Germans, and the native Whites had a satisfying sense of superiority toward them.... The chief element in the permission to be aggressive against the Germans was rivalry for jobs and status in the local woodenware plants. The native

Whites felt definitely crowded for their jobs by the entering German groups and in case of bad times had a chance to blame the Germans who by their presence provided more competitors for the scarcer jobs. There seemed to be no traditional pattern of prejudice against Germans unless the skeletal suspicion of all out-groupers (always present) be invoked in this place.[31]

38   Both experimental studies and historical analyses have added credence to the economic–competition theory. Muzafer Sherif directed several experiments showing how intergroup competition at a boys' camp led to conflict and escalating hostility.[32] Donald Young pointed out that, throughout U.S. history, in times of high unemployment and thus intense job competition, nativist movements against minorities have flourished.[33] This pattern has held true regionally—against Asians on the West Coast, Italians in Louisiana, and French Canadians in New England—and nationally, with the antiforeign movements always peaking during periods of depression. So it was with the Native American Party in the 1830s, the Know-Nothing Party in the 1850s, the American Protective Association in the 1890s, and the Ku Klux Klan after World War I. Since the passage of civil rights laws on employment in the twentieth century, researchers have consistently detected the strongest antiblack prejudice among working-class and middle-class Whites who feel threatened by Blacks entering their socioeconomic group in noticeable numbers.[34] It seems that any group applying the pressure of job competition most directly on another group becomes a target of its prejudice.

39   Once again, a theory that offers some excellent insights into prejudice—in particular, that adverse economic conditions correlate with increased hostility toward minorities— also has some serious shortcomings. Not all groups that have been objects of hostility (e.g., Quakers and Mormons) have been economic competitors. Moreover, why is hostility against some groups greater than against others? Why do the negative feelings in some communities run against groups whose numbers are so small that they cannot possibly pose an economic threat? Evidently values besides economic ones cause people to be antagonistic to a group perceived as an actual or potential threat.

Social Norms

40   Some sociologists have suggested that a relationship exists between prejudice and a person's tendency to conform to societal expectations.[35] **Social norms**—the norms of one's culture—form the generally shared rules defining what is and is not proper behavior. By learning and automatically accepting the prevailing prejudices, an individual is simply conforming to those norms.

41   This theory holds that a direct relationship exists between degree of conformity and degree of prejudice. If so, people's prejudices should decrease or increase significantly

---

[31]John Dollard, "Hostility and Fear in Social Life," *Social Forces* 17 (1938): 15-26.

[32]Muzafer Sherif, O. J. Harvey, B. Jack White, William Hood, and Carolyn Sherif, *Intergroup Conflict and Cooperation: The Robbers Cave Experiment* (Norman: University of Oklahoma Institute of Intergroup Relations, 1961). See also M. Sherif, "Experiments in Group Conflict," *Scientific American* 195 (1956): 54–58.

[33]Donald Young, *Research Memorandum on Minority Peoples in the Depression* (New York: Social Science Research Council, 1937), pp. 133–41.

[34]Andrew Greeley and Paul Sheatsley, "The Acceptance of Desegregation Continues to Advance," *Scientific American* 210 (1971): 13–19; T. F. Pettigrew, "Three Issues in Ethnicity: Boundaries, Deprivations, and Perceptions," in M. Yinger and S. J. Cutler (eds.), *Major Social Issues: A Multidisciplinary View* (New York: Free Press, 1978); R. D. Vanneman and T. F. Pettigrew, "Race and Relative Deprivation in the United States," *Race* 13 (1972): 461-86.

[35]See Harry H. L. Kitano. "Passive Discrimination in the Normal Person," *Journal of Social Psychology* 70 (1966): 23-31.

when they move into areas where the prejudicial norm is lesser or greater. Evidence supports this view. Thomas Pettigrew found that Southerners in the 1950s became less prejudiced against Blacks when they interacted with them in the army, where the social norms were less prejudicial.[36] In another study, Jeanne Watson found that people moving into an anti-Semitic neighborhood in New York City became more anti-Semitic.[37]

42   John Dollard's study, *Caste and Class in a Southern Town* (1937), provides an in-depth look at the emotional adjustment of Whites and Blacks to rigid social norms.[38] In his study of the processes, functions, and maintenance of accommodation, Dollard detailed the "carrot-and-stick" method social groups employed. Intimidation—sometimes even severe reprisals for going against social norms—ensured compliance. However, reprisals usually were unnecessary. The advantages Whites and Blacks gained in psychological, economic, or behavioral terms served to perpetuate the caste order. These gains in personal security and stability set in motion a vicious circle. They encouraged a way of life that reinforced the rationale of the social system in this community.

43   Two 1994 studies provided further evidence of the powerful influence of social norms. Joachim Krueger and Russell W. Clement found that consensus bias persisted despite the availability of statistical data and knowledge about such bias.[39] Michael R. Leippe and Donna Eisenstadt showed that induced compliance can change socially significant attitudes and that the change generalizes to broader beliefs.[40]

    Although the social–norms theory explains prevailing attitudes, it does not explain either their origins or the reasons why new prejudices develop when other groups move into an area. In addition, the theory does not explain why prejudicial attitudes against a particular group rise and fall cyclically over the years.

    Although many social scientists have attempted to identify the causes of prejudice, no single factor provides an adequate explanation. Prejudice is a complex phenomenon, and it is most likely the product of more than one causal agent. Sociologists today tend either to emphasize multiple-cause explanations or to stress social forces encountered in specific and similar situations—forces such as economic conditions, stratification, and hostility toward an outgroup.

---

[36] Thomas Pettigrew, "Regional Differences in Anti-Negro Prejudice," *Journal of Almormal and Social Psychology* 59 (1959): 28–36.

[37] Jeanne Watson, "Some Social and Psychological Situations Related to Change in Attitude," *Human Relations* 3 (1950): 15–56.

[38] John Dollard, *Caste and Class in a Southern Town,* 3d ed. (Garden City, N.Y.: Doubleday Anchor Books, 1957).

[39] Joachim Krueger and Russell W. Clement, "The Truly False Consensus Effect: An Interadicable and Egocentric Bias in Social Perception," *Journal of Personality and Social Psychology* 67 (1994): 596–610.

[40] Michael R. Leippe and Donna Eisenstadt, "Generalization of Dissonance Reduction: Decreasing Prejudice through Induced Compliance," *Journal of Personality and Social Psychology* 67 (1994): 395–414.

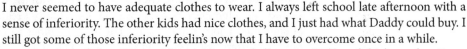

C. P. Ellis
Studs Terkel

1   *We're in his office in Durham, North Carolina. He is the business manager of the International Union of Operating Engineers. On the wall is a plaque: "Certificate of Service, in recognition to C. P. Ellis, for your faithful service to the city in having served as a member of the Durham Human Relations Council, February 1977."*

At one time, he had been president (exalted cyclops) of the Durham chapter of the Ku Klux Klan....

He is fifty-two years old.

Studs Terkel

2   My father worked in a textile mill in Durham. He died at forty-eight years old. It was probably from cotton dust. Back then, we never heard of brown lung. I was about seventeen years old and had a mother and sister depending on somebody to make a livin'. It was just barely enough insurance to cover his burial. I had to quit school and go to work. I was about eighth grade when I quit.

3   My father worked hard but never had enough money to buy decent clothes. When I went to school, I never seemed to have adequate clothes to wear. I always left school late afternoon with a sense of inferiority. The other kids had nice clothes, and I just had what Daddy could buy. I still got some of those inferiority feelin's now that I have to overcome once in a while.

4   I loved my father. He would go with me to ball games. We'd go fishin' together. I was really ashamed of the way he'd dress. He would take this money and give it to me instead of putting it on himself. I always had the feeling about somebody looking at him and makin' fun of him and makin' fun of me. I think it had to do somethin' with my life.

5   My father and I were very close, but we didn't talk about too many intimate things. He did have a drinking problem. During the week, he would work every day, but weekends he was ready to get plastered. I can understand when a guy looks at his paycheck and looks at his bills, and he's worked hard all the week, and his bills are larger than his paycheck. He'd done the best he could the entire week, and there seemed to be no hope. It's an illness thing. Finally you just say: "The heck with it. I'll just get drunk and forget it."

6   My father was out of work during the depression, and I remember going with him to the finance company uptown, and he was turned down. That's something that's always stuck.

7   My father never seemed to be happy. It was a constant struggle with him just like it was for me. It's very seldom I'd see him laugh. He was just tryin' to figure out what he could do from one day to the next.

8   After several years pumping gas at a service station, I got married. We had to have children. Four. One child was born blind and retarded, which was a real additional expense to us. He's never spoken a word. He doesn't know me when I go to see him. But I see him, I hug his neck. I talk to him, tell him I love him. I don't know whether he knows me or not, but I know he's well taken care of. All my life, I had work, never a day without work, worked all the overtime I could get and still could not survive financially. I began to say there's somethin' wrong with this country. I worked my butt off and just never seemed to break even.

9   I had some real great ideas about this great nation. (Laughs.) They say to abide by the law, go to church, do right and live for the Lord, and everything'll work out. But it didn't work out. It just kept gettin' worse and worse.

10   I was workin' a bread route. The highest I made one week was seventy-five dollars. The rent on our house was about twelve dollars a week. I will never forget: outside of this house was a 265-gallon oil drum, and I never did get enough money to fill up that oil drum. What I would do every night, I would run up to the store and buy five gallons of oil and climb up the ladder and pour it in that 265-gallon drum. I could hear that five gallons when it hits the bottom of that oil drum, splatters, and it sounds like it's nothin' in there. But it would keep the house warm for the night. Next day you'd have to do the same thing.

11   I left the bread route with fifty dollars in my pocket. I went to the bank and borrowed four thousand dollars to buy the service station. I worked seven days a week, open and close, and finally had a heart attack. Just about two months before the last payments of that loan. My wife had done the best she could to keep it runnin'. Tryin' to come out of that hole. I just couldn't do it.

12   I really began to get bitter. I didn't know who to blame. I tried to find somebody. I began to blame it on black people. I had to hate somebody. Hatin' America is hard to do because you can't see it to hate it. You gotta have somethin' to look at to hate. (Laughs.) The natural person for me to hate would be black people, because my father before me was a member of the Klan. As far as he was concerned, it was the savior of the white people. It was the only organization in the world that would take care of the white people. So I began to admire the Klan.

13   I got active in the Klan while I was at the service station. Every Monday night, a group of men would come by and buy a Coca-Cola, go back to the car, take a few drinks, and come back and stand around talkin'. I couldn't help but wonder: Why are these dudes comin' out every Monday? They said they were with the Klan and have meetings close-by. Would I be interested? Boy, that was an opportunity I really looked forward to! To be part of somethin'. I joined the Klan, went from member to chaplain, from chaplain to vice-president, from vice-president to president. The title is exalted cyclops.

14   The first night I went with the fellas, they knocked on the door and gave the signal. They sent some robed Klansmen to talk to me and give me some instructions. I was led into a large meeting room, and this was the time of my life! It was thrilling. Here's a guy who's worked all his life and struggled all his life to be something, and here's the moment to be something. I will never forget it. Four robed Klansmen led me into the hall. The lights were dim, and the only thing you could see was an illuminated cross. I knelt before the cross. I had to make certain vows and promises. We promised to uphold the purity of the white race, fight communism, and protect white womanhood.

15   After I had taken my oath, there was loud applause goin' throughout the building, musta been at least four hundred people. For this one little ol' person. It was a thrilling moment for C. P. Ellis.

16   It disturbs me when people who do not really know what it's all about are so very critical of individual Klansmen. The majority of 'em are low-income whites, people who really don't have a part in something. They have been shut out as well as the blacks. Some are not very well educated either. Just like myself. We had a lot of support from doctors and lawyers and police officers.

17   Maybe they've had bitter experiences in this life and they had to hate somebody. So the natural person to hate would be the black person. He's beginnin' to come up, he's beginnin' to learn to read and start votin' and run for political office. Here are white people who are supposed to be superior to them, and we're shut out.

18   I can understand why people join extreme right-wing or left-wing groups. They're in the same boat I was. Shut out. Deep down inside, we want to be part of this great society. Nobody listens, so we join these groups.

19   At one time. I was state organizer of the National Rights party. I organized a youth group for the Klan. I felt we were getting old and our generation's gonna die. So I contacted certain kids in schools. They were havin' racial problems. On the first night, we had a hundred high school students. When they came in the door, we had "Dixie" playin'. These kids were just thrilled to death. I begin to hold weekly meetin's with 'em, teachin' the principles of the Klan. At that time, I believed Martin Luther King had Communist connections. I began to teach that Andy Young[1] was affiliated with the Communist party.

20   I had a call one night from one of our kids. He was about twelve. He said: "I just been robbed downtown by two niggers." I'd had a couple of drinks and that really teed me off. I go downtown and couldn't find the kid. I got worried. I saw two young black people. I had the .32 revolver with me. I said: "Nigger, you seen a little young white boy up here? I just got a call from him and was told that some niggers robbed him of fifteen cents." I pulled my pistol out and put it right at his head. I said: "I've always wanted to kill a nigger and I think I'll make you the first one." I nearly scared the kid to death, and he struck off.

21   This was the time when the civil rights movement was really beginnin' to peak. The blacks were beginnin' to demonstrate and picket downtown stores. I never will forget some black lady I hated with a purple passion. Ann Atwater. Every time I'd go downtown, she'd be leadin' a boycott. How I hated—pardon the expression, I don't use it much now—how I just hated the black nigger. (Laughs.) Big, fat, heavy woman. She'd pull about eight demonstrations, and first thing you know they had two, three blacks at the checkout counter. Her and I have had some pretty close confrontations.

22   I felt very big, yeah. (Laughs.) We're more or less a secret organization. We didn't want anybody to know who we were, and I began to do some thinkin'. What am I hidin' for? I've never been convicted of anything in my life. I don't have any court record. What am I, C. P. Ellis, as a citizen and a member of the United Klansmen of America? Why can't I go to the city council meeting and say: "This is the way we feel about the matter? We don't want you to purchase mobile units to set in our schoolyards. We don't want niggers in our schools."

23   We began to come out in the open. We would go to the meetings, and the blacks would be there and we'd be there. It was a confrontation every time. I didn't hold back anything. We began to make some inroads with the city councilmen and county commissioners. They began to call us friend. Call us at night on the telephone: "C. P., glad you came to that meeting last night." They didn't want integration either, but they did it secretively, in order to get elected. They couldn't stand up openly and say it, but they were glad somebody was sayin' it. We visited some of the city leaders in their home and talked to 'em privately. It wasn't long before councilmen would call me up: "The blacks are comin' up tonight and makin' outrageous demands. How about some of you people showin' up and have a little balance?" I'd get on the telephone. "The niggers is comin' to the council meeting tonight. Persons in the city's called me and asked us to be there."

24   We'd load up our cars and we'd fill up half the council chambers, and the blacks the other half. During these times, I carried weapons to the meetings, outside my belt. We'd go there armed. We would wind up just hollerin' and fussin' at each other. What happened? As a result of our fightin' one another, the city council still had their way. They didn't want to give up control to the blacks nor the Klan. They were usin' us.

25   I began to realize this later down the road. One day I was walkin' downtown and a certain city council member saw me comin'. I expected him to shake my hand because

---

[1] *Andy Young:* Andrew Jackson Young, Jr. (b. 1932), prominent black leader and politician. Young was a friend and adviser of Martin Luther King, Jr., and served as President Jimmy Carter's ambassador to the United Nation. In the 1980s, he was twice elected mayor of Atlanta.

he was talkin' to me at night on the telephone. I had been in his home and visited with him. He crossed the street. Oh shit, I began to think, somethin's wrong here. Most of 'em are merchants or maybe an attorney, an insurance agent, people like that. As long as they kept low-income whites and low-income blacks fightin', they're gonna maintain control.

26   I began to get that feeling after I was ignored in public. I thought: Bullshit, you're not gonna use me any more. That's when I began to do some real serious thinkin'.

27   The same thing is happening in this country today. People are being used by those in control, those who have all the wealth. I'm not espousing communism. We got the greatest system of government in the world. But those who have it simply don't want those who don't have it to have any part of it. Black and white. When it comes to money, the green, the other colors make no difference. (Laughs.)

28   I spent a lot of sleepless nights. I still didn't like blacks. I didn't want to associate with 'em. Blacks, Jews, or Catholics. My father said: "Don't have anything to do with 'em." I didn't until I met a black person and talked with him, eyeball to eyeball, and met a Jewish person and talked to him, eyeball to eyeball. I found out they're people just like me. They cried, they cussed, they prayed, they had desires. Just like myself. Thank God, I got to the point where I can look past labels. But at that time, my mind was closed.

29   I remember one Monday night Klan meeting. I said something was wrong. Our city fathers were using us. And I didn't like to be used. The reactions of the others was not too pleasant: "Let's just keep fightin' them niggers."

30   I'd go home at night and I'd have to wrestle with myself. I'd look at a black person walkin' down the street, and the guy'd have ragged shoes or his clothes would be worn. That began to do somethin' to me inside. I went through this for about six months. I felt I just had to get out of the Klan. But I wouldn't get out.

31   Then something happened. The state AFL–CIO[2] received a grant from the Department of HEW,[3] a $78,000 grant: how to solve racial problems in the school system. I got a telephone call from the president of the state AFL–CIO. "We'd like to get some people together from all walks of life." I said: "All walks of life? Who you talkin' about?" He said: "Blacks, whites, liberals, conservatives, Klansmen, NAACP[4] people."

32   I said: "No way am I comin' with all those niggers. I'm not gonna be associated with those type of people." A White Citizens Council guy said: "Let's go up there and see what's goin' on. It's tax money bein' spent." I walk in the door, and there was a large number of blacks and white liberals. I knew most of 'em by face 'cause I seen 'em demonstratin' around town. Ann Atwater was there. (Laughs.) I just forced myself to go in and sit down.

33   The meeting was moderated by a great big black guy who was bushy-headed. (Laughs.) That turned me off. He acted very nice. He said: "I want you all to feel free to say anything you want to say." Some of the blacks stand up and say it's white racism. I took all I could take. I asked for the floor and cut loose. I said: "No, sir, it's black racism. If we didn't have niggers in the schools, we wouldn't have the problems we got today."

34   I will never forget. Howard Clements, a black guy, stood up. He said: "I'm certainly glad C. P. Ellis come because he's the most honest man here tonight." I said: "What's that nigger tryin' to do?" (Laughs.) At the end of that meeting, some blacks tried to come up shake my hand, but I wouldn't do it. I walked off.

---

[2] *AFL-CIO*: American Federation of Labor and Congress of Industrial Organizations—huge federation of independent labor unions in the United States, Canada, Mexico, Panama, and elsewhere.

[3] *HEW*: Health, Education, and Welfare—at the time, a department of the federal government.

[4] *NAACP*: National Association for the Advancement of Colored People.

35   Second night, same group was there. I felt a little more easy because I got some things off my chest. The third night, after they elected all the committees, they want to elect a chairman. Howard Clements stood up and said: "I suggest we elect two co-chairpersons." Joe Beckton, executive director of the Human Relations Commission, just as black as he can be, he nominated me. There was a reaction from some blacks. Nooo. And, of all things, they nominated Ann Atwater, that big old fat black gal that I had just hated with a purple passion, as co-chairman. I thought to myself: Hey, ain't no way I can work with that gal. Finally, I agreed to accept it, 'cause at this point, I was tired of fightin', either for survival or against black people or against Jews or against Catholics.

36   A Klansman and a militant black woman, co-chairmen of the school committee. It was impossible. How could I work with her? But after about two or three days, it was in our hands. We had to make it a success. This give me another sense of belongin', a sense of pride. This helped this inferiority feelin' I had. A man who has stood up publicly and said he despised black people, all of a sudden he was willin' to work with 'em. Here's a chance for a low-income white man to be somethin'. In spite of all my hatred for blacks and Jews and liberals, I accepted the job. Her and I began to reluctantly work together. (Laughs.) She had as many problems workin' with me as I had workin' with her.

37   One night, I called her: "Ann, you and I should have a lot of differences and we got 'em now. But there's somethin' laid out here before us, and if it's gonna be a success, you and I are gonna have to make it one. Can we lay aside some of these feelin's?" She said: "I'm willing if you are." I said: "Let's do it."

38   My old friends would call me at night: "C. P., what the hell is wrong with you? You're sellin' out the white race." This begin to make me have guilt feelin's. Am I doin' right? Am I doin' wrong? Here I am all of a sudden makin' an about-face and tryin' to deal with my feelin's, my heart. My mind was beginnin' to open up. I was beginnin' to see what was right and what was wrong. I don't want the kids to fight forever.

39   We were gonna go ten nights. By this time, I had went to work at Duke University, in maintenance. Makin' very little money. Terry Sanford give me this ten days off with pay. He was president of Duke at the time. He knew I was a Klansman and realized the importance of blacks and whites getting along.

40   I said: "If we're gonna make this thing a success, I've got to get to my kind of people." The low-income whites. We walked the streets of Durham, and we knocked on doors and invited people. Ann was goin' into the black community. They just wasn't respondin' to us when we made these house calls. Some of 'em were cussin' us out. "You're sellin' us out, Ellis, get out of my door. I don't want to talk to you." Ann was gettin' the same response from blacks. "What are you doin' messin' with that Klansman?"

41   One day, Ann and I went back to the school and we sat down. We began to talk and just reflect. Ann said: "My daughter came home cryin' every day. She said her teacher was makin' fun of me in front of the other kids." I said: "Boy, the same thing happened to my kid. White liberal teacher was makin' fun of Tim Ellis's father, the Klansman. In front of other peoples. He came home cryin'." At this point—(he pauses, swallows hard, stifles a sob)—I begin to see, here we are, two people from the far ends of the fence, havin' identical problems, except hers bein' black and me bein' white. From that moment on, I tell ya, that gal and I worked together good. I begin to love the girl, really. (He weeps.)

42   The amazing thing about it, her and I, up to that point, had cussed each other, bawled each other, we hated each other. Up to that point, we didn't know each other. We didn't know we had things in common.

43   We worked at it, with the people who came to these meetings. They talked about racism, sex education, about teachers not bein' qualified. After seven, eight nights of real

intense discussion, these people, who'd never talked to each other before, all of a sudden came up with resolutions. It was really somethin', you had to be there to get the tone and feelin' of it.

44   At that point, I didn't like integration, but the law says you do this and I've got to do what the law says, okay? We said: "Let's take these resolutions to the school board." The most disheartening thing I've ever faced was the school system refused to implement any one of these resolutions. These were recommendations from the people who pay taxes and pay their salaries. (Laughs.)

45   I thought they were good answers. Some of 'em I didn't agree with, but I been in this thing from the beginning, and whatever comes of it, I'm gonna support it. Okay, since the school board refused, I decided I'd just run for the school board.

46   I spent eighty-five dollars on the campaign. The guy runnin' against me spent several thousand. I really had nobody on my side. The Klan turned against me. The low-income whites turned against me. The liberals didn't particularly like me. The blacks were suspicious of me. The blacks wanted to support me, but they couldn't muster up enough to support a Klansman on the school board. (Laughs.) But I made up my mind that what I was doin' was right, and I was gonna do it regardless what anybody said.

47   It bothered me when people would call and worry my wife. She's always supported me in anything I wanted to do. She was changing, and my boys were too. I got some of my youth corps kids involved. They still followed me.

48   I was invited to the Democratic women's social hour as a candidate. Didn't have but one suit to my name. Had it six, seven, eight years. I had it cleaned, put on the best shirt I had and a tie. Here were all these high-class wealthy candidates shakin' hands. I walked up to the mayor and stuck out my hand. He give me that handshake with that rag type of hand. He said: "C. P., I'm glad to see you." But I could tell by his handshake he was lyin' to me. This was botherin' me. I know I'm a low-income person. I know I'm not wealthy. I know they were sayin': "What's this little ol' dude runnin' for school board?" Yet they had to smile and make like they're glad to see me. I begin to spot some black people in that room. I automatically went to 'em and that was a firm handshake. They said: "I'm glad to see you, C. P." I knew they meant it—you can tell about a handshake.

49   Every place I appeared, I said I will listen to the voice of the people. I will not make a major decision until I first contacted all the organizations in the city. I got 4,640 votes. The guy beat me by two thousand. Not bad for eighty-five bucks and no constituency.

50   The whole world was openin' up, and I was learnin' new truths that I had never learned before. I was beginnin' to look at a black person, shake hands with him, and see him as a human bein'. I hadn't got rid of all this stuff, I've still got a little bit of it. But somethin' was happenin' to me.

51   It was almost like bein' born again. It was a new life. I didn't have these sleepless nights I used to have when I was active in the Klan and slippin' around at night. I could sleep at night and feel good about it. I'd rather live now than at any other time in history. It's a challenge.

52   Back at Duke, doin' maintenance, I'd pick up my tools, fix the commode, unstop the drains. But this got in my blood. Things weren't right in this country, and what we done in Durham needs to be told. I was so miserable at Duke, I could hardly stand it. I'd go to work every morning just hatin' to go.

53   My whole life had changed. I got an eighth-grade education, and I wanted to complete high school. Went to high school in the afternoons on a program called PEP—Past Employment Progress. I was about the only white in class, and the oldest. I begin to read about biology. I'd take my books home at night, 'cause I was determined to get through. Sure enough, I graduated. I got the diploma at home.

54   I come to work one mornin' and some guy says: "We need a union." At this time I wasn't pro-union. My daddy was anti-labor, too. We're not gettin' paid much, we're havin' to work seven days in a row. We're all starvin' to death. The next day, I meet the international representative of the Operating Engineers. He give me authorization cards. "Get these cards out and we'll have an election." There was eighty-eight for the union and seventeen no's. I was elected chief steward for the union.

55   Shortly after, a union man come down from Charlotte and says we need a full-time rep. We've got only two hundred people at the two plants here. It's just barely enough money comin' in to pay your salary. You'll have to get out and organize more people. I didn't know nothin' about organizin' unions, but I knew how to organize people, stir people up. (Laughs.) That's how I got to be business agent for the union.

56   When I began to organize, I began to see far deeper. I began to see people again bein' used. Blacks against whites. I say this without any hesitancy: management is vicious. There's two things they want to keep: all the money and all the say-so. They don't want these poor workin' folks to have none of that. I begin to see management fightin' me with everything they had. Hire anti-union law firms, badmouth unions. The people were makin' a dollar ninety-five an hour, barely able to get through weekends. I worked as a business rep for five years and was seein' all this.

57   Last year, I ran for business manager of the union. He's elected by the workers. The guy that ran against me was black, and our membership is seventy-five percent black. I thought: Claiborne, there's no way you can beat that black guy. People know your background. Even though you've made tremendous strides, those black people are not gonna vote for you. You know how much I beat him? Four to one. (Laughs.)

58   The company used my past against me. They put out letters with a picture of a robe and a cap: would you vote for a Klansman? They wouldn't deal with the issues. I immediately called for a mass meeting. I met with the ladies at an electric component plant. I said: "Okay, this is Claiborne Ellis. This is where I come from. I want you to know right now, you black ladies here, I was at one time a member of the Klan. I want you to know, because they'll tell you about it."

59   I invited some of my old black friends. I said: "Brother Joe, Brother Howard, be honest now and tell these people how you feel about me." They done it. (Laughs.) Howard Clements kidded me a little bit. He said: "I don't know what I'm doin' here, supportin' an ex-Klansman." (Laughs.) He said. "I know what C. P. Ellis come from. I knew him when he was. I knew him as he grew, and growed with him. I'm tellin' you now: follow, follow this Klansman." (He pauses, swallows hard.) "Any questions?" "No," the black ladies said. "Let's get on with the meeting, we need Ellis." (He laughs and weeps.) Boy, black people sayin' that about me. I won one thirty-four to forty-one. Four to one.

60   It makes you feel good to go into a plant and butt heads with professional union busters. You see black people and white people join hands to defeat the racist issues they use against people. They're tryin' the same things with the Klan. It's still happenin' today. Can you imagine a guy who's got an adult high school diploma runnin' into professional college graduates who are union busters? I gotta compete with 'em. I work seven days a week, nights and on Saturday and Sunday. The salary's not that great, and if I didn't care, I'd quit. But I care and I can't quit. I got a taste of it. (Laughs.)

61   I tell people there's a tremendous possibility in this country to stop wars, the battles, the struggles, the fights between people. People say: "That's an impossible dream. You sound like Martin Luther King." An ex-Klansman who sounds like Martin Luther King. (Laughs.) I don't think it's an impossible dream. It's happened in my life. It's happened in other people's lives in America.

62   I don't know what's ahead of me. I have no desire to be a big union official. I want to be right out here in the field with the workers. I want to walk through their factory

and shake hands with that man whose hands are dirty. I'm gonna do all that one little ol' man can do. I'm fifty-two years old, and I ain't got many years left, but I want to make the best of 'em.

63   When the news came over the radio that Martin Luther King was assassinated, I got on the telephone and begin to call other Klansmen. We just had a real party at the service station. Really rejoicin' 'cause that son of a bitch was dead. Our troubles are over with. They say the older you get, the harder it is for you to change. That's not necessarily true. Since I changed, I've set down and listened to tapes of Martin Luther King. I listen to it and tears come to my eyes 'cause I know what he's sayin' now. I know what's happenin'.

POSTSCRIPT

64   *The phone rings. A conversation.*

65   *"This was a black guy who's director of Operation Breakthrough in Durham. I had called his office. I'm interested in employin' some young black person who's interested in learnin' the labor movement. I want somebody who's never had an opportunity, just like myself. Just so he can read and write, that's all."*

Part Four

Casebook: Reading and Writing Argumentative Texts

Crossing Borders of Immigration

Introduction to Part Four

Part Four explores the theme "Crossing Borders of Immigration" and uses texts and writing assignments in which authors argue different points of view on the topic.

- **Chapter 11** focuses on strategies for reading arguments.
- **Chapter 12** reviews a process that helps students develop, write, and polish argumentative paragraphs.
- **Chapter 13** prepares students to write argumentative essays.

At the end of Chapter 13 (p. 286), you will find the texts used for modeling the reading process and in the text-based writing assignments in Part Four: "Living in America: Challenges Facing New Immigrants and Refugees" edited by Katherine Garrett and "Aria" by Richard Rodriguez.

Introduction to the Casebook Theme: Crossing Borders of Immigration

Warm Up

DIRECTIONS: Look at this picture for a moment, then answer the following questions.

1. Explain why you think the children are dressed this way.

2. Explain what you think is the message of this photograph.

3. Write half a page about what you know and believe about immigrants to the US. Go beyond the first ideas that come to you.

Immigration means moving to a new country, usually with the goal of becoming a citizen of that country. The United States is a common destination for immigrants because many people in the world perceive the US as the land of opportunity—where good jobs, education, and other benefits abound. The children in the picture above look rather happy about wearing clothes with the American flag on them.

But leaving the country where you were born and grew up can be a difficult choice, and integrating into the United States can present hardships. Learning a new language, getting used to new ways of thinking and behaving, finding work, and so on means leaving the familiar. It means crossing a border into an unknown future. Many of us know immigrants or are immigrants ourselves. Learning about immigrants' experiences and about the various perspectives present in the conversation about it deepens our national understanding.

Casebook Texts

Immigration is a topic that many people have strong feelings and opinions about; therefore, it is a good topic for argumentation. This casebook includes two texts presenting two quite different perspectives on immigration. "Living in America: Challenges Facing New Immigrants and Refugees" is a research report based on interviews with hundreds of immigrants across the nation. It draws conclusions about their experiences and makes recommendations to reduce barriers many immigrants and refugees face. "Aria" by Richard Rodriguez is a narrative excerpt from his autobiography that tells about his experience learning English as a child and the effects it has had on his identity and family relationships.

This book also contains other texts on related themes of crossing borders, listed below, which you will find in Part Five. You may choose to use these readings to complete the reading and writing practices in this part of the book or your instructor may assign some of them for you to work on.

Introduction to Argumentative Texts

Argumentative writing, like most college reading and writing, communicates one central idea or thesis and then provides evidence to support or prove that thesis. Argumentation is organized around a thesis clearly stating a clear point of view, called a **claim**, on a controversial issue or problem.

In everyday language, an argument is when people disagree with each other and speak sharply about a topic, maybe even yelling. But argumentation in college reading and writing is not this negative, angry type of conversation. Although writers may feel strongly about a controversial issue, argumentative writing should be clear and not overly emotional. Argument in college means presenting reasons and evidence to support one point of view or position, sometimes with the purpose of persuading others to share the point of view or position.

In addition, good argumentative writing requires an understanding of more than one point of view on an issue. While it does put forward one particular position, good argumentation takes into account other perspectives so that the writing is informed and balanced. To read and write it well, you need to understand what others think in the larger conversation about an issue.

Purpose of Argumentation

The purpose of argumentation is always to explain the writer's reasons for taking a particular position on a controversial topic. In addition, the writer may seek to change readers' minds, to convince them of his or her point of view. People usually write argumentation because they think the issue is important and want to explain and perhaps convince others of their way of thinking about it.

Explicit or Implicit Main Ideas and Thesis Statements

When you read argumentative writing, the thesis can be clearly stated. It can also be implied—meaning you have to conclude for yourself what claim the author is communicating. When you compose argumentative college essays, you usually state the thesis. Because the purpose of this type of writing is sometimes to change the reader's point of view, or at least explain with clear evidence why the writer's position is valid, it is important that the reader understand the writer's position. Sometimes, this position may not be clearly stated until the end of the writing. However, you will probably be required to state your argumentative thesis early in your papers.

Organization of Ideas in an Argument Paper

Usually the body of an argumentative text is organized by the major reasons in support of the thesis, each reason being discussed in one or more paragraphs of information that support the reason. Many argumentative texts also include the major reason someone might disagree with the argument and then provide evidence about why the idea is untrue. This is called a rebuttal or refutation.

Types of Evidence Used in Argumentative Writing

Many writers use both information and personal experience (narrative) to support their argumentative thesis statements. Informational evidence is generally considered more valid for supporting opinions on controversial issues, but often, personal experience is used to illustrate a point. Combining informational and narrative evidence provides the best support because information appeals to the intellect while narrative appeals to the heart. Both types of appeal are legitimate strategies when arguing a point.

Types of Language Used in Argumentative Writing

The biggest danger with writing argumentation is to fall into using overly emotional language that turns off readers' attention. It is an easy mistake to make because we usually read or write argumentation because we feel strongly about the position we are taking.

This strong emotion is a great motivator for writing, but it can ruin the persuasiveness of an argument, so it is important to keep too much emotion out of the language used in an argumentative paragraph or essay.

Special Vocabulary for Argumentative Writing

There are a number of specialized terms that are used in argumentative writing. Here is a list of the most common ones with brief definitions of what each means.

- **Controversy** Controversy refers to a dispute or debate over an issue; people argue when they have different opinions about an idea, law, proposal, or other topic that can be understood or addressed in more than one way. All argumentative writing begins with a controversial issue or problem.
- **Problem-Solution Essay** A common type of argument essay, it explains a social problem or issue and its causes and recommends solutions.
- **Claim** The position that a writer takes on a controversial issue is generally called a claim, and this is also the thesis of an argumentative text.
- **Reasons** Reasons are the major supporting ideas for the claim made in a piece of argumentative writing. Often reasons form the topics of body paragraphs in argumentative texts you read and write.
- **Evidence** Each reason in an argument must be supported with concrete, convincing evidence or proof that it is true or right. Often evidence in support of an argument is based on information (facts, statistics, ideas, and examples). In most argumentative writing, personal experience (narration) can also be used as support.
- **Analysis** This is the part of argumentation where the writer explains how the evidence supports the thesis or claim. It is a very important part of argumentation as it connects specific evidence to more general supporting ideas and to the major claim or thesis of the text.
- **Assumptions** These are the unstated and probably unexamined opinions and ideas that underlie an argument and its reasons. It is important to understand your own assumptions on a topic, and to be able to find the unstated assumptions in what you read.
- **Multiple Perspectives** Good argumentation takes into account various perspectives or ways of looking at a controversial topic. Argumentation always offers a particular point of view, but it should also take seriously other viewpoints with different underlying assumptions.
- **Rebuttal/Refutation** Many argumentative texts you read and write contain a rebuttal or refutation section. This is where the writer outlines an opposing viewpoint and then explains why it is not as valid as the view he or she is presenting.
- **Evaluation** When you are reading and writing arguments, it is important to evaluate the validity and reasoning of the author's or your own claims and evidence.
- **Fallacy** A fallacy is a logically unsound reason in an argument, one which does not accurately support the claim.

11   A Reading Process for Argumentative Texts

LEARNING OBJECTIVES

In this chapter, you will learn to . . .

1   Preview before you read argumentative texts.

2   Actively read argumentative texts.

3   Consolidate your comprehension of argumentative texts.

Warm Up

DIRECTIONS: Look at the picture and answer the following questions.

1. What is the Ferris wheel's purpose?

2. How does its structure make it work?

3. How do the parts work together to help it fulfill its purpose?

MySkillsLab
Complete the Warm Up at
www.myskillslab.com

Phase One: Preview the Reading

Learning Objective 1
Preview before you read argumentative texts.

Reading and understanding a written argument requires looking at its structure as well as its ideas and evidence. In other words, you have to bring your critical thinking skills to the task. *Analysis* helps you divide the writing into parts to see the reasoning behind the argument and the evidence used to support it. *Evaluation*, another kind of critical thinking, helps you decide whether the argument is logical and the writer's claim is fully proven with valid evidence. *Considering different perspectives* helps you understand the many points of view on the topics about which you are reading and writing argumentative texts. *Reflection* helps you consider what the author believes but is leaving out—his or her assumptions and point of view.

To demonstrate how a reading process can help you do this thinking work when you read argumentation, this chapter uses "Living in America: Challenges Facing New Immigrants and Refugees," a 2006 research report for the Robert Wood Johnson Foundation, found on page 286. You can complete the practice activities based on "Aria" by Richard Rodriguez on page 307, an essay of your choice from Part Five (see the list of related themes and readings on p. 233), or one assigned by your instructor.

Because the purpose of argumentation is to prove a claim, when you read argumentative texts, you want to look for the claim the author is trying to prove. As you preview "Living in America," "Aria," or another reading, keep in mind the structure of arguments: the overall claim, the supporting reasons or main ideas, the evidence used, and the analysis of the evidence.

STEP 1: Get to Know the Text

The first step prepares you to read and understand an argumentative text by giving you a sense of its ideas and structure.

Scan and Skim the Text

A quick flip though the pages or paragraphs of an argumentative text gives you a feel for the author's claim and reasoning. Scanning helps you estimate how much time you need for reading, and will give you a basic framework for connecting the ideas and details you encounter when you actually read.

Familiarize yourself a bit more with the reading by skimming the introductory and concluding paragraphs, and perhaps the first or last sentences of several paragraphs throughout the piece. If a text does not use headings to identify big ideas in the article or essay, try reading the first sentence of each paragraph.

To explore an argumentative text, you can use the following strategies.

Strategies for Exploring Argumentative Text

1. **Title** Write down what it tells you about the text's topics. See if you can estimate what the author's main claim or point of view might be.
2. **Author** Do research on the author or source of the text, and write down what you find out. *Be sure to apply the CRAAP Test to both the text you are previewing and the online information you locate about the author.*
3. **Organization** Scan the text to look at the organization and structure. Where are the main reasons stated? Note where you find the main claim, reasons, and evidence.
4. **Purpose and Audience** Skim the text, and note what you can gather about its purpose and audience.
5. **Key Words** Choose several, and do some research on them. Write down what you learn about these words. *Remember to use the CRAAP Test when doing research.*

(Information Literacy:) **Key Words and Source Evaluation**

As you skim and scan an argumentative text, you will notice unfamiliar words and concepts that you will need to understand. As part of your previewing, research several of these key concepts using a Google or library search or by talking with a librarian.

Demonstration   Getting to Know the Text

This example shows how one student used the strategies on page 237 about "Living in America." Her use of information literacy skills is labeled.

1. <u>Title</u> The title says this report is about challenges or difficulties that immigrants and refugees face when they come to the US.

2. <u>Author</u> There does not seem to be an author. Something called Lake Snell Perry Mermin/Decision Research did the report for the Robert Wood Johnson Foundation—I have heard of that foundation somewhere before.

   Information Literacy: The Robert Wood Johnson Foundation Web site says it deals with health issues especially for vulnerable people.

   CRAAP Test: the RWJF seems like a legitimate, important group that spends a lot of money on helping the underdogs of this world.

3. <u>Organization</u> It's very helpful to look at the table of contents. I can't tell what the main argument in the report is yet, but the headings seem to show that it's about social issues affecting immigrants like education, jobs, housing, isolation, and discrimination. There are also recommendations at the end about what should be changed. There seem to be two introductions—an executive summary (one-page overview of the whole thing) and an introduction/background section.

4. <u>Purpose and Audience</u> The purpose seems to be telling people about the struggles of immigrants and what to do about it. Audience might be people who help immigrants to get situated when they first come here. It might be especially for people in health areas because that is the focus of RWJF's work.

5. <u>Key Words</u>

   Immigrant: The text uses this word in almost every sentence but never defines it. I believe it is a person who chooses to move to the US and plans to stay here for the rest of their life.

   — The Department of Homeland Security says there are 40 million immigrants in the US and about 1 million legal immigrants come each year.

   — Migration Policy Institute reports that 1 in 5 US children are immigrants or have immigrant parents. "In 2009, there were 32.5 million immigrants age 25 and older. Of those, 26.8 percent had a bachelor's degree or higher, while 32.3 percent lacked a high school diploma."

   Americanizing: becoming like other Americans (text)

   — Wikipedia says it means when people take on the culture and values of the US. Outside the US it means changing another country to be like the US.

— Merriam Webster online: "*to cause to acquire or conform to American characteristics*"

Undocumented: an immigrant who is living in the US without permission (text)

— Merriam Webster's Online Dictionary: "*lacking documents required for legal immigration or residence <undocumented workers>*"

— Internet: A New York Times article said 11 million undocumented immigrants live in the US.

Practice 11.1   Getting to Know the Text

DIRECTIONS: Look at "Aria" by Richard Rodriguez on page 307, or another reading from the list on page 233, or one you have been assigned. Then use the strategies on page 237 to get to know Rodriguez's text.

STEP 2: Check Your Attitude and Set Your Purpose

When reading argumentation, you want to pay attention to how you feel about the topics and ideas you discover. Usually argumentation is about controversial topics that evoke strong emotional responses in readers. Ranging from anger, dismissal, rejection, or fear to more positive ones like excitement, hope, validation, or conviction, strong emotions can affect understanding.

Critical Thinking: Examining Your Assumptions

Assumptions are unexamined, unquestioned beliefs. Often an idea provokes a strong reaction in you because it challenges or supports your beliefs. Assumptions influence how you think about and react to ideas and evidence, and these preformed ideas, biases, or perspectives can close your mind to an author's ideas. Thoughtfully examining your assumptions makes you a better reader and learner. Setting a purpose for reading also helps you focus on understanding an author's ideas rather than just reacting to or agreeing with them. Use the following questions to to check your attitude, examine your assumptions, and set your purpose.

Guide Questions for Checking Attitude, Examining Assumptions, and Setting Purpose

1. How do I feel about the argument I am discovering in this text?
2. What do I know about the argumentative topic?
3. What are my assumptions about the topic?
4. What is my attitude toward this assignment?
5. What is my purpose for reading?

Demonstration   Checking Attitude, Setting Purpose, and Examining Assumptions

The following provides a sample of one student's notes on getting to know the text, using the guide questions on page 239.

1. **How do I feel about the argument I'm discovering in this text?** I'm interested in learning about immigrants and refugees. After looking at this report, I can see that they struggle a lot. I hope that the report gives good suggestions for improving the lives of immigrants.

2. **What do I know about the argumentative topic?** I think immigration is when someone from another country wants to come live in America. Refugees are coming because they are threatened in their home country. They have a hard time when they come and live here, and there might be ways that their challenges can be solved.

3. **What are my assumptions about the topic?** I have heard people say "Everyone in the US is an immigrant, except Native Americans." I believe it is good to bring new people and cultures in. Not sure how I feel about people here illegally—I don't think they are as bad as some people say. There is a lot of unemployment. How do illegal immigrants affect jobs?

4. **What is my attitude toward this assignment?** My only concern is how long this report is. But I'm interested, so it shouldn't be too bad.

5. **What is my purpose for reading this?** My purpose for reading is to learn about immigrants and what struggles they experience.

Practice 11.2   Checking Attitude, Setting Purpose, and Examining Assumptions

DIRECTIONS: Based on your preview of "Aria" or another reading you or your teacher have chosen, answer the guide questions on page 239.

STEP 3: Connect Your Experience and Background Knowledge with the Text

When you read an argument, it is important to be aware of how your personal experiences and knowledge relate to the author's ideas. Examining past experiences and knowledge helps you to be more open-minded and interested in an author's ideas.

The writing assignments for this casebook ask you to build a good argument about immigrants' experiences in the US. The connections you make to your experience and knowledge can help you create strong reasons for the argumentative claim you will make in your paragraph or essay. Often it is useful to formulate more specific questions about the ideas you encounter as you preview. In the following Demonstration, we have modeled how you can create specific questions based on the topic you will read about.

Critical Thinking: Considering Multiple Perspectives

Arguments in readings exist within a bigger conversation. An argument arises out of its historical situation—what is going on politically and economically at the time it is made. An argument, and the reasons provided to support it, is also affected by other people's perspectives. A lot of people have a stake in the larger conversation of how immigrants integrate into US society.

As you come to understand the argument in the "Living in America" immigration report, consider what others might have to say about it. For example, some government officials might want to deport immigrants rather than provide them with better services. They might not want to solve problems that immigrants experience because it will cost more money. Lower-skilled US workers may fear that immigrants will take their jobs. Some health and social service providers might think having to learn about other cultures is impractical when they are already overwhelmed by the problems of the people they currently work with. Learning about other voices in a conversation helps you more fully understand the argument presented in the text, as well as the issue as a whole.

Understanding multiple perspectives usually requires you to do some research. If you start with a Google search, play around with different key words until you find useful information about other perspectives. If you go to the library, start with a list of search terms that your librarian can help you identify.

Guide Questions for Connecting to the Text and Considering Multiple Perspectives

1. What experiences have you had that relate to this text?
2. What do you know about the topic?
3. Taking Perspectives: Who might have an interest in the conversation about the topic of this text?

Demonstration Connecting to the Text and Considering Multiple Perspectives

Here the student reflects about her personal experiences and how they have shaped her ideas about immigration. She also considers alternative perspectives.

1. <u>**What experiences have I had that relate to this text?**</u> When I worked as a checker, lots of foreigners came through my line. Sometimes they spoke really good English and sometimes they couldn't understand me and I couldn't understand them. I felt kind of sorry for them. Here in college, there are lots of people who are immigrants—I think, anyway. There are lots of different languages that I hear spoken in the cafeteria and bookstore and library.

2. <u>**What do I know about the topic?**</u> Probably speaking English is the biggest problem for immigrants. I know that a lot of immigrants speak Spanish, and that some people think undocumented immigrants should be deported immediately. Asia is another place immigrants

(continued)

come from. I know there are 40 million immigrants in the US right now. I know that some people get really annoyed if somebody can't speak the language. I've heard people say stuff like "Go back where you came from."

3. **Who might have an interest in the conversation about the topic of this text?** Well, immigrants and refugees have an interest of course. Teachers I suppose would have a stake in how to teach immigrant children. Doctors and nurses should care about immigrants and refugees, although in the reading there's a lot of misunderstanding by the medical people. President Obama has talked about how broken immigration is in America.

Practice 11.3   Connecting to the Text and Considering Multiple Perspectives

DIRECTIONS: Using "Aria," or another reading, write your own answers to the guide questions on page 241 about connecting to the text and considering alternative perspectives.

Phase Two: While Reading

Learning Objective 2
Actively read argumentative texts.

All the work you do to preview an argumentative reading prepares you to really dig in and understand the author's argument about his or her topic. Learning vocabulary, taking notes, and paying attention to your responses to what you read will deepen your understanding of the author's message. They will also help you analyze, or break down, an author's reasoning and evidence to evaluate if it is accurate and convincing.

These steps are also *prewriting* strategies. For example, your notes on a reading could help you outline a paragraph or essay. Therefore, save all of your notes from this phase of reading because you may want to use them when you write.

STEP 4: Write Down and Define Vocabulary

All the texts you read for this casebook are challenging, and undoubtedly you will encounter words you do not know. Here are some strategies for learning new vocabulary.

Strategies for Learning New Vocabulary

1. **Find and note unknown words** Scan the reading for words you do not know. Highlight the sentences where the words appear. Write down your unknown vocabulary words on a piece of paper or in your Reading Process Journal.
2. **Context** Review the sentences in which the word appear and write down what you think the words mean based on how they are used.
3. **Dictionary** Look up the words in a dictionary (print or online), and write down the definitions.
4. **Internet** Finally, do an Internet search for the words to learn some additional information about them. *Be sure to apply the CRAAP Test to any Internet site used.*

Demonstration   **Defining Vocabulary**

Here is one student's vocabulary work on three words from "Living in America."

1. <u>Words I don't know or I'm not sure about</u>

— discrimination

— connector

— methodology

2. <u>Context/meaning</u>

— **discrimination:** This appears in the executive summary but is not defined. I know that it means treating people unfairly based on something about them like their race or if they have a disability, but I want to see how it's related to prejudice.

— **connector:** Seems to mean someone who connects with immigrants from the report.

— **methodology:** It's the title of a section in the appendix that explains how the researchers got the information. Must mean research methods.

3. <u>Dictionary definition from Merriam-Webster's online</u>

— **discrimination:** "3 a : the act, practice, or an instance of discriminating categorically rather than individually b : prejudiced or prejudicial outlook, action, or treatment <racial discrimination>"

— **connector:** Merriam Webster online says a connector is part of a dental plate!

— **methodology:** "1 : a body of methods, rules, and postulates employed by a discipline : a particular procedure or set of procedures 2 : the analysis of the principles or procedures of inquiry in a particular field." So I got that right.

4. <u>Internet information</u>

— **discrimination** online definition says it means to tell things apart. "Discriminate" means "to make a difference in treatment or favor on a basis other than individual merit." I thought it would be more negative. Googled "the difference between discrimination and prejudice." According to the Sociology Guide Web site, discrimination "is an action which is an unfair treatment directed against someone. It can be based on many characteristics: age, sex, height, weight, skin color, clothing, speech, income, education, marital status, sexual orientation, disease, disability, religion

(continued)

and politics." And prejudice is the attitude or belief that "involves prejudging a group as inferior."

CRAAP Test: The Sociology Guide site is for students studying sociology. It looks legitimate except that it has a place to hire a professional writer to write papers.

— **_connector_**: Online I found a couple of articles about connectors, people who help immigrants get health care or help them connect to community organizations.

Practice 11.4   Defining Vocabulary

DIRECTIONS: List the words you do not understand, and highlight the sentences in which you find them. For each word, record the meaning based on context, the dictionary definition, and any additional information from a brief Internet search. Use the list of strategies on page 242 as a guide.

STEP 5: Take Notes on Major Ideas and Important Details

Taking notes on argumentative writing helps you understand and evaluate the author's reasoning and evidence. When you take notes on an argument, start by writing down what the author is arguing for: the position, claim, or thesis. Usually writers state their major claim early in the article or essay but sometimes not until later. Do not worry if you cannot find it at once. It might take two or more readings to understand thoroughly what the author is advocating. You can always return to the start of your notes to state the author's claim.

Recording major reasons and supporting evidence is important when you take notes on argumentative texts. Mapping and Cornell Notes are effective strategies for taking notes on argumentative texts. We provide a demonstration of Cornell Notes here. Please remember that all notes should be written in your own words, not copied exactly from the text.

Note-Taking Strategy: Cornell Method

The Cornell note-taking system works well with argumentative writing because it helps you see the relationship between reasoning and evidence. In Cornell Notes, you divide a sheet of paper so that one-third of the page is to the left and two-thirds to the right. Then, general or big ideas go on the left, and smaller ideas and details go on the right. For arguments, we recommend putting the overall argument (the author's claim or thesis) at the top, the major reasons on the left, and the supporting evidence for each reason on the right. Put a summary of the notes at the end of each page of notes.

Demonstration   Taking Cornell Notes

The following example shows Cornell Notes for the "Living in America" report.

<u>"Living in America: Challenges Facing New Immigrants and Refugees," report for the Robert Wood Johnson Foundation</u>

Thesis: Immigrants and refugees report that they suffer many obstacles when they first come to the US. Improvements in services for learning English, finding jobs and housing, getting health care, and providing information will help them do better.

Reasons (General)	Evidence (Specific)
1. Hard time getting good education for themselves and their kids.	— ESL classes are valued but sometimes hard to find and get to.
	— Kids fall behind in school—often because of lack of English.
	— Parents can't help their kids in school.
2. Problems getting good jobs and finding good housing.	— Can't get good jobs because of lack of English and sometimes lack of education and sometimes prejudice.
	— Cheap housing that immigrants can get is unsafe and unhealthy.
3. They are isolated from services and communities.	— Most want to become US citizens.
	— Some fear deportation if they try to use services.
	— Immigrants lack health insurance and don't get preventive care.
	— Transportation is not available to get to services—cars are too expensive; public trans. does not serve where they live.
	— They are stressed but fear mental health services.
	— Many feel isolated from cultural traditions; kids Americanize while parents don't.
4. They are discriminated against.	— Mostly at work
	— From law enforcement
	— Also at school
	— In health care
5. Recommendations	— Integrate programs that serve immigrants
	— Make ESL easier; teach US culture
	— Create supports at kids' schools
	— Provide culturally sensitive health and mental health options
	— Add interpreter services and more activities for immigrant kids
	— Make information more easily available about legal rights, citizenship, jobs, starting businesses

(continued)

6. Appendix A: Study Methodology	— Pilot study: initial focus groups with service providers then with immigrants.
	— Providers were trusted
	— Types of questions asked
	— Providers reported services; immigrants reported now knowing about lots of them
	— Phase 2: chose new cities; chose new populations; did more background research on communities and service providers
7. Appendix B: Issues Ranked by Frequency and Prevalence	— 1. lack of legal documents, 2. Lack of English, 3. Exploitation and discrimination, 4. Stress, 5. Mental health issues, 6. Problems with schools, 7. Lack of good jobs, 8. Lack of transportation and physical isolation (especially for women), 9. Safety

Summary: "Living in America," a report by a research group for the Robert Wood Johnson Foundation, reports the findings of 32 focus groups with immigrants and refugees about their early experiences in the US, and 10 focus groups with service providers. They found 5 areas of challenge—education issues, troubles with getting good jobs and housing, isolation, and discrimination. The study recommends changes in services to help immigrants settle in the US with less damage and stress.

Practice 11.5   Taking Cornell Notes

DIRECTIONS: Create Cornell Notes on Rodriguez's essay or another reading of your choice or one that is assigned to you.

Practice 11.6   Taking Cornell Notes on Additional Material

DIRECTIONS: Find one article from your exploratory research in Practice 11.3; choose one that stands up to the CRAAP Test. Then take notes, again using the Cornell Method.

Critical Thinking: Synthesizing Multiple Perspectives

Understanding the bigger context or conversation about any controversial issue requires you to find and understand many sources. Taking notes on them ensures you have a more complete and well-rounded knowledge on the issue. The following Demonstration shows a grid one student created to align ideas from "Mute in an English-Only World" by Chang-rae Lee (p. 321) with ideas in "Living in America."

Demonstration   Synthesizing Texts

	"Living in America" for the RWJF	"Mute in an English Only World" by Chang-rae Lee
Argumentative Claim (thesis)	Immigrants and refugees encounter many obstacles when they first come to the US. Improvements in services for learning English, finding jobs and housing, getting health care, and providing information will help them do better.	Many Americans do not tolerate immigrants' speaking their own languages, and they do not understand the shame that immigrants feel when they cannot speak English—or speak it well.
Major Reasons	1. Poor educational opportunities for adults to learn English and poor help at school for kids. 2. No well-paying jobs or safe affordable housing. 3. Isolation from services. 4. Discrimination and lack of cultural understanding. 5. Better services and outreach will help.	1. Protest in NJ town when Korean businesses put up signs in Korean. 2. Kids have to translate for their parents in daily tasks. 3. Non-immigrants sometimes ignore and shame immigrants who do not speak English.
Types of Evidence	Personal experiences of immigrants and refugees based on focus group interviews; interviews with service providers	An immigrant child's personal experience; news accounts.
Author Perspective	The authors believe it is important to improve the experiences of immigrants and refugees to the US.	The author wants us to understand how painful it is for immigrants when other people ignore them or shame them when they do not speak English.

Practice 11.7   Synthesizing Texts

DIRECTIONS: Create a grid similar to the one above and fill it out based on "Living in America" and another text you have researched.

STEP 6: Write about Your Thoughts and Reactions, and Begin to Evaluate

Writing down your initial reactions to the reading can help you analyze the text. If you notice which ideas or details trigger a response of avid agreement or firm disagreement, then you can read that section more carefully to ensure you understand the author's points and evidence. Also, noticing these reactions can help you start to evaluate the author's claim or thesis, the strength of his or her reasons, and the effectiveness of the evidence. Here are some questions you can use to guide you through this process.

Questions to Guide Your Thoughts, Reactions, and Evaluation

1. What sections of the text cause strong reactions in you, and what are those responses?
2. Look back at your responses in Practice 11.2 on your assumptions. How have your assumptions changed as a result of reading the text?
3. Look back at your notes. Explain whether the evidence from the text convinces you of the author's argumentative claim.
4. If you have not done so, apply the CRAAP Test to the text to evaluate its reliability by noting your observations on its currency, relevance, authority, accuracy and purpose.

Demonstration   Writing about Your Thoughts, Reactions, and Evaluation

1. __What sections of the text cause strong reactions in me?__ The part about housing was upsetting. It does not seem right that immigrants have to live in small places with lots of people sharing, in bad areas with a lot of crime. The examples of discrimination were disturbing too, kids who get teased by classmates and ignored by teachers, people who cannot advance at work. I never really thought about what it would be like to move to a new country to get a better life and then have life be so hard.

2. __How have my assumptions changed as a result of reading the text?__ I still think immigration is basically a good thing. I am more upset by their hard experiences than I was before reading this. It seems that immigrants generally get jobs that pay poorly and have a hard time getting better jobs. I am not as worried about how immigrants affect unemployment.

3. __Does the evidence convince me of the author's argumentative claim?__ Yes, the evidence definitely convinces me that we need to make immigrants' experiences easier and safer.

4. __Apply the CRAAP Test.__ I did this in my reading process. "Living in America" stands up to the CRAAP Test.

| **Practice 11.8** | **Writing about Your Thoughts, Reactions, and Evaluation** |

DIRECTIONS: Answer the Questions to Guide Your Thoughts, Reactions, and Evaluation of "Aria" or another text you are reading for this chapter. Use the demonstration as a guide.

Phase Three: After You Read

Learning Objective 3
Consolidate your comprehension of argumentative texts.

Writing a summary, responding to an author's ideas, and reflecting on your reading process will help you solidify your understanding of the reading.

STEP 7: Write a Summary

Summarizing an argumentative article is a useful after-reading technique because it allows you to make sure you understand the author's claim, reasons, and evidence. It is also a good prewriting step because you may include parts of a summary in a paragraph or essay you will write. Use the following strategies.

Strategies for Writing a Summary

1. Start with a sentence that includes the author, title, and author's major claim.
2. Follow the first sentence of your summary with several sentences that explain the main reasons and evidence provided by the author to support his or her argument.
3. Look back at your notes to guide you as you write your summary.
4. Leave out your opinion about the article or its ideas; only include the author's points.
5. Express the author's ideas into your own words. Avoid copying directly from the reading.

| **Demonstration** | **Writing a Summary of an Argumentative Text** |

The example here shows one student's summary of the first half of the immigration report based on her Cornell Notes. Notice that her summary includes the major claim and the major supporting reasons, but examples are left out.

"Living in America: Challenges Facing New Immigrants and Refugees," is a study done for the Robert Wood Johnson Foundation that advocates for improvements to lessen obstacles to education, housing, and jobs, and decrease discrimination for immigrants. Challenges around education include difficulty getting to ESL programs to learn English, and trouble with the schools immigrants' children go to. Children of immigrants have to learn English before they can learn in school, and many fall behind because their parents cannot help them. Immigrants can often get a job, but it is usually low-paying and without benefits. Because of low pay, it is hard for immigrants to get good housing—they cannot afford safe comfortable places to live.

Practice 11.9   Writing a Summary of an Argumentative Text

DIRECTIONS: Review your Cornell Notes on "Aria" or another selection you are reading for this chapter. Write a summary; be sure to include the author's major claim and reasons. Refer to the list of strategies above the demonstration if you need a guide.

STEP 8: Write an Evaluative Response

Responding to what you read in writing gives you the chance to evaluate the ideas and evidence in the text, ask questions of the text, and make connections between the text and others you have read. It also helps you remember what you have read. However, it is important to keep your response clearly separate from the author's ideas.

Critical Thinking: **Evaluating Arguments for Logos, Pathos, and Ethos**

One aspect of arguments that we have not yet discussed is the type of reasoning that argumentative writers use. Most arguments use appeals to our intellect, our emotions, and our respect for the authority of the author.

- **Logos** refers to intellectual appeals—reasons and evidence that make logical sense or employ facts and verifiable knowledge. An example of logos in "Living in America" is its explanation of five categories of challenges, each supported with specific examples.
- **Pathos** means reasoning that reaches out to our emotions—such as when some immigrants' stories are included as examples in the report. These appeals ask us to feel sympathy and compassion. However, argumentative writers will sometimes appeal to strong negative emotions, such as fear, to convince us to agree with their argument. For example, the fear of crime might convince people to pay higher taxes to support a bigger police force.
- **Ethos** refers to the character and authority of the writer of an argument and whether he or she is reliable and authoritative. Clear organization and an appendix on research methods help to establish ethos in the research report.

Here are some questions you can use to evaluate the logos, pathos, and/or ethos of a piece of argumentative writing:

Guide Questions for Evaluating Logos, Pathos, and Ethos

1. **Logos:** Does the author's thesis seem reasonable? Do the examples, statistics, and other evidence provide enough support for the claim?
2. **Pathos:** What emotional appeals do you see in the text? What beliefs (assumptions) does the author hold that underlie the text's conclusions?
3. **Ethos:** What is the author's perspective or point of view on the topic? What evidence do you have that the author is reliable and trustworthy?

Demonstration   Writing an Evaluative Response of Logos, Pathos, and Ethos

Here is an example of a student's evaluative response to the report, "Living in America."

1. **Logos: Is the thesis reasonable?** It does seem reasonable that society and the government can do better at helping immigrants when they arrive here. **Does the evidence provide sufficient support for the claim?** The evidence here is what actual immigrants and refugees told interviewers during 32 focus groups. That is plenty of evidence to support the need for better services and more coordination.

2. **Pathos: Example of emotional appeals.** Many of the immigrants' and refugees' stories are really sad and some of them make me mad because it seems so unfair for these poor people to be treated harshly. It definitely appeals to my emotions. **What are the authors' assumptions?** The report writers clearly believe that it is important to listen to immigrants, that their experience matters. The authors also seem to assume that non-immigrants should know something about immigrants' cultures.

3. **Ethos: What is the authors' point of view?** This report is clearly based on the idea that immigrants have the right to be here—even illegal ones—and they have a right to good services to help them get settled. **How reliable are the authors?** From my research on authors, I know that the RWJF is mainly concerned about health care for vulnerable people. The RWJF is well known and has a lot of money that they give away for good causes, mainly health care. I could not find any information on the editor, Katherine Garrett.

Practice 11.10   Writing an Evaluative Response of Logos, Pathos, and Ethos

DIRECTIONS: Evaluate "Aria" or another reading for logos, pathos, and ethos using the guide questions on page 250.

STEP 9: Reflect on Your Reading Process

Looking back at your reading process helps you become an even better reader of your college materials. In this case, reflecting on reading an argumentative text helps you understand what steps are most effective for you in understanding and learning the argument in a text. Use the following questions to guide your reflections.

Questions to Guide Your Reflection on Your Reading Process

1. What steps helped you the most to understand the author's ideas and reasoning?
2. Which steps were more difficult and why?
3. What do you intend to do similarly or differently when you read argumentative texts in the future?

Practice 11.11   Reflecting on Your Reading Process

DIRECTIONS: Write a reflection on your reading process for "Aria" or another reading using the guide questions listed on the previous page.

✅ Chapter **Quick Check**   MySkillsLab   Complete the mastery test for this chapter in MySkillsLab.

Use the following questions and answers to check your understanding of this chapter.

QUESTION	ANSWER
Learning Objective 1: Preview before you read argumentative texts. *What steps are included in the first phase of the reading process, "Preview the Reading," that help familiarize you with an argumentative text?*	To preview an argumentative text... ✔ Skim, scan, and look at the title and headings in order to get a sense of the content and organization of the text. Try to determine the author's argumentative thesis. ✔ Check your attitude about and purpose for reading the argumentative text. Also examine your own beliefs and assumptions about the topic or thesis of the reading. ✔ Activate your background knowledge by thinking about what you already know about the topic(s) in the text. Increase your understanding of the larger conversation by researching a variety of perspectives on the issue.
Learning Objective 2: Actively read argumentative texts. *What steps are included in the second phase of the reading process, "While Reading," that help you fully understand argumentative texts?*	To actively read an argumentative text... ✔ Write down vocabulary words that you do not understand and look them up in a dictionary or research them on the Internet. ✔ Take notes on the author's argumentative claim, main reasons and supporting evidence. The Cornell Method is an effective way to take notes on argumentative texts because it clearly separates general reasons from specific evidence. ✔ Take notes on additional articles or other material that help you understand the larger conversation about the topic or issue. ✔ Make note of interesting or confusing information from the reading. Use your reactions to the text to begin evaluating its effectiveness.
Learning Objective 3: Consolidate your comprehension of argumentative texts. *What steps are included in the third phase of the reading process, "After You Read," that help you consolidate your understanding of argumentative texts?*	To consolidate your understanding of an argumentative text... ✔ Write a summary of the main ideas in the reading, making sure to include all the reasons in support of the author's argumentative thesis or claim. ✔ Respond to an argumentative text by evaluating it for logos, pathos, and ethos, and for the author's perspective. ✔ Synthesize various argumentative texts to see how each contributes to the larger conversation on the issue. ✔ Reflect on the effectiveness of your reading process.

A Process for Writing Argumentative Paragraphs

12

LEARNING OBJECTIVES

In this chapter, you will learn to...

1   Prewrite to compose an argumentative paragraph.

2   Draft an argumentative paragraph.

3   Revise and edit an argumentative paragraph.

Warm Up

DIRECTIONS: Take a moment to study the picture. Then answer the following questions.

1. Is this a good way to persuade someone of your point of view? Why or why not?

2. What are some effective ways to convince someone to agree with your point of view?

3. How could you create an image like this one to represent effective persuasion?

MySkillsLab
Complete the Warm Up at
www.myskillslab.com

Phase One: Prewriting

Learning Objective 1
Prewrite to compose an argumentative paragraph.

Doing the preliminary work of prewriting for an argumentative paragraph is more important than for any other type of writing. Arguments require careful planning to ensure that the ideas are clear and fresh, the evidence appropriate and valid, the analysis effective, and the organization logical.

In this chapter, we will illustrate the process of writing an argumentative paragraph using the reading selections introduced in Chapter 11: "Living in America: Challenges Facing

New Immigrants and Refugees" (The Robert Wood Johnson Foundation) on page 286 and "Aria: A Memoir of a Bilingual Childhood" by Richard Rodriguez on page 307. You can complete the practices in this chapter using these two casebook readings or find another reading on the topic of a barrier or challenge that new immigrants face in the US from this text (see list on p. 233), a resource such as a periodical, or your instructor.

STEP 1: Analyze the Assignment

The first step in preparing to write an argumentative paragraph is to look closely at your assignment to make sure that you understand your professor's instructions. Answer the following questions, either on paper or in your mind, to ensure you understand what is expected. If you are ever unsure about any of the answers to these questions, ask your instructor for help.

1. What is the purpose, goal, or objective of this assignment?
2. Who is the intended audience of the paper?
3. What is the central topic you will need to write about?
4. Can you imagine meaningful things to say about this topic?
5. What type of support are you supposed to use in this assignment?
6. What organizational structure will you need to use?
7. How will this assignment be graded?

Practice 12.1 Analyzing the Assignment

DIRECTIONS: Read the following assignment, and use the questions listed above to check whether you understand it. If you have any questions, ask your instructor to clarify.

Paragraph Assignment

PURPOSES: The first purpose is to understand the features of an argumentative paragraph: a topic sentence offering an argumentative claim, evidence, and analysis. The second is to write a thoughtful, developed, and cohesive argumentative paragraph. Finally, writing this paragraph will help you write an essay later, because the structure of a paragraph is similar to that of an essay, and you may be able to use your paragraph in the body of your essay.

AUDIENCE: Write your paragraph for an audience that you think would be interested or could benefit from your ideas. You may write your paper for other college students not in this class.

TOPIC: This paragraph will make an argument about an obstacle or barrier that US immigrants experience.

Assignment

- Submit one paragraph about a barrier or challenge that new immigrants face when they come to the US. The paragraph will argue in support of a claim (a clear point of view) about the obstacle. The claim should address a cause or a solution to a challenge. Please use at least two sources to provide evidence of your claim and reason.
- The paragraph needs a clear topic sentence that provides a focused topic for the paragraph, the claim, or point of view on that topic, and one reason why the claim is true.
- The paragraph should contain ten or more sentences that support, or develop, the topic sentence. It should use evidence from class reading(s) to develop the claim in the topic sentence. The supporting ideas and details should come from authors' texts, and you will need to explain or analyze how their ideas and evidence support your claim.
- Name the authors whose ideas you are using to avoid plagiarism. If you use quotations, provide the page numbers where the quoted sentences appear in the original texts. Put the page number in parentheses at the end of the quoted sentence.
- The paragraph needs to be edited for grammar, spelling, and punctuation.

How Your Paragraph Will Be Graded

1. **Topic Sentence** Argumentative paragraphs have a topic sentence that states the topic, the claim or position you are arguing for, and the reason(s) that will be supported in the paragraph. All other sentences in the paragraph should support the topic sentence with evidence and analysis of the evidence.
2. **Organization** The argumentative paragraph is cohesive: Each sentence connects to the topic sentence. The ideas and details in the paragraph follow a logical order such as deductive or inductive, most to least important, comparison–contrast, or process steps. The explanation and details work together to support or prove the topic sentence.
3. **Development and Support** The topic sentence is supported with enough evidence and analysis to convince readers. The paragraph should use at least two class readings and at least one direct quotation from each source. Credit should be given to sources used, including author and page number of every quotation.
4. **Editing** Grammar mistakes are corrected and the paragraph is proofread for missing words, extra words, or unclear meaning.

STEP 2: Generate Ideas

The next step in the process of writing an argumentative paragraph is to generate lots of ideas that you might use in your writing. This assignment tells you that you have to write about the challenges immigrants experience, so the topic or issue is provided. But you need to decide what part of this topic you will write about, and what your claim will be. You also must use the ideas of authors you have read in this casebook or for this assignment. A good place to start generating ideas is to review the ideas of the authors.

Critical Thinking: Considering Multiple Perspectives

The best argumentative writing takes into account more than one perspective on the topic as it presents evidence in support of its claim. Authors each have their own particular ideas and emphasis as they argue for a particular claim. Using more than one author's ideas in your writing helps establish your credibility and adds to the effectiveness of your argument.

Generate Ideas by Reviewing Reading Notes

Since your assignment requires you to use evidence from class readings, a good first step is to review your notes from Chapter 11 to see what ideas interest you and seem most convincing. Use the following list of guide questions to help you identify the ideas you are interested in writing about.

Guide Questions for Reviewing Reading Notes

1. List the authors whose ideas relate to your assignment. What claim does each of these authors make about your assignment topic? What evidence do they give to back up their conclusions? What is their perspective on the topic?
2. What do you think about these authors' arguments? Are the arguments logical and well supported? Is the evidence each presents convincing to you?
3. Does each author stand up to the CRAAP Test (p. 5)?

As you look at the Demonstration review of authors' ideas below, pay attention to the various perspectives that these authors put forward.

Demonstration   Generating Ideas by Answering Questions about Readings

Here the student answers the questions listed above for two readings: "Living in America" and "Aria."

1. <u>List Author's Claim, Evidence, and Perspective</u>

   <u>"Living in America" RWJF</u>

   — <u>Claim:</u> This report makes suggestions on how to improve immigrants' experiences when they first come to the US. The report describes the troubles they have and recommends solutions.

   — <u>Evidence:</u> Comes from focus group interviews with new immigrants and refugees from lots of other countries. The researchers did 32 focus groups in 10 different cities.

   — <u>Perspective:</u> The report is written from the perspective of people who work with immigrants and refugees.

   <u>"Aria," Richard Rodriguez</u>

   — <u>Claim:</u> His argument is that he is forced to give up Spanish in order to speak English.

   — <u>Evidence:</u> His evidence came from his own personal experience as the son of Mexican immigrant parents. He was born in the US, so he was a citizen, but he didn't feel like one because he could not speak English. He thought English was a public language and Spanish was a private language. He felt left out of public life—including in school. His family stops speaking Spanish at home to help Richard learn English. Then as he learns English and feels better at school, his family life changes. Home feels less close and warm when everyone speaks English not Spanish.

   — <u>Perspective:</u> Rodriguez's perspective is as the child of an immigrant family. He explains and analyzes his own experience.

2. <u>Evaluate Authors' Arguments and Evidence</u>

   These readings speak from the actual experience of newcomers to the US—that makes them valid in my mind. Their stories touch me. The report is probably the best argument because it is a research study with a clearly stated methodology. The researchers led focus groups with hundreds of immigrants and dozens of service providers.

3. <u>Apply the CRAAP Test</u>

   Yes. The authors stand up to the CRAAP Test, which I did during my reading process.

Practice 12.2   Generating Ideas by Reviewing Your Reading Notes

DIRECTIONS: Review the reading selections that you might use in your paragraph. Then write out your answers to the guide questions on page 255.

STEP 3: Focus Your Topic

For an argumentative writing assignment, you need to choose a topic and decide what claim you will make about it in your paragraph. This creates a main idea that is narrow enough to support in one paragraph. For the assignment in this chapter, your claim and reason should be about an obstacle that immigrants face.

Use the following strategies to help you focus your topic:

Strategies for Focusing Your Topic
1. Choose which authors you want to include in your paragraph.
2. Identify what ideas and evidence are most convincing.
3. Based on the ideas and evidence you have generated, identify the focused topic you want to write about, and your claim (point of view) about it.
4. List the reasons why your point of view is true, and choose the best ones.

Demonstration   Focusing a Topic by Reflecting on an Author's Ideas

In the following example, the student finds a focused topic by reflecting on the authors' ideas she just reviewed.

1. **Authors:** "Living in America" and "Aria" make strong arguments about barriers.

2. **Most convincing ideas and evidence.**

   — In "Aria," Rodriguez faced a lot of difficulty not speaking English. He gives lots of details about what school was like for him because he could not speak English—it is a touching story.

   — "Living in America" identifies lots of convincing reasons and evidence that immigrants face hardships and why. Lacking English is one of the hardships that lead to a lot of other problems. The report includes quotes from immigrants as evidence too.

3. **Focused topic and claim (point of view) about it:** I want to write about not knowing English. I think it is the hardest challenge because it causes so many problems for immigrants.

4. **List the reasons why your point of view is true, and choose the best ones.**

   ✔ It's hard on kids in school.

   It keeps people from feeling like they belong.

   ✔ Immigrants cannot get good jobs.

   It keeps immigrants from finding help with things like health care.

Practice 12.3   Focusing Your Topic

DIRECTIONS: Write down your responses to the focusing strategies listed above to find a focused topic for your argumentative paragraph.

Drafting a Topic Sentence

Each argumentative paragraph needs a controlling idea that all other ideas in the writing support. In academic writing, it is most often expected that you will state this point clearly in a sentence. In a paragraph, you put this idea in a topic sentence. Argumentative topic sentences should include the following:

Topic sentence = *topic* + <u>claim (opinion/point of view/argument about topic)</u> + *reason(s)*

You can draft your topic sentence at various points in the writing process. You may do so as you generate ideas or organize. You may have to draft the entire paragraph to find what you want to say in a topic sentence. Finally, you may write a topic sentence and then later revise it as you discover what you want to say in your writing.

Demonstration   Drafting a Topic Sentence

Here the student creates a topic sentence for her paragraph about a claim, or argument, about a challenge faced by immigrants.

1. **What is the focused topic of your paragraph?** Not knowing English

2. **What claim (opinion or argument) do you want to make about this topic?** Not knowing the English language is one of the biggest challenges that immigrants face.

3. **What reason or reasons will you include about why the claim is true?** Not knowing English keeps immigrants from learning in school and getting good jobs.

4. **Write a topic sentence that tells your topic, claim, and reason.**

         topic   claim

Not being able to speak English <u>is the biggest challenge immigrants face because it</u>

<u>keeps them from learning in school and getting good jobs</u>

                       reasons

5. **Consider whether your topic sentence is the right size for a paragraph—not too broad and not too narrow.** This might be a giant topic, but if I concentrate on how the report explains it and then use Rodriguez as my example, that should keep it focused enough for one paragraph.

Practice 12.4   Drafting a Topic Sentence

DIRECTIONS: Write down your responses to the prompts demonstrated above. Then write your topic sentence write a topic sentence for your paragraph.

STEP 4: Develop Support for an Argumentative Paragraph

The purpose of development in argumentative writing is to provide support to convince your readers that your claim is true. In argumentative paragraphs, support takes the form of reasons and evidence. Once you have determined the claim you want to convince readers of, you need to decide why it is true—your reasons. An argumentative paragraph can have one or two or even three reasons in support of the claim. The number of reasons you choose depends on how much explanation and evidence you need to fully support each reason. Each reason needs evidence: *quotations, facts, narrative examples, details,* or other information. Like any other academic paragraph, an argumentative paragraph needs analysis to tie the evidence to the main idea or claim.

Demonstration Developing Your Ideas by Listing Reasons, Evidence, and Analysis

The student writer tries out two reasons in support of the claim in her topic sentence. This exercise helps her decide that she has enough supporting evidence for a paragraph.

Topic Sentence: Not being able to speak English is the biggest challenge immigrants face because it keeps them from learning in school and getting good jobs.

Reason #1: Lacking English means it is hard to get good jobs.

— **Evidence for Reason #1:** The report says employers want workers who can speak English.

— **Analysis of Evidence:** Immigrants cannot get good housing or health care or even food if they do not find good-paying jobs.

Reason #2: Not speaking English makes it impossible for kids to learn in school.

— **Evidence for Reason #2:** Richard Rodriguez was silent in his classroom and dreaded when the teachers asked him questions. "Living in America" says that children sit in the classroom and do not understand what is going on.

— **Analysis of Evidence:** Immigrant kids will fall behind and lose the benefits of education.

Practice 12.5 Developing Your Ideas by Listing Reasons, Evidence, and Analysis

DIRECTIONS: Use the process of listing to decide whether you have enough evidence to write a well-supported paragraph. If it appears you need more evidence, you can add a third reason with evidence and analysis. Be sure to revise your topic sentence if you add a third reason.

Information Literacy: Using Quotations to Support an Argument

Most of the paragraph will be written in your own words, so it is expected that you will summarize authors' ideas, using your own words. However, sometimes using the exact words of authors can help you to provide a convincing argument. In order to use quotations effectively, keep in mind the following:

- *Select Quotations That Support Your Argument* Direct quotations should be used only to help your argument. In other words, they should help make your points crystal clear. A quote could provide important background information or information about your reason or evidence. It can also contribute to your analysis. In the following

Demonstration, our student writer considers possible sentences from "Living in America" and "Aria" to include in her paragraph.

- ***Tell Where Quotations Come From*** Whenever you use the ideas or exact words of someone else, you must give credit to the source of the words or ideas (see Part 6, p. 375). In the Demonstration, notice how the student includes the page numbers of the quotes in parentheses at the end of each one.

Demonstration   Developing Ideas by Selecting Quotations

Here the student listed some quotes she could use from "Living in America," evaluated the contributions they would make to her paragraph, and decided which ones to use.

<u>Source:</u> "Living in America: Challenges Facing New Immigrants and Refugees," edited by Katherine E. Garrett

- "Parents in this study expressed their most intense frustration on the issue of schooling in the United States. They value education highly and believe a good education is the key to success for their children" (287). <u>I like this quote because it tells how important education is to immigrant parents. But that's not really my point. Not this one.</u>

- "'The problem is we have arrived recently and the kids don't know the language, the teachers are Americans and [the children] might not even understand what the lesson is all about. They go to the same classes as the kids born here and they might end up sitting in the class without understanding anything,' said a Somali refugee from Minneapolis" (288). <u>This quote is good because it supports the idea that immigrant kids have language barriers at school. This one works.</u>

- "Even low-paying jobs that historically required little or no English are now demanding some language skills" (290). <u>Good quote about jobs and English. Use.</u>

- "Many immigrants and refugees who came to the United States equipped with advanced degrees and professional backgrounds are no more immune. Engineers spend years driving cabs; cabinet ministers work as security guards, 'jobs that Americans don't want' said one connector to refugees from Sierra Leone in Washington, D.C." (290). <u>This quote might be too long. May use.</u>

Practice 12.6   Developing Your Ideas by Selecting Quotations

DIRECTIONS: Follow the process demonstrated above to find quotes for your paragraph.

1. Make a list of possible sentences to quote in your paragraph from one or more readings (be sure to name each source).
2. Write about each quotation and the contribution it would make to the paragraph and whether you will use it.

STEP 5: Organize Your Ideas

Now you can consider how to organize your ideas and details. Usually argumentative paragraphs are organized from general to specific with analysis at the end. However, they can also be organized in the opposite way, from specific to general: The evidence and reason come first, and then analysis, and finally the claim. Deciding on the order of your ideas before you write makes writing the first draft much easier. It helps you determine whether your ideas and supporting details flow together well and if your reasoning makes sense. One way, as discussed in Chapter 10, is to use outlining. Another way is to map.

Mapping Claim, Reasons, Evidence, and Analysis

Mapping is particularly useful for organizing an argumentative paragraph because it helps you *see* the relationships among ideas and details.

Demonstration Organizing Your Ideas by Mapping Claim, Reasons, Evidence, and Analysis

Now that the student writer has written her topic sentence, chosen reasons and evidence, and written analysis, she is using mapping to decide how to order her information.

Claim
Not being able to speak English is the biggest challenge immigrants face because it keeps them from learning in school and getting good jobs.

Reason 1
Immigrants have a hard time getting jobs that pay well enough to actually support their families.

Evidence
"Even low-paying jobs that historically required little or no English are now demanding some language skills" (290). "Many immigrants and refugees who came to the United States equipped with advanced degrees and professional backgrounds are no more immune. Engineers spend years driving cabs; cabinet ministers work as security guards, 'jobs that Americans don't want' said one connector to refugees from Sierra Leone in Washington, D.C." (290).

Reason 2
Another reason that not speaking English is immigrants' biggest challenge is they cannot learn in school if they cannot speak the language.

Evidence
"Living in America": "The problem is we have arrived recently and the kids don't know the language, the teachers are Americans and they might not even understand what the lesson is all about. They go to the same classes as the kids born here and they might end up sitting in the class without understanding anything,' said a Somali refugee from Minneapolis'" (288). Richard Rodriguez: "But in part I couldn't believe that English could be my language to use. (In part I did not want to believe it.)" (307). "Silent, waiting for the bell to sound, I remained dazed, diffident, afraid" (307).

Analysis
Not being able to speak English causes huge problems for immigrants—it hurts them financially because it affects their job prospects. And it hurts them educationally. Since education and jobs are two of the most important ways of living a good life, helping immigrants learn English is important.

DIRECTIONS: Create your own map to plan out the order of your ideas or use another method of planning your paragraph, like outlining, if you prefer.

Phase Two: Draft

Learning Objective 2
Draft an argumentative paragraph.

At this stage in the writing process, you are finally ready to put all your ideas together into a well-written paragraph. This is your first full draft of an argumentative paragraph, but you still have time to make the paragraph better in the final polishing phase.

When you draft your paragraph, be sure to provide transitions to connect ideas. For example, when moving from your first to your second reason, use a word or phrase to signal the change to readers. For a review of transition words, see page 48 in Chapter 3. In addition, remember to add sentences that introduce or explain your quotations.

STEP 6: Draft Your Paragraph

If you have questions about the structure of a paragraph, review Chapter 3. Remember that paragraphs should have a topic sentence, support, and analysis.

Demonstration   **Drafting an Argumentative Paragraph**

Here is the students' first draft of her paragraph, based on her map on page 261.

> Not being able to speak English is the biggest challenge immigrants face because it keeps them from getting good jobs and learning in school. Immigrants have a hard time getting jobs that pay well enough to actually support their families. The report "Living in America: Challenges Facing Recent Immigrants and Refugees" states, "Even low-paying jobs that historically required little or no English are now demanding some language skills"(290). If immigrants can speak little or no English, employers will not hire them. Even immigrants with lots of education from their home countries can have trouble getting work. The report says, "Engineers spend years driving cabs; cabinet ministers work as security guards, 'jobs that Americans don't want' said one connector to refugees from Sierra Leone in Washington, D.C." (290). Another reason that

not speaking English is immigrants' biggest challenge is they cannot learn in school if they cannot speak the language. "Living in America" reports, "'The problem is we have arrived recently and the kids don't know the language, the teachers are Americans and [the kids] might not even understand what the lesson is all about. They go to the same classes as the kids born here and they might end up sitting in the class without understanding anything,' said a Somali refugee from Minneapolis'" (288). In his autobiographical essay "Aria," Richard Rodriguez tells about being a kid who could speak only Spanish when he started school. He did not feel like he belonged, and he was uncomfortable and unhappy in school. When his teachers asked him questions and told him to speak up loudly to the whole class, Rodriguez mumbled or stayed quiet. He writes, "Silent, waiting for the bell to sound, I remained dazed, diffident, afraid" (307). Not being able to speak English causes huge problems for immigrants—it hurts them financially because it affects their job prospects. It hurts their educational opportunities. Since education and jobs are two of the most important ways of living a good life, helping immigrants learn English is essential.

Practice 12.8   **Drafting Your Paragraph**

DIRECTIONS: Write the first draft of your argumentative paragraph using your map or outline.

Phase Three: Polish

Learning Objective 3
Revise and edit an argumentative paragraph.

Following the final three steps of the process for writing a good argumentative paragraph will help you to make sure you have written the best paragraph you can.

STEP 7: Revise

An excellent way to find what to improve in your first draft is to compare what you have written to the assignment to ensure you have met all the criteria. You start by creating questions based on the assignment. Then you (or a peer reader) can answer the questions to see how well the draft meets the requirements. The following demonstration shows one student's self-review based on the argumentative paragraph assignment on page 254.

Demonstration   Creating Guidelines for Self-Review

Our student created the following list of questions based on the assignment on page 254.

1. **Topic Sentence:** Does the topic sentence state the topic, the claim or position I am arguing for, and the reason(s) that will be supported in the paragraph? *Yes, my topic sentence states my topic and point of view plus my two reasons.*

2. **Organization:** Is the paragraph cohesive? Does each sentence connect to the topic sentence? Do the ideas and details in the paragraph follow a logical order such as deductive or inductive? Do the evidence and analysis work together to support or prove the topic sentence? *My paragraph is arranged deductively, with my claim first and reasons and evidence after. The order makes sense because all the sentences about jobs flow together, and then all the sentences on education. I will consider whether education should go before jobs. My analysis on both reasons is similar, so I decided to put all my analysis together at the end of the paragraph.*

3. **Development and Support:** Is the topic sentence supported with enough evidence and analysis to convince readers? Does the paragraph use at least two class readings and at least one direct quotation from each source? Is credit given to sources used, including author and page number of every quotation? *My evidence is good—I have two sources. I use two quotations from "Living in America" and one from "Aria," and I tell the author and page of each quote. There might be too many direct quotes—perhaps I should put one of the quotations from the report into my own words. I'll have to remember to give the page number even if I paraphrase it, though.*

4. **Editing:** Are grammar mistakes corrected? Is the paragraph proofread for missing words, extra words, or unclear meaning? *I worked with the instructor during office hours on my grammar. She helped me correct a couple run-ons and misspellings.*

Practice 12.9   Revising by Completing a Self-Review Questionnaire

DIRECTIONS: Using the Demonstration above as a model, complete a self-review based on the assignment on page 254. Use your self-review to make improvements to your first draft.

Critical Thinking: **Evaluating Logos, Pathos, and Ethos**

Another means of reviewing your writing to find ways to improve content is to analyze it for logos, pathos, and ethos (see page 250). Use the following questions:

- **Logos:** What parts of the argumentative paragraph use logic and facts to make intellectual appeals? How much of the paragraph is devoted to this type of reasoning?

- **Pathos:** What parts of the paragraph appeal to the emotions of the audience? How much of the paragraph uses this type of appeal?

- **Ethos:** How does this paragraph help the audience feel confident in your ideas? How do you establish your credibility as a writer?

Demonstration   Revising by Evaluating for Logos, Pathos, and Ethos

Here the student uses the questions above to evaluate her paragraph for logos, pathos, and ethos.

Logos: Every time I use the report "Living in America," the evidence is logical because the source is a research report from a respected foundation. The order of the sentences makes sense—they move from general to specific.

Pathos: The quotes and details from Rodriguez appeal to emotions. It is not overly emotional.

Ethos: This paragraph uses good sources: a report from a famous organization and the memoir of a famous writer, Rodriguez. I think it's well organized, and that helps people take me seriously. All of this establishes my ethos.

Practice 12.10   Revising by Evaluating for Logos, Pathos, and Ethos

DIRECTIONS: Write answers to the questions on page 264 to evaluate your use of the three appeals: logos, pathos, and ethos.

STEP 8: Edit and Proofread

Once you have reviewed and improved global issues—which include the topic sentence, support, organization, and use of logos, pathos, and ethos—it is time to edit your paper for grammar and spelling errors. Use your own writing to practice identifying and fixing grammar, punctuation, and spelling errors. This will help you move from finding errors in the writing of others to identifying it in your own writing. To edit your paragraph, try any of the following suggestions.

1. **Read your paper out loud to yourself.** Read slowly, and read every word. You will probably find some sentences that do not make sense or words that are missing. Fix these.
2. **Circle all of the punctuation, author names, and page numbers around each quotation you have used.** Check to see that you have given the correct information and that you have punctuated correctly.
3. **Have another person read the paper.** This should be someone who has not previously seen it. Have that person mark any sentences or words that do not make sense to him or her. While this person might not be a grammar expert, he or she can give you feedback about sentences that are not "reader friendly" and therefore could use editing.
4. **Work with a tutor in your school's writing center or other tutoring center.** Have this person read your paper and work with you to edit any sentences that are not clear.
5. **Have your instructor look at your paper and mark for grammar and spelling in one paragraph.** Then, look at his or her marks. Try to find similar errors in the remaining paragraphs and fix them.

Practice 12.11   **Editing and Proofreading**

DIRECTIONS: Choose at least two of the editing strategies listed above and use them to edit and proofread your paragraph. When you have made all the corrections to your paragraph, it is ready to turn in.

STEP 9: Reflect on Your Writing Process

In this final stage of the writing process, you think back on the steps you took to arrive at your final, polished draft. Reviewing your process is helpful so that the next time you write, you can change what did not work and repeat what did. Another approach is to discuss your process with a classmate. The following questions can act as a guide for your reflection.

1. **How did you grow as a writer through the process of composing this paper?** Are there phases or steps of the process that are getting easier or harder for you?
2. **How did this process of writing an argumentative paragraph help you grow as a reader?** Did it help you understand the readings more completely? Was it easy or hard to write about the authors' ideas?
3. **What do you see as the strengths of your essay?** Start with content (ideas and information), and then go to organization and style (organization, language, tone, etc.)
4. **What do you think are the weaknesses of your writing?**
5. **If you had more time or inclination, would you make any other changes to your writing?** If so, what?
6. **What will you do differently next time you write a paper?** Did you discover any new steps or strategies you would like to work on in the future?

Practice 12.12   **Reflecting on Your Writing Process**

DIRECTIONS: Write out answers to the questions above to reflect on your writing process.

✅ Chapter **Quick Check**   MySkillsLab   Complete the mastery test for this chapter in MySkillsLab.

Use the following questions and answers to check your understanding of this chapter.

QUESTION	ANSWER
Learning Objective 1: Prewrite to compose an argumentative paragraph. *How do I prewrite for an argumentative paragraph?*	To prewrite for an argumentative paragraph... ✔ Make sure you understand the assignment. ✔ Review reading process notes and think about the sources you will use in your writing. ✔ Choose your sources and focus your ideas by identifying the evidence. ✔ Create an argumentative topic sentence that includes the topic and an opinion or claim about the topic. ✔ Use mapping to plan your paragraph including topic sentence, reasons, evidence, quotations, and analysis.
Learning Objective 2: Draft an argumentative paragraph. *How do I draft an argumentative paragraph?*	To draft an argumentative paragraph... ✔ Write your first full draft based on a map or outline that lists your claim, reason, evidence, and analysis.
Learning Objective 3: Revise and edit an argumentative paragraph. *How do I revise and edit an argumentative paragraph?*	To revise and edit an argumentative paragraph... ✔ Use techniques such as a self-review based on the writing assignment to find ways to improve the paragraph's topic sentence, overall structure, development, and organization. ✔ Revise based on an evaluation of logos, pathos, and ethos. ✔ Have your teacher or a writing center tutor check your work to identify types of errors you made. ✔ Get to know the patterns of sentence errors you tend to make. ✔ Practice fixing your sentence mistakes, especially the ones you tend to repeat.

LEARNING OBJECTIVES

In this chapter, you will learn to...

1   Prewrite for an argumentative essay.

2   Draft an argumentative essay.

3   Revise and edit an argumentative essay.

Warm Up

DIRECTIONS: Look at the picture and then answer these questions to warm up for this chapter.

1. Make a list of ideas that this picture might illustrate (for example, "collaboration").

2. Write a short paragraph about how the picture might represent the process of learning or writing about a complex problem or issue.

3. Write a few sentences about how this image could help you write a good essay.

MySkillsLab
Complete the Warm Up at
www.myskillslab.com

Phase One: Prewriting

Learning Objective 1
Prewrite for an argumentative essay.

Preparing to write an argumentative essay requires exploration of ideas and careful planning. Following are prewriting steps that will help you create a convincing and thoughtful essay that argues a claim or point of view about the challenges immigrants face.

This chapter demonstrates the process of writing an argumentative essay using the texts "Living in America: Challenges Facing New Immigrants and Refugees" (p. 286) and "Aria: A Memoir of a Bilingual Childhood" by Richard Rodriguez (p. 307). You can complete the practices in this chapter using these two casebook readings, another reading on immigrants' experiences in this text (see list on p. 233), or a resource such as a newspaper or magazine article.

STEP 1: Analyze the Assignment

To make sure you fully understand what you are being asked to write, analyze your assignment using the guide questions listed here. This helps you get the best start possible on prewriting and drafting your essay.

1. What is the purpose, goal, or objective of this assignment?
2. Who is the intended audience of the paper?
3. What is the central topic you will need to write about?
4. Can you imagine meaningful things to say about this topic?
5. What type of support are you supposed to use in this assignment?
6. What organizational structure will you need to use?
7. How will this assignment be graded?
8. How do you feel about responding to this assignment (*eager and ready, afraid, unsure, etc.*)?
9. What questions do you have about this assignment?

Practice 13.1   Analyzing the Assignment

DIRECTIONS: Read the following assignment, and use the questions listed above to check whether you understand it. If you have any questions, ask your instructor to clarify.

Essay Assignment

PURPOSES This assignment is designed to encourage you to think carefully about the experience of immigrants. The second purpose is to practice using course readings to support your ideas about immigrants' experiences. The third purpose is to show you how to structure an argumentative essay written to persuade readers of your argumentative claim or thesis—in this case about a problem, its major cause, and a potential solution. Finally, the assignment asks you to apply what you are learning about grammar to your own writing to make it as correct as possible.

AUDIENCE Write this essay for other students like yourselves beginning their college education who could benefit from learning about immigrants.

ASSIGNMENT Write an argumentative problem-solution essay on a problem experienced by immigrants, a major cause of the problem, and a solution to the problem. In a problem solution essay, you aim to convince readers that the problem *is* a problem. You also persuade readers what is the cause of the problem. Finally, you advocate for a solution to the problem.

- **Thesis** Your paper will identify a problem many immigrants experience and your suggested solution to it. Your thesis, or your argumentative claim, needs to answer this question: *What hardship or barrier do immigrants experience, what is its primary cause, and how might the hardship or barrier be lessened or solved?*
- **Support** The body of your essay needs to provide evidence that the immigrants' problem or barrier exists, evidence of the cause, and evidence that your solution solves the problem. Most of your supporting evidence should come from the selections you have read for this casebook—"Living in America" and "Aria" or other selections you have read. You must use at least two sources in your paper, and body

---

(continued)

paragraphs must contain direct quotations from your sources with correct citations. Argumentative body paragraphs also need analysis to explain how the reasons and evidence work to support your thesis. Each body paragraph needs to illustrate strong paragraph structure.

> **Extension:** Add to the complexity of your essay by using an additional source of evidence. The source could be from an interview with an immigrant or someone whose parents or grandparents are immigrants. Or the source could be government documents that provide statistical information on immigration and immigrants' experience. You can also extend by adding an additional problem, cause, or solution to your paper.

- **Organization** This essay should have an introduction containing your thesis, at least three body paragraphs that support your thesis, and a conclusion. In your paper, you will want to use transitions to create connections between paragraphs. Your essay must be coherent in that each topic sentence and related paragraph contribute to supporting your claim or argumentative thesis. You may use any of the following organizational structures for your paragraphs and essay: general to specific, specific to general, or emphatic order (order of importance). Other modes of organization might also work well; ask your professor if you want to try a different one.

  > **Extension:** You may include one to two additional sources of evidence to provide more support. Or you may extend by adding up to three additional body paragraphs presenting additional causes and solutions.

- **Format** The length should be between two and four pages, typed, double-spaced, in 12-point font, with 1-inch margins. You do not need a cover page; instead, put your name, date, and class number at the top.

  > **Extension:** Your essay will be longer if you choose to write the extended paper. Plan on writing a three- to five-page essay.

How Your Essay Will Be Graded

1. **Thesis** Does your paper have a clear argumentative thesis that answers the assigned question *"What hardship or barrier do immigrants experience, what is its primary cause, and how might the hardship or barrier be lessened or solved?"* in one or two clear sentences?

2. **Support** Does the body of the essay support your thesis with body paragraphs on problem(s), cause(s), and solution(s)? Is there enough evidence from authors you have read to fully support your topic sentences and thesis? Does the body make use of direct quotations that are correctly cited?

3. **Paper Organization** Does the paper follow basic essay structure (introduction, body, conclusion)? Does each paragraph connect to the one previous to it and to the thesis? Are transitions used to show connections between ideas?

   - **Introduction and Conclusion** Does the introduction catch the reader's attention, provide necessary background information about sources, and state the argumentative thesis? Does the conclusion review your thesis, ideas, and evidence, reflect on their significance, and connect back to the introduction?

   - **Paragraph Organization** Does the order of body paragraphs lead the audience along a clear line of reasoning that includes problem, cause, and solution? Does each body paragraph have a topic sentence linked to the argumentative thesis? Are quotations carefully chosen and correctly inserted and cited? Does each paragraph contain analysis of the evidence?

4. **Grammar and Mechanics** Is the paper well edited and proofread for grammar and mechanics? Do the sentences convey meaning clearly to readers?

STEP 2: Generate Ideas

The next step in the process for writing an argumentative essay is to consider ideas that you could write about. The assignment in this chapter is to write an argumentative essay about hardships or barriers immigrants face, their causes, and solutions. Further, the essay must use the ideas of authors you have read. A good place to start getting ideas and evidence for your essay is to review the ideas of the authors.

In addition, you might gather facts from government sources, ideas from political or news organizations (be sure to understand their biases and assumptions), or visual media such as films. In the following Demonstration, the student reviews ideas from the reading selections in this casebook. In addition, he adds ideas from an interview with a family friend whose parents emigrated from Mexico.

Demonstration   Generating Ideas by Reviewing Notes

Here is the T-Chart the student compiled from the readings "Living in America" and "Aria," as well as from the student's interview of a family friend. He highlighted the ideas he decided to focus on in his paper.

	"Living in America"	"Aria"	Tonio, son of immigrant parents
Problems immigrants face	Lack of good education Lack of good jobs and housing Isolation from services and communities Bad transportation Discrimination	Lack of speaking English Feeling isolated Feeling like he did not belong	Dad (Luis) got fired for missing work when helping out in a family emergency Tonio believed he was not chosen for high school basketball team because of his ethnicity
Causes of the Problems	Lack of English skills Discrimination	Poor English instruction at school Parents' poor English skills	Lack of cultural understanding
Solutions	Better communication about services Good educational opportunities Teaching cultural awareness to service providers	Learning English and practicing English	Nonimmigrants learning about other cultures

Practice 13.2   Generating Ideas by Reviewing Notes

DIRECTIONS: Create a T-Chart like the one above and fill it out using the readings in this chapter or those you have chosen. If you are doing the assignment extension, include information from additional sources and/or an interview you have conducted.

STEP 3: Focus Your Topic

For an argumentative assignment, you need to decide what claim you will make in your thesis. For an essay, the claim must be focused but still broad enough to require several supporting paragraphs, so you need a claim that you can find several reasons for defending. For the assignment in this chapter, you want to focus on the causes of and solutions to barriers or challenges faced by immigrants to the US.

Demonstration   Focusing by Highlighting and Freewriting

Here the student finds his focus by reflecting on ideas and evidence from the sources that he has just reviewed.

1. **Highlight the ideas you want to use from your T-Chart or other brainstorming.** The student highlighted the ideas he wanted to use in his paper in his T-Chart above.

2. **What evidence do the authors use to support their ideas? Which evidence is most compelling?**

— "Living in America": This evidence is very solid because it is based on interviews with hundreds of immigrants and dozens of service providers. The conclusions are valid because the evidence is valid. The evidence is more informational.

— Rodriguez: His story is really detailed, and it describes how he felt not knowing English. This is narrative evidence that will put some emotion into my paper.

— Tonio: His stories about himself and his father are also narrative. They are also more recent.

3. **Choose which authors' ideas you want to write about and say why.**

I want to write about the challenges of speaking English and finding good jobs as the biggest barriers, and "Living in America," the report for the Robert Wood Jonhnson Foundation, and "Aria" by Richard Rodriguez provide really good support. I'm going to do the extension, so I will add my neighbor, Tonio, whose parents emigrated from Mexico to the US.

Practice 13.3   Focusing by Highlighting and Freewriting

DIRECTIONS: Follow the prompts below.

1. In the T-Chart you created to review ideas from your sources in Practice 13.2, highlight the ideas you want to use in your paper.

2. What supporting evidence do the authors use to support each of their claims? Which support is most compelling?

3. Choose which authors' ideas you want to write about and say why.

Create a Thesis

The thesis of an argumentative essay contains your *claim*, or the position you advocate about your topic. Your assignment is to write an argumentative essay about a problem immigrants experience, a major cause of the problem, and a solution. Therefore, your claim or thesis should identify these things and tell how they relate to each other. If you are planning to extend your essay by adding a second problem, cause, or solution, your thesis should include these too. By including these subtopics in your thesis, you let readers know what is coming in your essay. You can always adjust your thesis later if you find a new direction or new support.

Here is a formula for developing a thesis for an argumentative problem-solution essay:

Argumentative Thesis = *topic* + _point of view_ + *Problem(s)* + *Cause(s)* + *Solution(s)*

In a problem-solution essay, your point of view is expressed in the problem you choose, the cause you are proposing, and the solution you advocate.

Demonstration   Creating a Thesis for an Argumentative Essay

The student here has decided to extend his essay by offering two problems, two causes, and two solutions. Therefore, he creates a thesis that addresses the topics of his extended argumentative essay.

1. List the topic, problem(s), cause(s), and solution(s) you plan to include in your paper.

   Topic: Barriers or challenges that immigrants face

   Point of view: the barriers can be solved

   Problems: isolation and finding work

   Causes: lack of English and discrimination

   Solutions: education to learn English and job skills, and education of nonimmigrants about cultures and immigrants

2. Write a thesis that combines these things. Immigrants' worst barriers are isolation and difficulty finding work, which are caused mostly by their lack of English language skills and discrimination, **but these barriers can be lessened** with better education to improve English and cultural understanding.

3. Is this thesis the right size for an essay, not too narrow and not too broad? I think this is a great thesis! It includes all six paragraph topics: two problems, two causes, and two solutions.

Practice 13.4   Creating a Thesis for an Argumentative Essay

DIRECTIONS

1. List the topic, point of view, problem(s), cause(s), and solution(s) you plan to include in your essay.

2. Write a thesis that combines these elements.

3. Evaluate whether this thesis is the right size for an essay, not too narrow and not too broad.

STEP 4: Develop Your Ideas

In this casebook, your writing is argumentative, and the support you provide comes from the materials of the course. To create a well-developed essay, you must include enough support from the authors and other sources to convince your readers of your argument. Good argumentation often makes use of both informational and narrative supporting evidence.

Using Quotations

Since you must find support from the readings you are using to support your claim (thesis), using quotations is important. However, every supporting idea from an author cannot be quoted, so it is expected that you put some of the authors' ideas into your own words.

Direct quotes should be used only to help support your argument. In other words, they should help make your points crystal clear. Every time you use a direct quotation in a paragraph, make sure that you fully explain how it supports your ideas. The quote could provide important background information or support for your points. It can also contribute to your analysis.

Information Literacy: **Tell Where Quotations Come From**

Whenever you use the ideas or exact words of someone else, you must give credit to the original source. The following Demonstration shows how to add supporting quotations to develop an essay. Notice how the student includes source information (authors' names or the titles of sources) in his sentences and puts the page numbers of quotations in parentheses at the end.

Demonstration   Developing Ideas by Finding Quotations and Paraphrasing

This student has decided to do the full extension, writing two paragraphs each on problems, causes, and solutions and adding a third source. He includes informational and narrative evidence in all six body paragraphs. The demonstration below shows his development work for the first three paragraphs.

Thesis: Immigrants' worst barriers are isolation and difficulty finding work, which are caused mostly by their lack of English language skills and discrimination, but these barriers can be lessened with better education to improve English and cultural understanding.

— **Paragraph 1 Problem: Isolation**

Informational Support: "Living in America" – "isolation from services that could help them, as well as the emotional isolation caused by the stress" (286).

Narrative Support: Richard could not communicate with classmates and teachers since he didn't know any English.

— **Paragraph 2 Problem: Lack of good jobs**

Informational Support: In the report "Living in America," the researchers say, "Many immigrants and refugees feel stuck in low-level jobs and describe numerous barriers to advancing" (289).

— **Paragraph 3 Cause: Discrimination**

Informational Support: Researchers say, "Mexican and Central and South American immigrants in this study told many stories of harassment, poor treatment, inconsistent wages, and health and safety violations at work," say the researchers in "Living in America" (295).

Narrative Support: My neighbor Tonio tells a story about his father Luis who got fired from his job for missing too may days of work. Luis's boss did not understand that family comes first in Chicano culture, and Luis and Tonio's family had to help take care of relatives who were injured in a car accident.

Practice 13.5 — Develop Your Ideas by Finding Quotations and Paraphrasing

DIRECTIONS

1. List the problem(s), cause(s), and solution(s) your essay will present.
2. For each, find one supporting quotation. Be sure to include the page number in parentheses.
3. For each, write one paraphrase you want to include as support in your essay.
4. Where possible, choose *at least* one informational and one narrative supporting idea for each paragraph.

STEP 5: Organize Your Ideas

Now you can decide on the order in which you will present your ideas and paragraphs in the body of your argumentative essay. Deciding on the organization makes writing the first draft much easier. It helps you see whether your ideas and details flow together well and if your reasoning makes sense. Traditionally, body paragraphs in a problem-solution essay are used to first define the problem, then explain its cause, and, finally, offer a solution. If you are writing the extended essay with additional problems, causes, and solutions, you will need to decide the order of the additional paragraphs.

The following Demonstration offers an example of a formal outline which helps show the relationship between the student writer's ideas and the supporting evidence he uses from his sources.

Demonstration — Outlining an Argumentative Essay

This student writer gave careful consideration to the order of his body paragraphs. He wanted to make sure that his ideas built on each other and that he did not simply list the problems, causes, and solutions in his paper. Notice how each topic sentence builds from the ideas of the previous paragraph and keeps the thesis idea alive.

This demonstration provides topic sentences for all six body paragraphs, and supporting evidence and analysis for three of them.

I. **Introduction**

   a. Attention Getter

   b. Introduction to my topic and background information

   c. Thesis: Immigrants' worst barriers are isolation and difficulty finding work, which are caused mostly by their lack of English language skills and discrimination, but

(continued)

these barriers can be lessened with better education to improve English and cultural understanding.

II. **Body Paragraph 1: First Challenge – Isolation**

a. Topic Sentence: One of the biggest barriers immigrants face in the US is isolation from information about rights, from health care and other services, and from teachers and other students in school.

b. Support: "Living in America" – "isolation from services that could help them, as well as the emotional isolation caused by the stress" (286).

c. Support: Richard could not communicate with classmates and teachers since he didn't know any English.

d. Analysis: I will explain how isolation makes it harder for immigrants to fit in and be successful.

III. **Body Paragraph 2: Second Challenge – Lack of getting and keeping good jobs**

a. Topic Sentence: Another huge barrier for immigrants is getting and keeping well-paying jobs.

IV. **Body Paragraph 3: Cause 1 – Discrimination**

a. Topic Sentence: One of the main reasons that immigrants face isolation and problems with employment is discrimination.

b. Supporting Quote 1: Researchers say, "Mexican and Central and South American immigrants in this study told many stories of harassment, poor treatment, inconsistent wages, and health and safety violations at work" (Robert Wood Johnson Foundation 295).

c. Support 2: My neighbor Tonio tells a story about his father Luis who got fired from his job for missing work. Luis's boss did not understand that family comes first in Chicano culture, and Luis and Tonio had to help take care of relatives who were injured in a car accident.

d. Analysis: The general public often does not understand the cultural values of immigrants—like the family orientation of many Mexican immigrant families. The lack of understanding can lead to more hardships like feeling ashamed and losing jobs.

V. **Body Paragraph 4: Cause 2 – Lack of English skills**

a. Topic Sentence: Probably the biggest cause of hardships immigrants face is the lack of English skills.

VI. **Body Paragraph 5: Solution 1 – English education**

a. Topic Sentence: Immigrants—both parents and their children—need access to good English language education.

    b. <u>Support 1:</u> "Because learning English is a priority, ESL classes may be the most valued service for new immigrants and refugees" (Robert Wood Johnson Foundation 287).

    c. <u>Support 2:</u> The immigration report states, "Many instructors do much more than just teach English in their ESL classes: they teach about banking, how to interact with police, and how to obtain health care as well as dealing with immigration issues" (299).

    d. <u>Support 3:</u> In Richard Rodriguez's case, English improvement happened at home. Once his English improved, he felt like he could participate in school. One day he answered a question in class, and everyone understood him. "That day I moved very far from being the disadvantaged child I had been only days earlier. Taken hold at last was the belief, the calming assurance, that I belonged in public" (308).

    e. <u>Analysis:</u> English is the key for immigrants to participate in all aspects of life in the US and start to solve their hardships. If they can speak the language, they can start to ask for help, they can understand what is going on in classes, and they can take better care of their own needs.

VII. <u>Body Paragraph 6: Solution 2 – Cultural awareness education for nonimmigrants</u>

    a. <u>Topic Sentence:</u> To lessen the discrimination and isolation that immigrants often experience, nonimmigrants need to learn about the cultures of immigrants.

VIII. <u>Conclusion</u>

    a. Summary of thesis and supporting ideas

    b. Reflect on the importance of the issue; answer "so what?"

    c. Leave the reader with a point of significance or something to do

Practice 13.6   Outlining an Argumentative Essay

DIRECTIONS: Create a formal outline for your essay using the above model.

Phase Two: Draft

Learning Objective 2
Draft an argumentative essay.

In this phase you write out your first full draft, using all the preparation you did in the prewriting phase.

STEP 6: Draft Your Essay

During the drafting stage, you put together the ideas you have generated during prewriting into one complete essay. Remember that this is your first attempt at creating a strong essay, but it is not the final step. You will still have time to revise and polish your writing so it reflects your best work.

Introductory Paragraph

If you need to review how to write an introduction, look back at Chapter 3 on structuring essays. Even if you remember the basic structure of an introduction, you may have questions about how to write one for an argumentative paper. Here are some guidelines you can use:

Guidelines for Writing an Argumentative Essay Introduction

1. **Attention Getter**
   a. Brainstorm various perspectives in the current conversation about your topic. (Look back at the background research you did during your reading process, for example Practice 11.2 on page 240 and Practice 11.3 on page 242.)
   b. Brainstorm a list of stories you could tell to introduce your topic and thesis.
   c. Brainstorm a list of questions you could use to begin your introduction.
   d. Find or review statistics on your topic that you could use to start your essay.
2. **Background** Write one-sentence summaries of the sources you will use in your paper.
3. **Choose** which attention getter you will use, and write a draft introduction that includes an attention getter, background information, and your thesis statement.

Demonstration   Writing an Introduction for an Argumentative Essay

1. <u>Attention Getter</u>

   a. <u>Perspectives:</u> President Obama says immigration is broken, and he supports reform to help undocumented immigrants become citizens. Conservatives want closed borders to stop illegal immigration. Liberals want better programs to help immigrants succeed in the US, like the DREAM Act.

   b. <u>Stories:</u> Rodriguez's feeling like English was not his language to speak. A story from "Living in America," but those are not very detailed. Tonio's story about his high school basketball coach.

   c. <u>Questions:</u> What is it like to come to the US for the very first time, to leave family and culture behind? Why is the conversation about immigration often about what "we" should do about "them"? Shouldn't we be considering what immigrants experience, not just what to do about them?

   d. <u>Statistics</u>

   — The Department of Homeland Security says there are 40 million immigrants in the US, and about 1 million legal immigrants come each year.

   — The Migration Policy Institute says there are about 40 million immigrants in the US.

   — Children's Policy Initiative reports that one in five US children are immigrants or have immigrant parents. "In 2009, there were 32.5 million immigrants age 25 and older.

Of those, 26.8 percent had a bachelor's degree or higher, while 32.3 percent lacked a high school diploma."

2. <u>Background</u>

The report "Living in America: Challenges Facing New Immigrants and Refugees" presents what it is like for recent immigrants when they come to the US. Richard Rodriguez is a well-known author who wrote "Aria," an excerpt from his autobiography about learning English as a young child of Mexican immigrants. My neighbor Tonio is the son of parents who emigrated from Mexico 20 years ago; he has lots of immigration stories to tell.

<u>Draft Introduction</u>

Immigration is in the news a lot lately. Politicians like President Obama and members of Congress are debating on what to do about illegal immigrants who have been in the US for a long time working without the proper paperwork. There are 40 million immigrants in the US, 11 million of them undocumented, according to the Department of Homeland Security. That is about 12 percent of the US population. Shouldn't we be considering what immigrants experience, not just what to do about them? We don't usually hear directly from immigrants—illegal or legal—about what their experience is like coming here. The report "Living in America: Challenges Facing New Immigrants and Refugees" presents what it is like for recent immigrants when they come to the US. Richard Rodriguez is a well-known author who wrote "Aria," an excerpt from his autobiography about learning English as a young child of Mexican immigrants. My neighbor Tonio is the son of parents who emigrated from Mexico 20 years ago; he has lots of immigration stories to tell. All three of these sources helped me to understand how hard it can be to come to a new country and try to fit in and survive, much less succeed. Immigrants' worst barriers are isolation and difficulty finding work, which are caused mostly by their lack of English language skills and discrimination, but these barriers can be lessened with better education to improve English and cultural understanding.

Practice 13.7   Writing an Introduction for an Argumentative Essay

DIRECTIONS: Use the guidelines on page 278 to draft your argumentative introduction.

Body Paragraph Structure

Return to Chapter 3 if you need to review the basics of writing body paragraphs. In argumentative essays, each body paragraph should contain a clear main idea in support of the thesis, plenty of supporting evidence, and analysis to connect the support to the main idea or thesis. Use the first sentence of each body paragraph to connect it to the previous paragraph's idea and/or to the thesis. Paragraphs can be arranged in deductive (general to specific) or inductive (specific to general) order.

Practice 13.8   Writing the Body Paragraphs for an Argumentative Essay

DIRECTIONS: Use your outline to draft your body paragraphs. Organize them deductively or inductively.

Conclusion

Review Chapter 3 to refresh your memory on the structure of concluding paragraphs if necessary. Use the following guidelines to help you write a conclusion for an argumentative essay:

Guidelines for Writing an Argumentative Essay Conclusion

1. Write a three-sentence summary of the thesis and main supporting ideas in your paper.
2. Reflect on the importance of the issue; answer the question "so what?"
3. Connect back to the attention getter used in your introduction.
4. Write a final question or suggest a particular action to take based on the ideas in your essay.
5. Put these ideas together to write a full conclusion paragraph.

Demonstration   Writing a Concluding Paragraph for an Argumentative Essay

1. **Summary** Immigrants face a number of hardships and barriers when they come to the US, and the most difficult ones are being isolated and not getting good jobs. These problems are caused mainly by lacking good English language skills and by the discrimination they encounter. The solution is education, better, more accessible English instruction for immigrants, and education about immigrants' cultures and values to lessen discrimination.

2. **Importance** Immigrants make up 12 percent of the US population. They are a big part of our society.

3. **Connect to introduction** Instead of talking about what should be done about them, we should include them in our thinking of what it is to be American.

4. **Final thought or action** It is everyone's responsibility to help immigrants to adjust and become comfortable in their new land.

Conclusion Paragraph

   Immigrants face a number of hardships and barriers when they come to the US, and the most difficult ones are being isolated and not getting good jobs. These problems are caused mainly by *lacking good English language skills and by the discrimination they encounter. The solution is education, better, more accessible English instruction for immigrants, and education about immigrants' cultures and values to lessen discrimination. Immigrants make up 12 percent of the US population. They are a big part of our society. Instead of talking about what should be done about them, we should include them in our thinking of what it is to be American. It is everyone's responsibility to help immigrants to adjust and become comfortable in their new land.*

Practice 13.9 **Writing the Conclusion for an Argumentative Essay**

DIRECTIONS: Follow the guidelines on page 280 to draft your concluding paragraph.

Phase Three: Polish

Learning Objective 3
Revise and edit an argumentative essay.

Revising means you re-envision your paper by looking closely at its content and structure. On the other hand, editing means you look closely at your sentences to ensure they are correct and well written. Enlisting the help of your classmates, teacher, and tutors can help you to make your paper the best it can be.

STEP 7: Revise

An excellent way to get ideas to improve your first draft is to review your draft in relation to the assignment. Using the assignment, you can ask questions about how well an essay draft meets each requirement. We have created questions based on the argument essay assignment in this chapter. Answering these questions in writing, for your draft or for a classmate's essay, provides excellent guidance for revising an argumentative paper.

Guidelines for Self-Review Based on the Assignment

1. **Thesis** Does your paper have a clear argumentative thesis that answers the assigned question, *"What hardship or barrier do immigrants experience, what is its primary cause, and how might the hardship or barrier be lessened or solved?"* in one or two clear sentences?
2. **Support** Does the body of the essay support your thesis with body paragraphs on problem(s), cause(s), and solution(s)? Is there enough evidence from authors you have read to fully support your topic sentences and thesis? Does the body make use of direct quotations that are correctly cited?
3. **Paper Organization** Does the paper follow basic essay structure (introduction, body, conclusion)? Does each paragraph connect to the one previous to it and to the thesis? Are transitions used to show connections between ideas?
   Introduction and Conclusion Does the introduction catch the reader's attention, provide necessary background information about sources, and state the

(continued)

argumentative thesis? Does the conclusion review your thesis, ideas, and evidence, reflect on their significance, and connect back to the introduction?

Paragraph Organization Does the order of body paragraphs lead the audience along a clear line of reasoning that includes problem, cause, and solution? Does each body paragraph have a topic sentence linked to the argumentative thesis? Are quotations carefully chosen and correctly inserted and cited? Does each paragraph contain analysis of the evidence?

4. **Grammar and Mechanics** Is the paper well edited and proofread for grammar and mechanics? Do the sentences convey meaning clearly to readers?

Practice 13.10   Revising Using Self Review

DIRECTIONS: Review your own paper by answering the questions above, and on page 281, derived from the essay assignment. Alternatively, exchange your paper with a classmate and complete the questions as a peer review.

Critical Thinking: **Revise by Evaluating for Logos, Pathos, and Ethos**

Most arguments employ appeals to our intellect (logos), our emotions (pathos), and our respect for the authority of the author (ethos).

- **Logos** refers to intellectual appeals—reasons and evidence that make logical sense or employ facts and verifiable knowledge. Also, the logical order of paragraphs and evidence within paragraphs contributes to logos.
- **Pathos** means reasoning that reaches out to our emotions. These appeals ask us to feel sympathy and compassion. However, argumentative writers will sometimes appeal to strong negative emotions, such as fear, to convince us.
- **Ethos** refers to the character and authority of the writer of an argument and whether he or she is reliable and authoritative. Several things contribute to establishing a writer's ethos: the quality of evidence and sources, the clarity of organization, the careful use of pathos, educational credentials, and/or personal experience related to the topic.

Demonstration   Revising by Evaluating for Logos, Pathos, and Ethos

The student reviewed his essay using questions based on the concepts of logos, ethos, and pathos, looking for places he should revise.

> **Logos:** Every time I use the report "Living in America," the evidence is logical because the source is a research report from a respected foundation. The order of paragraphs is logical—first come two problems that immigrants experience, then two causes of the problems, and finally two solutions.
>
> **Pathos:** The quotes and details from Rodriguez appeal to emotions, and Tonio's story about his father also appeals to emotions. These parts are not overly emotional. In fact, more details might help this reach out to people's hearts more.
>
> **Ethos:** My essay uses great sources: a report from a famous foundation and the memoir of a famous immigrant writer, Rodriguez. I think my essay is well organized, and that helps people take me seriously.

Practice 13.11   Revising by Evaluating for Logos, Pathos, and Ethos

DIRECTIONS: Use the questions below to evaluate your use of the three appeals in your essay.

1. **Logos:** What parts of the argumentative essay use logic and facts to make intellectual appeals? Is the organization of paragraphs and evidence logical? How much of the essay is devoted to this type of reasoning?
2. **Pathos:** What parts of the essay appeal to the emotions of the audience? How much of the essay uses this type of appeal? Are these sections overly emotional?
3. **Ethos:** How does this essay help the audience feel confident in your ideas? How do you establish your credibility as a writer?

STEP 8: Edit and Proofread

Once you have looked at the content and structure of the essay—which include items like the thesis, support, and organization—it is time to edit your paper for grammar and spelling errors. Use your own writing to practice identifying and fixing grammar, punctuation, and spelling errors. This will help you move from finding errors in the writing of others to identifying them in your own writing. To edit your paper, try any of the following suggestions.

1. **Read your paper out loud to yourself.** Read slowly, and read every word. You will probably find some sentences that do not make sense or words that are missing. Fix these.
2. **Circle all of the punctuation, author names, and page numbers around each quotation you have used.** Check to see that you have given the correct information and punctuated correctly.
3. **Have another person read the paper.** This should be someone who has not previously seen it. Have that person mark any sentences or words that do not make sense to him or her. While this person might not be a grammar expert, he or she can give you feedback about sentences that are not "reader friendly" and therefore could use editing.
4. **Work with a tutor in your school's writing center or other tutoring center.** Have this person read your paper and work with you to edit any sentences that are not clear.
5. **Have your instructor look at your paper and mark for grammar and spelling in one paragraph.** Then, look at his or her marks. Try to find similar errors in the remaining paragraphs and fix them.

Practice 13.12   Editing

DIRECTIONS: Choose and complete two or more of the editing techniques above.

STEP 9: Reflect on Your Writing Process

Reflecting on your writing process as soon as you finish an assignment helps you to learn from the writing experience. It also provides your instructor with insight into where you are having trouble and what is going well in your writing. Here are sample reflection questions you can ask yourself before starting your next writing assignment:

1. **What did you learn from thinking about the topic of this paper?** Did reading and writing about prejudice help you or change you in any way?
2. **How did you grow as a writer through the process of writing this paper?** Are there phases or steps of the process that are getting easier or harder for you?

- If you completed the extensions in the assignment, comment on this. How was the experience of doing research on your topic and then adding this to your paper? What challenges did you face? What will you do the same or differently next time?

3. **How did the process of writing help you grow as a reader?** Did it help you understand the readings more completely? Was it easy or hard to write about the authors' ideas?

4. **What do you see as the strengths of your writing, starting with content (ideas and information) and then going to style (organization, language, voice, etc.).**

5. **What do you think are the weaknesses of your writing?** If you had more time or inclination, would you do anything else to your writing? If so, what?

Practice 13.13   Reflecting on Your Writing Process

DIRECTIONS: Answer the questions above to reflect on your writing process.

✓ Chapter **Quick Check**   MySkillsLab   Complete the mastery test for this chapter in MySkillsLab.

Use the following questions and answers to check your understanding of this chapter.

QUESTION	ANSWER
Learning Objective 1: Prewrite for an argumentative essay. *How do I prewrite to prepare for an argumentative essay?*	To prewrite for an argumentative essay... ✔ Analyze the assignment to ensure you understand it. ✔ Generate ideas by brainstorming and freewriting. ✔ Focus your topic and create a thesis statement. ✔ Review reading notes and summaries and do additional research to develop ideas. ✔ Organize your ideas using an outline. Remember the following as you prewrite... ✔ An argumentative problem-solution essay takes a clear position on a problem, its cause, and its solution. This forms the thesis of the essay. ✔ Body paragraphs need topic sentences and supporting evidence for why the thesis is true, followed by analysis. ✔ Argumentative essays need sufficient development. Support for argumentative papers often combines informational and narrative evidence. ✔ Argumentative problem-solution essays need to be organized so that the relationships between problem, cause, and solution are clear.

QUESTION	ANSWER
Learning Objective 2: Draft an argumentative essay. *How do I draft an argumentative essay?*	To draft an argumentative essay... ✔ Write an introduction that interests readers, provides enough background about the issue and sources, and states your thesis or claim. ✔ Write body paragraphs with topic sentences that each state a different supporting idea on why the thesis is true. Add supporting evidence, and analysis that connects the thesis with the evidence. ✔ Draft your essay from an outline or map of your thesis, topic sentences, and supporting information. ✔ Write a conclusion that reflects the ideas in your essay and thoughtfully ends the paper.
Learning Objective 3: Revise and edit an argumentative essay. *How do I revise and edit argumentative essays?*	To revise an argumentative essay... ✔ Use techniques such as a self-review of your draft using the assignment directions to evaluate your paper's thesis, overall structure, development, and organization. ✔ Evaluate your essay for use of logos, pathos, and ethos. ✔ Have your teacher or a writing center tutor check your work to identify types of errors you make. ✔ Get to know the types of sentence errors you tend to make. ✔ Practice fixing your sentence mistakes.

PART FOUR READING SELECTIONS

"Living in America: Challenges Facing New Immigrants and Refugees"
edited by Katherine Garrett, Robert Wood Johnson Foundation

1   In 2004, the Robert Wood Johnson Foundation's Vulnerable Populations Portfolio asked the research firm of Lake Snell Perry Mermin/Decision Research (LSPM/DR) to conduct a focus group study of immigrant and refugee communities in the United States. LSPM/DR conducted 32 focus groups between May 2004 and March 2005 in ten cities across the United States, speaking both with immigrants and refugees and with people who work with these populations.

2   There are many similarities in the stories that immigrants and refugees tell about their lives in America. It is striking that such diverse groups of individuals—coming from different countries and cultures and for different reasons—identify so many of the same needs and challenges. What is clear from this study is that life for immigrants and refugees can be extremely difficult. Most participants in this study said all they do in America is work and sleep, with little else in between. Commonplace tasks like grocery shopping, taking a bus, or finding a doctor can be overwhelming. Their family life suffers from numerous daily strains and parents feel they are growing apart from their children. And yet most remain optimistic and believe life will get better with time. They are most hopeful when talking about their children's lives and the opportunities for success they now have. In the end, few regret their decision to come to America.

3   This section of the report categorizes the challenges faced by immigrants and refugees by the underlying social issues that cause them:

- The type of education services available to these new residents—desperate to learn English—and to their children.
- Economic issues: the lack of secure jobs that pay an often undocumented population, and their resulting poor or crowded housing they can obtain.
- Isolation in immigrant and refugee communities: isolation from services that could help them, as well as the emotional isolation caused by stress.
- Prejudice and discrimination that new immigrants and refugees report they face, as well as the cultural differences that may deter them from seeking and receiving services.

4   Using the experience of new immigrants and refugees as well as their own words, this section of the report is intended to give a broad picture of how these social issues affect the lives, and especially the health status, of these vulnerable populations.

Learning English
Immigrants and refugees said that their lack of English proficiency is a barrier to a better life.

5   Language barriers are a fundamental hurdle for immigrants and refugees in this study and appear to stop them from making vital connections in their communities. Even daily tasks like taking a bus or grocery shopping can be overwhelming. One Arab immigrant from New Jersey described being unable to ask a simple question of an employee in a local grocery store and ended his story with: "So I cried, not for the food, but because I was unable to express myself in English."

6   Participants told many stories about the problems they have encountered in America due to language barriers. One Chinese immigrant in Chicago was in a car accident and could not describe his role in the accident to the investigating police officer. An Arab immigrant in New Jersey went to the hospital emergency room after she fainted and came home without treatment or medication because she could not communicate with providers about her health

condition. Immigrants and refugees reported facing language barriers when they went to the public library, saw a doctor, at their child's school, and when lost and seeking directions.

7   Research participants seemed motivated to overcome language barriers and to learn English. Most believe they cannot improve their lives and get a better job until they do so.

Immigrants and refugees value English as a Second Language (ESL) programs

8   Because learning English is a priority, ESL classes may be the most valued service for new immigrants and refugees. Most seemed to know about ESL programs in their community and many have actually attended these classes. "First of all I want to learn English so that I can choose a career. Get a better job. Language is the main thing," said a Central American immigrant in Prince Georges County, Md. Even though some immigrants and refugees said that learning English is very difficult, they seemed determined to succeed. "A lot of times I am not able to follow the lesson, so I self-study. I bought a dictionary and study myself," explained a Chinese immigrant from Orange County, Calif.

9   Some connectors in this study said that ESL classes often go beyond teaching English to include "how to" information. For example, one connector in Schuyler, Neb. who has taught ESL classes explained that he brought in guest speakers such as representatives of law enforcement to inform immigrants about other aspects of life in America. He also said that he was often asked to help fill out forms, accompany immigrants to appointments to interpret, and to explain issues like becoming a citizen and applying for government programs. He was not alone—other ESL instructors in this study say that their students ask them for advice on just about everything. A connector in Minneapolis who works with Somali refugees explained that her clients want more than just English classes: they want other topics taught in ESL and to receive a diploma that would be of value to an employer.

Accessing ESL programs can be difficult, however

10 Long work hours and busy lives can keep new immigrants and refugees from participating in ESL programs. "It takes time to learn English. There are very few schools that offer English classes and many times the schedules are not [compatible]. The number one priority is work and to support our families," explained a connector who works with Central and South Americans in Prince Georges County, Md. One connector in Schuyler, Neb. said, "The opportunities are there but it's not always convenient. I constantly have requests for classes at a different time." A few participants praised the convenience of ESL classes offered at their work site. One connector in Minneapolis pointed out that in some locations ESL programs are being cut back due to tight local and state budgets. "You have so many classes and there are so many students. Really, there is a problem now because of the budget this year. There will be a reduction on the certification programs. About 66 percent of Minnesota will not get that money. So, there might be a very big problem over there."

11   Lack of identification can also stand in the way of education. One research participant told how she came to America with a teaching degree, learned English, and then was unable to take her GED without a Social Security number.

Educating Their Children

Many immigrant and refugee parents described a variety of problems with schools

12 Parents in this study expressed their most intense frustration on the issue of schooling in the United States. They value education highly and believe a good education is the key to success for their children. Education is so important to Chinese immigrants in Orange County, for example, that some live three families to a house in order to live in a better school district. For this reason, many immigrant and refugee parents said they are frustrated that their children fall behind in U.S. schools, that schools lack bilingual teachers and aids, and that they are unable to help their children succeed. Some immigrant and refugee parents in this

study said that it is in schools that their children face discrimination and biases due to their different ethnic and cultural background. In addition, schools often are the site where the culture and traditions of immigrants and refugees are most challenged, and where children begin to adapt American values and customs, usually against their parents' wishes.

Immigrant and refugee children are not prepared for success in U.S. schools

13   One of the first problems mentioned is that immigrant and refugee children often fall behind in U.S. schools. "[I am] thankful to the government that our children are sent to school but the problem is we have arrived recently and the kids don't know the language, the teachers are Americans and they might not even understand what the lesson is all about. They go to the same classes as the kids born here and they might end up sitting in the class without understanding anything," said a Somali refugee from Minneapolis. The language barriers that children face–and the inconsistent schooling that some received prior to coming to America (particularly true of refugees)–means that immigrant and refugee children fall behind quickly at school.

14   Refugee children in particular seem in danger of failing at school. A connector who works with families from Sierra Leone explained that these children have not only been out of school for a considerable time, but they have also been exposed to the horrors of war which has traumatized them. She pointed out the need for school systems to work closely with parents of refugee children to find ways to help them succeed in school.

15   Another problem cited by parents and connectors alike is the lack of bilingual teachers and aids, interpreters, and counselors who can work with struggling or traumatized immigrant and refugee children. As a connector who works with Chinese immigrants in Orange County said,

> "[The schools] come to ask for translation, or they ask the kids to translate to counsel the kids. That is a problem, because we don't have these counseling services that can work with the schools. That is how I ran across some of the kids that were troubled...The school counselors come to us, because they don't have the facility to translate. They can't translate the problem to the kids. Sometimes you see the parents will say [to the child], 'Oh, you are stupid, why do you do that?' There is not a proactive plan for moving them from like getting an F in chemistry to a B."

16   Connectors who work with migrant farm workers from Mexico said the children of these families face many barriers to success in schools. They explained that these children move from state to state, rarely remaining in a school for the entire year. They said high school is particularly hard for these children. Because of feelings of displacement, high school students are more likely to join gangs and, according to this connector, about half drop out of school by the age of 16. A connector from North Carolina who works with migrant farm workers said, "The students are just waiting to turn 16, most of the students, to drop school. They say I do not want this and they join gangs and there is a problem with gangs now."

Parents find it difficult to help their children with homework and advocate for their children with the school

17   Parents in this study reported their regret that they are unable to help their children with schoolwork. Part of the reason is because their children tend to be more proficient in English than they are. "The homework...they go home, the parents don't speak the language, so they're behind the next year," said a connector in Dallas. Arab mothers in New Jersey seemed particularly upset about their inability to assist their children with school-related matters. Many said they felt "helpless" when it comes to helping children with schoolwork. While some said they have tried both print and electronic dictionaries as well as other aides, after a while these grow tiresome and the child is on their own.

18   In some cases, it is not so much the language barrier but also the lack of education of the parent. "Kids in the communities that I work with in low-income homes, they are not faring

well. A lot of it is because the immigrant family did not have that education themselves. It is not that they are not capable or don't care, they just don't have the resources to help tutor them when they fall down through the cracks," said a connector to Chinese immigrants in Orange County.

19   Parents also said they find it hard to get involved with schools or communicate their concerns to their child's teacher, and many feel intimidated interacting with school officials. "Typically the schools will encourage parents to volunteer in the classroom. Well, Somali moms…are not going to volunteer if they don't know the language," said a connector who works with Somali refugees in Portland, Maine.

A number of parents say their children face discrimination in schools

20   Immigrant and refugee parents said their children face discrimination at school from classmates and teachers alike. Their children feel like they do not belong, and language barriers and academic struggles only add to the problem. "I think the education is good, but there is some discrimination," said a Mexican immigrant in Schuyler, Neb. Another participant in that focus group added her own perceptions: "I think the same thing. There is a big difference between Americans and Hispanics. They pay more attention to Americans than Hispanics." Arab immigrants said their children frequently deal with harassment and taunting. "Some children sometimes say that when they say their names and it appears as Arab names, there is some tension," said an Arab immigrant parent from New Jersey. Another reported, "I wear the *hijab* in school and some people try and tell me to take it off…They keep on telling me to take it off, and then I say I can't take it off…so then they say, 'so is your father Osama Bin Laden?'" Some connectors in this study reported that the problem is so acute for some immigrant and refugee children that they drop out as soon as possible.

Somali and Arab immigrants worry about schools "Americanizing" their children

21   Both Somali and Arab parents in this study described a culture clash with American schools. As one Somali refugee parent from Minneapolis said,

> "We have also faced difficulties in adapting with the new environment and the culture of this country; also it's a major problem to come to new life with millions of people of different cultures, language and religion. The children go to schools with all these and they have to struggle adjusting and their mindset changes. When they come home they watch TVs and play video games and they get confused."

22   Arab parents in particular blamed schools for undermining their traditions and religion. Said one Arab parent in New Jersey, "They raise the children in a way that teaches them that a person is…selfish, they teach them selfishness and everyone is independent with a private life that we have nothing to do with. They consider our Islamic ideas old-fashioned."

23   Discipline, in particular, is a big issue for Arab parents in regard to schools. A few parents in this study said they have had problems with school officials who have accused them of child abuse. "Schools do not understand Muslim discipline," explained an Arab immigrant parent in New Jersey. A connector for the Arab community said that he plans to hold classes for Arab parents to explain American laws regarding discipline and school policies to avoid these kinds of misunderstandings.

Many immigrants and refugees feel stuck in low-level jobs and describe numerous barriers to advancing

24   The most important priority of many of the immigrants and refugees in this study is securing the next, better job. While appreciative of that first job when they arrive in the country—they say they are willing to take anything in order to start earning an income—the real problem is moving into a better paying job with more responsibility after they have been in the country a while.

25   A number of barriers exist to getting a better job, first and foremost being lack of sufficient language skills and education. In answer to what employers are looking for, one connector to Somali refugees in Minneapolis said, "The people I deal with it's language, language language." Even low-paying jobs that historically required little or no English are now demanding some language skills. This is especially true in cities where the job market is tight, like Minneapolis. One connector to Somali refugees explained, "There used to be a lot of [entry-level] industry jobs like packaging and jobs like that. That job isn't available now. Whenever you call them, they will tell you that the person has to speak or at least be able to follow the instructions of the supervisors. They have to read and write the English language."

26   Others believe that their lack of education—or lack of an American education—hurts them as well. Said one Chinese immigrant in Chicago, "[Employers are] very concerned about your work experience in the United States and also your education background in the United States. They emphasize your U.S. experience. Say for instance you're an accountant [in China], they will choose somebody with a U.S. diploma." Many immigrants and refugees who came to the United States equipped with advanced degrees and professional backgrounds are no more immune. Engineers spend years driving cabs; cabinet ministers work as security guards, "jobs that Americans don't want," said one connector to refugees from Sierra Leone in Washington, D.C.

27   Lack of identification and Social Security numbers can also make finding a job difficult. "If we were legal, we'd have better jobs," explained a Mexican immigrant in Dallas. A Mexican immigrant from Schuyler, Neb, told how she borrowed someone else's papers in order to obtain her job.

28   Many said they wanted to own businesses of their own one day, but few if any of the immigrants and refugees in this study knew of job training programs in their community or other ways to enhance their skill level to get a better job. The main way they seek advancement is by attending ESL classes and learning English as quickly as possible. A few pursue their GED. Many work within their own network of friends to learn of new job openings. Many also work a second job to offset the low pay of their primary job. Of note, few people outside their own network of friends seem to be helping these immigrants and refugees advance in the workplace.

Many immigrants and refugees lack safe, affordable housing in their communities

29   Finding appropriate housing can be challenging. Cost is the biggest barrier, since immigrant and refugee families say they usually obtain only low-paying jobs in their first years in America. Upon their arrival most spend anywhere from a few days to months sharing cramped quarters with family and friends. Eager to move from this often stressful environment, they have nowhere to turn. One connector to immigrants from South and Central America in Prince Georges County, Md., explained, "They can't leave because they don't have anywhere to go to. How do we solve this with the very little housing programs that exist?"

30   There is also the problem of zoning laws. Minneapolis, for example, places a ceiling on the number of individuals who can reside in one dwelling. One Somali refugee there recalled having to hide his child from the authorities. "I was paying 60 percent of my income towards rent and I was hiding my youngest child. If I didn't do that, they would have required me to rent a three bedroom apartment which I cannot afford. I was hiding my youngest for two years," he said. Landlords are also asking for job and rent histories, which many are unable to provide. Many families do not qualify for public housing assistance, with incomes slightly above the income limits because both parents work at least one job. If they do qualify, they report being put on waiting lists up to one-year long.

31   Immigrants and refugees said the housing they can afford is often in unsafe neighborhoods. The women in these focus groups expressed the most concerns about safety, since many must walk through these neighborhoods due to transportation problems. A number

of research participants said they have experienced vandalism and robberies. Many fear the gang activity in their neighborhoods and the easy access to drugs and alcoholism that appears to be increasing among the youth in their neighborhoods. Parents worry the most about raising their children in these environments.

32   In Benson, N.C., the dwelling structures themselves are unsafe. Connectors to migrant farm workers there say current codes are inadequate and do not require mattresses for sleeping, a telephone or more than one toilet for 12 people. For various reasons, they say inspectors allow uninhabitable dwellings to pass inspection. "A nail here, a nail there…16 people live there," explained one connector. "You can't ever think a person could live there." Health care providers say much of the health care concerns of migrant farm workers are due in large part to their unsanitary living conditions, which spread disease and poor health.

Becoming citizens is the shared goal

33   In just about every focus group participants said they wanted to become legal American citizens as soon as possible. Some believed that lack of documentation is the main impediment keeping them from realizing their goals. They want to own their own homes and businesses, scale back their work hours and spend more time with family, and yet they feel they cannot do any of these things until they are legal. For this reason, many said they wanted help in becoming a citizen. They are confused about the required steps and some explained that fulfilling basic needs like paying rent and getting a better job tend to take priority. This is one area where they would welcome assistance. "If I could get legal papers, I could get a real good job like working as an electrician, I could get my own help, or get a job working for the government or something working as an electrician. I could really, you know, get paid well, and I wouldn't have to kill myself," said a Mexican immigrant from Dallas.

Isolation from Government Services

Undocumented immigrants and refugees awaiting asylum find it hard to get access to social services

34   Lacking legal status blocks immigrant and refugee families from seeking assistance. The participants in this study, many of whom are undocumented, said it prevents them from taking even the first step to reach out for help or information. Instead, they hide and try to become "invisible" so that they do not run into trouble with the immigration authorities. This, in turn, makes them vulnerable to exploitation and extreme poverty.

Fear of being deported creates reluctance to seek assistance

35   Immigrants and refugees often fear taking steps to find assistance that might be available, for example, government programs that could help them with housing or health care. Some said they would not go to local health providers because they too have begun to ask for identification. One connector in Dallas explained that some local health clinics ask for Social Security cards before providing services. "There's a few of them right now especially [that say], 'Let me see your Social Security.' They walk out of the clinic…They are supposed to ask for it now. They cannot deny services, but you ask the question and you're instilling fear." A connector in New Jersey who works with Arab immigrants described a conversation with a client:

> "She said, 'But Susie, I don't have a green card, I'm not legal, but my husband's legal. My mom, she has breast and cervical cancer, and I'm scared to have it. I'm scared to have the doctor do a mammogram and pap smear.' I said, 'Listen to me. You come tomorrow to my center, and I'm going to go in with you and the doctor, and I'm going to ask if your doctor is female, because it's not allowed for you to see a man…' She called me on the second day, and said, 'I'm not going because my husband says immigration will deport me.'"

36   Others believe that if they accept services now while they are undocumented they will have to pay back services—or be denied citizenship—later on. "Because in the future they want to have their residency or citizenship... Their children are eligible for programs such as TANF but they are afraid this will affect them later on," said a connector who works with Central and South Americans in Prince Georges County.

Immigrants and refugees want information about their rights

37   Immigrants' and refugees' experiences with harassment, discrimination, and poor treatment in the workplace prompted a number of research participants to ask for more information about their rights. Because many are here illegally, they believe they have no rights at all. Even if they have legal status, many fear they will not be treated fairly due to widespread prejudice and discrimination. This keeps them from lodging legitimate grievances against employers, landlords, or even law enforcement. Many say they feel powerless. The answer, some believe, is more knowledge about laws in the United States and about their rights. As a Mexican immigrant from Schuyler, Neb. explained, "You think that you can do the same things here and that is where problems start. The culture is different and laws are stricter and they have to be respected. Over there you just have to know how to drive, but here you need a license; this is one of the problems one will find. Many obstacles. You get scared when the police stop you because you don't understand."

38   For many, the Immigration and Naturalization Service (INS)[1] also remains a mystery; interviewees knew very little about the laws governing their status, including the processes around work and travel. Some Mexican immigrants in Schuyler, said they find it difficult to keep up with the constant changes in immigration law. Other research participants complained about frequent delays in standard paperwork like work visas or residency. One connector to Arab immigrants in Union City, N.J., noted that many immigrants are "stuck—they cannot stay nor can they go back." Arab immigrants in particular talk at length about how the INS just tells them to "wait, wait" and many feel they are given "a hard time."

Isolation from Health Services

There are many barriers to obtaining health services

39   All of the issues mentioned in this report have an effect on access to and use of health care services. Lack of legal status discourages many immigrants and refugees from seeking medical care because they fear they will be turned in. Language barriers are a problem for many immigrants and refugees since they cannot effectively communicate with medical professionals when they do seek care nor can they learn about available health programs in their community. It is unclear whether immigrant and refugee children are accessing any of the health services available at schools. Experiences with discrimination also affect the willingness of immigrants and refugees to see providers outside of their culture or to generally reach out beyond their community when it comes to meeting health needs. Other barriers—such as transportation problems, stigma around discussing certain medical conditions, long work hours and holding on to precious jobs—also inhibit the ability and willingness of immigrants and refugees to seek out and use health services. Yet it is clear that all of these research participants value health care, are concerned about their health and that of their children, and want health insurance coverage if they currently lack it.

Most immigrant and refugees in this study lack health insurance and are not getting preventive care

40   Most immigrants and refugees in this study are uninsured. The exceptions include Mexican immigrants in Schuyler who receive coverage offered by the meat packing plant where they work, and the majority of Somali refugees in the Minneapolis focus groups

---

[1] Immigrants and refugees still refer to the "INS"—as opposed to the recently reorganized Department of Homeland Security—as the agency with jurisdiction over immigration matters.

who are enrolled in Medicaid. Most others, however, work for employers who do not offer health insurance, or cannot afford it even if the employer offers it, or do not work enough hours to qualify.

41   For most immigrants and refugees in this study, preventive care is an unfamiliar concept. One connector spoke to the vastly different medical culture from which Somali refugees hail: "The infrastructure that was in Somalia at that time was heavily focused on curative. If you had a fever or a headache or something, you could go wait in line and see a physician. They would give you something, tell you to take this medicine, or get an injection, then you go home and that's how it is." Most immigrants and refugees also cite a practical reason for not getting check-ups: they cannot afford to take the time off work. One connector in North Carolina pointed out that the migrant farm workers there "do not have sick days." Another added, "That is the key. Any day out of work is less money in their pocket so they do try and work even with a sore back or busted ankle, whatever, they are out there working."

42   Many immigrants and refugees said they turned to home remedies (herbs and teas, for example) and Tai Chi (in the case of some Chinese immigrants) to cure their ills, but rarely a doctor. "Even if I'm sick, I still stay at home, frankly, and you'll find me drinking tea and I don't know what...I don't go to the doctor, except as a last resort. I don't know why...I hate to go to doctors basically," said one Arab immigrant in New Jersey. This is also the case in Minneapolis, where the majority of Somali refugees have Medicaid. As one connector to the Chinese immigrants in Orange County, Calif., herself Chinese, notes, "We use the emergency room for health care rather than taking prevention." As connectors reported that immigrants and refugees suffer disproportionately from chronic illnesses such as diabetes, asthma, heart disease, and obesity, the reliance on episodic emergency room care is especially troubling.

Physical Isolation
Transportation is a major problem

43   In almost every location, immigrants and refugees reported concerns about their limited transportation options. Getting themselves to and from work and their children to and from school are their biggest concerns. Many immigrants and refugees in this study tell of walking long distances, sometimes late at night and through unsafe neighborhoods, because they have no other way to get home.

44   Even after years in America, many immigrants and refugees in the focus groups say they continue to rely on family and friends for transportation. One Mexican immigrant in Dallas, whose aunt had always driven her to their workplace, said, "And then she stopped working there. I didn't have a way to get there...many times I would walk." This demonstrates that carpooling only works if people share the same, regular hours and schedules. Many said they are often stuck at the end of the day and must find their own way home even when they do carpool. Women seem to suffer most from transportation problems, since the men normally drive the one car in the family.

45   Few own their own cars; those families that are able to afford a car have to share one among many family members. "They have to take a turn. They have to arrange the time," explained one connector to Chinese immigrants in Orange County. In these cases, say connectors, wives are entirely dependent on husbands (who often use the car to get to work), isolated during the day and at a loss if an emergency should arise.

There are barriers to driving legally

46   Immigrants and refugees reported it is difficult to obtain a driver's license. Navigating the Department of Motor Vehicles (DMV) is hard, particularly for those with limited English proficiency. According to one connector to refugees from Sierra Leone in Washington, D.C.: "It is a matter of educating the refugee, teaching the refugee to take the DMV classes, pass, and go for a learner's permit, pass and then learn how to drive.

Sometimes it takes over six months or a year." Some said the written test is too formal and confusing, even when provided in their own language and that even if they pass the written test, there are rarely bilingual instructors available for the road test. Still others applying for driver's licenses pointed out that their states are now demanding identification, like Social Security cards. As a result, many said they have no choice but to drive without a license. Others reported they cannot obtain auto insurance because they have no documentation.

Public transit does not provide an answer

47   Surprisingly few of these research participants use public transportation, either because it is unavailable in their communities or because schedules are limited. They said that traditional bus schedules often do not accommodate their erratic or late night work hours. Options are even more limited for those who have to travel to and from the suburbs. Most restricted, however, are the migrant farm workers in North Carolina who are usually camped in unpopulated and remote locations. As one connector said, they are "physically tied to their farms." For others the transportation system is simply too confusing, especially for those whose English is more limited. Newer immigrants and refugees are often unfamiliar with their surroundings, making public transportation even less appealing.

Transportation difficulties have a broad impact

48   Limited transportation options have implications that reach beyond just work and school. Although immigrants and refugees fear loss of employment, other important aspects of their lives are affected as well. One connector to Somali refugees in Minneapolis said, "It's an issue for accessing legal services or just any basic service, such as getting to a medical facility." Immigrants and refugees agree, pointing out that their children are often unable to participate in after-school activities. Another connector to migrant farm workers in North Carolina explained, "If they cannot stay after school to take those tutoring classes and all that, then they go back home. There are no computers to practice or anything like that so that is where the dropout rate [comes from]." Lack of transportation makes it harder to attend ESL classes, or meetings with Immigration officials, or appointments with health care providers.

Isolation of Families

Immigrant and refugee families are under stress

49   While this is not something that immigrants and refugees complain of directly in the focus groups, their comments—and the insights from connectors—show that these families are under enormous pressure. Long work hours, both parents working, children left alone after school, cramped living quarters often in unsafe neighborhoods, financial worries (including helping families back home), long commutes to and from work, daily language barriers, and other challenges are taking their toll. Research participants appear exhausted. Many are discouraged. They say they have no time to relax, socialize with other immigrants or neighbors, or to help each other. These pressures lead to fractured relationships within families, increased stress, and serious health issues.

Children embrace American culture while parents hold onto traditions

50   Perhaps the biggest strain on families is the growing gap between immigrant and refugee parents and their children who acculturate much more quickly. As one connector for Somali refugees in Minneapolis said:

> "The young are running away from the culture, running away from the parents, because that represents ignorance and it represents embarrassment. So, you see more and more of kids with the tennis shoes, with the hip-hop, and the gangs. We have drug use and teen pregnancy which I'm sure is an aberration in the Islamic culture. So, there is an age point

where the languages are no longer viable between parent and young. We have an adult very often who is speaking Somali or mostly Somali—maybe a little bit of basic English. Then, we have a young person who is speaking English and a little bit of Somali. Now, how's the parenting dynamic in that situation? It's very problematic."

51 Another connector in that same focus group added, "Mostly, the younger generation and the elders are what we would call a culture clash, the difference, the gap between the old and the young. The young want to become American and the old want to keep the tradition."

52 Arab immigrants in New Jersey and Chinese parents in Orange County raised similar concerns as the Somali parents. They claimed their children have become less respectful since coming to America and have grown increasingly uninterested in their own culture. They voiced serious worries about their children joining gangs and using drugs. They do not know their children's friends and do not know what is happening at their child's school. This saddens them but also frustrates them since they do not know how to reconnect with their children.

53 Finally, connectors said that some cultural norms discourage openness as a way to deal with family problems. Parents in many cultures are unused to talking with their children about problems. A connector who works with Chinese immigrants noted:

"I guess you kind of have a population where both parents are working their butt off and they are not getting paid. The kids are left on their own and they hope the kids will have a better opportunity and will strive academically. At the same time there is a gap and I think generally there is not enough communication. Let's talk about sex, let's talk about drugs, and let's talk about your mental issues. I think that is kind of a foreign concept in the immigrant community, talking about those issues and thinking about mental issues. In the Western community it may be a mental whatever but in the Asian community they might not see it as a mental issue. There are these cultural factors we need to consider and I think there is definitely a gap between the children and the parents in terms of certain issues, because it is not part of their lifestyle to talk about that."

Exploitation and Discrimination

The workplace is the primary site for exploitation and discrimination

54 Mexican and Central and South American immigrants in this study told many stories of harassment, poor treatment, inconsistent wages, and health and safety violations at work. Yet they said they do not complain. "They always think that they don't have any rights because they are here illegally. They don't know how to complain or whom to complain to," said a connector in Prince Georges County. The problem, said many immigrants and refugees, is that they do not know their rights and fear that if they were to press legal charges, they would lose their job and probably be sent back home.

55 Some also felt that immigrants are given the hardest, most dangerous jobs. A Mexican immigrant from Schuyler who works at a meat packing factory said, "There are undocumented workers at [the factory]. They can make them do the hardest jobs. Sometimes I think they are injured, but they don't say anything because they are afraid of being fired or getting more difficult jobs."

56 While some migrant farm workers may be familiar with the local Legal Aid's Farm Workers Unit, they are too afraid to use it. A connector who provides legal assistance to migrant farm workers in North Carolina said although he can help a client get back-pay owed to him, the worker will definitely be fired and probably be sent back to Mexico. Therefore, he gets few requests to pursue legal means to obtain back-pay. Ultimately, this connector said that it is easier for the farmer to replace a troublesome employee with another Mexican immigrant who will appreciate the job.

Immigrants and refugees report negative interactions with law enforcement

57   Many in this study said that they feel profiled by law enforcement officers and unfairly harassed. In Schuyler, Mexican immigrants feel police provide "harassment and not security," while Arab immigrants in New Jersey describe police as "the enemy." "That is the only problem. The police. Even if the person is driving well. There is racism here in Schuyler," asserted a Mexican immigrant. Another said, "They always stop Hispanics. They are on the lookout for us."

58   Some told stories of being victims of crime and how the police were not helpful. "Our car stereos have been stolen twice. I have never seen them show any follow-up. They just make the report and file it and they never tell you anything again," said a Mexican immigrant in Schuyler. Another participant in the same focus group added:

> "Last summer we were coming home from the football field, we were still wearing our uniforms. An unmarked car got next to us and followed us home. He said, 'Who is driving?' I said, 'I am.' He asked for my ID and called another policeman. They arrested us and took our fingerprints and pictures. Why did they arrest us? They said they got us confused with someone they were looking for."

59   Arab immigrants in New Jersey also told stories of police harassment. A woman in the focus groups reported:

> "I was in a car accident... The person who had the accident with me... He made me turn left and then he hit me. I had a witness, the guy behind me hit me between the two cars. My car was totaled. I told the police what happened. I heard the guy behind me tell the police what happened. Nothing of this was mentioned in the police report. And they blamed the accident on me. I am sure that all of this is because of my veil... they didn't pay any attention to me. Even in the ambulance they didn't take care of me. They put me in the ambulance and I sat on a seat like this one, and the ambulance was turning towards Palisades Hospital. I fell off the seat. They didn't... I mean the treatment was unbelievable. This is what I felt because I know that if someone has an accident that person may be injured and thus be placed in the ambulance in a certain way so as not move any bones in my body. They let me in and sat me on a seat without a seat belt even, they were very rude."

60   Troubles with police are also common for Chinese and Vietnamese immigrants in Orange County. A connector who works with this community said, "I see police harassment of our youth because... they dress like the other kids with baggy clothes. If you are Huntington Beach and you are white it would be no problem. But if you are a Vietnamese kid sitting at the mall waiting for your mother to pick you up, even though you are an "A" student, you get picked up by the police and typecast as a gang member."

Arab immigrants feel discrimination has increased since the events of September 11th

61   Arab immigrants in this study said that there has been a sharp increase in bias against them since 9/11. They must cope with open insults—one even reported being spat upon—when walking along the street. "I was standing at a red light and slowed down so someone could pass, he immediately yelled out 'terrorist' and did this to me [indicating a profane finger gesture]," recalled one Arab immigrant in New Jersey. Others said they felt a more subtle prejudice when dealing with government services. One connector explained, "I even noticed a lot of Social Service benefits are judgmental. The judgments are becoming stricter in terms of Muslims, in terms of accessing them. There is a rule book and in people's mind the book is tighter now." The focus group participants say that this has been hurtful and that they feel less comfortable and safe in America than they used to.

Lack of Cultural Understanding

Immigrants and refugees experience language barriers
and lack of cultural sensitivity from health care providers

62   Language issues cause frustration around access to health care services. Immigrant and refugee patients can have a hard time understanding medical correspondence, whether it be over the phone, on paper (e.g., children's vaccination records for schools), or verbal directions given in the doctor's office. Public hospital emergency rooms, where the uninsured in this study say they usually go for medical care, can have lengthy waits for an interpreter if there is even one available. Said one Chinese immigrant in Chicago, "If you're lucky [there's an] interpreter. Otherwise you're getting nowhere."

63   In addition, some pointed to a lack of cultural sensitivity from providers as an obstacle to seeking care. According to a conversation with one connector in Minneapolis, "most providers are still unprepared to deal effectively (with any cultural sensitivity) with the community." When doctors cannot connect effectively with their patients, she continued, "this increases mistrust and suspicion among the Somali community vis-à-vis medical professionals."

64   Some immigrants and refugees also have expectations about health care providers that are at odds with the American system. Many immigrants and refugees tell us that they prefer a provider who shares their background, while women from some cultures—particularly the Somali and Arab women in the focus groups—prefer to visit only another female provider, and yet this rarely happens. Many also expect to be cared for by a doctor and dislike the widespread use of nurses in the U.S. health system. A Somali refugee in Portland, Maine, for example, recalled a visit to a local emergency room where she felt insulted when treated by the nurse instead of a doctor.

The health care system needs to address cultural
stigmas around receiving mental health services

65   Mental health concerns were discussed primarily in the focus groups with connectors rather than in those with immigrants and refugees themselves; many immigrants and refugees have difficulty discussing mental health needs. Connectors explained that the immigrants and refugees they serve face significant stigma in discussing issues like trauma and depression. Connectors, and even a handful of immigrants and refugees, spoke of cultures that are averse to Western ideas of counseling and psychotherapy. Said a connector to Chinese immigrants in Orange County, Calif., "Even to go to a psychologist, people think you are crazy if you go to see a psychologist." One Arab immigrant in New Jersey suffering from post-traumatic stress disorder, recounted a confrontation with her parents: "I had to go to counseling and my parents could not accept that idea. It is something shameful."

66   The discussions in the focus groups suggest that many refugees—and some immigrants—arrive in the United States with special mental health needs: trauma and depression due to ravages of war, rape, and loss of loved ones.[2] Added to these are the culture shock and disorientation that come when one is suddenly put in a foreign environment. Connectors added that many of the refugees they see are unaware that they suffer from trauma. "A lot of them are coming here traumatized. They get here, they become re-traumatized. And the reason for that is because of [culture] shock...a lot of people are traumatized, a lot of people are depressed and they don't even know it," explained one connector who works with refugees from Sierra Leone in the Washington, D.C., area. Another connector said, "The woman finds herself in a peaceful environment, but believe me, she's still fighting the war that she left back home...there are no mechanisms upon which she can rely [for help]."

---

[2] According to one connector to Somali refugees in Minneapolis, "The Center for Victims of Torture along with the University of Minnesota conducted a...multiyear study of the Somali population in terms of assessing levels of torture and war violence in the population. They found extremely high levels of exposure to trauma, violence, or torture either directly or vicariously in the community both amongst men and women."

There is a great need in almost every community for mental health services that are both affordable and culturally relevant

67   One connector to Arab immigrants in New Jersey explained, "No one is there to take care of their psychological needs. There is a mental health issue as well and it is not being addressed. We clearly see this is affecting not only the first generation immigrants but their children as well." In Benson, N.C., representatives from Tri-County Community Clinic described their lack of enough specialists to meet the mental health demands of their growing community: currently they only have two mental health providers on staff and they serve over 12,000 migrant farm workers each year. Although the clinic provides mental health screening for migrant farm workers on-site (in the camps), there are no nearby agencies to which to refer people. Almost every community lacks enough mental health providers, according to these providers.

68   Connectors said that the American understanding of the refugee experience and of refugee attitudes toward mental health services is limited and can sometimes offend rather than heal. One connector to refugees from Sierra Leone offered some advice: "An African would hardly answer you in the first person singular when it really involves things that are personal... When you ask in the third person you say, 'how do they treat people back home during the war?' 'Oh they...,' they will start [talking]... Understand where this person is coming from. There you start building a relationship as trust." Connectors to Somali refugees in Portland agreed. One suggested that, "It is really important to have that bridge. In other words, to have somebody from that culture who understands the U.S. culture, and also understands the culture of the person."

69   Connectors said that most of the immigrant and refugees they see prefer to keep emotional problems hidden and rely only on family members for help. One connector to Arab immigrants in New Jersey—herself an immigrant of Arab descent, said, "There is a cultural issue we have that you are not supposed to talk about your problems. There is not an easy emotional release of your stress... We are trained by our culture to keep it to yourself and you cry in your bedroom and everyone is happy."

70   Others turn to spiritual counseling. As one connector to refugees from Sierra Leone explained, "If I come to a family and say, 'OK, family X, you need psychotherapy,' they're going to look at me as if I am crazy, but if I tell them, 'you need to pray,' or 'you need to go see the Pastor,' they would be more receptive." In Benson, N.C., a connector explained that one of her high school students was sent home to Mexico to see a witch doctor rather than see the school psychologist for emotional problems.

71   Using the information gained through these focus groups, LSPM/DR has identified two main ways to improve the services provided to immigrants and refugees:

- Work on the programs that serve this population: restructure or expand them, or develop new programs in key areas.
- Learn about and use the communications methods that are most valued by this population.

72   The issues facing immigrants and refugees are interconnected in ways that make solutions challenging. For example, legal status, lack of English proficiency, fear of discrimination, and poor transportation can all play a role in an immigrant's or refugee's ability to receive health care services. Programs that serve immigrant and refugee populations will be most successful if they can address this web of interconnected needs.

73   We have identified four categories of actions that could be taken to improve such programs:

- Restructuring existing services;
- Targeting immigrant and refugee needs more directly in current public services;
- Building new services; and
- Providing more and better information.

74   The following table presents the recommended actions for each of these categories and ideas on how to implement these recommendations.

TABLE 1
Actions and Implementation Ideas

Recommended Actions	Ideas for Implementation
Restructure existing services	
Integrate Services to Make them Easier for Immigrants and Refugees to Find and Use	Effective approaches to service integration include housing a range of services (e.g., legal services, ESL classes, services for school-age children, mental health counseling, help with housing) in the same building. The International Institute of New Jersey, for example, provides all of these services and more in one location. Mary Center in Washington, D.C., similarly combines health services with legal services, housing, and other assistance.
Use ESL as a Window to Other Services and Information	ESL classes provide an important opportunity to reach immigrants and refugees who might not use any other community service; ESL classes are perhaps the best known and best used service or program in many of the communities we visited.
	This study also found that the ESL instructor is one of a few highly trusted individuals that immigrants and refugees turn to for help. "It's the ESL instructors they feel comfortable with, not the regular teachers," said one connector to migrant workers in Benson, N.C.
	Many instructors do much more than just teach English in their ESL classes: they teach about banking, how to interact with police, and how to obtain health care as well as dealing with immigration issues. Others like to incorporate "softer" topics about American culture and customs, and may bring in guest lecturers and outreach workers to enlighten their students.
Target immigrant and refugee needs more directly in current public services	
Create More Supports for Immigrants and Refugees in Schools	Ideas from focus group participants on improving services in the schools include: • More bilingual school staff and more use of interpreters. • Written notices sent home in more languages. • More outreach to immigrant and refugee parents who may be too intimidated to participate in school activities. • Tutoring for their children to prevent them from falling behind. • Greater sensitivity among school staff for different cultures and traditions. • More vigilance against discrimination at schools by students and staff. • Seminars for immigrants and refugees explaining school rules and procedures. • School-based programs to bring refugee and immigrant parents into the life of the school. • More counselors and mental health professionals trained to work with immigrant children and, in particular, traumatized refugee children, to help them settle into school life.
Offer More Affordable and Culturally Sensitive Health Care Options	Most immigrants and refugees in this study appear to be receiving only infrequent health care, and almost no preventive care. Barriers to health care services include: • Lack of insurance. • Limited availability of free or low-cost care and concern that such programs are not available to undocumented people. • The desire to see a health provider from the same ethnic background who speaks the same language. • Limited knowledge of public programs such as Medicaid, SCHIP and WIC.

Recommended Actions	Ideas for Implementation
Use "Cultural Bridges" to Break Down Stigma Surrounding Mental Health	Connectors in many focus groups, especially those dealing with refugees, suggested that more attention be paid to understanding the cultural barriers to mental health services. Some recommended what they call "cultural bridges" or "cross cultural providers"—using community members to enlighten providers about cultural attitudes toward mental health. A similar model is the International Institute of New Jersey's "Pathways" program which encourages community leaders to engage and educate their own community members on mental health and other services.

Build new services

Make Interpreter Services More Widely Available	Immigrants and refugees in our focus groups ask for more interpreters in sites such as hospitals, doctors' offices, schools, local courts, banks, and the DMV. One Arab immigrant in Union City, N.J., said that having an interpreter in the courts is the "second best defense" they have after knowing their rights and laws. A fellow Arab immigrant said he knows of only one courthouse in their area that has a steady, reliable interpreter on staff. Chinese immigrants in Orange County, Calif., report that Spanish and Vietnamese interpreters tend to be available, but that they struggle to find Chinese-speaking help.
Create More Activities for Immigrant and Refugee Youth	The focus groups revealed a need for places where their children can congregate when school is out. Some parents say their child's public school does not offer any after-school programs; children may also be unable to attend such programs because they lack transportation. This is especially true in smaller cities. In Schuyler, Neb., for example, parents wish their children had a YMCA, "like the one in [nearby] Columbus."
	Parents and connectors worry about children, with so much time on their hands and little adult supervision, turning to drugs, alcohol and gangs. A connector to Chinese immigrants in Orange County said, "I think our kids get drawn into it, because we are not providing any alternative. We lack the youth centers. If the parents, or you, or the kids are not involved in church—some of the Vietnamese, our Buddhist churches they have something similar to a Boys and Girls kind of program, which is very good. In the Chinese communities in Irvine they have Chinese School so you can engage in those kinds of activities or...have music lessons. For some of the lower economic group what else do you do? You go to a park and get beat up by other ethnic groups."

Provide more and better information

Make Refugee Orientation Programs Ongoing and Address Longer-Term Needs	Some refugees and connectors suggest that more comprehensive, on-going orientation programs would be beneficial. They say that current, one-time programs only address the basic needs refugees have when they first arrive. Follow-up programs could help refugees with issues such as transportation, becoming citizens, obtaining health care services, dealing with discrimination, that emerge once refugees have been settled in America for some time.
	Refugees also say they retain little of what they learn in their orientation program due to the stress of arriving in the United States. As one connector to Somali refugees in Portland, Maine, noted, "People need constant orientation. People are not going to retain all this information."
	Others say the content of some refugee orientation programs could be changed to incorporate more "survivor skills." Orientation sessions focus on the immigration process and contain little information on acculturation skills such as shopping for groceries or using the telephone or public transportation. "There is a lot of education still to do with the kinds of things that we take for granted," explained one connector to refugees from Sierra Leone in the Washington, D.C., area. "We have instances where they use bleach to clean vegetables, because they don't know the safe use of some of the products...We still think that they know, but they don't know."

Recommended Actions	Ideas for Implementation
Provide More Information about Legal Rights	Immigrants and refugees would benefit from information about several specific areas of the law: • Labor law. With scant understanding of labor laws, many are working 16 hours or more each day; others say they are afraid to quit a job for fear of being sent back to their country of origin. • Traffic codes. Immigrants and refugees reported being in accidents and not knowing how to resolve them. This is an area where participants feel their limited English proficiency makes them especially vulnerable, and so information about the specific steps they should take if they are in a traffic accident would be valuable. • Discrimination. Many are unaware that they have any legal recourse when they face anti-immigrant discrimination in the work place, from law enforcement, in schools, and in their neighborhoods. Some communities we visited report holding informal seminars to bring law enforcement together with immigrants and refugees; such meetings enable participants to ask questions about rights and laws and for law enforcement to hear the concerns of these populations.
Offer Citizenship Instruction and Guidance on Immigration Problems	A shared goal of most of the immigrants and refugees in this study is to obtain U.S. citizenship. Most, however, are not familiar with the process of becoming a citizen and do not know how to get information on this topic. Others are not clear about immigration requirements. Without a source of reliable information about citizenship and residency, immigrants and refugees tend to rely on word of mouth and hearsay, and research participants therefore say they would like more information on these issues that they know is trustworthy. In one community we visited, information about citizenship was provided in ESL classes through a guest lecturer who provided legal advice to immigrants and refugees.
Supply Opportunities to Learn about Starting their Own Business and Obtain Job Skills	Many immigrants and refugees in this study express an interest in opening their own business, but few know how to do this. Others simply want to learn practical business skills that can help them obtain a better paying job. A resource that can help immigrants and refugees learn about these topics seems to be missing in the communities we visited and would be valued by research participants.

75 Immigrants and refugees can be invisible in communities. Research participants explain why they are often reluctant to reach out for help, but this reluctance is frustrating for service providers and others who want to help them. Immigrants and refugees need information about a range of topics on life in the United States. Their knowledge of the services and programs available in their communities is minimal.

76 In the focus groups, immigrants and refugees explain how they want to receive information. All service providers have an opportunity to improve their outreach by making better use of the communication networks that are used and trusted by immigrants and refugees.

77 First, the information must be in the appropriate language for each population. In every focus group, participants complain about the limited information they can find in their own language (although Spanish-speaking participants have more access to information than others in the study). Participants then describe the sources they use most often to get information:

• Family and friends
• In-language media
• Word of mouth, stories and personal connections
• Religious leaders

Family and Friends

78   The primary source of information for almost all of the immigrants and refugees in the study is family and friends, usually those who have been in America longest. These close-knit communities look to each other first and foremost to learn about life in the United States and about programs and services in the community. For example, Mexican immigrant mothers in Dallas knew from friends that their children could qualify for Medicaid and that they could qualify for WIC; word spreads quickly when there is a program or service that could benefit immigrant families. Other important information—about immigration, jobs, rides to and from work—is relayed from one to another, informally. Even those who have been in America for more than a few years say they turn to family first for information.

79   It is key to tap these informal family and community networks and to use them to disseminate important information about services and resources. Using local, trusted community members as messengers could be an effective way to get into these networks.

In-Language Media

80   Immigrants and refugees also rely heavily on in-language television and radio, and to a lesser extent newspapers, for information and entertainment. For most, television is the main source of news, especially updates on the political situation back home. Connectors agree. Said one in Orange County, Calif., "The radio and the TV are the best, because most of the people don't have transportation services to go to a seminar or a presentation." Another connector said, "You go right into the home with that." For many, especially seniors, television relieves boredom. Explained one connector to refugees from Sierra Leone (who watch mainly for war news), "I think that's the main thing they do 'cause they don't have any place to go." In Benson, N.C., radio is said to be the more popular medium, since many migrant farm workers are without television sets. The area boasts a radio station that serves the Hispanic community in North Carolina and two neighboring states. It provides public service announcements and many education programs in Spanish. Connectors in this community describe radio as an extremely powerful medium.

81   Connectors in every city suggest that lower literacy levels among the majority of their immigrant and refugee clients make television and radio more effective media and outreach tools than newspapers. The one exception is Chicago, where many of the Chinese immigrants we met with rely on Chinese language newspapers for important information, such as job listings.

82   The International Institute of New Jersey is one service agency that sponsors a regular radio program that addresses topics of concern to the immigrants and refugees they serve. They believe this is an effective way to broaden their reach into the community while raising awareness and providing useful information at the same time.

Word of Mouth, Stories and Personal Connections

83   Connectors urge greater use of active word-of-mouth networks, and to a lesser extent television and radio, because most of these immigrants and refugees hail from oral cultures. Connectors say talking and telling stories face-to-face are the most effective methods of communication. Connectors take this into consideration when attempting to educate the Somali community in Minneapolis. "Stories work," said one connector there, much more so than brochures or fliers. Refugees agree that they prefer to talk to one another, face-to-face, than to read or write.

84   Personal connections or at least some familiarity between the immigrant/refugee and the person providing them with help is essential for effective outreach. One connector to South and Central American immigrants in Prince Georges County, Md., said about her

clients, "I think they open up when they see Latin faces." A connector to migrant farm workers in Benson, N.C., shared similar thoughts: "They trust me…[They come to my office on Monday] and on Tuesday they see me in Wal-Mart." Connectors agree that immigrants and refugees tend to not only listen, but also talk more openly, if they are approached by someone they know. As a result, connectors often end up discussing issues that go far beyond their professional scope. A connector explained, "[Housing] is not the only thing you end up doing…you end up talking about taxes, health, immigration, everything…you become a counselor on everything."

85   Bilingual teachers, aides, counselors within the public school system provide valuable information and assistance to many immigrants and refugees, especially Hispanic immigrants. Said one connector to Mexican immigrants in Dallas, "The school is respected because that's [our] culture…the teacher walks on water."

86   In some communities, the agencies that sponsor refugees' arrivals, such as Catholic Charities in Portland, Maine, and Lutheran Social Services in Minneapolis and St. Paul, continue to be a trusted source of information for refugees even years after their initial arrival to the United States. Although these agencies are not always set up to provide services over the long term, refugees know and trust their staffs and may be willing to seek information from them, making these agencies a possible communication vehicle for other service providers as well.

Religious Leaders

87   Often coming from a highly religious background where religious leaders are greatly respected, many new immigrants and refugees turn to churches and mosques for spiritual support upon arrival. Religious organizations also provide practical help. Many offer ESL classes and other educational programs: a mosque we visited in Union City, N.J., for example, brings in speakers to discuss issues such as American parenting styles. Some serve as informal job banks, while others address needs such as food, clothing and shelter. Their church tends to be the main, and often first, meeting place for refugees from Sierra Leone living in the Washington, D.C., area. Its pastor said, "It is the church where they meet with their friends and then they go back home—and from that place we begin to show them the system. Most times we are the first people that will show them [a] McDonald's." It is clear that religious organizations are able to provide a source of comfort. Some Arab immigrants in Union City, N.J., describe their mosque as their second home.

88   For these reasons, organized religion in America can provide an effective opportunity for community outreach. Buddhist monks in Orange County, are already active in outreach with various social services, as are many Episcopalian and Evangelical ministries in and around Benson, N.C. In fact, in Benson, the majority of migrant farm workers are Roman Catholic and yet they are attracted to evangelical ministries because they fill a void: they provide much-needed services such as food, shelter, clothing and transport, as well as some sports and recreation opportunities for their children while the Catholic church does relatively little.

89   Immigrant and refugee communities have historically proven to be difficult to reach, making LSPM/DR's study methodology potentially useful to other researchers. The study had two parts:

- A pilot phase, involving five communities, primarily in large cities.
- Phase One, which incorporated refinements based on the pilot phase and involved five more diverse communities.

90   Pilot phase cities were chosen because:

- Census data showed they had a significant population of recent immigrants and/or refugees.

- RWJF grantees who work with immigrant and refugee populations recommended them.
- They provided representation from across the United States.

91   Table 2 contains a detailed breakdown of the locations and research participants in the pilot phase.

92   The process in each city had two parts:

1. Initially, before meeting any immigrants or refugees, LSPM/DR conducted one focus group with community "connectors" in order to learn about the needs of immigrants and refugees in that community as well as the kind of assistance available. Connector groups consisted of social workers, health care workers, housing managers, professional interpreters, mental health counselors, Medicaid enrollment workers, ESL teachers and other service providers. Connectors were recommended initially by local RWJF grantees; from these first contacts LSPM/DR staff were referred to other service providers who were asked also to participate in the focus group.
2. This focus group was followed by a series of group interviews with immigrant or refugee families. Local providers, sometimes RWJF grantees, helped identify and recruit research participants. Multi-generational families were selected in order to gain insight to the breadth of needs facing immigrant and refugee families. In most cases one family was interviewed at a time, although occasionally two families participated together. Roughly two to three group interviews were conducted in each city.

93   LSPM/DR staff made it a point to partner with trusted local providers who helped sponsor the focus groups and find comfortable settings and even local caterers. The focus groups took place in locations like a church hall, a local public library, a mosque, and a high school. Holding the focus groups in places where the participants felt comfortable helped ensure a good turnout for the focus groups. Equally important was using a moderator from the community, if possible, or of the same ethnic background. LSPM/DR staff identified and trained local community members to play this role, or contracted with a trained focus group moderator of the appropriate ethnic background.

94   All group interviews and focus groups were designed to be open-ended and informal to allow immigrant and refugee families as well as their providers to drive the conversation and raise issues of importance. The discussions (with both connectors and families) covered these topics:

- General experience settling in America;
- Goals, aspirations, daily routines;
- Specific or immediate needs as well as longer term needs, including employment, education, physical and mental health, transportation, housing, legal services, child care and language issues;
- Awareness of and access to programs and services; experiences seeking and enrolling in programs; and
- Sources of information and support.

95   In both the pilot phase and Phase One, connectors and the immigrants/refugees themselves at times provided a very different picture of services in their community. Connectors, for example, would describe the many services they provide and how many families they assist, yet immigrants and refugees would report being unaware of such services and unfamiliar with these very same service providers.

96   The experience in the pilot phase led to important changes in four areas for Phase One: the cities targeted (Table 3 lists the cities involved in Phase One), the background research conducted, the methodology used to interview the immigrants and refugees themselves, and the use of follow-up interviews.

TABLE 2
Pilot Phase Cities and Participants

Site	Population	Focus Group Type	Rationale
Prince Georges County, Md.	South and Central American Immigrants	1 Group w/ Connectors 2-3 Groups with Families	Emerging community; overextended local resources.
Washington, D.C.	Refugees from Sierra Leone	1 Group w/ Connectors 2-3 Groups with Families	Large refugee community; fairly strong infrastructure for dealing with refugee issues.
Chicago, Ill.	Chinese Immigrants	1 Group w/ Connectors 2-3 Groups with Families	Strong local service providers; established immigrant community.
Dallas, Texas	Mexican Immigrants	1 Group w/ Connectors 2-3 Groups with Families	Large immigrant population; experience dealing with immigrant concerns; resources possibly overwhelmed by demand.
Portland, Maine	Refugees from Somalia	1 Group w/ Connectors 2 Groups with Families	Emerging population; smaller city experience; fewer resources available.

Targeted Cities

97   Although our research populations largely remained the same (with the addition of migrant farm workers from Mexico), we expanded our criteria for site selection beyond density, RWJF recommendation and location. Our aim was to have diversity in:

- Size of city—smaller, less resources vs. larger, urban centers;
- Social services infrastructure—struggling vs. more resources;
- Dominant ethnic group vs. one of many newly arriving groups;
- First wave vs. second wave; and
- Immigration due to employment vs. community or family connections.

Background Research

98   In Phase One, the research team immersed itself in the community prior to any focus groups by gathering background information through interviews and then by spending about 6–8 hours touring the community and meeting with local leaders. Before arriving in the city we conducted 8–12 lengthy contextual interviews by telephone and reviewed recent articles and news stories about these communities. From this work we developed background memos on each city. We also added tours of ethnic enclaves, favored "hang-outs," and local clinics, which helped the research team to pick up on subtle undercurrents in the community and to know some of the locations, institutions, and people to which the focus group participants referred. The research team also conducted on-site informal interviews with various providers immediately before the focus groups. All these activities gave the research team a broader understanding of the community as well as a clearer picture of the social services infrastructure that was (or was not) in place.

Focus Group Methodology

99   We continued to start with one connector focus group although we broadened the definition of connector to include individuals in less formal positions, such as spiritual leaders, community advocates and members of the community who themselves became informal leaders. We also moved from the "family interviews" used in the pilot phase to more traditional focus groups. In Phase One, we conducted these focus groups with 8–12 immigrant/

refugee adults. We chose adults who were not related, so researchers could probe more deeply into sensitive issues and experiences which participants might have been reluctant to discuss with family members.

Follow-up Interviews

100   In Phase One, the research team conducted phone interviews with individuals who were important to the study but who were unable to meet with us on-site. In a few cases, we also followed up with certain focus group participants who were quiet during the focus groups, to ensure that we did not lose their voice. This was also done to be sensitive to cultural and other barriers that may have made it difficult for participants to participate during the larger group meetings.

101   In the body of this report, the issues shown by our research to be facing immigrants and refugees are organized by the social factors to which they pertain. In this Appendix, we instead present these issues in order of significance, based on the frequency with which these problems were raised in the focus groups, the degree to which they were widespread and affected all of the immigrant and refugee groups in this study, and the level of intensity with which they were discussed. Section 3 contains full descriptions of the nature and impact of each of these issues.

1. Legal status (lack of legal documentation)
2. Language—lack of proficiency with English
3. Exploitation and Discrimination
4. Stress
5. Undiagnosed and untreated mental health conditions
6. Problems with the schools
7. Lack of job mobility and low-paying jobs
8. Lack of transportation and physical isolation (especially for women)
9. Safety

TABLE 3
Phase One Cities and Participants

Site	Population	Group Type	Rationale
Schuyler, Neb.	Mexican Immigrants	1 Group w/Connectors 2 Groups w/Adults	Immigrants recruited by local meat packing industry to historically white rural community.
Orange County, Calif.	Chinese Immigrants	1 Group w/Connectors 2 Groups w/Adults	"Invisible minority" living among many other immigrant groups in crowded urban area. Many demands on local resources.
Union City, N.J.	Arabic Immigrants	1 Group w/Connectors 2 Groups w/Adults	Understudied population; second largest Arabic population in the U.S.; unique post 9/11 experience.
Minneapolis/St. Paul, Minn.	Refugees from Somalia	1 Group w/Connectors 2 Groups w/Adults	Largest Somali community in the U.S.; seen as successful transition; strong local providers.
Benson, N.C.	Migrant Farm Workers from Mexico	1 Group w/Connectors	Agricultural; fluid population hard to serve; unique needs.

Aria: A Memoir of a Bilingual Childhood
Richard Rodriguez

1   Supporters of bilingual education imply today that students like me miss a great deal by not being taught in their family's language. What they seem not to recognize is that, as a socially disadvantaged child, I regarded Spanish as a private language. It was a ghetto language that deepened and strengthened my feeling of public separateness. What I needed to learn in school was that I had the right, and the obligation, to speak the public language. The odd truth is that my first-grade classmates could have become bilingual, in the conventional sense of the word, more easily than I. Had they been taught early (as upper middle-class children often are taught) a "second language" like Spanish or French, they could have regarded it simply as another public language. In my case, such bilingualism could not have been so quickly achieved. What I did not believe was that I could speak a single public language.

Richard Rodriguez

2   Without question, it would have pleased me to have heard my teachers address me in Spanish when I entered the classroom. I would have felt much less afraid. I would have imagined that my instructors were somehow "related" to me; I would indeed have heard their Spanish as my family's language. I would have trusted them and responded with ease. But I would have delayed—postponed for how long?—having to learn the language of public society. I would have evaded—and for how long?—learning the great lesson of school: that I had a public identity.

3   Fortunately, my teachers were unsentimental about their responsibility. What they understood was that I needed to speak public English. So their voices would search me out, asking me questions. Each time I heard them I'd look up in surprise to see a nun's face frowning at me. I'd mumble, not really meaning to answer. The nun would persist. "Richard, stand up. Don't look at the floor. Speak up. Speak to the entire class, not just to me!" But I couldn't believe English could be my language to use. (In part, I did not want to believe it.) I continued to mumble. I resisted the teacher's demands. (Did I somehow suspect that once I learned this public language my family life would be changed?) Silent, waiting for the bell to sound, I remained dazed, diffident, afraid.

4   Because I wrongly imagined that English was intrinsically a public language and Spanish was intrinsically private. I easily noted the difference between classroom language and the language of home. At school, words were directed to a general audience of listeners. ("Boys and girls…") Words were meaningfully ordered. And the point was not self-expression alone, but to make oneself understood by many others. The teacher quizzed: "Boys and girls, why do we use that word in this sentence? Could we think of a better word to use there? Would the sentence change its meaning if the words were differently arranged? Isn't there a better way of saying much the same thing?" (I couldn't say. I wouldn't try to say.)

5   Three months passed. Five. A half year. Unsmiling, ever watchful, my teachers noted my silence. They began to connect my behavior with the slow progress my brother and sisters were making. Until, one Saturday morning, three nuns arrived at the house to talk

to our parents. Stiffly they sat on the blue living-room sofa. From the doorway of another room, spying on the visitors, I noted the incongruity, the clash of two worlds, the faces and voices of school intruding upon the familiar setting of home. I overheard one voice gently wondering, "Do your children speak only Spanish at home, Mrs. Rodriguez?" While another voice added, "That Richard especially seems so timid and shy."

6   *That Rich-heard!*

7   With great tact, the visitors continued, "Is it possible for you and your husband to encourage your children to practice their English when they are home?" Of course my parents complied. What would they not do for their children's well-being? And how could they question the Church's authority which those women represented? In an instant they agreed to give up the language (the sounds) which had revealed and accentuated our family's closeness. The moment after the visitors left, the change was observed. "*Ahora*, speak to us only *en inglés*," my father and mother told us.

8   At first, it seemed a kind of game. After dinner each night, the family gathered together to practice "our" English. It was still then *inglés*, a language foreign to us, so we felt drawn to it as strangers. Laughing, we would try to define words we could not pronounce. We played with strange English sounds, often over-anglicizing our pronunciations. And we filled the smiling gaps of our sentences with familiar Spanish sounds. But that was cheating, somebody shouted, and everyone laughed.

9   In school, meanwhile, like my brother and sisters, I was required to attend a daily tutoring session. I needed a full year of this special work. I also needed my teachers to keep my attention from straying in class by calling out, "*Rich-heard!*"—their English voices slowly loosening the ties to my other name, with its three notes, *Ri-car-do*. Most of all, I needed to hear my mother and father speak to me in a moment of seriousness in "broken"—suddenly heartbreaking—English. This scene was inevitable. One Saturday morning I entered the kitchen where my parents were talking, but I did not realize that they were talking in Spanish until, the moment they saw me, their voices changed and they began speaking English. The gringo sounds they uttered startled me. Pushed me away. In that moment of trivial misunderstanding and profound insight, I felt my throat twisted by unsounded grief. I simply turned and left the room. But I had no place to escape to where I could grieve in Spanish. My brother and sisters were speaking English in another part of the house.

10   Again and again in the days following, as I grew increasingly angry, I was obliged to hear my mother and father encouraging me: "Speak to us *en inglés*." Only then did I determine to learn classroom English. Thus, sometime afterward it happened: one day in school, I raised my hand to volunteer an answer to a question. I spoke out in a loud voice and I did not think it remarkable when the entire class understood. That day I moved very far from being the disadvantaged child I had been only days earlier. Taken hold at last was the belief, the calming assurance, that I *belonged* in public.

11   Shortly after, I stopped hearing the high, troubling sounds of *los gringos*. A more and more confident speaker of English, I didn't listen to how strangers sounded when they talked to me. With so many English-speaking people around me, I no longer heard American accents. Conversations quickened. Listening to persons whose voices sounded eccentrically pitched, I might note their sounds for a few seconds, but then I'd concentrate on what they were saying. Now when I heard someone's tone of voice—angry or questioning or sarcastic or happy or sad—I didn't distinguish it from the words it expressed. Sound and word were thus tightly wedded. At the end of each day I was often bemused, and always relieved, to realize how "soundless," though crowded with words, my day in public had been. An eight-year-old boy, I finally came to accept what had been technically true since my birth: I was an American citizen.

12   But diminished by then was the special feeling of closeness at home. Gone was the desperate, urgent, intense feeling of being at home among those with whom I felt intimate. Our family remained a loving family, but one greatly changed. We were no longer so close,

no longer bound tightly together by the knowledge of our separateness from *los gringos*. Neither my older brother nor my sisters rushed home after school any more. Nor did I. When I arrived home, often there would be neighborhood kids in the house. Or the house would be empty of sounds.

13   Following the dramatic Americanization of their children, even my parents grew more publicly confident—especially my mother. First she learned the names of all the people on the block. Then she decided we needed to have a telephone in our house. My father, for his part, continued to use the word gringo, but it was no longer charged with bitterness or distrust. Stripped of any emotional content, the word simply became a name for those Americans not of Hispanic descent. Hearing him, sometimes, I wasn't sure if he was pronouncing the Spanish word *gringo,* or saying gringo in English.

14   There was a new silence at home. As we children learned more and more English, we shared fewer and fewer words with our parents. Sentences needed to be spoken slowly when one of us addressed our mother or father. Often the parent wouldn't understand. The child would need to repeat himself. Still the parent misunderstood. The young voice, frustrated, would end up saying, "Never mind"—the subject was closed. Dinners would be noisy with the clinking of knives and forks against dishes. My mother would smile softly between her remarks; my father, at the other end of the table, would chew and chew his food while he stared over the heads of his children.

15   My mother! My father! After English became my primary language, I no longer knew what words to use in addressing my parents. The old Spanish words (those tender accents of sound) I had earlier used—*mamá* and *papá*—I couldn't use any more. They would have been all-too-painful reminders of how much had changed in my life. On the other hand, the words I heard neighborhood kids call their parents seemed equally unsatisfactory. "Mother" and "father," "ma," "papa," "pa," "dad," "pop" (how I hated the all-American sound of that last word)—all these I felt were unsuitable terms of address for *my* parents. As a result, I never used them at home. Whenever I'd speak to my parents, I would try to get their attention by looking at them. In public conversations, I'd refer to them as my "parents" or my "mother" and "father."

16   My mother and father, for their part, responded differently, as their children spoke to them less. My mother grew restless, seemed troubled and anxious at the scarceness of words exchanged in the house. She would question me about my day when I came home from school. She smiled at my small talk. She pried at the edges of my sentences to get me to say something more. ("What …?") She'd join conversations she overheard, but her intrusions often stopped her children's talking. By contrast, my father seemed to grow reconciled to the new quiet. Though his English somewhat improved, he tended more and more to retire into silence. At dinner he spoke very little. One night his children and even his wife helplessly giggled at his garbled English pronunciation of the Catholic "Grace Before Meals." Thereafter he made his wife recite the prayer at the start of each meal, even on formal occasions when there were guests in the house.

17   Hers became the public voice of the family. On official business it was she, not my father, who would usually talk to strangers on the phone or in stores. We children grew so accustomed to his silence that years later we would routinely refer to his "shyness." (My mother often tried to explain: both of his parents died when he was eight. He was raised by an uncle who treated him as little more than a menial servant. He was never encouraged to speak. He grew up alone—a man of few words.) But I realized my father was not shy whenever I'd watch him speaking Spanish with relatives. Using Spanish, he was quickly effusive. Especially when talking with other men, his voice would spark, flicker, flare alive with varied sounds. In Spanish he expressed ideas and feelings he rarely revealed when speaking English. With firm Spanish sounds he conveyed a confidence and authority that English would never allow him.

18   The silence at home, however, was not simply the result of fewer words passing between parents and children. More profound for me was the silence created by my

inattention to sounds. At about the time I no longer bothered to listen with care to the sounds of English in public, I grew careless about listening to the sounds made by the family when they spoke. Most of the time I would hear someone speaking at home and didn't distinguish his sounds from the words people uttered in public. I didn't even pay much attention to my parents' accented and ungrammatical speech—at least not at home. Only when I was with them in public would I become alert to their accents. But even then their sounds caused me less and less concern. For I was growing increasingly confident of my own public identity.

19   I would have been happier about my public success had I not recalled, sometimes, what it had been like earlier, when my family conveyed its intimacy through a set of conveniently private sounds. Sometimes in public, hearing a stranger, I'd hark back to my lost past. A Mexican farm worker approached me one day downtown. He wanted directions to some place. "*Hijito,...*" he said. And his voice stirred old longings. Another time I was standing beside my mother in the visiting room of a Carmelite convent, before the dense screen which rendered the nuns shadowy figures. I heard several of them speaking Spanish in their busy, singsong, overlapping voices, assuring my mother that, yes, yes, we were remembered, all our family was remembered, in their prayers. Those voices echoed faraway family sounds. Another day a dark-faced old woman touched my shoulder lightly to steady herself as she boarded a bus. She murmured something to me I couldn't quite comprehend. Her Spanish voice came near, like the face of a never-before-seen relative in the instant before I was kissed. That voice, like so many of the Spanish voices I'd hear in public, recalled the golden age of my childhood.

Part Five

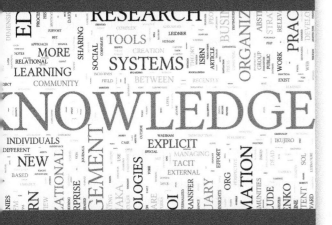

Reading Selections

Part Five includes selected readings from which you can draw to practice the reading and writing processes outlined in previous sections of the book. Each of the readings included in this section addresses the book's theme of crossing borders. For example, there are stories about immigrants, people actually crossing a physical border to come into the US, and other readings that address crossing the borders of culture, social class, education, and so on.

As you read from the selections in this section, remember the reading process outlined and demonstrated in Chapter 1.

The Naked Culture
Vincent G. Barnes

1   When I worked in Thailand in the mid-eighties, I often went to a border outpost, and peered over the no man's land into Cambodia, where alternating jungle and parched grass wavered in a gel of heat. Somewhere in the distance, at the ruins of ancient Angkor Wat, enigmatic smiles on faces carved in blocks of stone watched over incomprehensible violence—war and beauty in oxymoronic symbiosis. A delicate, sensuous Samsara dancer and a hideous Ramakian giant writhed in an inseparable union of paradox. Cambodia was an enigma, a mystery intensified by four years of silence in the seventies, when nothing went in and all that came out was a trickle of shocked refugees telling incredible tales of the bloody Khmer Rouge reign.

2   I also went to the nearby refugee camps that had swelled just inside Thailand after the Khmer Rouge were deposed in 1979. How could it come to be that the second largest Khmer city was now in Thailand? In the most prosaic terms, here was a land where nothing seemed to make sense—an odd, tragic country.

3   Having peeked once illicitly in Cambodia's veiled window, I wanted to see more. With the infatuation of a voyeur, I lustfully pursued what furtive glimpses I could get of the stricken yet forbidden country. I saw movies. I read books. Slowly, I learned the grisly details of how, under the terrible thunder of frenzied American bombing, on a stage built by the colonial French, with China and Vietnam as co-directors, Prince Sihainouk, Pol Pot and Khmer Rouge performed their dramas of violence.

4   I was just finishing graduate school when I heard about an English teaching job in Cambodia. I feverishly threw myself into the task of getting selected to go. Apparently there wasn't much competition for the job; forms for visas and immunizations started arriving. I would be going.

5   I brought along as many textbooks as I could, in addition to those I was assigned to transport for my employer. These were the usual fare: Betty Azar's grammar books, American Idioms, Pocket Dictionaries. But fresh out of graduate school, armed with a holster full of the latest language acquisition jargon, I was determined to temper this traditional approach with something innovative. In a moment of inspiration, I threw in a 1989 copy of the *Seattle Yellow Pages*.

6   My colleagues couldn't understand why I had brought the yellow pages, but in graduate school I had been taught how closely language and culture are tied. I had learned the importance of using materials which reflect the culture in which the language is used. What better window into American culture than a yellow pages? What better catalyst for conversation? It had pictures. It had written words. Pound for pound, it was a cultural, linguistic, and pedagogical bargain. It was also deeply profane.

7   What I remember most about flying into Phnom Penh was looking out the plane window at a bridge whose middle was missing. Something told me it was not a bridge under construction, but rather a victim in Cambodia's twenty years of war. I learned later that Khmer Rouge sappers had blown it up in 1973, and anyone under twenty years old knew no other bridge.

8   The bridge foretold what would become dismally clear. I soon saw that I had come to a country that was too shocked to know its own utter nakedness—a hot, dusty place not yet dead, whose inhabitants were like plane crash survivors, clothes burned off, wandering in a daze through the wreckage. Hospitals were crowded, dirty, and ill-equipped, filled with dying dengue-fevered children, jaundiced octogenarians who were probably only forty-five, and malaria-eyed farmers, who were lucky to find themselves in any hospital at all.

Electricity was intermittent. Roads were potholed, bridges broken. The monsoon flooded downtown at will.

9   Before starting work one afternoon, I opened my box of books, placed the yellow pages on my knee, and flipped through the flimsy parchment. With each turn of a page, I felt more and more as though I'd unwittingly smuggled a packet of pornography into a seminary. In the yellow pages were roof doctors, auto mechanics, service stations, sauna equipment, underwater sports, sign companies, carpet cleaners, sound systems, mini-storage, swimming pool contractors, cellular telephones and twenty-seven pages of restaurant listings—a saturnalia, a Marcosian shoe closet of opulence and excess. I felt relieved that our curriculum was so rigid that the distant calls from academia for tribute to the altars of curricular innovation could be ignored, and the Yellow pages put discreetly back in the box.

10   Here in the yellow pages was a big-headed, large-toothed Rescue Rooter logo rushing off in perpetual cheer to an eternity of clogged suburban bathroom drains, with a delightful smile chasing away the terrible angst Americans suffer when their sinks back up. In Phnom Penh, two-thirds of the country had no plumbing at all, and the only treated water got recontaminated through leaky pipes. Because of a lack of toilets, many went outside to the overgrown median strips or to vacant lots to relieve themselves; "dried airborne fecal matter" was a prominent cause of respiratory illnesses.

11   In the yellow pages were four pages of plush resorts; in Cambodia, the only equivalent diversion was to eat tough chicken on a stick in bamboo shelters over the parasite-infested waters of nearby lakes, or to visit some shot-up shrine under armed guard.

12   In the yellow pages were psychics, psychologists, psychotherapists, and counselors for marital and sexual crises, compulsive eating, co-dependency, addictive relationships—a panoply of treatments for a people too self-absorbed to know what misery really is. In Cambodia, polygamy was encouraged to make up for the understaffed male population, whose numbers had been depleted by war; thousands of widows remained, regardless. During Pol Pot time, rifle-faced cadre assigned complete strangers marriage partners and married them en masse. Nothing in the yellow pages for that.

13   Thousands of people have stepped on land mines in Cambodia. Lucky ones only lost a limb or two. One hot afternoon after teaching, I visited a prosthetics hospital in what was once a Buddhist temple. I stepped over and around young mothers practicing physical therapy on their children who would never walk because of diseases that common inoculations could have prevented. I stared at the obscenity of a young man straining to build up muscles to accommodate a new leg; I watched him sweat each stump raise, while deflecting his shame with contrived clinical distance. No less obscene was the workshop where men stood at power tools fashioning plastic, leather, and wooden legs for themselves and the thousands waiting for something better than metal crutches.

14   I left Cambodia ill and exhausted with a parasite infection, my voyeuristic thirst ruthlessly and abundantly quenched. I gave away most of the books I had brought. Anything printed in English was a hot commodity. The government printing office had pirated Azar's grammar book and was running off thousands of its own copies. They even reproduced the blue cover, right down to the yellow butterfly. Someone was probably going to profit handsomely, and it wouldn't be Betty Azar. If she could see the place, she wouldn't mind.

15   Perhaps there was a child somewhere who would enjoy shading in the funny figures in the yellow pages? But no. Somehow, the book could not be shown to anyone. It was a window through which I didn't want Cambodians to look. I could not let them see me in my culture's nakedness as I had them in theirs.

Don't Call Me a Hot Tamale
Judith Ortiz Cofer

1   On a bus to London from Oxford University, where I was earning some graduate credits one summer, a young man, obviously fresh from a pub, approached my seat. With both hands over his heart, he went down on his knees in the aisle and broke into an Irish tenor's rendition of "Maria" from *West Side Story*. I was not amused. "Maria" had followed me to London, reminding me of a prime fact of my life: You can leave the island of Puerto Rico, master the English language, and travel as far as you can, but if you're a Latina, especially one who so clearly belongs to Rita Moreno's[1] gene pool, the island travels with you.

2   Growing up in New Jersey and wanting most of all to belong, I lived in two completely different worlds. My parents designed our life as a microcosm of their *casas* on the island—we spoke in Spanish, ate Puerto Rican food bought at the *bodega*, and practiced strict Catholicism complete with Sunday mass in Spanish.

3   I was kept under tight surveillance by my parents, since my virtue and modesty were, by their cultural equation, the same as their honor. As teenagers, my friends and I were lectured constantly on how to behave as proper *señoritas*. But it was a conflicting message we received, since our Puerto Rican mothers also encouraged us to look and act like women by dressing us in clothes our Anglo schoolmates and their mothers found too "mature" and flashy. I often felt humiliated when I appeared at an American friend's birthday party wearing a dress more suitable for a semiformal. At Puerto Rican festivities, neither the music nor the colors we wore could be too loud.

4   I remember Career Day in high school, when our teachers told us to come dressed as if for a job interview. That morning, I agonized in front of my closet, trying to figure out what a "career girl" would wear, because the only model I had was Marlo Thomas[2] on TV. To me and my Puerto Rican girl-friends, dressing up meant wearing our mother's ornate jewelry and clothing.

5   At school that day, the teachers assailed us for wearing "everything at once"—meaning too much jewelry and too many accessories. And it was painfully obvious that the other students in their tailored skirts and silk blouses thought we were hopeless and vulgar. The way they looked at us was a taste of the cultural clash that awaited us in the real world, where prospective employers and men on the street would often misinterpret our tight skirts and bright colors as a come-on.

6   It is custom, not chromosomes, that leads us to choose scarlet over pale pink. Our mothers had grown up on a tropical island where the natural environment was a riot of primary colors, where showing your skin was one way to keep cool as well as to look sexy. On the island, women felt freer to dress and move provocatively since they were protected by the traditions and laws of a Spanish/Catholic system of morality and machismo, the main rule of which was: *You may look at my sister, but if you touch her I will kill you.* The extended family and church structure provided them with a circle of safety on the island; if a man "wronged" a girl, everyone would close in to save her family honor.

7   Off-island, signals often get mixed. When a Puerto Rican girl who is dressed in her idea of what is attractive meets a man from the mainstream culture who has been trained to react to certain types of clothing as a sexual signal, a clash is likely to take place. She is seen as a Hot Tamale, a sexual firebrand. I learned this lesson at my first

---

[1] A Puerto Rican actress, dancer, and singer. She is well known for her role in the movie musical *West Side Story*, a version of Shakespeare's *Romeo and Juliet* featuring Anglos and Puerto Ricans in New York City.

[2] Star of a 1966-71 television comedy about a young woman living on her own in New York City.

formal dance when my date leaned over and painfully planted a sloppy, overeager kiss on my mouth. When I didn't respond with sufficient passion, he said in a resentful tone: "I thought you Latin girls were supposed to mature early." It was only the first time I would feel like a fruit or vegetable—I was supposed to *ripen*, not just grow into womanhood like other girls.

8   These stereotypes, though rarer, still surface in my life. I recently stayed at a classy metropolitan hotel. After having dinner with a friend, I was returning to my room when a middle-aged man in a tuxedo stepped directly into my path. With his champagne glass extended toward me, he exclaimed, "Evita!"[3]

9   Blocking my way, he bellowed the song "Don't Cry for Me, Argentina." Playing to the gathering crowd, he began to sing loudly a ditty to the tune of "La Bamba"[4]—except the lyrics were about a girl named Maria whose exploits all rhymed with her name and gonorrhea.

10   I knew that this same man—probably a corporate executive, even worldly by most standards—would never have regaled a white woman with a dirty song in public. But to him, I was just a character in his universe of "others," all cartoons.

11   Still, I am one of the lucky ones. There are thousands of Latinas without the privilege of the education that my parents gave me. For them every day is a struggle against the misconceptions perpetuated by the myth of the Latina as whore, domestic worker or criminal.

12   Rather than fight these pervasive stereotypes, I try to replace them with a more interesting set of realities. I travel around the U.S. reading from my books of poetry and my novel. With the stories I tell, the dreams and fears I examine in my work, I try to get my audience past the particulars of my skin color, my accent or my clothes.

13   I once wrote a poem in which I called Latinas "God's brown daughters." It is really a prayer, of sorts, for communication and respect. In it, Latin women pray "in Spanish to an Anglo God/with a Jewish heritage," and they are "fervently hoping/that if not omnipotent, / at least He be bilingual."

Infographic: How the DREAM Act Helps the Economy
Juan Carlos Guzmán and Raúl C. Jara | October 1, 2012

How the DREAM Act Helps the Economy

Passing the federal DREAM Act would add a total of $329 billion to the American economy by 2030. This infographic explains how the act provides such a boost to the nation, by granting legal immigration status to 2.1 million young people and incentivizing higher education. The $148 billion in higher earnings that result from DREAMers being able to work legally and achieve greater education leads to increased spending on goods and services such as houses, cars, and computers. This spending ripples through the economy, supporting another $181 billion in induced economic impact, the creation of 1.4 million new jobs, and more than $10 billion in increased revenue.

---

[3] Eva Perón, wife of Juan Perón, President of Argentina in the 1940s and 1950s. She is the subject of the musical *Evita*.
[4] A song with Spanish lyrics popular in the late 1950s.

A CENTER FOR AMERICAN PROGRESS GRAPHIC

How the DREAM Act helps the economy

Passing the federal DREAM Act would add a total of $329 billion to the American economy by 2030. This infographic explains how the act provides such a boost to the nation, by granting legal immigration status to 2.1 million young people and incentivizing higher education. The $148 billion in higher earnings that result from DREAMers being able to work legally and achieve greater education leads to increased spending on goods and services such as houses, cars, and computers. This spending ripples through the economy, supporting another $181 billion in induced economic impact, the creation of 1.4 million new jobs, and more than $10 billion in increased revenue.

2.1 MILLION ELIGIBLE DREAMERS

= 50,000

Two ways in which this population will increase their earning:

Receiving legal status

This creates an aggregate 19 percent increasing in earnings by 2030, totaling

$148 BILLION

Pursuing higher education

Those earnings in turn trigger spending on goods and services:

THAT SPENDING RIPPLES THROUGHOUT THE ECONOMY CREATING:

$181 BILLION
in induced economic impact

1.4 MILLION
new jobs

$10 BILLION
in increased revenue

$329 BILLION

in total economic impact for 2.1 million eligible DREAMers

Source: Author's estimates based on American Community Survey Data 2006-2010, and 2010 IMPLAN Modeling

Center for American Progress

Using Learning Strategies in Various Disciplines
Laurie Kimpton-Lorence

1   Even though the various subjects share learning techniques, disciplines and cultures have acquired boundaries that separate and isolate one from another. One of the reasons may be because of the different questions they choose to ask. Scientists want to know what chemicals combine to make up sugar; social scientists wonder why the taste of sugar is so appealing. A mathematician looks to count the sugar grains, while an artist wants to explore the sugar's form. U.S. doctors ask how their patients can decrease their sugar intake while Somalian physicians look for ways to increase it.

2   The disciplines also differ in the ways they talk about a topic; in other words, their discourse differs. Each discipline has its own specific vocabulary and its own style of communication. Business and mathematics use bar graphs to illustrate their concepts, while geographers use maps and scientists use models. Social scientists use research studies to support their points while historians use stories. To give more specific examples of their differences and the different challenges they present to learners, we can look at five of the major disciplines: science, social science, mathematics, business and humanities.

Science

3   Science has a reputation for being one of the hardest disciplines to master because of its technical vocabulary and very formal style of communication. Steve Goetz, a science professor at a northwest community college, gives us some other reasons for this reputation:

> The main purpose of the natural and physical sciences is to seek a totally objective explanation for things. It is an incredibly precise field, attempting to include everything that needs including while leaving out anything that is even a little bit extra. Almost every word has an exact meaning and there is a distinct lack of flexibility in the procedures. Although the results and conclusions of an experiment can be open to discussions, the methods are careful and exact. Because learners are nervous about this precision, they want the reassurance of letter perfect definitions, which means they memorize everything exactly as it is stated in the book or lecture. They have difficulties trying to distinguish between the letter perfect definitions of things and the precision that results in really knowing the concepts. They also have problems knowing how to distinguish between the definitions and the examples, or how to get to the heart of an overwhelming amount of information. The less they understand, the more complex they write. Though scientific writing can appear lifeless, a well-defined, well-described study can be elegant in its simplicity, not complexity.
>
> Learners of science need permission to feel confused at first. They need to realize that scientific problems cannot be solved right away. They need to have patience and the confidence that their confusion will eventually sort itself out. Then they will finally be able to appreciate and duplicate the elegance of scientific precision and simplicity.

4   In its objective purpose, its numerous and specific terminology, and its precise writing style, the field of science separates itself from other disciplines. These subjects provide a difficult challenge for learners. They must personalize information that doesn't always seem to have a place in their world. To illustrate: What if the following information was presented to you. "One property of atoms is that they combine without changing their original structure. Even when hydrogen and oxygen combine, they still remain separate elements."

5   Does that concept seem difficult? Impersonal? What if you went to your kitchen and mixed sugar and water together, what would happen? The two would mix. On the other hand, if you tried to mix oil and water, they would remain separate. The same separateness is true when atoms combine. Bringing the theories into your kitchen is one way of personalizing them. This transfer from book to real life helps the concept "come alive" and thus becomes more easily learned.

6   Learners in the science field are not the only ones who struggle to personalize objective knowledge. Some scientists within the discipline question the objective, precise nature of science. In many of her essays, for example, scientist Evelyn Fox Keller reveals her concern about the language of science, suggesting that the way science discusses nature is masculine, and men possess a different culture from women. She insists that nothing can be truly objective, even science, if its answers are based on cultural beliefs. She and many other women have also talked about the myth of being objective in the science field, since by definition, objective thinking must radically separate the knowers from what is known, the experimenters from the experiment. As Fritjof Capra argues, "We can never speak of nature without, at the same time, speaking about ourselves." In science, as in many of the other disciplines, the ways of thinking and knowing are continually being challenged.

Social Science

7   Though termed a science, the social science discipline is called "social" because it concerns itself with the mixing of people rather than chemicals; with the feelings and perceptions of an event as well as the event itself. The subjects of anthropology, sociology, psychology, political science, economics, and often history and geography are included in this discipline. While each of these subjects focuses on a separate part of human nature, they share a common interest in the laws, principles and behaviors that govern humans throughout the world.

8   One way to reveal the "social" nature of this field is to consider an ongoing debate between scientists and social scientists concerning methods of experimenting. Researchers in the natural and physical sciences maintain that experiments are performed best in a laboratory setting where conditions can be controlled. For example, when mixing two chemicals or growing bacteria, science experimenters can establish and maintain the temperature, lighting and other factors. On the other hand, researchers in the social sciences argue that experiments have more "truth" or validity in a natural setting where events are allowed to take their own course. Anthropologist Jane Goodall observed gorillas in their natural environment without controlling or interfering with their movements. She described her results in a narrative, story-like discussion rather than using facts and numbers. Social scientists are often flexible, not only in their interpretations, but in their methods as well.

9   While learners of science have difficulties with the precision, beginners in the social science fields can have trouble wading through the various narrative opinions and stories that will lead them to new information. In social science, any one event can have a number of meanings: the world has war because violence is a basic part of human nature. The world has war because society has trained people to be violent. War occurs mainly because of economic reasons. Although both complex topics, the scientific reasons behind gravity can seem less confusing than the social reasons behind war.

10   The vocabulary used in the social sciences also can be as confusing as in science, not just because the words are new, but because they can differ from their normal meanings when used in a social science setting. For example, in social science research, the term "significant" does not mean quite the same as the popular meaning of the word. It is based on a specific mathematical formula.

11   Learners of the social sciences must struggle to determine which vocabulary meaning is appropriate, whose opinions have merit, and which experiments are valid, or more likely to get at the "truth." Since social science studies the relationships of living beings in their natural state, learners must accept that "truth" is social and contextual. It is social because it varies from one culture to the next. It is contextual in that it varies from one situation to the next.

12   Students can find help in clarifying the ideas and vocabulary of the social sciences by working in groups and by using organizing techniques. Since social science concerns social relationships, it follows that working with others can be used as both a study skill and a method of studying the discipline. Since social science involves a variety of opinions, it can be helpful to sort out the opinion using a cause/effect or comparison structure.

Mathematics

13   In contrast to the ambiguity of the social sciences, the math discipline reduces the world to its bare essence. Math has been called "the science of patterns" since it creates formulas for patterns that have been seen in life. For instance, the formula $x = 2y$ means that a pattern has been found: x is always twice as much as y. The word "always" can be a powerful one. In fact, one fear shared by math students stems from the expression, "There is only one right answer in math." That statement send chills down a learner's spine, but it is inaccurate. Mitchell Lazarus, who writes about "mathphobia," states that estimating and rough calculations are often very useful in math and don't always have to be exact. Math can have many "right answers," if the right answer is one that meets the problem's needs. In today's world of computers and calculators, the ability to estimate an answer is sometimes more important than knowing the answer itself.

14   Some mathematicians worry that the concentration on rules and right answers will be misinterpreted to mean that math stands for "simplified truth." Although an elephant walking down a hill can be simply represented in the single equation of an incline plane, the elephant still remains a complex animal. The incline plane is only one of the many "truths" that describe the elephant's situation. Students need to realize that math is only one piece of some purposeful end, but not usually the end itself. Just because a person accurately balances his checkbook doesn't guarantee he has any money left in his account.

15   Math is termed a "representational" system because it "represents" reality using symbols rather than words as its main form of communication. These non-word symbols present another reason for "mathphobia" among beginning math students who have difficulty translating numbers into language and real life. Even in math, students need to personalize and to make connections between math formulas and their own world. In his article "The Human Elements in Mathematics," Stephen Leacock approaches the job of translating symbols into reality by using his humor and imagination:

> The student of arithmetic who has mastered the first four rules of his art, and successfully striven with money sums and factions, finds himself confronted by an unbroken expanse of questions known as problems. These are short stories of adventure and industry with the end omitted, and, though betraying a strong family resemblance, are not without a certain element of romance.
>
> The characters in the plot of a problem are three people called A, B and C. The form of the questions is generally of this sort: A, B and C do a certain piece of work. A can do as much work in one hour as B can do in two, or C in four. Find how long they work at it.
>
> The occupations of A, B and C are many and varied. They have walking matches, ditch-digging contests, regattas and wood-piling races. At times they become commercial and enter into partnership. When they tire of walking matches, A rides on horseback, or borrows a bicycle and competes with his weaker-minded associates on foot.
>
> In the early chapters of arithmetic, their identity is concealed under the names of John, William and Henry. In algebra they are often called X, Y and Z. But to students like me, they have become more than symbols. They appear as creatures of flesh and blood, living people with their own passions, ambitions, and aspirations like the rest of us. Let us view them in turn. A is a full-blooded, blustering fellow. It is he who proposes everything. B is a quiet, easy-going fellow; afraid of A, but gentle and brotherly to little C. Poor C is an undersized, frail man with a plaintive face. His joyless life has driven him to drink. He has not the strength to work as the others; A can do more work in one hour than C in four.

16   Though written as a humorous essay, Leacock provides a way of translating math by viewing it as history, as sociology and as an adventurous tale. His writing also provides an example of how the disciplines and cultures can differ. Besides asking different questions, various disciplines and cultures differ in their terminology, their style of writing and their native expressions, also called colloquialisms. In his story about A, B and C, Leacock uses words that "math people" use. He uses a writing style that blends the more casual narrative

style, used abundantly in literature, with the more formal word phrasings, also called syntax, used in academic writing. And finally, because of his culture, many of his expressions stem from England, such as the phrase, "B and C had come in dead fagged." These specific vocabulary terms, the academic writing style, and/or the colloquial expressions can confuse a reader who might not know much about the subject or the writer's culture.

Business

17   The math, science and social science disciplines have gone through reevaluation of their content, their procedures and their beliefs about truth, yet none of them have experiences the dramatic change in philosophy that has affected the business field.

18   In the 1970s, there was concern that the future job market would require fewer highly skilled employees. Several researchers indicated that Americans were receiving more education than they needed and were becoming overqualified for the majority of available jobs. However, during the 1980s, this theory was found to be in error. Rather than requiring fewer skills, new technologies called for much higher level skills that required college degrees and certificates. Abilities such as self-assessment and communicating with others became (and are still) crucial to success in the workforce. Twenty-first century employers call for these workplace skills:

- Gather information through listening and reading
- Communicate effectively through speech and writing
- Use calculators and computers
- Acquire new skills and knowledge
- Solve problems
- Make thoughtful, open-minded decisions
- Be flexible and able to adapt to change
- Understand economics and culture in a global setting
- Work well in groups
- Be creative, innovative and self-initiating
- Set goals, plan and organize
- Tolerate uncertainty and ambiguity

19   Therefore, while business courses were previously restricted to accounting and shorthand, business has now become a broad division that parallels the content of many disciplines. The field includes classes in business communication, business math, technology and computers, interpersonal relations and leadership. Some of these courses, such as computers, may seem intimidating to students who haven't had much experience with them. Other courses, such as group dynamics, may seem uncomfortable to Americans who were raised with John Wayne's philosophy, "I can do it myself." Business communication classes can give a potentially confusing message: "Say what you mean, but be careful what you say."

20   In business as in many fields, there is an emphasis on cultural awareness. Being culturally literate is essential in the US where the population is becoming ever more diverse and where the business environment has become global rather than domestic. The US is now the leading importer of world goods. Also according to the census bureau, by the middle of the 21st century, the majority of the US population will consist of people who were once considered (and are still sometimes called) minorities. Their cultures could be at variance with mainstream business culture. For example, some Native Americans may be reluctant to work for companies that pollute or waste natural resources because their cultural beliefs promote deep respect for the earth. Many Japanese employees might prefer to work cooperatively rather than individually since their culture promotes this working style. For these reasons it is important for learners in the business discipline to be exposed to a variety of cultural work ethics and styles.

Humanities

21 The final discipline to be analyzed is the one whose purpose is analysis. According to Edwin J. Delattre, Director of the National Humanities Faculty in Concord, MA, the Humanities, also known as the liberal arts, were once called the liberating arts because they inform us of ideas and values that persistence and brilliance have created, which adds to the ideas we can think about and opens our minds. Mr. Delattre states, "No one is ever free to do anything that he cannot think of." He goes on to say that practice in reading, writing, speaking, listening and evaluating texts helps us to think harder, to analyze, and to imagine more freely. These activities show us possibilities that are new, at least to us, and expand our world. For example, we can learn through characters in stories without having to experience the glory or tragedy ourselves. This learning does not guarantee that we will become better human beings, but by putting ourselves in the place and viewpoint of others, we can expand our knowledge and opinions. In other words, although the subjects in the humanities such as literature, poetry, art, religion, languages, philosophy, and music may not free us from evil, the analysis that they require may help free us from being deceived by evil.

22 The difficulty of the humanities is for learners to be able to open themselves to the experience. Whether through writing, song or other forms, students of the humanities must expose themselves to the judgments of others. They must bare their souls, so to speak, in order to free their minds. For that reason, the criticisms are more difficult to endure. It's hard, for example, to be criticized for a paper that took so much personal agony to create. In other disciplines, the answers, right or wrong, originate from outside sources and those sources can share the criticism. In the humanities, however, the answers originate from within each individual and make him more vulnerable to the judgments of others. The strategy of writing-to-learn is especially valuable in this discipline because this technique allows writers to pull out their innermost thoughts and feelings without the worry of being judged.

Putting It Together

23 The humanities are related to the sciences, to math, and to business. It is not productive to know what is worth doing without having any idea of how to do it, which the other disciplines can teach. On the other hand, it is also not productive to know how to get things done without knowing what is important and meaningful, which the humanities can provide. The disciplines need one another and should walk hand-in-hand. Students who want full knowledge of any subject must view their topic from the eyes of many disciplines and cultures. Parker Palmer says it best: "Either eye alone is not enough. We need 'wholesight,' a vision of the world in which mind and heart unite 'as my two eyes make one in sight.' Our seeing shapes our being. Only as we see holistically can we and our world be whole."

Mute in an English-Only World
Chang-rae Lee

1 WHEN I READ OF THE TROUBLE in Palisades Park, New Jersey, over the proliferation of Korean-language signs along its main commercial strip, I unexpectedly sympathized with the frustrations, resentments, and fears of the longtime residents. They clearly felt alienated and even unwelcome in a vital part of their community. The town, like seven others in New Jersey, has passed laws requiring that half of any commercial sign in a foreign language be in English.

2 Now I certainly would never tolerate any exclusionary ideas about who could rightfully settle and belong in the town. But having been raised in a Korean immigrant family,

I saw every day the exacting price and power of language, especially with my mother, who was an outsider in an English-only world. In the first years we lived in America, my mother could speak only the most basic English, and she often encountered great difficulty whenever she went out.

3   We lived in New Rochelle, New York, in the early seventies, and most of the local businesses were run by the descendants of immigrants who, generations ago, had come to the suburbs from New York City. Proudly dotting Main Street and North Avenue were Italian pastry and cheese shops, Jewish tailors and cleaners, and Polish and German butchers and bakers. If my mother's marketing couldn't wait until the weekend, when my father had free time, she would often hold off until I came home from school to buy the groceries.

4   Though I was only six or seven years old, she insisted that I go out shopping with her and my younger sister. I mostly loathed the task, partly because it meant I couldn't spend the afternoon off playing catch with my friends but also because I knew our errands would inevitably lead to an awkward scene, and that I would have to speak up to help my mother.

5   I was just learning the language myself, but I was a quick study, as children are with new tongues. I had spent kindergarten in almost complete silence, hearing only the high nasality of my teacher and comprehending little but cranky wails and cries of my classmates. But soon, seemingly mere months later, I had already become a terrible ham and mimic, and I would crack up my father with impressions of teachers, his friends, and even himself. My mother scolded me for aping his speech, and the one time I attempted to make light of hers I rated a roundhouse smack on my bottom.

6   For her, the English language was not very funny. It usually meant trouble and a good dose of shame, and sometimes real hurt. Although she had a good reading knowledge of the language from university classes in South Korea, she had never practiced actual conversation. So in America she used English flash cards and phrase books and watched television with us kids. And she faithfully carried a pocket workbook illustrated with stick-figure people and compound sentences to be filled in.

7   But none of it seemed to do her much good. Staying mostly at home to care for us, she didn't have many chances to try out sundry words and phrases. When she did, say, at the window of the post office, her readied speech would stall, freeze, sometimes altogether collapse.

8   One day was unusually harrowing. We ventured downtown in the new Ford County Squire my father had bought her, an enormous station wagon that seemed as long—and deft—as an ocean liner. We were shopping for a special meal for guests visiting that weekend, and my mother had heard that a particular butcher carried fresh oxtails, which she needed for a traditional soup.

9   We'd never been inside the shop, but my mother would pause before its window, which was always lined with whole hams, crown roasts, and ropes of plump handmade sausages. She greatly esteemed the bounty with her eyes, and my sister and I did also, but despite our desirous cries she'd turn us away and instead buy the packaged links at the Finast supermarket, where she felt comfortable looking them over and could easily spot the price. And, of course, not have to talk.

10   But that day she was resolved. The butcher store was crowded, and as we stepped inside the door jingled a welcome. No one seemed to notice. We waited for some time, and people who entered after us were now being served. Finally an old woman nudged my mother and waved a little ticket, which we hadn't taken. We patiently waited again, until one of the beefy men behind the glass display hollered our number.

11   My mother pulled us forward and began searching the cases, but the oxtails were nowhere to be found. The man, his big arms crossed, sharply said, "Come on, lady, whaddya want?" This unnerved her, and she somehow blurted the Korean word for oxtail, *soggori*.

12   The butcher looked as if my mother had put something sour in his mouth, and he glanced back at the lighted board and called the next number.

13   Before I knew it, she had rushed us outside and back in the wagon, which she had double-parked because of the crowd. She was furious, almost vibrating with fear and grief, and I could see she was about to cry.

14   She wanted to go back inside, but now the driver of the car we were blocking wanted to pull out. She was shooing us away. My mother, who had just earned her driver's license, started furiously working the pedals. But in her haste she must have flooded the engine, for it wouldn't turn over. The driver started honking and then another car began honking as well, and soon it seemed the entire street was shrieking at us.

15   In the following years, my mother grew steadily more comfortable with English. In Korean she could be fiery, stern, deeply funny, and ironic, in English just slightly less so. If she was never quite fluent, she gained enough confidence to make herself clearly known to anyone, and particularly to me.

16   Five years ago she died of cancer, and some months after we buried her I found myself in the driveway of my father's house, washing her sedan. I liked taking care of her things; it made me feel close to her. While I was cleaning out the glove compartment, I found her pocket English workbook, the one with the silly illustrations. I hadn't seen it in nearly twenty years. The yellowed pages were brittle and dog-eared. She had fashioned a plain paper wrapping for it, and I wondered whether she meant to protect the book or hide it.

17   I don't doubt that she would have appreciated doing the family shopping on the new Broad Avenue of Palisades Park. But I like to think, too, that she would have understood those who now complain about the Korean-only signs.

18   I wonder what these same people would have done if they had seen my mother studying her English workbook—or lost in a store. Would they have nodded gently at her? Would they have lent a kind word?

Assimilation through Education: Indian Boarding Schools in the Pacific Northwest
Carolyn Marr

Introduction

1   The goal of Indian education from the 1880s through the 1920s was to assimilate Indian people into the melting pot of America by placing them in institutions where traditional ways could be replaced by those sanctioned by the government. Federal Indian policy called for the removal of children from their families and in many cases enrollment in a government run boarding school. In this way, the policy makers believed, young people would be immersed in the values and practical knowledge of the dominant American society while also being kept away from any influences imparted by their traditionally-minded relatives.

Part 1: Indian Boarding School Movement

2   The Indian boarding school movement began in the post Civil War era when idealistic reformers turned their attention to the plight of Indian people. Whereas before many Americans regarded the native people with either fear or loathing, the reformers believed that with the proper education and treatment Indians could become just like other citizens. They convinced the leaders of Congress that education could change at least some of the Indian population into patriotic and productive members of society. One of the first efforts to accomplish this goal was the Carlisle Indian School in Pennsylvania, founded by Captain Richard Henry Pratt in 1879. Pratt was a leading proponent of the assimilation through education policy. Believing that Indian ways were inferior to those of whites, he subscribed

to the principle, "kill the Indian and save the man." At Carlisle, young Indian boys and girls were subjected to a complete transformation. Photographs taken at the school illustrate how they looked "before" and "after". The dramatic contrast between traditional clothing and hairstyles and Victorian styles of dress helped convince the public that through boarding school education Indians could become completely "civilized". Following the model of Carlisle, additional off reservation boarding schools were established in other parts of the country, including Forest Grove, Oregon (later known as Chemawa).[1]

3   Seeking to educate increasing numbers of Indian children at lower cost, the federal government established two other types of schools: the reservation boarding school and day schools. Reservation boarding schools had the advantage of being closer to Indian communities and as a result had lower transportation costs. Contact between students and their families was somewhat restricted as students remained at the school for eight to nine months of the year. Relatives could visit briefly at prescribed times. School administrators worked constantly to keep the students at school and eradicate all vestiges of their tribal cultures. Day schools, which were the most economical, usually provided only a minimal education. They worked with the boarding schools by transferring students for more advanced studies.

4   In the Pacific Northwest, treaties negotiated with the Indians during the 1850s included promises of educational support for the tribes. For example, Article 10 of the Medicine Creek Treaty signed by members of the Nisqually, Squaxin, Puyallup and Steilacoom Tribes on December 26, 1854 called for the establishment of an agricultural and industrial school "to be free to the children of said tribes for a period of 20 years." The expenses of the school, its employees and medical personnel were to be defrayed by the federal government and not deducted from annuities. A similar clause appears in the Treaty of Point Elliott, signed by representatives of tribes living in the central and northern Puget Sound region.

5   The promised schools did not come into existence for several years. In the 1870s and 1880s a few small reservation boarding schools were established on the Chehalis, Skokomish and Makah Reservations. These institutions, which had fewer than 50 students, were all closed by 1896 and replaced by day schools. In Tacoma, a one-room shack served as a day school for young Puyallup Indians beginning in 1860. By 1873 students had begun boarding at the school and during the 1880s enrollment increased to 125 pupils. At the turn of the century, Cushman Indian School had become a large industrial boarding school, drawing over 350 students from around the Northwest and Alaska. The 1901 Report of Superintendent of Indian Schools praised Cushman for being well equipped for industrial training and photographs show a modern machine shop. Cushman remained one of the largest on reservation boarding schools in the region until it closed in 1920.

Part 2: Mission Schools

6   Meanwhile, on many reservations missionaries operated schools that combined religious with academic training. At Priest's Point near the Tulalip Reservation, Reverend E.C. Chirouse opened a school in 1857 for six boys and five girls. By 1860 he had 15 pupils and the school continued to grow under the auspices of the Sisters of Providence. At these missionary run schools, traditional religious and cultural practices were strongly discouraged while instruction in the Christian doctrines took place utilizing pictures, statues, hymns, prayers and storytelling.

7   Some missionary schools received federal support, particularly at times when Congress felt less inclined to provide the large sums of money needed to establish government schools. The Tulalip Mission School became the first contract Indian school, an arrangement whereby the government provided annual funds to maintain the buildings while the Church furnished books, clothing, housing and medical care. In 1896 Congress

[1] *Harper's Weekly*, v.26 (no. 1327), May 27, 1882: 324 (illus.), 327 (text).

drastically reduced the funding for mission schools and eventually, in the winter of 1900-01, the Tulalip school became a federal facility. The old school buildings were destroyed by fire in 1902. On January 23, 1905, exactly fifty years after the signing of the Point Elliott Treaty, a new and larger school opened along the shores of Tulalip Bay.

8   The Tulalip Indian School began under the supervision of Charles Milton Buchanan, a physician who also served as Indian Agent for the reservation. The first year it had only one dormitory, but by 1907 both girls' and boys' buildings were completed and the school had a capacity enrollment of 200 students. The children ranged in age from 6 to 18 years and came from many different reservations as well as some off reservation communities. It was not uncommon for teachers at day schools to recommend certain students for the boarding school. Because Tulalip offered a maximum of eighth grade education, some students transferred to Chemawa for more advanced training.

Part 3: Boarding Schools

9   In eastern Washington, a U.S. military fort near Spokane was transformed into a boarding school for Indians of the Spokane and Colville reservations. Fort Spokane Boarding School opened in 1900 with an enrollment of 83 pupils and grew to 200 by 1902. It operated only until 1914 after which time the children attended day schools closer to their homes. Similarly, the military facility at Fort Simcoe became a school for the Yakama and their neighbors.

10   The national system of Indian education, including both off reservation boarding schools, reservation boarding schools and day schools, continued to expand at the turn of the century. In the Pacific Northwest, Chemawa Indian School became the largest off reservation boarding school and drew pupils from throughout the region and Alaska. Chemawa had originally been located at Forest Grove, Oregon, but was moved to Salem in 1885 after officials determined that the original site lacked adequate agricultural land. By 1920 Chemawa enrolled 903 students from 90 different tribes, nearly a third coming from Alaska.

11   All federal boarding schools, whether on or off reservation, shared certain characteristics. The Bureau of Indian Affairs issued directives that were followed by superintendents throughout the nation. Even the architecture and landscaping appeared similar from one institution to the next. Common features included a military style regimen, a strict adherence to English language only, an emphasis on farming, and a schedule that equally split academic and vocational training. By reading the *Reports of the Commissioner of Indian Affairs* and other documents you can compare the official reports submitted by various schools.

Part 4: A Typical Daily Schedule

12   A typical daily schedule at a boarding school began with an early wake-up call followed by a series of tasks punctuated by the ringing of bells. Students were required to march from one activity to the next. Regular inspections and drills took place outdoors with platoons organized according to age and rank. Competitions were held to see which group could achieve the finest marching formation.

> Everything happened by bells, 'triangles' they were called. A triangle would ring in the morning and we would all run, line up, march in, get our little quota of tooth powder, wash our teeth, brush our hair, wash our hands and faces, and then we all lined up and marched outside. Whether it was raining, snowing or blowing, we all went outside and did what was called 'setting up exercises' for twenty minutes. (Joyce Simmons Cheeka, Tulalip Indian School, memoirs collected by Finley)

Conformity to rules and regulations was strongly encouraged:

> We went from the tallest to the littlest, all the way down in companies. We had A, B, C, D companies. E Company was the Lazy Company, those that just couldn't get up and make it. They had all kinds of demerits for those people. They thought

they'd shame them a little bit if they made an extra company and called it the Lazy Company. (Helma Ward, Makah, Tulalip Indian School, from interview with Carolyn Marr)

13　　The foremost requirement for assimilation into American society, authorities felt, was mastery of the English language. Commissioner of Indian Affairs T.J. Morgan described English as "*the language of the greatest, most powerful and enterprising nationalities beneath the sun.*" Such chauvinism did not allow for bilingualism in the boarding schools. Students were prohibited from speaking their native languages and those caught "speaking Indian" were severely punished. Later, many former students regretted that they lost the ability to speak their native language fluently because of the years they spent in boarding school.

14　　Another important component of the government policy for "civilizing" the Indians was to teach farming techniques. Although few reservations in the Pacific Northwest had either fertile land or a climate conducive to agriculture, nonetheless it was felt that farming was the proper occupation for American citizens. So boys learned how to milk cows, grow vegetables, repair tools, etc. and even had lessons on the various types of plows.[2]

15　　The boarding schools had what came to be called the "half and half" system where students spent half of the day in the classroom and half at a work assignment or "detail" on the school grounds. The academic curriculum included courses in U.S. history, geography, language, arithmetic, reading, writing and spelling. Music and drama were offered at most schools. Young women spent either the morning or the afternoon doing laundry, sewing, cooking, cleaning and other household tasks. Older girls might study nursing or office work. The young men acquired skills in carpentry, blacksmithing, animal husbandry, baking and shop. They chopped firewood to keep the steam boilers operating. The work performed by students was essential to the operation of the institution. The meat, vegetables and milk served in the dining room came from livestock and gardens kept by the students. The girls made and repaired uniforms, sheets, and curtains and helped to prepare the meals.

16　　A standardized curriculum for Indian schools emphasized vocational training. Estelle Reel, who served as Superintendent of Indian Education from 1898 to 1910, was a strong advocate of this curriculum which gave primary importance to learning manual skills. No amount of book learning, she felt, could result in economic independence for Indian people. Others would claim that by limiting education to manual training the educators were condemning Indian people to permanent inequality. A former student at the Fort Spokane boarding school described typical work done by the boys:

> Some of the boys were detailed to the garden… others were detailed to milk and care for the cows, feed the pigs and chickens and look after the horses, besides doing other chores. There was a large barn on the place, and the boys learned a lot about farming on a small scale. But for boys who had ambitions for becoming something else, Fort Spokane was far from being adequate. (Frances LeBret, as quoted in exhibit *They Sacrificed for Our Survival: The Indian Boarding School Experience,* at Eastern Washington Historical Museum)

17　　Mandatory education for Indian children became law in 1893 and thereafter agents on the reservations received instructions on how to enforce the federal regulation. If parents refused to send their children to school the authorities could withhold annuities or rations or send them to jail. Some parents were uncomfortable having their children sent far away from home. The educators had quotas to fill, however, and considerable pressure was exerted on Indian families to send their youngsters to boarding schools beginning when the child was six years old. Fear and loneliness caused by this early separation from family is a

---

[2] Curriculum records from National Archives and Records Administration, Pacific Northwest Region, RG75, Box 321: Tulalip Agency.

common experience shared by all former students. Once their children were enrolled in a distant school, parents lost control over decisions that affected them. For example, requests for holiday leave could be denied by the superintendent for almost any reason.[3]

Part 5: Negatives and Positives

18   For some students, the desire for freedom and the pull of their family combined with strong discontent caused them to run away. At Chemawa, for example, there were 46 "desertions" recorded in 1921, followed by 70 in 1922. Punishment of runaways was usually harsh, as the offenders became examples held up before their fellow students:

> Two of our girls ran away…but they got caught. They tied their legs up, tied their hands behind their backs, put them in the middle of the hallway so that if they fell, fell asleep or something, the matron would hear them and she'd get out there and whip them and make them stand up again. (Helma Ward, Makah, interview with Carolyn Marr)

19   Illness was another serious problem at the boarding schools. Crowded conditions and only the basic medical care no doubt contributed to the spread of diseases such as measles, influenza and tuberculosis. Tuberculosis was especially feared and at the Tulalip Indian School the dormitories were kept cold by leaving the windows open at night. Several students were sent to sanitariums in Idaho or Nevada. In a letter issued to superintendents in 1913, the Indian Office advised disinfecting all textbooks at the end of each school year to reduce the chance of spreading disease. Hospital reports for Tulalip indicate that boys spent a total of 110 days in the hospital during one month and girls 125 days. Death was not an unknown occurrence either. At Chemawa, a cemetery contains headstones of 189 students who died at the school, and these represent only the ones whose bodies were not returned home for burial.

20   Not all experiences at the boarding schools were negative for all students. In hindsight, former students acknowledge benefits they gained from their education, and there were happy moments for some. Sports, games and friendships are examples of experiences remembered in a positive light.

> The boys played baseball, broadjumping and ran foot races, played mumbley peg and marbles, spin the top and a lot of other things for entertainment. (Frances LeBret, Fort Spokane Indian School)
>
> We played baseball, football and a game we call shinney. They get two sticks and tie them together. You got a stick that was curved and you'd hit this and throw it. To score you had to hit a little pole. (Alfred Sam, Snohomish, interview with Carolyn Marr)

21   As the years went by and most students persevered, strong friendships developed. Occasionally a friendship might end up in marriage, although this certainly was not encouraged by the school. Young people from one culture group met boys and girls from other areas. Reflecting on her years spent in boarding schools, one elder stated:

> I think that the sharing in the government boarding school was an important part of that period. Just having the time to share with other Indian students a life that was completely different from your own was something that created a bond. (Vi Hilbert, Upper Skagit, interview with Carolyn Marr)

22   Another former student recognized the practical advantages offered by the schools but perceived deeper implications:

> On the reservations there was no electricity or running water. When kids came to the boarding school they had these things—showers and clean clothes—and they ate

---

[3] Correspondence from National Archives and Records Administration, Pacific Northwest Region, RG75, Box 321: Tulalip Agency.

decent food. My mom died when I was 13 months old. I stayed with my grandmother who wasn't well... My main criticism of the boarding school is that it didn't allow you to do your own thinking. You marched everywhere, you were governed by the bell and bugle, you were told when to go to bed and when to get up, your whole life was governed. As a result, you didn't learn how to become an independent thinker. (Arnold McKay, Lummi, interviewed by Carolyn Marr)

23   By the 1920s the Bureau of Indian Affairs had changed its opinion about boarding schools, responding to complaints that the schools were too expensive and that they encouraged dependency more than self-sufficiency. By 1923, the majority of Indian children nationwide attended public schools. A report on Indian education issued in 1928 revealed glaring deficiencies in the boarding schools, including poor diet, overcrowding, below-standard medical service, excessive labor by the students and substandard teaching. The 1930s witnessed many changes in federal Indian policy, among which was a shift in educational philosophy. Classroom lessons could now reflect the diversity of Indian cultures. States assumed more control over Indian education as more children enrolled in public schools. Most of the boarding schools were closed by this time, Tulalip in 1932 and Cushman in 1920, leaving Chemawa as the sole government boarding school remaining in the Pacific Northwest.

The Crossing
Rubén Martínez

1   I am, again, on the line.

2   I've been drawn to it my entire life, beginning with frequent childhood jaunts across it to Tijuana and back—that leap from the monochrome suburban grids of Southern California to the Technicolor swirl of urban Baja California and back. I am an American today because of that line—and my parents' will to erase it with their desire.

3   I return to it again and again because I am from both sides. So for me, son of a mother who emigrated from El Salvador and a Mexican American father who spent his own childhood leaping back and forth, the line is a sieve. And it is a brick wall.

4   It defines me even as I defy it. It is a book without a clear beginning or end, and despite the fact that we refer to it as a "line," it is not even linear; to compare it to an actual book I'd have to invoke Cortázar's[1] *Hopscotch*. This line does and does not exist. It is a historical, political, economic, and cultural fact. It is a laughable, puny, meaningless thing. It is a matter of life and death. And it is a matter of representation. It is a very productive trope[2] in both American and Mexican pop.

5   The cowboy crosses the line to evade the law, because he imagines there is no law in the South. The immigrant crosses the line to embrace the future because he imagines there is no past in the North. Usually rendered by the River (the Rio Grande/Río Bravo—its name changes from one shore to the other), the line appears again and again in film and literature and music from both sides.

6   Just a few: Cormac McCarthy and Carlos Fuentes, Marty Robbins and Los Tigres del Norte, Sam Peckinpah and Emilio "El Indio" Fernández, Charles Bowden and Gloria Anzaldúa.[3]

---

[1] *Cortázar:* Julio Florez Cortázar (1914–1986), Argentine writer known for his short stories.

[2] *trope:* Figure of speech such as a metaphor.

[3] *Cormac McCarthy... Gloria Anzaldúa:* Cormac McCarthy (b. 1933), American novelist known for writing about the Southwest; Carlos Fuentes (b. 1928), Mexican essayist and fiction writer; Marty Robbins (1925–1982), American country-western singer; Los Tigres del Norte, Grammy-winning musical group formed in the late 1960s; Sam Peckinpa (1925–1984), American writer, director, and producer of western films and television series; Emilio Fernández (1903–1968), Mexican actor, writer, and director; Charles Bowden (b. 1945), America non-fiction writer and editor; and Gloria Anzaldúa (1912–2004), Chicana writer and editor, best known for *Borderlands/La Frontera: The New Mestiza* (1987).

7   In the Western, the moment of the crossing (the lawless gang fleeing the lawmen, their horses' hooves muddying the muddy waters all the more) is heralded by a stirring musical figure, brassy and percussive, leaping several tonal steps with each note. Once we're safely on the other side, the melodic strings of Mexico take over. The swaggering American will have his way with a Mexican señorita. The post-colonial[4] representations of border lands literature—produced by Mexicans and Americans alike—have yet to soften the edges of this Spring Break syndrome. The whorehouse-across-the-river is there for a spurned Jake Gyllenhaal to get off with smooth-skinned brown boys in an otherwise liberatory *Brokeback Mountain*. Americans fictional and real always fantasize remaining in that racy, lazy South, but business or vengeance or a respectable marriage (the señorita is a puta, and you can't marry a puto[5] on either side of the border) usually call the cowboy back home.

8   The Mexican or Chicano production is an inverted mirror of the same. The climax of Cheech Marin's *Born in East L.A.* (and dozens of Mexican B-movies) fulfills every migrant's fantasy of a joyous rush of brown humanity breaching a hapless Border Patrol, the victory of simple desire over military technology that occurs thousands of times a day on the border and feeds the paranoid vision of a reconquista[6] (which, a handful of crackpot Chicano nationalists notwithstanding, has been largely invented by the likes of the Minutemen,[7] white dudes with real economic insecurities unfortunately marinated in traditional borderlands racism).

9   Every step across the line is a breach of one code or another. Some of these laws are on the books; some have never been written down; some are matters more private than public.

10   I've been drawn to that line my whole life. Sometimes it's a metaphor. Sometimes it's not.

11   This time, I am close to the line on the Buenos Aires National Wildlife Refuge in southern Arizona. It is a late August afternoon, a day that will not make headlines because there are no Minuteman patrols out hunting migrants, no Samaritans out seeking to save them. Nor is there, for the moment, any Border Patrol in the immediate vicinity. The land is as its public designation intended: a unique Sonoran desert habitat bizarrely and beautifully traversed by grasslands that are home to hundreds of unique species, including the endangered pronghorn antelope; it is also an outstanding birding location. But there are no birders in the dead of summer. The birders and the Minutemen have no wish to be out in temperatures that often rise to more than 110 degrees. (Some Samaritans who belong to a group called No More Deaths are indeed in the area, but the day's final patrol is probably heading back to the church-based group's campground near the town of Arivaca, which borders the refuge.)

12   I park at the Arivaca Creek trailhead. The interpretive sign tells of the possibility of hearing the "snap of vermilion flycatchers snatching insects on the wing." It also tells of another species, a relative newcomer to this "riparian ribbon."

13   "Visitors to BANWR are advised to remain alert for illegal activity associated with the presence of undocumented aliens (UDAs). There is also increased law enforcement activity by several agencies & organizations."

14   The bulleted visitor guidelines advise not to let the "UDAs approach you or your vehicle," a Homeland Security variation of "do not feed the wildlife."

15   The humidity from recent monsoonal deluges is stifling, making 100 degrees feel much hotter—and wetter. The reed-like branches of ocotillos have sprouted their tiny

---

[4] *post-colonial:* Refers to the time following the independence of a colony; postcolonial literature often deals with the impact and legacy of colonial rule.

[5] *puta/puto:* Whore

[6] *reconquista:* Reconquest; much of the American southwest once belonged to Mexico.

[7] *Minutemen:* Self-appointed anti-immigrant guardians of the U.S. borders, particularly in the southwest. This contemporary group has adopted the name of the well-known American revolutionary unit that fought in the Revolutionary War.

lime-green leaves, hiding their terrifically sharp thorns. Moss flourishes on arroyo stones. Mosquitoes zip and whine through the thick air. The desert jungle.

16   I tell myself that I'll take a short stroll; it's getting late. I climb the trail from the creek bed, which is dominated by mammoth cottonwood trees, south toward the red dirt hills—a trail used by birders and "UDAs" alike. I can imagine an Audubon guide leading a gaggle of khaki-clad tourists peering through binoculars, first at a vermilion flycatcher and then at a Mexican rushing through a mesquite thicket, *Profugus mexicanus*. On the line everything seems to attract its opposite or, more accurately, everything seems to attract a thing that seems to have no relation to it, not parallel universes but saw-toothed eruptions, the crumpled metal of a collision. These pairings occur not just near the political border—I am about 11 miles from the boundary between the United States of America and the United States of Mexico—but throughout the West. The border is no longer a line. Its ink has diffused, an ambiguous veil across the entire territory.

17   Take the microcosm of the BANWR and its immediate vicinity. The birders and the migrants, the Samaritans and the Minutemen. Hunters and stoners. A "dude ranch" that charges city slickers up to $2,500 a week. Retirees of modest means. Hellfire Protestants and Catholic penitents and New Age vortex-seekers. Living here or passing through are Americans and Native Americans and Mexicans and Mexican Americans and Mexican Indians, all of varying shades and accents, and there are Iranians and Guatemalans and Chinese. This kind of situation was once affectionately referred to as the Melting Pot. But no, it is more like speaking in tongues, speaking in Babel.[8] The tower is crumbling. Melting pot meltdown.

18   I climb into the red hills as the sun nears the horizon. The sky at the zenith is a stunning true blue. Reaching a saddle, I stumble on to a huge migrant encampment—water jugs and backpacks and soiled underwear and tubes of toothpaste and a brand-new denim jacket finely embroidered with the name of a car club, opened cans of refried beans, bottles of men's cologne, Tampax, tortillas curled hard in the heat. The things they carried and left behind because 11 miles into the 50-mile hike they'd begun to realize the weight of those things, and they'd resolved to travel lighter. If something was to go wrong and they got lost and hyperthermic, they might even begin stripping the clothes off their backs.

19   It is possible, too, that they've just broken camp; it is possible that they saw me coming and are hiding behind one of the saddle's humps. I call out ¡No soy migra![9] This is a line from the script of the Samaritan Patrol, who, like the activists of No More Deaths, scour the desert searching for migrants in distress. They call out so that the fearful migrants might reveal themselves to receive food and water. It is a good line in the borderlands; I can't think of a better one. The real problem is, what am I going to say if someone actually responds? Buenas tardes señoras y señores, soy periodista y quería entervistarles, si es que no les es mucha molestia[10]...the journalist's lame introduction. Of course, they would have no reason to stop and speak to me—just the opposite. Indeed, why would they believe that I am not migra? And what if the smugglers are hauling a load of narcotics instead of humans? What if they are carrying weapons? This is not idle paranoia—this desert is armed with Mexican and American government-issue sidearms and the assault rifles of the paramilitary brigades on both sides. It is no surprise that there is bloodshed. Assault, rape, torture, and murder are common.

---

[8] Babel: Refers to an ancient city whose inhabitants tried to build a tower to heaven, which God destroyed. He then made the people speak different languages so that they could no longer work together.

[9] *¡No soy migra!* I'm not immigration ("la migra" refers generically to any branch or agent of the U. S. immigration authority, such as the Border Patrol).

[10] *Buenas tardes...mucha molestia* Good afternoon, ladies and gentlemen, I'm a journalist and would like to interview you, if it's not too much trouble.

20   In any event, I have nothing to offer the trekkers; they have not run out of water yet (though by tomorrow, after 15 or 20 miles, they well might). I am suddenly ashamed, as if I've intruded on a tremendously private moment, as if I've stumbled upon a couple in erotic embrace, bodies vulnerable to the harshness of the landscape and my gaze.

21   The sun sets, a funnel of gold joining cerulean canopy to blood-red earth. The land is completely still. I hold my breath. I realize that I want them to appear. I want to join them on the journey. The Audubon birder needs the vermilion flycatcher; right now, the writer needs a mojado.[11]

22   The migrant stumbles through the desert and I after him—he's on a pilgrimage and I'm in pursuit of him. Thus I am the literary migra: I will trap the mojado within the distorting borders of representation—a problem no writer has ever resolved. But aren't I also representing the origins of my own family's journey? Don't I also return to the line because it was upon my parents and grandparents' crossing it that I became possible?

23   ¡No soy migra! I call out again.

24   There is no response. I sweat profusely, soaking through my UNM[12] Lobos T-shirt. Even
25   my jeans hang heavy with moisture. Swatting mosquitoes, I retrace my footsteps back to the car.

26   I drive west in the dimming light. There is no one on this road but me.

      Suddenly, a flutter in my peripheral vision. And now a figure stumbles out of the desert green to remind me that the border is, above all else, a moral line. He crawls from the brush and waves to me from the south side of the road. I stop the truck and roll down my window. He is a plaintive-looking fellow in his 30s, with thick black curls, a sweaty and smudged moon of a face. He has large brown eyes ringed by reddened whites. He is wearing a black T-shirt, blue jeans, and white tennis shoes. He carries a small blue vinyl bag.

27   ¿Qué pasó? I ask. What happened?

28   With the first syllables of his response I can tell that he is from El Salvador. It is an accent that splits the difference between the typically muted tones of the Latin American provinces and the urgent desire of urban speech. It is the accent of my mother and her family; it is the Spanish accent I associate most with my childhood.

29   He says his name is Victor and that he had hiked about 12 miles into U.S. territory and could not make it any farther. His migrant crew had traveled all night and started up again late in the afternoon—just a couple of hours ago—but he'd become extremely fatigued and his vision began to blur.

30   Soy diabético,[13] says Victor.

31   Immediately I grab my phone to dial 911. It chirps a complaint: There is no signal. I think: Hypoglycemia, he needs something sweet. I think this because of the hundreds of plot lines in television dramas I've watched since I was a kid. In the backseat I have enough supplies to keep a dozen hikers going for at least a day in the desert—power bars, fruit cups, tins of Vienna sausages, peanut butter crackers, bags of trail mix, several bottles of Gatorade and gallon-jugs of drinking water. I expect him to tear ravenously into the strawberry-flavored bar I give him, but he eats it very slowly, taking modest sips of water between bites.

32   I flip open the cellphone again. Still no signal.

33   The particulars of a problem begin to form in my mind. Although I am not a medical expert, it is apparent that Victor needs urgent attention. But there is no way to contact medical personnel. The only option is to drive Victor to the nearest town, which is Arivaca, about 10 miles away. I become aware that by doing so, both Victor and I will be risking apprehension by the Border Patrol. More than one border denizen has told me that merely giving a migrant a ride can place one in a tenuous legal situation.

---

[11]*mojado:* Wetback
[12]*UNM:* University of New Mexico
[13]*Soy diabético:* I am a diabetic.

34   U.S. Code (Title 8, Chapter 12, Subchapter II, Part VIII, Section 1324) stipulates that an American citizen breaks the law when "knowing or in reckless disregard of the fact that an alien has come to, entered, or remains in the United States in violation of law, transports, or moves or attempts to transport or move such alien within the United States by means of transportation or otherwise, in furtherance of such violation of law."

35   The ethical calculation is simple enough. The law might contradict my moral impulse, but the right thing to do is obvious. I also tell myself that in the event of apprehension by the Border Patrol, the truth of the situation will suffice. I am a Samaritan, after all, not a coyote. The truth will suffice at least for me, that is: I will go free, and Victor will be deported.

36   I tell Victor to get in the car.

37   The night falls fast. Soon the only things we can see through the bug-splattered windshield are the grainy blacktop ahead and the tangle of mesquites lining the road. I keep expecting more migrants to appear in the headlights and wave us down. At any given moment on this stretch of borderland there may be hundreds of migrants attempting passage.

38   It is a winding road and I'm a conservative driver, so there's time for small talk. Victor is much more animated now. He says he is feeling better.

39   He is from Soyapango, a working-class suburb of San Salvador that I remember well from my time in the country during the civil war, when it had the reputation of being a rebel stronghold. Right now, Victor is 1,800 miles from Soyapango.

40   ¿Y a qué se dedica usted? He asks what I do for a living.

41   I reply that I am a writer, and then there is silence for about a quarter of a mile.

42   The Border Patrol will appear any minute now, I think to myself.

43   His large round eyes glisten, reflecting the light from my dashboard. More questions. ¿Cómo se llama el pueblo al que vamos? ¿Qué lejos queda Phoenix? ¿Qué lejos queda Los Angeles? What's the name of the town we're heading to? How far is Phoenix? How far is Los Angeles? Phoenix: where the coyote told him he'd be dropped off at a safe house. Los Angeles: where his sister lives. He has memorized a phone number. It begins with the area code 818. Yes, he is feeling quite fine now, Victor says, and he realizes that I can't drive him all the way to L.A. But Phoenix is only 100 miles away. That's like from San Salvador to Guatemala City.

44   There is still no Border Patrol in sight. This does not make any sense. There are hundreds of agents on duty in what is called the Tucson Sector, the busiest and deadliest crossing along the U.S.–Mexico line. Is it the changing of the guard? Are the agents on dinner break? Are they tracking down Osama bin Laden, disguised as a Mexican day laborer?

45   Now, I realize, the problem is a bit different. Victor is apparently no longer experiencing a medical emergency, although I cannot be absolutely certain of this. The law is ambiguous on the matter of Samaritan aid. I am aware of a pending federal court case against two young No More Deaths activists, Shanti Sellz and Daniel Strauss, who recently attempted to conduct a "medical evacuation" by taking two apparently ailing migrants directly to a hospital rather than handing them over to the BP. Federal prosecutors decided that the activists were transporting the migrants "in furtherance" of their illegal presence in the U.S. and indicted the pair on several felony charges. The activists and their supporters say that the ethical imperative of offering aid in the context of a medical emergency supersedes the letter of immigration law—a moral argument without juridical precedent on the border. The activists are clearly hoping to set one.

46   But the law is decidedly less ambiguous about what Victor is now asking me to do. If I drive him to Phoenix and put him in touch with his sister, I will clearly have provided transportation "in furtherance of" his illegal presence. He is no longer asking for medical aid.

47   The air-conditioning chills the sweat on the wet rag that my Lobos T-shirt has become. It seems that there are now several possibilities, several problems. It seems that there are many right and wrong things to do. The scenarios tumble through my mind.

48   Risk the trip to Phoenix. (Where is that BP checkpoint on I-19? Is it north or south of Arivaca Junction? I look into the sky—are there thunder-heads? Checkpoints often close

when it rains.) What if Victor is actually still sick and on the verge of a seizure—shouldn't I turn him over to the BP? But will the BP give him the medical care he needs? And, not least of all, what of Victor's human right to escape the living hell that is Soyapango (poverty and crime there today are taking nearly as much a toll as the civil war did)? If Victor has that essential human right to seek a better life for himself and his family, what is my moral duty when he literally stumbles into my life on the border? Am I willing to risk federal charges to fulfill an ethical responsibility that I decide trumps the laws of my country?

49   I slow down to a crawl as we near the outskirts of Arivaca, a town famed for a '60s-era commune and the weed-growing hippies that hung on long past the Summer of Love. It will all end here in Arivaca, I tell myself. The BP trucks will be lined up outside the one small grocery store in town, or maybe up at the Grubsteak, which is presided over by a gregarious Mexican who waits on the graying hippies and handful of outsider artists who arrived years ago thinking they'd found the grail of Western living, long before chaos came to the border.

50   But when I pull up to the store, there is only the heat of the night and a flickering street lamp gathering a swarm of moths. I notice a few local kids—white, shaved heads—standing by a pay phone. Now it occurs to me that there is a possible solution to this mess. In the rush of events, I'd forgotten that No More Deaths had a camp about four miles east of town. Because it is a faith-based organization, the camp was baptized "Ark of the Covenant." Since 2004, No More Deaths had recruited student activists—like Sellz and Strauss, the pair under federal indictment—from around the country to come to southern Arizona and walk the lethal desert trails. There would be activists there with more experience than I in these matters. They could easily consult the doctors and lawyers supporting their cause to determine the right thing to do—or at least their version of the right thing.

51   I walk into the store. I tell Victor to stay inside the car. The clerk behind the counter is reading the newspaper, head cupped in her hands and elbows leaning on the food scale next to the cash register.

52   I briefly blurt out my story.

53   She asks me where Victor is. In the car, I say. Immediately she tells me that the BP can impound my vehicle, they can file charges. She tells me that she can call the Border Patrol for me. She seems to know exactly what the right thing to do is. The only thing to do. She places her hand on the phone.

54   A few seconds later I'm back in the heat of the night and I ask the first passerby, a young blond woman named Charity, for directions to the Ark of the Covenant. Do you have a map? She asks. She means a local map. No. Now she is drawing one on a page of my reporter's notebook. She draws many lines. Here there is a hill, she says; here, a llama ranch. She says a quarter of a mile, then a couple of miles, then three-quarters of a mile and left and right and across. It is a moonless night. Good luck, she says.

55   I climb back in the truck, I turn the ignition. I give Victor the notebook with the map. In a minute we're out of town and on to the first dirt road of the route. Still no BP in sight. The map is accurate. I pass by the llama ranch, barely catching the sign in the dimness.

56   For several minutes I ride on impulse—no thoughts at all. But as I turn left just where Charity told me to, a thought powerful enough to take my foot off the gas seizes me.

57   I can't ride into the Ark of the Covenant with Victor in the truck. What I'd forgotten in my haste was the political reality of the moment: The feds had called No More Deaths' bluff and were going after them in court. I remembered hearing from a couple of activists that before and since the arrests of Sellz and Strauss, there had been constant BP surveillance on the encampment.

58   If the BP were to see me dropping off Victor at the camp now, would they, could they use this as more evidence of running a de facto smuggling operation? Perhaps this could strengthen the federal case against Sellz and Strauss. And what if there was a conviction? And what if a judge ordered the camp closed?

59　　　　Now I was weighing Victor's singular rights and desire and the goals and strategy of an activist movement that had helped dozens of migrants in distress over the past two summers and that could continue to help many more. The problem was, my cellphone was dead. The problem was my desire to capture a mojado. The problem was, I didn't have enough information to know what the "right" decision was. I had placed myself on the line, and I wasn't ready for what it would ask of me.

60　　　　I slow down, and the dust kicked up by the tires envelops the truck. Victor and I turn to each other.

61　　　　Fifteen minutes later, I pull up, for the second time, to the convenience store in Arivaca. The clerk is still reading the paper. I tell her to call the Border Patrol. I tell her that Victor has diabetes and symptoms of hypoglycemia.

62　　　　She picks up the phone: "We've got a diabetic UDA."

63　　　　I walk out to Victor, who is standing next to my truck, staring into the black desert night. He asks me again how far it is to Tucson. I tell him that he'll die if he tries to hike.

64　　　　I tell myself that Victor is probably living and working somewhere in America now. It is quite possible that he attempted to cross over again after his apprehension by the Border Patrol, and that he succeeded. This thought does and does not comfort me.

65　　　　I tell myself I did the right thing. I tell myself I did the wrong thing. I tell myself that every decision on the line is like that, somewhere in between.

Now That You're Here
Sherrie L. Nist-Olejnik and Jodi Patrick Holschuh

1　Starting college! You may feel as if you have been preparing for this day forever. You've taken a college preparatory curriculum in high school, you've talked with friends or siblings who are already in college, and you may have visited several campuses before deciding which school to attend. Or you may be returning to college after several years of working, having already gone through careful life assessment and financial budgeting. Regardless of your situation, you are probably excited about what the next few years have in store for you. And some of you may even be a little wary and unsure of yourselves as you begin down the college path.

2　In this chapter, we will discuss some of the ways in which college differs from high school. In addition, we will present eight situations that you are sure to encounter in college sooner or later and will offer suggestions about how you might deal with them. Keep in mind as you read this chapter that campuses differ in size and in the expectations they have of students. For these reasons, some of the generalizations and solutions offered here might not apply exactly to your particular situation.

How Does College Differ from High School?

3　How many times since high school graduation have you heard one of your relatives say something like this: "Oh ____(insert your name)! Enjoy these college years. They will be the best of your life." Although this statement is probably true—college is enjoyable and memorable—it is also demanding and, in many instances, just plain different from high school. It's a time in your life when you will go through many changes as you prepare for the world of work that follows. In this section we will discuss some of the reasons why high school and college differ.

- **Reason 1: College Requires Greater Independent Learning.** Your high school teachers may have been willing to give you lots of test preparation help. They may have prepared study guides or even provided the exact questions that would be asked. Although college instructors also want you to be successful—we have never met a professor who wants students to fail—they don't give students as much study help.

Sure, most professors will answer questions about course content and things you don't understand, but they will not provide you with a variety of supplementary learning materials, and they certainly will not give you test questions. They expect that you know effective and efficient study strategies, and if you don't know how to study for their courses, they expect you to learn how.

- **Reason 2: College Courses Move at a Faster Pace.** If you ask first-year college students about the differences between high school and college, one of their most common responses would be that college courses move much faster than high school classes. What might have taken a full year to cover in high school will probably be covered in a semester in college. It's not uncommon for college professors to move through three, four, or more chapters in a week, expecting you to keep up. In addition, more topics are generally covered in greater detail. However, college professors may go into detail on just a few points and expect you to fill in the rest of the details on your own.

- **Reason 3: College Courses Require You to Think Critically.** In your high school classes, perhaps you were required to memorize lots of facts for exams. You may even have been discouraged from questioning either your high school textbooks or your high school teachers. But as you proceed through college, you will find yourself in classes where your professor wants you to do more than memorize. You might have to critique an essay on gun control, read and respond to a historian's view of the Vietnamese conflict, or compare and contrast conflicting scientific theories. All of these tasks require you to think critically because you need to go beyond memorization to applying or synthesizing the information.

- **Reason 4: College Classes Have Few Safety Nets.** Usually on the first day of a college class your professor will give you a syllabus. The syllabus outlines the course requirements and also generally tells you how your grade will be determined. Something that will become clear as you read your syllabus is that many of the safety nets that you had in high school, such as extra credit assignments or other bonuses to improve your grade, have all but disappeared. This means your course grade will be determined by the grade you earn on a limited number of tests or papers. So you'll need to give every assignment your best effort.

- **Reason 5: College Requires You to Study Longer and More Effectively.** You will probably find out pretty quickly that both the amount of time you put into studying and the way you study in college will have to change if you want to earn high grades. Many of our students tell us that they really didn't have to study in high school. "Studying" was reading over a study guide or reading over class notes for about a half-hour. Many students begin college without ever having to read their texts, and some have never taken essay exams. It is important to realize that studying in college requires not only more time, but also having a variety of study strategies at your disposal.

- **Reason 6: College Provides Fewer Chances for Evaluation.** In high school, it may have seemed as though you were always taking tests or writing papers. Chances are, you were tested over small amounts of material (only one or two chapters) and you had numerous chances for evaluation. If you did poorly on one test, you could usually make it up on the next one. In college, on the other hand, you will probably have fewer chances to be evaluated. At first, the idea of taking fewer tests per course in a term may seem appealing. But think about the big picture. If you have only three exams, you are going to be held responsible for much more information at one time than you were in high school. What at first seems to be an advantage—fewer tests, homework that goes unchecked, a longer period of time between exams—may actually work against you, unless you know how to stay on top of things.

- **Reason 7: College Gives You Great Freedom and Greater Responsibility.** Legally, you become an adult at age 18, which just happens to be about the same time you graduate from high school. In college, no one makes you stay on top of your school-work or keeps track of your comings and goings or checks to see that you have done all of your reading and studying before heading out for a night on the town. This free-dom comes with a tremendous amount of responsibility. It is your responsibility to prioritize the tasks you *have* to do against the things you *want* to do.

- **Reason 8: College Provides Greater Anonymity.** If you attend a moderate-sized to large college or university, you will be faced with being somewhat anonymous—and in some cases, very anonymous. By *anonymous* we mean that you can become just another face in the crowd. Most of you probably attended high schools where you got to know your teachers and your classmates fairly well. Your teachers not only knew your name, but also were concerned about whether or not you were learning and understanding the infor-mation presented in their classes. For the most part, in college, your professors have few opportunities to get to know you well. All is not lost, however. Most of the time, students are anonymous only if they want to be, regardless of how large or small their campus may be. You can become more than a "face" to your professors by making appointments to talk with them. You can join clubs that have faculty sponsors. You can take part in a variety of campus activities with other students who share your interests.

- **Reason 9: College Requires You to Be Proactive.** Being proactive means that it's your responsibility to take the initiative in a variety of situations. In high school, either your teachers or your parents may have insisted that you get help if you were having prob-lems with a particular course. And you may have followed their advice reluctantly. In college, however, it becomes your responsibility to know the resources that are available on your campus, so that if you do run into difficulties or need the services of some of-fice, you'll know how to find the information you need or where to go for assistance. If you are proactive and find out a little about them before you need their services, it will save you time in the long run. You don't want to wait until you are in dire need of these resources before seeking them out. Some of these services may include:

  - **The Library.** In addition to providing resources, the library is a great place to study, to do research online, or to meet your study group. Most campuses have li-brary orientations that help students learn to navigate large and complex systems.

  - **The Learning Center.** The campus learning center can be an excellent source of assistance because most offer a variety of services, from academic counseling to assistance with writing, studying, and mathematics.

  - **Tutorial Services.** Like learning centers, most campuses offer tutorial services for a broad range of courses. Generally, tutoring is provided by undergraduate stu-dents who earn top grades in the areas in which they tutor. This tutoring is usually free, but appointments are often necessary.

  - **Health Services.** Because getting sick enough to need the services of a doctor is inevitable, know where your campus health facility is and what the rules are to be able to see a medical professional. Don't wait until you feel as if you're on your deathbed. Find out where to go and what to do early on.

  - **Counseling Center.** More and more students are enlisting the help of a trained professional from their campus counseling center. If you find that you have prob-lems that are getting in the way of your academic success, you should seek out help. Sometimes talking with a friend works. If it doesn't, find out more about the services offered through the counseling center.

  - **Student Center or Student Union.** On most campuses, the student center is the hub of campus where you can meet friends, but most also offer a wealth of resources. Sometimes campus organizations and clubs have offices in the student center. Social event and concert tickets can be purchased there. You can get general information about the campus, such as bus schedules, campus maps, and event schedules. Often, the campus bookstore is located in or near the student center. When you don't know where else to turn, the student center is a good place to start if you need information about your campus.

4   So, college is different from high school in many ways. You must think differently about the expectations, learning conditions, level of responsibility, and studying methods than you did in high school. This is not bad. It simply means you will have to make some transitions in the way you learn and study in order to be successful.

What Special Situations Can You Expect to Encounter Sooner or Later?

5   Now that you have seen some of the ways in which high school and college differ, let's examine this transition from another perspective. We'll present eight situations that most college students will encounter sooner or later, and we'll also examine how you might cope with or handle each situation. All of these situations will be addressed again throughout this text, so you will be able to explore these ideas in greater detail.

6   In a perfect world, none of the following situations would occur. All students would go to class every day, distribute their study time over several days, stay on top of their reading, and make the dean's list every term. However, the world of college is an imperfect place. So, let's discuss some of the situations that you might encounter in college, some for which you might not be prepared. As you read each section, think about how you might handle the situation and what additional information might help you cope better.

- **Professors Who Take Roll.** Someone may have told you that the only time you really *have* to show up for classes in college is on test days, or that if you can get the information on your own, professors don't really care whether you are in class. Although many professors don't take attendance, eventually you will run across one who does, and, in reality, most actually do want you present in class. Many professors truly believe that attending class will help you learn. We believe this as well; so even if your professor does not take roll, it's still a good idea to attend class.

- **An Early Morning Class.** Most college students are not morning people. In fact, there's even scientific evidence to indicate that the biological clocks of college-aged people are preset to stay up late at night and to sleep late in the morning. However, the college officials who determine the times of class periods evidently are unaware of this research. Unfortunately (for most college students), a time will come when you will have to take an early morning class. If you do have that early class, try to juggle the rest of your schedule so that you can go to bed earlier than usual. Additionally, try to take one that meets only two or three days a week, thus allowing you a little more flexibility on other days.

- **A Course or Professor You Don't Particularly Like.** It's sad but true—there will be courses you don't like, and professors with whom you fail to connect. Even if you have a wide range of interests and you can get along well with almost everyone, at some point you'll probably have to make it through a rough class. You can take one of two routes when this happens.

    Route A: You can think of every excuse imaginable not to do the work or go to class. You can blame your attitude on the professor or the boring material that you are expected to learn.

    Consequences of Route A: You could receive a poor course grade, develop a bad feeling about yourself, or have to work doubly hard in another course to bring up your overall grade point average.

    Route B: Acknowledge that you really don't care much for the course or the professor. It's one course, however, and you can make it through. Study with

someone who seems to like the course. Try to motivate yourself with small rewards. Tell yourself that this is temporary and the course will soon be over.

Consequences of Route B: Perhaps you will not earn an A in the class but you
will emerge with your ego and your grade point average intact.

- **Cramming for a Test.** Imagine you have a big test in a couple of days (or worse yet, tomorrow) and you've done very little preparing. Now it's *cram time!* Personally, we've never
  met a student who didn't have to cram at some time. And cramming occasionally probably isn't a horrible thing, but it shouldn't become the way you live your academic life. If
  you have to cram occasionally, try to use the strategies you'll learn in this book to study to
  your advantage. And, as soon as possible, regroup so that you don't have to cram again.

- **Difficulty Maintaining Motivation for Academics.** Most college students experience
  motivation problems at some time or other. It usually doesn't last long, but for some students the decline in motivation is long enough and severe enough to interfere with their
  schoolwork. Other students experience a lull in motivation in just one class—generally
  a class with which they are experiencing difficulty. Still others begin the term with good
  intentions, yet quickly develop general motivation problems in every class. If you are
  having motivation problems, try setting some specific, reachable goals. Whether your
  lack of motivation is concentrated in one particular course, occurs at a specific period
  of time (such as around midpoint), or is generalized across all your academic courses,
  goal setting can help you stay focused and improve your motivation to learn.

- **Personal Problems and/or Illness.** No one plans on getting sick or having serious
  personal problems, but at some point you will likely experience both predicaments.
  However, there are some things you can do to salvage even a bad situation. First, as
  you plan your schedule for the term, build in some flexibility, just in case. If everything goes according to plan, the worst thing that can happen is you'll have some extra time to study, work, or play. Second, as mentioned earlier, use the services that are
  available on your campus. Third, develop a set of reliable peers who can be there for
  you in times of illness or other problems. Often, knowing that some other person can
  help you makes all the difference in the world.

- **Frustration.** It's a given that you will experience frustrations and stressful situations,
  but it's how you deal with them that makes the difference. Try not to let things build
  up to the point where you can't cope. As much as possible, deal with frustrations as
  they arise. Evaluate all the alternatives. And try not to become stressed by things you
  have no control over. So…take a walk. Go work out. Spend a few minutes venting to
  a friend. In time it will work out.

- **Juggling Too Many Responsibilities.** College students tend to be busy people—going to
  class, studying, attending meetings, working, exercising, taking part in campus organizations, and the list goes on. Add to all of this family responsibilities, social interactions,
  and some good old time to play, and you can easily become overcommitted. Although
  you certainly want to get the most out of your college experience, try to think about how
  new responsibilities will affect you. Remember that your primary job in college is to be a
  student. Then you can ask yourself: "What other kinds of responsibilities can I take on?"
  Will you have so much to do a month from now that you will constantly feel stressed out
  and frustrated? If you can think about this in advance and learn to say "No" when you
  find yourself maxing out, you will be able to keep all those balls in the air and be a much
  happier student.

- **Having Problems Organizing Course Materials Even If You Are a Very Organized
  Student.** With all of the advances in technology, more and more professors are making
  students responsible for a wider variety of materials from a broader range of sources. Rarely
  will you have just a textbook in your courses. The more likely scenario is that you will be
  responsible for information from not only one or more texts and lectures, but also any or all

of the following: WebCT, CD Rom supplements, on-line materials, workbooks, computerized homework assignments, and lab manuals. Being responsible for learning materials from a variety of sources in the same course requires you to keep up with a lot. You may have to be creative and find new ways to organize so that you can keep it all straight.

The Allegory of the Cave
Plato, translation by Thomas Sheehan

The Allegory of the Cave

1 SOCRATES: Next, compare our nature in respect of education and its lack to such an experience as this.

Part One: Setting the Scene: The Cave and the Fire

2 SOCRATES: Imagine this: People live under the earth in a cavelike dwelling. Stretching a long way up toward the daylight is its entrance, toward which the entire cave is gathered. The people have been in this dwelling since childhood, shackled by the legs and neck. Thus they stay in the same place so that there is only one thing for them to look at: whatever they encounter in front of their faces. But because they are shackled, they are unable to turn their heads around.

A fire is behind them, and there is a wall between the fire and the prisoners

3 SOCRATES: Some light, of course, is allowed them, namely from a fire that casts its glow toward them from behind them, being above and at some distance. Between the fire and those who are shackled [i.e., behind their backs] there runs a walkway at a certain height. Imagine that a low wall has been built the length of the walkway, like the low curtain that puppeteers put up, over which they show their puppets.

The images carried before the fire

4 SOCRATES: So now imagine that all along this low wall people are carrying all sorts of things that reach up higher than the wall: statues and other carvings made of stone or wood and many other artifacts that people have made. As you would expect, some are talking to each other [as they walk along] and some are silent.

5 GLAUCON: This is an unusual picture that you are presenting here, and these are unusual prisoners.

6 SOCRATES: They are very much like us humans, I [Socrates] responded.

What the prisoners see and hear

7 SOCRATES: What do you think? From the beginning people like this have never managed, whether on their own or with the help by others, to see anything besides the shadows that are [continually] projected on the wall opposite them by the glow of the fire.

8 GLAUCON: How could it be otherwise, since they are forced to keep their heads immobile for their entire lives?

9 SOCRATES: And what do they see of the things that are being carried along [behind them]? Do they not see simply these [namely the shadows]?

10 GLAUCON: Certainly.

11 SOCRATES: Now if they were able to say something about what they saw and to talk it over, do you not think that they would regard that which they saw on the wall as beings?

12 GLAUCON: They would have to.

13 SOCRATES: And now what if this prison also had an echo reverberating off the wall in front of them [the one that they always and only look at]? Whenever one of the people walking behind those in chains (and carrying the things) would make a sound, do you think the

14   GLAUCON: Nothing else, by Zeus!

15   SOCRATES: All in all, those who were chained would consider nothing besides the shadows of the artifacts as the unhidden.

16   GLAUCON: That would absolutely have to be.

Part Two: Three Stages of Liberation

Freedom, Stage One

A prisoner gets free

17   SOCRATES: So now, watch the process whereby the prisoners are set free from their chains and, along with that, cured of their lack of insight, and likewise consider what kind of lack of insight must be if the following were to happen to those who were chained.

Walks back to the fire

18   SOCRATES: Whenever any of them was unchained and was forced to stand up suddenly, to turn around, to walk, and to look up toward the light, in each case the person would be able to do this only with pain and because of the flickering brightness would be unable to look at those things whose shadows he previously saw.

Is questioned about the objects

19   SOCRATES: If all this were to happen to the prisoner, what do you think he would say if someone were to inform him that what he saw before were [mere] trifles but that now he was much nearer to beings; and that, as a consequence of now being turned toward what is more in being, he also saw more correctly?

The answer he gives

20   SOCRATES: And if someone were [then] to show him any of the things that were passing by and forced him to answer the question about what it was, don't you think that he would be a wit's end and in addition would consider that what he previously saw [with his own eyes] was more unhidden than what was now being shown [to him by someone else].

21   GLAUCON: Yes, absolutely.

Looking at the fire-light itself

22   SOCRATES: And if someone even forced him to look into the glare of the fire, would his eyes not hurt him, and would he not then turn away and flee [back] to that which he is capable of looking at? And would he not decide that [what he could see before without any help] was in fact clearer than what was now being shown to him?

23   GLAUCON: Precisely.

Freedom, Stage Two

Out of the cave into daylight

24   SOCRATES: Now, however, if someone, using force, were to pull him [who had been freed from his chains] away from there and to drag him up the cave's rough and steep ascent and not to let go of him until he had dragged him out into the light of the sun.

Pain, rage, blindness

25   SOCRATES:…would not the one who had been dragged like this feel, in the process, pain and rage? And when he got into the sunlight, wouldn't his eyes be filled with the glare, and wouldn't he thus be unable to see any of the things that are now revealed to him as the unhidden?

26   GLAUCON: He would not be able to do that at all, at least not right away.

27   SOCRATES: It would obviously take some getting accustomed, I think, if it should be a matter of taking into one's eyes that which is up there outside the cave, in the light of the sun.

Shadows and reflections

28 SOCRATES: And in this process of acclimitization he would first and most easily be able to look at (1) shadows and after that (2) the images of people and the rest of things as they are reflected in water.

Looking at things directly

29 SOCRATES: Later, however, he would be able to view (3) the things themselves [the beings, instead of the dim reflections]. But within the range of such things, he might well contemplate what there is in the heavenly dome, and this dome itself, more easily during the night by looking at the light of the stars and the moon, [more easily, that is to say,] than by looking at the sun and its glare during the day.

30 GLAUCON: Certainly.

Freedom, Stage Three: The Sun

Looking at the sun itself

31 SOCRATES: But I think that finally he would be in the condition to look at (4) the sun itself, not just at its reflection whether in water or wherever else it might appear, but at the sun itself, as it is in and of itself and in the place proper to it and to contemplate of what sort it is.

32 GLAUCON: It would necessarily happen this way.

Thoughts about the sun: its nature and functions

33 SOCRATES: And having done all that, by this time he would also be able to gather the following about the sun: (1) that it is that which grants both the seasons and the years; (2) it is that which governs whatever there is in the now visible region of sunlight; and (3) that it is also the cause of all those things that the people dwelling in the cave have before their eyes in some way or other.

34 GLAUCON: It is obvious that he would get to these things – the sun and whatever stands in its light – after he had gone out beyond those previous things, the merely reflections and shadows.

Thoughts about the cave

35 SOCRATES: And then what? If he again recalled his first dwelling, and the "knowing" that passes as the norm there, and the people with whom he once was chained, don't you think he would consider himself lucky because of the transformation that had happened and, by contrast, feel sorry for them?

36 GLAUCON: Very much so.

What counts for "wisdom" in the cave

37 SOCRATES: However, what if among the people in the previous dwelling place, the cave, certain honors and commendations were established for whomever most clearly catches sight of what passes by and also best remembers which of them normally is brought by first, which one later, and which ones at the same time? And what if there were honors for whoever could most easily foresee which one might come by next?

What would the liberated prisoner now prefer?

38 SOCRATES: Do you think the one who had gotten out of the cave would still envy those within the cave and would want to compete with them who are esteemed and who have power? Or would not he or she much rather wish for the condition that Homer speaks of, namely "to live on the land [above ground] as the paid menial of another destitute peasant"? Wouldn't he or she prefer to put up with absolutely anything else rather than associate with those opinions that hold in the cave and be that kind of human being?

39 GLAUCON: I think that he would prefer to endure everything rather than be that kind of human being.

Part Three: The Prisoner Returns to the Cave

The return: blindness

40   SOCRATES: And now, consider this: If this person who had gotten out of the cave were to go back down again and sit in the same place as before, would he not find in that case, coming suddenly out of the sunlight, that his eyes ere filled with darkness?"

41   GLAUCON: Yes, very much so.

The debate with the other prisoners

42   SOCRATES: Now if once again, along with those who had remained shackled there, the freed person had to engage in the business of asserting and maintaining opinions about the shadows – while his eyes are still weak and before they have readjusted, an adjustment that would require quite a bit of time – would he not then be exposed to ridicule down there? And would they not let him know that he had gone up but only in order to come back down into the cave with his eyes ruined – and thus it certainly does not pay to go up.

And the final outcome:

43   SOCRATES: And if they can get hold of this person who takes it in hand to free them from their chains and to lead them up, and if they could kill him, will they not actually kill him?

44   GLAUCON: They certainly will.

End

Equalizing Opportunity
Dramatic Differences in Children's Home Life and Health Mean That Schools Can't Do It Alone
Richard Rothstein

1   Public discourse about education pays great attention to the stubborn persistence of an achievement gap between poor and minority students and their wealthier white peers—and public schools come under great criticism for their apparent inability to close that gap. Some of this criticism may be justified. But there is more to the story than school reform. No society can realistically expect schools alone to abolish inequality. If students come to school in unequal circumstances, they will largely, though not entirely, leave school with unequal skills and abilities, in both cognitive and noncognitive domains. This is not a reason for educators to throw up their hands. Rather, in addition to efforts to improve school practices, educators, along with community partners, should exercise their own rights and responsibilities as citizens to participate in redressing the inequalities with which children come to school.

2   Income is more unequal and lower-class* families have less access to medical care in the United States than in any other industrial nation. The gap in average achievement probably cannot be narrowed substantially as long as the U.S. maintains such vast differences in socioeconomic conditions. Although some lower-class children can overcome these handicaps, and although more effective schools can help narrow the gap a little, it is fanciful to think that, on average, children from such different social classes can emerge at age 18 with comparable academic abilities.

---

*Throughout this article, the term "lower class" is used to describe the families of children whose achievement will, on average, be predictably lower than the achievement of middle-class children. American sociologists once were comfortable with this term, but it has fallen out of fashion. Instead, we tend to use euphemisms like "disadvantaged" students, "at-risk" students, "inner-city" students, or students of "low socioeconomic status." None of these terms, however, captures the central characteristic of lower-class families: a collection of occupational, psychological, personality, health, and economic traits that interact, predicting performance (not only in schools but in other institutions) that, on average, differs from the performance of families from higher social classes.

3   Nonetheless, many of the curricular and school organizational reforms being pursued to-day have merit and should be intensified. Repairing and upgrading the scandalously decrepit school facilities that serve some lower-class children, raising salaries to permit the recruitment of more qualified teachers for lower-class children, reducing class sizes for lower-class children (particularly in the early grades), insisting on higher academic standards, holding schools accountable for fairly measured performance, creating a well-focused and disciplined school climate, doing more to encourage lower-class children to intensify their own ambitions—all of these policies, and others, can play a role in narrowing the achievement gap.

4   Such reforms are extensively covered in public discussions of education, so it is not necessary for me to review them here. My focus is the great importance of reforming social and economic institutions if we truly want children to emerge from school with equal potential.

5   Readers should not misinterpret this emphasis as implying that better schools are not important, or that school improvement will not contribute to narrowing the achievement gap. School reform, however, is not enough. The social and economic conditions that lower-class children face must also be addressed. For example, the growing unaffordability of adequate housing for low-income families has a demonstrable effect on average achievement. Children whose families have difficulty finding stable housing are more likely to be mobile, and student mobility is an important cause of low student achievement. It is hard to imagine how teachers, no matter how well trained, could be as effective with children who move in and out of their classrooms as they are with children whose attendance is regular. In schools with high mobility, the nonmobile students are affected too, as classroom dynamics are disrupted and teachers must review material.

6   And yet, evidence indicates that schools, on average, are doing a great deal to combat the achievement gap. Most of the social class difference in average academic potential exists by the time children are 3 years old. This difference is exacerbated during the years that children spend in school, but the growth in the gap occurs mostly in the afterschool hours and during the summertime, when children are not in classrooms.[1] So children's out-of-school time offers an enormous—but needlessly neglected—opportunity to narrow the gap.

7   To better understand just how great the challenge is, this article reviews some of the key differences between lower- and middle-class families in childrearing and children's health. For a more detailed look at these issues, see *Class and Schools: Using Social, Economic, and Educational Reform to Close the Black-White Achievement Gap,* the book from which most of this article is drawn. Schools will not be able to address all of these differences on their own. But we, as a nation, can—and if we are serious about giving all children equal opportunities to succeed, we must.

8   Since the publication of *Class and Schools,* a growing number of national leaders, from across the political spectrum and with varied expertise, have advocated for combining school improvement with improvements in the social and economic conditions that prepare children to succeed in school. These leaders have sponsored a platform, "A Broader, Bolder Approach to Education," to which all Americans are invited to add their names at **www.boldapproach.org**. Yet despite this growing chorus proclaiming that schools alone cannot be expected to significantly narrow the achievement gap, opposition to the "Broader, Bolder Approach" persists. Therefore, it is necessary to reiterate the research establishing the importance of narrowing the gap in readiness to learn, if we are to succeed in narrowing the gap in learning.

Social Class Differences in Childrearing

9   To take full advantage of school, children should arrive every day ready to learn. But children differ in how ready they are, and these differences are strongly influenced by their social class backgrounds. Parents of different social classes, on average, tend to raise children somewhat differently. For example, more educated parents read to their young children more consistently and encourage their children to read more to themselves when they are older.[2]

10   How parents read to children is as important as whether they do; more educated parents read aloud differently. When low-income parents read aloud, they are more likely to tell children to pay attention without interruptions or to sound out words or name letters. When they ask children about a story, questions are more likely to be factual, asking for names of objects or memories of events.[3] Parents who are more literate are more likely to ask questions that are creative, interpretive, or connective. They ask questions like, "What do you think will happen next?" and "Why do you think this happened?" and "Does that remind you of what we did yesterday?"[4] Middle-class parents are more likely to read aloud to have fun, to start conversations, and to provide an entrée to the world outside. Their children learn that reading is enjoyable and are more motivated to read in school.[5]

11   Stark social class differences arise not only in how parents read but in how they converse. Explaining events in the broader world to children in dinner talk, for example, may have as much of an influence on test scores as early reading itself.[6] Through such conversations, children develop broader vocabularies and become familiar with contexts for reading in school.[7] Educated parents are more likely to engage in such talk and to begin it with infants and toddlers, conducting pretend conversations long before infants can understand the language. Typically, middle-class parents "ask" infants about their needs, then provide answers for the children ("Are you ready for a nap, now? Yes, you are, aren't you?"). Instructions are more likely to be given indirectly, such as, "You don't want to make so much noise, do you?"[8] This kind of instruction is really more an invitation for a child to work through the reasoning behind a command and to internalize it. Soon after middle-class children become verbal, parents typically draw them into adult conversations so children can practice expressing their own opinions.

12   Working-class parents typically maintain firmer boundaries between the adult and child worlds, and are less likely to conduct conversations with preverbal children. Except when it is necessary to give a warning or issue other instructions, these parents less often address language directly to infants or toddlers. Unlike middle-class parents, working-class parents are less likely to simplify their language (using "baby talk") to show preverbal children how to converse before the children are naturally ready to do so. If children need instruction, the orders are more likely to be direct, undisguised in question form.[9] Working-class adults are more likely to engage in conversation with each other as if their infants, and even their older children, were not present. These parents make less of a deliberate effort to name objects and develop children's vocabularies.

13   Twenty years ago, two researchers from the University of Kansas visited the homes of families from different social classes to monitor conversations between parents and toddlers. The researchers found that, on average, professional parents spoke over 2,000 words per hour to their children, working-class parents spoke about 1,300, and parents on welfare spoke about 600. So by age 3, children of professionals had vocabularies that were nearly 50 percent greater than those of working-class children and twice as large as those of welfare children. Indeed, by 3 years old, the children of professionals had larger vocabularies than the vocabularies used by adults from welfare families in speaking to their children. Cumulatively, the Kansas researchers estimated that by the time children were 4 years old, ready to enter preschool, a typical child in a professional family would have accumulated experience with 45 million words, compared with only 13 million for a typical child in a welfare family.[10]

14   Deficits like these cannot be made up by schools alone, no matter how high the teachers' expectations. For all children to achieve the same goals, those from the lower class would have to enter school with verbal fluency similar to that of middle-class children.

Social Class Differences in Children's Health

15   Childrearing practices play a role in school performance, but vast differences in children's health, and health care, are also important. Overall, lower-income children are in poorer health, suffering from undiagnosed vision problems, lack of dental care, poor nutrition, and more.

Vision

16 Lower-class children's higher incidence of vision problems has the most obvious impact on their relative lack of school success. Children with vision problems have difficulty reading and seeing what teachers write on the board. Trying to read, their eyes may wander or have difficulty tracking print or focusing. Tests of vision show that these problems are inversely proportional to family income; in the United States, poor children have severe vision impairment at twice the normal rate.[11] Juvenile delinquents especially have extraordinarily high rates of such problems; difficulties in seeing and focusing may contribute to their lack of mainstream success.[12] Foster children, who experience even more stress than most disadvantaged children, also have unusually high vision failure rates.[13]

17 Fifty percent or more of minority and low-income children have vision problems that interfere with their academic work.[14] A few require glasses, but more need eye-exercise therapy to correct focusing, converging, and tracking problems. In one experiment where therapy or lenses were provided to randomly selected fourth-graders from low-income families, children who received optometric services gained in reading achievement beyond the normal growth for their age, while children in the control group, who did not get these services, fell further behind.[15]

18 Children who are believed to have learning disabilities are also more likely to have vision impairment. Disproportionate assignment of low-income black children to special education may reflect, in part, a failure to correct their vision. Often, when children seem to have puzzling difficulties learning to read, the explanation is no more complex than that they cannot see. (Sometimes, vision difficulties remain undiagnosed in middle-class children as well, but more often, the failure to diagnose is a problem of the poor.)

19 Lower-class children are more likely to suffer from vision problems because of their less adequate prenatal development; typically, middle-class pregnant mothers have better medical care and nutrition.[16] Visual deficits also arise because poor children are more likely to watch too much television, an activity that does not train the eye to develop hand-eye coordination and depth perception.[17] Middle-class children are also more likely to have manipulative toys that develop visual skills.[18]

Hearing

20 Lower-class children also have more hearing problems.[19] These may result from more ear infections that occur in children whose overall health is less robust. If poor children simply had as much medical treatment for ear infections as middle-class children, they could pay better attention and the achievement gap would narrow a bit.[20]

Oral Health

21 Children without dental care are more likely to have toothaches; untreated cavities are nearly three times as prevalent among poor children as among middle-class children.[21] Although not every dental cavity leads to a toothache, some do. Children with toothaches, even minor ones, pay less attention in class and are more distracted during tests, on average, than children with healthy teeth.

Lead Exposure

22 Children who live in older, unrenovated buildings have more lead dust exposure, which harms cognitive functioning and behavior.[22] High lead levels also contribute to hearing loss.[23] Low-income children have dangerously high blood lead levels at five times the rate of middle-class children.[24] Although lead-based paint was banned from residential construction in 1978, low-income children more likely live in buildings constructed prior to that date and in buildings that are not repainted often enough to prevent old layers from peeling off. Urban children are also more likely to attend older schools, built when water pipes contained lead.[25]

Asthma

23   Lower-class children, particularly those who live in densely populated city neighborhoods, are also more likely to develop asthma.[26] A survey in New York City found that one of every four children in Harlem suffers from asthma, a rate six times as great as that for all children.[27] A Chicago survey found a nearly identical rate for black children and a rate of one in three for Puerto Ricans.[28] The disease is provoked in part from breathing fumes from low-grade home heating oil and from diesel trucks and buses (school buses that idle in front of schools are a particularly serious problem), as well as from excessive dust and allergic reactions to mold, cockroaches, and secondhand smoke.[29]

24   Asthma keeps children up at night; if they do make it to school the next day, they are likely to be drowsy and less attentive. Middle-class children typically get treatment for asthma symptoms, while low-income children get it less often. Asthma has become the biggest cause of chronic school absence.[30] Low-income children with asthma are about 80 percent more likely than middle-class children with asthma to miss more than seven days of school a year from the disease.[31] Children with asthma refrain from exercise and so are less physically fit. Drowsy and more irritable, they also have more behavioral problems that depress achievement.[32]

Medical Care

25   Children without regular medical care are also more likely to contract other illnesses—some serious, others minor—that keep them out of school. Despite federal programs to make medical care available to low-income children, there remain gaps in both access and utilization.[33] Many eligible families are not enrolled because of ignorance, fear, or lack of belief in the importance of medical care.

26   Even with health insurance, low-wage work interferes with the utilization of medical care. Parents who are paid hourly wages lose income when they take their children to doctors. Parents who work at blue-collar jobs risk being fired for excessive absence, so are likely to skip well-baby and routine pediatric care and go to doctors only in emergencies.

Use of Alcohol

27   Youngsters whose mothers drank during pregnancy have more difficulty with academic subjects, less ability to focus attention, poorer memory skills, less ability to reason, lower IQs, less social competence, and more aggression in the classroom.[34] On into adolescence, these children continue to have difficulty learning.[35] Fetal alcohol syndrome, a collection of the most severe cognitive, physical, and behavioral difficulties experienced by children of prenatal drinkers, is 10 times more frequent among low-income black children than middle-class white children.[36]

Smoking

28   Children of mothers who smoked while pregnant do worse on cognitive tests and their language develops less well. They have more serious behavioral problems, are more hyperactive, and commit more juvenile crime.[37] Because secondhand smoke causes asthma, children whose mothers smoke after pregnancy also are more likely to have low achievement.

Birth Weight

29   Low-income children are more likely to be born prematurely or with low birth weights and to suffer from cognitive problems as a result; low-birth-weight babies, on average, have lower IQ scores and are more likely to have mild learning disabilities and attention disorders.[38] Thirteen percent of black children are born with low birth weight, double the rate for whites.[39] Even if all children benefited from equally high-quality instruction, this difference alone would ensure lower average achievement for blacks.

Nutrition

30 Poor nutrition also directly contributes to an achievement gap between lower- and middle-class children. Low-income kindergartners whose height and weight are below normal for children their age tend to have lower test scores.[40] Iron deficiency anemia also affects cognitive ability; 8 percent of all children suffer from anemia, but 20 percent of black children are anemic.[41] Anemia also makes it more probable that children will absorb lead to which they have been exposed.[42] Compared with middle-class children, the poor also have deficiencies of other vitamins and minerals.[43] In experiments where pupils received inexpensive vitamin and mineral supplements, test scores rose from that treatment alone.[44]

31 Like social class differences in childrearing, each of these differences in health—in vision, hearing, oral health, lead exposure, asthma, use of alcohol, smoking, birth weight, and nutrition—has only a tiny influence on the academic achievement gap when considered separately. But together, they add up to a cumulative disadvantage for lower-class children that can't help but depress average performance.

32 To make significant progress in narrowing the achievement gap, three tracks should be pursued vigorously and simultaneously. First, school improvement efforts that raise the quality of instruction in elementary and secondary schools are essential. Second, comprehensive early childhood, afterschool, and summer programs must be implemented, so that lower-class children can have the same enriching experiences as their middle-class peers. And third, we must change our social and economic policies—and especially our approach to health care—so that all children can attend school more equally ready to learn.

33 For nearly half a century, the association of social and economic disadvantage with a student achievement gap has been well known to economists, sociologists, and educators. Most, however, have avoided the obvious implication of this understanding: raising the achievement of lower-class children requires amelioration of the social and economic conditions of their lives, not just school reform.

Endnotes

1. Meredith Phillips, "Understanding Ethnic Differences in Academic Achievement: Empirical Lessons from National Data," in *Analytic Issues in the Assessment of Student Achievement*, NCES 2000-050, ed. David W. Grissmer and J. Michael Ross (Washington, DC: U.S. Department of Education, National Center for Education Statistics, 2000); Richard L. Allington and Anne McGill-Franzen, "The Impact of Summer Setback on the Reading Achievement Gap," *Phi Delta Kappan* 85, no. 1 (2003): 68–75; and Doris R. Entwisle and Karl L. Alexander, "Summer Setback: Race, Poverty, School Composition, and Mathematics Achievement in the First Two Years of School," *American Sociological Review* 57 (1992): 72–84. One study (Roland G. Fryer Jr. and Steven D. Levitt, "Understanding the Black-White Test Score Gap in the First Two Years of School," NBER Working Paper 8975 [Cambridge, MA: National Bureau of Economic Research, 2002]) found no growth of the achievement gap during the summer, but this claim is at odds with most of the research literature.

2. Suzanne M. Bianchi and John Robinson, "What Did You Do Today? Children's Use of Time, Family Composition, and the Acquisition of Social Capital," *Journal of Marriage and the Family* 59, no. 2 (1997): 332–344; and Sandra L. Hofferth and John F. Sandberg, "How American Children Spend Their Time," *Journal of Marriage and the Family* 63, no. 2 (2001): 295–308.

3. Larry Mikulecky, "Family Literacy: Parent and Child Interactions," in *Family Literacy: Directions in Research and Implications for Practice*, ed. L. Ann Benjamin and Jerome Lord (Washington, DC: U.S. Department of Education, Office of Educational Research and Improvement, 1996), www.ed.gov/pubs/FamLit/parent.html.

4. See also Pia Rebello Britto and Jeanne Brooks-Gunn, "Concluding Comments," *New Directions for Child and Adolescent Development* 92 (2001): 91–98. Britto and

Brooks-Gunn report on a survey that included only poorly educated single African American mothers. Within this group, more expressive language use during book reading predicted children's achievement, but the survey does not lead to any reliable conclusions regarding whether the use of expressive language is related to social class.

5. Mikulecky, "Family Literacy."

6. Mikulecky, "Family Literacy."

7. Catherine Snow and Patton Tabors, "Intergenerational Transfer of Literacy," in *Family Literacy: Directions in Research and Implications for Practice*, ed. L. Ann Benjamin and Jerome Lord (Washington, DC: U.S. Department of Education, Office of Educational Research and Improvement, 1996), www.ed.gov/pubs/FamLit/transfer.html.

8. See Annette Lareau, *Unequal Childhoods: Class, Race, and Family Life* (Berkeley: University of California Press, 2003) for a general discussion of these childrearing pattern differences.

9. Shirley Brice Heath, *Ways with Words: Language, Life, and Work in Communities and Classrooms* (Cambridge, MA: Cambridge University Press, 1983).

10. Betty Hart and Todd R. Risley, *Meaningful Differences in the Everyday Experience of Young American Children* (Baltimore: Brookes Publishing, 1995); and Betty Hart and Todd R. Risley, "The Early Catastrophe: The 30 Million Word Gap by Age 3," *American Educator* 27, no. 1 (2003). The Hart-Risley findings have sometimes been misreported as meaning that the vocabularies of children of professionals were larger than the vocabularies of adults on welfare (not than the much smaller vocabularies that adults on welfare use when speaking to children). See Geoff Nunberg, "A Loss for Words," *Fresh Air* from WHYY, NPR, September 3, 2002, www-csli.stanford.edu/~nunberg/vocabulary.html; and Gerald W. Bracey, "The 13th Bracey Report on the Condition of Public Education," *Phi Delta Kappan* 85, no 2 (2003): 148–164.

11. Lisa Egbuonu and Barbara Starfeld, "Child Health and Social Status," *Pediatrics* 69, no. 5 (1982): 550–557; and Barbara Starfield, "Child Health and Socioeconomic Status," *American Journal of Public Health* 72, no. 6 (1982): 532–534.

12. Antonia Orfield, Frank Basa, and John Yun, "Vision Problems of Children in Poverty in an Urban School Clinic: Their Epidemic Numbers, Impact on learning, and Approaches to Remediation," *Journal of Optometric Vision Development* 32 (2001): 114–141.

13. Trudy Festinger and Robert Duckman, "Seeing and Hearing: Vision and Audiology Status of Foster Children in New York City," *Journal of Behavioral Optometry* 11, no. 3 (2000): 59–67.

14. The normal incidence of vision problems in children is about 25 percent. Clinicians and researchers have found incidences of more than 50 percent in some communities, although there has been no systematic nationwide survey of vision problems by race or social class. See Marge Christensen Gould and Herman Gould, "A Clear Vision for Equity and Opportunity," *Phi Delta Kappan* 85, no. 4 (2003): 324–328; Antonia Orfield, interview with author, November 11, 2003; Orfield, Basa, and Yun, "Vision Problems"; Robert Duckman (College of Optometry, State University of New York), interview with author, December 29, 2003; Paul Harris, interview with author, December 12, 2003; and Paul Harris, "Learning-Related Visual Problems in Baltimore city: A Long-Term Program," *Journal of Optometric Vision Development* 33, no. 2 (2002): 75–115.

15. Harris, "Learning-Related Visual Problems."

16. Surprisingly, there is no experimental evidence on the relationship between prenatal care and vision, and little good research evidence generally on the relationship between socioeconomic conditions and children's vision. In the following discussions, I was guided by personal correspondence and conversations with academic and clinical optometrists, including Professor Robert Duckman (State University of New York), Dr. Paul Harris, Dr. Antonia Orfield, and Professor Harold Solan (State University of New York). I also relied on the advice of Dr. Barbara Starfield at Johns Hopkins University. Sara Mosle, a

former teacher in a low-income school (and now a journalist and historian), stimulated this line of inquiry for me when she showed me her unpublished article, "They Can't Read Because They Can't See." See also Festinger and Duckman, "Seeing and Hearing"; Harris, "Learning-Related Visual Problems"; Orfield, Basa, and Yun, "Vision Problems"; and Harold A. Solan et al., "Effect of Attention Therapy on Reading Comprehension," *Journal of Learning Disabilities* 36, no. 6 (2003): 556.

17. National Center for Education Statistics, *Digest of Education Statistics, 2002*, NCES 2003-060 (Washington, DC: U.S. Department of Education, Office of Educational Research and Improvement, 2003), table 117.

18. Orfield, interview with author.

19. Egbuonu and Starfield, "Child Health."

20. Some medical authorities state that antibiotics have been overprescribed for young children's ear infections and that painkillers alone sometimes may suffice. However, without good access to personal pediatricians who know a child's history, parents themselves cannot determine whether antibiotics or painkillers are the proper treatment in any particular case. See Lawrence K. Altman, "Doctors and Patients Start to Curb Use of Antibiotics," *New York Times*, March 4, 2004.

21. U.S. General Accounting Office, *Oral Health: Dental Disease Is a Chronic Problem Among Low-Income Populations*, GAO/HEHS-00-72 (Washington, DC: GAO, 2000), 8, figure 1.

22. Egbuonu and Starfield, "Child Health"; U.S. General Accounting Office, *Lead Poisoning: Federal Health Care Programs Are Not Effectively Reaching At-Risk Children*, GAO/HEHS-99-18 (Washington, DC: GAO, 1999); Ulric Neisser et al., "Intelligence: Knowns and Unknowns," *American Psychologist* 51, no. 2 (1996): 77–101; and Ulric Neisser, "Never a Dull Moment," *American Psychologist* 52, no. 1 (1997): 79–81. There is scientific controversy regarding how much lead exposure is harmful to children.

23. Jeanne Brooks-Gunn and Greg J. Duncan, "The Effects of Poverty on Children," *Children and Poverty* 7, no. 2 (1997): 55–71.

24. GAO, *Lead Poisoning.*

25. Paul Barton, *Parsing the Achievement Gap: Baselines for Tracking Progress* (Princeton, NJ: Educational Testing Service, Policy Information Center, 2003); and Justin Blum, "High Lead Levels Found in Water at 9 D.C. Schools," *Washington Post*, February 25, 2004.

26. Christopher B. Forrest et al., "The Impact of Asthma on the Health Status of Adolescents," *Pediatrics* 99, no. 2 (1997): e1; and Neal Halfon and Paul W. Newacheck, "Childhood Asthma and Poverty: Differential Impacts and Utilization of Health Services," *Pediatrics* 91, no. 1 (1993): 56–61.

27. Associated Press, "Study: 1 in 4 Harlem Children Has Asthma," *New York Times*, April 21, 2003; and Roger D. Vaughan (associate professor, Mailman School of Public Health, Columbia University), personal correspondence, April 22, 2003.

28. Steven Whitman, Cynthia Williams, and Ami Shah, *Sinai Health System's Improving Community Health Survey: Report 1* (Chicago: Sinai Health System, 2004); and Scott Ritter, "Asthma Hits Record Rate among Minority Kids," *Chicago Sun-Times*, January 8, 2004.

29. Halfon and Newacheck, "Childhood Asthma."

30. Philip J. Hilts, "Study Finds Most States Lack System for Monitoring Asthma," *New York Times*, May 22, 2000.

31. Halfon and Newacheck, "Childhood Asthma."

32. Forrest et al., "Impact of Asthma."

33. Robert J. Mills and Shailesh Bhandari, *Health Insurance Coverage in the United States: 2002*, U.S. Census Bureau: Current Population Reports (Washington, DC: Government Printing office, 2003).

34. Susan Astley, "FAS/FAE: Their Impact on Psychosocial Child Development with a View to Diagnosis," in *Encyclopedia on Early Childhood Development*, ed. Richard

E. Tremblay, Ronald G. Barr, and Ray DeV. Peters (Montreal, Quebec: Centre of Excellence for Early Childhood Development, 2003), www.child-encyclopedia. com/ documents/AstleyANGxp.pdf; and Roger W. Simmons et al., "Fractionated Simple and Choice Reaction Time in Children with Prenatal Exposure to Alcohol," *Alcoholism: Clinical and Experimental Research* 26, no. 9 (2002): 1412–1419.

35. Gale A. Richardson et al., "Prenatal Alcohol and Marijuana Exposure: Effects on Neuropsychological Outcomes at 10 Years," *Neurotoxicology and Teratology* 24, no. 3 (2002): 309–320; and Ann P. Streissguth et al., "Maternal Drinking During Pregnancy: Attention and Short-Term Memory in 14-Year-Old Offspring—A Longitudinal Prospective Study," *Alcoholism: Clinical and Experimental Research* 18, no. 1 (1994): 202–218.

36. Ernest L. Abel, "An update on Incidence of FAS: FAS Is Not an Equal Opportunity Birth Defect," *Neurotoxicology and Teratology* 174 (1995): 437–443.

37. Astley, "FAS/FAE."

38. Maureen Hack, Nancy K. Klein, and H. Gerry Taylor, "Long-Term Developmental Outcomes of Low Birth Weight Infants," *The Future of Children* 5, no. 1 (1995): 176–196.

39. Kathryn Hoffman, Charmaine Llagas, and Thomas Snyder, *Status and Trends in the Education of Blacks*, NCES 2003-034 (Washington, DC: U.S. Department of Education, Office of Educational Research and Improvement, 2003), 15.

40. Robert Karp et al., "Growth and Academic Achievement in Inner-City Kindergarten Children," *Clinical Pediatrics* 31, no. 6 (1992): 336–340.

41. CDC (Centers for Disease Control and Prevention), *Pediatric Nutrition Surveillance 2001 Report* (Washington, DC: U.S. Department of Health and Human Services, 2002).

42. Larry J. Brown and Laura P. Sherman, "Policy Implications of New Scientific Knowledge," *Journal of Nutrition* 125 (1995): 2281S–2284S.

43. America's Second Harvest, *Differences in Nutrient Adequacy among Poor and Non-Poor Children* (Medford, MA: Center on Hunger, Poverty and Nutrition Policy, 2003), www.secondharvest.org; and Kathy Koch, "Hunger in America," *CQ Researcher* 10, no. 44 (2002): 1034–1055.

44. Neisser et al., "*Intelligence*: Knowns and Unknowns."

On the Uses of a Liberal Education as a Weapon in the Hands of the Restless Poor
Earl Shorris

1   Next month I will publish a book about poverty in America, but not the book I intended. The world took me by surprise—not once, but again and again. The poor themselves led me in directions I could not have imagined, especially the one that came out of a conversation in a maximum-security prison for women that is set, incongruously, in a lush Westchester suburb fifty miles north of New York City.

2   I had been working on the book for about three years when I went to the Bedford Hills Correctional Facility for the first time. The staff and inmates had developed a program to deal with family violence, and I wanted to see how their ideas fit with what I had learned about poverty.

3   Numerous forces—hunger, isolation, illness, landlords, police, abuse, neighbors, drugs, criminals, and racism, among others—exert themselves on the poor at all times and enclose them, making up a "surround of force" from which, it seems, they cannot escape. I had come to understand that this was what kept the poor from being political and that the absence of politics in their lives was what kept them poor. I don't mean "political" in the sense of voting in an election but in the way Thucydides used the word: to mean activity with

other people at every level, from the family to the neighborhood to the broader community to the city-state.

4   By the time I got to Bedford Hills, I had listened to more than six hundred people, some of them over the course of two or three years. Although my method is that of the bricoleur, the tinkerer who assembles a thesis of the bric-a-brac he finds in the world, I did not think there would be any more surprises. But I had not counted on what Viniece Walker was to say.

5   It is considered bad form in prison to speak of a person's crime, and I will follow that precise etiquette here. I can tell you that Viniece Walker came to Bedford Hills when she was twenty years old, a high school dropout who read at the level of a college sophomore, a graduate of crackhouses, the streets of Harlem, and a long alliance with a brutal man. On the surface, Viniece has remained as tough as she was on the street. She speaks bluntly, and even though she is HIV positive and the virus has progressed during her time in prison, she still swaggers as she walks down the long prison corridors. While in prison, Niecie, as she is known to her friends, completed her high school requirements and began to pursue a college degree (psychology is the only major offered at Bedford Hills, but Niecie also took a special interest in philosophy). She became a counselor to women with a history of family violence and a comforter to those with AIDS.

6   Only the deaths of other women cause her to stumble in the midst of her swaggering step, to spend days alone with the remorse that drives her to seek redemption. She goes through life as if she had been imagined by Dostoevsky, but even more complex than his fictions, alive, a person, a fair-skinned and freckled African-American woman, and in prison. It was she who responded to my sudden question, "Why do you think people are poor?"

7   We had never met before. The conversation around us focused on the abuse of women. Niecie's eyes were perfectly opaque—hostile, prison eyes. Her mouth was set in the beginning of a sneer.

8   "You got to begin with the children," she said, speaking rapidly, clipping out the street sounds as they came into her speech.

9   She paused long enough to let the change of direction take effect, then resumed the rapid, rhythmless speech. "You've got to teach the moral life of downtown to the children. And the way you do that, Earl, is by taking them downtown to plays, museums, concerts, lectures, where they can learn the moral life of downtown."

10   I smiled at her, misunderstanding, thinking I was indulging her. "And then they won't be poor anymore?"

11   She read every nuance of my response, and answered angrily, "And they won't be poor no more."

    "What you mean is—"

12   "What I mean is what I said—a moral alternative to the street."

13   She didn't speak of jobs or money. In that, she was like the others I had listened to. No
14   one had spoken of jobs or money. But how could the "moral life of downtown" lead anyone out from the surround of force? How could a museum push poverty away? Who can dress in statues or eat the past? And what of the political life? Had Niecie skipped a step or failed to take a step? The way out of poverty was politics, not the "moral life of downtown." But to enter the public world, to practice the political life, the poor had first to learn to reflect. That was what Niecie meant by the "moral life of downtown." She did not make the error of divorcing ethics from politics. Niecie had simply said, in a kind of shorthand, that no one could step out of the panicking circumstance of poverty directly into the public world.

15   Although she did not say so, I was sure that when she spoke of the "moral life of downtown" she meant something that had happened to her. With no job and no money, a prisoner, she had undergone a radical transformation. She had followed the same path that led to the invention of politics in ancient Greece. She had learned to reflect. In further conversation it became clear that when she spoke of "the moral life of downtown" she meant the humanities, the study of human constructs and concerns, which has been the source of reflection

for the secular world since the Greeks first stepped back from nature to experience wonder at what they beheld. If the political life was the way out of poverty, the humanities provided an entrance to reflection and the political life. The poor did not need anyone to release them; an escape route existed. But to open this avenue to reflection and politics a major distinction between the preparation for the life of the rich and the life of the poor had to be eliminated.

16   Once Niecie had challenged me with her theory, the comforts of tinkering came to an end; I could no longer make an homage to the happenstance world and rest. To test Niecie's theory, students, faculty, and facilities were required. Quantitative measures would have to be developed; anecdotal information would also be useful. And the ethics of the experiment had to be considered: I resolved to do no harm. There was no need for the course to have a "sink or swim" character; it could aim to keep as many afloat as possible.

17   When the idea for an experimental course became clear in my mind, I discussed it with Dr. Jaime Inclán, director of the Roberto Clemente Family Guidance Center in lower Manhattan, a facility that provides counseling to poor people, mainly Latinos, in their own language and in their own community. Dr. Inclán offered the center's conference room for a classroom. We would put three metal tables end-to-end to approximate the boat-shaped tables used in discussion sections at the University of Chicago of the Hutchins era,[1] which I used as a model for the course. A card table in the back of the room would hold a coffee-maker and a few cookies. The setting was not elegant, but it would do. And the front wall was covered by a floor-to-ceiling blackboard.

18   Now the course lacked only students and teachers. With no funds and a budget that grew every time a new idea for the course crossed my mind, I would have to ask the faculty to donate its time and effort. Moreover, when Hutchins said, "The best education for the best is the best education for us all," he meant it: he insisted that full professors teach discussion sections in the college. If the Clemente Course in the Humanities was to follow the same pattern, it would require a faculty with the knowledge and prestige that students might encounter in their first year at Harvard, Yale, Princeton, or Chicago.

19   I turned first to the novelist Charles Simmons. He had been assistant editor of *The New York Times Book Review* and had taught at Columbia University. He volunteered to teach poetry, beginning with simple poems, Housman, and ending with Latin poetry. Grace Glueck, who writes art news and criticism for the *New York Times,* planned a course that began with cave paintings, and ended in the late twentieth century. Timothy Koranda, who did his graduate work at MIT, had published journal articles on mathematical logic, but he had been away from his field for some years and looked forward to getting back to it. I planned to teach the American history course through documents, beginning with the Magna Carta, moving on to the second of Locke's *Two Treatises of Government,* the Declaration of Independence, and so on through the documents of the Civil War. I would also teach the political philosophy class.

20   Since I was a naïf in this endeavor, it did not immediately occur to me that recruiting students would present a problem. I didn't know how many I needed. All I had were criteria for selection:

Age: 18–35.
Household income: Less than 150 percent of the Census Bureau's Official Poverty Threshold (though this was to change slightly).
Educational level: Ability to read a tabloid newspaper.
Educational goals: An expression of intent to complete the course.

---

[1]Under the guidance of Robert Maynard Hutchins (1929–1951), the University of Chicago required year-long courses in the humanities, social sciences, and natural sciences for the Bachelor of Arts degree. Hutchins developed the curriculum with the help of Mortimer Adler, among others; the Hutchins courses later influenced Adler's Great Books program.

21   Dr. Inclán arranged a meeting of community activists who could help recruit students. Lynette Lauretig of The Door, a program that provides medical and educational services to adolescents, and Angel Roman of the Grand Street Settlement, which offers work and training and GED programs, were both willing to give us access to prospective students. They also pointed out some practical considerations. The course had to provide bus and subway tokens, because fares ranged between three and six dollars per class per student, and the students could not afford sixty or even thirty dollars a month for transportation. We also had to offer dinner or a snack, because the classes were to be held from 6:00 to 7:30 P.M.

22   The first recruiting session came only a few days later. Nancy Mamis-King, associate executive director of the Neighborhood Youth & Family Services program in the South Bronx, had identified some Clemente Course candidates and had assembled about twenty of her clients and their supervisors in a circle of chairs in a conference room. Everyone in the room was black or Latino, with the exception of one social worker and me.

23   After I explained the idea of the course, the white social worker was the first to ask a question: "Are you going to teach African history?"

24   "No. We'll be teaching a section on American history, based on documents, as I said. We want to teach the ideas of history so that—"

25   "You have to teach African history."

26   "This is America, so we'll teach American history. If we were in Africa, I would teach African history, and if we were in China, I would teach Chinese history."

27   "You're indoctrinating people in Western culture."

28   I tried to get beyond her, "We'll study African art," I said, "as it affects art in America. We'll study American history and literature; you can't do that without studying African-American culture, because culturally all Americans are black as well as white, Native American, Asian, and so on." It was no use; not one of them applied for admission to the course.

29   A few days later Lynette Lauretig arranged a meeting with some of her staff at The Door. We disagreed about the course. They thought it should be taught at a much lower level. Although I could not change their views, they agreed to assemble a group of Door members who might be interested in the humanities.

30   On an early evening that same week, about twenty prospective students were scheduled to meet in a classroom at The Door. Most of them came late. Those who arrived first slumped in their chairs, staring at the floor or greeting me with sullen glances. A few ate candy or what appeared to be the remnants of a meal. The students were mostly black and Latino, one was Asian, and five were white; two of the whites were immigrants who had severe problems with English. When I introduced myself, several of the students would not shake my hand, two or three refused even to look at me, one girl giggled, and the last person to volunteer his name, a young man dressed in a Tommy Hilfiger sweatshirt and wearing a cap turned sideways, drawled, "Henry Jones, but they call me Sleepy, because I got these sleepy eyes—"

31   "In our class, we'll call you Mr. Jones."

32   He smiled and slid down in his chair so that his back was parallel to the floor.

33   Before I finished attempting to shake hands with the prospective students, a waiflike Asian girl with her mouth half-full of cake said, "Can we get on with it? I'm bored."

34   I liked the group immediately.

35   Having failed in the South Bronx, I resolved to approach these prospective students differently. "You've been cheated," I said. "Rich people learn the humanities; you didn't. The humanities are a foundation for getting along in the world, for thinking, for learning to reflect on the world instead of just reacting to whatever force is turned against you. I think the humanities are one of the ways to become political, and I don't mean political in the sense of voting in an election but in the broad sense." I told them Thucydides' definition of politics.

36   "Rich people know politics in that sense. They know how to negotiate instead of using force. They know how to use politics to get along, to get power. It doesn't mean that rich

people are good and poor people are bad. It simply means that rich people know a more effective method for living in this society.

37   "Do all rich people, or people who are in the middle, know the humanities? Not a chance. But some do. And it helps. It helps to live better and enjoy life more. Will the humanities make you rich? Yes. Absolutely. But not in terms of money. In terms of life.

38   "Rich people learn the humanities in private schools and expensive universities. And that's one of the ways in which they learn the political life. I think that is the real difference between the haves and have-nots in this country. If you want real power, legitimate power, the kind that comes from the people and belongs to the people, you must understand politics. The humanities will help.

39   "Here's how it works: We'll pay your subway fare; take care of your children, if you have them; give you a snack or a sandwich; provide you with books and any other materials you need. But we'll make you think harder, use your mind more fully, than you ever have before. You'll have to read and think about the same kinds of ideas you would encounter in a first-year course at Harvard or Yale or Oxford.

40   "You'll have to come to class in the snow and the rain and the cold and the dark. No one will coddle you; no one will slow down for you. There will be tests to take, papers to write. And I can't promise you anything but a certificate of completion at the end of the course. I'll be talking to colleges about giving credit for the course, but I can't promise anything. If you come to the Clemente course, you must do it because you want to study the humanities, because you want a certain kind of life, a richness of mind and spirit. That's all I offer you: philosophy, poetry, art history, logic, rhetoric, and American history.

41   "Your teachers will all be people of accomplishment in their fields," I said, and I spoke a little about each teacher. "That's the course. October through may, with a two-week break at Christmas. It is generally accepted in America that the liberal arts and the humanities in particular belong to the elites. I think you're the elites."

42   The young Asian woman said, "What are you getting out of this?"

43   "This is a demonstration project. I'm writing a book. This will be proof, I hope, of my idea about the humanities. Whether it succeeds or fails will be up to the teachers and you."

44   All but one of the prospective students applied for admission to the course.

45   I repeated the new presentation at the Grand Street Settlement and at other places around the city. There were about fifty candidates for the thirty positions in the course. Personal interviews began in early September.

46   Meanwhile, almost all of my attempts to raise money had failed. Only the novelist Starling Lawrence, who is also editor in chief of W. W. Norton, which had contracted to publish the book; the publishing house itself; and a small, private family foundation supported the experiment. We were far short of our budgeted expenses, but my wife, Sylvia, and I agreed that the cost was still very low, and we decided to go ahead.

47   Of the fifty prospective students who showed up at the Clemente Center for personal interviews, a few were too rich (a postal supervisor's son, a fellow who claimed his father owned a factory in Nigeria that employed sixty people), and more than a few could not read. Two home-care workers from Local 1199 could not arrange their hours to enable them to take the course. Some of the applicants were too young: a thirteen-year-old and two who had just turned sixteen.

48   Lucia Medina, a woman with five children who told me that she often answered the door at the single-room occupancy hotel where she lived with a butcher knife in her hand, was the oldest person accepted into the course. Carmen Quiñones, a recovering addict who had spent time in prison, was the next eldest. Both were in their early thirties.

49   The interviews went on for days.

50   Abel Lomas[2] shared an apartment and worked part-time wrapping packages at Macy's. His father had abandoned the family when Abel was born. His mother was murdered by his

---

[2]Not his real name.

stepfather when Abel was thirteen. With no one to turn to and no place to stay, he lived on the streets, first in Florida, then back in New York City. He used the tiny stipend from his mother's Social Security to keep himself alive.

51   After the recruiting session at The Door, I drove up Sixth Avenue from Canal Street with Abel, and we talked about ethics. He had a street tough's delivery, spitting out his ideas in crudely formed sentences of four, five, eight words, strings of blunt declarations, with never a dependent clause to qualify his thoughts. He did not clear his throat with badinage, as timidity teaches us to do, nor did he waste his breath with tact.

52   "What do you think about drugs?" he asked, the strangely breathless delivery further coarsened by his Dominican accent. "My cousin is a dealer."

53   "I've seen a lot of people hurt by drugs."

54   "Your family has nothing to eat. You sell drugs. What's worse? Let your family starve or sell drugs?'

55   "Starvation and drug addiction are both bad, aren't they?"

56   "Yes," he said, not "yeah" or "uh-huh" but a precise, almost formal yes."

57   "So it's a question of the worse of two evils? How shall we decide?"

58   The question came up near Thirty-fourth Street, where Sixth Avenue remains hellishly traffic-jammed well into the night. Horns honked, people flooded into the streets against the light. Buses and trucks and taxicabs threatened their way from one lane to the next where the overcrowded avenue crosses the equally crowded Broadway. As we passed Herald Square and made our way north again, I said, "There are a couple of ways to look at it. One comes from Immanuel Kant, who said that you should not do anything unless you want it to become a universal law; that is, unless you think it's what everybody should do. So Kant wouldn't agree to selling drugs *or* letting your family starve."

59   Again he answered with a formal "Yes."

60   "There's another way to look at it, which is to ask what is the greatest good for the greatest number: in this case, keeping your family from starvation or keeping tens, perhaps hundreds of people from losing their lives to drugs. So which is the greatest good for the greatest number?"

61   "That's what I think," he said.

62   "What?"

63   "You shouldn't sell drugs. You can always get food to eat. Welfare. Something."

64   "You're a Kantian."

65   "Yes."

66   "You know who Kant is?"

67   "I think so."

68   We had arrived at Seventy-seventh Street, where he got out of the car to catch the subway before I turned east. As he opened the car door and the light came on, the almost military neatness of him struck me. He had the newly cropped hair of a cadet. His clothes were clean, without a wrinkle. He was an orphan, a street kid, an immaculate urchin. Within a few weeks he would be nineteen years old, the Social Security payments would end, and he would have to move into a shelter.

69   Some of those who came for interviews were too poor. I did not think that was possible when we began, and I would like not to believe it now, but it was true. There is a point at which the level of forces that surround the poor can become insurmountable, when there is no time or energy left to be anything but poor. Most often I could not recruit such people for the course; when I did, they soon dropped out.

70   Over the days of interviewing, a class slowly assembled. I could not then imagine who would last the year and who would not. One young woman submitted a neatly typed essay that said, "I was homeless once, then I lived for some time in a shelter. Right now, I have got my own space granted by the Partnership for the Homeless. Right now, I am living alone, with very limited means. Financially I am overwhelmed by debts. I cannot afford all the food I need…"

71   A brother and sister, refugees from Tashkent, lived with their parents in the farthest reaches of Queens, far beyond the end of the subway line. They had no money, and they had been refused admission by every school to which they had applied. I had not intended to accept immigrants or people who had difficulty with the English language, but I took them into the class.

72   I also took four who had been in prison, three who were homeless, three who were pregnant, one who lived in a drugged dream-state in which she was abused, and one whom I had known for a long time and who was dying of AIDS. As I listened to them, I wondered how the course would affect them. They had no public life, no place; they lived within the surround of force, moving as fast as they could, driven by necessity, without a moment to reflect. Why should they care about fourteenth century Italian painting or truth tables or the death of Socrates?

73   Between the end of recruiting and the orientation session that would open the course, I made a visit to Bedford Hills to talk with Niecie Walker. It was hot, and the drive up from the city had been unpleasant. I didn't yet know Niecie very well. She didn't trust me, and I didn't know what to make of her. While we talked, she held a huge white pill in her hand. "For AIDS," she said.

74   "Are you sick?"

75   "My T-cell count is down. But that's neither here nor there. Tell me about the course, Earl. What are you going to teach?"

76   "Moral philosophy."

77   "And what does that include?"

78   She had turned the visit into an interrogation. I didn't mind. At the end of the conversation I would be going out into "the free world"; if she wanted our meeting to be an interrogation, I was not about to argue. I said, "We'll begin with Plato: the *Apology,* a little of the *Crito,* a few pages of the *Phaedo* so that they'll know what happened to Socrates. Then we'll read Aristotle's *Nicomachean Ethics.* I also want them to read Thucydides, particularly Pericles' Funeral Oration in order to make the connection between ethics and politics, to lead them in the direction I hope the course will take them. Then we'll end with *Antigone,* but read as moral and political philosophy as well as drama."

79   "There's something missing," she said, leaning back in her chair, taking on an air of superiority.

80   The drive had been long, the day was hot, the air in the room was dead and damp. "Oh, yeah," I said, "and what's that?"

81   "Plato's Allegory of the Cave. How can you teach philosophy to poor people without the Allegory of the Cave? The ghetto is the cave. Education is the light. Poor people can understand that."

82   At the beginning of the orientation at the Clemente Center a week later, each teacher spoke for a minute or two. Dr. Inclán and his research assistant, Patricia Vargas, administered the questionnaire he had devised to measure, as best he could, the role of force and the amount of reflection in the lives of the students. I explained that each class was going to be videotaped as another way of documenting the project. Then I gave out the first assignment: "In preparation for our next meeting, I would like you to read a brief selection from Plato's *Republic:* the Allegory of the Cave."

83   I tried to guess how many students would return for the first class. I hoped for twenty, expected fifteen, and feared ten. Sylvia, who had agreed to share the administrative tasks of the course, and I prepared coffee and cookies for twenty-five. We had a plastic container filled with subway tokens. Thanks to Starling Lawrence, we had thirty copies of Bernard Knox's *Norton Book of Classical Literature,* which contained all of the texts for the philosophy section except the *Republic* and the *Nicomachean Ethics.*

84   At six o'clock there were only ten students seated around the long table, but by six-fifteen the number had doubled, and a few minutes later two more straggled in out of the

dusk. I had written a time line on the blackboard, showing them the temporal progress of thinking—from the role of myth in Neolithic societies to *The Gilgamesh Epic* and forward to the Old Testament, Confucius, the Greeks, the New Testament, the Koran, the *Epic of Son-Jara,* and ending with Nahuatl and Maya poems, which took us up to the contact between Europe and America, where the history course began. The time line served as context and geography as well as history: no race, no major culture was ignored. "Let's agree," I told them, "that we are all human, whatever our origins. And now let's go into Plato's cave."

85   I told them that there would be no lectures in the philosophy section of the course; we would use the Socratic method, which is called maieutic dialogue. "'Maieutic' comes from the Greek word for midwifery. I'll take the role of midwife in our dialogue. Now, what do you mean by that? What does a midwife do?"

86   It was the beginning of a love affair, the first moment of their infatuation with Socrates. Later, Abel Lomas would characterize that moment in his no-nonsense fashion, saying that it was the first time anyone had ever paid attention to their opinions.

87   Grace Glueck began the art history class in a darkened room lit with slides of the Lascaux caves and next turned the students' attention to Egypt, arranging for them to visit the Metropolitan Museum of Art to see the Temple of Dendur and the Egyptian Galleries. They arrived at the museum on a Friday evening. Darlene Codd brought her two-year-old son. Pearl Lau was late, as usual. One of the students, who had told me how much he was looking forward to the museum visit, didn't show up, which surprised me. Later I learned that he had been arrested for jumping a turnstile in a subway station on his way to the museum and was being held in a prison cell under the Brooklyn criminal courthouse. In the Temple of Dendur, Samantha Smoot asked questions of Felicia Blum, a museum lecturer. Samantha was the student who had burst out with the news, in one of the first sessions of the course, that people in her neighborhood believed it "wasn't no use goin' to school, because the white man wouldn't let you up no matter what." But in a hall where the statuary was of half-human, half-animal female figures, it was Samantha who asked what the glyphs meant, encouraging Felicia Blum to read them aloud, to translate them into English. Toward the end of the evening, Grace led the students out of the halls of antiquities into the Rockefeller Wing, where she told them of the connections of culture and art in Mali, Benin, and the Pacific Islands. When the students had collected their coats and stood together near the entrance to the museum, preparing to leave, Samantha stood apart, a tall, slim young woman, dressed in a deerstalker cap and a dark blue peacoat. She made an exaggerated farewell wave at us and returned to Egypt— her ancient mirror.

88   Charles Simmons began the poetry class with poems as puzzles and laughs. His plan was to surprise the class, and he did. At first he read the poems aloud to them, interrupting himself with footnotes to bring them along. He showed them poems of love and of seduction, and satiric commentaries on those poems by later poets. "Let us read," the students demanded, but Charles refused. He tantalized them with the opportunity to read poems aloud. A tug-of-war began between him and the students, and the standoff was ended not by Charles directly but by Hector Anderson. When Charles asked if anyone in the class wrote poetry, Hector raised his hand.

89   "Can you recite one of your poems for us?" Charles said.

90   Until that moment, Hector had never volunteered a comment, though he had spoken well and intelligently when asked. He preferred to slouch in his chair, dressed in full camouflage gear, wearing a nylon stocking over his hair and eating slices of fresh cantaloupe or honeydew melon.

91   In response to Charles's question, Hector slid up to a sitting position. "If you turn that camera off," he said. "I don't want anybody using my lyrics." When he was sure the red light of the video camera was off, Hector stood and recited verse after verse of a poem that belonged somewhere in the triangle formed by Ginsberg's *Howl,* the Book of Lamentations, and hip-hop. When Charles and the students finished applauding, they asked Hector to

say the poem again, and he did. Later Charles told me, "That kid is the real thing." Hector's discomfort with Sylvia and me turned to ease. He came to our house for a small Christmas party and at other times. We talked on the telephone about a scholarship program and about what steps he should take next in his education. I came to know his parents. As a student, he began quietly, almost secretly, to surpass many of his classmates.

92   Timothy Koranda was the most professorial of the professors. He arrived precisely on time, wearing a hat of many styles—part fedora, part Borsalino, part Stetson, and at least one-half World War I campaign hat. He taught logic during class hours, filling the blackboard from floor to ceiling, wall to wall, drawing the intersections of sets here and truth tables there and a great square of oppositions in the middle of it all. After class, he walked with students to the subway, chatting about Zen or logic or Heisenberg.

93   On one of the coldest nights of the winter, he introduced the students to logic problems stated in ordinary language that they could solve by reducing the phrases to symbols. He passed out copies of a problem, two pages long, then wrote out some of the key phrases on the blackboard. "Take this home with you," he said, "and at our next meeting we shall see who has solved it. I shall also attempt to find the answer."

94   By the time he finished writing out the key phrases, however, David Iskhakov raised his hand. Although they listened attentively, neither David nor his sister Susana spoke often in class. She was shy, and he was embarrassed at his inability to speak perfect English.

95   "May I go to blackboard?" David said. "And will see if I have found correct answer to zis problem."

96   Together Tim and David erased the blackboard; then David began covering it with signs and symbols. "If first man is earning this money, and second man is closer to this town...," he said, carefully laying out the conditions. After five minutes or so, he said, "And the answer is: B will get first to Cleveland!"

97   Samantha Smoot shouted, "That's not the answer. The mistake you made is in the first part there, where it says who earns more money."

98   Tim folded his arms across his chest, happy. "I shall let you all take the problem home," he said.

99   When Sylvia and I left the Clemente Center that night, a knot of students was gathered outside, huddled against the wind. Snow had begun to fall, a slippery powder on the gray ice that covered all but a narrow space down the center of the sidewalk. Samantha and David stood in the middle of the group, still arguing over the answer to the problem. I leaned in for a moment to catch the character of the argument. It was even more polite than it had been in the classroom, because now they governed themselves.

100   One Saturday morning in January, David Howell telephoned me at home. "Mr. Shores," he said, anglicizing my name, as many of the students did.

101   "Mr. Howell," I responded, recognizing his voice.

102   "How you doin', Mr. Shores?"

103   "I'm fine. How are you?"

104   "I had a little problem at work."

105   Uh-oh, I thought; bad news was coming. David is a big man, generally good-humored but with a quick temper. According to his mother, he had a history of violent behavior. In the classroom he had been one of the best students, a steady man, twenty-four years old, who always did the reading assignments and who often made interesting connections between the humanities and daily life. "What happened?"

106   "Mr. Shores, there's a woman at my job, she said some things to me and I said some things to her. And she told my supervisor I had said things to her, and he called me in about it. She's forty years old and she don't have no social life, and she's jealous of me."

107   "And then what happened?" The tone of his voice and the timing of the call did not portend good news.

108   "Mr. Shores, she made me so mad, I wanted to smack her up against the wall. I tried to talk to some friends to calm myself down a little, but nobody was around."

109   "And what did you do?" I asked, fearing this was his one telephone call from the city jail.

110   "Mr. Shores, I asked myself, 'What would Socrates do?'"

111   David Howell had reasoned that his co-worker's envy was not his problem after all, and he had dropped his rage.

112   One evening, in the American History section, I was telling the students about Gordon Wood's ideas in *The Radicalism of the American Revolution*. We were talking about the revolt by some intellectuals against classical learning at the turn of the eighteenth century, including Benjamin Franklin's late-life change of heart, when Henry Jones raised his hand.

113   "If the Founders loved the humanities so much, how come they treated the natives so badly?"

114   I didn't know how to answer this question. There were confounding explanations to offer about changing attitudes toward Native Americans, vaguely useful references to views of Rousseau and James Fenimore Cooper. For a moment I wondered if I should tell them about Heidegger's Nazi past. Then I saw Abel Lomas's raised hand at the far end of the table, "Mr. Lomas," I said.

115   Abel said, "That's what Aristotle means by incontinence, when you know what's morally right but you don't do it, because you're overcome by your passions."

116   The other students nodded. They were all inheritors of wounds caused by the incontinence of educated men; now they had an ally in Aristotle, who had given them a way to analyze the actions of their antagonists.

117   Those who appreciate ancient history understand the radical character of the humanities. They know that politics did not begin in a perfect world but in a society even more flawed than ours: one that embraced slavery, denied the rights of women, practiced a form of homosexuality that verged on pedophilia, and endured the intrigues and corruption of its leaders. The genius of that society originated in man's re-creation of himself through the recognition of his humanness as expressed in art, literature, rhetoric, philosophy, and the unique notion of freedom. At that moment, the isolation of the private life ended and politics began.

118   The winners in the game of modern society, and even those whose fortune falls in the middle, have other means to power: they are included at birth. They know this. And they know exactly what to do to protect their place in the economic and social hierarchy. As Allan Bloom, author of the nationally best-selling tract in defense of elitism, *The Closing of the American Mind,* put it, they direct the study of the humanities exclusively at those young people who "have been raised in comfort and with the expectation of ever increasing comfort."

119   In the last meeting before graduation, the Clemente students answered the same set of questions they'd answered at orientation. Between October and May, students had fallen to AIDS, pregnancy, job opportunities, pernicious anemia, clinical depression, a schizophrenic child, and other forces, but of the thirty students admitted to the course, sixteen had completed it, and fourteen had earned credit from Bard College. Dr. Inclán found that the students' self-esteem and their abilities to divine and solve problems had significantly increased; their use of verbal aggression as a tactic for resolving conflicts had significantly decreased. And they all had notably more appreciation for the concepts of benevolence, spirituality, universalism, and collectivism.

120   It cost about $2,000 for a student to attend the Clemente Course. Compared with unemployment, welfare, or prison, the humanities are a bargain. But coming into possession of the faculty of reflection and the skills of politics leads to a choice for the poor—and whatever they choose, they will be dangerous: they may use politics to get along in a society based on the game, to escape from the surround of force into a gentler life, to behave as citizens, and nothing more; or they may choose to oppose the game itself. No one can predict the effect of politics, although we all would like to think that wisdom goes our way. That is why the poor are so often mobilized and so rarely politicized. The possibility that they will adopt a moral view other than that of their mentors can never be discounted. And who wants to run that risk?

121   On the night of the first Clemente Course graduation, the students and their families filled the eighty-five chairs we crammed into the conference room where classes had been held. Robert Martin, associate dean of Bard College, read the graduates' names. David Dinkins, the former mayor of New York City, handed out the diplomas. There were speeches and presentations. The students gave me a plaque on which they had misspelled my name. I offered a few words about each student, congratulated them, and said finally, "This is what I wish for you: May you never be more active than when you are doing nothing…" I saw their smiles of recognition at the words of Cato, which I had written on the blackboard early in the course. They could recall again too the moment when we had come to the denouement of Aristotle's brilliantly constructed thriller, the *Nicomachean Ethics*—the idea that in the contemplative life man was most like God. One or two, perhaps more of the students, closed their eyes. In the momentary stillness of the room it was possible to think.

122   The Clemente Course in the Humanities ended a second year in June 1997. Twenty-eight new students had enrolled; fourteen graduated. Another version of the course will begin this fall in Yucatán, Mexico, using classical Maya literature in Maya.

123   On May 14, 1997, Viniece Walker came up for parole for the second time. She had served more than ten years of her sentence, and she had been the best of prisoners. In a version of the Clemente Course held at the prison, she had been my teaching assistant. After a brief hearing, her request for parole was denied. She will serve two more years before the parole board will reconsider her case.

124   A year after graduation, ten of the first sixteen Clemente Course graduates were attending four-year colleges or going to nursing school; four of them had received full scholarships to Bard College. The other graduates were attending community college or working full-time. Except for one: she had been fired from her job in a fast-food restaurant for trying to start a union.

On Being an Excellent Student
Donald E. Simanek

An ex-president of this institution, when it was a college with an enrollment of several thousand, was asked how many students the school had. He quipped "Oh, perhaps a dozen." He was making a joke which is as old as the hills. The president of a large corporation used it when he was asked by a reporter (during a strike) how many workers there were in his plant. One of my junior-high teachers used to remind us that to be a student meant more than merely being a pupil.

Times change. The definition of "student" once was "one who studies something". Today it can mean merely "one who attends a school, college or university". This modern definition doesn't even suggest that the person does more than "attend". College and university professors still use the first definition, and schools have ways (such as requirements, exams and grades) to attempt to ensure that those who attend will also study and learn something.

So what distinguishes a student? What makes the student stand out from the rest of the class? The four As: attitude, academic skills, awareness, and accomplishment, certainly are a large part of it, and a student who has them will be very likely to earn As:

- Attitude is primarily a genuine desire to learn, and the willingness to do hard intellectual work to achieve understanding. It is also shown by how well you apply yourself even to subjects in which you have little interest, and how much you can achieve even when a professor's style isn't to your liking.

- Academic skills include the ability to read with comprehension, intelligent use of resources (including library resources), logical and mathematical skills, efficient study habits, and the ability to communicate clearly and fluently in speaking and writing.
- Awareness of what's going on in the world around you, and the habit of intelligently relating it to your academic courses. For example, when taking a course in political science, you should relate what you are learning in class to what's happening on the national and world political scene. When taking a science course, you should relate scientific principles to phenomena you observe in everyday life, and go out of your way to find applications and examples of science in the real world.
- Accomplishment is demonstrated by successful application of understanding. The evidence of that is:

  1. correct and confident application of what you've learned to new problems and challenges,
  2. clear and effective communication of your understanding through speaking and writing, and
  3. possession of a base of information, skills and understanding sufficient to allow you to continue your education outside of the classroom, throughout your life.

All of these add up to a fifth A: ability, a word frequently used above. The goal of education is to achieve the ability to apply one's knowledge in new, creative, and correct ways. Abilities are not entirely innate; some are achievable through dedicated and focused effort.

Other symptoms and qualities of a good student include:

1. **Self-discipline.** The successful student has learned to budget time, and use it efficiently, and will do the things that need to be done, when they must be done, whether or not he or she feels like it at the time.
2. **Initiative.** In short: doing things without being told. The student doesn't wait for assignments to read ahead in the textbook, or to seek out and study related books to gain understanding. The good student does more problems or exercises than assigned, and does them even when none are assigned. The good student working in the laboratory does not merely follow instructions (though that is an important skill) but looks for opportunities to discover new things, try new things, or find better methods. When an opportunity arises to do a project outside of class, the good student jumps at the chance and doesn't even ask whether it will earn extra credit.
3. **Breadth of interests.** College provides a great opportunity to broaden your interests and explore new things. You may never again have available to you such a convenient and comprehensive library, such diverse and inexpensive cultural events and academic activities.

   Much education can occur outside of class, if you seek it. But if you confine yourself to the things you've always done, avoiding anything new and unfamiliar, you will have squandered a valuable opportunity.
4. **An open mind is a mind receptive to examination of new ideas and facts.** Having an open mind does not mean that one jumps on the bandwagon of every new fad. A better characterization of an open mind is one, which is willing to dispassionately and rationally analyze new ideas, weighing them objectively against established knowledge and the facts at hand.
5. **A critical habit of mind.** Education is more than the acquisition of information. It includes the ability to acquire new information, to critically evaluate that information, and to correctly and effectively use it. With so many information sources at our disposal in this computer age we are awash in information, and in danger of information

overload. But much of that information is fraudulent, worthless, incomplete, or just plain wrong. It has always been so.

Probably 95% of the books in any library could be lost with no harm to human knowledge. But it's not easy to determine just which books are worth keeping. We are assaulted through every medium by folks trying to sell us something (with impressive claims of its value), to persuade us to accept some political or social idea, to convert us to some religion or philosophy, or to convince us of the value of some medical panacea. Most of this is humbug.

One of the values of a good education is the ability to see through false and un-founded claims and outright deceptions. By this criterion, education has largely been a failure, for many people who have college degrees are still suckers for the snake-oil and perpetual-motion-machine peddlers.

6. **Perceptiveness.** The more you learn, the more perceptive you become. You can, as necessary, "read between the lines." You no longer need everything spelled out; you can fill in missing details. You aren't dependent on being shown; you can puzzle things out for yourself. You perceive quickly what a writer or speaker means, without misinterpreting.

You learn to seek the intended meaning of what you read or hear rather than try-ing to impose your own preconceived meaning. You can see through complexity to the heart of a matter. You are able to distinguish the important from the trivial in a serious discussion.

7. **Objectivity.** Most of us begin our education with an "egocentric" view, expecting ev-erything to have some relevance to our needs or desires. We even impose such inter-pretations on things we learn, and avoid learning some things because they don't seem important at the time. Education can broaden that view, encouraging us to set our egos aside and objectively evaluate facts and interpretations. We find out that mere unsup-ported personal opinions have no value in an academic discussion. We learn to recog-nize the validity of facts and ideas, which we may not like. We learn that other people and other cultures interpret things differently, and that fact is not a-priori evidence that they are wrong. We learn that the world does not revolve around us, and the universe cares not one bit whether we exist, or what we do. Education can give us humility.

8. **Humility.** However much one knows, one must realize there's a lot more to be learned, and that some of what one 'knows' may turn out to be wrong. For this reason intellec-tual arrogance is unbecoming in an educated person. Knowing lots of things is good, but knowing the limitations of one's knowledge is essential to using it properly. Many of the classic errors of history were made by people over-confidently going beyond what they knew and understood.

Work to be educated, not merely trained.
1997

Reclaiming Native Education
Christina Twu

1   When Colville tribal member Laurie Sison became a mother at 16 in White Swan, Wash., she dropped out of high school and received her GED.

2   Later in her adult life, Sison wanted to get an associate's degree at Yakima Valley Community College, but her abusive ex-husband threatened to slash her face if he ever saw her talking to another man on a school campus.

3   She became shy, nervous, alienated.

4   Later, when she moved to Auburn and remarried, she tried taking a few courses at Green River Community College.

5   But nothing seemed to stick until she came across Antioch University Seattle's First Peoples' Native educator program at the Muckleshoot Tribal College. The tribal college is one of the region's emerging efforts to help fight the persistent barriers facing Native students.

6   Still, Sison's debut presentation at First Peoples proved to be a daunting task.

7   "It lasted like 45 seconds," Sison recalls. "I rushed through it, and then, I was done. Now I can get up and do a presentation and speak to people to their faces like a teacher. They've made a teacher out of me. And people tell me that that was always there, they just got it out of me."

8   Her newfound confidence was a result of the personal nature of class structure, where the stories, experiences and perspectives of each student were drawn upon to enhance group learning:

9   Historically, the American school system has had a dismal track record in relation to Native American students. As late as the 1930s, Native children were forcibly taken from their communities to attend federally funded boarding schools.

10   Capt. Richard Pratt, who opened the first off-reservation Indian school in 1879 at an abandoned Pennsylvania military post, famously said that his goal in forcing assimilation upon Native American children was to "kill the Indian, not the man" in them. For decades, his reprehensible legacy would be replicated at other boarding schools where young children were forbidden from speaking their language, and parenting's closest cousin resembled a rigid, disciplinarian and often abusive hand, as Native youth suffered a bleak existence away from the warmth and education of family and culture.

11   But lately more culturally specific educational resources have been available to Native American and Alaskan Native children, as well as Native adult learners. The landmark Indian Education Act of 1972, which was amended to support teacher training programs the following year, paved the way for more Native educators in school systems.

12   In more recent years, the success of Native education has been bolstered by national advocacy efforts, such as The Early College High School Initiative, which Antioch University Seattle's Center for Native Education (CNE) has applied in seven high-school sites across Washington state since 2004 and at four other sites in three additional states: two in Oregon, and one each in California and Alaska. It is the first college-access effort of its kind specifically designated for Native American youth.

13   Another, the First Peoples' Program, launched in 2002 and housed at Muckleshoot Tribal College in Auburn, is designed primarily for adult learners who are seeking post-secondary education to become teachers in tribal and public schools and other Native youth communities.

14   Not only do these secondary and post-secondary education models prove to be culturally relevant and seated in the heart of Native communities, they also play a part in combating Native dropout rates and making degrees more accessible for adults who wish to continue to pass on Native teachings as educators.

15   At Ferndale High School near the Lummi Reservation in Bellingham, where the Early college model program was implemented in 2004, dropout rates of Native high school students decreased from 69 percent to 16 percent after the first semester, according to Ferndale High School records. On the WASL test that year, 92 percent of Native students met reading standards, compared to 73 percent of the general student population. WASL test scores overall increased over 2004–2005 scores the following school year, although exact percentages are still unknown. Even when Native students were taking more challenging early college courses, grade point averages also rose after the program was implemented.

16   "We have seen Native students accruing anywhere from five to 40-some college credits during their high school years, which is a phenomenon that has not been observed

before," says Linda Campbell, a St. Regis Mohawk descendent who is the executive director of the CNE.

17   In 2004, Antioch received a $6.1 million grant from the Bill & Melinda Gates Foundation to expand its refined "Early Colleges for Native Youth" model nationally, adding 10 sites throughout states such as California, Texas, New York, Alaska, North Carolina, Oregon and New Mexico. The process of developing these sites started this year and is expected to be complete by 2008.

18   Next year, the U.S. Department of the Interior will contribute $157.4 million to the construction and maintenance of tribal schools across the nation, and a portion of it will go towards a new K-12 tribal school on the Muckleshoot Reservation slated for construction in 2008.

19   Early College High School program is supported by grants and the First Peoples' programs receive no direct grants or funding.

Early College Focus

20   Before the new wave of programs catered to Native American learners, the need for high school dropout intervention as well as post-secondary educational support was glaringly obvious. Nationally, Native American students have the highest dropout and lowest college completion rates of all ethnic groups. Researchers in a 2003 Manhattan institute study found that only three in five Native American students graduate from high school. Of those who do go on to higher education after high school, less than 3 percent complete a four-year degree. In contrast, about 30 percent of Caucasian students who pursue bachelor's degrees complete them, according to research by the National Center for Education Statistics for the same year.

21   The Early College High School Initiative Program caters to this specific and dual dilemma, which under the design model, exists as a partnership between tribal leaders, school districts and local colleges. The emphasis is culturally infused curriculum geared toward students who do not necessarily see themselves on the road to college, and many courses rely heavily on local tribal narrative and perspectives.

22   According to Susan Given-Seymour, who develops and runs special programs at Northwest Indian College on the Lummi Reservation, the early college sites across the state do not function like dual-credit systems such as the Running Start program. For starters, Running Start and Early College High School serve different needs.

23   "Running Start students are usually students that already think of themselves as college-bound, so they can just fit right into the existing college classes, whereas Early College is deemed for those students who don't think of themselves as college-bound," Given-Seymour explains. "And so the school district will start working with kids and learn to start identifying them as young as fourth or fifth grade, to start talking to them and try to get them to start seeing themselves as college material. They give them extra classes in the middle school years. And then by high school, the belief is that they'll be ready to be taking some actual college courses."

24   CNE school development specialist Dawn Stevens, who is a Steilacoom tribal member and a longtime educator and administrator in the Shelton school district, attributes the success of the early college model to all-inclusive curriculum and partnerships that balance the interests of tribal elders, the college and the high-school site. She especially commends tribal involvement in the classroom.

25   "The (early college) learning process builds on community, builds on Native students having a guest speaker come in—someone from their own tribe—and having pride, or having an adult person from the tribe visit and walk across campus," Stevens says.

26   At the end of the day, a strong sense of cultural identity and pride woven throughout lectures, coursework and extracurricular activities are the very cornerstones by which Native education programs succeed.

The Role of Cultural Identity in Education

27 Even before Northwest Indian College offered early college courses at Ferndale High School, Victor "Turtle" Johnson, 26, was taking extended-learning courses.

28 At the time, he attended an accredited summer program called NASA Seaquest, organized by Northwest Indian College. This was designed to help students catch up on high-school credit and gain job experience while engaging in their community. The hands-on summer course put special emphasis on environmental science and water quality.

29 Johnson's father always encouraged higher education for his children. Before he died 12 years ago, his father suggested that Johnson look into NASA Seaquest. He took his father's advice, but his desire to pursue higher education had not been fully realized.

30 During the majority of the school year at Ferndale High School, he "slipped through" his classes. "It didn't really seem like I had an identity there," says Johnson, who now attends Northwest Indian College and serves on the Lummi Indian Business Council in Natural Resources. "At any rate, I just kind of learned to blend in. I didn't really make the best grades ever. I think I graduated (in 1999) with a 1.98 (GPA)."

31 He remembers very little about any mention of Native Americans in his history classes.

32 "It seemed like in history, we only learned about Europeans and the Industrial Revolution," Johnson remembers. "It was like those were the two greatest things ever. (Native Americans) didn't really have an identity there."

33 Another "greatest thing ever" he remembers discussing in school was the California Gold Rush.

34 "In history (class), they don't show that when the '49-ers were coming into this area, they were killing everyone in sight that wasn't a gold miner; they were killing Native Americans for target practice," Johnson says. "They didn't show that they were being kicked off their own lands. I wasn't even shown anything like that up until now. That just gives me more fuel to try and find out who I am and what I need to do to stop making it feel like I don't exist, like Native Americans don't exist."

35 The Seaquest program was another story.

36 "For me, I always had Northwest Indian College to fall back on," Johnson remembers. "They always had a cool program where I learned all week Monday through Thursday and went on a field trip on Friday. To me, that was more interesting. It was more focused...You're reading and learning about what's going to happen on Friday. There was a goal at the end of the day. We're closer to getting to know more about whales, and we're learning about how to write about whales, and that sort of thing."

37 His summer experience at NASA Seaquest got him a two-year internship at the 29 Palms Band of Mission Indians in California, where he learned Geographic Information Systems (GIS), water sampling and techniques in a state certified laboratory.

38 When he came back to Lummi Reservation in 2001, he immediately came on board in the Natural Resources department of its business council, where he started out as a restoration technician. Meanwhile, his son Kamron Johnson, now 5, had just been born. After Johnson and Kamron's mother split a year later, he went to court to be awarded partial custody of his son.

39 The long nights with his lawyer discussing child custody laws were over, Johnson says he "had nothing to fight for," and nothing to keep him on his toes. So, he went to school. In fall 2005, Johnson relearned history and discovered unknown treasures in his community.

40 "Learning about plants and geology and having a lot of that here in our own backyard, you can't get that in LA," he laughs. "You can't go in LA and see plants growing right next to someone's house that was natural. Here, you can drive down to the beach and see where all of our ancestors lived. If you go to Portage Island, you can still see where some of the small houses, some of the structure floorboards or corners of the houses are still there. Going to

high school in Ferndale High School, I didn't even know that that was even there, and then when I came to Northwest Indian College, they kind of just said, 'Stop closing your eyes to all of this. This is right here in your backyard. Why aren't you looking?' "

41   Another perk was having local elders come speak in the classes. "Sometimes when we were learning about history and stuff, we had some of the living history come in like (longtime activist and elder) Billy Frank, who's one of the main voices for fishing rights," Johnson says. "When he came in to speak, everyone was in awe."

42   Unlike Johnson, his classmate Charene Alexander, 25, didn't get any encouragement to go on to higher education.

43   She always knew she was "book smart." That's what her peers told her growing up on the Lummi Reservation in Bellingham, Wash. She was an honor student until her freshman year at Ferndale High School, when she started drinking heavily.

44   "My grades kind of decreased and no one ever really paid attention to it," Alexander recalls.

45   High school was a blur. She doesn't remember much of it, being "preoccupied with partying and living it up," she explains. Her parents, both alcoholics, had split when she was 13. By then, she was already an alcoholic herself.

46   While Alexander's father was off the reservation attempting sobriety, her mother was frequently out drinking. Alexander spent much of her time staying with friends and for the most part, without parents.

47   For the remainder of high school, she just "slid through," graduating with a 1.88 GPA. Within the next few years, she started trafficking cocaine in her community. By the time she gave birth to her son Kainan in 2001, she had become notorious for her role in the OxyContin narcotic epidemic that made headlines regionally. By 2002, she was actively smuggling the prescription drugs from Canada. As Alexander relates it, she was a forerunner of "an entire empire" in the local drug ring.

48   But she hit a dead end. At the U.S.-Canadian border in 2002, she was finally caught smuggling. Washington state charged her with possession of a controlled substance, while the Lummi Reservation charged her with delivery of a controlled substance as it considered banishing her off the reservation.

49   At 22, Alexander was incarcerated. By February of 2004, she was out on probation by and in transitional living for 10 months. Kainan was back in her care and she wanted to provide for him. By then, he was 2, and barely spoke. At the transitional living center, Alexander realized that she had to identify her goals before she got out.

50   In 2005, she decided to try Northwest Indian College. "People at Northwest Indian College know where I come from," she explains. "I'm a felon, I'm an alcoholic, I'm an addict and I'm a single parent."

51   Reclaiming her roots at Northwest Indian College and learning who she is as a Lummi woman gave her the direction she always lacked in youth. "To be Native American is to know your identity, to know who you are and where you're going," she explains. "Without that, you're just lost."

52   When Alexander started classes in 2005, she gained exposure to a part of her culture that had always been lost in her adolescence. "I know that tribal schools really work on that: teaching students their ancestors, their language, the types of food we used to live off of," she elaborates. "All those important things were just drowned out for me and my family, by alcohol. There were just generations and generations of depression. It was hard to break that cycle. It still is today."

53   Reflecting back on her high-school education, she saw that part of what was holding her back from "breaking the cycle" and investing in education was how she viewed herself and her people.

54   "There were always so many stereotypes that I felt were going on," she says. "I remember points in my life where I was ashamed of living on the reservation and sometimes

ashamed of being Native American because all of the things that were stated in the stereo-types: '(They're) nothing but drunks,' 'they're dumb Indians,' 'they're weak.' That's what I saw...Right now, I'm just really learning to identify who I am and to be proud to be Native American and to learn how to walk in a way that's going to bring pride to, not only myself and my family, but to all my people."

55   Alexander is pursuing a human services degree at the college, and hopes to apply it towards vocational counseling within her Lummi community.

First Peoples' Program

56   Operating under Antioch's wide umbrella and about 110 miles south of Northwest Indian College, many education degrees are being pursued. The First Peoples' students make their learning homes at Muckleshoot Tribal College, a cedar-sided building located on the reservation.

57   There, students earning bachelor's and graduate teaching degrees can grow and learn in the same classroom and graduate at the same time, a cohort model that emphasizes community-driven learning.

58   Sherri Foreman, 39, and a mother of two, has been teaching technology courses for eight years at the tribal college, and now teaches sixth grade at the K-12 Muckleshoot Tribal School nearby. As a part of First Peoples' first graduating cohort where she acquired her K-8 teacher certification for her bachelor's in elementary-school preparation, she understands that learning should not be driven by competition. In her sixth-grade classroom, she applies the principles of diversity and acceptance.

59   "We should have expectations for our kids to do things, but the reality is, each student is different," Foreman explains.

60   She likes to acknowledge those differences to build community in her classroom by saying to her students: "Right now, you're at about this level. You read at this level, because that's who you are...Your level of knowledge you have and what you know how to do will help your neighbor."

61   "We don't need to think that we all will test the same, that I'm not as good as you, because I didn't get this grade," she says. "They need to feel successful wherever they're at and whatever they're doing. When you individualize the learning, you're asking them to improve themselves. You're not asking them to be better than or to compete with their neighbor...but it's: 'Let's look at where you're at.'"

62   Sison, too, prefers the cohort system for the same reason Foreman does: a more collectivistic approach in teaching.

63   Sison, 43, graduated from First Peoples' bachelor's teaching program in June and recently started on her Master's Program for Experienced Educators. She says that community-building is essential.

64   "(Cohort two) started together, and we ended together, and by the end of it—I mean, not even by the end of it—we were family," Sison explains.

65   Before she started the program, Sison had never graduated from anything before, she says. During an education issues course she took focusing on the boarding school experience, Sison was able to personally identify with what she was learning about. The course shed light on her alcoholic mother's troubled and hidden past, which she always wondered about growing up in White Swan, Wash.

66   "She lived up on the Colville Indian Reservation, and she went to St. Mary's Mission School (now a tribal school), a Catholic boarding school," says Sison. "And she ran from that school. She spoke our language and she left it there at boarding school because they don't let you do that. It really scarred her."

67   Sison's mother would continue her "running away" act for the rest of her life, leaving a family behind. "She would leave us and we never knew why," Sison remembers.

68   In light of her childhood experiences, Sison made the connection, however.

69   "She had a loving mom that she was taken from. There's a lot of coercion in it. If you didn't send your children (to boarding school), you didn't get your food rations," she explains. "And the land that my tribe was on was desert, not land that you can farm. So it was really a dire situation. If you didn't send your kids, none of them ate…That's one of the main things that angers me and saddens me. There wasn't that family connection—that loss of learning how to be a mom. Sure they taught them how to sew, they taught them how to cook, they taught them how to build wagons or whatever, and work on farms…they were teaching them to live like white farmers and white settlers. But those kids didn't learn how to be a parent."

70   The reading and films documenting boarding school abuse and unjust education policy had a profound effect on everyone in her cohort, so much that it inspired Sison to leave a box of tissues in the classroom for the next cohort.

71   Tracy Rector, 35, attended in the same cohort as Sison. An active storyteller herself and an award-winning filmmaker through the Seattle-based Native Lens/Longhouse Media, Rector says that the cohort model, more than other models, is designed as a support system for those who may not be inclined toward education.

72   "If you look at the First Peoples' program, we don't sit in rows, we sit in a circle so we can all face each other," says Rector. "Everybody gets a chance to speak, everybody knows to listen, so if someone has something to say, we all listen, we don't interrupt. If there's an issue that comes up in a cohort, oftentimes we'll have a talking circle, so we'll all sit together, we'll pass the feather along and everyone has a chance to speak. In that classroom, as a cohort, I think we're close-knit because we took time to recognize each others' stories. And I don't think that's always encouraged in traditional classrooms. (Here) everybody's individual story contributes to the group's success. And for our cohort, that's how we made it through."

73   Shared experience was also a connecting point between the cohort students.

74   "A large percentage of us never imagined themselves either in school or getting their master's, so a lot of us started off really nervous and we came through it," she explains. "If we're in any other educational setting where it's your standard classroom, you're in rows, not everybody has a voice, not everybody knows that your auntie just passed or your child's sick—what's the incentive of putting yourself through something so rigorous as a master's education in the middle of working full-time, raising kids, serving your community, and dealing with your own personal issues?…So for us, we're able to make it through because we supported each other. We were that network that said, 'Nope, you gotta keep going on. Nope, you're doing this. It's not just for you, it's for your kids, it's for your people.'"

Teaching—Not Just a Day Job

75   For Will Bill Jr., involvement in Native education is in his blood. His father, Will Bill Sr., was the former director of education for the state, and the first certified teacher in the Auburn School District from the Muckleshoot Tribe.

76   Bill Jr. is also evidence of the historic gains of Native Americans in education. If it were not for the Indian Education Act of 1972, for example, Bill Jr. would not have money solidified for his position as the program director of the Huchoosedah Indian Education Program, funded by Seattle Public Schools.

77   Known for his hard-hitting and in-your-face curricula as an instructor with First Peoples' (he tackles the boarding school experience in one of his education courses), Bill Jr. knows that teaching is all-encompassing, and a lot of it should happen outside of the classroom.

78   His work with the Huchoosedah Indian Education Program—which includes summer work/education courses for high school students, WASL prep classes, summer camp and free preschool—also includes seeing his students on the weekends on a canoe trip or something else equally culturally relevant.

79   Before students are ready to dive into difficult benchmark tests such as the WASL, they must culturally identify with and trust their teachers, Bill Jr. says. "I think

students relate with me," he says. "I use quite a bit of disclosure about who I am and where I'm from."

80   A down-to-earth educator, Bill Jr. decided to pursue education at Antioch University Seattle, where he received his teacher's certification in 1997. He says that being a distinguished professor who touts his accolades and research credentials is not going to yield respect and trust from Native youth. "In our community, that doesn't impress people. That just turns them off," he explains.

81   Gaining trust outside of the classroom is essential to student success, he says. "(Teaching) is something that I live and practice," he says. "It's not just a day job for us (teachers)...I see my students on the weekends."

Empowering the Next Generation

82   For Tracy Rector, a First People's graduate student and executive director of Native Lens/ Longhouse Media, environmental justice and education are intertwined.

83   "We are rooted in this environment more than any other race of people," says Rector, who is also a Native naturalist and education specialist at Seattle Art Museum. "Native American people came from this land, and I think that's our first teacher. And so Native education—respecting one another, honoring community, recognizing diversity—these are all teachings from the tree people and the plant people. I always refer back to the teachings of the environment."

84   In a modern world where youth are constantly on MySpace, listening to iPods and watching TV, Rector utilizes technology and filmmaking as a storytelling device to help empower youth and take back their media.

85   "Are there a lot of positive Native images out there in media? No, so let's change that," she tells them. "If you have a kid that watches TV six hours a day, we tell them, 'You know what? You are an expert. You watch TV. You know what the shots are. You know how to tell a story. How do you tell your own story and reach out to the broader public? You know what needs to be said.' So we use that experience of being connected in technology and encourage them to shape it in their own way to tell their own story from a cultural perspective, and encourage them to take back those images and stereotypical presentations of what being Native American is or what being Indian is, and put their own images out there...We've figured out a way to infuse modern technology with cultural tradition."

86   Longhouse Media's most recent project is a documentary led by three teenage boys from the Swinomish tribe near La Conner. Assigned by the Environment Protection Agency and National Geographic to foster youth advocacy in preserving the environment, the film "March Point" investigates oil refineries on reservations. The film focuses on biotoxins from the refineries that seep into salmon and shellfish, traditional coastal foods that are now destroyed cultural resources for Native communities.

87   By interviewing elders in the Swinomish community, the three boys uncover the crucial connection points between resource degradation, cultural disintegration and poor health in Native communities, says Rector.

88   "The kids are making the link that that pollution is also part of cultural degradation: 'So people can no longer eat traditional foods and their bodies react negatively to junk food. Why is that? Well, it's because First People in the Puget Sound, you know, Coast Salish people, never ate hamburgers and Big Macs and French fries. They ate salmon and clams and oysters.'" Rector explains. "And so (the kids) saw the direct link to help diabetes, to depression, and from that depression link, they saw people not being able to have traditional jobs because the salmon is so depleted, and then that linked to drugs and alcoholism, for instance. When there's drugs and alcoholism, who's there to support the youth and what are those role models telling the youth? And so the youth start doing that. And so the youth are making that direct link."

89   In June, Rector taught an intertribal and intercultural digital filmmaking workshop in partnership with Seattle International Film Festival, where 36 youth received college credit from Northwest Indian College. They only had 36 hours to film the resulting "Fly Filmmaking."

90   Rector, who has worked with youth in film since January of 2005, believes that self-empowerment and education start with higher expectations and raising the bar for Native youth, as demonstrated in the workshop.

91   "We set the bar really high, and that's something I learned in my education program," she says. If you dumb down the education process, who does that serve? If you set the bar really high and offer a ton of support for the student or participant to reach that level, they're going to make it. And it's just like proving that with Native kids. They're natural storytellers, they're natural observers. It's like they totally get this stuff quickly, and it's very powerful for them. Even the fly filmmaking festival at SIFF, I think the adults got something like 10 days to make their films and our kids got 36 hours. So we totally treated them like adults. We set that bar high. We told them what was expected of them. It was scary how smoothly it went...but the thing was, they said that they felt respected because we knew that they could do it, and we gave them something that was challenging."

92   The youth she has been working with, says Rector, are already challenging stereotypical images of Native Americans in film and TV just by being behind the lens.

93   "A great majority of people feel that Native Americans are antiquated figures of the past like the dinosaurs or the wagon trains," she says. "Oftentimes, it always deals with stereotypes: 'Native Americans were here. Native Americans did this.' Native Americans always wear huge feather headdress regalia, always have war paint on, are always on a horse. All of them live in tipis...A lot of stories that we tell are traditional stories, yeah, because that's important and that's part of cultural reclamation. But we also tell stories that say, 'Yeah, we're here, we're a thriving culture, we have cultural ways that reflect tradition, but we also live in homes that have electricity.'...So our stories show that our youth are smart, are active, are creative, are dealing with issues that many other kids deal with, and also are culturally engaged in their communities."

94   Not only are they culturally engaged and dealing with contemporary issues, Rector also believes that the generation of youth she works with is moving past the addictions and historical grievances of their parents and grandparents.

95   "Sherman Alexie speaks really well to this. Every time you get a call in the middle of the night, someone's died. And it's been part of reservation experience in the last few decades. There's lots of deaths that occurred and it's due to the trauma, and I feel it's due to the trauma of the boarding school experience, so our kids are speaking to this," she observes. "They're speaking to the fact that no 10-year-old kid should have already been through treatment, no 10-year-old kid should have already been to 50 funerals in their lifetime. So our kids really address that in their films and this (represents) their experience...This is the first generation of students who are working out of that cycle."

Stepping Forward

96   In providing culturally specific programs for indigenous communities, and helping to close the access and achievement gap for many Native students, educators also give students a strong cultural identity and the resources to stand tall.

97   As the younger generation rises up to reclaim their land and history, they also redefine what it means to be a contemporary Native American. New words are birthed: Achievement, pride and progress.

98   Not that the haunting images of abuse and boarding school scandals are gone. But they're beginning to be overcome.

From The School Days of an Indian Girl
Zitkala-Sa

I. The Land of Red Apples

1   There were eight in our party of bronzed children who were going East with the missionaries. Among us were three young braves, two tall girls, and we three little ones, Judéwin, Thowin, and I.

2   We had been very impatient to start on our journey to the Red Apple Country, which, we were told, lay a little beyond the great circular horizon of the Western prairie. Under a sky of rosy apples we dreamt of roaming as freely and happily as we had chased the cloud shadows on the Dakota plains. We had anticipated much pleasure from a ride on the iron horse, but the throngs of staring palefaces disturbed and troubled us.

3   On the train, fair women, with tottering babies on each arm, stopped their haste and scrutinized the children of absent mothers. Large men, with heavy bundles in their hands, halted near by, and riveted their glassy blue eyes upon us.

4   I sank deep into the corner of my seat, for I resented being watched. Directly in front of me, children who were no larger than I hung themselves upon the backs of their seats, with their bold white faces toward me. Sometimes they took their forefingers out of their mouths and pointed at my moccasined feet. Their mothers, instead of reproving such rude curiosity, looked closely at me, and attracted their children's further notice to my blanket. This embarrassed me, and kept me constantly on the verge of tears.

5   I sat perfectly still, with my eyes downcast, daring only now and then to shoot long glances around me. Chancing to turn to the window at my side, I was quite breathless upon seeing one familiar object. It was a telegraph pole which strode by at short paces. Very near my mother's dwelling, along the edge of a road thickly bordered with wild sunflowers, some poles like these had been planted by white men. Often I had stopped, on my way down the road, to hold my ear against the pole, and, hearing its low moaning, I used to wonder what the paleface had done to hurt it. Now I sat watching for each pole that glided by to be the last one.

6   In this way I had forgotten my uncomfortable surroundings, when I heard one of my comrades call out my name. I saw the missionary standing very near, tossing candies and gums into our midst. This amused us all, and we tried to see who could catch the most of the sweet-meats. The missionary's generous distribution of candies was impressed upon my memory by a disastrous result which followed. I had caught more than my share of candies and gums, and soon after our arrival at the school I had a chance to disgrace myself, which, I am ashamed to say, I did.

7   Though we rode several days inside of the iron horse, I do not recall a single thing about our luncheons.

8   It was night when we reached the school grounds. The lights from the windows of the large buildings fell upon some of the icicled trees that stood beneath them. We were led toward an open door, where the brightness of the lights within flooded out over the heads of the excited palefaces who blocked the way. My body trembled more from fear than from the snow I trod upon.

9   Entering the house, I stood close against the wall. The strong glaring light in the large whitewashed room dazzled my eyes. The noisy hurrying of hard shoes upon a bare wooden floor increased the whirring in my ears. My only safety seemed to be in keeping next to the wall. As I was wondering in which direction to escape from all this confusion, two warm hands grasped me firmly, and in the same moment I was tossed high in midair. A rosy-cheeked paleface woman caught me in her arms. I was both frightened and insulted by such trifling. I stared into her eyes, wishing her to let me stand on my own feet, but she

jumped me up and down with increasing enthusiasm. My mother had never made a plaything of her wee daughter. Remembering this I began to cry aloud.

10   They misunderstood the cause of my tears, and placed me at a white table loaded with food. There our party were united again. As I did not hush my crying, one of the older ones whispered to me, "Wait until you are alone in the night."

11   It was very little I could swallow besides my sobs, that evening.

12   "Oh, I want my mother and my brother Dawéel I want to go to my aunt!" I pleaded; but the ears of the palefaces could not hear me.

13   From the table we were taken along an upward incline of wooden boxes, which I learned afterward to call a stairway. At the top was a quiet hall, dimly lighted. Many narrow beds were in one straight line down the entire length of the wall. In them lay sleeping brown faces, which peeped just out of the coverings. I was tucked into bed with one of the tall girls, because she talked to me in my mother tongue and seemed to soothe me.

14   I had arrived in the wonderful land of rosy skies, but I was not happy, as I had thought I should be. My long travel and the bewildering sights had exhausted me. I fell asleep, heaving deep, tired sobs. My tears were left to dry themselves in streaks, because neither my aunt nor my mother was near to wipe them away.

II. The Cutting of My Long Hair

15   The first day in the land of apples was a bitter-cold one; for the snow still covered the ground, and the trees were bare. A large bell rang for breakfast, its loud metallic voice crashing through the belfry overhead and into our sensitive ears. The annoying clatter of shoes on bare floors gave us no peace. The constant clash of harsh noises, with an undercurrent of many voices murmuring an unknown tongue, made a bedlam within which I was securely tied. And though my spirit tore itself in struggling for its lost freedom, all was useless.

16   A paleface woman, with white hair, came up after us. We were placed in a line of girls who were marching into the dining room. These were Indian girls, in stiff shoes and closely clinging dresses. The small girls wore sleeved aprons and shingled hair. As I walked noiselessly in my soft moccasins, I felt like sinking to the floor, for my blanket had been stripped from my shoulders. I looked hard at the Indian girls, who seemed not to care that they were even more immodestly dressed than I, in their tightly fitting clothes. While we marched in, the boys entered at an opposite door. I watched for the three young braves who came in our party. I spied them in their ranks, looking as uncomfortable as I felt.

17   A small bell was tapped, and each of the pupils drew a chair from under the table. Supposing this act meant they were to be seated, I pulled out mine and at once slipped into it from one side. But when I turned my head, I saw that I was the only one seated, and all the rest at our table remained standing. Just as I began to rise, looking shyly around to see how chairs were to be used, a second bell was sounded. All were seated at last, and I had to crawl back into my chair again. I heard a man's voice at one end of the hall, and I looked around to see him. But all the others hung their heads over their plates. As I glanced at the long chain of tables, I caught the eyes of a paleface woman upon me. Immediately I dropped my eyes, wondering why I was so keenly watched by the strange woman. The man ceased his mutterings, and then a third bell was tapped. Every one picked up his knife and fork and began eating. I began crying instead, for by this time I was afraid to venture anything more.

18   But this eating by formula was not the hardest trial in that first day. Late in the morning, my friend Judéwin gave me a terrible warning. Judéwin knew a few words of English; and she had overheard the paleface woman talk about cutting our long, heavy hair. Our mothers had taught us that only unskilled warriors who were captured had their hair shingled by the enemy. Among our people, short hair was worn by mourners, and shingled hair by cowards!

19   We discussed our fate some moments, and when Judéwin said, "We have to submit, because they are strong," I rebelled.

20   "No, I will not submit! I will struggle first!" I answered.

21   I watched my chance, and when no one noticed I disappeared. I crept up the stairs as quietly as I could in my squeaking shoes—my moccasins had been exchanged for shoes. Along the hall I passed, without knowing whither I was going. Turning aside to an open door, I found a large room with three white beds in it. The windows were covered with dark green curtains, which made the room very dim. Thankful that no one was there, I directed my steps toward the corner farthest from the door. On my hands and knees I crawled under the bed, and cuddled myself in the dark corner.

22   From my hiding place I peered out, shuddering with fear whenever I heard foot-steps near by. Though in the hall loud voices were calling my name, and I knew that even Judéwin was searching for me, I did not open my mouth to answer. Then the steps were quickened and the voices became excited. The sounds came nearer and nearer. Women and girls entered the room. I held my breath, and watched them open closed doors and peep behind large trunks. Some one threw up the curtains, and the room was filled with sudden light. What caused them to stoop and look under the bed I do not know. I remember being dragged out, though I resisted by kicking and scratching wildly. In spite of myself, I was carried downstairs and tied fast in a chair.

23   I cried aloud, shaking my head all the while until I felt the cold blades of the scissors against my neck, and heard them gnaw off one of my thick braids. Then I lost my spirit. Since the day I was taken from my mother I had suffered extreme indignities. People had stared at me. I had been tossed about in the air like a wooden puppet. And now my long hair was shingled like a coward's! In my anguish I moaned for my mother, but no one came to comfort me. Not a soul reasoned quietly with me like my own mother used to do: for now I was only one of many little animals driven by a herder.

Part Six

Grammar Essentials

Part Six will help you when you are ready to edit your writing. It consists of short divisions that cover the most **prejudicial grammar errors**—errors that cause readers to judge writing poorly—and how to avoid them in your final written drafts. It also provides some exercises, so you can practice each element of grammar covered. For further practice, we direct you to MyWritingLab (MyWritingLab. com), an online, interactive program that provides numerous exercises with these and other grammar points.

Contents

Introduction

While grammar is a component of strong writing, it should not be thought of as *the only* component of strong writing; finding what you want to say so your writing conveys significant ideas is the center of strong writing. Grammar should serve this larger purpose by helping you communicate your ideas clearly. Think of editing for grammar, mechanics, and spelling as a final polish.

A. Foundations of the Sentence

Imagine that it is a crisp October Sunday, and you are headed to a home NFL football game. The excitement builds as you near the stadium and find your seat. The referees blow their whistles, and the game begins. However, there is no quarterback to throw the ball. Then a quarterback sprints onto the field, but there is no ball. Finally a ball is found, snapped, and the quarterback throws. However, the running back who is supposed to catch the ball does not complete the pass.

Like an NFL game, a sentence needs a subject, or something that will do the action. In the scenario above, the *subject* is the quarterback *who does the action* of throwing the ball. A sentence also needs a verb, or an action. In the football story above, the *quarterback's throw* is *the action*. Finally, a sentence needs a *complete thought.* Just as in football, sometimes there can be a quarterback (subject) and a throw (verb), but this does not mean that the pass will be completed (complete thought). While a sentence can have more than these three elements, it will not be a sentence if it is missing any of these three elements.

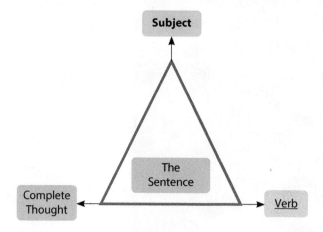

NOTE: In examples throughout Part 6, subjects are shown in bold and verbs are underlined.

A.1 The Subject

1. **What is a subject?** A subject is a person, place, or thing that is doing the action in the sentence.

   Simone <u>went</u> to the Writing Center.

2. **How many subjects can there be in a sentence?** There can be multiple subjects in a sentence.

   Simone and Mandy <u>went</u> to the Writing Center.

3. **Does the subject have to come in a certain place in the sentence?** Subjects usually come at the beginning of a sentence, and your writing will generally be clearer if you keep your subjects at the beginning of your sentences. However, there are a couple of exceptions.

   - **Sentences that begin with "There" or "Here":** When sentences begin with *there* or *here*, the subject will come after the verb.

     Here is the **Writing Center**.

   - **Sentences that form a question:** When you have a question, your subject and verb move. Sometimes your verb will split and the subject will come in the middle. Other times the verb will come before the subject.

     Are **you** going to the Writing Center?

4. **Can a subject ever be implied?** Yes, when you give a command, the subject is often implied. This means that it isn't directly stated in the sentence because it is already understood from the context.

   Get me some coffee! (*The subject, "you," is implied.*)

5. **Can a verb ever be a subject?** Occasionally you see a sentence that starts with a word ending in "ing." This looks like a verb but really is not. It functions as a thing in your sentence and can be your subject.

   Reading is my favorite hobby. "Reading" is the subject of the sentence.

6. **Finding the subject in sentences.** The following are some tips for finding subjects in sentences. Remember that you want to find these because they are key players in your sentences. As you check for subjects in your writing, also try to place them at the beginning of your sentences. This will make your writing easier to understand and more engaging for the reader.

Tips for Finding the Subject of a Sentence

- Ask **"Who or what is doing the action in the sentence?"** This should be your subject. (Remember that if there is more than one subject, they should be placed together in the sentence.)
- **Look at whether your sentence starts with *here* or *there*.** If it does, your subject may fall at the end of your sentence, after the verb.
- **Look at whether your sentence is a question.** This may cause your subject to come after or in between your verb.
- **Find and temporarily cross out prepositional phrases.** A **prepositional phrase** begins with a **preposition** (a word that relates a noun or pronoun to other words in a sentence) and is followed by a short group of words. It usually gives more information about an idea in the sentence. As a subject will *never* fall in a prepositional phrase, eliminating them can simplify your sentence, making it easier see the subject, as shown here:

  ~~Beside Mandy in the Writing Center,~~ **Simone** worked ~~on her English paper~~.

Prepositions				
about	behind	during	on	to
above	below	except	onto	toward
across	beneath	for	out	under
after	beside	from	outside	underneath
against	besides	in	over	unlike
along	between	inside	past	until
among	beyond	into	since	up
around	but	like	than	upon
as	by	near	through	with
at	despite	of	throughout	within
before	down	off	till	without

A.2 The Verb

1. **What is a verb?** A verb is a word or group of words that expresses the action or state of being of the subject. Actions are usually easy to identify. They are words like *runs, rushes,* or *dodges.* State of being verbs can be harder to identify because they do not seem so active. They are forms of "to be" such as *is, are, was, were,* and *will.* While these words might not seem to be doing anything, keep in mind that the act of being is still an act. For example, your simple presence in a room is an act.

   Action Verb: Simone <u>rushed</u> to the Writing Center.

   State of Being Verb: Carly <u>is</u> a tutor in the Writing Center.

2. **Are verbs always single words, or can they come in phrases?** Verbs can be either single words such as *runs,* or they can form phrases. When verbs form phrases, they usually include **helping verbs** (words like *can, do, might*) which help to indicate different verb tenses and other information. The following are some common helping verbs that may be linked with a main verb in your sentences followed by an example.

Helping Verbs					
am	being	do	have	must	were
are	can	does	is	shall	will
be	could	had	may	should	would
been	did	has	might	was	

   Simone and Mandy <u>should have gone</u> to the Writing Center.

3. **How many verbs can be in one sentence?** Just as there can be more than one subject in a sentence, so, too, can there be more than one verb.

   Simone and Mandy <u>went</u> to the Writing Center and <u>revised</u> their papers.

4. **Does the verb have to come in a certain place in the sentence?** Just as the subject usually comes at the beginning of the sentence, verbs usually come after the subject in the sentence. However, the same exceptions that exist for subjects also exist for verbs. Remember, if a sentence begins with *here* or *there,* the subject and verb will exchange

places. Also, if a sentence is a question, the subject and verb will move out of their traditional places in a sentence.

5. **Can a verb ever be implied?** No. A verb needs to be explicitly stated in a sentence.

6. **Finding the Verbs in Your Sentences.** Here are some tips for finding verbs in your sentences. As you look for and find verbs in your sentences, also work on making them active, engaging, and fresh. A good way to improve your writing is to use a variety of verbs that express specific actions.

Tips for Finding Verbs in Your Sentences

- **Ask *"What is happening in this sentence? What is the action?"*** This should help you identify action verbs. (Remember that there can be more than one verb.)

- **Ask *"Is there a state of being in this sentence?"*** This should help you identify "to be" verbs.

- **Look at whether your sentence starts with *here* or *there*.** If it does, your verb may come first, before your subject.

- **Look at whether your sentence is a question.** This may cause your verb to come before your subject.

A.3 Complete Thought

Once you have found the subject and the verb in a sentence, you need to make sure that your sentence forms a complete thought. Like the quarterback who throws the ball in the game of football with the intention of completing the pass and making a touchdown, you want to make sure that your ideas connect with and make sense to your reader. The following are some things that can keep you from completing your ideas in your sentences. Use this as a checklist as you do one final check of your sentences.

Checklist for Avoiding Incomplete Thoughts

1. **Do I have a properly conjugated verb?** Verbs need to be in their correct form in order to do their job. When a verb is not complete or is in an incorrect form, it does not act as a fully functioning verb in your sentence. One of the most common mistakes is using a verbal instead of a verb. **Verbals** are often words that end in "ing" or begin with "to." For example, *running, talking, to run,* and *to talk* are all verbals. They are tricky because they look active; however, they do not form a complete action. You need to add words to them to make the action complete.

> *Incorrect:* **Simone and Mandy** to go to the Writing Center.

> *Corrected:* **Simone and Mandy** want to go to the Writing Center.

2. **Do I have an incomplete thought?** Certain words called subordinating conjunctions (see list on p. 383) or relative pronouns (*that, what, which, who, whom, whose*) create incomplete thoughts when they are not properly added to a sentence. These words are like a needy child. Whenever they are present in a sentence, they demand two subject and verb pairs, or two "parent" sentences, to balance them.

> *Incorrect:* If **Simone and Mandy** go to the Writing Center.

> *Corrected:* *If* **Simone and Mandy** go to the Writing Center, **they** will get help with their English papers. *(Another subject and verb pair helps to complete the idea in this sentence.)*

Practice 1   Identifying Subjects and Verbs

DIRECTIONS: Cross out prepositional phrases, highlight subjects, and underline verbs.

1. My most valuable lesson from this class was learning about my writing potential.

2. In high school I detested English and essay assignments.

3. I had little faith in my writing abilities because I had never really tried to improve.

4. When I first started attending this class, I feared the five essays worth 20% of my grade.

5. My first essay about a life lesson was hard for me, especially deciding which topic
   to write about.

6. It was a terrible essay until we shared in groups, and I got a lot of valuable criticism.

7. The next essay, on communities, was easier to write by following the writing process.

8. Plus, the teacher gave me valuable suggestions to revise my paragraphs.

9. When I got to essay three, I knew exactly what to do.

10. Now I am writing this essay, and I am prepared and confident.

B. Identify and Correct Sentence Fragments

Imagine that you drop a plate onto a concrete floor. What will most likely happen? It will break into fragments, or parts, right? The same thing can happen with sentences. Sometimes they, too, break, leaving only a fragment of the complete sentence. When that happens, you want to find the missing piece and add it back to the sentence in order to form a complete sentence that your reader will clearly understand.

1. **What is a sentence fragment?** A sentence fragment is a sentence that is missing one of the key elements—a subject, a verb, or a complete thought.

> *Missing Subject:* Was trying very hard to revise her paper. *(Who was trying?)*
>
> *Corrected:* **Donicha** was trying very hard to revise her paper.

> *Missing Verb:* The student with the red hair, glasses, oversized purple Jansport backpack, and the silly grin on her face. *(What was she doing?)*
>
> *Corrected:* **The student** with the red hair, glasses, oversized purple Jansport backpack, and the silly grin on her face, stared at her "A" paper with delight.

> *Incomplete Thought:* Because I studied all week for that Chemistry exam. *(What happened because of studying all week?)*
>
> *Corrected:* Because **I** studied all week for that Chemistry exam, **I** had deeply learned the material and scored a solid grade for my work.

2. **How can you fix a sentence fragment?** You first need to find what is missing from the sentence. Then you need to add that missing element, or elements, back to the sentence. There is no one way to do this; there are usually several correct ways to fix a sentence fragment such as adding a verb, adding a subject, adding a subject and a verb, removing a subordinating conjunction or relative pronoun, or attaching the fragment to a complete sentence or independent clause.

3. **Why is it important to fix sentence fragments?** Sentence fragments make it hard for your reader to understand what you are saying because they represent incomplete ideas.

| Practice 2 | **Identifying and Correcting Fragments** |

DIRECTIONS: Identify what is missing from each sentence fragment below and then fix it by adding it to the sentence.

1. Another important lesson learned during this class.

2. What motivates me to do well.

3. In my previous schooling.

4. Because I felt like I was being forced to attend.

5. Made me skip and never do my work.

6. A new beginning for people to judge my abilities by.

7. Poor attendance and grades in high school my transcripts worthless as a resume tool.

8. What I love about college.

9. I complete control of what classes I take, how many, and what time of day they are.

10. I also think that part of the reason I am doing so well.

C. Identify and Correct Run-on Sentences and Comma Splices

Have you ever had a conversation with someone who talked very fast and non-stop? How have you felt when you talked to such a person? Did you feel rushed? Ignored? Tired? Run-on sentences and comma splices are similar versions of this, but they are in written form. They happen when you have too many **subject/verb pairs** (also known as **independent clauses**; statements including a subject and verb that comprise a complete thought and can stand as a complete sentence) in one sentence and without the proper words or punctuation to connect them. The difference between run-on sentences and comma splices is that one places a comma between subject/verb units while the other has no punctuation that separates the clauses.

1. **What is a run-on sentence?** A run-on sentence is when there are too many subject/verb pairs in one sentence without the proper words or punctuation to connect them. Run-on sentences do not place any punctuation in between subject/verb units.

> **Tyler** <u>finished</u> reading Fredrick Douglass's essay then **he** <u>went</u> to work at Starbucks **work** <u>was</u> busy. *(This sentence has three subject/verb pairs with no punctuation or connector words in between. Therefore, it is a run-on sentence.)*

2. **What is a comma splice?** A comma splice is similar to a run-on sentence in that it also has too many subject/verb pairs in a sentence without the proper punctuation or words to connect the ideas. However, in a comma splice, there are commas in between the subject/verb units.

> **Tyler** finished reading Fredrick Douglass's essay, then **he** went to work at Starbucks, **work** was busy. *(This sentence has three subject/verb pairs with commas in between each pair. While the comma shows that there needs to be some breaks in the sentence, it is not a strong enough punctuation mark to complete the job. Therefore, it is a comma splice.)*

3. **Why is it important to fix run-on sentences and comma splices?** Run-on sentences and comma splices make it hard for your reader to understand what you are saying because there is no clear indication of where one idea begins and the other ends.

4. **How can you fix run-on sentences and comma splices?** There are four ways to fix run-on sentences and comma splices, and each way works to fix either error. Each "fix" can be equally good depending on your sentence and what you are trying to say. Therefore, choose the one that fits your style and the content of your sentence. You might want to use a variety of these suggestions in your writing, so that your sentences vary in style and length.

   - **Solution #1: Add a Period.** Put a period in between each subject/verb unit. When you use the period, you indicate a clear and strong break between the ideas in each subject/verb pair. Therefore, make sure the ideas you are separating are each distinct from the other.

   > *Incorrect:* **Alexis and Sonith** worked on the presentation until 10:00 then **they** got a good night's sleep before the presentation at 9:00 the next morning.
   >
   > *Corrected:* **Alexis and Sonith** worked on the presentation until 10:00. Then **they** got a good night's sleep before the presentation at 9:00 the next morning.

   - **Solution #2: Add a Comma and a Coordinating Conjunction.** Another way to fix run-on sentences and comma splices is to add a comma and a coordinating conjunction between the two subject/verb pairs. **Coordinating conjunctions** are words that connect two ideas, and there are only seven of them (*for, and, nor, but, or, yet,* and *so;* easily remembered using the acronym FANBOYS). Remember that you have to use *both* the comma *and* the coordinating conjunction, not just one or the other. The comma and coordinating conjunction properly connect ideas that are of equal importance.

   > *Incorrect:* **Tamera** previewed the assigned psychology chapter **she** wrote down all of the words she didn't understand.
   >
   > *Corrected:* **Tamera** previewed the assigned psychology chapter, *and* **she** wrote down all of the words she didn't understand.

   - **Solution #3: Use Subordination.** Subordination is when you create a relationship of dependence between sentences by using either a **subordinating conjunction** (a word that introduces and links a subordinate clause to an independent clause, see box below) or a **relative pronoun** (a word such as *that, which, what, whatever, who,* and *whoever* that relates groups of words to nouns or pronouns). The subordinating conjunction or relative pronoun makes one idea in the sentence dependent on or secondary to the other.

Incorrect: **Ben** completed his first math course **he** registered for the next math course.

Corrected: After **Ben** completed his first math course, **he** registered for the next math course.

or

Corrected: **Ben** completed his first math course, *before* **he** registered for the next math course.

Subordinating Conjunctions			
after	before	since	when
although	even though	so that	when-
as	if	than	ever
as if	in order that	though	where
as soon as	once	unless	wherever
because	rather than	until	whether
			while

- **Solution #4: Add a Semicolon.** The semicolon has as much grammatical power as a period, so it can be used to separate sentences. However, while a period indicates a strong break between ideas, a semicolon indicates that there is still a close relationship between the ideas it separates.

Semicolon with Conjunctive Adverb	
; also	; moreover
; besides	; nevertheless
; consequently	; similarly
; finally	; still
; furthermore	; then
; however	; therefore
; instead	; thus
; meanwhile	

When you fix comma splices and run-on sentences with a semicolon, make sure that the ideas in the sentence relate closely to one another.

Incorrect: **Allyson** submitted her Financial Aid Form **she** met with a Financial Aid Officer and established a college payment plan.

Corrected: **Allyson** submitted her Financial Aid Form; then **she** met with a Financial Aid Officer and established a college payment plan.

Practice 3   Identifying and Correcting Run-Ons and Comma Splices

DIRECTIONS: Use any of the four ways of fixing run-ons and comma splices to correct the "sentences" below. Pay special attention to punctuation.

1. The third most important lesson learned was sentence structure, improving the sentences of my essays significantly improved the clarity of my writing.

2. I have the problem of repeating a word many times throughout my paper I also tend to add a lot of filler into my writing this leads the reader away from what I have to say.

3. You can see in essays one and two I had some ugly sentences, activities like reading backwards, reading aloud, and carefully examining with a checklist have dramatically improved my writing.

4. This class taught me numerous lessons I have learned how to study effectively, read actively, and write fluently.

5. The most significant to me are my writing potential, motivation and sentence structure I will use these a lot over the next couple of years.

6. This was an excellent first class to take it greatly improved my reading and writing abilities that I have not used for months.

7. I always used to say to myself that all my writing was bad, bad, bad, learning how to quiet my judgmental inner voice was especially helpful.

8. In the end, I am satisfied with what I learned my improvements in reading and writing will go a long way to make me successful in college.

9. Reading Shorris and Plato helped me I now realize that the classes I have to take for my VCT degree are not all unrelated to my future work.

10. I actually like to read books now my living room needs a shelf or bookcase for all the books sitting on the floor waiting to be read.

D. Use Coordination and Subordination

Coordination and subordination are not grammar errors. Rather, they are ways that you can show relationships between ideas in your sentences. They are also methods through which you can build more complex and interesting sentences in your writing.

While the terms "coordination" and "subordination" may be new to you, their meanings and the relationships they represent aren't new. **Subordination** represents a relationship of dependence. The relationship between parent and child represents subordination as does one between boss and employee. **Coordination** represents a relationship where all parties are equal in importance and power. Relationships between siblings can represent coordination. You might mow the lawn while your brother weeds the beds, but both of you are equally important to the care of the yard.

The same relationships can exist between ideas in a sentence. For example, you can make one idea more important than another if you use subordination. In contrast, you can show your reader how two ideas are of equal importance if you use coordination to link ideas in a sentence.

1. **What is subordination?** Subordination is a sentence pattern in which you have at least two subject/verb pairs, and one is made to depend on the other. A subordinating conjunction or relative pronoun can be added to link the subject/verb pairs in a way that makes one depend on the other. (See p. 383 for a list of subordinating conjunctions.)

> *Subordinating Conjunction: Since* **Ron, Allyson, and Marcelino** registered for classes together, **they** were all able to get into the learning community class.
>
> *(This sentence has two subject verb pairs, **Ron, Allyson, and Marcelino** registered and **they** were able linked with the subordinating conjunction "since," which comes before the first subject/verb pair, making that part of the sentence dependent on the next part.)*

> **Or**

> *Subordinating Conjunction:* **Ron, Allyson, and Marcelino** registered for classes together *so that* **they** were all able to get into the Learning community class. *(Here the subordinating conjunction comes before the second subject/verb pair in the sentence, which also creates subordination, but it makes the second part of the sentence dependent on the first part.)*

> **Or**

> *Relative Pronoun:* **Ron, Allyson, and Marcelino** *who* **each** took this quarter's learning community class registered for classes together and successfully got into the next Learning community class in the sequence.
>
> *(Here a relative pronoun* who *and the subject/verb pair "**each** took" is spliced into the middle of another complete sentence. The subject/verb pair "**Ron, Allyson, and Marcelino** / registered and got" is subordinated to the subject/verb pair "**each** took" because the relative pronoun "who" comes before this subject/verb pair, making it dependent on the first pair.)*

2. **What is coordination?** Coordination is a sentence pattern which has at least two subject/verb pairs, and each subject/verb pair is equal in importance to the other(s). A comma + coordinating conjunction (*for, and, nor, but, or, yet, so*) or a semicolon can be added to link the subject/verb pairs so that all ideas are equal in weight and importance.

> *Two Sentences:* **Kelley** bought the books for her chemistry class. **She** completed her first night's homework.

Comma + Coordinating Conjunction: **Kelley** <u>bought</u> the books for her chemistry class, *and* **she** <u>completed</u> her first night's homework.

Semicolon: **Kelley** <u>bought</u> the books for her chemistry class; **she** <u>completed</u> her first night's homework.

Notice how you can use a semicolon instead of the comma + coordinating conjunction to create coordination. A semicolon also shows that the two ideas are linked and equal in importance. You can use the semicolon alone or with a conjunctive adverb (see semicolon with conjunctive adverbs box on p. 383).

A common mistake: Remember that you need to have two subject/verb pairs in order to create coordination. Simply adding a comma + a coordinating conjunction to a sentence does not automatically create coordination.

3. **Why should I create subordination and coordination in my sentences?** Coordination and subordination can help you to *express certain relationships between ideas* that might not be possible if you used simple, standalone sentences.

Consider the difference in meaning between these examples.

- *Example 1:* **Angela** <u>brainstormed</u> ideas for her American Literature paper. **She** <u>drafted</u> her paper with her idea brainstorm as a guide.

- *Example 2 (Subordination):* **Angela** <u>brainstormed</u> ideas for her American Literature paper *so that* **she** <u>could draft</u> her paper with her idea brainstorm as a guide.

- *Example 3 (Coordination):* **Angela** <u>brainstormed</u> ideas for her American Literature paper, *and* she <u>was able to draft</u> her paper, using her idea brainstorm as a guide.

Coordination and subordination also allow you to make your sentences *more engaging* for your reader. By linking sentences in different ways, you change the rhythm of your writing, which results in a more interesting read. Read the next two examples and notice the difference it can make when a writer adds subordination and coordination to his/her writing.

- *Example 1:* Angela had a three-page paper due for her American Literature class. To begin her paper, Angela brainstormed ideas. She drafted her paper with the brainstorm as a guide. She took the draft to the Writing Center to get feedback on her ideas and organization. She revised her draft using the comments from her peer conference at the Writing Center. She read the paper out loud to herself to find missing words and grammar errors. She made final editing corrections. She turned in the paper.

- *Example 2:* Angela had a three-page paper due for her American Literature class. To begin her paper, Angela brainstormed ideas *so that* she could draft her paper with the brainstorm as a guide. She took the draft to the Writing Center to get feedback on her ideas and organization; *then* she revised her draft using the comments from her peer conference at the Writing Center. *Since* she read the paper out loud to herself to find missing words and grammar errors, she could make final editing corrections; *finally* she turned in the paper.

Practice 4   Using Coordination and Subordination

DIRECTIONS: Use coordination or subordination to combine the pairs of sentences below to create more interesting writing.

1. I used to believe I was a good reader and writer. After this class, I realize that how I used to read and write is not very effective and scientific.

2. I took the class. I just read without thinking.

3. Words flew by. After reading, I had only a very general idea of what the article said.

4. At first, I regarded the reading process assignment as busy work. I was not willing to take notes. It took too long.

5. Reading is reading. Why make it so complex?

6. However, I did the assignment. I found out its advantages.

7. It is good for concentrating on the author's development and tone. It is most important for remembering.

8. I did the reading process for Donna Beegle's essay I could easily tell her process of growth as she gained a formal education.

9. I read each paragraph twice. I put the ideas in my own words.

10. Now I can think more critically when I read. I write before, during, and after reading.

E. Use Parallel Structure

Parallel means to keep similar, to keep equal, and to keep proportionate. For example, train tracks have to be parallel, so the train can stay on the tracks. If the tracks are not parallel, the train may derail or not be able to move forward. Similarly, series of words and phrases in your writing need to be parallel, so the ideas are clear to your reader.

1. **What is parallel structure?** Parallel structure means that you have presented a series of words or phrases in a similar form, so that each one matches the structure or form of the others.

2. **What are some different situations in which I should check for parallelism in my sentences?** You need to make sure you have correct parallel structure when working with words in a series (three or more words in a list), phrases (two or more short phrases), or words connected by correlative conjunctions (word pairs such as "either/ or" or "both/and" that connect items).

- **Parallel Structure with Words in a Series:** A series applies to any three or more words you provide in a list. When you have a series, you want each word in the series to be in the same form.

  > *Incorrect:* To start his paper, Jorge will brainstorm, outline, and to sit at his computer as long as it takes to write something.
  >
  > *(Notice how the first two items in the series are verbs, <u>brainstorm</u> and <u>outline</u>. The final item, though, is not a verb. It breaks the structure and the parallelism of the sentence.)*
  >
  > *Correct:* To start his paper, Jorge will brainstorm, outline, and draft.
  >
  > *(This correction makes the final item in the series like the other items in the series. Now there are three verbs in the series, and each one is in the same form.)*

- **Parallel Structure with Phrases in a Series:** A phrase is a short group of words that expresses an idea. When there are two or more phrases listed in a sentence, the phrases need to stay in parallel structure.

  > *Incorrect:* The shorter Writing Center hours affected those in my coordinated studies class who needed help with their paper, those in GED preparation who were preparing for the weekend GED exam, and leaving out night students who couldn't come to campus until after 5 p.m.
  >
  > *(The first two phrases begin with a noun, but the final phrase does not. It breaks parallel structure.)*
  >
  > *Corrected:* The shorter Writing Center hours affected students in my coordinated studies class who needed help with their paper, students in GED preparation who were preparing for the weekend GED exam, and students in night classes who couldn't come to campus until after 5:00 p.m. *(To correct the sentence so it demonstrates parallel structure, we changed the final phrase in the list. It now begins with a noun and follows the structure of the other phrases listed before it.)*

- **Words Connected by Correlative Conjunctions:** Make sure ideas are parallel when they are connected by correlative conjunctions. Correlative conjunctions include the following word pairs.

Correlative	Conjunctions
both/and	not only/but also
either/or	whether/or
neither/nor	

Incorrect: Whether you register before you finish your current class or you will register after the end of the quarter, you should be able to take Math 101.

(Each phrase you compare with "whether/or" needs to be the same in structure and form. This sentence does not achieve that parallel structure because the second phrase doesn't match the first.)

Corrected: Whether you register before you finish your current class or after the end of the quarter, you should be able to take the next course.

(By changing the second item being compared in this sentence, the structure becomes parallel.)

3. **Why is it important to have parallel structure in writing?** Parallel structure helps your reader to follow your ideas and understand what you are saying.

Practice 5   Ensuring Parallel Structure

DIRECTIONS: Correct the parallel structure mistakes in the following sentences.

1. The teacher recommends an organized writing process: generate ideas, focusing, organizing, drafting, and edit.

2. Taking notes is good for concentration, understand, and memory.

3. Both a careful reading process and writing are important for getting good grades in college.

4. I made sure that each paragraph had a topic sentence or main idea, with enough evidence, and analysis.

5. I would not mind at first small matters such as grammar, spelling the words right, and punctuation.

6. However, it is important not only to check for good paragraph structure, but also editing for spelling and punctuation.

7. We searched the Internet for information on global issues and how to research.

8. I got practical ideas from the class: looking not only at myself, but also examine communities I belong to and issues in the world.

9. As members of society, we need to know more about what happens around us and become advocates.

10. I feel more confident and organization in reading and writing.

F. Ensure Subject/Verb Agreement

Imagine that you and three of your friends take a road trip. You gather on the agreed upon day, get in the car, get gas, and head out to the freeway. Then the trouble begins. No one in the car can agree upon where to go for the road trip, so you pull over, turn around, and go home. Without agreement, you cannot go anywhere. The subjects and verbs in your sentences are similar. They, too, need agreement in order to communicate meaning and move your reader forward in understanding what you have to say. When the subject and verb do not agree, it is like having a driver that does not know where to direct the car.

1. **What is subject/verb agreement?** Subject/verb agreement is when the subject(s) and verb(s) in your sentences agree in number. If the subject is singular, the verb also must be singular, and if the subject is plural, the verb also must be plural.

2. **How can I make my subjects and verbs agree?** To make your subjects and verbs agree, you want to make sure you pair singular subjects with singular verbs and plural subjects with plural verbs. For common subjects and verbs, you can use the "One S Rule" to help you make the subject and verb agree. The "One S Rule" means that you have only one "s" to use on either the subject or the verb. By doing this, you will keep singular subjects matched with singular verbs, and plural subjects matched with plural verbs.

   > *Plural:* **Candles** <u>burn</u> brightly on the table.
   >
   > *(The subject gets the "s," so the verb does not)*
   >
   > *Singular:* **A candle** <u>burns</u> brightly on the table.
   >
   > *(The verb gets the "s," so the subject does not.)*

3. **Other Subject/Verb Agreement Rules** Sometimes subjects and verbs do not follow a regular form that allows you to apply the "One S Rule." In these cases, refer to the list of rules below.

   - **Rule #1:** When the subject is compound, use a plural verb. The only exception is when the compound subject is thought of as a unit.

     > *Compound Subject:* **Sherri and Tanner** <u>study</u> together often for their Biology class.
     >
     > *Compound Subject as a Unit:* **A peanut butter and jelly sandwich** <u>is</u> my favorite "brain food" when reading for my philosophy class.

   - **Rule #2:** Make sure subject and verb agree when the subject follows the verb. A subject will follow the verb when sentences start with *here* or *there*. A subject will also follow the verb when the sentence is a question.

     > There <u>are</u> **five people** on the waitlist for the class.
     >
     > <u>Is</u> **Kevin** on the waitlist for the class?

   - **Rule #3:** Make sure subject and verb agree when words come in between them. Crossing out prepositional phrases can help you make sure that the subject and verb agree. Crossing out subordinate clauses that come between the subject and the verb can also help you make sure the subject and verb agree. (For a list of prepositions that begin prepositional phrases, see p. 378.)

Prepositional Phrase: Ellie, ~~in the red coat and pink sneakers,~~ is waiting to see a Writing Center tutor.

Subordination: My friend ~~who always follows a writing process when writing her college papers~~ is now a confident writer.

- **Rule #4:** When the subject is a singular word that ends with "s," use a singular verb. Some words that end in "s" are not plural; rather, they are one unit or thing. These include such words as *politics, economics, mathematics,* and *news.*

  Politics is Jamie's favorite class.

  ("Politics" ends in an "s," but it is a singular word. Therefore, it needs a singular verb.)

- **Rule #5:** Use singular verbs when the subject expresses measurement, time, money, or weight. Words that express these things can look plural, but they work as a unit. Therefore, they are singular.

  Seventy-five dollars is a lot to pay for a textbook.

  (The subject "seventy-five dollars" is a unit. Therefore, it should be matched with a singular verb.)

- **Rule #6:** When the subject has the same singular and plural form, use a singular verb when you mean "only one" and a plural verb when you mean "more than one." Since the subject will not make it clear, the reader will look at your verb to see how many you mean. For example, words that have the same singular and plural form include *moose, fish, species,* or *deer.*

  Fish is my favorite dish for dinner.

  Fish are my favorite topic to write about in Biology.

- **Rule #7:** When subjects are collective nouns, make sure you use a singular verb. Collective nouns refer to groups of people or things. While there may be many people in the group, there is only one, singular group. Collective nouns include such things as *team, faculty, herd,* or *swarm.*

  The class listens intently to the lecture.

- **Rule #8:** Make sure subjects and verbs agree when using indefinite pronouns. Indefinite pronouns are pronouns that replace specific nouns. They can be tricky because some of them are plural while others are singular. Some can be either plural or singular.

Singular Indefinite Pronouns

another, anybody, anyone, anything, each, either, everybody, everyone, everything, much, most, neither, nobody, no one, nothing, one, somebody, someone, something.

Everyone wants to remember more of what they read and study for college.

Plural indefinite pronouns: both, few, many, several.

> **Many students** <u>learn</u> a reading and writing process in college.

Either plural or singular pronouns depending on use: all, any, more, most, none, some.

> **All of the books** for this class <u>are</u> at the used book store.
>
> (All *is referring to* books, *which are plural. Therefore the verb should also be plural.*)
>
> **Most of the group** <u>is</u> ready for the presentation.
>
> (Most *is referring to the* group, *which is a collective noun and is singular. Therefore, the verb should also be singular.*)

- **Rule #9:** Use cue words to help you determine whether a subject is singular or plural.

Singular cue words: a, an, another, each, either, ever, neither, one.

> **Each person** in the group <u>is</u> reviewing a partner's paper.

Plural cue words: all, both, few, many, several, some.

> **Many of the students** <u>improve</u> their papers after peer review.

Practice 6   Correcting Subject/Verb Errors

DIRECTIONS: Correct the subject/verb agreement errors in the following sentences.

1. Steak and eggs are my favorite breakfast. Pancakes are yours.

2. The room behind the science labs need to be cleaned.

3. Knowledge of economics create a better understanding of the world.

4. Five dollars, which I borrowed from my parents, are in my wallet.

5. The middle of the semester before midterms are the best time to check your grades.

6. Most students in college cares about their grades.

7. All members of the philosophy study group needs to participate in the project.

8. Each of the students who complete the service learning requirement receives a certificate.

9. Professors Smith and Backer, who teach English and history, respectively, is teaching a class on literature from the WWII era.

10. Too much cramming and not enough paced study over time hurt your chances for the best grades.

G. Use Commas Correctly

At some point in my education someone taught me that you put a comma anywhere you take a breath in a sentence. This seemed reasonable enough to me until I realized that everyone breathes at different times. My grandpa who smokes two packs of cigarettes a day has to take a lot of breaths. On the other hand, my cousin, who is a long distance cyclist, can make it through an entire sentence without having to take more than one breath. This led me to question the "take a breath" rule. Whose breath was I supposed to follow when I wrote? What if my reader did not need so many breaths?

When I got to college, I realized that there were set and consistent rules for using commas. These rules help readers to understand what you are saying by systematically separating ideas. While there are many comma rules in existence, the following are some of the main ones you will encounter as you write for college.

Comma Rules

1. **Rule #1: Use commas to separate items in a list of three or more.** The list can be individual words or short phrases.
   Note: There is flux in this rule. You may also see the comma omitted between the final two items in the list. This is also acceptable.

   > *Three or More Words*: **Joseph** ate, exercised, and studied.

   > *Three or More Phrases*: **Candice** previewed her textbook chapter, wrote down vocabulary words she did not understand, and annotated as she read.

2. **Rule #2:** Use commas to indicate pauses between clauses that are connected by conjunctions.

   - *Comma with Coordinating Conjunctions:* Use a comma with a coordinating conjunction (*for, and, nor, but, or, yet, so*) when you are separating two subject/verb pairs.

     > **Margo** met with her group, *and* **she** completed her part of the presentation preparation.

   - **Comma with Subordinating Conjunctions:** Use a comma when a subordinating conjunction comes before two subject/verb pairs. Do not use a comma when a subordinating conjunction comes between the subject/verb pairs. (See p. 383 for a list of subordinating conjunctions.)

     > *Even though* **Margo** met with her group, **she** still had time to complete her part of the presentation preparation.

   - **Comma with Correlative Conjunctions:** Use a comma to separate two subject/verb pairs that are linked with correlative conjunctions such as *either/or, neither/nor, whether/or, both/and,* and *not only/but also.*

     > *Either* **Margo** will present her material, *or* **her group** will present what she prepared.

3. **Rule #3:** Use commas to set off material that interrupts the sentence. The material that interrupts should not be vital to the meaning of the sentence; it should be extra information. Remember: Always use a pair of commas to set off interrupters.

> **Miguel**, *the boy wearing the blue shirt and sitting by the window*, is focused on his test.

4. **Rule #4:** Use a comma to set off introductory material. Introductory material should come before the subject of the sentence and should be used to set up or introduce the content of the sentence.

   - *Introductory material is a single word:* Therefore, **you** should study when **you** are alert.

   - *Introductory material is a short phrase:* On the other hand, if **you** have to study late into the night, **caffeine** can help.

   - *Introductory material is a verbal or prepositional phrase:* Working late into the night, **Patty** was able to finish the PowerPoint presentation for her group project the next day.

5. **Rule #5:** Use commas with conventional material such as numbers, names, dates, correspondence, and addresses.

   - **Numbers: My horse** weighs a little over 1,000 pounds.

   - **Names/titles: Dr. Howard**, PhD, is our guest speaker today.

   - **Openings and closing of correspondence** (Note: For formal letters, use a colon and not a comma to set off the opening salutation.)

   Dear Laura,

   [insert letter here]

   Sincerely,

   Lisa

   - **Dates: September 11, 2001**, will remain in our memories forever.

   - **Addresses: I** live at 19817 Hollow Street, Kent, WA 98731.

Practice 7   Using Commas Correctly

DIRECTIONS: Put in or take out commas in the following sentences to punctuate them correctly. Also, indicate the comma rule or rules you use to correct each sentence.

_____ 1. This class had taught me a lot about writing reading and social skills.

_____ 2. While the readings and research have prepared me for my college degree which is in English the most important lesson is having confidence in my work.

_____ **3.** When writing my introduction to my essay I found the cluster brainstorm process brought out new details.

_____ **4.** The story initially did not have many details and I did not know how to describe things very well.

_____ **5.** After adding details from the cluster I felt that the reader would get an excellent sense of Monet's appearance personality and passions.

_____ **6.** We tend to relate more to one community in our lives than others but each person belongs to many communities.

_____ **7.** Emulating me my daughter Bless sat reading beside me and I realized that what I do has more impact than what I say.

_____ **8.** I was unsure of my success when enrolling in college but thanks to the teacher my classmates and my personal determination I have gained confidence to accomplish my goals.

_____ **9.** The prime minister of England lives at 10 Downing Street London.

_____**10.** My dentist whose name is Joseph Smiley retired on September 30 2008.

H. Use Quotation Marks Correctly

Have you ever had the experience of someone else taking what you have said and sharing it as their own idea rather than as yours? Did you feel angry when credit was not given to you?

Quotation marks allow us to give credit in our writing to ideas that come from other people. They show our readers where the ideas came from, so there is no confusion between what you said and what someone else said. They are also a way of honoring the ideas of others, and they add credibility to our writing by showing that we can back up what we have to say with support from the ideas of others.

The following are some basic rules for using quotation marks in your writing. We have used MLA guidelines.

1. **Quotation Marks with a Short Quotation** If the passage you are quoting is fewer than four lines of your typed prose, follow these directions. Note that you need to include the author and page number for each quote, but this information can also come before the quote, or you can give the author before the quote and page number after it in parentheses. The important part is that you provide the author and page number immediately around the quotation.

   - Introduce the passage with a tag or signal phrase that tells the reader where the quote comes from or who is talking.
   - Then put a comma followed by an opening quotation mark.
   - Write the passage you are quoting, making sure to reproduce it word for word and with spelling that is true to the original.
   - End with a closing quotation mark, a parenthetical citation that includes the author and page number or just the page number if the author was mentioned in the introduction, and the final end mark of punctuation that closes the sentence.

Author + page number at end: According to an expert gardener, "Fertilizer is a key component of growing a dynamic garden" (McGrath 79).

Author + page number at beginning: According to McGrath, an expert gardener, on page 79 of her book, "Fertilizer is a key component of growing a dynamic garden."

Author + page number split around quote: According to McGrath, an expert gardener, "Fertilizer is a key component of growing a dynamic garden" (79).

2. **Quotation Marks with a Longer Quotation:** If the passage you are quoting in your writing is longer than four lines of your typed prose, the rules change. In this case, do the following.

- Introduce the passage with a tag or signal phrase that tells the reader where the quote comes from or who is talking.
- Put a colon (:) following your signal phrase to introduce the quote.
- Start a new line, indent 10 spaces, and type the passage you are quoting making sure to represent it word for word and with accurate spelling that is true to the original. Double space throughout the quotation.
- *Do not put quotation marks around this passage as the indenting takes the place of the quotation marks and signals to your reader that this is a quote.*
- End the quote with the end punctuation for the sentence. Then put the parenthetical citation with author and page number or just the page number, if you have already cited the author.
- Resume typing your paragraph flush with the left margin. (Do not indent again as the reader will see this as a new paragraph.)
- All of the other rules listed above for shorter quotations apply here.

I have been working on building a stronger garden this year. My efforts started last winter when I spread manure on all of my garden beds and covered them with burlap sacks. This spring, I continued my work by putting down a layer of compost below the new seeds I planted. However, I need to keep up my efforts this summer as well. According to McGrath, an expert gardener, fertilizer is crucial to gardening success:

> Fertilizer is a key component of growing a dynamic garden. Compost adds nutrients to soil, improves its texture and structure, attracts beneficial earthworms, and helps control insects and diseases. Commercial fertilizers are useful because they are premixed, but gardeners can cultivate their own brew by using things in their cupboards such as Epsom salts or food leftovers like banana peels. (79)

This seems like great advice and will help my earlier efforts pay off with a beautiful garden.

3. **Quotations within Quotations** Sometimes you will quote a passage that has a quotation in it. This can happen when the author you are quoting has referenced

someone else in his or her text or when the text you are quoting includes dialogue. In this case, you will want to start your quote with double quotation marks. When the quote within a quote happens, signal that with a single opening quotation mark. Make sure to close out both the single and double quotation marks.

> When Dr. Fulford asked Donna Beegle if she would like help learning academic English, she responded, "I said, 'Yes. Please teach me how to talk like you, because no one thinks I am smart. No one asks my opinion. I feel like no one can hear me'" (Beegle 140).

4. **Omitting Information in Quotes Using Ellipses:** If you are quoting a passage and you need to omit part of it, you can use ellipses (. . .) Ellipses should be used sparingly and only to omit information that may be redundant or not necessary given what you have already said in your writing.

> **Original passage:** "McGrath is an expert gardener who has her PhD in Botany, over sixteen years of experience working in the fields with farmers, and has published numerous books on gardening. She confirms that fertilizer is a key component of growing a dynamic garden" (Monroe 105).
>
> **Example with ellipses:** "McGrath is an expert gardener who has . . . published numerous books on gardening. She confirms that fertilizer is a key component of growing a dynamic garden" (Monroe 105).

5. **Adding Information to Quotes Using Brackets:** If information is missing from a quote but is needed to clarify the meaning for your reader, you can add it by using brackets [ ]. You can then put the information that is needed within the brackets. This signals to the reader that you added information and that it is not part of the quote.

> "She [McGrath] gives clinics on how to effectively raise a dynamic garden" (Monroe 106).

Practice 8   Using Correct Punctuation with Quotation Marks

DIRECTIONS: Add punctuation around the quotes where they are needed in the following sentences. Highlight your additions, so they are easy to see.

1. She said It is easy to fertilize your garden effectively (McGrath 78)

2. Caring for a garden in the winter is key to its success. This is something I never realized until I read about it in an article in *Sunset* magazine. In this article, expert gardener, McGrath, talked about winter garden care

> Winter garden care is often overlooked, but it is vital to your garden's success in the summer. Pruning is easier in the winter when leaves are off the trees, and it helps them grow more vibrantly come spring. Fertilizing with compost is also a good idea to

(continued)

do in the winter as rain will help the compost penetrate the deeper layers of topsoil and build a rich garden dirt for spring (78)

This article made me realize that I need to garden year round for success.

3. In an interview with McGrath that is published in *Sunset*, she said I learned key strategies for success from my mentor in college who always told me Time is not wasted in the garden. Garden year round for success (Monroe 104)

4. In the *Sunset* article, McGrath also encourages planting a diverse number of plants in your garden. She said Add color from different plants like Coleus to add drama to any garden! (Monroe 103).

5. McGrath has this to say about slugs in the garden Avoid strong poisons and use natural deterrents such as beer in a dish. Slugs will crawl into this and die, and your plants will not be harmed by pesticides (80)

6. *Sunset* magazine's interview with McGrath went on to relate what she says about composting and the garden

   The best compost is natural. Visit your local coffee house and get used coffee grounds. Then sprinkle them over your garden. Or you can find a farm that has animals and ask if you can have some of their manure. This also makes wonderful compost that will feed plants all summer. Finally, if you live near a chocolate factory, purchase chocolate nubs. They make fantastic fertilizer, and your garden will smell like chocolate (Monroe 106)

This interview made me realize that gardening need not be expensive. There are natural and free ways to build my soil.

7. The most important thing says McGrath is to water regularly throughout the dry summer months (78)

8. McGrath said The most important thing I learned about pruning was from a local tree expert who said Prune in the spring or winter. Avoid the fall when plants are struggling to survive the long summer drought (78)

9. Weed regularly so plants and not weeds get the nutrients in your soil says McGrath (78)

10. The joy of gardening says McGrath is worth all of the trouble (80)

Credits

Text Credits

Copyright © 1998 by Julia Alvarez. From *Something to Declare*, published by Plume, an imprint by Penguin Group (USA), in 1999 and originally in hardcover by Algonquin Books of Chapel Hill, 1998. By permission of Susan Bergholz Literary Services, New York, NY and Lamy, NM. All rights reserved.

Excerpt from "The Naked Culture" by Vince Barnes, Spindrift. Copyright © 1993 by Vince Barnes. Used by the permission of Vincent Barnes.

Dr. Donna Beegle. "An Insider's Perspective: The Donna Beegle Story" from *See Poverty... Be the Difference* by Dr. Donna Beegle, p. 3–19. Copyright © 2007. Used by permission of Dr. Donna Beegle, leading poverty expert, author, public speaker and president of Communications Across Barriers, Inc.

Katherine E. Garrett, "Living in America: Challenges Facing New Immigrants and Refugees." Copyright © 2006. Permission to reprint this publication is provided by the Robert Wood Johnson Foundation.

Infographic: How the DREAM Act Helps the Economy by Juan Carlos Guzman and Raul C. Jara from *Center for American Progress*. Copyright © 2012. Used by permission of Center for American Progress.

"Using Learning Strategies in Various Disciplines" by Laurie Kimpton-Lorence. Copyright © 1995 by Laurie Kimpton-Lorence. Used by permission of Laurie Kimpton-Lorence.

"Assimilation through Education: Indian Boarding Schools in the Pacific Northwest" by Carolyn J. Marr. Copyright © by Carolyn J. Marr. Used by permission of the author.

Sherrie L. Nist and Jodi Patrick Holschuh, "Now that You're Here" from *College Success Strategies* 2nd Ed. Copyright © 2006. Reprinted and Electronically reproduced by permission of Pearson Education, Inc., Upper Saddle River, New Jersey.

Parrillo, Vincent N., *Strangers to These Shores*, 10th Ed. Copyright © 2011. Reprinted and Electronically reproduced by permission of Pearson Education, Inc., Upper Saddle River, New Jersey.

Richard Rothstein, "Equalizing Opportunity: Dramatic Differences in Children's Home Life and Health Mean That Schools Can't Do It Alone" Reprinted with permission from the Summer 2009 issue of *American Educator*, the quarterly journal of the *American Federation of Teachers*, AFL-CIO and by Richard Rothstein.

Earl Shorris, "The Uses of Liberal Education: As a Weapon in the Hands of the Restless Poor," *Harper's Magazine*, September, 1997. Copyright © 1997 by *Harper's Magazine*. All Rights Reserved. Reproduced from the September issue by special permission.

Donald E. Simarek. "On Being a Student." Reproduced by permission of the author.

Katherine Kellegher Sohn, "Whislin' and Crowin' Women of Appalachia: Literacy Practices since College" from *College Composition and Communication*, Volume 54, Number 3, February 2003, pp. 423–452. Copyright © 2003 by the National Council of Teachers of English. Reprinted with permission.

"C.P. Ellis" by Studs Terkel. Reprinted by permission of Donadio and Olson, Inc. Copyright © 1980 by Studs Terkel.

"Reclaiming Native Education" by Christina Twu from *Colors Magazine*, September 2006. Copyright © 2006 by National Indian Education Association. Used by permission of National Indian Education Association.

"The School Days Of An Indian Girl," *Zitkala-Sa, Atlantic*. Feb. 1900.

From "Hunger of Memory: The Education of Richard Rodriguez" by Richard Rodriguez. Reproduced by permission of David R. Godine, Publisher, Inc. Copyright © 1982 by Richard Rodriguez.

Judith Ortiz Cofer, "The Myth of the Latin Woman: I Just Met a Girl Named Maria" from *The Latin Deli: Prose and Poetry* pp. 148–154. Copyright © 1993 by University of Georgia Press. Used by permission of University of Georgia Press.

"Mute in an English-Only World" by Chang-rae Lee from *Dream Me Home Safely*. Copyright © 2003 by Chang-rae Lee. Used by permission of author.

Frederick Douglass, "Learning to Read and Write" from *Narrative of The Life of Frederick Douglass*, New York: Penguin, 1982.

"The Allegory of the Cave," Plato, Dialogues.

Photo Credits

Critical Thinking icon John_Woodcock/iStock Vectors/Getty Images **p. 1** aihumnoi/Fotolia **p. 19** Digieye/Fotolia **p. 41** Photo courtesy of Olympic Sculpture Park **p. 43** M.studio/Fotolia **p. 47** Gresei/Fotolia **p. 57** dimdimich/Fotolia **p. 61** AkunaMatata/Fotolia **p. 63** Chlorophylle/Fotolia **p. 66** Nenov Brothers/Fotolia **p. 68** Torsten Paris/Fotolia **p. 73** Library of Congress **p. 77** aihumnoi/Fotolia **p. 78** kikkerdirk/Fotolia **p. 81** kikkerdirk/Fotolia **p. 96** Alfonso de Tomás/Fotolia **p. 113** Jut/Fotolia **p. 135** Donna Beegle **p. 145** Katherine Kelleher Sohn **p. 161** aihumnoi/Fotolia **p. 162** ollyy/Shutterstock **p. 166** Scanrail/Fotolia **p. 166** diez-artwork/Fotolia **p. 182** saschi79/Fotolia **p. 195** Friedberg/Fotolia **p. 213** USA.gov **p. 215** Darrin Bell **p. 223** Nancy Kaszerman/ZUMAPRESS/Newscom **p. 231** aihumnoi/Fotolia **p. 232** Ariel Skelley/Blend Images/Getty Images **p. 236** nueng/Fotolia **p. 253** frenta/Fotolia **p. 307** Christopher Felver/Corbis **p. 311** aihumnoi/Fotolia **p. 375** aihumnoi/Fotolia **p. 380** PhotoSG/Fotolia **p. 381** alphaspirit/Fotolia **p. 384** leremy/Fotolia **p. 387** arsdigital/Fotolia **p. 390** coramax/Fotolia **p. 393** Daisuke Ito/Fotolia **p. 395** AKS/Fotolia

Index